"No man is an island, entire of itself; every man is a piece of the continent, a part of the main; if a clod be washed away by the sea, Europe is the less, as well as if a promontory were, as well as if a manor of thy friends or of thine own were; any man's death diminishes me, because I am involved in mankind; and therefore never send to know for whom the bell tolls; it tolls for thee." JOHN DONNE (Devotions XVII)

"Men never do evil so completely and so cheerfully as when they do it from religious conviction." BLAISE PASCAL (Pensees)

"Life is not a spectacle or a feast. It is a predicament." GEORGE SANTAYANA

"To sin by silence when they should protest makes cowards of men." ABRAHAM LINCOLN

"I am a citizen of the world, and so I defend my right to speak about anything . . . . The sickness is not of the state, the system or the government. It is the civil society that is sick. We have placed too many responsibilities on politicians. There must be other ways to express our will and solve our needs." JOSE SARAMAGO, 1998 winner of the Nobel Prize in Literature, after a visit to Chiapas, Mexico.

SPEAKING OUT!
YOUR OPINION COUNTS!

SPEAKING OUT! YOUR OPINION COUNTS!

Toward an Ethic of Personal Integrity and Citizen Responsibility in a Democratic Society

Meyer Rangell

Copyright © 2004 by Meyer Rangell.

ISBN :   Hardcover   1-4134-4876-3
            Softcover   1-4134-4875-5

All rights reserved. No part of this book may be reproduced or transmitted in any form or by any means, electronic or mechanical, including photocopying, recording, or by any information storage and retrieval system, without permission in writing from the copyright owner.

This book was printed in the United States of America.

To order additional copies of this book, contact:
Xlibris Corporation
1-888-795-4274
www.Xlibris.com
Orders@Xlibris.com

FOR EVELYN

(and for Lea, in loving memory)

And, uniquely, for our very special Annie

Things fall apart; the centre cannot hold;
Mere anarchy is loosed upon the world,
The blood-dimmed tide is loosed, and everywhere
The ceremony of innocence is drowned;
The best lack all conviction, while the worst
Are full of passionate intensity

WILLIAM BUTLER YEATS

It is difficult to condense in a few words the significance of all the letters to the editor Meyer Rangell has written over the years. "SPEAKING OUT!" is an historical account of the most significant issues and events of the last half of the 20th. century which he brought to public attention with logic and clarity. A must reading for those who want to review issues and events in context as they unfolded."

> AARON BINDMAN, PH.D.
> Professor Emeritus, Sociology
> Suny, New Paltz, New York

"I received your 'magnum opus' and stayed up until 3:30 am reading the fascinating material. The fervor of your emotions on behalf of the angels is most gratifying in an otherwise narrow and egocentric world."

> *Alexander Bassin, PH.D.*
> *Professor Emeritus, Criminology*
> *Florida State University*
> *Tallahassee, Florida*

Dedication

Dedicated to my children, grandchildren, and great grandchildren, in the hope that their generations will improve upon the world that we bequeath them.

Dedicated, also, to all those other letter-writers across the nation-cranks, freethinkers, non-conformists all—who dare not only to think for themselves but to put their controversial opinions into print, mixing it in the marketplace of public opinion.

Risking the disfavor of their neighbors, they uphold the true meaning of a free press and a free society.

Helping to form, rather than be formed by, the prevailing winds of public opinion, they validate the concept that a free people must also be a responsible people.

Refusing to go with the herd, they force a social and political responsiveness from the powers that be. They stimulate others to come out of the closet where so many hide their individuality in abject obeisance to the almighty god of popularity and conformity.

They encourage the process that seeks integrity and the fulfillment of each individual's worth and meaning.

They respond positively to Edmund Burke's famous dictum, "ALL THAT IS REQUIRED FOR THE SUCCESS OF EVIL IS THAT GOOD MEN REMAIN SILENT."

Meyer Rangell
Bloomingburg, New York
January, 2004

December 20, 1962
Letter to 100 friends at Christmas/Chanukah

Dear Friend,

I am sending you a copy of Norman Cousins' IN PLACE OF FOLLY because I am sure that you will be as aroused and as stimulated by it as I was.

I know that you, as a thinking person, are vitally concerned with the dangers of nuclear war and the problems of a durable peace.

I am sure too, that there are many more like us who see the danger of a horrendous war of unimaginable destructiveness, but are overwhelmed and silenced by the enormity of the war machine, the hugeness of the military juggernauts, the seemingly insurmountable power of governments and states and alliances moving inexorably toward conflict and disaster. Against this formidable array we tend to think that any individual effort we might make for peace would be puny and insignificant . . . and so we do nothing . . . and by our inactivity we allow (or indeed invite) inevitable war and death.

I think that this book, if distributed widely enough, can exert an influence in the opposite direction. I agree with Cousins that every single individual is possessed of an important power, THE POWER TO ADVOCATE what he thinks is right, and by such advocacy to influence the course of national policy.

WE CAN HELP SPREAD THE IDEA OF PEACE.
WE CAN HELP ESTABLISH A CLIMATE OF PEACE.
WE CAN HELP CREATE A WORLD PUBLIC OPINION FOR PEACE.

Toward this end I am sending 100 copies of this book to people like yourself, to help spread its clear, persuasive, timely, and URGENT message. I ask that you read it and pass it along. AND, if you wish, send nine more copies to friends (along with this, or a similar letter of your own.)

You and I can thus make ourselves heard and get others to join us in ever-increasing numbers, until our combined voices help return the world to the road of sanity and peace.

CONSIDER THIS: *If each of us takes on the responsibility for just ten others, we can reach 1,000 people in the first stage, 10,000 in the second, 100,000 in the third, and ONE MILLION PEOPLE in the fourth!! (And even if our effectiveness is only ten percent, we will have done a hell of a lot more than just sitting around waiting for destruction!)*

Read the book and see if you don't agree with me. And then let us start our own SELF-SUSTAINING CHAIN REACTION . . . this time FOR PEACE!

PS: A good idea would be to include your Congressman and Senator on your list. A million letters to Congress would surely not go un-noticed.

June, 1962
Random Thoughts on Spontaneity
GROUP PSYCHOTHERAPY, JUNE, 1962

It may very well be that the major contribution of psychodrama, and allied group therapy techniques, lies in the vitality of its attack on the *passivity* that has come to characterize the intellectual and emotional climate of our time.

Too much of our educational experience, from high school through college and university and even graduate school, consists of sitting and listening (with some furious note-taking, to be regurgitated—half-digested—at examination time), and with the lines of communication, when they are successfully established, running from lecture platform to supine, absorptive, sponge-like receptors. And in society at large, whether at television or at the movies, at theaters, at concerts or lecture halls, in the football stadium or at the prize ring, we have become a nation of watchers, of listeners, of spectators, of non-participants who sit on the outside looking inside, while attempting to live vicariously the experiences of the small minority of doers and performers.

Spectatoritis has become a national disease; watching, instead of doing, a national preoccupation!

The entire underlying philosophy and approach of psychodrama, role-playing, and group therapy, represent a force in the opposite direction. Countering passivity, psychodrama places the highest premium upon action and participation. It boldly postulates the concept that within every individual there resides an inner spark of creative potential—a spark that has been all but extinguished by the conformist pressures of society—a spark that we once knew in childhood, but which we have allowed to dim as we bowed to the mores and customs of our milieu—but a spark that stubbornly continues to exist, a latent promise of potential yet untapped. It is the function and the goal of psychodrama to fan that spark, and to activate that potential.

It does so by placing participation ahead of passivity, doing ahead of watching, living in substance and in reality ahead of vicariousness. One has only to observe a dynamic psychodramatist in action to recognize the catalytic role it can play in overcoming entrenched patterns of repression, withdrawal, and conformity.

Where our culture is characterized by timidity and the unquestioned acceptance of the already-accepted, psychodrama acts as a gadfly, stimulating thought, spontaneity and creativity, originality and newness of perception. Action methods and techniques in general can play a re-vitalizing role in many fields—in education, in psychotherapy, in personnel training in industry, in guidance and counseling, in correction—in all the varied forms and areas of human communication. To the extent that psychodrama and group therapy do this—to the extent that they counter the stultifying trend toward a passive, absorptive, sponge-like, non-participating populace of receptors with a dynamic concept of humanity alive to its inherent potential—active, thinking, feeling, responding, participating, living creatively and spontaneously—to that extent will they make a lasting contribution.

October 27, 1968
The New York Times Magazine

Nathan Perlmutter's strained analogies, unsupported generalizations, and erudite rhetoric (which prove to be more often obfuscating than illuminating) do precious little either to provide new understanding or to chart new directions in the black-white crisis which confronts us.

While attacking "the liberal intellectual community" (which he conveniently neglects to identify, either as individuals or groups) for engaging in what he calls "liberal stereotypy," Mr. Perlmutter proceeds to his own exercise in stereotyping by tarring all "liberals" with one sweeping brush, ascribing to them an oversimplified "position," and proceeding with the semantic skill of an experienced college debater to shoot down the straw man he has just set up.

The liberal, he avers, condones the "up-ending of law and order" because "it must be understood in the light of 300 years of white racism." With one fell swoop he thus saddles the liberal with the burden of supporting disorder and violence, and gets in a sneer at the white community's belated recognition of its responsibility for the black condition.

It is a well-known phenomenon that if you repeat certain words or phrases over and over again their meaning is often blurred. Instead of repeating "300 years of white racism," try, "the black man's 300-year experience of the unspeakable brutality, barbarism and dehumanization of chattel slavery, followed by years of beatings, torture and lynching, accompanied by the systematic discrimination, deprivation, humiliation and exclusion which has kept him from sharing in America's affluence to this very day."

If white liberals are only now beginning to understand blacks in the light of this stark reality, it is a much-to-be-desired, if belated, development.

April 1969
White Racism
Commentary

... It is difficult to see how Mr. Friedman arrives at his conclusion that because white Americans are divided into a variety of ethnic groups that are at times in conflict with one another they are exempt from participation as whites in the black-white confrontation, or how he thinks he can convince blacks that because white America is diverse it ceases to be white vis-à-vis the blacks.

In what has by now become an all too familiar litany on the part of liberal critics of the Kerner report, Mr. Friedman is more critical of the report than of the conditions it portrayed, and even blames this long-overdue recognition of the extent and depth of the black-white crisis for "helping to provoke the current backlash." It would be more constructive if Mr. Friedman directed his attention to the meaning and quality of that backlash, with particular reference to its social and *moral* significance....

One wonders to whom this piece is directed, with what purpose, and to what effect. Insofar as it is directed to liberals (to those who are still vocal and active in support of what they conceive to be legitimate black causes), Mr. Friedman urges that they "dispense with liberal rhetoric," which means divest themselves of any notion that they are doing anything particularly right or noble or just. Here, rather than in the Kerner report, is a real backlash overtone.

Insofar as it is directed to Negroes, Mr. Friedman urges that they stop "pointing the finger of guilt either at Americans in general or at special groups" in the interest of "the development of strategies which can lead to a necessary accommodation." Just what these accommodations are, Mr. Friedman does not reveal, but presumably they would be in the direction of black understanding and concern for the needs and fears of other groups.

In this regard, Mr. Friedman would be in a much stronger position to exhort the blacks had he addressed himself with equal, or indeed with greater, vigor to the "in" groups.... It is the white power structure which needs the prodding, which still must be convinced of the reality of the black condition and the desperate necessity for immediate remedial programs.... If "power has to be shared," ... the process out of which such sharing will eventually materialize must surely begin with ... the present holders of power—and it is to them that Mr. Friedman should direct his appeal for accommodation rather than to the deprived and the powerless....

September 1, 1973
Time for everyone to speak up
The Times Herald Record

I could not resist a letter of congratulations and support for your forthright, direct, and unequivocal editorial of 8/17/73 "The President and the presidency are on trial" you state, "That means the democratic system is on trial" You are so right!

If anything, you understate. President Nixon may not merely be an "obstacle to the orderly conduct of the nation's business," he may be the forerunner of a type of American fascism that brings on the police state (under the pretext of "national security," of course,) by the gradual development of a political atmosphere that first condones, and eventually encourages, surveillance, spying, wire-tapping, blackmail, burglary, forgery, hush-money, kidnapping, prostitutes, sex scandals, enemy-lists, millions of dossiers of private and public figures, bribing of judges, patronage, White House "horrors", plumbers and secret police accountable only to the "boss," illegality and corruption . . . all at the highest levels of our national government.

"Someone must make him see," you state, "that he alone stands as the obstacle to orderly conduct of the nation's urgent business."

"Someone," I suggest, is everyone of us . . . everyone who cares about the American heritage of democracy.

That means, first and foremost, that we all speak up. Let the President know. Let our senators and congressmen know. Let a great outpouring of public outrage and public anger pour out in a way that cannot be ignored.

If the people, and their representatives in Congress, cannot get the President to acknowledge, confront, and correct the glaring evidence of corruption and malfeasance that is all about him, let them face up to the need, for the sake of our very survival as a democratic republic, to do what is necessary: If the President will not change, then let us change the President.

That is democracy . . . in action.

September 15, 1973
Nixon and Thomas More
The Times Herald Record

By an ironic, but instructive, juxtaposition in TV programming, viewers were treated one afternoon last week to President Nixon in his live news conference, and, in the evening, to Sir Thomas More (in "A Man For All Seasons").

The contrast was an education!

More, in language that rang with an astonishing current relevance, spoke eloquently of justice and morality and, above all, of adherence to principle, even at the eventual cost of his life.

Mr. Nixon, back at his old stand, was still blaming "the leers and sneers of commentators" (not the corruption of his appointees!) for the erosion of confidence in his administration.

He was still reserving his most bitter language not to castigate the corrupters and the moral sewer into which they were leading us, but to attack those who have exposed them.

Sir Thomas More and Richard Nixon . . . a study in Contrast Morality and principle versus expediency and opportunism.

September 29, 1973
"Durable" programs at Daytop
The Times Herald Record

Amid the furor raised by Governor Rockefeller's new get-tough drug policy, I should like to call attention to the durable, successful, on-going, rehabilitation program of Daytop Village, which operates two important centers in our area, one in Parksville, the other at Swan Lake.

Daytop, which stresses creative rehabilitation rather than sterile punishment, is now in its tenth year, and is the forerunner of that type of treatment known as the drug-free therapeutic community. Setting ambitious goals both for itself and for its residents, Daytop seeks not only the immediate goal of quitting the dependence on drugs, but the more difficult and far-reaching goal of creating new human beings—with new values, a new sense of self-worth, and a new commitment both to oneself and to society.

It attempts the re-socialization of the anti-social drug addict through a process that aims at total human renewal.

The Daytop process, based on its slogan, "Helping Man to Help Himself", uses the group encounter to focus on individual attitudes and behavior, to encourage the ex-addict to face himself as he never has before, to examine himself, his values, his goals and his prospects with a naked and ultimate honesty, and through this in-depth process to change for the better.

Daytop's philosophy, based on peer-group pressure and indigenous leadership, attests to the great potential for good of the humanizing group process, not only in the treatment of drug addiction, but in many other areas of human relationships.

For it is a modern, affirmative, answer to the Biblical question, "Am I my brothers's keeper?" And by this affirmative answer, Daytop re-asserts that man's humanity to man can still provide the basic force to counter our all too prevalent penchant for violence and destructiveness.

(Member of the Board of Trustees,
Daytop Village, Inc.)

October 6, 1973
Hits columnist on Watergate
The Times Herald Record

William Safire (column 9-28-73) obviously believes that a strong offense is the best defense.

Hence he attempts to paint the Ervin Watergate Committee as villainous rather than focus attention on the villainies they have uncovered.

"The committee," he says, " . . . threatens the political freedom of every group." Balderdash! The central fact, which Mr. Safire would like to obscure, is that our political freedom was seriously threatened by the outrageous election abuses of Liddy, Hunt, et al, and by the criminal machinations of the burglars, the plumbers, and their mentors in high places.

This is what brought the Watergate Committee into existence in the first place.

To hold up Pat Buchanan, who is still busy trying to justify those vile tactics, as a champion of liberty, is sheer effrontery.

Fortunately, we can rely on the good sense of the American people, despite Mr. Safire, to be able to distinguish between those who would endanger our democratic system and those who would defend it.

December 10, 1973
A LETTER FROM CRETE . . .
on Henry Miller, Greece and Israel

I am writing this from a Paradise, otherwise known as the island of Crete, the last stop in what has turned out to be a varied and fantastic journey. We are on the north shore of the island, in a cottage of sun-drenched white cement on Minos Beach, near the fairyland sea-coast town of Agios Nikolaos. The furnishings are blue, like the waters of the Mediterranean Gulf of Merabello which lap gently on the rocks at the foot of our veranda. The small, protected cove is warm and dazzling bright in the sunshine, and the small, white cottages that dot the shore, as well as the magnificent main house where we take our sumptuous suppers, are Spanish-Mexican in architecture and feeling—like Santa Fe, or Lake Chapalla in Mexico. It is off-season here and the place is practically empty (half-rates also make it a great tourist bargain). There are only six other guests here in this utterly elegant, magnificent resort that always has a capacity crowd of two hundred or more in season, and we move around the superbly gardened grounds (hibiscus, bougainvilla, exotic tropical plantings and the most hardy and huge and abundant and varied geraniums I have ever seen) as though it were all our own private preserve. It is peaceful, tranquil, a balm to the soul—nirvana, in which one is almost seduced into forgetting the madness, the stupidity, the greed and the folly, the violence and avarice, the false values that abound in the world outside.

We came here last week on an overnight ship from Piraeus, (an experience in itself,) after a few days in Athens, where we had come from Israel (another story which we'll get to a little later).

In Athens we stayed at a small hotel in Constitution Square. From our window we could see the great rising presence of the Acropolis, dominating the Athenian landscape, with the Parthenon at the top outlined in magnificent relief against the blue sky beyond. We trudged around those ancient and impressive ruins until our feet, and my wind, could hold out no longer, but we walked back, tired as we were, down the slopes and through the old and interesting, relatively unchanged old quarter known as the Plaka. Despite the touristy character of many of the shops, there is much excitement in the winding streets and sloping alleys and the old stone stairways leading down to the newer part of the city.

The overnight ship (the Minos) that brought us from Piraeus should not be missed. After a night's voyage, an evening on a moonlit deck, a sound sleep in a comfortable first-class stateroom, you sail serenely into the ancient harbor of Heraklion at seven-thirty in the morning, with the sun coming up over the sloping mountains all around, casting a beautiful and wondrous light on the white, clean, welcoming harbor. It is unforgettable! Evelyn and I exult in what seems much more than the beginning of a bright new day.

As I write, I look up at two small islands that sit out there, almost close enough to touch, right in front of our cottage. One, a gentle rising hill, looks only about ten blocks long. A small white house is perched near its summit. The other, about a half mile long, lies softly in the water, its gentle hillocks and graceful curving spine could be a whale at rest. If it slowly heaved out of the water and quietly drifted away, I would not in the least be surprised!

While in Athens, I chanced upon Henry Miller's COLOSSUS OF MAROUSSI, in which he describes his feelings and emotions upon his first visit to Greece in 1939-1940. It became an exciting dimension to read Miller's description every evening of the very places we had visited that morning or afternoon—the Acropolis, Piraeus, the Zapion, Crete, Knossus, Heraklion, the museums, etc.

I have always liked Miller, though not unreservedly. The curious thing is that what I find objectionable in him (aside from his unforgivable anti-semitic lapses in the Tropic books) are a direct consequence of the precise qualities that arouse my admiration, even my enthusiasm. That is to say, Miller has the rare quality of ebullience, enthusiasm, gusto, zest. He is brimful of the juices of life; he is not namby-pamby about anything; he goes whole hog for this business of living. He lives wildly, freely, joyously. He is direct, open, spontaneous, candid, outspoken. Words spill out of him like a gushing waterful. He never uses just one adjective where five or ten or twenty might say it better. He wants to make sure that his overflowing senses really get over to you, so he expresses himself with a super-abundance of words and a true largesse of imagery: his emotions fairly spill onto the page until you feel inundated by his vibrance and his energy. If he dislikes something or someone, he hates it, or him, from his guts, and tells you so without censorious inhibition, in marvelous language that rings with passion, strength and vigor. And if he likes something, he goes mad about it and acts as though he were the first man in the whole world to discover it, and proceeds to bowl you over with his exuberance and enthusiasm. It might be sex, or literature, or the crummy English, or the magnificent Greeks, Miller goes whole hog and the devil take those who disagree with him! It is this very ebullience, which strikes such a happy and responding chord in me, that leads him so frequently to outrageous generalizations and utterly wild conclusions on the grand scale, which he states with appropriate, and delicious, bombast, without any regard whatsoever to the possibilities of subsequent, more sober judgments either by himself or by others. It is as though the depths of his uninhibited feelings and emotions as he *experiences* something makes the exact truth unimportant and trifling, as he wildly soars from fact to fiction to fantasy. ("I say it sincerely and deliberately: he writes, "I would a thousand times rather be that poor Greek than an American millionaire.", or "if I had my choice between being the president of an American tyre company or the prison keeper of the old fortress at Nauplia, I would prefer to be the prison keeper . . . I would take twenty years in jail, too, as part of the bargain!") What does it matter if it is not exactly true? It's the *feeling* that counts. And, of course, I am always with him all the way when he lambasts as no one else can all that he sees as sham and hypocrisy, money and power, status and pride, arrogance and vanity, show and pretense, war and violence, greed and selfishness and materialism, and the mad follies of Western man who thinks he is the be-all and end-all!

The *Collossus of Maroussi* will always be a part of our Greek experience, although I part with Miller on the notion that what he describes is exclusively and uniquely Greek. What he describes, and what he happened to find and to experience in Greece, is the *human experience*, the sense of an untapped human potential for cooperation and love and warmth and decency and brotherhood and peace and tranquility. And the understanding that the deepest meanings of life lie in the human qualities of the heart as it reaches out to others (what the Greeks, incidentally, called "agape") . . . all of which I had found before coming to Greece, (in the opening-up processes of the group experience and in the humanizing qualities of the encounter group process in Daytop and elsewhere), and which I felt much more keenly a few weeks ago in the *living* experience of Israel, especially in the Kibbutz, than in the *imagined* experience of Greece of 2500 years ago in Athens, or almost 5000 years ago in the Cretan civilization of King Minos at Knossus. Knossus and the Parthenon are *dead* and for Miller they are glorious *past* reminders of man's potential. Israel is *alive*, and stands as a *present* monument to the best in man!

As you can see, we did get to Israel after all. When we started our trip early in October, it seemed that the sudden outbreak of war would upset our plans to visit there, with the result that we spent more time in France than we had intended. We followed the war news from Israel closely, as we toured the lovely valleys and mountains of central and Southern France. We drove along the breathtaking Corniches from St. Raphael, along the Mediterranean coast, to the border town of Menton, and into Italy. When we reached Rome, we visited the El Al office at once. Strict security prevailed there, on a busy street near the Via Veneto, because one of their people had been killed just a short time before by an Arab terrorist. The El Al official, however, assured us that flights were going in and out of Tel Aviv, that relative calm had returned, and that we could go if we wanted. There would be a shortage of services, and none of the luxuries tourists could normally expect, but things were relatively safe. We decided to chance it. It turned out to be the highlight of our trip, the *gut experience*, where we became emotionally involved from surprising depths of feeling, where I felt a sudden sense of identity, of continuity, of coming home, of kinship, and yes, of pride in what our Jewish people have accomplished against unbelievable obstacles in an unbelievably brief space of time, and in the nobility and bravery and courage and self-sacrifice and altruism that they exhibit on all sides in this terrible time of trial and terror.

You know how I have always hated chauvinism and nationalism and jingoism and racial pride. I think now, however, lest you think me a throwback to chauvinism in some of these remarks, that love of country, and patriotism, and pride in one's people, need not be chauvinistic in the derogatory sense. One can have a *justifiable* pride in one's people, a passionate love for one's land, (like Miller attributes to the Greeks whom he has suddenly found and suddenly adores), a self-sacrificing behavior for one's group, without necessarily diminishing the virtues and qualities of others. Without, in other words, assuming that the other side of the coin of that pride is a derogation of others, or a vain and dangerous sense of "uber mensch". *Justifiable pride is not racism.*

In Israel we found more that the beauties of landscape, or the intellectual stimulus of historicity, or the aesthetic thrills of art and tradition. We had been to Paris and the south of France, to Arles and Avignon, to Cannes and Antibes, to the magnificence of Florence and the excitement of Rome. We had visited the Pitti Palace, and the Uffizzi galleries, the Ponte Vecchio and the Piazzale de Michaelangiola. We saw the David in Florence and the Moses in Rome, and castles and chateaux in France, and churches in Paris and Chartres and Florence and Aix en Provence and Rome, and statues and monuments all over France and Italy, and beautiful rivers and landscapes and mountains and high gorges. All of it very thrilling, believe me. I don't think you can find a more enthusiastic tourist than I am. But all of it was involved with seeing *things*—beautiful things, historic things, landmark things, exciting things, artistic things, and the environmental beauty all around. But in Israel we were immediately drawn not to things (although Israel abounds in beauty of landscape and environment, in artifacts and history and tradition and art), but to the essential, *people*—people in continuous struggle for that which has been the concern of man since time began. Israel immediately and forcefully strikes you as dynamic, fluid, open-ended, diverse, argumentative, questioning, experimental, seeking, tolerant, and intolerant—like America may have been before and during our Revolution of 1776, or before the Western frontier was closed. Our covered-wagon people may have had some of the qualities of modern Israel. The difference between the visit to Israel and anywhere else is the difference between being an observer, even an enthusiastic and appreciative one, and getting personally and emotionally involved in a deep and transcendental way.

We arrived in Tel Aviv on November 15, just a few weeks after the cease fire was signed. Tourism was at a standstill. The peace was (and still is) very fragile. Full mobilization still prevailed and the streets were empty of young men and women, except the few one saw on leave, tired looking and dressed in tired battle fatigues, tommy gun slung over one shoulder, trying to hitch-hike a ride home. Our hotel, like all the others, had only a handful of guests. Services were cut to the bone, but that did not prevent them from setting out their famous Israeli breakfast for us (a long smorgasbord of delicacies) in the dining room where only four of us sat among tables that could accommodate three hundred. "We're ready, just in case", the waiter said, "soldiers drop in, who knows, we like to be ready." We were welcomed warmly wherever we went, as people thanked us for having the courage to visit them at this time, and to show our solidarity in this way!

We rented a car and drove by ourselves around the country—Tel Aviv, Jerusalem, the Masada on the Dead Sea, Haifa, Caesaria, Netanya, Tiberias, the Sea of Galilee, the mountain town of Safad, Nazareth, even to the military lines on the Golan Heights, where we were turned back by Israeli soldier patrols just a few miles from the Syrian front. We picked up hitch-hiking soldiers all the time (there were always many of them on the road, crowding every bus stop, as the limited transportation facilities tried vainly to meet the need.) We spoke with them when we could, in Yiddish, or French, or English, and developed a strong admiration for these brave and courageous people, rising again to the need to defend their country, and performing incredible feats of heroism on both fronts against fantastic odds. They were attacked, caught unaware on their holiest day, by a fanatic and heavily-armed foe of over one million, on two separate fronts, the enemy had the important element of surprise on its side, yet the Israelis came up again with what was nothing less than a military miracle, turning the invaders back, defeating the attacking forces and pushing them back into their own territory, all in just a few weeks. And then, unheard of in any war ancient or modern, they permitted a defeated army of twenty thousand invaders, who had been hell bent for their destruction, to remain intact. Unable to fight, defeated and surrounded, Egypt's third army was nevertheless saved from surrendering, and was further allowed to be succored and fed without any assurance whatsoever that they will not, after their rest and recuperation, be attacking Israel again! The politics of this anomaly are too complex to enter now, but will certainly be the subject of analysis and argument for a long time to come.

On the home front people carry on as usual, life bustling in the lively cafes on the Dizengoff in Tel Aviv, political discussion everywhere and all the time—a vital evidence of the grass-roots nature of this democracy, where, during a war that might very well end their existence, a free-for-all political discussion goes on with passionate intensity on every level, in the Knesset, in the papers, on the streets, in the cafes, everywhere people gather; no holds are barred and all opinions are heard, including strident calls for the resignation of the government, loud and persistent demonstrations on the prisoner of war issue (Israel has returned over 8,000 Egyptian prisoners in return for under 300 Israelis captured by the Egyptians, while Syria still refuses even to give the names of its prisoners to the Red Cross or to anyone else! Moshe Dayan says that there are no prisoners on the Syrian front, that the Syrians, butchers like the Nazis, have tortured and killed all they held. Mutilated bodies discovered on the Golan Heights after the Syrians retreated seem to support this view.) All manner of opinions are heard about the captured Third Army, the occupied territories, doves, hawks, the talks at Km 101, America's position, the enmity of Soviet Russia, the responsibility of the Government, or its irresponsibility, Kissinger (was he a friend who sent arms in the nick of time, or an enemy who forced them to stop fighting just when victory seemed within their grasp?), and so on, and on, and on. But all, everywhere, are supremely dedicated to Israel, to their country, to their Statehood, to the justice of their cause, and determined to fight on, alone if necessary, to whatever end. This determination stands out above all else. It is visible, palpable, everywhere. The sad thing is that once again, mankind is short on morality; the rest of the world is indifferent to the Jewish people, justice or no justice, and just as they gave only lip-service to the six million victims of the Nazi holocaust, they will no doubt find it possible to view with equanimity the murder of another three million for the sake of Arab oil. But one thing is sure: Israeli Jews will not go meekly into the gas ovens of their enemies!

We had a beautiful visit, warm and moving, with two old friends from New York, who, with their four young children, settled in Israel eleven years ago, at their house on a cooperative agricultural settlement in Avihail. They have three kids at the front (their daughter in the medics and two boys in "Africa"). Like all the others they are firm and brave. But like all other parents they suffer the pangs of anxiety and the torment of waiting for news, as this period of no-war and no-peace, of indecision and anxiety, continues to drain the patience and to test the endurance.

The highlight of our stay in Israel was the week we spent on a Kibbutz. This was the showplace Kibbutz of the country, Ginosar, situated near the old city of Tiberias, on the shore of the beautiful Sea of Galilee. Across the lake (called Kinneret because it is shaped like a harp) lie the pink mountains of the Golan Heights, from which we could still hear the occasional sounds of exploding shells. This Kibbutz of over 500 members in normal times, now manages, with its best young people off at the fronts, with the invaluable help of a group of young international volunteers. Ginosar lies only ten miles from the furthest Syrian advance in the first days of the Yom Kippur war and it is only by a miracle that it was not taken. We were practically the only guests there at the time, and were so warmly received and taken in by these hospitable, dedicated, marvelous people— both the regular kibbutzim and the young volunteers (English, Danish, Dutch youths, Australians, South Africans, and a few Americans) who come to spend a month, or a year, living, working, learning and growing in this communal atmosphere.

More than half the volunteers, incidentally, are non-Jewish. Most are non-Zionist. Their reasons for coming are diverse. But whatever the original stimulus, they are quickly caught up in the spirit of the enterprise, the humane-ness of the Kibbutz. We became particularly friendly with a young girl from Cleveland, who had come originally for six months, has been there now for over a year, and finds that she cannot leave now, during this war crisis, because it would be deserting her friends and betraying her self-imposed sense of responsibility. "When peace comes," she says, "and they no longer need me as they do now, I'll think of going home."

The Kibbutz itself is an astounding phenomenon. Its basic slogan and guide for living is actually Marx's ideal: "From each according to his ability, to each according to his needs." When one considers that this is taking place sanctioned, and indeed assisted, by a capitalist government, with the complete tolerance of others in the vast majority, who may find this communal existence abhorrent to them, in a tiny nation of only three and one half million people, completely voluntarily, with members free to leave whenever they decide they would prefer another type of life, with membership available as a privilege only to those accepted by the Kibbutz itself acting in complete and open democracy, within a society that offers more diversity of living styles than our own large and secure country, it gives you some idea of the vitality of Israel, the choices open to its citizens, and the dynamic quality of its search for new and better forms of human relationships. Kibbutzim, moshavim, city dwellers, shopkeepers, factory workers and factory owners, land developers, speculators, builders, farmers, students, teachers, academicians and scientists, and 45 different cultures drawn from all parts of the world (from the sophisticated and educated Westerners to the masses of refugees from North Africa, Tunisia, Morocco, Iraq, Iran) building a vibrant, stable, and open society— in a fantastically short space of time, all the while under the guns of implacable and unreasonable foes.

If Karl Marx were alive today, I am sure he would find the Kibbutz of Israel closer to his humanistic dream than the repressive "Marxism" of the Soviet Union.

I could go on and on . . . the Hebrew University, with its campus, fantastic and impressive, artistic and beautiful, on a magnificent height overlooking all of Jerusalem; the new and stately Knesset; the Israel Museum, with the most exciting sculpture display anywhere in the world, outdoors, in a magnificent natural setting, the pieces silhouetted against the blue sky—Rodin, Picasso, Maillol, Jacques Lipschitz, Calder (in what is called the Billy Rose Garden, by the way, contributed by our own Billy Rose); the jewel-like city of Haifa on the Carmel mountain range, overlooking the Mediterranean. And the unforgettable memorial to the six million victims of Hitler, a place called Yad Vashem, high on a windy hill, somber and haunting, where a Hall of Remembrance documents in terrifying photographs and grisly memorabilia of the death camps and the ovens, the greatest crime in the long brutal history of man, and where an eternal light glows in a dimly lit chamber in memory of these dead.

How many still remember? Most, I am afraid, have already forgotten. And now there is the danger that all of these accomplishments, built with the blood, sweat, and unquenchable spirit of a people that would not be destroyed, might be wiped away in an orgy of violence and irrationality.

Will the still unfulfilled potential that is Israel become a dead relic—like the remains of the Parthenon, and Knossus . . . for the wonderment of future visitors, if there are any of us left?

These were some of our thoughts as we left Israel, on the day after the death of Ben-Gurion. It seemed symbolic. The truly noble figure, the giant of Israel, dead at the very moment his people are engaged again in the life and death struggle to continue what he helped to establish.

We have one more week here in Crete. We are happy for the opportunity to rest and to enjoy the beauty and the tranquility and the unbelievable opulence of these surroundings. But I already miss reading the Jerusalem Post and the news of Israel and the fast moving events in the Middle East, and the sense of involvement (more wishful than actual, in point of fact) in the vital, seminal, intense Israeli scene. What the world lacks most is the sense of humanity. Brotherhood is still so far away, while petty and vain and self-seeking concerns, competitiveness and status, still hold sway over the hearts of men.

The Israeli Kibbutz, I feel, is at least a tentative movement in the opposite direction. If it were destroyed, along with the rest of vibrant Israel, it would be still another crime against humanity, and we would all, all of us, be the poorer.

February 11, 1974
The Addicts' Cycle
The New York Times

Consider this:

(1) An aroused public, properly alerted to the dangers of drug addiction, clamors for, and succeeds in establishing, rehabilitation projects for the treatment and cure of addicts. This, eventually, results in . . .

(2) " . . . tens of thousands of rehabilitated addicts emerging from treatment programs in New York City alone." When these cured addicts look for work they find . . .

(3) " . . . widespread, irrational discrimination" against their employment, according to a special report of the Temporary State Commission to Evaluate the Drug Laws. "Most major corporations will not consider reformed addicts for jobs on their merits," the report states. This results in . . .

(4) " . . . the grave risk that the money expended for treatment will have been wasted." They may have to resort to welfare and "through forced inactivity some of them are bound to slip back to unlawful drug use."

Which brings us back full cycle to number 1.

This despite the fact that the same study found that rehabilitated addicts who had "spent a period of time in treatment are either indistinguishable from or even better than other workers with similar capacities."

If it is too naive in these times to look for compassion and humaneness to correct this patent absurdity, is it also too much to hope that ordinary, practical common sense will prevail?

July 6, 1974
Nixon stock 'hardly rising'
The Times Herald Record

It was astonishing to read, in William F. Buckley's column that "at this moment his (President Nixon's) stock is rising, very fast."

Either Mr. Buckley has access to public opinion polls not available to the rest of us, or, more likely, this is a feeble attempt to minimize the deep fundamental difficulties of the Nixon administration through the wildest flights of wishful thinking.

Jeb Magruder and Charles Colson are in jail, Dwight Chapin is appealing his jail sentence, Egil Krogh has just come out, Ehrlichman and Haldeman are facing trial as burglars and soon, along with John Mitchell and others, they will face another jury for their part in the Watergate cover-up; President Nixon himself is being investigated on several levels for, among others things, his role in the unauthorized bombing of Cambodia, his personal tax returns, his role in the ITT and the milk cases, his possible use of the IRS to harass political opponents, and, unprecedented in the history of the American presidency, he has been named by a grand jury as an "unindicted co-conspirator!"

But, according to Mr. Buckley "his stock is rising very fast!"

Since Mr. Buckley suggests a comparison between President Nixon and Henry Kissinger to sustain his tenuous logic, let us pursue his own analogy further:

Kissinger reacted to an attack on his credibility by offering, indeed threatening, to resign unless he secured what amounts to a vote of confidence from the government he serves. Perhaps Nixon, whose credibility has all but disappeared and whose presidency has suffered an erosion of confidence unprecedented in our history, might be advised to do likewise.

Or could it be, as The New York Times suggested, that those who should not resign threaten to, while those who should, do not?

July 13, 1974
PLO blocks just peace
The Times Herald Record

Amid reports that the Arab League has agreed to assist Lebanon and the Palestine Liberation Organization against Israel, and "unconfirmed reports" of U.S. pressure on Israel, it is important to reiterate that the best, and perhaps the only, way to stop the Israeli attacks on the PLO guerrilla bases in Lebanon is to stop the unprovoked PLO attacks on innocent civilians, women, and schoolchildren in Israel.

All responsible reporters have referred to the Israeli actions as "retaliatory," as "reprisal attacks," that have taken place only in response to PLO terror and murder. Quiryat Shmono, Nahariya, where seven were killed only last week, and Maalot, where school children were held hostage and then murdered in their classroom, are only the latest in a series of PLO outrages and slaughters, that included the murder of Israeli athletes at the Olympics, murders in airports in Rome, Athens, and around the world, and in Khartoum where two American diplomats were killed.

It must be remembered that Israeli attacks have taken place against the Lebanese camps only in response to these PLO murders and as a direct consequence of what your recent editorial (TH-Record 7/2) described as the PLO "commitment to terrorism against civilian targets," and their persistent "use of Lebanon as a staging area for raids into Israel." (NY Times 7/7).

It is not so long ago that world public opinion was either too impotent or too indifferent to prevent the slaughter of six million Jews in Europe. Although the martyred millions cannot be restored, the world-wide pressure of decent humanity today can and must be brought to bear on that minority of Arab murderers and terrorists in the PLO who stand in the way of a just, peace in the Middle East.

July 20, 1974
Israel & the PLO
The Times Herald Record

The difference between the approach of the Israeli government and the leadership of the Palestine Liberation Organization to the problems that divide them was thrown into sharp and illuminating relief last week.

The Israeli government, through its minister of information, Aharon Yariv, offered to negotiate with the Palestinians, to start the process that would eliminate the disastrous raid and counter-raid situation that is wreaking such havoc on both sides.

The Israelis, Mr. Yariv said, are ready to negotiate if the PLO "declared its readiness to enter negotiations while acknowledging the existence of a Jewish state here in Israel," and terminated all hostile actions against Israel. (NY Times, 7/14). A Palestine leader responded by calling the conditions "impossible" and a "mockery" and by referring again to the PLO "goal of the liberation of Palestine."

Israel's conditions are, in fact, no more than would be put forward by any sovereign state in the world (unless it were expected to negotiate its own destruction!) The negative PLO response, on the other hand, reflects the rigid and discredited position of "no recognition, no peace, and no negotiations" which has for so many years characterized the Arab stance, and which has always been the major obstacle to a mid-East settlement.

With major Arab nations (Egypt, Syria, Jordan) softening their position, and with the upcoming Geneva Conference holding forth the promise, at last, of mutual accommodations leading toward a lasting peace, the initiative of Israel vis-a-vis the Palestinians deserves widespread applause.

It is to be hoped that the PLO official response turns out to be more rational, that it abandons its rigid turn-the-clock back view of the "liberation of Palestine" (which sounds like it means the destruction of the state of Israel), and that it enters the negotiations that are proffered for a just solution for both the Arab and the Jewish people.

August 3, 1974
Insight into Nixon ethic
The Times Herald Record

William Safire's column of July 19, which he calls "A lesson in political loyalty," is a provocative example of amorality, unbridled cynicism, and a studied ethical obtuseness that strikes a new low even in these days of Watergate revelations. It should give us all much food for thought.

Mr. Safire seeks to present President Nixon as a man of uncommon virtue because he believes in "political loyalty." Unlike Eisenhower, who fired an aide (Sherman Adams) when he was found to be influence-peddling (Nixon saw this, we are told, not as a moral act on the part of Eisenhower, but as "abandoning a loyal supporter"), Nixon, when faced with similar problems, "loyally, sentimentally, wrongly, dug in his heels," saying, "We're going to protect our people, if we can."

No matter that "his people" were guilty of obstruction of justice, that they lied to grand juries and to congressional committees, that they committed burglary and robbery, perjury and bribery, that they had subverted the electoral process by illegal campaign activities and misuse of election funds, that some had already been convicted of crimes against the people of the United States. Nixon saw it as more important "to protect our people" than to carry out his constitutional mandate to "take care that the laws be faithfully executed."

Safire sees merit in John Mitchell's behavior, when, "his memory conveniently fuzzy on most matters", he nevertheless "reaches heights of total recall" to help the President from being implicated in the Hunt payment matter. Nowhere does Safire mention Truth, or Justice, or Morality, or the welfare of the country.

Unwittingly, perhaps, Safire has provided us with a profound insight into the fundamental ethic of Richard Nixon. It is the ethic of the self-serving politician and opportunist, the manipulator, the power-broker. It is the kind of ethic that makes it inevitable that he give more importance to the "political loyalty" required of and to his henchmen (no matter what their crimes) than to the welfare of the people of the United States whom he was sworn to serve.

August 17, 1974
Doesn't appreciate Buckley 'lecture'
The Times Herald Record

William F. Buckley Jr., who only a few weeks ago exhibited his skill at prediction by stating that "Mr. Nixon's stock is rising . . . fast," now, even after the deluge, has the unmitigated gall to lecture those who would apply the American principle of equal justice under the law to private citizen Nixon, as failing to "understand the moral character of the problem!"

Anyone who still has the temerity to refer to Watergate as "a little scandal in his household" is hardly qualified to lecture the rest of us on "morality."

For it is precisely "moral character" that is at the heart of the issue. President Ford sensed it keenly when he referred not to "a little scandal" but to "our long national nightmare" and when he received prolonged applause in his first major address as he spoke of "a higher plane of public morality" and of "exemplary official conduct."

Mr. Buckley's continued sleazy defense of Nixon is an outrageous affront to our intelligence. And his casual assumption of a magisterial and judicial stance (with what authority one can only wonder!) as he seeks to place Mr. Nixon above the ordinary processes of law, should alert us all to the continuing need to see to it that the real lessons of Watergate are not lost.

We must never forget how perilously close we came to losing our democratic heritage and our liberties to a corrupt and power-hungry cabal, whose stock in trade was exactly that double standard of law and accountability that Mr. Buckley now seeks to perpetuate a little longer. The only way to keep our liberties and our system of justice intact is to hold fast to one rule of law and to see to it that it applies to all citizens equally and fairly. That means that it must apply to ex office-holders just as well as to all the rest of us.

September 21, 1974
Calls pardon a 'mockery'
The Times Herald Record

President Ford's injudicious and untimely pardon of Richard Nixon has dashed our hopes for a return to some semblance of "domestic tranquility," and has aroused ugly suspicions of a continuing cover-up—this time by our new President acting in collusion with our disgraced ex-President on the very same issues on which the latter was forced from office.

It is difficult to conceive an act more calculated to discredit President Ford's new regime, unless it is the horrendous implication that all the Watergate defendants are also to be pardoned!

What a mockery of justice! The very meaning of the word, pardon, is turned on its head. "Pardon," which has always been a means of mercy applied to the guilty, is here applied to a man who steadfastly and in the face of known facts, refuses to admit any criminal guilt.

And Ford, playing Nixon's game, is careful not to impute any guilt as he pardons Nixon in advance of any legal determination of the issue, thus preventing forever the definitive verdict of guilt or innocence which history demands and which the American people deserve. Ford's pardon has the calculated effect of preventing any disclosure of just what Nixon was, or was not, guilty of, in the Watergate and in other criminal matters.

Reasonable men, of course, can make some reasonable assumptions: A pardon, by definition, is needed only if one is guilty. Where there is innocence, no pardon is necessary. And it is precisely this determination, which can be made unequivocally only by the due process of law, that President Ford seems bent on preventing.

Pardon before the full and open establishment of the facts in the case smacks of a continuing cover-up and will stick in the public's craw. Even President Ford's old friend, and first appointee, J.F. terHorst, couldn't stomach it. His immediate disgust, and his quick resignation in protest, will reflect the reaction of millions of Americans.

November 10, 1974
Toward Morality in Government
The New York Times

F. E. Masland Jr., in suggesting in a recent letter that "what this nation needs are far more managers in government," implies that our problems are technical and managerial and would be readily solved if only the proper technological know-how were applied. This know-how, he assumes, is in the hands, and heads, of the managerial and technological elite, and it is to them that we ought to turn for solutions.

I suggest that Mr. Masland misses the central point of our age, which is that while we have no lack of technological skill (enough to put a man on the moon, or to increase food production on an unprecedented scale if we chose to, rather than subsidize farmers *not* to produce), what we lack is a clear recognition of our moral imperatives. It is morality and purpose, humanism and a profound sense of the needs of all of our people, that this nation needs in government—not simply "managers" skilled in the ways of assembly-line production and dedicated to the holiness of corporate growth.

Last November, at Congressional hearings on his nomination for the Vice-Presidency, Gerald Ford was asked what he thought were "the characteristics most needed by a President." His profound reply was that "he should be a person of great truthfulness" and that "the people should know he is telling the truth." The country, in other words, desperately needed a President who was not a liar. What a commentary on the political morality to which this country had sunk—and from which it has not yet recovered.

No, it is not managerial skill this country needs. All the skills we possess have not yet solved the problems of inflation, unemployment, poverty amid plenty and corruption in government, to name but a few. What we need, and desperately, is a massive infusion of honesty and morality both in government and in our national life in general—a morality that places the highest priority on the welfare of all of our people, rather than favor the interests of the privileged few.

March 1, 1975
'An absurd arms control'
The Times Herald Record

The absurdity of that quaint and curious human custom known as war was never more sharply illuminated than by two recent events:

First was the signing by President Ford and Soviet Party chief Brezhnev of an accord in Vladivostok agreeing to a limitation of 1320 MIRV nuclear missiles each. Defense Secretary Schlesinger has already announced that the Soviet Union is beginning to deploy these multiple warhead nuclear bombs, while the United States, which already has 800 in position, will presumably build up to the maximum 1320 allowed under the agreement.

The second event is our signing—finally—of a 1925 treaty prohibiting the use of poison gas.

The logic here truly boggles the mind. We calmly approve of weaponry which, even with the limitations so solemnly imposed, can result in 100 million deaths in both the United States and Russia (according to Pentagon estimates), while we piously outlaw poison gas because it causes "unnecessary suffering, particularly upon civilian populations."

Presumably the 100 million people who will be killed by MIRVs, Minutemen and Poseidon missiles, and by the new Russian SS 19s, will not suffer "unnecessarily," or "cruelly," as would those done in by poison gas!

The operative morality here is worth pondering: A misguided sense of self-interest, plus the corruption and cynicism that seem to accompany enormous power, appear to override both morality and rationality, so that otherwise sensible men approve of a means of human genocide, while the disturbing demands of at least a minimum morality impels them, simultaneously, to outlaw the "cruelties" of an infinitely less threatening method of killing.

March 15, 1975
Haldeman, CBS and morality
The Times Herald Record

One looks in vain throughout the length of James Reston's recent column on "CBS And Haldeman" for any mention of the moral issues involved. Morality as a consideration is, in fact, conspicuously absent.

But is it not obscene when a convicted felon, perjurer, and corrupter of the political and governmental process at the highest level, is rewarded with a $25,000 fee for a one hour TV appearance, and, perhaps even more important, is given access to millions of American homes to polish up his tarnished image and to ingratiate himself with the American public?

If reward and punishment are viewed in balance, the punishment meted out in Judge Sirica's courtroom will almost seem like a mere token when compared with the emoluments and status conferred on Haldeman by CBS.

But Reston seems to be concerned only with the monetary-commercial aspects of the affair. "Haldeman has every right," he states, "to sell his story to the highest bidder." He is worried only about the "little stations that can't afford to pay the freight."

But the issue, I suggest, goes far deeper than this crass commercialism—a commercialism so morally blind and ethically corrupt it will compete unashamedly for any performer as long as he can turn a corporate profit on a sponsored broadcast.

The issue goes to the enormous opinion-molding and character-molding power of television, pointed up a long time ago by Professor Marshall McLuhan when he stressed the role of the media in actually "altering the way we think and act." "All media work us over completely," he wrote, "The medium is the massage."

In granting this tremendous power to mold opinion and character to a convicted expert in political and ethical perversion, CBS does a grave injustice to the American people.

Those responsible should not be allowed to escape their moral accountability.

March 29, 1975
Inflexibility called myth
The Times Herald Record

It would be morally unjust and politically indefensible if, as a result of the breakdown of the Egypt-Israeli disengagement talks, the United States were to retreat from its firm and just policy of support for the State of Israel.

Since this possibility is tied to the question of blame in the failure of the talks (no matter how much Kissinger may publicly deny it), it is relevant to consider those facts we do have and to scotch once and for all the destructive and false myth of "Israeli inflexibility."

In all the columns of print, what emerges clearly and unequivocally is this: Israel is willing to return the strategic Sinai passes, and the Abu Rudeis oil fields (which supply Israel with about half its current oil consumption). In return Egypt is asked only to issue a statement "ending the state of war." This Egypt refuses to do. It demands the passes, the oil fields, and other territorial concessions, but, even if granted, refuses even then to end the "state of belligerency."

If language means anything at all, the "non-belligerency" statement Israel demands is, and has always been, the goal of all peace negotiators in any war, anywhere, in all history. Granting "non-belligerency," or an end to the "state of war" is not a concession one side makes to the other. It is a mutually necessary condition for peace, the sine-qua-non on which all other concessions, compromises and agreements are based.

It is an agreement each side makes to the other, without which no settlement is possible. After all, what sort of "peace settlement" would it be if one side insists on maintaining a "state of war."

It should be crystal clear to the American people that it is not "Israeli inflexibility" that persists in this untenable and unreasonable position. It is the paradox of Egypt attempting a "peace settlement" that insists on continuing a "state of war" with a nation whose very existence it steadfastly refuses to recognize.

April 12, 1975
'Thieu lacks viability'
The Times Herald Record

Congratulations. Your Sunday editorials were first rate.

The debacle of U.S. policy in Vietnam and the chilling emergence of the United States as the number one arms merchant to the world, are surely not unconnected phenomena.

It has become clear to most Americans that American policy in Vietnam addressed itself almost exclusively to the military situation and responded in purely military terms, while we ignored, to our own peril it turned out, the essential political realities and the moral-ethical considerations involved.

South Vietnam's disaster resulted not from a lack of U.S. arms or because America had turned traitor, as a desperate Thieu would have the world believe, but because Thieu has simply been unable to establish a viable regime which could command the respect and support of his own people.

In our over-all foreign policy position as number one arms merchant of the world, supplying huge amounts of weaponry to nations of disparate policies and purposes, we again stress militarism and destructive capacity, rather than morality, values, and human purpose. Like the profiteering gun merchant whose only concern is the volume of business, we sell arms to friend and potential foe alike. In the past year alone we sold five billion dollars in arms and training services to Iran and Saudi Arabia, our major adversary in the oil cartel. Either side in many conflicts around the world can buy their arms from the number one dealer, our even-handedness and unconcern about purpose a glaring exposure of our moral pretensions. It is pretty difficult, after all, to be the big gun seller and the big peacemaker at one and the same time!

May 17, 1975
Bicentennial barrages
The Times Herald Record

Now that the Bicentennial has begun, we can look forward to a barrage of oratory from both the right and left. The former will mouth emptily the noble ideals of the American Revolution; while the latter will extend justified criticism about America's shameful role in Indochina.

But, perhaps, the Bicentennial may yet serve as an impetus to a more rational re-examination of America's history; not as a phony Fourth of July oration by an aspiring politician nor as a slashing indictment born of disillusionment with our recent foreign policy.

Now may be a time to rediscover the truly revolutionary role once played by a young American republic in a world of monarchical rule and aristocratic privilege. And, it could be a time to revive the original American sense of the common man.

With the end of the disgraceful war in Indochina, an end brought about in no small part by the mobilization of the common man in America, we are at another historical crossroad. We have an opportunity to turn away from the imperial American image created in Vietnam and Cambodia, as well as the decadent image of Watergate. We can return to an America reminiscent of the populist, democratic era of Jefferson and Paine, Jackson and Lincoln, Emerson, Thoreau and Whitman.

June 11, 1975
Malpractice: Toward a Solution
The New York Times

Dr. Bernard Jacobs' remark that "the best interests of our patients and our profession . . . are essentially identical" (letter June 4) belongs alongside the statement of that other famous altruist who said, "What's good for General Motors is good for the country."

For who can be so cynical as to doubt that it was the doctors' fervent concern for their patients' welfare that prompted their powerful A.M.A. to fight tooth and nail throughout the years against Social Security, against H.I.P or any other form of prepaid group health insurance, public or private? Who can doubt that the doctors' only concern was to preserve and protect the uniquely independent joy experienced by their patients as they paid their astronomical private fees, happy, secure and free from the Marxian specter of government control, Bolshevism and, Heaven (and the A.M.A.) forbid, socialized medicine.

The doctors' passionate complaints against high legal fees sounds curiously like the pot calling the kettle black. And their pious call for government action to regulate and reduce insurance fees and legal fees would be more persuasive if they went a step further and included medical fees as well. As the old saying goes, "People in glass houses . . . ." or should it be, "Physician, heal thyself!"

What we need is a Carey "high-level commission" to investigate the high malpractice insurance fees and the high legal fees with special regard to their impact on high medical fees—not to protect one of these rip-off artists from the other two, but to protect the long-suffering public from all three.

July 26, 1975
'Buckley continues defense of Nixon'
The Times Herald Record

William F. Buckley Jr., still relying on his fabled skill at word—mongering and obfuscation, and on his supreme confidence in the short memory of the American people, continues his determined and hypocritical defense of Richard Nixon.

"The sin of Richard Nixon", he insists (column of July 11) was that he was simply "clumsy and tasteless." No more!

Can Mr. Buckley seriously ask us to believe that is all? After the convictions of Haldeman and Ehrlichman and Mitchell? After the imprisonment of Dean and Magruder, Colson and Krogh, among others? After Nixon himself was named as an "unindicted co-conspirator" and was spared trial and probable conviction only by a merciful pardon by the man he named to succeed him? After his own humiliating resignation in the face of imminent impeachment?

Mr. Buckley is either audacious, or insulting to our intelligence, or both, to expect us to accept his assessment.

If the post-Watergate re-examination of our national morals and ethics is to be meaningful and illuminating, the sleazy defenses of Mr. Buckley ought to be exposed for what they are—a shameless repetition of the moral bankruptcy so shockingly revealed by both Haldeman and Ehrlichman when they suggested in the hearings that anything was justified, no matter how immoral or illegal, as long as it perpetuated the power of their leader, Richard Nixon. As they saw it, any means justified their particular ends.

Mr. Buckley's column illustrated again that there are those who, impervious to the lessons of history, will attempt to manipulate and distort the past in order to emasculate our peoples' victory over Nixonian corruption.

One can only hope that our memory and our vigilance will make this impossible. Only thus will the ordeal and the agony of Watergate not have been in vain.

August 9, 1975
'Daytop story: Hope & trust'
The Times Herald Record

The Daytop Village message is a message, essentially, of hope and trust: Hope for those caught in the quicksands of drug addiction, and trust in the continuing viability of the old virtues of honesty, love, caring, and human concern.

For it is on the solid ground of these old (but, alas, neglected) values that Daytop has built its "therapeutic community" and forged its therapeutic program. In the process, it has rediscovered that warm human involvement, and loving human support, given authentically one to the other, can overcome seemingly insoluble difficulties.

In rediscovering these values in the process of curing drug addiction. Daytop may be rediscovering for us all some long neglected axioms of humane behavior.

For if "responsible love" and a humanizing group experience can change and rehabilitate a junkie's character and personality, perhaps they also contain a message of importance for all the rest of us.

Member, Board of Trustees,
Daytop Village

April 24, 1976
'Drug cuts sham & delusion'
The Times Herald Record

The New York State Legislature has voted a cut of almost one-third in the funding of anti drug-abuse treatment centers. Not only does this represent a callous indifference to human need, but it is also irresponsible and deceptive from a purely hard-nosed, fiscal point of view.

The budget cuts will return thousands of addicts either to prison or to the streets. In prison they will cost the taxpayers $18,000 each per year. In state juvenile detention centers like Goshen, they cost $28,000 each per year for "what amounts to custodial care," according to The New York Times. While out on the streets, back on drugs, they will add to the frightening increase in crime.

In sharp contrast, the anti-drug, therapeutic community treatment centers cost about $6,000 per year per resident and have shown a remarkable success in rehabilitation. (92 per cent of the graduates of Daytop Village, for example, have remained free of drugs and are pursuing useful lives in the community. Many are devoting their lives to helping other addicts.)

Presented as a savings to the taxpayer, the budget cuts are thus a sham and a delusion. They will not save the taxpayer a dime. On the contrary, they will cost us millions more in increased prison costs and in the cost of street crime. And they will condemn thousands of young people, caught in the misery of drug abuse, to lives of despair and hopelessness—and to early death.

It is not too late for the Legislature to restore the cuts, in the name of both humanity and of common sense. Let us not play politics with human lives.

Member, board of trustees,
Daytop Village

Podhoretz and COMMENTARY

Dear Sir:

Norman Podhoretz, in his autobiographical "Making It", tells the story of his friend William Phillips who "once told the New Left-minded English critic Kenneth Tynan that he could not argue with him about politics, because Tynan's arguments were so old that he, Phillips, could no longer remember the answers." One gets a similar feeling in reading Podhoretz' article in the April Commentary. But along with this weird sense of déjà vu and a growing irritation at Podhoretz' glib Monday-morning quarterbacking, there emerges the gnawing fear, and finally the certainty, that in "retrospectively justifying McCarthyism for having brought home the Communist threat", as Christopher Lehmann-Haupt put it in the New York Times (4/15), Podhoretz is sounding the call for a repeat performance. To paraphrase Podhoretz himself, he appears to be indulging, if not wallowing, in a "return of the repressed clichés" of the fifties.

It is surely no accident that Podhoretz was promptly and enthusiastically embraced by William F. Buckley, Jr, who patronizingly presented him in his widely syndicated column as "the lesson for today", while making sure to point out that he, Buckley, was "five years" ahead of him in the same endeavor. In this atmosphere, Vice-President Rockefeller "revealed" that Senator Jackson's staff had been "infiltrated" by a Communist and that "another aide had Communist leanings". When he found it necessary to apologize to the Senate and to Senator Jackson, he did so not because of any revulsion at the renewal of this McCarthyist character assassination or its implications, but only because his charges were "unsubstantiated"!

Was it not Podhoretz who said, in *Making It*, that he had been "caught up on the side of the hard anti-Communists . . . and it shames me to say that I shared fully in their brutal insensitivity on this issue . . . the persecution to which so many people were being subjected in the early fifties . . ."? Can Mr. Podhoretz now be unaware that his new anti-Communism is the very same "hard anti-Communism" he ascribed to Elliott Cohen and the old Commentary, of which he was later to be "ashamed" and which inexorably leads him now to similar dilemmas?

Having decided that, after all, the anti-Communists were more in the right (no pun intended) than the anti-anti-Communists, as the anti-McCarthy liberals were dubbed, Podhoretz, in retrospect, bemoans the liberal victory over the "imperial Presidency" of Richard Nixon, laments the exposure of the lawlessness of the CIA, finds our support of fascists like Franco, Salazar, Park and Thieu "prudential", and even "moral", applauds the CIA when it intervenes in Italian electoral politics, and finally suggests that the United States was "not wrong in the purposes" for which it fought the Vietnam War (although he does not make it too clear how the "purpose" was right while the war was wrong).

Of course, there is a certain consistency in all this, just as there was a consistency in Elliott Cohen's "Grand Design" for the old Commentary of the fifties—which Podhoretz vowed to change and which he was later to criticize for its "crippling rigidity". If the Communists are indeed "the most determined and ferocious and barbarous enemies of liberty ever to have appeared on the earth" (is Hitler losing this honor, is the Holocaust being downgraded in the hierarchy of evil? Or does Podhoretz intend here a posthumous rehabilitation of Hitler as the most reliable and prescient anti-Communist of them all?), then anti-Communists of all kinds would do well to grab allies wherever they may find them. And it would be foolish to undermine such valuable and powerful allies as the CIA (Buckley joins Podhoretz here in lauding "the CIA's role in helping the anti-Communist fraternity everywhere in the world during the post-war years"), as well as the "imperial Presidency"—both powerful weapons indeed. Maybe we were also foolish to have destroyed such steadfast anti-Communists as the friends and supporters of our "prudential" ally Franco, Mussolini (who might have saved us from those Italian Communists!) and Hitler himself?

Podhoretz recommends a familiar scenario: suppression at home and reckless adventurism abroad, including interference in the internal affairs of other countries whenever and wherever we, or our unaccountable CIA, deem it advisable, all in the name of the anti-Communism of old, and with an amazing replication of the attitudes and stances of that other era: We must be wary of those who are "soft on Communism" and forgive the sins of those who can be relied upon to fight "Communists and their sympathizers, real and alleged, inside the government and out." The Podhoretz-Buckley-Commentary-National Review alliance will rally us to fight the Communist enemy, and we are not to worry excessively about our personal and political liberties here at home, or about pro-Communist (read here all who are not actively anti-Communist) casualties abroad.

Finally, the logic by which the so-called "literary intellectual" assumes a posture of expertise in matters far removed from literary criticism has always eluded me. "I had become a New York literary intellectual", Podhoretz exulted in *Making It*, having progressed from being a mere "Leavisian". Having attained that exalted station, mainly by the approval of his peers in "the family", the modifying "literary" is soon dropped, and lo and behold the former "literary intellectual" is now firmly installed as a full-fledged expert on political and economic theory, capitalism and socialism and communism, the problems of diplomacy, power politics, international relations, foreign policy, philosophy, ethics and history, with prognostication and evaluation of future events thrown in for good measure. How a background in Shakespeare, Joyce, Yeats and Proust, in the Romantic poets and the Victorian novelists, qualifies one for such a role is never quite explained.

Or may we not be persuaded that Podhoretz' opinions on these non-literary matters ought not to carry any greater weight than those of the rest of us—"literary intellectuals" and otherwise?

The fact is that Podhoretz' piece does a grave disservice to the cause of democracy in general and to the Jewish people in particular (when repression comes are we not always among the first victims?) by encouraging the forces of reaction both at home and abroad. While failing to advance a single viable suggestion for a policy of extending democracy and opposing Communist spread, he offers the best of ammunition to those who would destroy democracy wherever it exists.

August 1976
Commentary

... It is surely no accident that Norman Podhoretz's 'article' was promptly and enthusiastically embraced by William F. Buckley, Jr., who patronizingly presented him in his widely syndicated column as "the lesson for today" while making sure to point out that he, Buckley, was "five years" ahead in the same endeavor....

Mr. Podhoretz recommends a familiar scenario: suppression at home and reckless adventurism abroad, including interference in the internal affairs of other countries whenever and wherever we, or our unaccountable CIA, deem it advisable, all in the name of the anti-Communism of old, and with an amazing replication of the attitudes and stances of the 50's. We must be wary of those who are "soft on Communism" and forgive the sins of those who can be relied upon to fight "Communists and their sympathizers, real and alleged, inside the government and out." The Podhoretz-Buckley-COMMENTARY-*National Review* alliance will rally us to fight the Communist enemy, and we are not to worry excessively about our personal and political liberties here at home or about pro-Communist ... casualties abroad ...

The fact is that Mr. Podhoretz's piece does a grave disservice to the cause of democracy in general and to the Jewish people in particular (when repression comes, are we not always among the first victims?) by encouraging the forces of reaction both at home and abroad. While failing to advance a single viable suggestion for a policy of extending democracy and opposing Communist spread, he offers the best of ammunition to those who would destroy democracy wherever it exists.

NORMAN PODHORETZ writes:

Let me say, first of all, how grateful I am for the generosity with which so many of these letters treat "Making the World Safe for Communism" and how gratified I have been by the thoughtfulness of the response in general. I had, frankly, expected that there would be much name-calling and much vituperative misrepresentation of my argument, but very little of that kind of thing has turned up either in the letters I have received (of which the ones printed above are a representative sample) or the published comments I have seen. This in itself can be taken as a sign that things may not be quite as bad as Mr. Varon, Mr. Cox, and Mr. Grun all fear. A year or two ago an article as outspokenly anti-Communist as mine would almost certainly have been greeted with many more letters like Mr. Rangell's accusing me in effect of calling for a new McCarthyism, or like Mr. White's accusing me of hysteria and paranoia, or like Dr. Abramson's accusing me of failing to place sufficient emphasis on the sins and crimes of the United States. Today, however, it is evidently becoming possible to raise the issue of Communism without being shouted down or merely vilified and dismissed by McCarthyites of the Left.

August 5, 1976
Reply to Mr. Podhoretz—
not published by COMMENTARY

Dear Sir:

Mr. Norman Podhoretz's response to my letter criticizing his article, "Making the World Safe for Communism", deserves, in the interest of fairness, still another response.

Although he states that he was "gratified . . . by the thoughtfulness of the response in general", after he had "frankly, expected that there would be much name-calling and vituperative misrepresentation of my argument", Mr. Podhoretz proceeds to precisely such name-calling and vituperative misrepresentation of his own. He selectively emasculates my letter, and then "answers" it, not by addressing the issues raised, but, blithely unconcerned with the paradox in terms, by calling me a "McCarthyite of the left."

It is ironic, and perhaps instructive, that his only critical response (complaining of "Mr. Rangell's accusing me in effect of calling for a new McCarthyism") is directed toward that portion of my letter which Mr. Podhoretz saw fit to delete in the first place! (My original comments on Mr. Podhoretz and McCarthyism were in fact based in part on an evaluation by the admirable book-critic, Mr. Christopher Lehmann-Haupt, whom I had quoted as saying of Mr. Podhoretz that he "retrospectively justified McCarthyism for having brought home the Communist threat" [New York Times, 4/15/76]).

Mr. Podhoretz also saw fit to omit the larger portion of my communication which concerned itself with the attitudes of both COMMENTARY and of Mr. Podhoretz in the fifties and their possible relevance to his current piece. Although he has every right to use his editorial blue pencil, it would have been more fair, and surely more ethical journalism, if Mr. Podhoretz had allowed his readers to read and to judge for themselves what it was that had piqued him so. His name-calling diminishes his own argument and does little service to the cause of rational debate.

August 14, 1976
On Agnew's return
The Times Herald Record

It is not surprising that the re-entry of ex-Vice President Agnew into political life, from which he was expelled in disgrace in 1973, should occur with his re-emergence as a strident spokesman for the extreme right and as a representative of scurrilous anti-semitism.

Agnew's vicious attacks on "Jews in the media" and his uninformed and ill-conceived attacks on Israel have been properly repudiated by responsible Jewish organizations and others.

It is astonishing that this unspeakable blight on American political life, who, as Theodore White reported in "Breach of Faith," "remained on the take all the way through his career . . . even as vice president," now has the audacity to come before the American people as a patriot and a savior, as president of a new group called "Education for Democracy"!

The only "education" Agnew is fit to discuss is education for corruption and betrayal of trust; and as for "democracy," he understood it only as an opportunity for bribery, thievery and venality.

Surely his propaganda efforts and his demagoguery will be rejected by all thinking people, and he will be reconsigned to the obscurity that is more than he deserves!

August 18, 1976
"New Political Ritual"
The New York Times

When Richard Nixon a few years ago solemnly told the American people that "I am not a crook," he may have been bequeathing us a political legacy that will remain to plague us for some time to come.

In his recent acceptance speech, Walter Mondale saw fit to announce that he and his running mate "solemnly pledge to restore Government that tells the truth and obeys the law." In other words, in case anyone was asking, neither he nor Carter was a liar or a crook! The convention responded with wild applause.

It will be interesting to see whether the Republicans find it necessary to make a similar pledge at Kansas City. Perhaps such a statement is on the way to becoming the new political ritual—something like the loyalty oath of other days (which, it is worth noting, has been abandoned: it has, apparently, become more important to affirm one's honesty than one's loyalty). Accordingly, the Presidential candidate will ask of potential running mates not only the now-accepted questions about their stocks and bonds and mental condition, but a new question: "Are you now or have you ever been a liar or a crook?"

At least it's a change from, or an improvement over, the classic question of the 1950's.

August 24, 1976
Higher goals for campaigns
The Times Herald Record

It will be a sure sign of improvement in our political and moral climate when candidates for high office no longer find it necessary to assure us, as vice-presidential candidate Mondale did in his acceptance speech, that, "We solemnly pledge to restore government that tells the truth and obeys the law."

As long as candidates advance a devotion to truthfulness and a willingness to obey the law as qualifications for the presidency (with the implicit assumption that these are such rare qualities among the American people as to recommend the highest office in the land to one who possesses them!), so long will the disastrous legacy of "I Am Not A Crook" Richard Nixon continues to foul our political life.

The real issues of 1976 are crucial. Their resolution will determine the quality of American life for years to come. A high order of innovative leadership is called for, one that is based not only on an unquestioned integrity, but that is keely responsive to the unmet needs of our people, as well as a statesmanship in foreign policy that will restore America to a position of respect and integrity abroad.

The schoolboy naivete with which a candidate, albeit with a winning smile, assures us that he is neither a liar nor a crook, is surely not a sufficient recommendation.

It is to be hoped that the campaign will move on to higher ground.

August 28, 1976
Who's right in campaign?
The Times Herald Record

The problem for today's voter is to be able to distinguish between demagoguery and authenticity.

The modern candidate has his speeches written for him by expert speech writers, his campaign managed by expert PR men, his public appearances staged by expert TV consultants, and his image carefully molded by image-making professionals. Under these circumstances, it becomes increasingly difficult to tell what is authentic with the candidate and what is merely technique for vote-getting.

F. Clifton White, for example, hailed as a "consummate tactician," is chief of Gerald Ford's "communications team" and received much credit for Ford's victory at Kansas City. A few years ago the same Mr. White was consultant to Richard Nixon's Committee to Re-elect the President.

Was he aware, incidentally, of CREEP's corruption and illegalities? Does it even matter? He is a professional political consultant, and a client is a client. Today he is selling Ford, just as he sold other clients before him: Nixon, Eisenhower, Goldwater, Buckley. Like the ad agency that is equally tireless and enthusiastic whether selling cars, catsup or cat food—or political candidates!

Can we get through this mirage to any real sense of authenticity? Can we distinguish between technique and substance, between strategy and principle? This is the problem for all of us, as voters and as citizens in a participatory democracy.

January 2, 1977
Cabinet Choices
The New York Times

 Once again, as President-elect Carter reveals in his decision-making process, our Government leadership is being selected, in the main, on the basis of technological skill, managerial expertise and the elitism of the successful in corporate enterprise. Would it not be a magnificent new departure if at least one position on the Cabinet level were reserved for one whose eminence rested on moral leadership and ethical stature rather than on technology?

 The early church, I am told, had a position known as Keeper of the Deposit of the Faith. Perhaps the Cabinet ought to have a similar post, reserved for one whose ethical judgment, moral leadership, and dedication to the ideals of justice and humanity could serve as an inspiration and guide. Such a person, balancing the technologists, would serve as a sort of Conscience of the Cabinet, Protector of the Public Weal, Keeper of the Faith of Democracy. He would infuse our leadership with a continuing passion for justice and a sense of the welfare of the common man and would direct attention and concern to the specifically moral and human components of public problems.

 It would be interesting to speculate whom President-elect Carter would interview for such a post. Any suggestions?

February 23, 1977
How Not to Deter Heroin Addiction
The New York Times

If, as Clifford S. Fishman states (Op-Ed Feb. 12), "heroin addiction is not a law-enforcement problem," it is difficult to understand his conclusion that "we must . . . commit adequate resources to existing enforcement . . . ."

On the contrary, his cogent declaration that "it is a societal problem" and that "human misery—poverty, occupational and educational discrimination, sub-human housing—is the fundamental cause of heroin addiction" would seem rather to support his other conclusion: "To deter heroin addiction, we must eradicate the conditions that breed addiction" and that until then we must support rehabilitation programs.

In this context it is important to note that last year's cuts of about 30 percent in public funding for drug-treatment programs (and the threat of additional cuts this year) move addicts from hopeful treatment facilities (where the cost is an average $6,000 each per year) to hopeless prison warehousing (average cost about $18,000 each per year). This makes absolutely no sense from either a fiscal or a human point of view. It saves neither lives nor money; on the contrary, it squanders the latter and further dehumanizes the former.

The answer is a long-range effort to alter the decaying social milieu that breeds addiction, while at the same time we increase, not decrease, effective efforts to treat and reclaim its current victims.

Humane social treatment offers all of us, the public and the addicts alike, more hope than archaic "law enforcement."

March, 1977
What is Your A.Q. (Altruism Quotient)?

Isn't it time we stopped bending our knees to the dominance of pure I.Q.? Although many educators are no longer as sanguine as they used to be about the Intelligence Quotient as the most reliable measure of human potential, as a society we still pay an enormous, and probably undue, homage to pure so-called intelligence per se, especially when attested to by high scores on tests, and academic degrees, or simply imputed by high status and position.

The mess we are in, from urban chaos to global nuclear anxiety, from widespread personal alienation and despair to international instability and the constant threat of war and violence, attest to the failure of our leaders with the high I.Q.s. Something, obviously, is missing. Maybe we need another measure, another guide to human behavior, one that concerns itself with *morality and quality*, and not exclusively with pure analytic intelligence.

We need, in short, a guide that concerns itself with ALTRUISM. It is a word and a concept that is sorely in need of resuscitation, if not complete rehabilitation.

The dictionary defines altruism as *"selfless devotion to the welfare of others; motivation for the good of others, rather than for one's own gain."*

The question, in its broadest sense, is "how much of human behavior is motivated by altruism, so defined, and how much by pure self—interest?" Or, to put it another way, how widespread is the "What's-in-it-for-me" syndrome?

This question, and its moral and practical implications, permeates every area of our society.

Let's look at a few examples: We were all brought up to believe that, whatever else, the "helping professions"—doctor, psychotherapist, psychiatrist—surely were exemplars of altruism. Surely our Drs. Kildare and Marcus Welby were concerned only with the welfare of their patients. Today we are not so sure. Experts on the workings of the AMA, the hospital system, and organized medicine in general, are not so certain in the belief that the system is designed with the best interests of the patient in mind. And the recent exposures of gross manipulations of medicaid, medicare, and even methadone maintenance clinics, for the enrichment of rapacious medical entrepreneurs, reflect an ethical illness that has changed the public image of the profession. And when the doctor's bill arrives for most of us, it pretty well confirms that dictionary definition of altruism just does not apply!

And elsewhere, is it altruism or self-interest? What motivates the politician seeking public office? Does he have a burning desire to serve the needs of the public through the powers of the office he seeks? Or is it quite the other way around: does he manipulate the public by any means at hand in order to achieve the office, the goal-in-itself? Which are the means and which the ends? (As the "savvy pols" would have it, the first requirement of a politician is to get elected, the second to stay in office. If the public interest happens to be served in the process, it is purely coincidental!).

Do all of our teachers have as their primary interest the welfare of the children-or their own? The repeated strikes in New York and elsewhere, for reasons that have often seemed frivolous, surely gave us cause to question.

Or the criminal justice system. Is it really interested in either the criminal or in justice? James Baldwin once made the bitter comment that it is a system which is interested in neither, but in which "the poor, the black, and the ignorant, become the stepping stones of careers."

Is there room for altruism in the business and commercial community? To ask the question is almost to answer it!

In short, is it altruism or self-interest that prevails? How right was William James in his famous observation that "the exclusive worship of the bitch-goddess SUCCESS is our national disease"? Does that characterization still obtain?

It is a hopeful sign that this question is, at long last, being addressed. In a new book on the corporate personality, Michael Maccoby, ("THE GAMESMAN"), comments that "the new industrial leader can recognize that his work develops his head but not his heart." "Given our socioeconomic system" he writes, "with its stimulation of greed, its orientation to control and predictability, its valuation of power and prestige above justice and creative human development, these fair-minded gamesmen may be as good as we can expect from corporate leaders."!

Socrates, more than 2,000 years ago, said that he "*sought to persuade every man that he must . . . seek virtue and wisdom before he looks to his private interests . . . and this should be the order which he observes in all his actions."* Is that still valid as a moral guide?

Other, more recent, voices have begun to stress the importance of warmth, caring, and altruistic concern for others as abiding values, over the ethic of personal-success-at-any-price.

The famous Menninger Clinic recently celebrated its 50th. anniversary with a convocation in New York held under the title, TOWARD A CARING SOCIETY, at which "caring among people" was seen as an essential component, not only for mental health, but for all the needs of a truly human society.

Alcoholics, long considered untreatable, have found in Alcoholics Anonymous a path to personal redemption through a regimen of mutual concern and deep human support one for the other. Altruism and self-interest here seem to merge. In pursuing a dedicated course of vital help and concern for another alcoholic, the ex-alcoholic strengthens his own resolve and maintains his own responsible sobriety.

And hard core junkies, the despair of traditional treatment disciplines, have developed the concept of *responsible love and concern* as they help each other change their whole system of morals and behavior in their remarkably effective *"therapeutic communities"* (Synanon, Daytop Village, and many others across the country and abroad.).

If love and an altruistic concern for others cured falling-down drunks and hardcore drug addicts where all else seemed to fail, perhaps there's a message there for all of us!

College President Josiah Bunting 3d, in discussing the problem of an equitable college admissions policy, said something very profound for all of society:

"We don't need more brains. We have plenty of brains. We need young men and women imbued with the notion of *service*, young people prepared to efface personal egoisms in larger causes, people prepared to do the drudgework that brings neither lucre nor public recognition, people who can lead because they have been willing to follow, people whose intellectualism is not cynical and overweening, young people who understand that the most overrated decision they shall be called upon to make in their young lives is the decision about where they will go to college. We have plenty of young good minds; we have far fewer tender hearts and brave souls."

Of course the idea suggests itself that many acts defy pure characterization, that there is no sharp polarity, and that much of our behavior contains a mix of both altruism and self-interest. Perhaps we can clarify, and quantify, the altruistic component by the following formula:

Altruism (A) equals Concern for Others (CO) divided by Self-Interest (SI). Or, stated mathematically, $A = co/si$. Thus, the amount of altruism which adheres to a given act is in inverse proportion to the self-interest involved, where the Concern for Others remains constant. The more the self-interest, the less the altruism.

Along these lines, perhaps we can begin to become more conscious of one's ALTRUISM QUOTIENT, or A.Q., and its deep moral significance, instead of paying exclusive attention to I.Q.

And perhaps then we can approach the profundity of the observation of the Hebrew sage, Hillel, when he said: *"If I am not for myself, who then shall be for me? If I am only for myself, then what kind of man am I?"*

It is a good sign that many are now beginning to see this question as relevant.

May 2, 1977
'Malfeasance' Rewarded
The New York Times

Is it not ironic that ex-President Nixon will be receiving in the neighborhood of $1 million for an interview on television on the very subject he would have been obliged to discuss for free on the witness stand, were it not for the pardon so magnanimously granted by Gerald Ford?

In the latter instance he would at least have been under oath and would have been subjected to cross-examination. And we would not be witness to this spectacle, of dubious morality, in which Mr. Nixon is able to turn his malfeasance into such a windfall. Only in America.

May 14, 1977
Understanding race hatred
The Times Herald Record

Mr. Malwald's violent attack on Alex Haley and "Roots" is a curious combination of emotion and contradiction.

On the one hand, in what almost appears as an apologia for slavery, he states that institution was not as evil as has been painted, while on the other hand he stoutly denies any guilt on his or his ancestors' part because they arrived in America long after the crime was committed!

His injudicious attack on Haley's account as "lies" is patently unfair. Like other historical novels, "Roots" vividly re-creates an era (just as Dickens portrayed the slums of London in "Oliver Twist" or as John Steinbeck portrayed the depression Okies in "Grapes of Wrath"), and its authenticity lies in the description of the characteristics of that era, rather than on specific details of fact.

The significance of "Roots" lies ultimately in the manner in which it illuminates with stunning impact, the value of freedom in human affairs and the extent of man's capacity for inhumanity to man. He has challenged us, disturbed us, and goaded us into a fresh and deeper realization of the inner, personal, meaning of freedom, and of the enormity of the crime of denying that freedom to others. The Nazi holocaust and other recent events amply demonstrate that this variety of evil did not die with abolition.

If our reaction to "Roots" is neither a paralyzing guilt nor an emotional denial of historic fact but a heightened understanding of the evil of race hatred and of the theories of "racial inferiority" which support it, Haley will have served us well. For the problems of living together are still with us and will more readily be solved if we face the past honestly and learn from it to live the present more nobly.

May 28, 1977
'The king can do no wrong'
The Times Herald Record

It was only by cowardly hiding behind the shield of immunity granted him by the Ford pardon that ex-President Nixon dared to assert the pernicious and dangerous doctrine: When the president does it, that means it is not illegal."

Even more dangerous, he maintained with unparalleled arrogance that this could be a matter of opinion, rather than of law!

The fact is that John Ehrlichman advanced this thesis before the Ervin Committee, but neither he nor his co-conspirators Mitchell and Haldeman, nor indeed any of the Watergate criminals, were able to invoke this defense successfully before a court of law.

It was only the Ford pardon that made it possible for Nixon to put forward, with unmitigated gall (and with a tidy financial profit!) this modern-day version of "The king can do no wrong." His immunity from prosecution permitted him once again to poison the political and moral atmosphere, in the certain knowledge that his anti-democratic views, and his criminal actions, would be free of a final judicial determination.

Thus, the pardon by Gerald Ford, in direct consequence of which we are made victims again of Nixon's continuing attempts to subvert the Constitution and the Bill of Rights, may very well turn out to be the most iniquitous "obstruction of justice" of them all.

July 22, 1977
$100 Deductible
The New York Times

When the House ethics committee surveyed 700 Congressmen and former Congressmen to find out about Korean bribery, the survey questionnaire asked whether they had "received anything worth more than $100 from a representative of the Korean Government.'

The ethics committee was apparently applying the principle of the $100 deductible from the field of insurance to the practice of corruption. Congressmen were thus put on solemn notice that bribes under $100 are O.K., but that's just about as far as they can go!

To many it will appear very much like the diagnosis of only "slightly pregnant."

July 30, 1977
Of weapons & war
The Times Herald Record

    Recoiling from the ghostly memory of Hiroshima and Nagasaki, some have hailed the neutron bomb as an "advance," since it will only "kill people while preserving buildings, tanks and artillery"; others argue that, being less frightful and more easily used, it will serve to deter an aggressor; while a professor of international law solemnly warns that we ought first to consider whether this bomb will cause "needless suffering"!

    Glaringly absent is a discussion of the moral aspects of this exclusive attention to weapons per se, and a neglect of the only real alternative to mutual suicide: the elimination of war itself.

    History amply demonstrates that the development and sophistication of armaments have never deterred the war-makers, nor have they ever prevented war. There is no reason to believe now that the modern weapons researcher will be any more successful.

    From the Roman phalanx to modern artillery and tanks, from the hand-hurled spear with a burning torch at its end to the atomic warhead on a guided missile, weapons have succeeded in maiming, killing and destroying, with increasing deadliness—but they have not moved us one inch toward eliminating war.

    As for "needless suffering", shall we argue which is worse, the ancient sword in the belly or modern death by radiation?

    The crying need is for the best brains and the moral leadership of all mankind to be directed toward the essential problem of the elimination of the institution of war itself. This is the area of man's most glaring failure.

1978
Traveling Through Mexico And Guatemala

I. Spontaneity, involvement, and a capacity for open-ness to people and to experience, are the magic ingredients which can transform a journey from a sterile "sight-seeing trip" into a profound exercise in personal growth and a new sense of human interconnectedness.

Add to this a willingness to set aside pre-judgements (otherwise known as prejudice) and a determination to cast off the rigidities and inhibitions born of urban, middle-class life, and you have the formula: spontaneity, involvement, a new openness. For my wife and myself, on a three month, unplanned, freewheeling trip through Mexico and Guatemala, by plane, train, car, boat, rinky-dink bus, and foot, this formula led to stimulating, often exhilarating, times with a wide variety of fellow-travelers and fellow-adventurers, and, in our contacts with Mexicans and Guatemalans and with indigenous Indians in remote regions of both countries, a renewed awareness of the diversity of human cultures and the richness therein, as well as a healthy respect for the infinite varieties of human experience.

We criss-crossed Mexico from the Western coast (the lovely fishing village of Manzanillo with still-unspoiled Pacific beaches) to the Eastern coast (the island of Cozumel, off the Yucatan), from the central mountains around San Miguel de Allende and Guanajuato to Oaxaca in the South, from sea-level heat to the cool mountain air at 7,000 feet, from sophisticated Mexico City and American-colony, bohemian, arty San Miguel to primitive villages of potters and weavers in the mountains and countryside.

It was Guatemala, however, which proved the most exciting, giving us a sense of time-travel, back to one or two thousand years ago, in unchanged Indian villages in the highlands around Lake Atitlan and its surrounding volcanoes, and especially in visits to the pre-Columbian archaeological sites, the vast and unbelievable cities of the Mayans in Tikal, in the jungles of Northeastern Guatemala, and at Chichen-Itza, near Merida in Mexico's Yucatan. One's whole conception of the America that existed before Cortes and the Spanish Conquistadores must be changed when one sees the architecture, sculpture, mathematics and astronomy ("One of the most astonishing civilizations the world has ever seen", according to University of Pennsylvania archaeologist William R. Coe, who headed the excavation team which uncovered Tikal), which are evident in the restorations at Tikal, Chichen-Itza, Monte Alban, Mitla, Uxmal, Palenque, and elsewhere. I climbed to the top of Pyramid 1 at Tikal and stood in awe of the vista—public squares, temples, ball fields, stellae—the ruins are believed to cover an area of 25 square miles—evidence of an astonishing urban expanse, existing for perhaps 2500 years and achieving a high sophistication in art and in science when Europe was still in the Middle Ages. Hardly the naked savages destined to be tamed, Christianized, and introduced to civilization by the Europeans, as most of us were taught to believe.

At Lake Atitlan, which glistens like a blue jewel nestled in the mountains, we visited villages of the descendants of these Mayans, living much like their ancestors— weaving the most magnificent cloth on their hand looms in an atmosphere which gives one the impression of having been untouched by time. Chichicastenango, Solola, Santiago-Atitlan, San Lucas de Tolliman, Huehuetenango, Quetzaltenango. Their native markets are as exotic as their names and we were caught up in the hustle-bustle, the energy, the verve, and the irresistible enchantment of the whole scene as the local craftspeople exhibited their colorful weavings and handcraft. We tramped from market to market, from village to village, or rode with the Indians and their children and chickens and baskets and produce (and once a huge pig who was being taken to market on the roof-rack) in rinky-dink, third class buses over winding, climbing mountain roads (no railings around perilous curves, but with magnificent views of lake and ravines and distant volcanoes) . . . and we still have not sorted out the multitude of impressions and stimuli, of color and people and costumes, and of values and priorities and ways of life.

Again, it all confirms for me that the human family is so diverse, has so many ways to go, so many patterns around which to organize life, so many different systems of values and purposes. Who is to say which is "better"? Is "different" necessarily "better" or "worse"? "Are they happy?", people have asked me of the Indians living their barefoot lives in the "backward" villages. "How should I know?", I respond, "Are the New Yorkers we see in the subways from Brighton Beach to Manhattan to the Bronx, happy? With their cars and television sets, and shoes and inside plumbing and hot and cold running water on tap? Look at their faces. And ask a few." Which of the two groups sees his family more? Who is closer to nature and to his own place in the nature of things—to the past and the future, as well as the present? Who has greater gratifications of a truly meaningful kind? I don't know. But I think the questions are open, as they should be—and we are better advised to relinquish our smug and arrogant assumption that we are in the best of all possible civilizations, and that technological achievement and human happiness are one and the same. To witness the close family orientation of Mexico's and Guatemala's Indians (from the babe at its mother's breast carried continuously within the warm folds of the rebozo, and given the loving breast whenever it wants and needs it, in public or in private, in the market place or on the bus . . . to the obvious respect and concern shown for the aged) is to be reminded of some of the values we have neglected or forgotten in our "advanced" culture.

II. Another aspect of our experience was the sense of community with other travelers. We had left New York alone, but . . . . we climbed the inspiring pyramid of Teotihuacan near Mexico City in the company of an engineer from London who was on his way to Canada from the island of Jamaica. And we were joined by a professor from Bulgaria on leave from his teaching post in Trinidad.

. . . we toured the ancient Maya ruins at Chichen-Itza with a German physicist and his artist—wife. And discussed the meaning of it all later that evening in the exotic Hotel Maya land together with a couple from Oakland, California.

. . . we dined and discussed archaeology and philosophy and the many ways of people with a Swiss biologist at Uxmal,

. . . and joined a group of young back-packers in the primitive campground in the jungle area of Tikal. Although they slept for fifty cents a night in hammocks hung in open "palapas", while we enjoyed the relative luxury of the Jaguar Inn, we met and ate together and climbed together over the magnificent pyramids and temples and plazas of the ancient Mayan civilization which flourished here over one thousand years ago.

. . . We spent an afternoon with a Swedish sociologist in the old square at Oaxaca,

. . . and a few weeks with the artists, writers, sculptors, of many nationalities, in the beautiful colonial city of San Miguel de Allende,

. . . and three delightful days with a diamond dealer and his wife from Capetown, South Africa, with whom we explored the old Spanish city of Antigua-Guatemala, and the villages around Lake Atitlan, surely one of the most beautiful places in the world.

. . . We met psychologists from New York, and dentists, doctors and teachers from Los Angeles, New York, Chicago, Detroit—and Kalamazoo, Michigan. And students from Montreal, Toronto, and Miami—and Paris, France. And Peace Corps workers from El Salvador and Costa Rica.

. . . And above all, we met, talked with, ate with, traveled with, and were stimulated by, a host of the exuberant young—the backpackers and campers, ever curious, ever interested, traveling for one month or one year, tasting life in Mexico and Guatemala, in El Salvador and Belize and Costa Rica, in remote villages and cities, exploring, asking questions, reading and discussing, and absorbing new environments, exuding a joie-de-vie which proves infectious, and learning and growing, it seemed to me, in dimensions never possible in the halls of formal academia.

They form a sort of traveling camaraderie, these kids, and, if you are open to it and sensitive to it, you can hook into it (even if you are a bit over-age), with exhilarating results:

The kids we met at Tikal turned up again at Panajachel, up on Lake Atitlan. The couple we dined with in Oaxaca, Mexico, we met two weeks later in Guatemala City. The lovely lady we met at the Teatro Delgollado in Guadalajara we met again on the beach in Manzanillo. And all along this grapevine we picked up ideas and suggestions for places to visit, hotels and pensions to stay in, restaurants to eat in, special trips to take, books to read, and books swapped,—all of which proved more valuable than any of the guide books. And, a wonderful additional bonus, we made friends we are certain to meet again, in New York or in future travels.

Should all this be surprising? Or is it not a confirmation of the on-going human need for community, a need which is often frustrated by the traditional, almost institutionalized travel experience? At home the search for community takes many forms. Away from home, who has not experienced the sense of unconnectedness, of not belonging, of what may be called "separation anxiety" upon the loss of familiar supports and the absence, to borrow a phrase of Carl Rogers', of the "significant others" in one's life?

Octavio Paz[*], the highly respected Mexican poet and intellectual, touched on something profoundly universal when he wrote that ". . . every separation causes a wound . . . any break with ourselves or with those around us creates a feeling of solitude."

Traveling with a daring spontaneity, with respect for others in strange places and strange cultures, and with an openness which leads to involvement, opens the way toward reversing that solitude, and in so doing enriching and deepening both your experience and yourself.

So when you go traveling, let yourself really go. Loosen up. (Maybe, even, grow a beard!) Perhaps you can make your journey one not only of place-discovery, but, through a process of re-examination of values, one of self-discovery as well.

February 18, 1978
Three Questions
The New York Times

Inasmuch as a Mideast accord seems to be stalemated on two issues—the return of conquered territory and the question of self-determination for the Palestinian Arabs—the following three questions may not be irrelevant:

- *To the P.L.O.:* If a Palestinian state is established, would the P.L.O. expunge from its covenant that clause which calls for the destruction of the state of Israel, and would the new state establish normal, friendly relations with Israel and with all other states in the Middle East?
- *To President Sadat:* Is it possible for Egypt to exert its influence to accomplish the above, and, along with others, to act as guarantor for such a vital Israeli security requirement?
- *To Prime Minister Begin:* In the event of an affirmative answer to the above two questions, along with appropriate guarantees, would Israel agree to self-determination for the Palestinians, even if this results in an independent state?
- Affirmative replies to all three questions would go a long way toward breaking the deadlock and establishing some necessary conditions for peace.

April 15, 1978
'PLO doesn't deserve U.S. hospitality'
The Times Herald Record

The State Department has decided that the New York office of the Palestinian Liberation Organization (PLO) is operating legally and can remain open, but it must observe the law and make periodic reports of its activities to the Justice Department." One wonders whether these reports would cover PLO plans to murder Israeli athletes at future Olympics, to hijack aircraft and kill innocent passengers of any nationality, including Americans, to murder Arab editors or Arab moderates who might oppose their plans, or to slaughter Israeli civilians, women, and children in schools, on the streets, or in buses—and to continue this wanton terrorism until they achieve their openly stated objective of annihilating the state of Israel.

For the PLO disdains to conceal its allegiance to terrorism as its chief modus operandi. On the contrary, it flaunts it in the face of the civilized world, and directs it not only toward Jews but toward any who oppose its aims, including the increasing number of Arabs who would promote peace and coexistence with Israel.

In these circumstances, instead of the pious, and ineffective, statements against international lawlessness and terrorism we issue after each horrendous event, we would be more effective if, at the very least, we withdrew our hospitality from the terrorists' organization and urged other friendly nations to do likewise.

We could thus at least refrain from enhancing their image, if not their operational efficiency, and remove the semblance of legitimacy they now enjoy in our country.

May 6, 1978
Arms, peace 'contradiction' seen
The Times Herald Record

The moral contradictions which ensue when one attempts the dual role of arms merchant to the world and peace-maker are nowhere more in evidence than in the Mideast arms package President Carter is attempting to foist upon a recalcitrant Congress.

Congress, and the public, are understandably confused:

1. The United States, on firm moral as well as political grounds, is firmly committed to the State of Israel and to its right to exist within secure and defensible borders.
2. Saudi Arabia is just as firmly committed to the opposite position, that of the PLO, which it recognizes as the "sole legitimate representative of the Palestinian people," and which openly calls for the destruction of Israel. The Saudis, in fact, contribute millions a year to aid the PLO recruit and train and arm its bands of terrorists.
3. The United States now proposes to provide Saudi Arabia with F-15 fighter planes, the most advanced combat planes in the world, without the slightest indication of any change in this hostile Saudi Arabian policy.

We would thus support the enemies of our friends and even provide them with the means of pursuing a policy which directly opposes our own, which flouts international law and decency, and which threatens world peace.

Morality is thus drowned in a sea of oil. We do not serve our own interests or those of our ally, we do not placate our foes, while we lose credibility in a drifting and dangerous world.

July 15, 1978
'Freedom of speech not absolute'
The Times Herald Record

Nazi Frank Collin in Chicago last week attempted to re-kindle a virulent race hatred, issued a ghastly call for another round of genocide, and revealed the totalitarian's tendency to rewrite history, so brilliantly predicted by George Orwell in his prophetic novel, "1984."

Surrounded by uniformed storm-troopers and a Nazi flag, Collin declared, "I don't believe there was a holocaust. But if there was, they deserved it—just as they're going to deserve it this time." Another Nazi spokesman proclaimed: "Do you want us to put you in the ovens? We will . . . We say one more time, all you Jews are going to get it."

One wonders whether the American Civil Liberties Union, after the event, still considers such provocation as legitimately protected by the free speech guarantees of the First Amendment? Or should this frightening Nazi audacity not remind us, and alert us, to the fact that the right of free speech has never been absolute.

It is not an abstract principle to be considered academically and in a social vacuum. Free speech was designed as an instrument for social good and its preservation is closely bound up with its abuse.

There is no inherent "right," for example, to falsely yell fire in a crowded theater. Or to use free speech in order to abolish it.

Acquiescence in, or public indifference to, such activities, in the name of free speech, may be a greater risk to our survival as a free people than we can afford. For free speech will never be preserved by an ostrich policy of ignoring its avowed enemies.

August 2, 1978
All-American Smokescreens
The New York Times

In the time of the unlamented Senator McCarthy, the show-stopping question was: Are you now, or have you ever been . . . a red?

In the immediate post-Nixon era, the question was changed to: Are you now, or have you ever been . . . a crook?

After the Bourne affair, today's question has become: Do you now, or have you ever, smoked marijuana or used other drugs?

Mutatis mutandis, there appears to be no end to which hypocrisy, stupidity and prejudice can go to throw up the particular smokescreen which is in fad at the moment to obscure reality and to divert us from the real problems which confront the nation and the world.

Unemployment, inflation, racism, the burden of armaments, the threat of nuclear war? Are you now, or have you ever been . . . ? Do you now, or have you ever smoked . . . ?

One wonders what would happen if President Carter's ultimatum to his staff—"Obey the law [i.e., do not smoke marijuana] or seek employment elsewhere"—were to be applied, as presumably it should be, to that "elsewhere"; to industry, advertising, the arts and academia. We would surely expand hypocrisy to widespread paranoia, add to the ranks of the youthful unemployed and, in the process, lose the talents and the contributions of millions of young Americans.

As the French say, *"Plus ca change, plus c'est la même chose,"* or, loosely translated, the smokescreen differs from era to era, but the smell remains the same.

February 4, 1979
Understanding The Cults
The New York Times Magazine

    We have, at our own peril it turns out, not sufficiently appreciated the vital significance of nurturing loving connections in our daily lives. To win back the alienated, the disaffected and the dropouts, *we must make it unnecessary for them to feel that they have to look elsewhere for the love and sense of self-worth they so desperately seek.* To accomplish this, we must re-examine our own values, and not fall back on the strangely comforting psychiatric assurances that we are all O.K. but our dropouts are, certifiably, "mentally ill."

April 25, 1979
All Hail the Spiderwort!

(According to a New York Times report (April 25), "recent studies by a Japanese scientist indicate that the spiderwort, a common roadside wildflower . . . could be an ultra-sensitive monitor of ionizing radiation." Observing that hairs on its stamens "mutate from blue to pink when exposed to as little as 150 millirems of radiation", Dr. Sadao Ichikawa "said he found the spiderwort a more reliable indicator of the effects of low level radiation than the currently used mechanical counters such as the dosimeter.")

> All hail the spiderwort,
> Nature's most congenial sport,
> Its stamens turn from blue to pink
> To warn of radioactive stink—
> The common peril Man has wrought.
>
> Blue to pink? A blush of shame?
> A blush from nature at the game
> Pursued by Man, in Mankind's name,
> While all creation feels the stain?
>
> Is the lowly spiderwort
> Giving us some food for thought:
> CONCERN—concern for all that lives
> Or all the earth may come to naught?
> ALL HAIL THE SPIDERWORT!

(The Times concludes its report with the statement that "scientists hope eventually to be able to plant spiderworts around nuclear facilities in the United States"!)

July 30, 1979
Start disarming
The Times Herald Record

Although the SALT II treaty must be supported as a step in the right direction, we will continue to remain victims of the vry real threat of huge nuclear stockpiling until we move, or at least begin to move, from arms limitation to meaningful disarmament.

Under the treaty a vast arsenal of 2250 missiles will be maintained by each side, including bombers ICBMs, and the devastating multiple warheads. The destructive power of this arsenal is unimaginable. Expert studies, prepared for the Senate Foreign Relations Committee, have indicated that nuclear war, with present technology, will kill 165 million Americans, and as many Russians, and leave the living even worse off than the dead on a scorched and radiated earth.

It may be reassuring to get a treaty to prevent that technology from increasing even further its murderous potential, but as long as we (on both sides) fail to face up to mankind's urgent need for immediate steps to move from mere limitation to real disarmament, we remain morally deficient, politically inept, and dangerously impotent in a frightening and vulnerable world.

August 29, 1979
The American Way And Tongsun Park
The New York Times

No more trenchant comment on American political morality has been uttered recently than the remark of Tongsun Park as recorded in the Aug. 17 issue of The Times: "I thought I was taking part in the American political process. So far as I was concerned, I was helping Congressional friends who were loyal to me."

Thirty-one members of Congress, he testified, readily agreed with him that their loyalty was worth about $850,000.

It will, furthermore, escape no one that after a costly two-year investigation, at the taxpayers' expense, only one Congressman was convicted. The chief culprit, Mr. Park himself, not only had all the charges against him dropped but got away with $4.5 million in back taxes in addition to the huge profits netted him by his illegal activities.

After all, there were good precedents. The chief culprit of Watergate, unindicted and pardoned, has just purchased a New York apartment for $1 million with the proceeds of the sale of his San Clemente estate, the value of which was considerably enhanced by the taxpayers' dollars.

Plus ça change, plus c'est la même chose, or, who said that crime does not pay?

As that astute observer, Mr. Tongsun Park, might say, "It's the American way, isn't it?"

September 8, 1979
'Analysis of Carter fraudulent'
The Times Herald Record

Jack Anderson quoted two psychoanalysts who, without benefit of a single personal consultation, offered several psychiatric "insights" into President Carter's "innermost feelings." Carter, we are told, "undergoes periods of intense contemplation," and suffers from "temporary despair and disillusionment" from which he emerges "with an almost compensatory aggressive tone."

When these opinions are offered as the "scientific" findings of "experts" they smack of fraudulence. Firstly, psychiatric examinations and conclusions from afar should be viewed with a healthy sketicism. Secondly, the application of psychiatry to the political process is at best a dubious enterprise.

Since neither psychiatrist offered anything which even vaguely approaches scientific evidence for their generalizations, the imputation of a special political "expertise" deriving from psychiatric training is misleading. As citizens, the two "experts" have a right to their opinions of Mr. Carter. But nothing in the Anderson column indicates that their special "insight" ought influence the rest of us in our own evaluation of Carter on the basis of his political actions and performance, his influence for good or for evil, and his capacity to address the nation's problems.

These are all political matters, on which there is no established psychiatric "truth" (psychiatrists will differ politically, from radical to conservative, in just about the same proportion as the rest of the population), and we are all, therefore, left to form our own independent judgments in political affairs—Anderson's two "experts" notwithstanding.

September 29, 1979
'Daytop idea has caught on'
The Times Herald Record

Over 300 delegates from 47 countries gathered in New York last week to take part in a conference of therapeutic communities and to discuss further how this relatively new community approach can be applied not only to drug abusers, alcoholics and delinquents, but to a wide variety of mental health problems.

It may be of special interest to our community to know that this world-wide gathering was planned and hosted by Daytop Village which has rehabilitation facilities here in Swan Lake, Parksville and Millbrook. Monsignor William B. O'Brien, who is president of Daytop, is also president of the world body.

The therapeutic community idea, conceived originally by ex-alcoholics (inspired by Alcoholics Anonymous) and by ex-drug addicts determined finally to do something for themselves, is less than 20 years old. Originally scorned by skeptical professionals, the idea has caught on around the world, inspiring many other types of effective self-help groups.

People joining together to help each other overcome difficulties seem to work, and the success at Daytop, Samaritan House, Phoenix, Odyssey, and a host of others has added a new dimension not only to mental health theory, but to the revival of a new sense of brotherhood and mutual responsibility.

The therapeutic community movement has reminded all of us that a resounding "yes" to the question, "Am I my brother's keeper?" can create significant changes in the moral atmosphere of our time.

May 10, 1980
'Let psychiatrists treat, not testify'
The Times Herald Record

The Fischer murder trial offers a classic example of the pernicious effect of the intrusion of psychiatry into the processes of the criminal justice system.

Operating presumably from the same "scientific" base, the defense psychiatrist concludes that the defendant was suffering from "psychopathic intoxication, a mental illness," while the prosecutor's psychiatrist stated that he was only "drunk and angry, not mentally ill."

It is a frightening thought that the contention of the psychiatrist for the defense, which would relieve the defendant of any responsibility for the alleged murder (and even prevent a determination as to whether he did or did not commit the crime), could be extended to cover any act by anyone, no matter how heinous, while drunk.

All that would be needed is a "diagosis" of "psychopathic intoxication," and anyone could get away with anything, including murder.

On the other hand, the psychiatrist who, on the same evidence, found the defendant simply "drunk and angry," was also making a judgment that does not require dubious psychiatric expertise to authenticate. The ultimate irony is that the final decision was made, as is proper by 12 laymen on the jury, none of whom is equipped with any special psychiatric training.

Although psychiatrists, along with other social forces, ought to be part of the treatment process, after the determination of guilt (or innocence), a responsible criminal justice system should avoid these shabby courtroom duels, which tend to obstruct rather than advance the primary determination of guilt or innocence.

August 3, 1980
The New York Times Magazine

　　Ronald Reagan, we are informed, "doesn't have an internal mechanism to help him judge." Behavioral scientists as well as biologists, will surely wonder just what that "internal mechanism" is and what the lack of it could do to a person. How will such a lack influence his judgments on poverty, inflation, unemployment and whether or not to push that nuclear button that could destroy us all?

　　All of us, after all, are called upon to make judgments, large and small, every day of our lives. It is to be hoped that we have that "internal mechanism" to help us out.

July 22, 1980
'Carter drifts on hostages'
The Times Herald Record

As the American hostages in Iran enter their ninth month of captivity, our government's policy appears to be more one of drift than of direction.

'The administration has chosen . . . to let others not readily identified with the United States do the negotiating with the Iranians.' (news item 5/26). Why, indeed, must others be doing the negotiating for us?

'Let us never negotiate out of fear,' said the late president, John F. Kennedy, in what now appears a prescient admonition. 'But let us never fear to negotiate.' What more pressing moral obligation falls upon President Carter at this time? Instead of criticizing Ramsey Clark for focusing the world's attention on the hard realities of the problem, why does President Carter not come forward with a bold initiative of his own?

The missing initiative, the only initiative which contains the possibility of an early release of the hostages, is that from the president of the United States to his opposite number, the Ayatollah Khomeini.

The president must seize the initiative by proposing an immediate, direct meeting with Khomeini and by indicating his readiness to discuss not only Iran's unconscionable kidnapping of diplomats, but to address also their grievances against the U.S.: our support of their hated enemy, the shah, both before and after his overthrow, and the crucial question of alleged U.S. interference in Iranian affairs.

Our national honor would not suffer from direct and open negotiations in this spirit. On the contrary, a direct presidential appeal that stresses the moral issues on both sides would increase our world stature and offer the best hope of resolving the stalemate.

August 13, 1980
Not only Jews oppose tyranny
The Times Herald Record

There it is again! This time from the president of the United States, who confided to his diary that his bother Billy's affection for Libya would prove "embarrassing . . . particularly with American Jews"!

Only the Jews, presumably, would find it obnoxious that the president's bother would celebrate the terrorist regime of Muammar el-Qaddafi, who supported murder and terror not only in Israel, but also subsidized the unspeakable Idi Amin in Uganda, presided over the burning of the U.S. Embassy in Tripoli, and encouraged the practice of terror as state policy.

Although Jews have a long and bitter history of first-hand experience of terror, persecution and injustice, decent people of all faiths and persuasions all over the country will share their revulsion at attempts to legitimize and promote a regime that is as repressive and morally corrupt as it is anti-semitic.

You don't have to be Jewish to condemn tyranny and torture and those who elevate these obscenities to national policy.

September 5, 1980
If Carter Proposed To Meet the Ayatollah
The New York Times

As the hostages in Iran pass their 300th day of an unjust captivity, I ask again why President Carter does not publicly propose a conference with the Ayatollah Khomeini to discuss the real issues that keep our people captive.

A bold initiative by the President for personal negotiation at the highest level would expose these issues, on both sides, for the world to see. This would not compromise our national honor, and would offer the best hope for early resolution of the problems and the freedom of our fellow citizens.

October 11, 1980
What a Debate Can Be Like
The New York Times

The greatest political debate in American history was arranged by a simple exchange of letters between Abraham Lincoln and Stephen Douglas, without the help (or interference) of media consultants.

Douglas, replying to Lincoln, wrote on July 30, 1858: "I agree to your suggestion that we shall alternately open and close the discussion. I will speak at Ottawa one hour; you can reply, occupying an hour and a half, and I will then follow for half an hour . . . We will alternate in like manner in each successive place." Simple, reasonable and effective—an hour and a half each to address each other and the issue, not two and a half minutes to respond to reporters' canned questions!

Their audience was a mere trifle compared with TV's 50 million, but over the years their words reached more people and affected more issues than the bland, slick, media-produced non-debate of Anderson and Reagan.

The failure of the major candidates to agree to meaningful debates does a great disservice to the voters and represents a disgraceful capitulation to their media experts, who apparently advise that the less they say the better. This fateful election may be remembered not for its deathless prose but for the debate about the debate, or perhaps the debate about the debate about the debate.

The candidates ought to be required to read Lincoln-Douglas to learn what a debate can be like.

June 13, 1981
'Reagan avoided problem of peace'
The Times Herald Record

In an unusual concordance, both Ellen Goodman and William Safire (Record, June 4) pan President Reagan's West Point speech, the former decrying his "Cold War words" while the latter calls it "a mishmash . . . a themeless pudding on a platter of platitudes."

It is a matter of no small significance, however, that neither saw fit to address the most glaring, and frightening, weakness of the speech: Although it was heralded as a major foreign policy address, President Reagan studiously avoided the major foreign policy problem of our time—the search for peace in a world facing nuclear disaster.

He failed to even mention our, and the world's, most critical problem, how to save ourselves, humanity, and the earth we all share from thermonuclear annihilation.

In sharp contrast, the recent remarks of Mr. George F. Kennan on the occasion of his receiving the Albert Einstein Peace Prize stand forth as a beacon of hope and sanity. Mr. Kennan, former ambassador to Moscow and an experienced expert on Soviet affairs, warned that we are drifting toward nuclear collision, "piling weapon upon weapon, missile upon missile" resulting in a situation of "overkill" that "reaches such grotesque proportions as to defy rational understanding." He recommends "an immediate across-the-board reduction by 50 percent" of the nuclear arsenals of both superpowers. The search for even more nuclear fire power, he states, is "a form of madness" bringing us "very close to the point of no-return."

President Reagan's silence on this issue is either an unforgivable lapse, or an ominous indication of a lopsided sense of priorities.

Equally disturbing is the casual reporting, or non-reporting, in the media of Mr. Kennan's highly significant message, and of the general under-reporting in the press on the life and death issues of nuclear danger and the threat posed by nuclear war to human survival.

At a time when the "United States and the Soviet Union have in their nuclear stockpiles more than one million times the destructive power of the American bomb that destroyed Hiroshima in 1945," we avoid this question only at our own risk—and the risk of all mankind.

July 7, 1981
'Military exalted over disadvantaged'
The Times Herald Record

Amid all the lamentations concerning the imminent bankruptcy of the Social Security system, there is an appalling lack of attention to the context within which this bankruptcy is supposed to take place.

That social-economic context is characterized by the contrast between the wild, runaway, staggering expenditures for military hardware proposed by the Reagan administration on the one hand, and the mean-spirited, harsh and callous reduction in human services on the other. Senator Mark O. Hatfield recently called it "budgetary surgery without the benefit of anesthesia on the handicapped, the old, the hungry."

Can it be that a government that plans to spend up to $1.7 trillion on the military in the next five years can plead poverty when it comes to the needs of its elder citizens?

Can we afford as much as $50 billion on new bombers and $100 billion on new missiles while the Senate Agriculture Committee, in the name of economy, votes to end free school lunches for low-income children and special milk subsidies for schools?

Can we justify the cuts in student loans to a million needy college students, the slashing of education, welfare, Medicaid and Medicare benefits, the drastic denial of food stamps to the hungry, the betrayal of aid to our Vietnam War veterans, while we plan the largest peacetime military spending in the nation's history?

The answer does not lie in the glib claim of military necessity. There are qualified voices which question the easy assumption that more money spent means more security. (Indeed, a runaway nuclear buildup would, in the opinion of many, add to the world's insecurity and to the possibility of nuclear collision.)

The answer is more to be sought in the realm of morality and responsibility. We must reappraise and reorder our national priorities, and call a halt to what has become an abject obeisance to the military at the expense of our most disadvantaged.

August 15, 1981
'Move spurs arms buildup'
The Times Herald Record

With perfect journalist timing, just one day after President Reagan announced his intention to build the neutron bomb, which has the virtue of killing people through high radiation while safeguarding surrounding property, your two columnists. Jack Anderson and Anthony Lewis informed us that "anywhere form 80 million to 150 million Americans would probably be killed outright in a nuclear exchange with the Soviet Union" (Anderson), that one bomb dropped on an American city would cause an "estimated two million deaths" (Lewis), and that "unless the two super powers act quickly to renew negotiations on limiting their nuclear weapons, it soon may be impossible in a practical sense to stop the accelerating arms race" (Lewis).

It was in this atmosphere that Reagan decided to go ahead with the controversial neutron bomb, which had been opposed by European leaders during the Carter Administration as increasing the danger of catastrophic nuclear collision.

Predictably, the immediate Russian response was a threat to do likewise. Thus, instead of taking a much-needed step to prevent nuclear proliferation. Mr. Reagan has set in motion another round of nuclear buildup, an upward spiralling of the arms race in an already tense and explosive world.

Instead of more nuclear bombs (and another billion dollars added to our already crushing burden of armaments) the world stands in need of fresh ideas and bold leadership for peace, such as the establishment of a Peace Academy, meaningful arms limitations, a rollback of nuclear weapons as recently proposed by George Kennan—to prevent the ultimate disaster of nuclear holocaust to us all.

September 14, 1981
The Neglected Half of the Drug Problem
The New York Times

Although your Aug. 28 editorial focuses on a major social problem ("A new heroin trade . . . is sweeping the Eastern Seaboard and drug abuse of all sorts is an increasingly common fact of life in all parts of the country"), you address only half the problem. That is, you address only the problem of *drug enforcement* while ignoring the equally important problem of *rehabilitation* for the ever-growing number of drug abusers.

Drug abuse is a complex problem, insidious in its effects not only on the lives of hundreds of thousands of addicts but also on their families and the communities in which they live. Drug abuse adds up to broken homes and broken lives, to deteriorated neighborhoods and crime. It blights not only the inner city but reaches into wealthy neighborhoods and affluent suburbs as well.

It is simply not enough to stress drug enforcement to prevent further drug casualties. It is equally imperative that we treat the addict and address the here-and-now human consequences of unchecked drug abuse, not only to save countless young lives from ruin but also to prevent further social deterioration.

The thrust of the Reagan Administration, however, is to pay lip service to the problem (President Reagan declared a few months ago that drug abuse would be a high priority), while drastically cutting essential funding for rehabilitation programs. The current budget slashes appropriations for mental health and drug and alcohol abuse by 25 percent, a cut of about $1 billion.

How can we talk of drug enforcement while cutting funds for treating the abuser and salvaging the community? Logic, morality and a decent concern for people demand a more rounded, humane approach. Drug enforcement? By all means. But let us not abandon the victims of our previous enforcement failures.

Spring, 1975
If Love and Concern Can Cure the Addict, What Can They Do For Us All?

The Addiction Therapist
(The international journal for the advancement of addiction therapists and therapeutic communities.)

Say the word, junkie, or drug-addict, and most people recoil in horror. Junkie means mugging, assault, robbery and violence. Junkie means the streets are not safe, from Needle Park to Washington Square. Junkies are responsible for everything from crime in the streets to the alienation of our youth. Wipe out the junkies, many people feel, and the streets will be safe once again, kids won't run away from home, and a lot of our problems will disappear.

But the cure, as well as the diagnosis, has proved too elusive. How astonishing, therefore, that out of the despair and suffering of this group of social pariahs, this rabble of modern day lepers, there has emerged nothing less than a social phenomenon—in the form of a *method of treatment* than is nothing less than a *method of living*. This method, or Concept, as the ex-addicts call it, has discovered, or re-discovered, the healing power of Love—a discovery which has the deepest implications for us all.

They have found that honesty and openness and the responsible concern and love of one suffering individual for another, have been able to accomplish what the best efforts of well-meaning professionals were unable to achieve: changing hopeless, destructive, amoral junkies into concerned and upright human beings.

Daytop Village, in New York, is a leading example of that type of anti drug-abuse treatment facility that has come to be known as the "drug-free therapeutic community", where some of these miracles of change have occurred. Stressing creative rehabilitation, rather than sterile punishment, Daytop seeks not only the immediate goal of quitting the dependence on drugs, but the more difficult and far-reaching goal of creating new human beings—with new values, a new sense of self-worth, and a new commitment to oneself and to society. Through the workings of a total environment, carefully planned down to the last detail for positive therapeutic influence, it attempts the re-socialization of the anti-social drug addict through a process that aims at nothing less than total *human renewal.*

This process, based on the slogan "Helping Man To Help Himself", uses the group encounter (a kind of group therapy refined and shaped to meet the special needs of the drug user) to focus on individual attitudes and behaviour, to encourage the ex-addict to face himself as he never has before, to examine himself, his values, his goals and his prospects for growth with a naked and ultimate honesty, and through this in-depth process to change for the better.

In the encounters, the new member learns to confront his feelings, no matter how much it hurts. "From the guts" as they say, coming to grips with emotions of fear, anxiety, anger, rage, depression. "Drop your image," he is told, "Abandon your carefully built up facade, your false front. Get in touch with your true inner feelings. Your bad feelings won't go away just because you ignore them. Don't be ashamed of these feelings. Express them. We'll understand. We all have had similar feelings, but we have learned how to deal with them." He hears all this, not from social workers, or probation officers, or psychologists, (all of whom he has learned to distrust and to manipulate and to con), but from ex-addicts, his peers in age and in experience. He feels way down in his belly their love and concern and support, and he is able to relate to them as he never has to the best-meaning of professionals.

With the relentless, but consistently loving, pressure and guidance of these experienced and gifted ex-addicts, who "have been there before" and who act as role models and examples, the new member gradually comes to face himself and to begin to understand the destructive nature of his behavior. Slowly he relinquishes his lying and self-defeating posture (it gets him nowhere in this environment) and eventually he recognizes and confronts his feelings for what they are, develops a new understanding of himself, and takes the first steps toward changing his behavior and outlook on the basis of a new self-knowledge and a new set of values and goals. He takes the first steps towards maturity.

What is striking about all this, and what gives it such wide significance, is the fact that its accomplishments are based, not on influence from the outside by professionals armed with professional knowledge and techniques (the very existence of the ex-addict therapeutic community is itself a response to the widespread failure of traditional methods), but that its core, its spirit, its most basic ingredient is the deep and authentic mutual concern among suffering individuals whose only bond is their common despair, their newly found common hope, and their common humanity. Like the early Christians, who suffered together and taught each other and the world a new morality. Or the modern day Alcoholics Anonymous, which cured more alcoholics through love and caring and a mutual bondedness than all M.D., Ph.D., "qualified" and high-priced therapists put together.

It is this which suggests that this method, this Concept, has the deepest implications in areas of human relationships far beyond the drug-abuse problem. For if a regimen of honesty and responsible love and deep, authentic caring and mutual concern, can cure the addict (Daytop's latest figures show that 95% of its graduates in the last three years are successful, using the criteria of complete drug abstinence, no arrests, and social productivity as evidenced by school attendance or employment), then it surely contains a clear message for all of us in a troubled world.

The late Dr. Abraham Maslow, former president of the American Psychological Association, after a visit to Daytop and after taking part in their encounters, caught the quality of this community as a re-educational enterprise, rather than a narrow "treatment facility", when he observed that "The lessons of Daytop are for education in the larger sense of learning how to become a good adult human being." One of the graduates with whom I talked put it this way: "Daytop gave me back my life!"

And the soft-spoken and compassionate priest, Monsignor William B. O'Brien, who heads the program and has been its guiding inspiration for many years, expressed it this way: "We must return to the important concerns of involving more people more intensely in the more substantive issues of life-living itself, values, growth, honesty, love and concern, community, family, friends and the strength-bond woven therefrom."

Now in its eleventh year, Daytop, as well as other therapeutic communities around the country, are still exploring the humanizing aspects of the group process, suggesting that love and concern may not only be the most effective means of curing the addict, but may also be the best means of curing us all, and in the process creating not only better people, but a better and more humane society.

Autumn, 1975
Daytop Village—Treatment by Peers
The Addiction Therapist

In New York City and in other large urban centers throughout the country, the problem of drug addiction has reached epidemic proportions, with estimates of the addict population in New York City alone ranging as high as 150,000, and twice that number for the country as a whole.

Many of the causes of addiction, stemming from an essentially social pathology, in addition to the personal and the familial, have been found to lie outside the parameters of traditional medicine and have continued to resist traditional medical approaches. Experience has further indicated that traditional approaches from the fields of psychology and social work, although wider in scope, have proved equally ineffective. Drug addiction continues to grow faster than rehabilitative efforts, while steps in the broad area of prevention, which must, perforce, encompass the personal-familial-social scene as a whole, lag pathetically behind.

Dr. Nils Bejerot, an international authority on addiction, states that:

> *With the exception of paranoia, there is hardly any psychiatric condition that is more resistant to treatment than addiction.* Many call for adequate treatment measures, but no one listens to the specialists when they declare that, despite hundreds of years experience and widespread international research, there is still no successful medical method of curing addiction. This has been stated most clearly by the American professor of psychiatry, Alfred Freedman at a conference on addiction in 1963: '. . . it is scarcely necessary to point out that the psychiatrist using conventional psychotherapeutic methods finds himself in general little more successful than other physicians, or even law enforcement officers, in coping with the problems presented by this group of patients.' (1969)

It was into this atmosphere that Daytop Village was born, representing a response to the failure of traditional approaches to the frightening growth of the drug-abuse problem.

Daytop is an off-shoot of Synanon, which in turn, was born out of the crying needs of a suffering and anguished and neglected group of social outcasts who, slowly, pragmatically, but perceptively, forged an instrument for change that came to be known as the "therapeutic community". Peer group influence, they discovered, was more effective in bringing about change, "kicking the habit" and learning how to live again, than the efforts of professionals, with whom they had found it difficult, if not impossible, to relate. But they were able to relate deeply and emotionally on the basis of shared experience to each other, and on this foundation, they built a therapeutic process.

Drawing on their own experience and learning from their own suffering, Synanon, and later Daytop, developed techniques calculated to radically change a complete human being. The goal was not simply, or only, to break the drug habit, or to detoxify or to cure the addiction, but in fact, to create a new human being, equipped with a new set of morals and values, prepared to rejoin the larger community not only as a functioning and contributing member, but also as a role-model for others.

The basic technique of treatment at Daytop is known as the encounter, or the encounter of confrontation, a distinctive form of group therapy designed to force the ex-addict to face himself as he never has before, to come to grips with the reality of his behavior and to face his emotions of fear, anger, rage, depression and anxiety. Surrounded by a loving "family" and with relentless but loving pressure from his peers in experience as well as in fact, the ex-addict is encouraged to commit himself to a process of self-examination and self-exploration. He is gradually moved along by the dynamics of this encounter process until he is able to relate feelings to behavior, to relinquish his lying and self-deceiving posture, to recognize and to confront his feelings and behavior for what they are, to face up to their self-destructive character, and eventually to change his behavior on the basis of a new self-knowledge and a new set of values and goals.

If there is one word to indicate the thrust of this innovative therapeutic endeavor it is "Honesty". Honesty and responsible love. "Honesty" represents not only a goal and an aspiration for future behavior, but is deeply embedded in the everyday activities of the community, and is the hallmark of all relations within the house. And "responsible love" embraces each and every member of the "family", putting on each the responsibility for pointing up the destructive facets of each others' behavior, within the context of a love that makes them all responsible, individually and collectively, for taking steps to alter that behavior for the better. In a very real sense, every member of the community is a therapist for every other member. Each learns to accept that responsibility as he grows and matures. Helping others becomes a key component in the process of helping oneself.

At Daytop it has been shown again, that when A takes the responsibility for helping B to change his ways, whether or not he succeeds in changing B, A is invariably strengthened in his own resolve.

The nature of the group process and the underlying dynamics of its effectiveness as a change-agent remain areas for continued study and research. Daytop is contributing to this research, as well as performing a service by its very existence, by the maintenance of a new, bold, open and inquiring approach to the addiction problem.

In a visit to the Daytop therapeutic community, the late Dr. Abraham Maslow, former president of the American Psychological Association, observed that:

> *The lessons of Daytop are for education in the larger sense of learning how to become a good adult human being . . . Somehow the group is a help . . . From the kind of talking that we did last night, I very definitely have the feeling that the group would feed back things that you could not get in a hundred years of psychoanalysis from one person. (1965)*

Daytop's experience also seems to reinforce the observations of Dr. Carl Rogers, a leading figure in the development of group methods and concepts:

> *A striking aspect of any intensive group experience is the manner in which group members show a natural and spontaneous capacity for dealing in a helpful, facilitative and therapeutic manner with the pain and suffering of others. This shows up so often in groups that I am led to believe that healing ability is far more common than we suppose. In order to come into play it frequently needs only the permission granted by a free-flowing group experience. Individuals totally untrained in the helping relationship often exhibit a sensitive capacity to listen, an ability to understand the deeper significance of some of the attitudes expressed, and a warmth of caring that are truly helpful. (1970)*

These, then, are the thrusts, and the direction of Daytop: therapeutic community, honesty, responsible love, self-help, a "new direction in helping man to help himself."

Along with Daytop, it is increasingly evident that any effective confrontation of the drug-abuse problem must be inter-disciplinary, representing not only medicine and psychiatry, but also the insights of psychology, social work and cultural anthropology. To these professional disciplines there must now be added the new, dynamic and vital input of experienced ex-addicts, adding a dimension of new understanding and modalities of approach that could prove crucial.

This approach seems to us to be a persuasive response to the keen observations of Dr. Donald Louria:

> Recurrent or chronic illicit use of drugs, however, is often a reflection of our troubled society—a society in which respect for laws is disdained, which at least temporarily appears to have lost the capacity to make its visions a reality, which appears to be dominated by a technology it cannot or will not control, and in which idealism and achievement appear to have been subverted by an ever-quickening rush to sensate pleasures. Laws can be passed, preventive education undertaken and millions spent on rehabilitation, but until this society regains its vigor, direction and integrity, the promiscuous, indiscriminate and illicit use of mind-altering and other dangerous drugs will remain a major problem. (1968)

Daytop's philosophy, both in theory and in practice, addresses itself to this broad view. By creating, in microcosm, a community that strives for "vigor, direction, and integrity", as well as molding individuals dedicated to a personal integrity that is concomitant to such a community. Daytop may be pointing up vital lessons for us all, both as individuals and as citizens of the larger society.

For if concern and love and caring and honesty can cure the addict, perhaps they can cure us all, and in so doing, create not only better people, but a better society for all of us.

REFERENCES

Bejerot, N. Premises for the treatment of addictions. *British Journal of Addiction*, 1969, 64, 87-93.
Louria, D.B. *The drug scene*. New York: McGraw-Hill, 1968, 187-188.
Maslow, A. From a Daytop tape. 1965.
Rogers, C. On encounter groups. *Psychology Today*, 1969, 3 (7).
Rogers, C. *On encounter groups*. Harper & Row, 1970, 21-42.

Summer 1976
On Altruism and T.L.C.
(Therapeutic Love and Concern)
The Addiction Therapist

Altruism

Funk and Wagnalls defines altruism as "selfless devotion to the welfare of others; motivation for the good of others, rather than for one's own gain".

"And just what does your 'warm person' do, sit in a room and exude warmth?"

We had been discussing the subject of altruism, and the relative importance in human affairs of warmth and caring and a genuine concern for others. How much of our conduct, I wondered, is motivated by altruism (dictionary definition above) and how much by pure self-interest? I was dismayed by the cynical responses given by most of the people to whom I had put this question, and had just suggested to my friend that genuine caring, warmth and concern were all too conspicuous by their absence in our society, victims of the undue homage we have come to pay to technological skill and specialization, and to the notion that objective expertise is its own justification, free of the requirement of what is perceived as a subjective, expendable, superfluous, even detrimental quality of human warmth and concern. If the doctor alleviates your pain by means of his surgical skill, what does it matter if he is a cold bastard or a warm human being? And if he happens to be the latter, what good is his warmth if his skill is inadequate? So ran the argument.

My friend happens to be a psychologist, part of the "health-care delivery system", and his impatient retort. "What does your warm person do, sit in a room and exude warmth?", hit me like ice-water in the face. That angry and cynical response (in an effort to prove that skill was more important than human warmth; that warmth was, in the last analysis, unnecessary) struck me as illuminating a central question of our time. How much of our conduct is motivated by altruism, and how much by self-interest? And to what extent are we justified in judging a society by the extent to which it fosters the former by placing human considerations high on its list of priorities, or the latter by giving its greatest rewards to aggression and self-assertion and by an emphasis on personal goals rather than, and often at the expense of, the social good?

To put it another way, does the social ambience encourage people to treat other people as fellow-humans, or as objects to be manipulated and used for one's own private ends?

A young doctor friend, fresh out of medical school, told me that his three year intensive course was so pressured, so arduous, so competitive, so impersonal, that it was counterproductive in terms of the humane attitude. What it produced were doctors trained to treat diseases, not people. Their thrust was toward a disease that happened to reside in a person, rather than toward a person who happened to have a disease. Many of them, too, were all set to make their patients pay forever to compensate them for the "sacrifice and deprivation" they had "suffered" during their training.

My wife died recently of cancer. In the course of a long and painful period of treatment, we met a parade of skilled specialists,—surgeon, radiologist, anesthesiologist, chemotherapist, neurologist, breast cancer man, bone cancer man, etc., etc. Each directed his attention to a cancer, or that small portion of it that fell within his narrow purview. Not one had the time or the interest to pay attention to the special and unique human being in whom the cancer happened to be growing. My wife expressed a keen sense of this de-humanization when, after a series of examinations, she whispered to me, "I don't feel like a person anymore!" But she warned me, almost in panic, not to say anything about this for fear that the doctors might be offended and that matters would get even worse!

Her doctors had been taught, no doubt, never to get "emotionally involved" with the patient. Warmth and a sense of personal caring were not only not encouraged in their training, they were actually discouraged as a detriment to objectivity and as a threat to "efficiency". The quest for efficiency (or were other, less admirable motives at work?) had produced a counterproductive de-humanization.

Is the situation different in the field of psychotherapy, where warmth and caring would seem to be an obvious component of the therapeutic attitude? Is the therapist more humanly concerned with his patient, or with his fifty, or hundred, dollar an hour fee? To what extent does the high fee corrupt the "helping relationship"? With unusual if not extraordinary candor, a famous analyst, Dr. Thomas Szasz (1965), gives this advice to therapists: "You need not show that you are humane, that you care for him . . . Your sole responsibility to the patient is to analyze him." The two, in this view, do not necessarily go together. It is not surprising that the same analyst states further that "it is paying the analyst, more than anything else, that enables the patient to be a responsible, negotiating party to a contract with him." Not humanity, not concern, not love, he states, but money "more than anything else", is at the heart of the analytic contract.

When the entrepreneurial ethics of the health care delivery system makes us wonder whether the "helping professions" are designed more to help their practitioners than their clients, there is surely cause for alarm.

Altruism or self-interest? The question permeates every area of our society. Its moral and practical implications are all around us, affecting us all.

In politics and government, is the aspiring office-holder motivated to seek the office in order to use its power to actualize the promises of his campaign, or is it the other way round: is the program only a means, a snare by which the candidate gains the office, the end in itself? Which are the means, and which the ends? The parade of successful-candidates-turned-office-holders who cannot or will not deliver on their campaign promises suggests a dismal answer. James Baldwin (1972), in a bitter comment on our criminal justice system, once wrote that "the poor, the black, and the ignorant become the stepping stones of careers." Are the human needs of all of society merely the "stepping stones of careers" for ambitious politicians?

More than 2,000 years ago, Socrates, defending his life before the Athenian court, said that he "sought to persuade every man that he must look to himself and seek virtue and wisdom before he looks to his private interests . . . and this should be the order which he observes in all his actions." Since the time of Socrates, the development of science, technology and specialization has moved us away from this essentially humane, societal concept. At the same time we have moved away from the model of the Renaissance man with his holistic concept of knowledge and growth, and have moved instead toward a working-thinking-acting approach that is task-oriented and artificially separated from human consequences. Today's specialist tends to know more and more about less and less and considers it not only necessary, but entirely proper, that he concerns himself only with the narrow confines of his specialty. Anything else, including warmth and human concern and genuine caring, would interfere with "efficiency".

But there are other voices, other trends. In a recent convocation in New York to celebrate the fiftieth anniversary of the Menninger Clinic, the future development of mental health was seen as depending on "people learning to care more for one another". The meeting itself was conducted under the title "Toward A Caring Society". Dr. Roy Menninger (1975) commented that "people are increasingly coming to question whether the old goals of success, continuing technological achievement and efficiency are synonymous with happiness and personal satisfaction." "Caring among people" was seen as an essential for future social development, affecting a wide range of problems, from global concerns of war and peace to individual questions of personal adjustment and happiness.

Erich Fromm (1968) writes that "tenderness, compassion, and empathy" are central to the "human experience."

A. H. Maslow (1971), spokesman for humanist psychology, has stated that "that society is good which fosters the fullest development of human potentials, of the fullest degree of humanness." This means, in his view, the struggle to create "the Good Person and the Good Society."

In a recent book, widely read by young people on and off campus, Robert Pirsig (1974) speaks of "caring as a necessary component of Quality". "He has to care. This is an ability about which formal traditional scientific method has nothing to say." He was talking about mechanics and other workmen, but the message is for all of us. We have to care.

The thrust of the youth counter-culture, more vocal and visible in the sixties but nonetheless present in the seventies as well, is away from self-centeredness, alienation, and the single-minded pursuit of personal and often essentially selfish goals, toward a new sense of social commitment, involvement with others, community, family, and a concern for the social good—for the old-fashioned virtues of love and concern and brotherhood.

However groping, however unformulated, the feeling of this movement confronts "pure" science with its social implications, "pure" skill with the need for humanness, "pure" objectivity with the element of human concern. How we treat our fellow human beings is becoming a central, if not critical cultural concern. The effect on another human being or on society is becoming an important measure of the quality of a person's act.

In a world that is dangerously divided and hostile, while developing at the same time a technology capable of total destruction, it may very well be that this movement toward altruism, toward caring and warmth, may turn out to be our only hope. It may in fact be our road to survival itself.

And if we do not as yet have all the right answers, we can and must, like Socrates, start asking the right questions.

FROM ALTRUISM TO T.L.C. (Therapeutic Love and Concern)

What has all this to do with the Therapeutic Community? Everything! For it is the modern therapeutic community that has raised the concept of warmth, and love and concern, from a pious abstraction to a position of centrality in the therapeutic process. (We refer here not to the tender-loving-care of old, but to the more incisive, dynamic and meaningful concept of Therapeutic Love and Concern—A TLC that is therapeutic because it cares, a TLC that dares to be honest and even temporarily cruel in confrontation, a TLC that acts as the midwife to change, and that offers the maximum of human support during the agonizing period during which the change is taking place.)

The Therapeutic Community suggests that such TLC is not merely a fringe benefit, a relatively unimportant and even dispensable "bedroom manner", but is a central component, perhaps even the central component, the sine-qua-non of a treatment procedure that attempts the difficult task of basic behavioral change.

This dynamic TLC flows in all directions—laterally from one resident to another and back again, and vertically, between resident and therapist, whether lay, paraprofessional or professional. It is that which distinguishes the modern therapeutic community (Synanon, Daytop Village, Portage) from its predecessors, as well as from other treatment modalities.

It may also be that it is the difference in basic attitude toward TLC and its profound implications, which is at the bottom of the conflict between the paraprofessional and the professional groups discussed by Bassin (1973), Devlin and Vamos (1975), Vamos and Devlin (1975), Lakoff (1975), Casriel (1971), and others. This continues to be a major problem in the internal dynamics of the Therapeutic Community, and its future successful development may depend to no small extent on its constructive resolution.

Lest one conclude that the ex-addict spokesmen are extreme when they state that "the majority of psychotherapists are impotent role-models" and that "the traditional professional training for psychotherapists results in a deterioration of their ability to help" (Vamos and Devlin, 1975), one might turn to an evaluation from professional sources: Drs. Filstead and Rossi (1973) state that "The traditional professional role is quite inappropriate to the therapeutic community. Therefore, in order to operate an effective therapeutic community, the professionals have to lose their professionalism. This means that the program becomes the prime identity; the profession becomes secondary." Even Dr. Maxwell Jones (1973) respected pioneer in the history of the therapeutic community movement, whose aim was to improve the effectiveness of the psychiatric hospital, as well as the medical hierarchy, rather than to initiate an original therapeutic community de novo, as we know it today, questioned "the dominance of the medical profession and the passive recipient role of the patient" as well as "the abuse of authority within the medical profession, particularly within the hospital system". He further stated that "many of the traditional attitudes and beliefs of the medical world were found to be inappropriate or actually harmful."

It is by now a truism to state that both the ex-addict paraprofessional and the professional each make a singular and significant contribution to the total viability and effectiveness of the Therapeutic Community program. Their joint effort is required to make the total effort work. But it cannot be overemphasized that this effort must be under the general ambience of TLC as a guiding principle, or the Therapeutic Community loses that which makes it work and which distinguishes it from other forms of treatment.

For the ex-addict this does not raise any particular problem. The fact is that peer group TLC and its effectiveness as a change-agent is the essence of the recovered addict's contribution. It is precisely this ingredient, which the addict life-experience was able to provide, which transformed the drug-abuse treatment scene from one of utter confusion and conspicuous failure to one of hope and the promise of human renewal. And as the Therapeutic Community emerged from its infancy to its present position of acceptance, or relative acceptance, (due to its astonishing success and the subsequent change of attitude by the professional community from one of undisguised hostility to tolerance and finally to cooperation), the ex-addict began to learn that "love is not enough". He learned that, in addition to TLC, he must have training and an expansion of therapeutic skills and knowledge for maximum effectiveness. And he learned that in order to achieve this a modus vivendi between himself and the professionally trained psychiatrist or psychologist was essential—despite the difficulties involved.

I suggest that the touchstone of these difficulties lies in the basic attitude toward altruism in general and toward TLC in particular which characterizes each of these two groups. (Although an acceptance of the principle of TLC may not derive solely from altruism as defined, it surely contains within it a very large altruistic component.) The professionals, as I have indicated in Part 1, from the beginning of their training, perhaps even from a period before that, in the very motivation that led them to medical, professional, or graduate school, gave scant attention to TLC as a significant concept. To the extent that this quality did exist, it was ground out in the course of training, as my young medical friend described, while subsequent immersion in the milieu of professional success and status, material and otherwise, did very little to assign a high priority to TLC as an abiding value.

(When the paraprofessionals "regarded the professional as valuing material welfare . . . and asserted that the professionals valued leisure and comfort for themselves above that of the delinquent", as reported by Bassin (1973), were they not, in fact, mirroring the prevailing view of society in general toward the medical profession as a whole?)

With the addict, on the other hand, it was just the other way. Basically unfulfilled, unloved, alone and alienated, without the sustenance of human warmth or support, utterly devoid of any sense of self-worth, the ex-addict lucky enough to find himself in a Therapeutic Community and treated with massive doses of TLC, found that commodity as literally life-saving—like water to a desert-parched throat, or sunshine to a hungry plant. Where all else had failed, it was TLC that literally brought him back to life. It became a lesson he would never forget. The importance of TLC, as the professionals would put it, had become "internalized".

TLC—the ex-addicts recognize its value from the deepest levels of their experience, from the gut, as they would say. While the professionals, belatedly and tentatively, from an essentially theoretical and intellectual approach, are only now just beginning to understand its real significance. But old habits, professionals' as well as addicts', die hard. Dr. Lakoff (1975), in discussing "the training requirements of the ex-addict therapists", complains that "there is often a bitterness toward the 'straight' professional community, especially doctors and psychiatrists who they feel have failed to help them . . ." As a result, he writes, the ex-addict isolates himself until he has "adequately learned to control his impulses, and although his resentment of the professional is quickly repressed, it often surfaces in a passive resistance to the suggestions given him . . ." Dr. Lakoff's analytic training, and bias, is only too clearly in evidence. The ex-addict's attitude is unrealistic "resentment", his accommodation is "repression", and his critical suggestions, if he has the temerity to make any, are "passive resistance" to the professional! Does Dr. Lakoff even consider the possibility that the addicts' "bitterness" is not pathological but based on reality, that doctors and psychiatrists have in actual fact "failed to help", as all evidence indicates (Casriel, 1971; Bassin, 1973; Devlin, 1975; Vamos, 1975; Bejerot, 1969; etc.), and that this attitude represents an understandable response to reality and not a distorted, unrealistic posture, or just a neurotic "feeling" on the addicts' part? And could it not just possibly be that the professional "suggestions" Dr. Lakoff refers to might be subject to discussion, and even change, and that the ex-addict input, his point of view, deserves more than an arrogant dismissal as "passive resistance" or as evidence of a need to "control his impulses"?

The mutual respect so necessary for a healthy and productive exchange of views will not be fostered by such a posture of superiority and infallibility.

Nor will the paraprofessional, or indeed any other worker of any discipline in the drug field, be impressed by the necessarily superior wisdom of professional opinion, when the celebrated analyst, Dr. Bruno Bettelheim (1975), calling on a special insight deriving from psychoanalytic theory, can write that "many of the young people who today suddenly seek escape in drug-induced dreams" . . . owe some of their problems to having been deprived in their childhood of the beneficent values of fairy tales!

Only if movement takes place on the part of both groups—if the ex-addict paraprofessional can overcome the reality of his past negative experience and move forward to assimilate the skills and techniques available to him through the professional—and if the latter can overcome his long-nurtured and ego-sustaining stance of superiority, if he can genuinely relinquish his posture of omniscient M. Deity, if he can "lose his professionalism", as Drs. Filstead and Rossi (1973) suggested, can mutual respect be established. And it is only on the basis of such a genuine mutual respect that an effective addict therapy rationale can be constructed.

Here again, I believe, the concept of TLC is central. The ex-addict moves toward greater knowledge and depth of understanding to expand and deepen the TLC which he almost automatically brings to the program, while the professional who is willing to learn and to grow in a dimension he never even envisaged while in medical school, will move toward a genuine incorporation of TLC as an essential component of his technical skills, useful and important not only in his work with drug addicts, but in all of his life experience.

If the addicted are not to be added to those other disadvantaged groups who have provided "stepping stones to careers" for those who would manipulate their needs for private ends, then TLC, Therapeutic Love and Concern, deriving from a basic altruism, an ipsum bonum in life in general, must remain the basic building block upon which the Therapeutic Community is fashioned, and the measure of all who participate in its work.

REFERENCES

Baldwin, J. *No name in the street*. New York: The Dial Press, 1972.

Bassin, A. Taming the wild paraprofessional. *Journal of Drug Issues*, 1973, 3, 338.

Bettelheim, B. Reflections (fairy tales). *The New Yorker*, 1975, p. 63.

Bejerot, N. Premises for the treatment of addiction. *British Journal of Addiction*, 1969, 64, 87-93.

Casriel, D. H. *Daytop: three addicts and their cure*. New York: Hill and Wang, 1971.

Devlin, J. and Vamos, P. The addiction worker: a crisis in identity. *The Addiction Therapist*, 1975, 1, 20-23.

Fromm, E. *The revolution of hope*. New York: Bantam Books, 1968.

Jones, M. In *The therapeutic community*. New York: Behavioral Publications, 1973.

Maslow, A. *The farther reaches of human nature*. New York: The Viking Press, 1971.

Menninger, R. *The New York Times*. November 13, 1975.

Pirsig, R. *Zen and the art of motorcycle maintenance*. New York: William Morrow and Company, 1974.

Plato. *The apology of Socrates*. New York: P. F. Collier & Son Corp., 1937.

Rossi, J. and Filstead, W. *The therapeutic community*. New York: 1973.

Szasz, T. *The ethics of psychoanalysis*. New York. Basic Books.

Vamos, P. and Devlin, J. The evolution of the addiction therapist: a training imperative. *The Addiction Therapist*. 1975, 3, 27.

Winter, 1978
Some Social Implications of the Therapeutic Community Concept
The Addiction Therapist

Although the modern Therapeutic Community and its concept of changing behavior through the building and nurturing of a special relationship with fellow-human beings developed as a response to the particular needs of drug addicts and alcoholics, the accumulated experience of Synanon, Daytop Village, Portage, etc., points to profound lessons for all of society. What began as an innovative experiment to cure addicts, in the face of the continued failure of the traditional disciplines of medicine, psychiatry, and social work, has now become an exercise in human and social engineering with the most significant implications for us all.

It may once have been comforting to think that "treatment" is something required for those with "character disorders" and that "rehabilitation" is something required only by the "anti-social" and the "deviant". The Therapeutic Community experience, with its emphasis on love, responsible concern, involvement with other human beings in an open mutuality, and growth, has brought home to many of us that we all have characters that can stand improvement, that we all face the problem of growth (or decline), that we all are social beings, that "no man is an island", and that we need, to varying degrees, the identical human support and involvement which proved to be the essential ingredient of the process of rebirth and renewal which saved the lives of so many lost and alienated addicts. We all need love, especially that "responsible love and concern" which is the hallmark of the TC. We all need involvement with others. We can all experience growth through a process of openness, honesty, and self-exploration, as individuals and as members of society.

In its quest for a new and more effective approach to the special problems of the drug addict, the TC movement discovered, or more accurately re-discovered, a whole set of principles and values that are inspirational, if not revolutionary. Love and concern, sharing and involvement, the truly authentic giving of oneself to other suffering individuals without thought of personal gain or profit or fee, this process, at the very core of the *modus operandi* of the TC, stands in the sharpest contrast to the selfishness, the cynicism, the what's-in-it-for-me syndrome which permeates the rest of our society.

Compare the uncaring, self-oriented, look-the-other-way, mind-your-own-business, and above-all-don't-get-involved mentality which is characteristic of most of our society with the TC encouragement, indeed pressure, on each and every participant, resident or staff, to get involved and concerned with the suffering and the needs of others. *The ethic of the Therapeutic Community stands in sharp contrast to the ethic of the larger society, and it is the latter which has more to learn from the former.* For the ethical and cultural value of altruism (love my neighbor), which has always been a central feature of the Judaeo-Christian ethic, is surely more in evidence in the TC than in the community at large. In the TC, in fact, altruism has been rescued from oblivion and from the platitudinous mouthings of the pious, to a position of centrality in the therapeutic process, to the basic ethical value of the community, and recognized as the *sine-qua-non* of the TC way of life. Where, in the real world, altruism in practice has given way to the drive for material success, it has been re-discovered and enshrined in the TC world as the best means of personal success and renewal, in its deepest and humanistic sense.

As Dr. Sugarman put it:

> "*The (TC) movement rejects the materialism of modern America, not only the emphasis on material success but also the emphasis on "externals" such as lifestyle, status symbols, wealth, fame, and so forth. Instead it upholds the values of altruism or concern, honesty, and responsibility—essentially "internal" or "moral" qualities... Yet, unlike the hippies, the (TC) movement does not totally reject the Protestant Ethic. On the contrary, it embodies a very strong commitment to the notion that each person has the responsibility of overcoming his problems so that he can lead a responsible life....*
>
> *To have brought together again the emphasis on mastery of one's own life situation and the value of altruism is a remarkable achievement. It is an achievement of profoundly important implications...*" (1)

Compare this with the recent remarks of a venerated elder stateswoman of psychoanalysis, Dr. Helene Deutsch, colleague of Freud himself, in an interview in the NEW YORK TIMES MAGAZINE (7/30/78):

> "*I am not very satisfied with the psychoanalytic movement here. It is not very idealistic. It's too concerned with money.*" The article continues: "*The lack of idealism in America is partly due, Dr. Deutsch feels, to the character of current analytic candidates*". "*The quality of people,*" she said, "*is different. In the time we started there were people who were very much interested in* analysis. Now

there are people who are very much interested in money, money, how much money can they make?" (2)

If this cynicism and materialism is true of the most prestigious branch of a "helping profession", what can one say of its truth in other areas of American life, in business, politics, academia and the arts? Dr. Rene Dubos, renowned biologist, humanist and social philosopher, made the following revealing comments:

> "Many anthropologists and sociologists have taken a gloomy view of the effects that the modern conditions of life have on human relationships; they see in the present scene little chance to satisfy the essential need for the intimate kind of contact with a very few persons that can occur only within a small primary group ... All the evidence of psychiatry shows that membership in a group sustains a man ... The civilization that, by its very process of growth, shatters small group life will leave men and women lonely and unhappy."

> "Man is alienated not only from other men, not only from nature, but more importantly from the deepest layers of his fundamental self."

"I doubt that mankind can tolerate our absurd way of life much longer without losing what is best in humaness."

> "At heart, we often wish we had the courage to drop out and recapture our real selves. The impulse to withdrawn from a way of life we know to be inhuman is probably so widespread that it will become a dominant social force in the future."

> "The most poignant problem of modern life is probably man's feeling that life has lost significance ... The search for significance is the most important task of our times." (3)

The Therapeutic Community movement, almost alone among modern developments, seems to address all these problems vigorously and imaginatively as a natural and inevitable consequence of its operative philosophy: It strives to give "significance" to the lives of its participants; it recognizes and combats the pervasive "alienation" with which most of the addicts come into the program; it accentuates and nurtures the essential "humaness" of each individuals; it faces squarely and openly the fact that the addict has indeed "dropped out" and encourages him to take the difficult road toward exploring "the deepest layers of his fundamental self", to "recapture his real self"; and above all, it re-emphasizes the tremendous importance of "small group life" and the "intimate kind of contact". The TC seems to incorporate, in microcosm, answers to the problems Dr. Dubos so cogently raises.

Herein lies the making of an historic irony: A corrupt, and corrupting, dehumanized society produces a group of amoral, destructive junkies, who, alienated and dropped out, are fortunate to find a renewing experience in the ethical-moral atmosphere of the Therapeutic Community, and who then re-join the larger society as role-models of humaneness and altruism—bringing with them a philosophy and an ethic which can remake society in a new and more human form!

The Therapeutic Community, an oasis of humanization in the midst of a dehumanized society, points the way to a whole new approach to a wide gamut of human problems. Indeed, "if love and concern can cure the addict, what can they not do for us all?" (4)

One of the concept's most socially significant characteristics is the way in which it views people and the attitude it fosters toward the central concepts of honesty and integrity. In encouraging and demanding honesty within the TC as a tool for self-understanding and for growth, the movement sets up as a paramount virtue the pervasive value of honesty in general—in the selection and promotion of staff, in the development of the theory and practice of the TC modality, in the pursuit of the characteristics, the what and the how, of becoming effective change-agents for people in trouble. It sets up a whole new way of looking at people in general.

This means an end to cant and hypocrisy. It means that a person must be judged on the value of his contribution or potential contribution, the sincerity of his motives, the effect he has on others, his tendency to manipulate or not—and not pre-judged on the basis of traditional credentials, or the lack of them. This means a reversal of the process by which so many hide behind their credential, their title, their MD, PhD, Professor or President of this or that, academic, political, business, even religious titles. The basic TC *group encounter*, which forces the addict to "drop his mask", to come out from behind his facade, to reveal himself and to confront himself as the authentic person he is, to face the question of his selfishness or his generosity, his coldness or his warmth, his alone-ness versus his potential for loving involvement with others—is applicable on a wider scale to all of us, in or outside the TC, with or without titles. *The only "accreditation" the TC recognizes is the accreditation of a person striving to become a full human being.* This entirely honest and open way of looking at people, of accepting them for what they are, of judging them in a new light, can, if spread to the outside society, have a most profound effect on human relations. That might very well be, over and beyond the curing of drug addicts, the TC's most significant contribution of all.

This attitude toward "accreditation" reflects, confirms, and deepens the posture of Dr. Carl Rogers, often called the "dean of the encounter group movement". In describing the qualifications he considers important for candidates for his training program, The La Jolla Program of the Center for Studies of the Person, Dr. Rogers states that "little attention is paid to the paper credentials . . . the Program emphasizes the humanness of the person", and, after the program is completed, "the staff completely avoids putting any formal stamp of approval on those who have participated". He explains this as follows: "If he has no diploma to put on his wall, no certificate of expertise, individuals will judge him for what he is and will make the decision as to whether he is helpful to a group. If he is not, there will be little demand for his services. *He cannot awe people by his diploma.*" (5)

The TC experience also confirms that altruism (love and concern for others) is not necessarily to be found in greater abundance among members of the "healing professions" than in the population at large. And, along with Rogers, discovered "what incredible potential for helping resides in the ordinary untrained person, if he only feels the freedom to use it." (6) These qualities of human empathy, and the willingness to give of oneself, are not limited to any occupational group, or any class, or any income group. They are just as apt to be found among factory workers and farmers as among doctors, among salesmen, carpenters and musicians as among psychologists, social workers or teachers. The difficulty lies in the fact that our society does not cherish, encourage or nurture these qualities, or understand their abiding importance. The TC does, and therein lies another profound contribution.

If this ethic—honesty, integrity, responsible love and concern, and altruism, virtues exalted above all others in the TC, superseding status, title, and position, were to prevail in society as a whole, what mind-boggling changes might not be wrought? We can, at least, speculate: Would Watergate and the myriad scandals and corruption in government be possible? And the corruption in business—payoffs, kick-backs, bribery, nepotism, fraud? And the corruption even in the "hallowed" professions—the Medicaid scandals? And the hundred and one problems in families, in organizations large and small, in unions and in corporations, and in the supposedly virtuous halls of academe? The very nurturing of love and concern, of honesty and integrity, as abiding values deserving of the most careful nourishment, to counteract the personal-success-at-any-price philosophy which predominates in our world, is an idea of tremendous importance—which can be crucial to human development if not to human survival itself. Yet there are few movements outside the TC which even address this problem (I can think of Ethical Culture as another). The very raising of this cluster of ideas, first as an important component of the rehabilitative process and then as a set of social postulates with profound philosophical and practical implications is another major TC contribution. For it addresses each and every one of us with the admonition, "Look to your values".

Characteristically, the charismatic, intense and eloquent David Deitch, who must be credited more than other single person with the early success of Daytop Village, hit the nail on the head (and proved himself disturbing to many others), when he said:

> "... our real job ain't got nothing to do with just overcoming drugs. Our real job ... is confronting a racist community and challenging them to live the life we show by example." (7)

A final observation: The name Therapeutic Community, it seems to me, may not be the best to describe Synanon, Daytop Village, Portage, and all the other self-help communities which constitute our movement. It might indeed be a significant mis-nomer. Webster defines therapeutic as *"to take care of, to treat medically; concerned with remedies for diseases"*. The word is traditionally medical. It was, therefore, the appropriate word for the older Therapeutic Community pioneered by Dr. Maxwell Jones (8), which was originally designed by physicians, to be administered by physicians and their staff, in hospitals and other medicalsettings. Although patients were encouraged to get more involved, the total authority was with the doctor and the enterprise was completely medical in philosophy and outlook. The modern TC, on the other hand, was from the beginning, and is today, a non-medical enterprise. It was born, in fact, as a result of the failure of medicine and allied professional groups to deal effectively with the growing problem of drug-abuse. It's *raison d'être* still resides in that failure. Where medical and psychiatric approaches had failed, the new approach, based on ex-addicts and the human encounter, seemed to succeed. Instead of traditional "diagnoses, etiologies, classifications, and prescriptions for treatment", instead of futile medication and advice, the dynamic of the self-help process, with the recovered addict as catalyst and role-model, introduced a completely new dimension, the success of which spurred the development of a new movement. This dimension and this movement was, and is, thoroughly non-medical. Its early stages were made more difficult, in fact, by the overt hostility of the medical establishment, and if they had their way the TC movement would have died a-borning. Even today, when professionals join a now-respectable TC endeavor, Charles Devlin, Executive Director of Daytop Village, can write:

> "The rhetoric is about professional qualifications; the reality is turf. We cannot ignore the fact that there is a whole establishment world out there which will go to any lengths to keep their monopoly. Thus, we in the therapeutic community

> *field must realize that the professionals working with us are probably considered as bastards by many of their peers, let alone the ex-addict, who is undoubtedly seen in a contemptuous manner by that establishment."* (9)

The theory and practice of the modern Therapeutic Community derive their substance, their strength, and their vitality through the repudiation of the Medical Model, and its substitution by a broad humanitarian model, an educational model, a model based on a holistic concept of human renewal, rather than on the narrow model of medical disease. Since this is so, and since our communities disdain narrow medical explanations (and the narrow medical path of medication and advice) but address themselves rather to the areas of ethics, value, honesty, integrity, love, responsible concern, and human involvement, a more descriptive name, certainly a name more in keeping with its concerns and its outlook, would be The Ethical Community, or the Caring Community, or the Human Community, or the Community for Honesty and Integrity, or the Valued Community. These are surely more reflective of what goes on, rather than the narrow, essentially medical term "Therapeutic" Community. For experience has taught that all that is medical is not necessarily therapeutic, and all that is called therapeutic is not necessarily medical.

But whatever its name, the Therapeutic Community movement is not only a breakthrough in the treatment of drug-abuse, it is also a message of transcending significance to a society which is sorely in danger of losing its human bearings.

REFERENCES

Sugarman, B. *Daytop Village: A Therapeutic Community.* New York: Holt, Rinehart, & Winston, 1974, p. 131.

Gordon, S. *Helene Deutsch and the Legacy of Freud.* The New York Times Magazine (July 30, 1978) p. 25.

Dubos, R. *So Human and Animal.* New York: Charles Scribner's Sons, 1968, p. 184, p. 16, p. 217-218.

Rangell, M. *If Love and Concern can cure the Addict, what can they do for us all?* The Addiction Therapist (Spring, 1975) Vol. 1, No. 2, p. 63-65.

Rangell, M. *On Altruism and T.L.C. (Therapeutic Love and Concern).* The Addiction Therapist (Summer, 1976) Vol. 1, No. 4, p. 59-65.

Rogers, C. *Carl Rogers On Encounter Groups.* New York: Harper & Row, 1970, p. 151.

Rogers, C. *Carl Rogers On Encounter Groups.* New York: Harper & Row, 1970, p. 58.

Quoted in Sugarman, B. *Daytop Village: A Therapeutic Community.*

Rossi, J. and Filstead, W. *The Therapeutic Community.* New York: Behavioral Publications, 1973.

Devlin, C. *The Trial Marriage in the Modern Therapeutic Community: The Relationship between the Ex-Addict Paraprofessional and the Traditional Professional in Drug Free Therapeutic Communities.* Paper delivered at the National Drug Abuse Conference, San Francisco, Cal.: May 5, 1977.

Photo by Meyer Rangell

Photo by Meyer Rangell

Photo by Meyer Rangell

Photo by Meyer Rangell

Photo by Meyer Rangell

February 24, 1982
Mexican Impressions
(writing from San Miguel de Allende, Mexico, GTO.)

The road from San Miguel de Allende, the beautiful colonial town that is a favorite of American artists and writers, takes you along the high central plain to the lovely city of Guadalajara. Thence, heading westward to the coast, you enter a high mountain range with hairpin curves up steep, spiral grades. You hug the mountain and honk your horn against the fear of oncoming buses careening around the bend, while you try to overcome your vertigo and enjoy the magnificent vistas of distant peaks and enchanting valleys. Then it is gradually around the bends and tranquilly down to the sea.

In the countryside you pass the thatched huts of the *campesinos*—primitively built, no windows, no electricity, no running water, no toilets. Barefoot children in rags often share the dusty front yard with chickens and a few pigs. You are reminded of a news item in today's NEWS, of Mexico City: *"In a recent publication, the Inter-American Development Bank reported that approximately three million families in rural Mexico live below the breadline, and cannot produce enough food to meet their daily needs."* (THE NEWS, Jan. 26, 1982)

The road along Mexico's Pacific Coast, from the charming fishing villages of Punta de Mita, Bucerias, Cruz de Huanacaxtle to the bustling resorts of Puerto Vallarta, Manzanillo, Zihuatenejo and the fabled Acapulco, is one of the most stunning mergers of mountain and sea anywhere in the world. Magnificent views greet the eye on your right as you turn with the mountain on your left. White sand beaches come into view—Mismaloya, Desiderios, many still "undiscovered" and free for the time being of creeping development. Along the rim south of Puerto Vallarta where the mountain comes down to the sea in an abrupt and breathtaking joining, the landscape is dotted with high rise hotels and glittering condominiums where, at about $ 125.00 a night, you can stay in dripping opulence.

At Manzanillo, the fairy tale village of Las Hadas, a white Arabesque Disneyland for the ultra rich, with its magnificently ordered streets and lanes lined with bougainvilla and exotic plantings, offers the international jet set the height in luxury—private golf, tennis, swimming pools, sophisticated restaurants, and lavishly furnished condominium apartments and villas conveniently adjacent to a stunning cove and marina for their yachts.

Just across the road from Las Hadas' guarded gates, and a few miles inland, the real Mexico faces other problems.

"*For all the wealth coming into the country—from oil exports and borrowing—Mexico, has, according to a report from the University Alimentary program made by researchers from Mexico's University (UNAM), 18 million people suffering from chronic malnutrition . . . Malnutrition affects between 18 and 21 million Mexicans who live in villages with populations of less than 1,000, where they lack medical attention, electricity, running water and access to education.*" (NEWS, 1/26/82)

This is election time, and everywhere, in small villages and in larger towns and cities, huge signs proclaim the candidacy of the Portillo-designated successor, Miguel de la Madrid Hurtado. A whitewashed wall a hundred yards long in Manzanillo proclaims in letters six feet tall, "*LA JUVENTUD DE MANZANILLO CON MIGUEL DE LA MADRID HURTADO.*" Also, "*POR LA REVOLUCION y CON LA REVOLUCION CON MIGUEL DE LA MADRID.*" Everywhere. In Nayarit, Bucerias, Puerto Vallarta, Guadalajara. The signs are huge, compelling, ubiquitous.

But our waiter in a rough and ready fish joint on the beach, serving us freshly-caught *huachinango* (red snapper), scoffed at the election. "*The outcome is certain,*" he said. "*Portillo and the PRI guarantee the victory of their selection.*" "*And,*" he smiled, "*the mordida (graft) will continue unabated, an ongoing and unchanging characteristic of the bureaucracy in power.*"

In what is seen here as tacit admission of the widespread prevailing corruption, De La Madrid promises a "*moral revolution*" and urges workers to keep a sharp eye on government officials and to report bribery and corruption.

Under the headline, "*DE LA MADRID PLEDGES TO PROVIDE CAMPESINOS WITH HOUSES, FOOD,*" it is reported that "*The candidate received a large applause when he solemnly promised to bring the destitute and desperately poor out of their state of miserable existence.*" (NEWS, 1/26/82)

Meanwhile, "*Nutritionally speaking, Mexico rates at the same level as India, a country with a per capita income ten times lower than Mexico . . . . It is regrettable, the report says, that a country with such vast resources as ours can be compared to one of the worst-fed countries in the world.*" (ibid)

At Mismaloya and at the enchanting, isolated beach at Yelapa, tourists are drawn on high in colorful parachutes, strapped to seats dangling below the supporting cords, wafted into the air behind the tow rope of a swiftly moving motor boat, high over the beach, out to sea, soaring above picturesque rock formations, along the shore line and back to a gentle landing on the beach or in the shallow surf. Freshly broiled fish-on-a-stick is available for an exotic seaside lunch. The south-sea island shop nearby will sell you a T shirt with *YELAPA* on it to maintain the memory.

Despite the fact that "Mexico is the fourth largest oil producer in the world... half of Mexico's people are unemployed, and its inflation rate last year was over 28%... So far, Mexico's oil wealth hasn't benefitted a third of the population that still lives in conditions similar to those of pre-revolution days... Another significant fact is that 10% of the country's population receives 40% of the country's GNP, while more than 40% of the population receives approximately 10% of it." (NEWS, 1/26/82).

At the beautiful waterfalls up the mountain road from Mismaloya Beach daring young divers leap from a high ledge, barely miss the outjutting rock, and land gracefully in the small deep pool below. Tourists gasp as they sip their (expensive) margueritas. The waiters barely notice.

The real Mexico, meanwhile, shows every sign of turning, however slowly, to its real problems: inflation, grinding poverty, widespread malnutrition, and a vast social, economic and educational inequality.

Every appearance is that of a country on the verge of crucial decisions and far-ranging changes.

April 17, 1982
'Survival is the issue'
(In response to a letter that attacked the doctor group, Physicians For Social Responsibility, for their activities against nuclear war.)
The Times Herald Record

It is difficult to take Mr. Philip M. Schmer seriously when he states in his letter that "Whether or not we or the Soviets can survive a nuclear war is not the issue." Is he really asking us all to be as unconcerned as he appears to be about the survival of our country, our civilization, the human race itself, and even our planet as an inhabitable environment?

A study prepared for the Senate Foreign Relations Committee in 1979 reported that 165 million Americans, and as many Russians, would be killed in a nuclear exchange. The living would be even worse off than the dead on a scorched and radiated earth!

A distinguished scientist, Prof. Henry Kendall of the Massachusetts Institute of Technology, as reported in the Congressional Record (Senate) of May 12, 1981, stated that in the event of nuclear war, "there would arise the strong possibility that mankind, and indeed all life, would no longer continue as it always had . . . the principle target nations would be obliterated . . ." There would follow "disease epidemics both of crops and animals on a global scale . . . increased rates of lethal cancer worldwide . . ."

Incredibly unmoved by these prospects, or by human survival as an issue, Mr. Schmer states that "What each side perceives to be the truth is the issue." Alas, differences in perception of "the truth" have caused war and bloodshed since history began. The dead are no longer with us; the differences are. Does Mr. Schmer suggest that we now risk the human race itself and the earth we share because of such differences?

The fact that physicians are speaking up is all to their credit. They have the right, indeed the duty as citizens as well as doctors, to join the growing number of people in all professions and occupations who are opposing the nuclear threat . . . groups like Clergy and Laity Concerned, Pax Christi, a Catholic organization that includes dozens of bishops as members, the Union of Concerned Scientists, as well as educators, students, writers, artists and people in all walks of life.

All of these groups and individuals see it as both patriotic and moral to stop the drift toward an unimaginable nuclear annihilation for us all.

To make light of mankind's survival, on the other hand, as Mr. Schmer does, is the ultimate in cynicism and irresponsibility.

May 17, 1982
Einstein's Warning For the Nuclear Age
The New York Times

       Jeremy Bernstein's excellent Op-Ed piece (April 28) brings to mind a curious puzzlement:
       Albert Einstein, undoubtedly the greatest intellectual force of his time, or indeed of any time, was able to re-examine the existing "verities" of scientific thought and to produce a totally new conception of space-time-velocity that altered permanently the way in which we perceive the universe and man's place in it.
       Is it not strange, therefore, that the insights of this extraordinary mind on the vital questions of war and, M peace and human survival should be forgotten or ignored?
       Einstein believed that the discovery of atomic weapons changed forever the nature of war and, consequently, required a re-examination of the tolerance of war as an instrument of international policy.
       At the very beginning of the Atomic Age, Einstein warned ["Out of My Later Years"] that "unless another war is prevented it is likely to bring destruction on a scale never before held possible and even now hardly conceived, and little civilization would survive it." This must be prevented at all costs, he said, "if man is to prove himself worthy, at least to some extent, of the self-chosen name of Homo sapiens."
       Turning to the problem, Einstein came to the conclusion that there was "only one way out":
       "Our situation is not comparable to anything in the past," he declared. "We must revolutionize our thinking, revolutionize our actions, and must have the courage to revolutionize relations among the nations of the world . . . We must overcome the horrible obstacles of national frontiers."
       "Mankind can only gain protection against the danger of unimaginable destruction and wanton annihilation if a supranational organization has alone authority to produce or possess these weapons."
       Einstein remained a passionate and eloquent advocate of world government to the end of his life. That national sovereignty is an anachronism in the nuclear age and supranational world government our only hope may be the most important message Einstein left us. And he is surely a hard man to ignore.

June 11, 1982
The road to disarmament
The Times Herald Record

Editor's note: In the last year, disarmament has become an important political issue in the U.S.

This Saturday, many mid-Hudson region residents will be among the hundreds of thousands attending a New York City rally for disarmament timed to coincide with the second United Nations conference on that subject.

For months, support has been building for a freeze of nuclear weapons and delivery systems. President Reagan opposes the call for a freeze but has announced his own arms control proposals. Talks between Russia and the U.S. are scheduled to start this summer.

The Times Herald-Record asked its readers to assess the danger of nuclear war and to suggest ways of alleviating the peril. Today's letters represent the second part of the series.

* * *

An exchange of letters on nuclear disarmament will serve a useful purpose if they help to spark a serious, sober and rational discussion throughout the community and within its organizations on what is widely viewed as the most important and pressing issue facing the world today: the peril of nuclear war.

Such a discussion could not be more timely. It comes at a time when the awareness of the destructive potential of nuclear war, and the growing sense that such a war is not outside the realm of possibility, that it is in fact a real danger, is beginning to permeate every stratum of society both in the United States and abroad. After years of comparative silence on the issue, a groundswell of concern is gathering strong momentum as people are becoming aware of the "horror beyond comprehension," as the New York Times called it (April 11).

This is not a partisan issue: people of all political parties are aroused.

This is not a class issue, or an ideological issue; people from every walk of life and of all persuasions are joining the chorus of opposition voices.

This is not an exclusive religious issue: People of all faiths are making their voices heard.

In the week of April 18-24, a new grassroots organizations, Ground Zero (the term refers to the spot on which a nuclear bomb explodes) conducted demonstrations, seminars, workshops and teach-ins in 650 towns, 350 colleges, and 1,000 high schools across the country to bring the dangers of nuclear war to public attention. It is estimated that one million people participated.

Among a growing number in the scientific community, Professor George Kistiakowsky of Harvard University, formerly chief science adviser for President Eisenhower, stated that "the Reagan Administration is launching a massive escalation of the nuclear arms race . . . This is an escalation that dramatically increases the likelihood of a nuclear war that will destroy our life and the lives of your children and grandchildren . . . pushing the military budget of the Pentagon to $1.5 trillion in five years . . . enough money to pay for all of the needed social programs that the Reagan Administration has maimed and killed."

It is not my position that the road to peace is easy. Or that nuclear disarmament is a simple goal to achieve. But it is my position that nuclear weapons have made obsolete all hitherto held conceptions of war-as-usual, with winners and losers. At the very beginning of the Atomic Age, Albert Einstein stated that another war "is likely to bring destruction on a scale never before held possible and even now hardly conceived, and that little civilization would survive it."

Concern for each other, for humanity, for unborn generations must bring us all together to search out new paths of cooperation, new roads to compromise, new solutions to the problem of living together on our common planet.

For it we do not find such paths the alterative is surely that we will face the prospect of being incinerated together.

July 10, 1982
'Israel aims for self-defense, not genocide'
The Times Herald Record

The violent attack on Israel by Messrs. Gidaly, Klein, et al, (Letter, July 6) and their passionate call for a negotiated peace in Lebanon would have been more persuasive had they addressed with equal ferver the harsh realities of PLO terrorism and PLO purpose. For it is only in the context of the PLO's goal for Palestine and their plans for Israeli Jews that Israel's policy can be evaluated and understood.

That goal, boldly emblazoned in the PLO Covenant, calls for nothing less than the destruction of the State of Israel. The Palestinian National Covenant, the PLO's ruling document, as amended in Cairo in July, 1968, spelled out with utmost clarity their intention to expel or "dispose of" over 2 million Israeli Jews after the liquidation of the Israeli State. Article 18 further stated that "Warfare against Israel is legal, whereas Israel's self-defense is illegal."

Officially recognized and supported by the Arab states at their summit meeting in Rabat in 1974, that goal has never been repudiated or altered and remains to this day the bedrock of PLO philosophy and purpose. Toward this end, an unremitting and unrelenting campaign of terror and murder has been directed against Israeli towns and villages, against schools and children, against civilians and others, launched from sanctuaries in Lebanon and elsewhere. Insofar as statehood is concerned, the PLO goal is not an independent state that would live peacefully with Israel, but one that would be a springboard for further pursuit of its ultimate goal, Israel's liquidation.

Succeeding Israeli governments have thus found it impossible to negotiate with a PLO which did not hesitate to demand its destruction. As Golda Meier put it in a speech at Princeton in 1974, the question of "to be or not to be" can never be put on the agenda, for no sovereign state could reasonably be asked to negotiate itself out of existence! The PLO position which prompted that remark (no recognition, no peace, continued guerrilla warfare) remains unchanged today and remains the major obstacle to peace. Every PLO spokesman, from Arafat in Beirut to Terzi at the UN, openly confirms it. A long record of brutal terrorism and murder inside and outside of Israel, at Quiryat Shmone, Nahariya, Maalot, at the Olympic games at Munich, to cite but a few, attest to it.

Much has been said about so-called "moderates" in the PLO. But the search for such "moderates," who might lead in the direction of peaceful Arab-Israeli coexistence, has thus far proved fruitless. And the anguished cries of outrage by the PLO and its

Arab supporters against the Egyptian peace accord with Israel at Camp David confirmed once again their intransigent, hard-nosed position of enmity, hatred and continued guerrilla warfare against the Israeli people.

In these circumstances it is outrageous obfuscation and hysterical hyperbole to accuse Israel of "genocide." To equate the hideous racial murder of 6 million Jews by Hitler with the attempt on the part of the survivors and their descendents to defend themselves against a declared and determined enemy is sheer obscenity. The problem is complex enough without such wilfull, dangerous and untruthful semantics.

As for the deplorable cost in Lebanon in civilian lives and property, is the blame solely with Israel, or with the PLO terrorists who choose to hide in civilian neighborhoods where, in fact, they are better protected and better provisioned than the civilians among whom they cover themselves and whom, in effect, they hold hostage?

How does it happen that Messrs. Gidaly and Klein are "appalled" at "this war of extermination against the PLO," but have not one single word to say about the PLO's uninterrupted record of murder, assassination, brutal warfare and terror in their attempt to exterminate Israel?

What is called for at this juncture is neither the destruction of the Palestinians or of the State of Israel, but the encouragement of a process, on both sides, that would lead to peaceful coexistence.

This means, first and foremost, the abandonment by the PLO of its announced intention to liquidate Israel. Unless and until this is done, any foreseeable government in Israel will of necessity place at the top of its agenda the security and survival of the state and the maintenance of defensible borders against marauding PLO guerrillas.

If, on the other hand, a moderate successor to Arafat comes forward, whose aspirations for Palestinian statehood envision peaceful coexistence with, and official recognition of, Israel, a beginning can be made.

There are ample signs that such a prospect would find great support on the Israeli side.

August 31, 1982
Letter to the Editor
The Times Herald Record

Yes, "Israel Must Win The Peace," as you state in your editorial of August 24, but, since peace is two-sided and in the case of the Middle East many-sided, would it not be more accurate to say that the peace must be won by Israel and the PLO and the Palestinian people and the rest of the Arab world? Is it fair to imply that the burden is only Israel's?

The key question, of course, is whether the Palestinians and the Arab world truly seek peace, mutual recognition and friendly coexistence (the path embarked upon by Egypt and Israel at Camp David), or do they obdurately stick to the PLO Covenant's declaration of intent to destroy the State of Israel? That always has been, and remains today, the heart of the matter.

"The legitimate aspirations of the Palestinians" can only be served if a moderate leadership dedicated to recognition, coexistence and peace emerges in the wake of the Beirut debacle and the humiliation of the Arafat leadership following their military trouncing. Such an outcome would mark Beirut as a milestone in Mideast history.

It is disconcerting, therefore, to read your statement that "the PLO has gained prestige (in Beirut) . . . a prestige strengthened by Israel's failure to kill or capture the organization's most prominent leaders." How ironic. It is the general consensus of most observers that the PLO's survival was a result not of any special virtue on their part, but of the unprecedented restraint of the Israeli military, which could have taken West Beirut at its choosing but did not do so out of concern for the cost in Lebanese, civilian, and Israeli casualties. Military history has recorded very few such examples of restraint in warfare, and unfortunately many examples of the reverse (witness the Allied destruction of Dresden in World War II, not to mention Hiroshima). One might note Israeli restraint in Beirut rather than PLO "prestige."

It is also worth noting that these same guerrillas, upon leaving Beirut, are exhorted by their leaders to continue "merciless underground war" against Israel, according to today's New York Times.

Can we, under these circumstances, expect Israel alone to "win the peace"? Is the burden exclusively Israel's?

September 4, 1982
Senator East's Culprits
The New York Times

Senator John P. East of North Carolina is quoted in The Times of Aug. 25 as saying that the Federal budget is "hemorrhaging" and that the "single biggest cause" is in "the entitlement programs . . . such as welfare, food stamps, Medicaid, Medicare and Social Security."

Some therapeutic blood-letting appears to be the Senator's answer. Transfusions for the national health are sorely and immediately needed—from the poor, the hungry, the sick and the aged.

You don't have to be English to label this ultimate Reaganomic prescription as bloody cynical nonsense.

October 10, 1982
Vogue Word Watch
New York Times Magazine

Over in the Senate, John East of North Carolina—our only multidirectional Senator—was using another hot word in worrying aloud about the *hemorrhaging* of the Federal budget. Writes an irate Meyer Rangell of Bloomingburg, N.Y.: "To cure the hemorrhage he wants to *cut* (or should it be *leech* or *blood-let*) the budget . . . bloody nonsense!"

August 30, 1982
William Safire
New York Times Magazine

Dear Mr. Safire:

The medical metaphor, as we all know, has been done to death. Witness the indiscriminate use of the word *sick* to describe everything from the common cold to the state of the world.

The ultimate (or can it be the penultimate?) may be Senator John P. East's diagnosis of the Federal budget as "*hemorrhaging*" (NYTimes, 8/25). To cure the hemorrhage he wants to *cut* (or should it be *leech* or *blood-let?*) that portion of the budget designed for the poor, the hungry, the sick (here used in a straightforward way) and the aged. Apparently, since these programs are not hemorrhaging, they must be made to do so. This would restore the budget as a whole to good health.

The whole thing reeks of *bloody* nonsense!

November 12, 1982
'Strident' elderly have rights
New York Times Magazine

Given William Safire's powerful penchant for political punditry and pontification, plus his egregious erudition in emendation and exactitude in the use and mis-use of language, one is nonplussed at his referral to our elderly as the "strident retiring" in his column of November 5.

Does he mean that all those who retire are "strident" (Webster definition: "harsh-sounding, grating, shrill")? Or only those who have the temerity to expect that they will get what they are entitled to after years of work and payroll deductions, namely that the government will fulfill the obligation it undertook under the Social Security Act in the same manner that an insurance company redeems a policy after the premiums have been paid?

Could the government renege just when its obligation becomes payable? What would we think (and do) about an insurance company that refused to pay on a policy come due?

Or should the retiring who are now "strident" have been previously more prudent and invested their premiums (payroll deductions) elsewhere?

April 16, 1983
Letter to the Editor
The New York Times

> In this, the penultimate year before *Nineteen Eighty-Four*, one reads with a sense of fear and foreboding, in an AP report buried on an inside page of the New York Times of April 14, that a new Government decree in Rumania will "prohibit the possession or use of typewriters by Rumanians who have a criminal record or pose 'a danger to public order or state security'". The decree will require "private citizens to register with the police any typewriters they own or want to purchase."
>
> George Orwell's ghastly warning—he always insisted that his was a warning, not a prophecy—is mirrored in this obscene, and inherently idiotic, step toward a more thorough thought control. After typewriters, what? Pens and pencils? And what about crayons? Who can foretell the potential dangers to "state security" that lurk in the untutored minds of children? Away with their crayons! At least until we can be sure of what they are thinking—and soon might be writing!
>
> And what about the fingers that do the writing? And the minds that guide the fingers? And the persons who shape the minds? When one considers the use of psychiatric institutions, as recently related in the New York Times Magazine, to "rehabilitate" dissidents, whose activity against such thought-control is itself seen as a symptom of Soviet-defined schizophrenia, we have the Orwellian nightmare almost upon us.
>
> But it is not yet 1984 and one can only hope that sanity will yet prevail and that the world-wide forces of human rights and human dignity will yet be heard against the totalitarian spirit that seeks to shackle man's freedom.

4/14/83:
Rumania Bans Typewriter Use By Persons Who Pose Threat
News Item, New York Times

BUCHAREST, Rumania, April 13 (AP)—A new Government decree prohibits the possession or use of typewriters by Rumanians who have a criminal record or pose "a danger to public order or state security," according to an official publication issued today.

The decree takes effect April 28. It requires private citizens to register with the police any typewriters they own or want to purchase.

The reasons for the decree were not given, but it was believed to be prompted by a spate of clandestine typewritten leaflets, critical of the Communist Government, which have circulated in recent years.

United States Senate
WASHINGTON, D.C. 20510

May 12, 1983

Mr. Meyer Rangell
Mountain Rd.
Bloomingburg, New York 12721

Dear Mr. Rangell:

Thank you for your petition urging me to support a mutual U.S./Soviet halt to the arms race. I agree that this should become—and remain—the first foreign policy objective of the United States. This is why I am an original cosponsor of Senate Joint Resolution 2, calling on the United States and the Soviet Union to

> pursue an immediate and complete halt to the nuclear arms race

and to

> decide when and how to achieve a mutual verifiable freeze on the testing, production, and further deployment of nuclear warheads, missiles, and other delivery systems.

I am happy to know that you and I share the same position.

Sincerely,
Daniel Patrick Moynihan

June 29, 1983
Reagan 'doublethink'
New York Times Magazine

"Doublethink," wrote George Orwell, "means the power of holding two contradictory opinions in one's mind simultaneously, and accepting both of them."

In this, the penultimate year before "Nineteen Eighty-Four," George Orwell's description and dire warning of how corruption in language could be used as a weapon in the hands of those who would corrupt the body-politic seems to have found its apogee in the utterances of President Reagan.

Speaking in Albuquerque before the Parent-Teachers Association, the president seemed to be calling for increases in teachers' salaries as he urged a program of "merit pay." In fact, he resolutely defends his reckless cuts in federal educational commitment not only for the education of disadvantaged children but for the entire educational establishment, including teachers' salaries.

In the same speech, Reagan "denounced drug and alcohol abuse among students as a "dark and dangerous enemy." The fact is, however, despite Nancy Reagan's token visits to drug rehabilitation centers and her expressed enthusiasm for their programs, President Reagan has slashed appropriations for the very programs Mrs. Reagan had lauded, including a $9 million cut this year in New York alone and a crippling cut of 33 percent nationally since he took office.

A Congress that recently voted a resolution calling for a nuclear freeze now approves the world's most destructive missile because the president promises "arms reduction flexibility" and a "build-down" if only he could get approval now for a "buildup." The MX missile, meanwhile, threatening destruction and devastation on an unprecedented scale, is put forward as a "peace missile."

Big Brother, in George Orwell's masterpiece of prophetic satire, used the language of *Newspeak* to convince his people that *War is peace, freedom is slavery and ignorance is strength*. "Newspeak," Orwell wrote, "was designed not to extend but to diminish the range of thought."

"Newspeak" was the language, "doublethink" the method.

Reaganspeak seems to have taken the cue.

July 31, 1983
'We trust you, trust us'
Times-Herald Record

    Congressman Benjamin A. Gilman, as reported in The Record of July 12, returned from a visit to Mexico to report that Mexicans "differ from us on foreign policy, and attitudes toward Central America." Viewed in the context of the Reagan Administration's current policies, Mr. Gilman's remark raises some profound questions. Particularly, Mr. Gilman described what he called "a very moving moment" when a message was displayed on cards from the packed stands of the closing ceremonies of the conference which read "We trust you; trust us." I suggest a profound meaning in this dramatically delivered message which goes to the heart of the saber-rattling policies currently espoused in Washington. May I provide some background?

    I was living in Mexico, in a small town north of Mexico City, this past winter when I was appalled to read in the Mexican press that Senator Henry Jackson, on CBS's "Face The Nation," had warned of "the extremely serious" danger of a Castro-Soviet takeover in Mexico and of the likelihood of a "clamor to bring our troops back from overseas to defend our border" on the Rio Grande! Dismayed by these statements, "the Mexican Senate denounced remarks by U.S. Sen. Henry Jackson . . . assured that Mexico is not headed toward communism" and suggested that Jackson spoke for "transnational interests who seek to benefit from the charge." (Mexico City NEWS, 2/22/83).

    The most influential English-language daily in Mexico, the Mexico City NEWS, in an editorial titled "Easy Now, Sen. Jackson," suggested that Jackson would "resurrect a Manifest Destiny psychosis" and summed up a widespread sentiment as follows; "In a case like this one doesn't know whether the real menace seems from north or south . . . nor whether the senator is speaking for himself or trial-ballooning some official version. While we prefer to believe the former, please, NO NOS AYUDES, COMPADRE (do not help us, comrade)! We've got trouble enough as it is." (2/22/83). This, Mr. Gilman, is what I think the demonstrators meant by their slogan, "We trust you; trust us."

    Unfortunately, Sen. Jackson's "trial-ballooning" soon emerged as the official domino theory applied to Central America by President Reagan, Secretary Weinberger, and U.N. spokeswoman Jeanne Kirkpatrick, a policy which has escalated to an ominous military blockade of Nicaragua, a CIA "covert" build-up of an army of up to 15,000 men dedicated to the overthrow of the established government of Nicaragua, an increase of military aid to the repressive government of El Salvador and the fear, expressed in

Mexico today, as reported in the New York Times, "that the Reagan Administration could provoke a war between Honduras and Nicaragua, settling back diplomatic efforts for months or years" (7/26).

At the heart of the problem is the need to recognize that appalling local conditions-social, economic, political—not "outside importation"—lie at the root of the unrest in El Salvador and in other countries of Central America. As John B. Oakes reported (The New York Times, 7/23), "The majority of Salvadorans are hungry, illiterate, infested with parasites, malnourished, poorly housed, underemployed, and have little opportunity for self-improvement." Efforts to change these circumstances, efforts that are bitterly opposed by a privileged minority backed by a savagely repressive government, constitute the reality that is El Salvador today.

The ongoing problem, in El Salvador, Nicaragua, Guatemala, and in Mexico itself, is the problem expressed in the faces of these children I photographed in Guatemala and Mexico, faces that challenge the humanity in all of us. Will their hunger and their need be met—or will they continue in their turn the century-long pattern of poverty, malnutrition, illiteracy, and oppression that has been the lot of generation after generation before them?

This, not the "importation of revolution by outsiders," or the domino theory, or the "threat" to the Rio Grande border, is what the crisis in Nicaragua and in El Salvador is all about.

October 26, 1983
CIA a government unto itself
New York Times Magazine

What is the CIA? Is it purely an intelligence gathering organization, as its name implies? Or is it more? To whom is it responsible? To Congress? To the Secretary of Defense? To the President?

Or is the CIA a government unto itself?

Your news article of Oct. 16 reports that "the Central Intelligence Agency (CIA) recommended and helped plan recent rebel attacks . . . in Nicaragua." The CIA, in other words, is directly engaged in waging war against the government of Nicaragua, with whom we have normal diplomatic relations, and with whom we share membership in the United Nations. Both nations, presumably, are solemnly pledged to the principles of the U.N. Charter, pledged to honor each other's sovereignty, pledged not to interfere in each other's internal affairs.

What is one to make, then, of the CIA's secret, illegal and dangerous undeclared war? To whom is the CIA accountable? How can it assume war-making authority? What is the legal and moral situation after the vote in the House of Representatives on July 28 to cut off further "covert" aid (more than $50 million), only to have the CIA blatantly continue that aid in an open effort to overthrow the Nicaraguan government?

And what is the significance of the "covert" nature of this involvement, except that it was carried out without the approval or knowledge of the American people . . . and now against the stated judgment of the House of Representatives?

Aroused by the danger to peace inherent in this CIA military adventurism, the House in July finally made the issues public, with the only result that the CIA now operates, at least in this area, "overtly"—but still without the approval of the American people.

To whom is the CIA accountable? How long will the Congress, and the government, permit it free reign to conduct illegal war?

October 21, 1983
The Risk in Culling Aristotle's Thoughts
The New York Times

In his attempt to place Aristotle on the side of those who would support "proper moral indignation and its logical consequences, *including war if need be*" (my emphasis) in the aftermath of the Soviet attack on the Korean airliner, Ken Masugi [letter Oct. 12] demonstrates that it is just as dangerous to quote the ancient masters as it is to quote Scripture.

For example, Aristotle, who died in 322 B.C., in another age and another time, said that "some men are by nature free and others slaves," and that for the latter "slavery is both expedient and right." ("Politics," Book 1). Or how about this one: ". . . the male is by nature superior, and the female inferior; and the one rules, and the other is ruled; this principle, of necessity, extends to all mankind." (*Ibid.*) Or this nugget: "The courage of a man is shown in commanding, of a woman in obeying." (*Ibid.*)

On the subject of anger, and the proper response to the downing of the K.A.L. plane, Mr. Masugi finds a quote to substantiate his thesis that The Times mistook "pusillanimity for prudence" when it soberly stated that "our first, and mutual, problem in the nuclear age is survival." Had he read further, as he advised The Times to do, he would have come to Aristotle's remark that "the angry are more impetuous in starting an attack, for they do not listen to reason." ("Politics," Book 5).

Selective quotation, from Aristotle as well as from Scripture, can be a facile and nonproductive enterprise. It is hard to imagine, however, that if, as Mr. Masugi states, Aristotle thought about politics "in a commonsense way," he would have risked the very survival of our planet as he sought "a life of excellence."

On the contrary, had he lived in our time, he would surely have understood the nature of all mankind's life, if any survived, that would follow nuclear holocaust.

October 5, 1983
Linguistic imperialism
Times-Herald Record

At a time when President Reagan ominously threatens a military blockade of Nicaragua, when the CIA is planning to mount an even larger army of 12,000 to 15,000 for "covert" aid to help overthrow the Nicaraguan government, when an increase of military aid to the repressive government in El Salvador is being pushed through Congress, when four Latin American presidents are meeting to discuss "the increase in conflicts in Central America" and when President Reagan finds it necessary to appoint a high-level commission to consider "the freedom and independence of the countries of Central America," it may be useful to examine what might on the surface appear a minor semantic quibble but may, in fact, on further examination turn out to have profound significance.

I refer to the linguistic imperialism by means of which we residents of the United States have assumed a total and complete monopoly over the word "American."

In his recent speech to the longshoremen, President Reagan stated that, "We send to forget sometimes that here in the Western Hemisphere we are Americans from pole to pole." Yet anyone who has lived or traveled in Mexico, Central or South America knows for sure that the word "American" or its Spanish counterpart, "Americano," refers exclusively to residents of the United States and to no others. This linguistic arrogance (and injustice) is an accepted fact of life and communication "from pole to pole."

Is it not strange that all other residents of the North American continent are known with greater national and geographic specificity as Canadians or Mexicans; that Central Americans with equal specificity are known as Guatemalans, Salvadorans, Costa Ricans, Hondurans; while South Americans, equally entitled to the name "American" are Chilean or Argentinian or Brazilian?

Residents of the continent of Europe also choose the place-specific Frenchman or Italian or German rather than the non-specific "European," which properly covers them all.

How did the United States manage to monopolize the name "American" to refer to its residents alone? And how did the other Americans, North and Central and South, and, indeed, the whole world, come to permit it and to accept it?

It is instructive and significant that there is not a single word in the English language to refer specifically to a resident of the United States as distinguished from others in the Hemisphere. There is such a word in Spanish, "Estadounidense" (University of Chicago Spanish-English dictionary), derived logically from Estados-Unidos and signifying precisely "from the United States." The word is scarcely used, however . . . never in ordinary conversation and rarely in print. "Americano" is preferred and used by all. All other Americans, "from pole to pole," North, South and Central, had better be more specific if they hope to be properly understood!

Has an appropriate English word ever been offered to fill the void? Would it be "United Stateser," or "United Statesian?" The eminent architect Frank Lloyd Wright, borrowing from the English novelist Samuel Butler, coined "Usonian," an acronym for United States of North American, but it never caught on. Might I suggest, with humility, "United Statesmen?"

Since language, as the semanticists are fond of pointing out, is the mold into which we pour our thoughts and our attitudes, this might not be a bad starting point for the Kissinger Commission.

January 29, 1984
Lettes To The Editor
Mexico City—The News

Dear Sir:

Mr. Amnon Kapeliouk's piece on "ARAFAT THE NOUVEAU DIPLOMAT" (1/11), is so replete with subtle bias and selective misinterpretation that, in the interest of balance, it deserves a reasoned reply.

In a stunning display of "even-handedness" Arafat is characterized as a "diplomat" ("nouveau," to be sure, but a diplomat nonetheless), while the Israeli Government is described as "hysterical" and led by "narrow-minded politicians." As is so often the case, underlying bias shows itself in the choice of words; the positive word, "diplomat," for the erstwhile terrorist, while the pejoratives are reserved for the elected leadership of a recognized and sovereign state.

The central fact remains, however it is disguised, that if indeed Yasser Arafat has become a "diplomat" it is not because of newly-discovered principle or because of a sudden conversion to the superior moral position of civilized negotiation. It is, rather, a move dictated by the desperation of defeat and a last-minute attempt to snatch a victory through dissimulation and deceit that he could not accomplish by terror, bloodshed and assassination.

The charter of the PLO boldly proclaims that its goal is nothing less than the destruction of the State of Israel. The "Maximalists" in Syria, as Mr. Kapeliouk calls them, still adamantly adhere to that aim, while the "moderate" Arafat, touted by Mr. Kapeliouk as reaching a "decision to emphasize diplomacy rather than armed struggle," has yet to repudiate that same goal. Nor has he ever indicated his willingness to have the Palestinian state he urges pledge recognition of Israel and peaceful coexistence.

Mr. Kapeliouk, berating Israel and the United States, states that "the key is first of all in the hands of the United States" and that it must recognize "Palestinian wishes for self-determination." But the demands of both morality and practicality, I suggest, would indicate that this is putting the cart before the horse. It is first and foremost incumbent upon Mr. Arafat, or any subsequent leadership that may emerge, to renounce the use of indiscriminate terror and that provision of the PLO charter that calls for the destruction of the Jewish State before he, or the PLO, can claim the legitimacy of diplomatic discourse. For no responsible government, Israel included, could pretend a normal diplomatic exchange with a group that is dedicated to its extermination!

In the absence of such a renunciation, Arafat's "diplomacy" is not only "nouveau' but a sham—the clutching at straws by a defeated and desperate, but still intransigent, terrorist clinging stubbornly to his original goal.

When, finally, Mr. Kapeliouk states that unless we meet Arafat's blackmail, "violence will multiply", he is unwittingly confirming that Arafat has not changed, that his diplomacy, however "nouveau," falls far short of diplomatic standards, that his time has passed and that he has nothing more but continued violence to contribute to the history of the Middle East.

(In response to an Op-Ed article published originally in the New York Times and reprinted in the Mexico City NEWS.)

February 19, 1984
Letter to the Editor
Mexico City—The News

    Displaying his vaunted skills as a powerful and prestigious purveyor of polysyllabic political punditry, William F. Buckley Jr., in his News column of January 22, commits egregious errors in logic and violates a decent approach to morality in an effort to obfuscate rather than illuminate the moral/political issues involved in El Salvador. (You see, Mr. Buckley, anyone can play the language game!)
    In other, simpler, words (which Mr. Buckley avoids like the plague!) he states that it is quite moral, if not essential, that we crawl into bed with murderers and terrorists and support a repressive regime, death-squads and all, in El Salvador, because they are "geopolitically allied with us in the great cosmic effort . . . to give freedom and democracy and decency a chance against the communist monolith."
    He is wrong on at least three counts: To call the effort he describes as "cosmic" is sheer Buckleyan hyperbole, unless he is referring to the recent Reagan moves to extend his military exercises into outer space!
    As to the "communist monolith," serious students of the Soviet Union and of world communism (like Averell Harriman and George Kennan, to name only two) have long ago discarded the archaic notion of an all-powerful Kremlin dictating the moves and calling the shots in a world-wide communist plot. The differences in the various policies of Marxist nations (Russia, China, Yugoslavia, Cuba, Nicaragua, Hungary, Poland) both in their solutions to internal economic problems and in their foreign policies (witness the China-Soviet mutually hostile rhetoric) is today's reality, while the "communist monolith" is a no longer credible myth left over from the past.
    The revolutionary movements in Cuba and in Nicaragua, as in El Salvador, as well as the Marxist and reformist movements of Allende in Chile and Arbenz in Guatemala (both brought down by CIA intervention, to be followed by repressive military dictatorships), are less expressions of Kremlin directives and control than they are of inevitable and predictable responses to brutal oppression, inequality, disease and grinding poverty—and to the Batistas, and Somozas and the military dictatorships that supported and imposed these intolerable conditions.
    The most outrageous argumentation of all, however, is Mr. Buckley's call for support to El Salvador's murderous regime in the name of "freedom and democracy and decency". No matter that there is no freedom in El Salvador, that democracy is neither

valued nor practiced, and that the use of the word "decency" for a government that tolerates, if not directly supports, the sadistic murder and torture of political opponents, as well as non-political missionary nuns, by "grisly death squads", is sheer obscenity!

Most of us, however, will not be swayed by Mr. Buckley's linguistic virtuosity and will see perversity rather than logic in his attempt to advance "freedom and democracy and decency" by supporting a regime that is openly and viciously opposed to all three.

March 19, 1984
Death Squads
Mexico City—The News

It is difficult to read column after column of William F. Buckley Jr. without coming to the conclusion that there is a consistent "modus operandi" throughout, a consistent strategy which can be summed up thusly: If you cannot persuade your readers with logic, or convince them with facts, then befuddle them with a dazzling, and seemingly impregnable, linguistic barrage. Mr. Buckley's fame, in fact, seems to rest more upon this singular virtuosity as a wordsmith than upon any profundity as a political ideologue.

A case in point resides in today's column (The Mess In the Middle East, 3/1), in which Buckley refers to "that grand old word so popularly associated with American foreign policy, tergiversation." I conducted an on-the-spot survey of a round dozen of educated and literate people here in San Miguel and, lo and behold, not one had ever heard of the word, much less of its relevance to American foreign policy. Most opined that in all probability Mr. Buckley had made it up! So I rushed off to my favorite resource in these matters, Roget's Thesaurus, therein to learn that tergiversation means "motion backwards; backsliding", or "change of mind; renunciation; recantation", and even "reversal, repentance; defection; apostasy." Well, if that is what Mr. Buckley thinks of President Reagan's foreign policy, why doesn't he come right out and say so? Tergiversation, indeed!

Meanwhile, however, while I was busy in Roget's, Buckley's agile mind had leaped ahead of at least this reader and, in the next paragraph was linking Reagan to the illustrious Franklin D. Roosevelt and the Immortal Abraham Lincoln who, Mr. Buckley now informs us, also based their policies on tergiversation. So if you respected Roosevelt and revered Lincoln, why don't you like Ronald Reagan?

Moving right along, hoping that the reader in his befuddlement is not lagging too far behind, Buckley next excoriates Anthony Lewis for daring to criticize Reagan's policy in Grenada and in Lebanon. It's all right for Buckley to carry on with his "tergiversation," but Lewis, according to Buckley, "positively sputters"! If you seriously criticize Reagan policy, it appears, you "sputter," whereas if you praise it fulsomely even when it falls flat on its face you become eligible for a Buckley accolade as an eloquent, knowledgeable (and elitist) tergiversationalist.

Almost fifty years ago, in an essay that has since become a classic of its kind; George Orwell, who loved direct, straight, unadorned speech, wrote ("Politics and the

English Language) of the tendency of politicians and political hacks to use the English language to confuse and mislead their readers rather than to inform them. He might have been writing of William F. Buckley Jr. and his penchant for intellectual trickery.

May 5, 1984
Reagans' split message on drugs
The Times Herald Record

It was especially poignant to watch the television production of *The Chemical People* while on a cross-country trip through the small towns and cities of middle America. I caught the program in a small town in northern Texas. It had a greater impact on me there, I felt, than it would have had comfortably at home.

Inspired and graciously hosted by Nancy Reagan, *The Chemical People* boldly and courageously cut through the complacency, the benign facade which masks so much of American life, to focus attention on the dangerous epidemic of alcohol and drug abuse—an epidemic that corrodes our youth, wreaks untold havoc on families, and corrupts our communities.

Nancy Reagan's interest in this problem is admirable, and no one can quarrel with the program's excellent prescription for "community responsibility and involvement." But is it not a supreme irony that while Mrs. Reagan is urging community responsibility and involvement, President Reagan is all but abandoning federal responsibility and reducing federal involvement in the same cause!

Soon after taking office President Reagan cut the nation's mental health budget, including funds for drug and alcohol abuse, by 25 percent—a drastic slash of about one billion dollars across the country.

Thus, while Mrs. Reagan urges responsibility, President Reagan cripples effective prevention and treatment programs by irresponsible budget cuts that have forced many worthwhile treatment centers to close their doors and curtailed the effectiveness of others by forced reduction of services. Many troubled youths who today seek treatment must wait for openings as overcrowded programs lack the facilities to accommodate them—thanks to Reagan administration policies.

Perhaps Mrs. Reagan ought to be talking with President Reagan in the first place about "responsibility and involvement," with particular reference to the moral responsibility of government as role model and leader, so that we can mobilize effectively all of our resources, both private and governmental, in this pressing social crisis.

Otherwise, Nancy Reagan's initiative in *The Chemical People* leaves a central area inexcusably unaddressed.

May 7, 1984

President and Mrs. Reagan
The White House
Washington, D.C.

Dear Mr. President and Mrs. Reagan:

I am sending along the enclosed clipping, a Letter that appeared in our local paper, the Times-Herald RECORD of Middletown, New York, because I think that it expresses a widely held feeling that the American people are receiving a double message from the White House on the important issue of drug-abuse:

While Mrs. Reagan wages a laudable and passionate campaign, culminating in the persuasive television production, The Chemical People, urging national awareness, responsibility and involvement, President Reagan cuts crucial federal funding from programs designed for education, prevention and treatment.

Most people working in the field at the grass roots agree that New York's Mayor Edward I. Koch put the problem in perspective when he said, "It is now clear that we cannot achieve final victory unless we get help. And that means help from President Reagan." Mayor Koch boldly called for "a commitment by President Reagan to ask Congress for an emergency appropriation of $10 million to combat the drug epidemic on the streets of New York." (NEW YORK TIMES, 4/27/84).

What is the message from the White House? Nancy Reagan's passionate advocacy, or President Reagan's crippling of worthwhile programs by the slashing of critical funding?

Will the White House respond with the funding so desperately needed . . . or will it continue to undercut programs?

The question is too important to the youth of our country, and to our country's future, to remain unanswered!

June 18, 1984
Mines are not moot
The Times Herald Record

When the World Court recently, in a stunning unanimous decision, condemned the United States for laying mines in Nicaraguan ports (almost without precedence the American representative on the court, Judge Stephen M. Schwebel, concurred in the decision, voting against his own government), the Reagan administration blandly responded that the question was "moot" because the mining operation had been discontinued a month before and no new explosives had been set in the harbor.

This is like a convicted mugger insisting before the court that had tried him and found him guilty that his crime was "moot" because he had not mugged anyone since his arrest! If the mugger also added that he would not do it again, unless he felt that it was absolutely necessary, he would be closely approximating the Reagan position.

Law and order apparently is a selective concept.

August 23, 1984
Creeping bigotry
The Times Herald Record

It was appalling to read in The Record of July 26, the Rev. Jesse Jackson's startling statement that the Democratic National Convention "acted to mollify women, organized labor, the West, the South *and Jews*" (my emphasis) while "Blacks and Hispanics were told to wait."

Certainly, anyone who followed the convention could not note the slightest "mollifying" (unfortunate choice of words!) of Jews as a particular and separately identifiable group, and Jackson's singling out Jews in this respect is, to say the least, expressive of a vulgar bias, hardly the path he so eloquently suggested in his "conciliatory" convention speech ("We must redeem each other and move on," he had said.).

How, indeed, were Jews "mollifed" at the convention? Why not the Irish, or Italian Catholics (who in fact were more widely represented on the speakers' platform), or any other ethnic group? Why the Jews? Why this singling out of Jews particularly among all our diverse ethnic groups? Why, again, this divisive, ugly, negative and untrue comparison?

As long as Jackson persists in this obscene rhetoric, whether through carelessness (recall his "Hymie" and "Hymietown" references to Jews and New York City) or design (he repeated that "Jewish groups got what they had wanted" at the convention, in Washington on July 25 and yet again before the National Urban League on Aug. 1), plus his persistent refusal to unequivocally condemn the rampant anti-Semitism of his supporter, Louis Farrakhan, he does a grave disservice to the cause of the "Rainbow Coalition," whose colors become soiled and tarnished by such continued, outrageous displays of creeping bigotry.

September 29, 1984
Laxalt's letter, Kennedy's words
The Times Herald Record

A most ominous portent of things to come in a Reaganite future was revealed in the recent effort of Sen. Paul Laxalt, as chairman of the president's re-election committee, to mobilize "Christian leaders" in the president's behalf. Wrapping himself (and the president) in the mantle of "God's authority." Sen. Laxalt unashamedly suggested that Christian leaders use their pulpits, and the authority they derive as religious spokesmen, to pressure their parishioners to work for the re-election of Ronald Reagan, the choice, presumably, of "God's authority." Some 45,000 ministers in 16 states were contacted in this fashion in the hope that such pressure, emanating from high political sources operating through powerful religious figures upon captive audiences in churches throughout the country would have the effect of a kind of political-religious blackmail upon millions of people who are accustomed to treat the utterances of their religious leaders with confidence and respect. Many people would find it hard to resist such pressure coming from the pulpit with the force of a religious injunction.

Such a tactic does a grave injustice to our multi-ethnic, multi-religion society. It must surely be viewed as an egregious violation of our constitutional separation of church and state as well as a blow to the spirit of religious liberty so important to our first settlers. Sen. Laxalt's letter was addressed, one notes, to "Dear Christian Leader." What about the non-christian, the Jew, the Moslem, the secular humanist, the un-religious, the atheist or agnostic—or those millions of Americans who prefer to keep their religious philosophy personal and private? The Laxalt-Reagan tactic is a scary, dangerous trend toward a state religion, creating an atmosphere of religious dictation and intolerance, and pandering to the worst possibilities of religious prejudice.

That President Reagan and his men can dare this tactic is a measure of the extent to which they seek to avoid the real issues of 1984: poverty and unemployment, peace and war, nuclear holocaust or disarmament.

Sen. Laxalt's appeal stands in sharp contrast to the position taken by then-Sen. John F. Kennedy when he ran for the presidency in 1960:

"I believe in an America where the separation of church and state is absolute—where no Catholic prelate would tell the president, should he be a Catholic, how to act, and no protestant minister would tell his parishioners for whom to vote—where no church or church school is granted any public funds or political preference—and where no man is denied public office merely because his religion differs from the president who might appoint him or the people who might elect him."

Kennedy's words in 1960 are equally relevant today.

February 17, 1985
Letter to the Editor
Mexico City—The News

Mr. William F. Buckley, in his piece of Feb. 2, "Concern Over Concerned Scientists' Union", reaches a low point in public argumentation not seen, at least in this writer's memory, since the unlamented days of the late Sen. Joseph McCarthy. Attacking one of the most prestigious organizations of scholars, thinkers and scientists in America, the Union of Concerned Scientists, Mr. Buckley's sneering reference to their careful and well-thought out appeal for a sane peace policy as a "Dear Comrade" letter, and his subsequent reference to Linus Pauling as a "senior fellow traveler," and to the respected George Wald, who has courageously fought for nuclear disarmament for years, as "choking in his own tears," bring to mind the rasping voice of Joseph McCarthy as he ruthlessly and irresponsibly calumnied and defamed some of America's best-known heroes in the Army-McCarthy hearings in the fifties. And one is also reminded of the rejoinder, heard by millions on television, by the gentle attorney from Massachusetts. Mr. Welch, as he leveled his eyes on the glowering McCarthy and said: "Sir, have you no decency?"

One is inclined to say the same to Mr. Buckley. Unable to accept, or to comprehend, the magnitude and the intellectual significance of the support given the Concerned Scientists' proposals by 46 Nobel Laureates and by 500 members of the National Academy of Sciences, Mr. Buckley attempts to befuddle his readers with the nonsensical speculation that it was "fresh air and clean water" that the scientists must have favored, not the peace proposals put forward. Buckley's delusion that he can always gull his readers with fancy foot-work is, apparently, unbounded.

Wrapping himself in the mantle of "duty, honor, and patriotism" (one must be on special guard with such an introduction!). Mr. Buckley exclaims, with wide-eyed incredulity, that he cannot understand why Admiral Noel Gayler and economists Paul Samuelson and Wassily Leontief, and the brilliant and eminent bio-medical researcher Dr. Lewis Thomas "associate themselves" with such a document. The answer may escape Mr. Buckley, but is not so mysterious to the rest of us:

Along with millions of other Americans, these realistic and socially responsible scientists favor the five proposals of the UCS. (No first strike; a comprehensive test ban; massive reductions in nuclear arsenals; a bilateral freeze; a non-proliferation policy) as the best means by which to prevent nuclear catastrophe. Buckley may sneer that this does not sound "like the fruit of ratiocination," but to most of us Messrs.

Pauling and Wald and Gayler and Samuelson and Leontief and Thomas, and their colleagues in science, know more about "ratiocination" (they would probably prefer the words "scholarship" and "thinking" and "careful research" to Buckley's befuddling vocabulary) than does the oracular Mr. Buckley, whose forte resembles more a spurious punditry than any consistent profundity.

For, when it comes to thoughtfulness, clear thinking, and above all an understanding of the ghastly consequences of a nuclear exchange (such as the "nuclear winter" predicted by Carl Sagan and his associates and confirmed by many others in the scientific community), the evidence adduced by science, and the remedies proposed here by these men and women of science, are more persuasive and responsible than the red-baiting, *ad hominem* smears indulged in by the flamboyant Mr. Buckley.

February 22, 1985
Creativity and Crticism
Atencion San Miguel

The talk was warm and flowing on a lazy afternoon in San Miguel, open and candid talk, the kind one likes, uninhibited, and with aspontaneity that is so much more revealing and expressive than the guarded rhetoric meant more to impress than to express.

"If someone would only tell B. to quit writing and to try her hand at something else they'd be doing her a great favor. My God, her tortured prose would be bad even for a not-too-bright eight year old." Heads shook sympathetically.

"Did you see the paintings, if you can call them that, that H. is turning out? Really!"

Going farther afield, one critic opined that it was just awful, enough to make Emily Dickinson turn over in her grave, to see the kind of stuff written these days in the name of poetry, and getting printed, no less—not to mention "novels" that do not deserve the name.

I listened for a time, and finally entered the lists, revving up the conversation and heating up the afternoon by proclaiming, with an equal amount of assurance and fervor, that we were in the presence of one of my pet peeves, *intellectual snobbery*, evidenced by that smug, self-assured, look-down-the-nose criticism by self-appointed arbiters of quality, taste and talent, who delight in derogating, demeaning and diminishing the work of all who, in their lofty opinion do not qualify as "great". As much to parade their own erudition as to address the subject at hand, they offer references to, and comparisons with Dostoievsky, Proust and Stendahl, Emily Dickinson and William Blake, DaVinci, Bernini, Cezanne and Picasso, and even throw in for good measure the novels of Anthony Trollope—the latter, I surmise, just to throw you off base. Of course the lowly unknowns struggling to write or paint or sculpt in the studio classes of San Miguel must shrivel before such an array of genius and, squelched and beaten to a pulp, crawl unobtrusively into the night.

But what was my point, someone asked. "Are you in favor of no-talent or mediocrity? Do you think an attitude of suspension of judgment is either honest or helpful?"

"Good question," I replied, and was off and running on my theme. Here it is, if you will bear with me:

Much of our modern American, and indeed Western, culture, I suggest, suffers from the widespread and malignant disease of Spectatoritis. Watching instead of doing has become the national pastime. Millions of people experience life vicariously, derivatively, their emotions stirred by the emotional output of others, while they themselves live passively, absorptively, spongelike receptors soaking up the creativity of the few. On any Sunday afternoon millions are glued to their idiot-boxes watching a few hundred performers on the gridiron or basketball court or baseball diamond. Like zombies they drink their beer and pass the pretzels while others play and perform—just as others act and talk and love and debate and analyze and elucidate problems and solutions and attitudes. The very stuff of life is experienced secondhand by multitudes, their own creativity and powers of expression and performance withering away from atrophy and disuse. Even sex, through the proliferation of pornography and how-to-do-it books, is being robbed of its creative, individual, explorative beauty, to become voyeuristic and imitative.

This is due in part to a rampant technology that offers us too much too fast too effortlessly, and in part to the dominance of the star-system in our society, which reinforces the importance of Success and Celebrity and makes shameful their lack. Technology makes it easy to be a non-performer, a watcher instead of a doer, while intellectual snobbery, the handmaiden of the star system, reinforces the tendency.

Does this mean that I am advocating the suspension of judgment or that I approve bad painting or bad writing or bad anything? Not at all. It does mean that honest evaluation is properly conducted within the proper frame of reference, its purpose to help and encourage, not to squelch, to destroy, or to suggest that if you are not Dostoievsky you have no business writing; if not Michaelangelo, no business sculpting. Such criticism, in addition to implying that "talent and good taste" reside exclusively in the already-accepted values of others, has the effect of squelching spontaneity, crushing self-expression and smothering that free and untrammeled expression of new ideas and new forms that is the essence of creativity.

What I am suggesting, and what the exuberant example of San Miguel projects, is the opposite of that spectatoritis that threatens to turn so many into amoeba-like blobs. The San Miguel example, encouraging doing instead of watching, suggests that there is a potential for creativity in everyone. It is our human inheritance. More in evidence in our pre-socialized childhood, it is all but extinguished as we are put through the society-factory that stamps out acceptable forms like cookie-molds on a baker's pan. The countervailing influence to a derivative plastic culture lies in the direction of turning around that mass of absorptive human receptors living vicariously, and moving in the direction of living openly, freely, spontaneously, creatively, alive to oneself and to others, unafraid of our impulses toward originality, undaunted by the haughty censuring of others, ready to take a position in the marketplace of ideas in free communion with our fellowmen.

Finally, the Romans were most profound when they said: "De gustibus non est disputandum." (There is no arguing taste.) The French, as usual, said it with insouciance, "Chacun a son gout!" To me it means that performance, quality, talent, and that elusive something called "taste", so arrogantly assumed by some as their exclusive property, are usually defined by culture-bound biases, and those who superciliously assume a cavalier and uppity proprietorship serve themselves and their unbridled egos, but do a grave disservice to the cause of free expression.

So, San Miguel, continue on your exuberant path; paint, write, play, act, sculpt, photograph, do your thing in music, theater and art in all its variegated forms. Full speed ahead—and the critics be dammed!

March 8, 1985
Professionalism vs Amateurism
Atencion San Miguel

Reaction to my essay, "Creativity and Criticism," in the ATENCION of Feb. 22, ranged from accolades (unexpected) to brick-bats (expected). Most of the discussion centered upon the use, or misuse, of the terms "professional" and "amateur" and the conceptualization of "professionalism" versus "amateurism". Many saw my spirited defense of what they called "amateurism" as an abandonment of "standards", without which ART would surely suffer and CHAOS, in the form of untutored anarchy and unbridled license, rear its ugly head.

The issue of professionalism versus amateurism does indeed raise some profound questions, reaching into the realm of the usage of language and the way in which it affects thought and behavior, as well as reflecting the sociology of modern attitudes. The semanticists, Marshall McLuhan among them, are fond of pointing out that language is the mold into which we pour our thoughts, and which, in turn, helps shape the subsequent thinking and behavior of society as a whole. Language, thought, attitudes and behavior are inextricably linked.

Examine the meaning, the aura, that surround the words "professional" and "amateur": The former is almost always used as a compliment (He, or she, is a 'pro'", one says), while the latter is commonly used in a pejorative sense (What an amateur!" Or, "His, or her work is amateurish.")

But what is the essential, rock-bottom, distinction between the professional and the amateur? Both Webster and common usage are in agreement that the essential distinction is that *the professional gets paid for what he does while the amateur does not*. And it is not accidental that the final criterion in our commercially-oriented society is just that. If you make money out of it, whatever you do, it makes you a professional (therefore, good); if you do not make money, you are, by definition, an amateur (therefore less-than, not-so-good—otherwise why aren't you being paid?) This is the way it is.

But what is the deeper meaning of "amateur"? As every student of Latin 1 knows, after having been forced to decline amo, amas, amat, amamus, amatis, amant, the verb is AMARE, to love, and the noun form that derives from that verb is AMATEUR, one who loves. Thus, the amateur follows his creative urges for the sheer love of doing it, (in his Dictionary of Contemporary American Usage, Bergen Evans states that "an amateur is one who takes an interest in something, usually in an art or sport, for the pure love of it.") while the professional does it for the money: Now which, I ask you, is nobler? Which should stand higher in the moral scale of things? Which is a compliment, and which a pejorative? Which leads to more integrity? Is the professional, writing or painting with his eye always on the main chance, on the market, on saleability, truer to a nobler standard? Or is the amateur, who ignores the market and saleability and writes or paints only because he loves to do so and is for that reason less impressed by professional criticism or by the often sordid requirements of the market place? Which leads to more honesty of purpose, more integrity of performance?

Our language and its contemporary usage continuously inform us, and thus shape us to believe as revealed truth that the "professional" is "better" and the "amateur" lower down on the scale. But does a more thoughtful inquiry into motivation and its consequences substantiate such a facile conclusion? Does doing something for money necessarily make it better than doing it for love?

Take the example of LOVE, itself. What do we call the person who does it for money? Is that "professional" higher or lower than the "amateur", who literally does it for LOVE?

Finally, if we strip the work itself—painting, writing music—from the impediments of its money-making aspects (its professionalism), might we not then be in a better position to re-examine its real attributes, in terms of quality and integrity? And might not such an approach lead to a truer appreciation of the dedicated "amateur", literally *one who loves*, rescuing him or her from the bad-mouthing he or she now receives, and restoring him or her to the position of lovingness-in-creativity rather than the present image of hopeless dilettante or inept bungler to which our modern usage has unfortunately consigned them.

Tuesday, April 23, 1985—
Will Nancy Reagan Talk of Drug-Program Cuts?
The New York Times

When Nancy Reagan discusses "ways of combatting the use of narcotics" with "the numerous wives of heads of state" she has invited to Washington on April 24-25 (Washington Talk page, March 26), will she tell them of the disastrous cuts in Federal funds for drug-abuse treatment and prevention programs initiated by her husband?

Will she inform them that since Mr. Reagan took office, "There has been a 40 percent erosion in Federal dollars going to the nation's treatment system," according to Karst J. Bestman, executive director of the Alcohol and Drug Abuse Association of North America ("Some Flaws in the Presidential Rivals' Drug Plans," news story, Oct. 16, 1984)?

Will she tell them that as a result of these cuts many programs across the country have been forced to close their doors and most have had to curtail their services, while treatment centers experience heartbreaking waiting lists for our most troubled drug-addicted youth?

With her much-publicized interest in drug rehabilitation, will Mrs. Reagan explain to her guests, and to us all, why she has not raised her voice against this calamitous budget cutting and program slashing?

It would surely raise her credibility were she to urge rescinding the crippling cuts in Federal funding and the return by the Government to the moral responsibility so needed in this area.

April 25, 1985
Reagans pay lip service to drug ills
The Times Herald Record

Sydney Schanberg, in his column "Our Kids and Cocaine" (Record, 4/8), performed a sorely needed community service when he focused attention on the frightening use of cocaine and other drugs by young people across the country. The seriousness of this situation was further underscored by the recent survey by our state Division of Substance Abuse Services which revealed that an astonishing 43 percent of high school students, or an estimated 675,000 students, were multiple users of alcohol and drugs and at considerable risk of "dangerous side effects . . . and even death."

At a time when funding for drug-abuse treatment and prevention programs is being cut across the country (the Reagan administration has slashed appropriations for treatment centers almost 33 percent since taking office in 1981), it is imperative that we take a closer look at what has to be done, and at the consequences of doing nothing, or not enough. Those consequences, in the opinion of most observers, are to be found in broken lives, crumbling families, destroyed neighborhoods, increased crime, and a tangled web of social deterioration and decay.

Mr. Schanberg does not here address the problem of treatment and rehabilitation. "There is no easy way to turn around the teenage drug scene," he states. But he does touch on the direction we must take in his concluding sentence: "We'll have to set a better . . . role model for them."

In this, Mr. Schanberg is on the right track: If the last two decades of treatment experience in this difficult and frustrating field has taught us anything, it is that the most effective catalyst for change is the role model of the recovered addict, who provides the addict-in-treatment a sense of hope and a method of rearranging his values and priorities. When he comes to the realization that someone truly cares and is deeply concerned about his return to a productive and satisfying life, the addict takes his first step toward recovery. And when that someone, in addition, is one who has painfully traveled the same route, progress is enhanced.

On a larger scale, the rest of us also have a duty and a responsibility: to set "role models" that are free from the cant and hypocrisy which often form the background of that moral decay which the young and cynical addict is quick to cite as a rationale for his own behavior. The adult world cannot behave in an immoral and asocial manner and expect our youth to develop acceptable social patterns. "Do as I say, not as I do" is not an acceptable formula for influencing the young.

It is in this connection that we might examine the attitudes and the performance of society as a whole and of the federal government in particular. While loudly proclaiming its concern with the problem of drugs and its effect on the young, the Reagan Administration has consistently undercut programs for treatment and prevention. From the very beginning of his administration, President Reagan has sought to dissociate the federal government from responsibility in this area as he shifted the burden to local communities and to the private sector. As early as 1981 the federal budget cut appropriations for mental health and drug and alcohol abuse by 25 percent, a cut of about $1 billion, and additional cuts have taken place since. The philosophy of the federal government is to pay lip service to the problem, while shifting the practical responsibility elsewhere.

In an interview last year, Karst J. Besteman, executive director of the Alcohol and Drug Abuse Association of North America, said, "There has been a 40 percent erosion in federal dollars going to the nation's treatment system" since Mr. Reagan took office (New York Times, 10/16/'84). At the same time, Representative Charles B. Rangel, then-chairman of the House Select Committee on Narcotics, stated that his committee hearings had indicted that "private resources cannot fill the void left by federal abandonment of the treatment and prevention field."

In this climate, how can we view the activities of Nancy Reagan who, while making drug-abuse a major and well-publicized area of interest, has never raised her voice against these crippling cuts? What are we to make of Mrs. Reagan's stated concern, while President Reagan scuttles urgently needed funding? Is it simply public relations? A White House pollster recently reported that Mrs. Reagan's involvement in drug-rehabilitation activities was a major reason for "a 20-point increase in her approval rating." And now Mrs. Reagan is inviting "numerous wives of heads of state" (as though this were a special problem for the wives rather than for the heads of state themselves!) to come to Washington "to discuss ways of combatting the use of narcotics."

One wonders whether Mrs. Reagan will inform her guests, and explain to them as well as to the rest of us why the federal government is in the process of abandoning the treatment and prevention field, and how she sees her role in that betrayal. For it would surely raise her credibility before her guests, as well as before the nation if she were to urge her own "head of state" to rescind those cuts and return the federal government to that moral responsibility that is so needed in this area.

This is the kind of "role-modeling" that Mr. Schanberg may have been talking about, on both a personal and a governmental level, that would represent a sensible advance in addressing the problem of "Our Kids And Cocaine."

Meyer Rangell of Bloomingburg is a retired social worker. He has been active in drug rehabilitation for many years and is a member of the Alcohol and Drug Abuse Planning Committee of the Sullivan County Department of Social Services.

July 2, 1985
Times demand new approaches to peace
The Times Herald Record

In his effort to discredit those who advocate a halt in the nuclear arms race, Mr. Phillip M. Schmer (Deterrence, not freeze, keeps peace, 5/31), offers, with an exquisite indifference, a contradiction of his own: Pessimistically asserting that "Man has been slaughtering man for 6,000 years" (a "simple fact," he states), Mr. Schmer nevertheless optimistically assures us that "the nuclear umbrella over Europe and the strength of the United States" will be able to keep the peace in the future.

After proving that no arms race in the past has had the effect of preventing war, he goes on to urge our reliance on the most dangerous arms race in all history to prevent war in the future.

Understandably, Mr. Schmer is not willing "to gamble my children or my country" on a "theory that has never worked." But is he willing to gamble on a destructive power that would render our planet uninhabitable for all of us and for all living things?

Albert Einstein, a hard man to ignore, stated ("Out of My Later Years") that "unless another war is prevented it is likely to bring destruction on a scale never before held possible and even now hardly conceived, and little civilization would survive it . . . our situation is not comparable to anything in the past."

The character and the consequences of all previous wars compared to the character and the consequences of a 20th century nuclear war make all previous thinking about war obsolete. Einstein, again, warned that "We must revolutionize our thinking, revolutionize our actions, and must have the courage to revolutionize relations among the nations of the world . . ."

Mr. Schmer singles out the Physicians for Social Responsibility (PSR) for his special criticism. Yet it is the PSR that has continuously and informatively warned the American people, on the basis of sound research and the collective wisdom of such scientists and scholars as Dr. Jonas Salk, Dr. Carl Sagan, former Secretary of State Cyrus Vance, presidential science adviser George Kistiakowski, and an array of scientists whose credentials Mr. Schmer would not deny, that there can be no medical planning for nuclear war, "that there is no possible effective medical response; that recovery from nuclear war would be impossible, that there can be no winners in a nuclear war, that worldwide fallout would contaminate much of the globe for generations and atmospheric effects would severely damage all living things as well as food and water supplies; that there is no cure for nuclear war, only prevention."

That this is not the hysterical opinion of a small band of alarmists was evidenced last year when a majority of the House of Representatives, agreeing with this assessment, voted to support a bilateral, verifiable nuclear weapons freeze. Representing millions of Americans, the House thus asserted that the road to peace is not still another dead-end and deadly arms race, but a new approach that is in keeping with the demands of a new age—beginning with arms control and arms reduction on both sides, before it is too late.

August 13, 1985
A double response in the nuclear debate
The Times Herald Record

With the 40th anniversary of the dropping of the first atom bomb over Hiroshima, on Aug. 6, 1945, it is altogether fitting that we address the awesome problem of nuclear weaponry and its potential for destruction in the modern age. Estimates are that 340,000 deaths resulted from the two bombs over Hiroshima and Nagasaki. A recent study ordered by the Senate Foreign Relations Committee revealed that over 300 million would be killed in a thermonuclear exchange between the United States and the Soviet Union. We have come a long way!

It is in this light that we view the recent exchange of letters and "my view" articles by Mr. Philip Schmer, Mr. Ben Schlamm and myself. The subject is complex; no one has a corner on the wisdom needed here, and nowhere, at no time, has there been a more urgent need for reasonable, responsible discussion of the literally earth-shaking issues involved.

It is, therefore, regrettable that Mr. Schmer chose to descend to name-calling and calumny in his response (7/24) to my previous "my view" article (7/2), which attempted a reasoned plea for "arms control and arms reduction on both sides, before it is too late."

Mr. Schmer calls me "deceitful" and accuses me of misquoting, although he does not offer (nor, indeed can he offer) a single example of misquotation.

Mr. Schmer also calls the Physicians for Social Responsibility (PSR) "deceitful" because of their conviction, based on scientific studies and medical evidence, that "recovery from nuclear war would be impossible."

In a recent issue of Manhattan Medicine (2/83), official organ of the New York County Medical Society, the society's president wrote: "I believe physicians are virtually united in their effort to convey an urgent message to all Americans and to the administration about nuclear war. The message is clear. Nuclear war of any kind would cause death and suffering on a scale never seen before on this planet, and modern medicine with all its skills could do little or nothing to help." Is this medical spokesman, according to Schmer, also being "deceitful?"

The essential difference between Mr. Schmer and myself is his contention that nuclear war is winable. "The effects of any disaster can be mitigated," he writes. Nuclear war, in this view, is thinkable, an option to be entertained and to prepare for.

I, on the other hand, stand with those scholars, scientists, and statesmen around the world who contend that there can be no "winners" in the aftermath of nuclear war—only a devastated and unlivable Earth. I stand with the revered Albert Einstein, who warned that "little civilization would survive a nuclear exchange." Or was Einstein, according to Schmer, also "deceitful?" Do we believe Professor Einstein, or Mr. Schmer?

Outdoing Mr. Schmer, Mr. Ben Schlamm's letter on 7/27 was nothing more than a vicious, intemperate, personal attack. He accuses me of calling for the "collapse of the capitalistic system," supporting "Marxist power," harboring deep and dark ulterior "motives," and even being in favor of the Russian "Gulag" prison system! Of course, I said nothing of the kind, and when this type of "argument" is used to address the central issue of our time—the danger of nuclear war to us all and to all humanity—the demands of honesty and integrity require that we sit up and take notice.

What I did call attention to was the danger that nuclear war had the potential of visiting unimaginable death and devastation on us and on generations yet to come, and even the potential to destroy our Earth as a livable environment.

Mr. Schlamm's vituperative personal attack is beneath contempt. His is the real red-herring, the cover-up to an hysterical refusal to address the facts. Calling names is so much easier!

Finally, I would offer a prophetic poem, entitled "Future," by Joseph Brodsky, who left the Soviet Union in 1972, and now lives and teaches in the United States:

> "High stratosphere winds with their juvenile whistle.
> A thought-like white cloud in search of mankind.
> Oh, where are you flying?, said missile to missile.
> There is nothing ahead and nothing behind."

October 21, 1985
Nothing says it better than the Nobel Prize
The Times Herald Record

Were Philip Schmer's statement of Sept. 23 that "peace movements bring on wars" merely an example of absurd hyperbole, one could ignore it and accept his intention to end the "nuclear debate." But the statement is too destructive and pernicious to go unchallenged, and the nuclear debate too important to be abandoned at this crucial time. On the contrary, what is needed is a broadening and expanding of responsible discussion to include every group in the community. Attempting to build a world climate of peace, encouraging citizens on every level to make his/her input, rather than leaving this life-and-death issue to the politicians alone, may make all the difference between human extinction and survival.

May I respond specifically to some of Mr. Schmer's arguments:

1. Mr. Schmer stated (July 24) that Dr. Carl Sagan's theory of widespread famine caused by a "nuclear winter has been discredited by the scientific community." Inexplicably, he repeats this falsehood in the face of precisely opposite scientific findings: Under the headline, "Study Says 4 Billion Could Starve In 'Nuclear Winter' After Attack," The New York Times reported (Sept. 13) that "billions of people who survived the explosions of a nuclear war would face drawn-out deaths by starvation, an international scientific group said today in a new study supporting the theory of a global 'nuclear winter' that would ruin agriculture." It was further reported that "the new report's conclusions don't represent the views of political activists or environmental extremists or people with any particular policy position, but rather we feel this is a sober assessment by 200 of the top world scientists on agriculture and ecologic systems." So much for Mr. Schmer's shedding the light of truth on Dr. Sagan's nuclear winter theory!

2. Impervious to mounting evidence, Mr. Schmer repeats (Sept. 23) that nuclear war in winnable and "with proper prior planning," survivable. Contrary evidence, however, was adduced by the prestigious Institute of Medicine of the National Academy of Sciences, which reported (Sept. 22 New York Times) that "epidemics of diseases are likely in the months and years following nuclear attack. Such diseases include tuberculosis, leprosy, pneumonia, Legionnaire's disease and probably cancer. . . . The three-day symposium has furthered recent

studies that have concluded a nuclear war would be much more destructive than original estimations by scientists." While defaming the Physicians for Social Responsibility, Mr. Schmer gives no indication of the kind of planning his little-heard-of "Doctors for Disaster Preparedness" propose to respond to this predictable scenario of chaos and rampant disease.

3. Mr. Schmer invokes the name of Albert Einstein to bolster his argument for increased nuclear armaments, stating correctly that Professor Einstein initiated the atom bomb project with his letter to President Roosevelt during World War II in order to defeat Hitler's Germany. Yes, that much is ture. But it also cannot be ignored that Einstein, after Hiroshima, clearly foresaw the immense destructiveness of nuclear warfare, was appalled at the unprecedented danger it represented to civilization itself and spent the rest of his life advocating the elimination of nuclear weaponry. To use his name to advocate an unrestrained nuclear escalation is to distort Einstein's position and to deliberately misrepresent his final message to posterity.

Finally, if ever confirmation were needed of my position with respect to the medical disasters that would follow a nuclear exchange, that confirmation came this month in stunning fashion with the granting of the Nobel Peace Prize to the International Physicians for the Prevention of Nuclear War.

The Nobel Peace prize is certainly the most eloquent answer to the outrageous attack by Mr. Schmer on the Physicians for Social Responsibility (PSR), the American wing of the international group. He called that honored group "deceitful" when it alerted us to the impossibility of mounting an effective medical response to the chaos, disease and famine that would follow a nuclear exchange by the super powers. The Nobelists thought otherwise!

The Nobel Prize Committee reconfirmed the message that Dr. Bernard Lown, founder of the PSR in the United States, and his associates in 41 nations, including the Soviet Union, rang out to all peoples that "nuclear winter" is a dread reality to be reckoned with and that famine, disease and horrors yet unimaginable make nuclear war unwinnable and unthinkable. In so doing, the Nobel Prize Committee has struck a powerful blow for sanity and peace.

Monday, Dec. 30, 1985
Tolerating apartheid only perpetuates its evil
Tallahassee Democrat

In a celebrated essay, "Politics and the English Language," George Orwell demonstrated almost 50 years ago the tendency of politicians and some political writers to corrupt the process of language in order to corrupt the process of thinking. This is accomplished by the deliberate use of emotionally charged words specifically designed to deflect the reader from rational thought and to appeal instead to his prejudice, his fears and his angers.

Language is thus used to obfuscate rather than illuminate the real issues, while facts and logic are avoided, or twisted, in favor of a hysterical orgy of panic-mongering.

A case in point is the Nov. 25 My View column by Steve Brockerman. In a relatively brief space, Mr. Brockerman manages to use the following pejorative words and phrases, each of which is deliberately calculated to inflame rather than to inform: "opportunistic," "racist," "anti-capitalistic," "collectivist mob of stooges," "statist," "reactionary," "butchers," "planned economic slavery," "deacons of virtue," "puppeteers," "enslavement," "mob of stooges" (again) and "altruistic verbiage." All of these well-thought-out and carefully selected epithets are directed at those who oppose the repressive Botha regime in South Africa on straight moral grounds, and against the now widespread attempt to withdraw support from that regime by economic sanctions and divestiture.

If one can survive the heat and smoke of Mr. Brockerman's linguistic assault and still manage some rational thought, one arrives at his main arguments; that those who oppose the evils of the Botha government of South Africa are hypocrites because they do not also oppose the inequities and evils in the Soviet Union, North Korea, Red China, Afghanistan, Nicaragua, Ethiopia and all Marxist regimes, with particular reference to other black nations in Africa where "white oppression" flourishes. Mr. Brockerman passionately opposes all of those evils and feels for their victims, but successfully restrains his compassion with regard to South Africa and its millions of black victims. His reason is that South Africa is a "quasi-free nation."

His logic, and his ultimate philosophy, is contained in the following wistful universal declaration: "The greatest political statement anyone can make is to make a profit." Thus, if we only refrain from preventing the Botha government and its white corporate supporters from making a profit, or conversely, if we actively support them economically and socially, we make the optimum in virtuous political statements and help to keep South Africa a good and desirable "quasi-free nation."

Presumably, according to Brockerman, that state is "quasi-free," which permits 3 million whites to prosper and to enjoy the freedom to disenfranchise, exploit and oppress 23 million blacks. The loss of freedom by the overwhelming majority, the harassment and humiliation, the summary jailing without charges or bail, the murder of school children, the enforcement of odious laws that destroy families, prevent free movement, stifle free speech and freedom of assembly and deny the most elementary civil liberties in order to keep minority in power and privilege— all this, apparently is Mr. Brockerman's concept of "quasi-free." "Quasi means partly, so I imagine he means free for some but not for others—which is not, after all, that completely bad!

Because South Africa is thus "quasi-free," Mr. Brockerman opposes all efforts to influence the Botha government in the direction of democratic change. Presumably, the best contribution we can make is to help them (the white upper class, that is) "make a profit," the cost in human life and human degradation notwithstanding.

Mr. Brockerman accuses the supporters of the campaign against apartheid of a hypocritical indifference to the evils found in Marxist regimes, as well as in other African governments. There is, however, no evidence whatsoever of such an equation. Indeed, if evil is to be fought wherever found (the soundest of moral positions), Mr. Brockerman should be equally passionate on the side of the anti-apartheid movement as he is on the side of the anti-Marxists.

As it is, a paranoid, monomaniacal fear of "communism," however loosely defined, permits him to tolerate, even support, the most evil of regimes and practices on the ground that he anticipates greater evil in any regime that may follow. Ignore the present evil before us, he suggests, because future evil may be worse. It is a facile reasoning, simplistically appealing to many, but its consequences are an acquiescence in, and a perpetuation of, existing evil, disarming those who would oppose oppression and supporting the oppressors, while millions languish under conditions of patent injustice and intolerable deprivation.

The argument, finally, that we ought to tolerate state-sanctioned murder and a fascist social structure and do nothing to oppose them because injustice also exists elsewhere, just won't wash in anyone's morality.

Meyer Rangell is a retired social worker.

March 26, 1986
Letter To The Editor
Mexico City—The News

You know, William Buckley Jr. is really a sweet guy. Despite the carping critics (I among them) who are wont to fault him for the acidity of his pen, the sharpness of his tongue and the venom of his vocabulary, underneath it all he is really a sweetheart.

Take his column of March 2 for example ("Reflections On Marcos' Departure"). While everyone else stands aghast at the proportions of the revealed corruption in which his regime was steeped, Buckley, all heart, calls Marcos a "prince" who bravely stepped down to save his people from bloodshed. Bill can also find it in his heart to stand up and say kind words about other dictators, like Salazar and Franco, who, he informs us, with an exquisite generosity of spirit, "ruled their countries rather permissively"! And with what sensitivity, empathy, and just sheer sweetness he defends the honor and virtue of Imelda Marcos as he chides those who would churlishly deny her collections of jewels and of priceless masterpieces of art, no matter how obtained. Yes, Bill can be very sweet and thoughtful when he wants to.

The fact is that while Mr. Buckley employs his heavy artillery and fabled skill at invective in passionate tirades against labor unions, strikers, union musicians and mushy liberals (see Jan. 24), he can always be counted upon to draw on an unsuspected reserve of human sympathy and kindness for the Francos and Duvaliers and Marcoses of this world—at the same time that he self-righteously inveighs against the "Jacobinical" mobs that insist on storming the palaces for a chance at a better life.

April 11, 1986
Passover Starts April 24
Atencion San Miguel

The Passover Seder which we celebrate at present means different things to different people.

It is a time when Jewish families gather in warmth and solidarity, in closeness and in love to be together and to celebrate together their unity within the family circle—while they dedicate themselves once again, through the medium of an age-old ritual, to the meaning and the spirit of a profound aspect of Jewish history.

But I like to think that Passover is also a time for a wider coming together and a wider compassion, encompassing not only the family but the community in which we reside and the world in which we live . . . indeed, a reaching out in compassion and brotherhood to all humanity.

And I like to think that this Seder in particular here in San Miguel de Allende, far from home, including not only our Jewish brothers and sisters but also our many non-Jewish friends who have come to celebrate with us, reflects in a special and beautiful way the universality of the Seder spirit.

For the Seder, to me, is not only a religious ritual. So many rituals, by their very repetition and their very ritualization, stand in danger of losing their deep moral and philosophic significance. Our Passover Seder does, of course, rest on a bedrock of religiosity. But it also appeals to the non-religious Jew, and our Jewish brothers and sisters all over the world come together at Passover regardless of the extent of their religiosity or their lack of it.

I like to think that they, we, come together at Passover to remind ourselves that we are Jews, to seek the deeper meaning of our common Jewish heritage, and to explore together the unique contributions that Judaism and Jewish history have made to civilization and to all humanity.

How much more significant and important and profound this has become because of the Holocaust, and the lessons of the Holocaust! Albert Einstein, no observer of ritual, was profoundly insightful when he said, "Hitler made me a Jew!"

Performed in the privacy of the family circle, the Seder has, among other things, a bonding effect, bonding the family together once again. Ritual and love affectively cohere. Performed in a community, however, in the presence of a larger social unit and including non-Jewish friends, the Passover Seder seems to me to provide an even more profound experience, emotionally and spiritually, as we re-commit ourselves in each other's presence—bearing witness as it were—to the larger meaning of Passover.

And what is that larger meaning?

To me, the Exodus from Egypt represents the start of the first FREEDOM MARCH. And the forty years in the parched desert represent the travail, the doggedness, the perseverance, and the dedication to freedom of those first FREEDOM MARCHERS. Sustained by a fierce opposition to slavery and an unquenchable dedication to their self-determination as a people, the Exodus marchers fought on against all adversity, until they reached their "promised land." In so doing they set an eternal example for all future freedom fighters . . . and for freedom marchers yet to come.

When Martin Luther King, Jr. and his brave band of followers marched from Selma to Birmingham, Alabama, braving the water-hoses and the snarling dogs of Bull Connors, theirs was the spirit of the Jewish marchers across the arid Sinai desert years before.

When Harriet Tubman and her gallant supporters, black and white, led runaway slaves to freedom along the underground railway, they were in the same tradition.

When Northern students defied the cruelties of Southern' sheriffs to help bring the vote to disenfranchised blacks in the Civil Rights movement of the sixties (they, too, were called Freedom Riders), they were in the same tradition and the same spirit.

When two Jewish young men, Andrew Goodman and Michael Schwerner, and their black comrade, James Chaney, were viciously tortured and murdered as they took part in this freedom campaign, they also were carrying the torch in this same tradition.

When the modern sanctuary movement, encompassing many religious faiths, ours among them, assists today's Salvadoran and Guatemalan' refugees in flight from cruel oppression in their native lands, that is also in the same tradition.

When the Chinese engaged in their Long March in 1948 for their own self-determination against the tyranny of their day, they were also engaged in a FREEDOM MARCH, in the same tradition.

When Father Hidalgo and Ignacio Allende marched down with their ragged band from Dolores to San Miguel and on to the Spanish garrison at Guanajuato in 1810, they were also in the same tradition. And when, along with the heroic Pipila, their severed heads were hung in the ramparts of the Spanish Granary in Guanajuato as a warning (a vain warning, it turned out!) to other freedom fighters, they were being slaughtered by their Pharaoh in the same struggle.

Yes, the Jews of the Exodus may be viewed as the first of a long line of FREEDOM MARCHERS, and their exploit resounds down through history—wherever people rise to fight the tyrant and to stand up for freedom.

From this inspiring and joyous Seder, here in San Miguel, Jews and non-Jews together (and I especially toast our non-Jewish friends!) I would like to lift glasses to toast our brothers and sisters everywhere, in close family circles and in communities all over the world, as we come together to remember, through ritual and religious symbols, yes, but also with a sense that we are moving beyond ritual, and transcending symbols and religiosity, to remember forever that freedom is never a gift handed to us by others without payment or struggle, but an everlasting good, to be cherished and protected and fought for again and again, and preserved and extended by us all.

This, to me, is the meaning of the Passover Seder we have come to celebrate today.

SHALOM!

July 12, 1986
Sad road from Bitburg to Vienna
The Times Herald Record

What President Reagan started at the Bitburg Cemetery just one year ago, 53 percent of the voters of Austria completed recently. The moral pathway is not difficult to discern: If the most powerful political figure in the world could honor the graves of the Waffen SS, how can one criticize the Austrian voter who decides to forgive the Nazi past of Kurt Waldheim? If the president of the United States could reveal a moral obtuseness that proclaimed that "most of the German soldiers buried in the cemetery were as much victims of the Nazis as the Jewish inmates of the concentration camps" (New York Times, April 20, 1985), how can we expect a more discerning moral posture on the part of the average Austrian voter?

The message sent out by President Reagan from Bitburg was received loud and clear in Vienna. In the name of "reconciliation," the message ran, play down or ignore the unimaginable horrors of the Holocaust. With this rationale, a generation of Austrians has been carefully shielded from the unspeakable truth.

The shocking election of an ex-Nazi to the presidency of Austria (Sen. Daniel P. Moynihan, D-N.Y., aptly stated that Waldheim's "election amounts to an act of symbolic amnesty for the Holocaust") raises once again the problem of how the people of the world, Jew and Christian alike, view the Holocaust and come to terms with its monumental depravity. How do we view, and how does history view, the Josef Menegeles, the Adolph Eichmanns, the Klaus Barbies, and the system in whose name they committed their crimes? In his famous speech last year in which he implored President Reagan not to go to Bitburg, Elie Wiesel asked, "How does life continue in the face of this crime against humanity?" One way, he said, is to "teach each new generation of Americans the story of the Holocaust." (New York Times, April 20, 1985). It is clear that the Austrians felt no such need. An Austrian school teacher informed us (New York Times, June 14, 1986) that "The Growth of Austria," a high school history text . . . has one sentence about the Austrian persecution of Jews and Gypsies in World War II!"

President Reagan chose to ignore Mr. Wiesel's plea, and that of 53 senators led by Sen. Howard Metzenbaum. He displayed, said Sen. Moynihan at the time, "a measure of moral insensitivity that we must not permit in our Presidency." (It is instructive and ironic that the presidential aide who planned the details of the Bitburg trip was none other than Michael Deaver, now under investigation for moral, and perhaps legal, indiscretions of his own.)

The message from the cemetery at Bitburg in 1985 had its effect in Vienna in 1986: The American president who honored Nazi graves helped to pave the way for the election of an ex-Nazi to the presidency of Austria, and even now continues on that shameful path by sending him a congratulatory telegram on his victory.

The lesson of Bitburg and of Vienna must be added to the lesson of the Holocaust for all of us to ponder.

August 7, 1986
D'Amato comes late to the drug-abuse fray
The Times Herald Record

Even if Sen. Alfonse D'Amato, the "make-believe narc," as you so aptly put it in your cogent editorial of July 11, does not take kindly to your advice to "Campaign on your record, senator," his less-than-brilliant record of non-performance in the area of drug abuse and prevention will not escape the voting public.

Over a year ago, I wrote in a Record "my view" (Reagans pay lip service to drug ills, 4/25/85) that "as early as 1981 the federal budget cut appropriations for mental health and drug and alcohol abuse by 25 percent, a cut of about $1 billion" and that "there has been a 40 percent erosion in federal dollars going to the nation's treatment system since Mr. Reagan took office." Since then, despite the well-publicized activities of Nancy Reagan, drug abuse has continued to be a major national health problem of epidemic proportions, while a report by the National Institute on Drug Abuse reports "dramatic increases in cocaine-related injuries and deaths in recent years" (7/11/86). All this time, the federal government has been dragging its feet, cutting appropriations for treatment, education, and prevention, while drug-treatment centers across the country report increasing waiting lists of addicts who desperately need and want help but cannot get into underfunded and overcrowded facilities.

The problem was dramatically underscored when Julio A. Martinez, director of the New York State Division of Substance Abuse Services, reported that 1,079 people languish on waiting lists while federal aid to New York state for drug treatment has declined from $28 million in 1982 to $19 million in 1986.

Where has Sen. D'Amato been during this period? In announcing his candidacy for re-election recently, the senator bravely promised that the "scourge of drug abuse" will be a major concern in his next term. And he astutely makes the front pages with a dramatic undercover buy of "crack" in upper Manhattan to prove what we all have known for years—that drugs are freely available on our city streets! But D'Amato has been in office for almost six years, the very period during which drug abuse has flourished in New York and in urban centers throughout the country, despite repeated federal attempts at interdiction, despite publicized raids and arrests, despite the much heralded "war on drugs," resuscitated whenever a headline is needed or when the problem is thrust into the view of a fearful public by such tragic deaths as those of Len Bias and Don Rogers.

But during this entire period, the record of the Reagan administration insofar as treatment, rehabilitation, education and prevention are concerned has been one of callous budget-cutting and the abandonment of this field to the private sector. This has been the thrust of the carefully publicized efforts of Mrs. Reagan—covering the scandalous federal cuts by directing and urging the private sector to assume the burden. What Rep. Charles Rangel, chairman of the House Select Committee on Narcotic Abuse, said a year ago still holds: "Private resources cannot fill the void left by federal abandonment of the treatment and prevention field."

And Sen. D'Amato? Where has he been? What is his record? Has he spoken up against the federal cuts? Has he urged Mrs. Reagan, and the president, to restore federal funding and federal responsibility? Has he attempted to secure emergency funding for the inner cities, as urged by Mayor Koch and Rep. Rangel? (Rangel recently called for an immediate grant of $100 million to spearhead a renewed campaign of treatment and education). Has Sen. D'Amato given meaningful support to the efforts of Rep. Rangel and our own Ben Gilman, minority leader of the House Select Committee, to rally support behind their hill (H.R. 526) that would restore $125 million in each of the next five years for treatment, rehabilitation and prevention programs?

Or has D'Amato conveniently "discovered" the drug issue just in time for his next election campaign, on the theory that, just as he rode into office in 1980 on Ronald Reagan's coattails, he can accomplish the same thing this time around by jumping on the anti-drug abuse bandwagon and riding into office on Nancy Reagan's train?

The press now reports that President Reagan plans to establish a "high-level commission to find ways to curb drug abuse." (Commissions to study issues seems to be the favorite device of this administration to give the impression of action while urgently needed remedies are postponed or withheld). And the pathway is already evident when White House spokesman Larry Speakes emphasizes "private sector programs" rather than the full reestablishment of federal responsibility and federal funding as urged by Rep. Rangel. A front-page New York Times story Aug. 2 states that "the White House indicated that a new administration anti-drug campaign would not include additional aid for drug treatment programs."

We can only wait and see the direction of this new study, while drug abuse continues to fester on all levels of society, while new and improved "crack" continues to take its dreadful toll in destroyed lives and sudden deaths, while the administration continues to cut budgets and to "study" the problem.

Sen. D'Amato's past record in this area {"Campaign on your record, senator"} leaves much to be desired, while his cheap, attention-getting tricks, in an election year, seem to be more a play for the grandstand and the front pages than a serious professional attempt to approach a problem that demands attention at the earliest possible moment.

Meyer Rangell of Bloomingburg is a member of the Alcohol and Drug Abuse Planning Committee of the Sullivan County Department of Community Services.

September 23, 1986
'Rejectionist' label is aptly applied to the PLO
The Times Herald Record

One cannot help being moved by Professor Frederick Madeo's plea in his "my view" of Aug. 22: "Let it not be written in the annals of history that the Jews, who have made stunning contributions in the sciences, the arts, and industry, who have throughout the world been in the forefront of humanitarian causes for peace and justice, let it not be written that the oppressed became the oppressor." A passionate plea, moving and inspirational, and articulating an aspiration with which we can all identify.

The problem is, however, that Professor Madeo offers a simplistic view of the complex problems that surround the concept of a Palestinian homeland and burdens an "oppressive" Israel alone with full responsibility for the Arab condition. He attacks Israel's "rejectionist policy," as though the homeland solution for the Palestinians is a problem that is exclusively Israel's, to be addressed only by Israel alone. Scholars and students of Middle-East politics, on the other hand, have documented many times over the fact that the homeland envisioned by the PLO has as many obstacles to overcome in the Arab world as it has in Israel. Despite the apparent consensus reached at the Arab Summit in Rabat in 1974, when the Arab League designated the PLO as "the sole legitimate representative of the Palestinian people," there has been little agreement among the Arab nations as to the actual political/territorial/demographic constituency of the proposed state. Where, for example, was the cry for a homeland during the 19 years of Palestinian residency under Jordanian rule, from 1948 to 1967? During all that time, Jordan exhibited no eagerness to establish an independent Palestinian state, nor was the issue pursued. Where were the Arabs, and the Palestinians, when an independent homeland was actually granted them by the United Nations at the time of the Partition plan, on Nov. 29, 1947? The Jews accepted that Partition compromise, despite an inadequate and indefensible border, and were ready to live in peace with the proposed Palestinian state. On May 15, 1948, the State of Israel was born. And, on the very next day, five Arab states attacked the fledgling Israel and bombed Tel Aviv. They preferred a war of extermination rather than the homeland that was theirs for the asking—the same homeland which Professor Madeo states now would be the only valid answer to their problem.

It is curious that Professor Madeo repeats over and over again the phrase "Israel's rejectionist policy." Most writers, on the contrary, have used the term to represent the Arab position, as stated in the PLO's Charter, the Palestine National Covenant, "rejecting" the legitimacy of the State of Israel and its right to exist—a position unchanged to this day.

The problem is far more complex than the simple question of support or non-support for an independent Palestinian state. The problem goes to the heart of Arab-Israeli relations, to different visions of the future. What would be the goal, and the posture, of a Palestinian state? As envisioned by the PLO, and openly proclaimed in their Covenant, such a state would have as its goal the liquidation of the state of Israel. In his recently published monumental review of Israel history, "The Siege," Conor Cruise O'Brien, a respected historian and diplomatist, refers to "the uncompromising terms of the Palestinian National Covenant of 1960 and a whole series of resolutions ruling out any idea of negotiations or peace with the 'Zionist entity.'" One can hardly propose a Palestinian homeland while ignoring this reality.

"Rejectionist" is a term that is far more aptly applied to the PLO position than to that of Israel, among whose population there exists a substantial body of opinion that would trade territory for peace, as was demonstrated in the Egyptian accord. But the problem, as Conor Cruise O'Brien posed it, remains: "Would the Palestinian state be based on compromise with Israel, or would it be a springboard for the overthrow of Israel?" Applying an impartial and rigorous scholarship, O'Brien concludes that, "solidly based as they (the Palestinians) are on the movement's fundamental charter, the Palestinian National Covenant . . . it seems clear that PLO moderation and the Jewish State are incompatible." Even where PLO "moderates" are concerned, not to mention the radical extremists, O'Brien continues, "It seems to follow that the Palestinian State, which these "moderates" seek to establish "on any part of Palestinian land to be liberated" would be dedicated to the destruction of the Jewish State."

In this context, the first step in the direction of a solution that would include an independent Palestinian homeland lies not with Israel but with the Arab spokesmen, in or out of the PLO. It is they who must remove the major obstacle: their intransigent and persistent campaign, through terrorism, war, and diplomacy where possible, to destroy the state of Israel. Conor Cruise O'Brien puts it even more starkly: "The reality, as most Israelis see it, is that most Arabs yearn not merely to get rid of the Jewish State but also to get rid of its inhabitants, in one way or another."

No amount of rhetoric is likely to reconcile that reality, and Professor Madeo's one-sided attack on Jewish "injustice" while, incredulously, ignoring the very real and ever-present Arab hostility does not contribute to a fair understanding of the problem.

Meyer Rangell of Bloomingburg is a frequent contributor to these pages.

October 18, 1986
Too little, too late
The Times Herald Record

President Reagan's "war on drugs" is too little, too late, too naive, too shallow and too lacking both in understanding and in resolve.

The causes of drug abuse have both short-range and long-range components. A proper response would direct attention to both, addressing the short-range aspects at once while taking at least the first steps in addressing the long range.

In the short range, the immediate problem is the easy availability of the drug of current choice (alcohol, marijuana, heroin, crack or the newer synthetics that are undoubtedly in process at this very moment in the drug-creators' world). The short-range response must also address the small army of current user-victims, the fallout of our past failures in prevention, treatment and education.

The long-range component is the social fabric—poverty, racism, unemployment, slum housing, homelessness, the conditions of despair and of hopelessness that together spawn the breakdown of values, the apathy, anomie, ennui and boredom that spell an emptiness which the addict tragically attempts to fill with a short-term answer—the conquering and temporarily satisfying fix.

Rooted in social determinants, drug abuse thus spells itself out in the personal tragedies of its failed victims. *It spans the social-psychological arc, from a failed social milieu to failed individuals.* Understanding, profoundly, both the social surroundings and the personal/psychological components is a must if the problem is not only to be met in the short term, but to be resolved in the long.

Against this background, the administration offers Nancy's pathetic homilies ("Just say 'no'"), and the president's grandstand urine tests. Lip service is paid to the pressing problems of treatment in overcrowded facilities with token, inadequate grants, while no one even mentions meaningful, long-range efforts that would address the social deterioration, the ghastly ghettos, the minority slums that lie at the long-term root.

The gamut runs from futility to farce to a continuation of political fakery!

January 4, 1987
Letter to the Editor
Mexico City—The News

Even for one so skilled in the slippery art of polysyllabic obfuscation as William F. Buckley Jr., his column of December 17 (A Letter to Colonel North) is nothing less than astonishing.

It is Mr. Buckley's "tangentially relevant view" (how modestly he puts it!) "that if the president, in his role as commander in chief, and in anticipation of acquiescent congressional action a few months later, contrived to bring relief to the contras, hurray for him."

Consider the import of that paragraph, "tangentially" slipped in as though 'en passant' as he offers Col. Oliver North some unwelcome advice. It is just fine, Mr. Buckley says, if the president "contrived" (no matter how) to come up with funds for guns for the contras at a time when the Congress had specifically barred such military aid. It is of no import, says Mr. Buckley, whether this presidential "contrivance" specifically violated the Boland amendment, flouted the express legislation of Congress, went against the wishes of the American people and skirted the law, if not violated it outright. The specious rationale offered by Buckley is that this is acceptable behavior by a president because he acted "in anticipation of acquiescent congressional action a few months later."! Which is to say that it is OK to break the law as long as one anticipates that law will be changed at a future date. Mr. Buckley does not claim to be a lawyer, although he does frequently posture as a philosopher of law. But I doubt that even he would dare to advance this fake argument in defense of a lawbreaker in any court before any jury.

"But of course," Buckley quickly continues as though to change the subject, "that is no longer the point the people are wondering about." Says who? Evidence by all the polltakers indicated that the people are not only wondering about it but are deeply concerned about a president who takes so lightly the rule of law, as it applies to all of us—presidents and high officials like North and Poindexter and Casey included. Even Mr. Buckley's erstwhile companion-in-apologia-for-Watergate, William Safire, has the simple honesty to state that "knowledge of the diversion was guilty knowledge of lawbreaking". Further, it was a "theft of government property" (*News*, 12/19).

It is hard to believe that Mr. Buckley believes his own flawed rationale as he comes to the aid of his beleaguered president in a repetition of his tortured logic in 1973 and 1974, when he rallied to Richard Nixon under similar circumstances.

January. 19, 1987
Newsweek

* * *

What leaps out from John Ehriichman's article (U.S. AFFAIRS, Dec. 8) is the sense that even in hindsight, even after 14 years, there is a total lack of ethical and moral reappraisal of Watergate and its relevance to Iran-contragate. That is the arrogance of power assumed by Richard Nixon and his men. Now Ehrlichman provides Ronald Reagan with advice that is purely tactical and strategic how to avoid public wrath and manage to stay in office. On the moral issues involved [Ehrlichman] remains as obtuse as ever.

February 24, 1987
Nicaragua 'threat' less menacing in Mexico
The Times Herald Record

Sometimes, when a problem is viewed from a distance, or from another geopolitical environment, new insights and new understanding emerge. It is like viewing a large canvas by stepping back: a larger view presents itself and suddenly one gets a new perspective on the whole painting.

Living in a small town in Mexico (San Miguel de Allende, in the mountains north of Mexico City), talking to Mexicans of varying persuasions, reading the Mexican press, gives one another perspective on the Reagan administration's Nicaraguan policy—which is to say on its policy toward all of Central America. In a word, President Reagan is convinced (some have gone so far as to call it his "obsession") that a Marxist Nicaragua is a menace and a direct threat to the security of the United States. It is the domino theory again, this time in a Central American version: the dominoes fall from Nicaragua to Honduras to El Salvador to Costa Rica to Mexico and, presto, communism is at the Rio Grande, just across the river from Texas. Such is the Reagan logic. The "Evil Empire" is at our back door.

One would think that this scenario would feature a Mexico trembling in fear of the communist hordes and looking to the United States for succor and protection. The reality here, for anyone to see, shows no such thing. On the contrary, the fear here is not of a communist threat from Managua, but of the destabilizing influence of a United States policy that is seen as interfering in the internal affairs of Central American nations and undermining their Independence. United States support and financing of the Nicaraguan contras is seen as an illegal external attempt to overthrow a legal, established and recognized government—a lesson not lost on all the other governments in the region. Most significant is the fact that even the strongest pressures from the United States have failed to enlist the other governments in Central America in support of the U.S.-contra effort. The communist threat, it seems, is more a construct of U.S. policy than a perceived reality in the neighboring countries supposedly threatened.

ITEM: "In his annual speech before the Senate, Secretary of Foreign Relations Bernardo Sepulveda reaffirmed his confidence in the Contadora Group. Referring indirectly to the United States' support for rebels fighting the Nicaraguan government, Sepulveda said that 'Mexico does not want to be an accidental victim of foreign conflicts . . . and we cannot leave to alien forces the defense of national integrity and the stability of the area to which we belong . . . The actions of Contadora and its support group offer the only peaceful alternative, while also supporting non-intervention and the free determination of Central American people.'" (Mexico City News, 11/25/86).

ITEM: "Thousands of demonstrators marched down the Paseo de la Reforma to the U.S. Embassy in protest of United States involvement in recent violence along the Nicaraguan-Honduran border." (Ibid, 12/12/86).

ITEM: "Guatemala will not allow Nicaraguan rebels to train on its territory, the country's interior minister said. . . . Minister of the Interior Juan Jose Rodil Peralta said the government 'will not permit the training of armed men in its territory' to fight other countries." (Ibid, 12/16/86).

ITEM: "Costa Rica, which professes neutrality in the Nicaraguan conflict, reportedly refused . . . to allow a clandestine air operation to use a remote airstrip in northern Costa Rica from funneling arms to U.S.-backed so-called contra rebels in Nicaragua." (Ibid, 12/10/86).

ITEM: "The retired bishop of Cuernavaca, Sergio Mendez Arceo, stated at a University of Mexico theology conference: "We on this platform wish to manifest our opposition to the Reagan Intervention in Nicaragua . . ." (Ibid, 12/11/86).

ITEM: "The four-nation Contadora Group received the annual peace prize of the Beyond War Foundation. . . . In their acceptance speeches all the presidents (of Mexico, Panama, Colombia and Venezuela) agreed that military interventionism adds to the region's problems and in no way contributes to regional peace or security." (Ibid, 12/15/86).

It is evident here that participation by other Central American governments in the United States-contra efforts to overthrow a neighboring regime is avoided like the plague, even in the face of open U.S. threats and arm-twisting. Mexico's problems, like those of most of Central America, are concerned with pervasive poverty, ailing economies and galloping inflation. A United States policy that spends hundreds of millions of dollars in an illegal attempt to overthrow a government with which it does not agree (but with which it continues to have diplomatic relations!), is seen here as an attempt to divert attention from these real and pressing problems, and as dangerous to the peace and security of the entire region.

Meyer Rangell of Bloomingburg wrote this piece from San Miguel de Allende, Mexico.

February 27, 1987
Letter to the Editor
Mexico City—The News

Norman Podhoretz demonstrates in his column of Jan. 10 that it is possible to be eloquent and wrong at the same time.

Never mind that the trail of illegal arms *dealing, law-breaking, violation of the Boland* amendment, cynical disregard of Congressional legislation, unaccounted moneys in Swiss banks under CIA control, unspecified commissions for avaricious arms merchants, led from Reagan's men in the National Security Council to Reagan's men in the CIA (not a single congressman among them). Never mind that, as Podhoretz so gingerly states, "members of this administration did what they could to get around congressional restrictions." Mr. Podhoretz' keen mind ignores this obvious trail of violation of law and of public trust by officials who now, incredibly, refuse even to report to their chief, the President, even as they refuse to report to the American people. The real problem, Mr. Podhoretz informs the rest of us, who may be so naive as to think that something was very wrong with the actions of the president and his men, is "not an Imperial Presidency but an Imperial Congress."

Thus does Mr. Podhoretz fulfill the neo-conservative role, that of providing intellectual justification, no matter how spurious, for those who, in the name of anti-communism, violate our democratic tradition of the rule of law.

April 28, 1987
Letter to the Editor
The New York Times

Will future generations, if there are any, wonder why, in the critical years of the 20th. century, the profession of soldiering was held in higher esteem than the profession of peace-seeking? Why, in fact, *there was no recognized profession that could be called peace-seeking* or even a name to designate one who dedicates himself to the study of peace—how to attain it and how to preserve it—unless one counts the sneering and pejorative "peacenik"?

Where is the West Point of peace studies? Why the prestige and honor accorded to students of the advanced science of mass killing, while there exists no counterpart for the scholarly study of peace and its requirements? With peace the most critical issue in a world on the brink of nuclear disaster, with the very future of the human race in jeopardy, with trillions being spent on the means of destruction while military preparations wreak havoc on the economies of nations around the globe, why is there so little thought given to the possibilities of genuine, structured, on-going peace studies?

Why are there no Peace Institutes, equivalent to our War Schools: West Point, Annapolis, Air Force Academy, professional schools to prepare professional warriors, as well as the myriad of military academies around the country whose express purpose is to lay the psychological groundwork that will prepare our youth to accept a militaristic outlook?

Why are there no Peace Departments in our universities with courses of study leading to undergraduate and graduate degrees in peace (a Ph.D. in Peace!)? Why is there no professional school specifically designed to pursue courses of study in the complex area of peace, its requirements and its maintenance? Why is there no recognized, established profession, equal in prestige to the military, the law, medicine, as well as the various disciplines of academia, dedicated specifically to peace studies in all its aspects and ramifications? Such a school, establishing the *profession of peace-professional* or peace-seeker or peace-advocate, would include in-depth studies of problem-solving, arbitration, the political and economic roots of conflict, nationalism, mediation and conflict-resolution, the history of warfare among nations with a view toward discovering causes, trends and possible solutions. History would be studied with a new outlook—where were the opportunities for peace that were overlooked or never seized? Law, psychology, anthropology, religion, biology, diplomacy, international relations, political science, the significance of the rivalries of past societies and their primitive solutions, would be studied, as well as past and current efforts at peace-keeping, the League of Nations, the United Nations, the World Court (from which President Reagan withdrew in a huff when their decision on Nicaragua went against U.S. policy). Such schools and such studies can contribute new understanding and new insights that might form the basis of new efforts to rid the world of war.

Why not a new profession, in short, with all the prestige accorded to other professions, that would build upon a continuing accumulation of a body of scholarship to lay the basis for an assault on the problem of war?

An INSTITUTE FOR PEACE STUDIES, peace departments in every university, a B.A., M.A., and Ph.D. in Peace Studies, the stimulation and encouragement required to attract the best and the brightest and the most dedicated of our young men and women into this field of research and study, would be a great, and long overdue, start. Sometime down the road our accumulated knowledge of ourselves and our society, our social institutions, the way we live and the way we govern, the way we relate to each other individually and as nations . . . somewhere, sometime in the future these studies may lead to the key, which has somehow eluded us up to now, that will teach us how we can live together in peace—before we die together in war.

United States Senate
WASHINGTON, D.C. 20510

July 1, 1987

Mr. Meyer Rangell
Mountain Rd.
Bloomingburg, New York 12721

Dear Mr. Rangell:

Thank you for writing regarding the activities of the United States Institute of Peace.

As you may know, I was an original cosponsor of an amendment to create the Institute in 1983. The Institute was finally established in 1984 as a provision of the Department of Defense Authorization for 1985.

Shortly, the institute will submit a report to Congress, of their activities in the first two years of operation. I eagerly await this report and will review it when completed. In addition, I have taken the liberty of forwarding your address to the Institute of Peace so that they will send you a copy of the same report.

Sincerely,

Daniel Patrick Moynihan

May 1, 1987
College should not reward McFarlane for role in scandal
Times-Herald Record

I was appalled to read in The Record of April 16 that the Sullivan County Community College will be paying former National Security Adviser Robert McFarlane the sum of $10,000 for an hour's talk on America's foreign policy in the Middle East.

College President John Walter explained that "He is hot right now, and we want to have someone of his stature speak to the community"!

Mr. McFarlane is "hot," of course, not because of any particular moral excellence or because of outstanding performance in high office, but because he has achieved a certain media celebrity, along with a dubious reputation, as a result of his involvement in the outrageous Iran-Contragate scandal. He was smack in the middle of secret machinations, along with Oliver North, involving arms-to-terrorists-for-hostages, as well as secret, illegal funding for the contras in Nicaragua. The implications for Mr. McFarlane within this scandal were such as to force his retirement from his high post as presidential adviser.

McFarlane has not yet told the full story of his involvement, but there is enough information emerging to indicate that we have only seen the tip of the iceberg.

Even a casual reading of the Tower Commission Report (the president's special review board) reveals the following: ". . . studying what went wrong in the National Security Council, the president's own foreign-policy staff apparatus, which under the leadership of Robert C. McFarlane and then Vice Adm. John Poindexter appears to have run wild . . ." "The report pictures a National Security Council led by reckless cowboys . . ." "a kind of parallel government came into being, paying scant heed to laws, deceiving Congress and avoiding oversight of any kind," "the President's aides willfully ignored legal restraints." In its futile efforts to trace the diversion of money from the arms deal, the board stumbled upon a vast network of private assistance to the contras being run out of the Security Council offices in apparent defiance of a congressional ban.

Summarizing the board's findings, former Secretary of State Edmund S. Muskie stated that "neither the National Security Adviser Robert C. McFarlane and Vice Adm. John M. Poindexter nor the other NSC principals deserve high marks." Further, "The National Security Adviser failed in his responsibility to see that an orderly process was observed."

Under these circumstances, for a college president to refer to the disgraced Mr. McFarlane as a man "of stature" indicates a moral obtuseness wholly unbecoming in an educational role model.

In an age when morality and ethics in government are under the heaviest siege, especially in Washington, President Walter and Mr. Lamber send precisely the wrong message to their students and to the community, as they aid a failed public servant reap unexpected profit from his alleged wrong-doing in office, commanding a huge fee from gullible college officials because "he is hot right now"!

Whatever Mr. McFarlane has to say, whatever light he can cast on the worst moral disaster to shame this country since Watergate, he ought to be saying before the appropriate committees of Congress and before the American people—without a fee!

Messrs. Walter and Lamber can perform a real public service if they refused to allow Mr. McFarlane to profit from the notoriety he has gained through a dubious performance while in office. Instead, a community forum could be held on the moral and political consequences of the Iran-Contra scam, with appropriate speakers (McFarlane included) and with public participation . . . without rewarding a failed Reagan adviser with a bonus of $10,000.

A decent sense of morality and prudence calls for such a more thoughtful approach to scholarship and to public education.

July 16, 1987
Deniable Plausibility?
The New York Times

To the Editor:

Lieut. Col. Oliver L. North may have added a memorable phrase to the lexicon of political obfuscation at the Iran-contra hearings when he referred to his concern for "plausible deniability" as he carried out his covert activities. The simplest interpretation of this arcane language is what used to be called, simply and with less pretension, a cover story: a scenario carefully prepared in advance with which one can lie oneself out of a tight spot. What he was most concerned with, he stated, was the "plausible deniability" of a direct connection with the United States Government.

This may be an updated version of Catch-22, or Colonel North may have invented something new: a consistent oxymoron.

July 12, 1987
Monarch butterflies on their way
The Times Herald Record

One summer, from the deck of our house on the Shawangunk Mountain near Bloomingburg, we saw a large group of distinctive and beautiful monarch butterflies gracefully fly overhead. We hadn't the faintest idea that we would meet up with them again the following January in distant Mexico.

Spending the winter in the small town of San Miguel de Allende, in the mountain range that forms the spine of the center of Mexico, 200 miles north of Mexico City, one of the exciting excursions my wife and I took was to the southerly state of Michoacan, where, for reasons that are still debated by scientists, millions of monarch butterflies (and only this distinctive and beautiful specie out of 135,000 different kinds of butterflies) gather each winter in the high pine forest to carry out their courtship and mating.

They come from far-away Canada (those are the ones we observed flying over our house as they headed south) as well as from the northern and eastern United States. Estimates of their numbers range from 50 to 100 million. In huge hordes they come, with a whirring, buzzing, purring, murmuring sound as they zoom in to cover branches and entire trees from trunk to soaring tops, creating a unique and spectacular sight.

Orange and gold provide stunning backgrounds of vivid color for black veins and white dots on papery wings, outspread in a magnificent harmony of color, shape and form.

The ground is covered by a living, quivering mass, creating a moving carpet on the forest floor. The monarch (Its scientific name is Danaus Plexxipus Linneo), considered to be the most beautiful butterfly in the world, seems genetically programmed to return each year to the oyamel trees located in these Mexican mountains.

The climb to the butterfly sanctuary begins at Anganguo, a beautiful, quiet little village that nestles like an alpine gem 10,000 feet high, surrounded by lovely green slopes and forests. The trip there is an experience in itself, taking you through some of Mexico's loveliest mountain terrain. We came by bus from San Miguel. The five-hour trip included a charming stop at the town of Acambaro, where an unexpectedly exciting local museum offers a spectacular mural depicting the Rev. Hidalgo and his associates at the time of 1810 revolution that freed Mexico of its Spanish conquerors.

An overnight rest at the charming Hotel Albergue Don Bruno, in picturesque Anganguo, prepared us for the climb the following morning up another 2,000 feet to the butterfly grounds. The trip begins in an open-back truck. We stand, holding the wooden sides, as the truck makes its perilous way up a rutty, narrow road on a dangerous-looking ledge overlooking steep drops. We are thoroughly bounced around as we try to maintain our footing and stand upright, trying at the same time to take pictures of the breathtaking views of mountain, slope and valley.

Soon the road becomes too narrow for the truck: We have to get out and climb the rest of the way up the steep slope on foot. The going is tiring, but suddenly the appearance of myriads of black and gold and orange whirring wings on all sides make one forget fatigue. The spectacle is overwhelming.

Why the monarchs make the long trip each year—more than 3,000 miles from their woods in Canada—to their annual family reunion in Mexico, is the subject of debate and study among scientists.

As far as we are concerned, however, we'll be looking for them again from our Bloomingburg deck. Perhaps we'll see the same butterflies we saw in Angangueo, on their way back to their spring and summer quarters in the Canadian woods!

July 18, 1987
The Cardinal trivializes the Holocaust
The Times Herald Record

In Newburgh last week, Cardinal John O'Connor, archbishop of New York, referred to the official audience granted recently to ex-Nazi Kurt Waldheim by Pope John Paul II and the subsequent outcry of criticism and hurt on the part of Jewish leaders. In what must surely be the understatement of the year, the cardinal said "There will always be squabbles in families." (June 29 Record.)

Thus did the cardinal join the ranks of those who in recent years have seen fit to trivialize the Holocaust, the most monstrous obscenity in modern history.

The 6 million Jewish dead, murdered by Nazi hands, cannot be revived, nor can their ghastly humiliation and tortures be revoked. All that is left is the searing memory of their horrible fate, and the sober obligation we all bear to examine and evaluate the kind of society in which it occurred and the kind of people who permitted it. The American Jewish Congress, in an open letter to Pope John Paul II in The New York Times of June 26, put it with exquisite clarity: "Surely the most sacred command of our generation is memory; not to forget how silence became indifference became complicity, and finally turned into a nightmare of slaughter for millions upon millions. Surely that much—that debt of memory—we owe not only the victims, but ourselves and our children."

When French justice convicted Klaus Barbie, the Butcher of Lyon, just last week for crimes against humanity and for his part in the deaths of hundreds of Jews and resistance fighters, his lawyer also trivialized his behavior and its significance, stating that massacres had also occurred in other countries at other times. On this issue, columnist Flora Lewis wrote in the July 7 Record: "The important lesson wasn't so much the Nazis' extraordinary evil but that it could happen with the participation of so many, the indifference of many more, that humanity has no guarantees against its vicious streaks except its own conscience, for which each individual is responsible . . . the effort for decency and justice must go on every day, everywhere."

Also instructive is the case of Primo Levi, himself a survivor of the Auschwitz concentration camp who later became a celebrated Italian author and novelist. Mr. Levi could not outlive the despair born of his Auschwitz torture. In the midst of what appeared to be a successful career, he committed suicide. "By the end of his life," reported the New York Times (July 5), "Levi had become increasingly convinced that the lessons of the Holocaust were destined to be lost as it took a place among the routine atrocities of history." He was "troubled by the collective amnesia of those responsible for the exterminations."

In this context, the pope's audience with Waldheim seemed to provide a mantle of respectability for this unrepentant ex-Nazi and raised again the specter of a world unable to comprehend the depth and the reach of the depravity that was the Holocaust. And for Cardinal O'Connor to dismiss the anguish of the Jewish people with a flippant, "there will always be squabbles in families" is to remind us, painfully, once again that the lessons of the Holocaust may indeed be lost, that it could happen again, unless its hideousness is burned indelibly into the memory and the conscience of us all.

When, in a world sadly lacking in moral imperatives, those we expect to provide moral leadership, like the pope and the cardinal, abdicate their responsibility—the pope by providing a protective respectability to an ex-Nazi whose past has caused the United States government to bar him from this country, and the cardinal who fails to respond to the legitimate Jewish outcry but issues instead a statement of unfeeling banality—then the pope and the cardinal become part of the problem rather than part of the solution.

September 29, 1987
Please, Ben, reconsider your position
The Times Herald Record

An open letter to Congressman Gilman.

Dear Mr. Gilman:

I feel free to write this public letter because you have always been open, forthright and available to your constituents. It is, in fact, your responsiveness to your people that stands out as a major reason for your success in re-election time after time. Most of us feel that you listen, and maintain an open mind to our concerns. For that, you have earned our great respect.

That is why some vital direct questions should be put forward now, at a moment that is crucial to the foreign policy now being forged with respect to Central America.

Do you not think that the time is at hand for a new, hard look at your position on aid to the Contras? Recent developments suggest that this may be the time for you to change your vote from a consistent support to the Contras to a vote against continuing military aid.

What do you make of the recent Iran-Contra hearings, which revealed, if nothing else, that high government officials shredded official documents, lied to Congress and to each other, transferred significant elements of foreign policy control to private enterprises for their own profit, sought aid for the Contras in a humiliating and demeaning, and probably illegal way from foreign governments and private individuals with their own axes to grind, and did all they could to ride roughshod over the express wishes of Congress and the American people?

And after all this was exposed to a startled public, what moral purpose is served when the president meets with Contra leaders, as he did recently in Los Angeles, to encourage them to continue their efforts to overthrow their government—a government with which we have official diplomatic relations?

Do you not think that such behavior on the president's part has the effect of throwing a monkey wrench into the Arias peace process? We have called many times for the five Central American nations to attempt solutions to their problems and the problems of the region without violence and without outside interference. Now that such an attempt appears possible, how do you assess the president's bellicose contribution:

he meets with rebel forces to encourage their violent insurgency, but is not available to meet with official Nicaraguan leaders of state to discuss peace.

The world is thus witness to the unedifying sight of a powerful head of state using his long (and illegal) reach to overthrow another head of state—while maintaining official diplomatic relations!

You are surely too astute, Ben, to believe that the self-serving, ex-Somosista Contras have become sanctified "freedom fighters" just because that title was bestowed upon them by Reagan, by the discredited Col. North and John Poindexter and by the "patriotic" war profiteers Hakim and Secord. To the contrary, news reports abound which testify to their vicious anti-democratic character. Here are just a few:

From The Record of July 29: "Contra rebel forces have executed prisoners, forcibly recruited soldiers and killed civilians, according to the first report of a human rights association that Congress mandated as a condition of U.S. aid . . . other cases involved allegations of kidnapping and attacks on civilians including the deaths of children and unarmed individuals."

From The New York Times of July 19: "United States backed Nicaraguan guerrillas killed nine Sandinista soldiers, three children and a pregnant woman but failed to capture their target . . ." The report details indiscriminate attacks on civilians, women and children in poverty ridden villages without the slightest military significance, as the Contras impress their U.S. supporters.

Your own House Narcotics Committee, Ben, is reviewing "allegations of drug smuggling by the Contras" according to your chairman, Charles Rangel (Record, June 24).

It is entirely likely that by Sept. 30, the president will be requesting more than $200 million with the audacious suggestion that this money be held in escrow for the Contras to use when they decide that the Arias plan is not working. An astonishing proposal that grants a veto power over war or peace, and a carte-blanche of our support, to the rebel side!

Now is the time, Ben, for you to face these issues—before the opportunity for peace presented by the Arias plan evaporates, victim of the Reagan obsession to have Nicaragua "cry uncle" at all costs. Reagan apparently will not take peace for an answer as long as the Managuan regime remains in office.

This is the time, Ben, if ever there was one, for statesmanship that rises above party.

Congressman Guy Vander Jagt was quoted as saying recently that your re-election is certain no matter who takes Reagan's place on the 1988 ticket. "I don't think Congressman Gilman needs to worry about the lack of Reagan," he said, "Ben was really carrying Reagan on his coattails in this district."

You should give careful thought, Ben, to the possibility that continuing to support a failed and dangerous' Reagan policy in Nicaragua may result in your carrying an albatross on your coattails instead.

Your vote against continuing Contra aid will be a sign of outstanding independence and integrity; it will be looked upon on all sides as statesmanship of the highest order.

October 3, 1987
Many thanks to Chinese guides
China Daily

I feel impelled to write this brief letter of thanks and deep appreciation for the beautiful, warm hospitality shown to our American Elderhostel group in our visits to Beijing and Shijiazhuang.

Our Chinese guides, each and every one of them, have overwhelmed us with their warmth, their caring, their kindness, their sensitivity, and their generosity of spirit, as well as their knowledge of the region and the over-all philosophy of the People's Republic of China. Their wit, humour, and patience have made every minute of our stay here a memorable one.

Such people-to-people visits—getting to know each other and each others' values—with mutual respect and a deepening understanding of each others' problems and goals would be a step in the direction of that lasting peace and friendship between our countries that we all cherish.

October 23, 1987
Letter to the Editor
The New York Times

Today's announcement of the selection of the exiled Soviet poet, Joseph Brodsky, for the Nobel Prize in Literature is in the splendid tradition of the previous prizes awarded to Bishop Tutu, President Arias of Costa Rica, and, in 1985, to the International Physicians for the Prevention of Nuclear War.

The Nobel signature has thus firmly established itself as perhaps the most socially aware symbol in a world that has all but lost its moral bearings. Bravo to the Nobel Committee!

May I recall the following, written by Brodsky (no ivory-tower poet he!) as reported in the New York Times of Dec. 20, 1984:

"High stratosphere winds with their juvenile whistle.
A thought-like white cloud in search of mankind.
Oh, where are you flying?, said missile to missile,
There is nothing ahead and nothing behind."

Relevant then, and still relevant now.

January 27, 1988
Letter to the Editor
Mexico City—The News

Leave it to Buckley! At a time when the gilded image of Ronald Reagan is plummeting with the speed of a falling star in the Republican heaven, William F. Buckley Jr., in shining intellectual armor brings his fabled skill at hyperbolic deflection to the rescue, as he squeaks out a limp defense for his floundering hero (State-Loving in the G.O.P.). It is not, after all, Buckley informs us, the policies of the Reagan Administration that are responsible for the various crises that beset the nation and the world. It is "statism" that is at the bottom of it all. Not specifically the present Republican state, but "statism" in general.

Thus war and the threat of war, poverty, crime, taxation, racism, educational impoverishment, are all the result not of any particular policies of the Reagan Administration but the natural result of "statism." If there were no powerful—central government, he explains, if problems were left to individual solutions and efforts, rather than to the concentrated power of government, things would be better. Ronald Reagan is off the hook!

If the world is faced with the threat of nuclear war, it is not due to the bungling of the administration in international affairs, to Reagan's years of "evil empire" rhetoric, to the near-destruction of "detente," to the disastrous obsession that demands the overthrow of the recognized government of Nicaragua, to the Reagan mentality that results in the invasion of Grenada, the mining of Nicaraguan harbors, the disgraceful walk-out from the World Court, when it found our behavior in Nicaragua unlawful. It is not the arming of a rebel army to terrorize the Nicaraguan people or the shameful conducting of foreign policy through the likes of Oliver North and Richard Secord and Albert Hakim. None of these are at fault, Mr. Buckley solemnly instructs us. "Statism" is the villain.

Reagan and his policies are off the hook, saved by the theoretical poppycock of his favorite apologist. The fault lies with "statism," not with Reaganism. The problem is in the individual, not the government.

There is, ironically, a measure of truth here, but not in the sense intended; Individuals elected Ronald Reagan, and if the last few years have taught us anything it is that the electorate must be newly alerted and aroused to understand substance instead of style, to value the ability to govern over the Hollywood ability to win votes, to reinstate a respect in government and in our national leadership, to demand responsibility instead of Teflon—and to see through the rhetorical and semantic apologetics of the Buckleys of our time.

March 17, 1988
Letter to the Editor
Mexico City—The News

Israel-bashing has emerged in recent months as the most popular sport in American journalism. Editorialists, columnists, political pundits and armchair analysis, most of whom were content to remain on the sidelines while Israel fought desperately for its existence against an array of determined and ferocious enemies, now seem eager to get off the bench to get their licks in.

To be sure, Israel has never lacked for enemies, from the day that David Ben Gurion and his followers accepted the U.N. Partition Plan of 1948 in the interest of peace and justice for both sides, while the Arab states rejected the plan, thus also rejecting the Independent Palestinian State which they now declare to be their primary goal. They chose, instead, to declare war and to invade the new-born Israel with the intent to destroy it. After 40 years, the Arab world, with the single exception of Egypt (whose President paid with his life for making peace), is still at war with Israel and the official Covenant of the P.L.O. still calls for the destruction of the Jewish State.

The significance of the latest phase in the bash-Israel game is that now "Friends of Israel," the title of Anthony Lewis' column of March 7, have joined the chorus. Lewis, who is usually fair and insightful when dealing with other problems, seems to abandon both fairness and balance when discussing Israel. In a piece distinguished by its one-sidedness, he assigns blame solely to Israel, holding it unilaterally responsible for the Middle East dilemma. Not one word does he write about the PLO record of terror and assassination, both within Israel against public buses, school children, and civilian targets, as well as outside Israel in airports, on the high seas, in synagogues—wherever they could murder Jews to advance their political aims. Not one word does he write about the responsibility and the culpability of Arab nations for the condition of the Palestinians, who were murdered and driven from Jordan and Lebanon by their fellow-Arabs and who persist to this day in a policy of no-recognition and no-peace with Israel.

If the solution lies somewhere in the direction of "land for peace," as almost half of the Israeli people themselves seems to believe, there still remains the problem of who among the Palestinians possesses the power, the capacity and the willingness to negotiate such a settlement. And who can guarantee that an Independent Palestinian State will not be a springboard for continued assaults on Israel? After 40 years of unabated terrorism, is Israel not justified in seeking assurances for its security?

Responding to current criticism, Israeli President Chaim Herzog recently raised this central question: With what responsible Palestinian leadership, he asked, can Israel meet in order to discuss peace with justice and mutual security? As yet, no one, including Anthony Lewis, has provided an answer.

In these circumstances, Lewis' unbalanced attack on Israel, while completely ignoring the role a responsible Palestinian and Arab leadership must play in the peace process, emerges as yet another exercise in Israel-bashing that adds obfuscation rather than illumination to the problem.

May 7, 1988
The Finger of Blame for Drugs Points to Us
The New York Times

I read your excellent editorial on the drug problem "Too Soon to Back Down on Drugs" (April 14), which was timely reprinted in The Mexico City News on April 18. Timely because on the previous day, The News reported the angry reactions of Mexican officials to the recent Senate vote proposing economic sanctions against Mexico for "failing to cooperate 'fully' in the fight against drug trafficking."

Your editorial hits the nail on the head and, incidentally, agrees with Mexican criticism when it notes the "voracious appetite for drugs in the U.S." (Mexican critics point out that "the U.S. constitutes the largest drug-consuming market in the world"), and that a major element in any anti-drug effort must concentrate on controlling and reducing that ever-increasing demand.

As long as we continue to put all the blame on the distant producer; as long as we use the drug issue as a political football; as long as we refuse to recognize our responsibility as a society for the root causes, the problem of drug abuse will stay with us.

Your editorial suggests, among other cogent ideas, a "national commitment to drug treatment programs." After almost eight years of the Reagan Administration's callous slashing of budgets for such programs in favor of the cheap but ineffective sloganeering of Nancy Reagan ("Just Say No!"), it is doubtful that a turnaround in funding now can take place. Do we hear any such voices in Congress? How about our own Senator Alfonse D'Amato and his pre-election promises?

The deplorable fact is that there is nowhere to be seen the zeal, the dedication, the passion that is necessary to face up to the real issue: Why, in the richest and most powerful nation in the world, with the world's highest standard of living, with the greatest opportunities for self-advancement, with the most effective popular democracy, are so many millions of people, of their own free will, ready to risk their careers, their families, their jobs, their freedom, even their lives, to subsidize a vast criminal empire that is undermining our society in order to seek out mind-altering drugs at any price that the criminals demand?

From the most degraded of ghettos to the highest reaches of Wall Street, from neighborhood high schools to the stately colleges of the Ivy League, from Hollywood and the world of entertainment and sports to political circles in Washington, no aspect of our society is totally free. Drug abuse is on the increase, almost sanctioned, if not by law then by widespread social acceptance and usage. Why? What are the wellsprings, the subsoil, of this pervasive national behavior?

No approach to this problem promises any success unless it includes basic research into this staggering, puzzling phenomenon. Such research must be multidimensional and interdisciplinary with real commitment on the national level. Until that is done, one can view only with contempt the attempts to avoid our responsibilities by placing the blame on distant shores.

July 2, 1988
Time is right for U.S.-Soviet anti-war pact
The Times Herald Record

Last year in Washington President Reagan and Chairman Gorbachev took a first significant step toward peace by signing the Treaty on Intermediate-Range Nuclear Forces (the INF Treaty). This year, in Moscow, they had the opportunity to take a giant step forward. They had the opportunity to seize the high moral ground together, to ease the anxieties of a world at the brink of nuclear disaster and to assure their place in history. They could have accomplished this by lifting their discussion, in a spectacular quantum leap, to a higher lane by boldly addressing the real problem: the specter of war itself rather than the danger of armaments. They would thus address the disease rather than the symptom, the problem of the human race rather than the arms race alone.

They could have, and still can provide the world with an example of wisdom and statesmanship by articulating on center stage that the enemy is war itself not the implements of war. Von Clausewitz' hoary dictum that "war is a continuation of political intercourse, a carrying out of the same by other means" can no longer be accepted as a guide to international behavior in the nuclear age. The problem of our time is to confront the inadmissibility of war in the nuclear era and to take meaningful steps toward banning war as an instrument of national policy.

The two most powerful statesmen in the world can take such steps by initiating a Washington-Moscow Peace Pact, or a Reagan-Gorbachev Anti-War Pact of 1988. They could stun the nation, electrify the world, and shatter the complacency with which the world has been drifting toward a U.S.-U.S.S.R. nuclear confrontation and its cataclysmic consequences.

Such a pact might include:

1. A solemn declaration by the two super-powers pledging not to engage in acts of war against each other.
2. A pledge not to interfere in each others' internal affairs, respecting the sovereign right of each nation to the social system of its own choosing.
3. A declaration pledging not to resort to war as a means of settling differences in ideology.

4. A declaration inviting all peace-loving nations to join such a pact—in effect outlawing war as a means of furthering national policy, solemnly declaring that, in the nuclear age, war is an unacceptable method by which to solve our problems: We must assert that human problem is worth the destruction of our planet Earth!

Of course, this will remind many of the Kellogg-Briand Pact of 1929. Originally proposed by Aristide Briand, minister of foreign affairs of France, and worked out with Frank B. Kellogg, the United States secretary of state, the Pact "renounced war as an instrument of national policy and agreed not to seek the settlement of any dispute or conflict except by peaceful means." It was subsequently ratified by 63 additional nations. The fact that it failed to achieve the peace that it sought does not negate its high moral purpose or the breadth of its noble vision.

The Kellogg-Briand ideas are not only still relevant, they are ideas and purposes whose time has come. What Kellogg-Briand promoted as ideal statesmanship in the pre-nuclear age is, in the nuclear age, a necessity for survival, the sine-qua-non of human existence.

That neither Reagan nor Gorbachev made such proposals in Washington last year or in Moscow this year, is sad proof of the timidity of world statesmanship in this, the most dangerous time in the history of man.

For, welcome as the INF Treaty is as a first step in the reduction of nuclear arms, the reality remains that a 4-percent reduction in nuclear weaponry on the part of two mutually hostile and heavily armed giants is not sufficient to make the world sleep easy, as long as that deep hostility continues unabated. And when one observes the rage of important political figures and shapers of public opinion even to this small step toward nuclear sanity, it becomes clear that the world is not out of danger. The shrill voices raised in the Senate in opposition to ratification testify to a widespread cynicism and hostility throughout our body politic, as though they were afraid to see our mutual hatred diminish.

Countering this cynicism, a Reagan-Gorbachev Anti-War Pact could grasp the hope and the imagination of the world in a brilliant moment of sanity and lucidity. It could be the spark that illuminates the sensibilities of the best minds in every country to the ultimate responsibility of the human race: the elimination of war. Such a step would mark the maturing of humankind, a final turning away from the disasters of war and violence. The removal of the crushing burden of armaments on all peoples would enable man to direct his attention and his resources to the real problems that face us: poverty, hunger, disease.

The billions now spent for war or for the preparation for war could end starvation in the Third World, provide a real base for worldwide education, and address the pressing needs of environmental and ecological research and development.

The world would literally gain a new lease on life, lifting mankind to new levels of achievement and well-being.

Now is the time for President Reagan and Chairman Gorbachev to seize the day and grasp the opportunity!

United States Senate

WASHINGTON, D.C. 20510
August 24, 1988

Mr. Meyer Rangell
RD # 1, Box 445
Bloomingburg, New York 12721

Dear Mr. Rangell:

Thank you very much for having taken the time to write and to send a copy of your editorial on the need for a U.S.-Soviet anti-war pact. I am glad to have it, and I anticipate that it will prove to be of use.

Sincerely,

Daniel Patrick Moynihan

October 20, 1988
Surely Lincoln-Douglas Roll in Their Graves
The New York Times

When Abraham Lincoln wanted to discuss the issues in the fateful election of 1858 he simply wrote to his opponent, Stephen Douglas, who answered: "I agree to your suggestion that we shall alternately open and close the discussion. I will speak at Ottawa one hour; you can reply, occupying an hour and a half, and I will then follow for half an hour . . . We will alternate in like manner in each successive place."

Thus, without the help (or interference) of media consultants the greatest political debate in American history was arranged. For an hour and a half each, without the filter of pre-arranged questions, Lincoln and Douglas confronted each other and the issues of the day. One can only wonder what they would have thought of today's "debates," with each candidate responding in two or three minutes to reporters' canned questions.

Instead of thoughtful process we get political theatricality. The robotic performances of today's "debaters" as they put out their carefully preprogrammed responses stand in sharp contrast to the comment on Lincoln-Douglas made by the great Charles Evans Hughes, who said: "Lincoln made himself the apostle of thinking America in its opposition to the extension of slavery" and that "there has never been an illustration . . . within the memory of man where intellect has exerted so potent a magnetism."

The candidates ought to be required to study Lincoln-Douglas to learn what a real debate might be like.

November 20, 1988
The people speak
The Santa Fe New Mexican

    An election can be an educational experience. It can teach us something about our country, our leaders, and above all about ourselves. What did we learn this time around?

    After almost two years of the most intensive electioneering, from the primaries through the conventions to the campaign itself, after millions of dollars of TV commercials and reams of newsprint, and all manner of polls, on election day it all boiled down to this: 47,917,341 people voted for George Bush (54 percent of the vote cast); 41,013,030 people voted for Michael Dukakis (46 percent). And 92,179,181 people, representing 50.9 percent of the eligible voters, did not vote at all.

    How can we say "the American people have spoken" when half the eligible voters did not choose to open their mouths? More important, how can we interpret their silence?

    Was the massive non-vote a result of apathy, or of disgust with the lying, distortion and shoddiness of the campaign? Fifty percent of the voters of America cannot be easily dismissed or ignored. The extent to which honest answers are sought to this question will indicate the extent to which integrity still exists in our political leadership. That may be the most important lesson of this election.

January 27, 1989
Letter to the Editor
Mexico City—The News

In the general euphoria following what William Safire called Yasser Arafat's "Three Yesses," pundits, editorialists, columnists and even statesmen professed to breathe easier because, dragged kicking and screaming to the staged performance, Arafat seemed to renounce terrorism—not all terrorism, to be sure (he still gave his blessing to the violence of the Palestinian uprising)—but enough to make wishful thinkers proclaim a basic change even while other significant PLO factions said it isn't so.

I wonder how many noticed the bit of historical irony that the first United States-PLO contact between U.S. Ambassador Robert Pelletreau and four PLO representatives took place in Carthage, now a suburb of Tunis. The name of Carthage, you will remember, rings down the corridors of history because of the echoing phrase of Cato the Elder in the Roman Senate, "Cartago Delenda Est!". "Carthage Must Be Destroyed!", Cato reared at the end of every speech he gave on any subject, no matter how irrelevant, until the phrase became the hallmark of the persistent non-sequitur. His jingoistic bombast was ultimately successful: Carthage was sacked and destroyed by the Romans in 146 BC in the Third Punic War.

Does this remind us of Yasser Arafat's strident and persistent "Israel Delenda Est!", screamed repeatedly over the last twenty-five years? After all, that clause in the PLO Charter, the Palestine National Covenant, that calls for the destruction of the State of Israel has yet to be removed, renounced or altered. Or are Israelis being too sensitive when they see in the retention of that repudiated clause a signal of the continued ultimate goal of the PLO? "Cartago Delenda Est"? Not this time, say the Israelis.

February 7, 1989
Letter to the Edtior
Mexico City—The News

    Old habits die hard, if at all. William F. Buckley, Jr., in his column of Dec. 19 ("Gorbachev's Triumph") writes like one who, after years of attacking his "evil enemy" and urging him to show some small shred of decency, is taken aback when his arguments seem to prevail. He is shocked. He is dismayed. He can't take yes for an answer. The possible end of the cold war leaves this cold-warrior with cold shivers up and down his spine!

    With a mean-spirited cynicism that represents a new low even for him, Mr. Buckley refers to the ghastly earthquake in Armenia as "an ironic master stroke"—as though Gorbachev had fiendishly planned it all as a nefarious PR production! With an unbridled obscenity, Buckley compares the earthquake to the "genocide in Afghanistan," which he lays at Gorbachev's door, while at the same time detracting from the credit Gorbachev should receive for bringing that intervention to an end. Coming or going, Gorbachev can't win. Nor does Buckley mention, in balance, the role of the United States and the CIA in encouraging, arming and supporting the anti-government side in that civil conflict.

    Gorbachev seems to irk Buckley more by doing what the world, and even Ronald Reagan, perceives to be right than by doing wrong. Does Gorbachev announce an unprecedented unilateral reduction in Soviet armed forces? Terrible, says Buckley. We must beware these sinister attempts to begin a world reduction in armaments, and especially the nuclear reduction that now appears closer through a revitalized START. That Gorbachev touched a universal chord in reviving the hopes and aspirations of mankind for a release from nuclear tensions is anathema to the old rhetorician. How much more simple things would be if the "Evil Empire" remained evil, if the cold war remained the touchstone of world politics, and if William F. Buckley Jr. didn't have to entertain the possibility of changing, even tentatively, the heated inflammatory rhetoric upon which he has built a career.

March 24, 1989
Letter to the Editor
Mexico City—The News

It is an irony of the political process that will no doubt be endlessly explored by future historians that Ronald Reagan, who spent the first seven years of his administration rousing the world to a pitch of feverish alarm and hatred for the "Evil Empire" and building a foreign policy whose touchstone from Moscow to Managua was the necessity of the Cold War, declared upon leaving office that his greatest accomplishment may have been his ending of the Cold War—and his winning of it! He embraced Gorbachev and left the presidency in an aura of reduced tension and the promise of detente.

But, like her colleague William F. Buckley Jr., (see his column of Dec. 19) and other ideologues of the right, Jeane Kirkpatrick just won't abide it. No amount of attractive *perestroika*, or policy changes, or concessions ought to lull us, she warns, into the dangerous belief that peaceful co-existence might indeed be a goal more worthy than permanent hostility. Analyzing the recent Soviet withdrawal from Afghanistan (*The News*, Feb. 19)—unilaterally and without conditions, it must be noted, since the United States promptly announced that it would continue its policy of arming and encouraging the rebel *mujahedeen*, thus prolonging the conflict—Mrs. Kirkpatrick concludes that the Soviet move is suspect, in fact more menacing than pacific. The new flexible and compromising Soviet foreign policy, characterized by a unilateral reduction of troops in Europe, unilateral withdrawal from Afghanistan and a new willingness to overcome the impasse at the start negotiations, is viewed by Kirkpatrick as a cause for alarm rather than a hopeful development.

She gives away her basic position; against co-existence and peace and in favor of permanent hostility—by her choice of the chess metaphor. "The reason for withdrawal," she writes, "is that Gorbachev, playing for high stakes on a global board, concluded that sacrificing a pawn would improve his overall strategic position." In chess, of course, there is no room for arbitration, no conciliation, no peaceful concession, no peaceful, voluntary detente. The chess goal is firm and immutable: the total destruction of the other side. All moves are calculated to that end and to that end alone. Nothing else will suffice.

That, Mrs. Kirkpatrick reveals, is how she views foreign policy and global politics. No Soviet foreign policy position can be viewed as other than a ploy, a pretext, a gambit (like the suspicious sacrifice of a pawn) that conceals an evil and nefarious motive. Nothing Mikhail Gorbachev can do, short of rolling over and dying, can satisfy her.

In this view, any reduction of Cold War tension is dangerous and suspect. Peace and detente become the enemy. Permanent, escalating hostility is the preferred Kirkpatrick scenario. In a world that yearns for surcease from the tensions of confrontation and war, from the overwhelming burden of arms and from the ghastly threat of nuclear disaster, this Kirkpatrick prescription for permanent armed hostility is not good news!

April 5, 1989
Our Mexican Experience

We first came to Mexico ten years ago—and it was love at first sight. Since then we have spent four to five months each year here, enjoying the sun, the weather, the sights, the sounds, the smells, the cool mountain air and the warm tropical seashore, the forests, the stunning archeological sites and the ghosts of pre-Hispanic culture at Chichen Itza and Uxmal and Monte Alban and Mitla and countless reminders of ancient Indian culture in remote villages. Above all, we return to the warmth and hospitality of the Mexican people.

With San Miguel de Allende, Guanajuato, as home base, we have roamed from Cancun and Quintana Roo in the East to the magnificent Pacific shore at Manzanillo and Puerto Vallarta and the tranquil fishing village of Bucerias. We have driven across the mountains in our trust Mexican VW bug over the horse-shoe curves and perilous drops from San Miguel to Guadalajara to the coast, always stopping en route to savor the flavor of Mexico's small towns: Magdalena and its opal salesmen, Tequila, Atotonilco, lakeside Chapala and Ajijic. We have visited the butterfly fishermen at Patzcuaro and the fascinating island of Janizio, as well as the butterfly sanctuary in the oyamel trees high up in the cool forests of Angangueo in Michoacan. Oaxaca and Morelia and Cuernavaca and Merida each provided its unique ambience and excitements. We have climbed the hilly streets of old Guanajuato, with its challenging El Pipila raising his hand in eternal defiance of the Spanish conquerors; and Dolores Hidalgo where the famous Grito de Dolores by Father Miguel Hidalgo marked the beginning of Mexican independence.

But beyond and above all, when all is said and done, it is the remarkable warmth and hospitality of the Mexican people that bring us back year after year, eager for new experience, and never disappointed.

In San Miguel, the cobbled streets and the innumerable "calle jons" that twist up and down the mountain slope along which the old town sprawls provide endless stimulation for the walker, while the exquisite Jardin in front of the Parroquia provides a unique center for a vigorous outdoor social life. Behind every door on every street in San Miguel lies a surprise and an adventure. You may be greeted by a simple Mexican dwelling or a mansion of marble and glass and beautifully tended gardens, rivalling the most elegant homes anywhere in the world.

So when winter's grip begins to tighten its icy fingers in New York, and Election Day in November brings surcease, at least for another year, from the brawling hypocrisies of overloud politicians, it is time to head to the warmth of another Mexican experience.

It is part of the transformation, or transition that we seek from the stress-producing aspects of fast-lane American culture, that we make every effort to accept and to appreciate, and to come to terms with the vastly different culture of Mexico and its varied people. Too many of us fail to make that transition. How often do we hear American and Canadian and European visitors loudly rail at Mexican habits they deplore: the lack of punctuality, the "mañana" syndrome, the unconcern of the plumber or the electrician or the gas-man or the carpenter or the TV repairman when he arrives days later than promised. Americans who have not bothered to learn even kitchen Spanish are quick to blame Mexicans who speak little or no English for their deficiencies in communication! While understanding and appreciation of Mexican cultural values and priorities are sadly lacking.

Instead of loud complaints and "gringo" condescension, how much better it would be if we sought to understand at least a little of the culture and history of our Mexican hosts! For me, it was Octavio Paz who opened doors to such understanding. His LABRYNTH OF SOLITUDEZ (1961) is still, to my mind, a brilliant and thought-provoking introduction for any who would try to comprehend the Mexican reality.

"The Mexican hides behind a variety of masks", writes Paz . . . "The mask of an old man is as indecipherable at first glance as a sacred stone covered with occult symbols; it is the history of various amorphous features that only take shape, slowly and vaguely, after the profoundest contemplation. Eventually these features are seen as a face, and later as a mask, a meaning, a history." . . . "The history of Mexico is the history of a man seeking his parentage, his origins."

"The Mexican", Octavio Paz continues, "whether young or old, criolles or mestizos, general or laborer or lawyer, seems to me to be a person who shuts himself away in order to protect himself. His face is a mask and so is his smile. In his harsh solitude, which is both barbed and courteous, everything serves him as a defense: silence and words, politeness and disdain, irony and resignation."

An attempt to understand the character of this "solitude" that Paz describes so eloquently, to comprehend the "variety of masks" as history, and the deep meanings of Mexican attitudes would be a good starting point from which to make our sojourn in Mexico not only a brief experience in living abroad but a profound exercise in human relations and an appreciation of the wide variety and possibilities of human responses to the conditions of life.

June 1, 1989
What's in a name?
The Times Herald Record

How does it happen that leaders selected to head government departments such as education, HHS, defense, justice, etc., are called secretaries or attorney general, whereas the leader selected to coordinate activities in the area of drug-abuse is called a "czar"—more specifically the "drug-abuse czar"?

There is no "czar" at HHS or at education or even at defense (which used to be called the War Department). Why a "czar" at the helm in drug abuse?

Historically, czars (and other tyrants like kings and monarchs and emperors) were not especially noted for enlightened social policy or for a passionate concern for the welfare of their subjects. That is why they have been eliminated in most civilized societies. So why was William Bennett only a secretary of education but is now a "czar" at drug-abuse?

What's in a name, you might say? Is it only semantics? Or is it more? Our thoughts and our ideas are shaped to no small extent by the words we use to express them, students of the science of semantics tell us. Perhaps the so-called "war on drugs" has been so abysmally fought and so disgracefully lost because we have been relying on "czars" rather than on the abiding values of diversity and democracy.

The problem of drug-abuse will not be successfully addressed until it is recognized as a problem requiring the scope of all the social sciences—medicine and law, psychiatry and psychology, education and penology, anthropology, diplomacy, economics and politics and government. It is hardly likely that this will be achieved, or sought after, by the "czar" mentality.

June 24, 1989
America's Phony War
The Times Herald Record

If the United States had waged all its wars, beginning with the American Revolution of 1776, in the same way it is waged its "war on drugs," we would still be colonies of the British Empire.

The plain truth is that nothing that could remotely be fled a war has ever been waged against the culture of drugs in the United States. The so-called "war on drugs" has been a gigantic fraud on the American people. The murder, violence, and carnage on our streets and the racial and moral decay resulting from a narcotic culture continue virtually unabated.

"War on drugs" has been an empty battle cry, a cynical began for political careerism. Image has supplanted substance.

In terms of epidemiology and social control, our 30-year war can only be judged a dismal failure. In 1963 official estimates held that 500,000 heroin addicts, about half of them in New York, constituted the main problem. Is astonishing that almost the same figure is put forward today. In addition, count the 5.8 million who use cocaine, the 20 million who smoke marijuana, and the 100 million who imbibe alcohol legally, not to mention the millions on time, which Surgeon-General Koop recently declared to an "addictive drug" causing 300,000 deaths each year, and the vision of a nicotine society emerges in all its terror. Just recently a 13-year-old child was executed in Brooklyn by drug trade rivals, a minor episode in a billion dollar traffic that is clearly out of control.

The question is: do we, as a society, really want to do something about it? It does not seem so. The illegal drug industry is among the largest, if not the largest multi-national capitalist enterprise in the world. Larger than our largest corporations, larger than the total operating budgets of most countries, it seems almost too big and too powerful to take on.

Yet, it has been cogently argued, it would begin to topple if the insatiable market in the United States were to disappear or to appreciably diminish. It is the American consuming public that keeps the drug lords in business. The problem is America's demand first, and only then foreign supply. The enemy is at home, not abroad. It is clear that if a beginning is to be made toward the eradication of the scourge of drugs it must be in efforts to reduce the demand in our own country.

That means basic research into the primary causes of addiction, anti-drug education at every level, meaningful prevention programs, and the immediate establishment of a nationwide network of treatment facilities for all those who are ready and willing to enter treatment. Until these components of a comprehensive program are put in place, our "war on drugs" will remain a charade and a convenient political football for cynical political deception.

But is there any evidence that we, or our leadership, really want to do what is necessary? The evidence is doubtful. Our new "drug czar," William Bennett, has suddenly made the discovery that, right under his nose in Washington, it is the nation's capital that merits designation as the "first high-intensity drug-trafficking area" in the country! And his solution, grandly called a "landmark plan," is a call for more prisons. After 30 years of "war" his "new" solution is the old failed road of futile incarceration. No new funds to expand treatment facilities, or serious new prevention programs or education, or basic research. Instead, the "new solution" by the new "czar" after 30 years of the "war on drugs" is the hackneyed, sterile, oldest and most unsuccessful route of the failed past: more prisons. So what else is new?

Meanwhile, on the treatment front a pitifully inadequate struggle is being waged against gigantic odds. A tiny number of facilities tries vainly to stem the deluge. And they have their own problems: Dependent on government funding, they are reluctant to confront the failures of official policy. In the first four years of the Reagan Administration, budgets for drug treatment were slashed by almost 50 percent with hardly a peep of protest out of the treatment community. Practical politics and opportunism reigned. Nancy Reagan mesmerized them with her pathetic "Just Say No" while President Reagan mercilessly cut their operating budgets. A major battle in the "war on drugs" was lost during the Reagan years. Lost by default. The forces of decency and concern never even showed up. We are now paying dearly for that lost battle. Even now, opportunism still wins over principle, as a well-known treatment center honors the disgraced Richard Nixon as an exemplar of virtue. The phony war produces its own phony political twists and turns.

When George Bush was vice-president and himself in charge of the "war on drugs," Panama's Noriega was a kingpin in the international drug route. He still flourishes. Ronald Reagan is reported to have suppressed efforts to investigate drug trafficking by the Nicaraguan Contras at the same time they were receiving hundred of millions of dollars of American aid. Was the "war on drugs" conveniently on hold, or called off? Was it principle or opportunism that lost that battle as well?

Do we really want to end this charade? Or is this the sort of national theater the public craves? "Give them circuses," the Romans said. Today's version, it appears, is "Give them drugs . . . and a phony war to ease our collective conscience."

Meyer Rangell of Bloomingburg is a member of the Alcohol and Drug Abuse committee of the Sullivan County Department of Community Service.

July 16, 1989
North's Sentence Teaches Wrong Lessons
The New York Times

The "punishment" in Oliver North's $150,000 fine is nonexistent; prominent Republicans have already offered to pay it, and Mr. North's lecture fee of $25,000 (made possible by his criminal behavior) could pay the whole thing off in six appearances.

But the worst of this "sentence" is the notion that somehow Mr. North will pay for his crimes by 1,200 hours of "community service" in a drug program. What are true and authentic volunteers to make of this?

Thousands give their time and skills to programs all over the country with no incentive other than service. The volunteer's altruism has been placed in the same bag as the felon's punishment.

August 7, 1989
Democratic socialism and Deng
The Times Herald Record

The horrendous massacre of hundreds of pro-democracy demonstrators in Tiananmen Square and the brutal repression that followed, and still continues, came as no surprise to those aware of Deng Ziaoping's political position in the recent past. We were in Beijing in November, 1987 and picked up a widely-distributed volume titled "FUNDAMENTAL ISSUES IN PRESENT-DAY CHINA" (Foreign Languages Press, 1987).

We quote therefrom:

"Firm measures must be taken against any student who creates trouble at Tiananmen Square" (he was referring to previous student demonstrators) . . . "No concessions should be made in this matter" . . . "We cannot do without dictatorship." Thus spoke Deng on Dec. 30, 1986.

Before that, in May 1985, Deng unequivocally denounced "bourgeois liberalization." "Its exponents", he stated, "worship the 'democracy' and 'freedom' of the Western capitalist countries." (!) . . . "China must absolutely not liberalize or take the capitalist road." . . . "To check bourgeois liberalization is therefore a matter of principle and one of key importance to us."

The warning was clear, and ominous.

It came, therefore, as no surprise that Deng saw the Tiananmen Square demonstrators as a direct challenge to his dictatorial rule. Democratic freedoms were definitely not on his agenda. The ferocity of the government's reactions to peaceful demonstrators and the subsequent repression, arrests and executions underscore the point.

Tiananmen Square, June 1989, is in the tradition of the campaign for "socialism with a human face," led by Alexander Dubcek in Czechoslovakia in 1968. In American history, it inherits not only the symbolism of the Statue of Liberty and the Populism of Lincoln's "of the people, by the people, and for the people," but also the "democratic socialism" of Eugene V. Debs and Norman Thomas, a concept endorsed by Mikhail Gorbachev in Paris, where he expressed his faith in the "ultimate democratization" of socialism. This is more in line with China's students than with Deng!

November 25, 1989
Too little, too late
The Times Herald Record

President Bush is to be commended for putting the issues of drug-abuse on the front burner. He has focused the nation's attention on this killer-scourge, the bubonic plague of our time.

But his remedies are too little, too late and too shallow. Too little: compared to the monies available to the drug-gangsters, the $7.9 billion allotted is pitifully inadequate. Too late: *remember that George Bush himself was in charge of drug abuse management for the eight years of the Reagan administration and in a sense is responsible for the enormity of the problem we now face.* And too shallow; nowhere in the voluminous vocabulary of the drug debate is the basic climate of drug abuse addressed.

Drug abuse did not just grow, like Topsy, out of nothing. It was, and is, a result of poverty, homelessness, squalor, racial discrimination, despair, hopelessness, unemployment, boredom, lack of opportunity, lack of skills, lack of education. It results from the loss of moral and spiritual values, deteriorated neighborhoods, destroyed families, lovelessness, alienation, aloneness, selfishness and meanness of spirit. It is a result of parents who don't tune in to children turned off by what they perceive to be a barren wasteland empty of promise or fulfillment.

Bush's plan seems oblivious to this basic climate of abuse. His figures indicate his priorities: major attention to foreign supply; punishment and prisons for addicts and traffickers; lip service to prevention, treatment and education; and zero to basic causes.

When will our priorities come home? The problem is heartbreak and heroin in Harlem, not coca in Columbia; disillusion and despair in Detroit, not marijuana in Mexico; anguish and lawlessness in Los Angeles, not the pot crop in Peru; bitterness in Boston and Brooklyn not the barrios of Bolivia.

The drug-gangsters are here at home, feeding on our failure of social will and the failed agenda of a society that has lost its moral bearings. And they will continue to be here as long as we pay more attention to relieving the rich of capital gains taxes than to relieving the poor of rat-infested slums.

December 31, 1989
The Buckley Line
Mexico City—The News

Pity poor William F. Buckley, Jr! How can he be consoled? How can one not feel some degree of sympathy for him as he sees his "raison d'etre" suddenly snatched from under him in an onrush of events that he could neither predict nor stem nor welcome. The possibility that peace may break out leaves him in a cold sweat! He would much prefer the Cold War!

"Careful! Careful!", he warns in his column of Nov. 15. Gorbachev's sinister moves toward a Soviet withdrawal, his "perestroika" and "glasnost" catching on like a prairie fire in Eastern Europe, where Communist power, flying in the face of all previous history, seems to be dismantling itself without the shedding of a single ounce of blood, is, in Mr. Buckley's wisdom, a lure, a snare and a delusion. Only the foolish and the unwary will fall for it. Even as his ideological colleague, Mrs. Jeane Kirkpatrick, concedes that "The dramatic events of recent days confirm beyond reasonable doubt that Mikhail Gorbachev and his collaborators in Eastern Europe have abandoned the totalitarian project" (The News, Nov. 19); Mr. Buckley clings to his perennial enemy, the "Evil Empire." Nothing will persuade him to give it up. He cannot do without it. He apparently prefers what Eric Alterman described in the New York Times of Nov. 12 as "the remarkably stable and predictable" admosphere of the cold war, stubbornly endorsed by many within the foreign policy establishment Buckley excoriates Mr. Alterman for supporting the emergence of a new less threatening Soviet foreign policy. With withering Buckleyite sarcasm he sneers at "the possibility that the Holy Ghost has descended on Mikhail Gorbachev," while he, Buckley, does his best to perpetuate hostility, distrust and the belicose, and profitable arms race. Peace is as distasteful to Buckley as the sudden diminution of the Soviet threat is to defense contractors.

The Malta Summit and its aftermath hold forth the promise of historic and monumental change. This could include a nuclear free, even a demilitarized Europe, a major withdrawal of both NATO and Warsaw Pact forces, a new approach for reducing strategic weapons on both sides, and a declaration of non-interference in the internal affairs of all nations.

The question is, will President Bush rise to the occasion, join Gorbachev to lead the world in that direction, and establish a new era of peace and stability?

Or will he follow the Buckley line that patterns foreign policy on the old and dangerous construct of permanent confrontation and enmity?

The time for change, for statesmanship, and for greatness is at hand.

February 27, 1990
The German Threat
Mexico City—The News

In a fortuitous concert of programming, William Styron's SOPHIE'S CHOICE was re-run on television on the same day that A.M. Rosenthal's trenchant article on German unification (GERMANY; HIDDEN WORDS) appeared in *The News* (Feb. 4). In that piece Rosenthal, in fact, had asked for Styron's views among others. They were given, it seems to me, in that powerful, poignant, heart-breaking saga of Nazi evil. Sophie's choice, now, for Germany may not be difficult to imagine.

It would center around the imperative to understand and to eradicate the virulent anti-semitism, and what remains of it, that spawned the horrors of the Holocaust, and to defuse the remnants, or the return, of German revanchism.

To ignore these central issues, while praising the new "unity" of the German nation, is to court disaster. The current generation of Germans, while not responsible for the crimes of their parents, must nonetheless face their history and their heritage. Hitler, the Holocaust, the barbarity of invasion, murder and aggression on "untermenschen," are crimes that do not enjoy a statute of limitations and cannot be swept under the historical rug.

The issue is not simply "unification." The issue is the kind of Germany that is being unified.

Although admittedly complex, some things are clear: The new Germany must be a neutral Germany, aligned neither to NATO nor the Warsaw Pact. The new Germany must be a disarmed Germany; a nuclear-free Germany. The new Germany must never again be allowed to be a threat to its neighbors or to the peace of Europe. Whatever the mechanisms necessary to accomplish this, either through agencies of the United Nations, or special action by the Allies of WW II, this goal must be unambiguously articulated and actively pursued.

Domestically, intensive, thorough, no-holds-barred education at every level on the roots of anti-semitism and racism must be pursued. Their re-emergence is always a fearsome threat. Ask Sophie!

Unification? Yes. But only if it furthers thorough de-Nazification at home and a removal of any German threat abroad.

March 12, 1990
A cozy couple
The Times Herald Record

President George Bush and Czar William Bennett have their own cozy mutual admiration society, each supporting the other in his own private never-never land. The president loudly proclaims that his czar is "winning the war on drugs" while the czar provides the president with an intellectual anti-drug rationale for his naked aggression against a small sovereign nation.

None of this, however, washes south of the border!

There is universal condemnation in Central America of what is generally perceived as brutal interference in the internal affairs of an independent nation and a growing fear of the return of gun-boat diplomacy. They see the military might of the world's most heavily armed power directed against a tiny country in the name of democracy. Czar Bennett adds the rationale of fighting the drug war. This may fly in Peoria, but surely does not fly in Mexico City or in the capitals of Central and South America. The opposition to American militarism and high-handedness is almost universal.

Former Panamanian Ambassador to Mexico Jorge Turner Morales, struck a common chord when he said here, "President Bush justifies his aggressions with the combat of drug trafficking. This concept can be a very dangerous weapon against Mexico" and other Central American countries. There is strong support here for this position. (Mexico City NEWS, Jan. 17, 1990).

As to the drug war itself, the prevailing opinion is that the problem lies with the insatiable demand for drugs in the United States, which remains the world's prime market. If the powerful U.S., with all its resources, cannot control or reduce its own user population, how can it be expected to control foreign suppliers thousands of miles away and beyond its jurisdiction? As the Washington Post reminded us in a recent cogent editorial, "runaway American demand created the drug plague in the first place."

The fact is that one year into Czar Bennett heroics, drug demand and drug use in the United States show no signs of diminishing. William Bennett and his boss hope to distract us from this failure (Washington, D.C., still remains the drug murder capital of the country) by a bravado, swashbuckling display of vigilante violence abroad. At home they advocate more prisons, more jail cells and boot camps while the basic causes of the plague of addiction continue to elude them.

What is needed, and without delay, is an honest appraisal of America's responsibilities at home rather than guns and bullets and deaths in Central and South America.

March 30, 1990
Criticizing Buckley
Mexico City—The News

In his analysis of the Nicaragua election "Was February 25 A 'Triumph'?" (*The News* 3/13), William F. Buckley, Jr. treats us to some convoluted logic (heads I win, tails you lose!) and a sorry discourse that unblushingly reveals his low regard for democracy.

Far from being jubilant over the victory of the anti-Sandinista forces in what was generally agreed to be an honest election (attested to by Jimmy Carter among others, as well as our own Phil Roettinger of San Miguel), Buckley is dismayed that the Sandinistas were able to 'crank up 45 votes out of every 100." So, he warns, let us not be so "incontinent in our faith in democracy"! He is depressed by the fear that "we could have democracy to thank for marshaling the sanctions of the world to honor the verdict if the Sandinistas had won." How Buckleyian! According to his lights a democratic process which might permit the other side to win is too dangerous. Democracy he infers, is not an "ipsum bonum," a good in itself, but is of value only if our side wins. And wins big!

It requires no extraordinary insight to realize that what really rankles Mr. Buckley is that the military 'solution' so dear to the heart of his idol, Ronald Reagan, never came even close to success and now Buckley cannot resist resurrecting the ghost of that evil enterprise. His obvious message is that a Contra victory in which the Sanidinistas and their supporters, and the country of Nicaragua in general, would have been pulverized beyond repair, would have been more to his liking than this anti-Sandinista victory at the polls, Don't rely on frail democracy is his message . . . even when we win!

(Discussing democracy, it is worthy of note that George Bush won the presidency in an election in which 51% of the registered voters stayed away from the polls. Of the 49% who voted, slightly more than half voted for Bush, making him President by the votes of only one-fourth of the electorate. That American democratic politics need vast improvement and more participation is self-evident.)

In this context, Mr. Buckley's derision of democracy as not much of an abiding value does not contribute to the search for the best possible vehicle for man's improvement either in Nicaragua or at home. Imperfect as it is, most of us would prefer to place our hopes on the expansion of democratic thought and practice while Buckley can only sneer at the democratic process and its aspirations.

April 21, 1990
On Anti-Semitism
Mexico City—The News

The resurgence of anti-Semitism in the Soviet Union, ably reported and commented upon in *The News* (A.M. Rosenthal, 3/23, 3/26, William Safire, 3/29, and frequent news articles, 3/24, 3/27, 3/29) should serve to alert those whose historical memories are short and to rekindle the conscience of those who would prefer to forget. The profound admonition of philosopher George Santayana, "Those who refuse to learn from history are doomed to repeat its mistakes," is perhaps the best text for our time.

Among the many questions on the root causes of prejudice, racism and anti-Semitism that demand continued examination is why, after 70 years of Socialism, a system under which, in theory at least, racial and religious hatreds were supposed to disappear, does the specter of widespread anti-Semitism now arise, a specter that impels hundreds of thousands, perhaps as many as a million Jews to flee for safety?

Is it the scapegoat theory once again, as suggested by Safire? Can it be that the same propaganda technique, holding the Jews responsible for Germany's plight in the thirties, is now being resurrected to hold the Jews responsible for the Soviets' plight in the nineties?

Do we never learn? Hitler blamed the Jews; the German people acquiesced; and the world watched in silence as the ovens roared.

Now the Russians hound the Jews: are they responsible for the failures of socialism now, as they were responsible for the failures of capitalism then? The Arab nations, meanwhile, work overtime employing their usual weapons of oil and bomb threats to close off the escape routes via Hungary and Eastern Europe. The Soviets, under Arab pressure, prohibit direct flights from the USSR to Israel. And the world watches again, in complicitous silence.

Only Israel holds forth a welcoming hand, their historic Law of Return offering hope and the promise of safe haven.

May 4, 1990
Refuting Buckley
Mexico City—The News

Dear Editor: In his column of April 18, William F. Buckley employs again his fabled capacity to twist and confuse, this time as he addresses the problem of Soviet anti-Semitism. The column's title, "Israel's Problems" gives the game away. Anti-Semitism in Russia, we are informed, is a problem after all not for the Soviet Union, or for decent people all over the world who do not want to see a replay of Germany's "final solution"; the problem, it turns out, is "Israel's Problem": The victims, and those who wish to help them, turn out to be the villains of the piece. Buckley's wrath and ire, and fire and brimstone, are directed not at those who are responsible for the desperate flight of Jews from Russia (at the rate of 1500 per week!), but at the easy and perennial enemy, the Jewish State of Israel.

Buckley complains that those who flee Russia "do not know Hebrew, have never been in a synagogue, and feel no calling whatever to the practice of the Jewish religion." Somehow this is supposed to cast doubt on the authenticity of their persecution, their honesty in taking flight, and their integrity as they seek emigration to Israel. What arrogance, even for Buckley. Is he suggesting that Israel qualify its Law of Return, that it require credentials, like a letter from their Rabbi confirming that they were in good standing at the Temple, before they are let in? Hitler made no distinctions when he set out to exterminate all Jews, religious or not. And Israel's supreme ethic is to save all Jews, atheist or orthodox, Hebrew-speaking or not. Buckley's spurious and irrelevant reasoning on this score has no basis whatever either in logic or in compassion. It is an insult to reality and to the beleagured emigres.

The Law of Return was promulgated when Israel was born in 1948, long before the present Russian exodus, and represents more than any other single factor the meaning of Israel and its "raison d'etre." It requires no revision or re-interpretation by W.F. Buckley.

Buckley prefers to sneer that Israel's welcoming hand represents "a high degree of cynicism," providing not "religious sanctuary" but merely "importing manpower" to settle the West Bank. Thus he comes full circle, aiming his fire at the victims and their helpers, as though they seek to conceal some interior evil, while he draws attention away from the anti-Semitism that caused them to flee for their lives in the first place. Here, too, he plays fast and loose with the facts in his attempt to paint Israel as the evil party: The truth is that Soviet and other immigrants in Israel are free to travel and to settle wherever they choose; Israel does not command them to settle in the West Bank. As clearly enunciated by Israel's Prime Minister, "Every Jewish immigrant has complete freedom to choose where he wants to live." (*The News*, 3/29). Further, "Government figures show that only 0.5 percent of the Soviet Jews arriving in Israel last year settled in the occupied West Bank or Gaza strip." (*The News* 3/29).

In his eagerness to vilify Israel and to derogate it in its role of Jewish sanctuary, does Mr. Buckley seriously suggest a religious "means test,' and does he demand that the Government impose travel and living restrictions upon new arrivals? Russian Jews seeking refuge, and Israel authorities seeking to help them, clearly and properly reject such advice. They can do without consultants like Buckley!

May 17, 1990
Letter to the Editor
The New York Times

Dear Sir:

Leonard Kriegel is to be applauded for his cogent, brilliant attack on the professors at the City College who, under the cover of academic "science" and faculty protection, fan the fires of race prejudice and hatred with their retrograde obscenities.

I must agree, however, with the letter of Dr. Alvin Poussaint (5/16), who, while agreeing with the diagnosis offers a more reasonable and appropriate response. "The competence of these men to teach effectively," he states, "is undermined by their untenable racist diatribes that spread bigotry rather then open-mindedness." It is, therefore, "a proper concern of the university."

It is also a concern of the student body. When I attended CCNY in the thirties, when the moral and intellectual climate was informed by such teachers as Morris Raphael Cohen and Dean Morton Gottschall, whose breadth and intellectual vigor and honesty stand in sharp contrast to the Neanderthal crudities of Messrs. Levin and Jeffries, the student body that I remember would hardly have remained silent in the face of such faculty-sponsored racism.

CCNY's anti-fascist students of the thirties fought racism decades before the civil rights movement. They tried to alert an almost indifferent nation to the dangers of Hitler and Mussolini when it was not popular to do so. For this, later historians were to characterize them as "premature anti-fascists" (!), as they foreshadowed the campus activism of the sixties.

It is sad to see that the same old tired rubbish about race is still alive and poisoning the well, and good to see that teachers like Kriegel and Poussaint are at their posts to speak out for reason and common sense in the face of renewed bigotry.

July 2, 1990
Law of the Land
The New York Times

When John Cardinal O'Connor officially warns Roman Catholics that they "risk being excommunicated from the Catholic Church" if they persist "in supporting a woman's right to abortion" (news article, June 15), he is using his not inconsiderable power to pressure his constituency into breaking the law. As Gov. Mario M. Cuomo was quick to point out, the right to abortion is, after all, the law of the land. By threatening religious punishment, the Cardinal seeks to employ his unusual power to interfere in the legislative process. Not only Catholics but all citizens who believe in our time-honored principle of the separation of church and state, will greet this incursion with dismay.

 The Cardinal's audacity in this matter may cause a review of the tax-exempt status enjoyed by church institutions. Many of us have never been able to fathom why large real estate holdings of religious institutions should be exempt from taxation, thus forcing every citizen, religious or otherwise, to bear an extra burden and, in a way, to support religious purposes.

July 28, 1990
"Who Won the War, Anyway?"
The Times Herald Record

Will some historian or statesman step forward to explain why World War II, the most destructive war in history, ended without a German/Allied Peace Treaty? Why there was no document to spell out the result of a conflict in which 40 million people lost their lives? Why there was no Peace Conference to set down for the historical record what exactly the 40 million died for?

In a purely personal and anecdotal poll, I conducted among a group of usually well-informed people, almost all said that I must be mistaken, that there was, indeed, such a treaty. "It was at Yalta, wasn't it?" some said. Or "At Potsdam," others said. The latter were closer to the truth, but no cigar as they say in the TV game shows.

In fact, there never was a peace conference or a peace treaty with Germany. In July, 1945, as Germany lay prostrate, Churchill, Truman and Stalin met at Potsdam to establish guidelines for the post-war world. When they disagreed, as they did on the German/Polish border, on the transfer of populations in countries overrun by Hitler, and on other issues, temporary settlements were reached. The permanent solution was left to a future peace conference. *Only that conference never took place.* As a consequence, there is no peace treaty to ring down the corridors of history and to establish for future generations Hitler's and Germany's, responsibilities for the murderous aggressions, the genocidal slaughters, the murder of millions of Jews and other "undesirables" in the infamous death camps. At war's end, the victors never did impose long-range conditions designed to prevent a recurrence of the Nazi horror. "Unconditional surrender" did not address the conditions for a future world of peace.

The result is that now, after 45 years, we are supposed to dance with joy when a German chancellor (who did win the war anyway?) states that the two Germanys, upon reunification, would be willing to accept the Oder/Neisse line established at Potsdam as the permanent border with Poland.

We are supposed to cheer the establishment of a democratic, peace-loving Germany, where even now a powerful German organization, called the Leagues of Expellees, which claims a membership of 2.3 million, clamors for the return of the lost Polish territories. As the New York Times reported it (Magazine, April 15, 1990), " . . . he (head of the Silesian Patriots' Club,) sticks to the right-wing position that the Oder-Neisse line can't be recognized until the Allies and Germany sign a peace treaty, deferred since 1945!" Was Winston Churchill prescient when he stated at Potsdam, "One day the Germans would want their territory back and the Poles would not be able to stop them"? (Triumph and Tragedy; Vol. 6, p. 648.) Who did win the war, anyway?

If we had a peace conference at the war's end, would we have left it to the defeated Germans to decide what part of ravaged Poland to withdraw from or what part to keep? Would we have left it to the Germans to decide whether or not to join a military alliance directed against one of the victorious allies? (President Bush now uses all his power to push for full membership in the North Atlantic Treaty Organization for a united Germany). Who won the war anyway?

Would we have left it to the Germans to decide whether or not Nazism and racism were acceptable and what means we deemed necessary to prevent their resurgence? Who won the war, anyway?

Where is a peace treaty, where are Terms of Surrender, where is acknowledgement of guilt and responsibility? Where, and what is the monument to the memory of 40 million victims?

Is a peace conference, and with it a peace treaty, still possible? Or did history miss forever a watershed opportunity?

A peace treaty was signed, finally, on September 12, 1990!

Postscript: News Item (July 17): West German Chancellor Helmut Kohl said "he had told Moscow that a united Germany would seek to become a member of the North Atlantic Treaty Organization. . . . In exchange, Mr. Kohl said, the Germans agreed to negotiate a treaty with the Soviet Union covering all aspects of their relations—political, economic, military, cultural and scientific . . ."

Strange! Forty-five years after the conclusion of the war, defeated Germany "agrees to negotiate a treaty!" with the country that it murderously invaded, almost succeeded in conquering, and where it did succeed in murdering 20 million men, women and children before it was driven back. One for the books *Who won the war, anyway?*

December 1990
The Big Religious Give—Away
Freethought Today . . . .

"I would also call your attention to the importance of correcting an evil that, if permitted to continue, will probably lead to great trouble in our land . . . it is the accumulation of vast amounts of untaxed church property . . ."

The speaker was not a wild-eyed atheist reformer, but the President of the United States, in his annual message to Congress. The year was 1875; the President, Ulysses S. Grant; the immediate stimulus a 900-foot petition presented to Congress, containing $5,000 signatures, stating, "We demand that churches and other ecclesiastical property shall be no longer exempt from taxation."

"In 1850," the President continued, "the church properties in the United States which paid no taxes, municipal (churches do not die), that churches may own and operate business and be exempt from the 52% corporate income tax, and that some property used for church purposes (which in some states are generously construed) is tax exempt, it is not unreasonable to prophesy that with reasonably prudent management the churches ought to be able to control the whole economy of the nation within the predictable future."[2]

The Most Reverend Fulton J. Sheen, shortly after assuming the post of Roman Catholic Bishop of Rochester, New York, stated, "There never should be a new church built here that costs more than, say, $1 million. If a diocese insists on spending more for a church, it ought to pay something like a 20% tax for mission. The right of the poor to have a decent house enjoys priority over our right to erect a tax-exempt structure which exceeds the minimum."[3]

If it was not evident at its inception, the legal tax-exemption soon revealed or state, amounted to about $83 million. In 1860, the amount had doubled; in 1875 it is about $1 billion. By 1900, without check, it is safe to say this property will reach a sum exceeding $3 billion . . . . So vast a sum, receiving all the protection and benefits of government without bearing its portion of the burdens and expenses of the same, will not be looked upon acquiescently by those who have to pay the taxes . . . . I would suggest the taxation of all property equally, whether church or corporation."[1]

As it turned out, the President did not exaggerate. By 1971, experts calculated that the amount of real and personal property owned by US churches had grown far beyond President Grant's "vast sum" of $3 billion. It was now $110 billion! In New York City alone, tax exemptions for religious properties, clergy and parsonages had reached over

$750 million, according to the City of New York Annual Report of the Tax Commission for the fiscal year 1968-69. The Tax Commission's latest report, for the fiscal year 1981-82 (a spokesperson at the Commission could not explain why this "annual report" has not been issued since then) listed religious tax-exempt properties at over $1 billion. And by March, 1989, the New York State Board of Equalization and Assessment listed religious exemptions *in New York City alone*, at a staggering $3,022,475,000. Thus, the fearful expectations of President Grant that religious exemptions would reach $3 billion for the nation as a whole by the year 1900 came true in a single city less than a century later.

This rapid accumulation of colossal wealth by church organizations and its implications for the community at large did not escape thoughtful clergy. Doctor Eugene Carson Blake, leader of the United Presbyterian Church in the United States and general secretary of the World Council of Churches, said, "When one remembers that churches pay no inheritance tax the ease with which abuses could grow under the clause "for religious purposes," whose broad interpretation could, and did, give rise to many opportunities for lucrative abuse. In a study published by the Russell Sage Foundation in 1971 ("The Free List," by Alfred Balk), one example among many is cited:

"In one action . . . the Catholic Archdiocese of Hartford purchased 121.5 acres of vacant land in New Britain, Connecticut, for $23,500. The land then was classified as a cemetery and exempted; a body was buried there, and in 1966, when the land had appreciated to $607,000, the body was removed and the 'cemetery' was sold. According to Americans United for Separation of Church and State, the exemption saved the church $200,000 in taxes in the years it owned the land." The church's "savings," of course, added an additional burden of $200,000 to the general taxpayer.

It is of historic and philosophic interest that the "acquiescence" of the taxpayer noted by President Grant has lasted, without effective challenge for more than 100 years. It seems to point to an essential religiosity in our people. Religion, like politics, cannot be discussed without raised voices often emitting more heat than light. Most citizens have been prone to look acquiescently on the special tax favors enjoyed by religious institutions. Those who have the audacity to raise the question as a significant issue in the realm of public policy are looked upon as party spoilers. Who but a quibbler would want to question the religious about their (God-given?) exemptions?

And yet there is ample justification for re-examining any area where tax revenue might be justly and equitably increased, when the federal government is struggling under the weight of the largest budget deficit in history; when local governments all over the country strain to the breaking point to meet human needs with shrinking and inadequate funds, when in New York City, with violence and crime almost out of control, the Mayor cannot find the money to put more police officers on the streets (he is struggling for 1,000 more cops at a cost of $80 million, when the need is clearly for at least 5,000, according to the New York Times and the Police Commissioner); when more cells are needed for a prison system that is almost unmanageable; when sensitive probation efforts are hamstrung; when thousands of drug addicts languish on waiting lists, unable to gain admission to overcrowded and underfunded treatment programs; when the homeless are without shelter and the poor without affordable housing.

Under these circumstances how can we not look with a more critical eye on the millions of dollars of tax forgiveness given year after year to religious institutions? How can we countenance this give-away of public money while crying human needs go unmet? Should the public interest be denied while the private interests of religious groups are served?

What is the justice of forcing atheists, agnostics, humanists, freethinkers and others who follow the private dictates of their own conscience in matters of theology to pay for the practice, and the ornate trappings, of organized religion? (It is obvious, of course, that the narrowing of the tax base by exemptions forces a compensatory, involuntary tax increase for those property owners who are not tax-exempt).

This has nothing to do with religious freedom. True religious freedom, in fact, would be better served if believers carried their own weight and if religionists and nonreligionists shared equally in bearing public burdens.

Let organized religion pay its own way, according to the tastes of its members, no special favors asked or granted, for a true ambience of free choice for all. That would be true freedom of religion in a fair and unbiased democracy.

Meyer Rangell, a Freethought Today reader from New York, is a graduate of the University of Chicago School of Social Work. He has worked as a social worker and business executive. His social activism has included many years in anti-drug abuse activities. His frequent essays and letters on drug abuse, racism, nuclear war, and civil rights have appeared in the New York Times, Times-Herald Record; Mexico City News, and elsewhere.

December 1, 1990
Washington Plan?
The New York Times

    Your Nov. 11 editorial in praise of William J. Bennett was simply underwhelming. Mr. Bennett did what a wag once suggested we do about the Vietnam War: "Declare a victory and go home."

    He quit, you write, just when there appear "glimmers of hope that the nation's crack epidemic may have peaked." Surely, to say that drug addiction and abuse came to their highest point during William Bennett's watch is nothing for him to brag about.

    But, you imply, with more wish fulfillment than credible scientific evidence, after this "peak" we'll see a decline, for which there are those "glimmers of hope."

    A more sober evaluation of Mr. Bennett's 19-month reign gives less cause to cheer. Some basic questions are still to be answered:

    When he took office, Mr. Bennett was quoted as designating the District of Columbia as "the first high-intensity drug-trafficking area" in the country, and he proposed a "landmark plan" (chiefly relying on more prisons). As he leaves, one might ask whatever happened to that plan? Or is Washington still a "high-intensity drug-trafficking area"?

    How much more do we know now, after Mr. Bennett's 19 months, about the cause of drug abuse? What research has been conducted and with what results? How much more do we know about treatment methods? The "solid intellectual base" you refer to is less than visible.

    As to those "encouraging statistics," still with us are drug-related crime, violence and turf wars in the inner cities, and overwhelmed and underfunded treatment centers.

    Officeholders come and go (and make hay for future careers), but drug despair, drug violence, drug crime and drug misery stay with us, impervious to grandstanding and politics.

December 7, 1990
(In response to an editorial in the New York Times, reprinted in NEWS.)
Mexico City-The News

Your *New York Times* editorial of Nov. 9 properly condemns "THE LEGACY OF HATE" that lies at the root of the bloody assassination of Rabbi Meir Kahane in New York City recently. But in its eagerness to be even-handed as between the assassin and his victim the piece focuses almost exclusively on the (discredited) policies of Kahane in Israel, with hardly a word about the virulent Arab hatreds that infused the murderer, created his motivation and led him inexorably to the executioner's deed.

Blaming the victim is always an easy out, but one that will be rejected by those with an honest regard for history. The editorial asks, "Why this reverberating crime was committed . . ." and whether it was "the fruit of a deeper conspiracy." The history of unabated Arab hatred for Israel and their denial of its legitimacy provides the answer. From the very beginning, Palestinian Arabs rejected the independent state that was offered to them in the United Nations Partition Plan of November, 1947. Along with their Arab neighbors they preferred war and invasion in order to destroy the new State of Israel. The Palestine National Covenant, official Charter of the PLO, has not altered that official stance to this day. Incursions, murder, assassination and terror toward Israelis and toward Jews anywhere has been their modus operandi. Olympic athletes at Munich, civilians of all nations in the air, in airports and on the high seas, Jews at prayer in synagogue in Istanbul, innocent women and children and non-combatants, have been the indiscriminate targets of PLO murder and terror. Whether the Kahane assassin belonged to a specific conspiratorial group or acted alone, one does not have to look far for "the fruit of a deeper conspiracy." That "deeper conspiracy" is the 42-year-old war waged by the Arab states in order to exterminate Israel. With the single exception of Egypt, whose President Sadat was also assassinated (by an Arab), that state of war and that purpose still exist.

That Meir Kahane was a political extremist does not legitimize his assassination. It is significant that Kahane met with little success in Israel. His KACH party attracted only a small group of supporters. And the State of Israel disqualified him for the Knesset because he was "racist and undemocratic." By contrast, what Arab state ever condemned any terrorist, anywhere for murder and violence against Jews? The contrast is clear: Israel, its people and its State, condemned and contained the extremism of the

Kahanes, while the Arab States, and the PLO, officially encouraged, rewarded and abetted violence and terror as instruments of political process. The assassin of Kahane in New York was a moral and ethical product of that disastrous Arab policy.

January 2, 1991
Letter to the Editor
Mexico City—The News

    Gerald F. Uelmen's phrase, "the drug-abuse industrial complex," (in his column, A New Drug Czar, 12/13) may serve to illustrate the complexities, and the hypocracies, of the so-called "war on drugs" in the same way that Dwight D. Eisenhower's memorable phrase, "The military-industrial complex," served to illuminate the intertwining relationships between war and peace, patriotism and defense contracts.
    After more than 30 years of a "war on drugs" that has always seemed more hype than substance, "the march of folly rolls on," Mr. Uelmen so aptly puts it. William J. Bennett leaves drug-abuse for greener fields and Florida Gov. Bob Martinez is granted the consolation prize as national drug czar after losing the race for Governor in his home state. Qualifications? Expertise? Special training and insight into the problems of addiction and their social consequences? Don't be naive! After 19 months, Bennett left the job, his sights set on more lucrative assignments, with the praises of President Bush ringing in his ears and the scourge of drug-abuse still pretty much where he had found it when he started. Now, Bob Martinez, rejected by his constituency for another term as Governor, is rewarded and rescued by President Bush with Bennett's old job, to carry on in the same tradition. A job is a job is a job!
    Professionals who have devoted years of training and study, as well as the general public, which has had it up to its eyeballs with increasing drug crime, drug violence, and the waste of young lives to drug despair, look with dismay as another political appointment makes a mockery of the seriousness and depth of the problem.
    A huge bureaucracy which, like all bureaucracies, tends to place its own survival interests at the top of its list of priorities, remains muted in its criticism of the federal government, to which it looks for support and grants, money and jobs.
    The only thing missing, again, is a fresh approach and the courage to seek answers to the problems of chemical abuse in the social fabric that spawned it: deteriorating slums, joblessness, despair, educational failure, family disintegration, miserable housing, and a host of problems ranging from the societal to the personal/psychological that our leaders in Washington are determined to avoid.
    They would rather build a "drug-abuse industrial complex"—a new and growing source of jobs and political patronage which has every potential of providing a political

gravy-train for years to come, while doing next to nothing for the basic problem for which it was ostensibly created.

January 7, 1991
Newsweek

*   *   *

Simply to ask the question "Must Our Wars Be Moral?" testifies to how low morality and ethics have fallen in modern political discourse. The word moral, as defined by Webster, deals with "the principles of right and wrong" and is concerned with conduct that is "good or right." The Center for Defense Information in Washington recently estimated that even three months of heavy fighting in the Persian Gulf would leave 10,000 U.S. soldiers dead and 35,000 wounded. For what? To restore a feudal monarchy in Kuwait? For oil? For "jobs," as Secretary of State Baker has stated? Must our wars be moral? Must we even ask the question?

*   *   *

February 7, 1991
Letter to the Editor
Mexico City—The News

When that great moral arbiter, Richard Nixon, who reduced the U.S. Presidency to its nadir, who made Watergate and its White House conspirators synonymous with lying, deceit, disinformation and disgrace, takes it upon himself to lecture us about our "highly moral commitment" in the Persian Gulf (OpEd Jan. 8), readers who weren't born yesterday must sit up and beware.

"We must first be clear about what the conflict is not about," Nixon pontificates. Doesn't this ring a bell? "Let me be perfectly clear" once again? Once again, predictably, Nixon is anything but "perfectly clear"!

In an article replete with contradiction; Nixon supports Senator Bob Dole when he says "we were in the gulf for oil," as well as Secretary of State James Baker when he said "We were there for jobs." But, Nixon says, unflappable in his contradictoriness, our war against Iraq will not be "about oil," nor about "a tyrant's cruelty," nor "about democracy." "It will be a war about peace." That is why it will be "a highly moral enterprise."

"War about peace" is almost a direct crib from George Orwell's satiric masterpiece, "1984," in which Big Brother brainwashed his people into believing that "war is peace; freedom is slavery; ignorance is strength." Orwell would be sardonically amused.

Nixon is opposed to continuing sanctions. He prefers a war "to stop him (Hussein) now." But nowhere does he examine, or criticize, the disastrous policies of the West (including the U.S., the USSR, Germany, France, et al) that supported and armed Saddam Hussein for oil and profit. Nor does he have faith that policy can be changed. Indeed he does not anywhere even suggest such change. "Because he (Hussein) has the oil he has the means to acquire the weapons he needs," Nixon writes. But it is precisely that disgraceful policy on the part of the West, the United States included, (give him anything he wants as long as he sells us oil and we make a handsome profit on armaments), that has brought us to the present danger. Is that policy not yet seen to be changed? MUST IT NOT BE CHANGED? Sanctions are a welcome step in the direction of such change.

If we do win the war (a bloody war "about peace") will it not be necessary to make that change thoroughly and consistently so that we do not again have to send thousands of U.S. soldiers to grisly deaths and many thousands more to mutilation and destroyed lives, when another Hussein sells us oil for arms and profit?

The answer lies in political and economic and diplomatic change, from a posture of oil/arms trafficking with Iraq (and Kuwait and Saudi Arabia) to a moral posture that isolates the oil-rich blackmailers, strangles them in the international marketplace, and exposes them on the world diplomatic stage.

We will surely have to adopt such a policy after Nixon's war (if we win it), why not do it now, before the body bags start coming in and before incalculable death and destruction are visited upon us all.

February 12, 1991
Letter to the Editor
Mexico City—The News

Mr. Rami G. Khouri's Arabist narrative of the historical antecedents of Saddam Hussein's Gulf War (*The News*, 1/26) deserves a response.

Mr. Khouri's claim to scholarly objectivity is forfeited at once by his shallow and unbalanced treatment of the central issue of Arab/Israeli relations since November, 1947, when the United Nations established the State of Israel and when, at the same time, the Palestinian Arabs refused their own equally independent state offered to them under the same Partition Plan. Instead, the Arab world preferred to launch a war of annihilation against new-born Israel, a war they have not abandoned, with the single exception of Egypt, to this day. In his assiduous avoidance of the centrality of this issue, Mr. Khouri forfeits any pretensions he may have had to impartial scholarship.

With a gallows humor that is supposed to substitute for profundity, Mr. Khouri writes that Saddam "may be a son-of-a-bitch, but he is our son-of-a-bitch."! When Saddam drops Scud bombs on residential areas in Tel Aviv, Jerusalem and Haifa, killing and injuring hundreds of innocent civilians, destroying thousands of homes, and terrorizing a non-combatant people, whose son-of-a-bitch is he then? When he creates the world's worst ecological disaster by a calculated oil-spillage in the Persian Gulf, whose s.o.b. is he then? When three and a half million men, women and children in Israel are forced to wear gas-masks to counter Saddam's threat to incinerate their country with chemical and biological warheads, whose son-of-a-bitch is he then?

Mr. Khouri's moral indignation, so glaringly absent in the face of Saddam's wanton attack on Kuwait, is opened full throttle against Israel, the non-combatant major target! When he cannot refrain from gloating that "it is a source of pride to Arabs that Saddam hit Israel with missiles," he reaches a new low in audacious amorality.

Does Mr. Khouri really think that he can paper over the evil intent of the Iraqi tyrant and aggressor by blaming all Arab troubles "on the wishes of the Israeli lobby in Washington"? Saddam's attempt to distract the world community, and his own people, from his pillage, rape and plunder in Kuwait by turning the war into a holy war (Jihad) against Israel may serve well as Arab deceit and disinformation, but will fool no one but those die-hard anti-Israel forces that have been waiting and hoping for Israel's destruction for over 40 years.

May 16, 1991
Injury to Insult
The New York Times

Small events, perhaps insignificant in themselves, sometimes serve to illuminate the larger picture. Such an event was the recent refusal of Saudi Arabia to honor the United States passport of Senator Frank Lautenberg because it contained an Israeli stamp. The Senator had traveled to Israel; he was therefore persona non grata in Saudi Arabia. The Saudis thus demeaned the official, solemn document of travel—issued by the United States Government to its free citizens to protect their rights while abroad—to pursue the policy of nonrecognition, embargo, boycott and hatred toward the State of Israel.

And how did the United States respond to this insult? By a shabby device: the State Department issued the Senator a new passport in which the Israeli stamp did not appear! The Saudis must have smugly smiled in their small victory: the deceitful new passport was a moral victory for their policy.

The irony will escape no one. A half million American soldiers risked their lives to defend Saudi Arabia in the recent war. Were fresh passports, conveniently free of any evidence or taint of Israeli travel, issued to our fighting men and women? Or were they allowed to fight without passports? Can it be that Americans who come to fight and die to defend Saudi Arabia are welcome? But those who come only for a friendly visit (even a Senator) must show evidence that they support the Saudis' embargo and boycott against Israel?

The craven and obsequious response of the State Department to this unconscionable state of affairs is an insult to the common sense of the American people as well, as to the integrity of our policy in the Middle East. In effect, the Saudis are successfully compelling American acquiescence in their policy of embargo and boycott (and official belligerency) toward Israel. This was always reprehensible. In the aftermath of the Persian Gulf war, however, after we saved them from the brutalities of Saddam Hussein, its continuance is a slap in the face and a monstrous insult. In the interest of justice and of self-respect, the State Department must move, immediately, for change.

May 29, 1991
Senator Lautenberg Responds: Bring Arab Passport Bigotry to an End
The New York Times

To the Editor:

Meyer Rangell (letter, May 16) writes about the refusal of Saudi Arabia to accept my passport because it had an Israeli stamp in it. He notes that the State Department's response was to issue me a new passport, which he characterizes as a shabby device. I agree.

In Congress, Representative Howard Berman and I introduced legislation to require Secretary of State James A. Baker 3d to instruct our Middle Eastern diplomatic corps to commence negotiations with Arab countries to reverse their passport policy. If, within 90 days of enactment, negotiations have not resulted in a commitment from each Arab country to reverse this policy, the State Department will be prohibited from issuing duplicate passports to United States Government officials traveling in the Middle East.

For nondiplomatic United States travelers, our legislation would prohibit so-called Israel-only passports. Thus, if the Arabs continue this policy, American travelers would be issued Saudi-only passports, and suffer the stigma and isolation that United States acquiescence in the Arab boycott imposes on Israel. This legislation has been adopted by a Senate subcommittee, and hearings are scheduled in the House of Representatives shortly.

Saudi Arabia and Kuwait welcomed American soldiers to fight for their sovereignty, but they refuse to admit Americans who have committed the "offense" of having visited Israel. To accept this Arab behavior gives tacit approval to the Arab League policy of isolating Israel and refusing to accept its right to exist.

American law and policy reject the Arab League boycott. The Arab practice of denying entry to United States citizens with Israeli stamps in their passports is an extension of the boycott. It is an insult to every American, and every American soldier who fought in Operation Desert Storm. The Administration can act to reverse this archaic and misguided Arab policy. If not, I hope Congress will enact our legislation and end this practice.

May 31, 1991
Restrict U.S.-Arab arms sales
The Times Herald Record

At the end of the Gulf War, the headline in the New York Times read:
"BUSH, PROCLAIMING VICTORY,
SEEKS WIDER MIDEAST PEACE,
HINTS AT PRESSURE ON ISRAEL."

I'm confused. Wasn't Israel on our side? Did it not refrain, at our insistence, from retaliating against the Arab aggressors even as its cities were being bombed by Scud missiles and an entire non-combatant population was forced to wear gas masks in response to Saddam Hussein's threat to "incinerate" their country?

Now that the war is over, is it back to square one? Back to "pressuring Israel", while we re-arm the Arab world and continue the disgraceful policy of confusing our friends with our enemies in the Mideast?

The philosopher George Santayana warned that those who do not learn from history are doomed to repeat its mistakes. Have we learned nothing from the disastrous policy of arming a Saddam Hussein, supporting him with oil money, never "pressuring" him on his maintaining a state of war with Israel, acquiescing in fact, while he trained and financed PLO terrorism?

Now the Bush administration plans to sell $18 billion worth of arms to the Middle East in the coming year (New York Times, 3/22)! Should we use our power to put "pressure on Israel", while the Arab states insist on maintaining an official state of war against Israel, continue to support the PLO Charter position of destroying Israel's statehood, finance and encourage terrorism via the so-called Intafada and frequent border raids, murder and assassination? In short, while the Arab states maintain the position they adopted in 1948 in their first, and continuing, war of extermination against Israel: "No Recognition; No Negotiations; No Peace!"

In these circumstances, is it logical or moral for U.S. policy to arm Arab states to assist them in their plans for Israel's destruction? Is it overstatement to consider the possibility that Syria's Hafez al Assad may in due time become another Saddam Hussein? Our lack of trust in Assad as an ally was clearly evident when we chose to do without Israel's military strength rather than risk the danger of Syria (and Saudi Arabia) betraying our alliance of expediency in preference for their unabated hatred for and designs upon Israel.

Who are our friends and who our enemies in this region? Where is principle and where expediency?

Shall we continue to provide the Arab states with oil money, providing the means with which we can sell them arms, while we remain indifferent to their war-making potential with each other and, jointly, against our ally Israel? (Before the Kuwait invasion, Egypt, Iran, Iraq, Kuwait, Libya, Saudi Arabia and Syria bought about $125 billion in arms since 1983.) (New York Times, 3/25/91).

A sane and modest moral position, and one that would at the same time represent the national interests of the United States, would be:

1) Sell no arms to Arab states as long as they maintain an official state of war with Israel.
2) Make the ending of that state of war, and the establishment of peace with Israel a requirement, a sine-qua-non, before any arms are sold.
3) Thereafter, with peace established, sell only those arms that are required for self-defense.
4) Abolish all nuclear, biological, and chemical weapons in the region.
5) Limit and restrict the total flow of conventional arms to all states in the region to the minimum required for self-defense.

These goals could be monitored by appropriate organs of the United Nations.

June 10, 1991
Letter to the Editor
The Atlantic

I was chagrined to see, in the otherwise penetrating article, "CAN POETRY MATTER?", by Dana Gioia (May, Atlantic), the casual coupling of Ezra Pound and George Orwell as writers who both valued "good writing" and "efficient language". Pound is quoted as saying "good writers are those who keep the language efficient . . . It doesn't matter whether a good writer wants to be useful, or whether the bad writer wants to do harm" (!). While Orwell is quoted, "One ought to recognize that the present political chaos is connected with the decay of language . . ." Both are cited as wanting "to keep the nation's language clear and honest . . ." It is hard to imagine a less felicitous juxtaposition. Pound was a self-declared fascist, anti-semite, and traitor to the Allied cause in WW II, who used his dexterity with language, and his reputation as a poet, to support Mussolini and Hitler and to engage in a scurrilous antisemitism that has little equal in modern literature. George Orwell, on the other hand, was a philosophic socialist, a trenchant critic of Pound, am anti-fascist (he fought on the Loyalist side in the Spanish Civil War) and a writer, columnist and propagandist who used his not inconsequential talents to support libertarian causes. To couple the two as "good writers" is like coupling Hitler and Goethe because they both wrote German.

In *The Roots of Treason*, (1984), Dr. E. Fuller Torrey demonstrates Pound's anti-semitism beyond doubt: "In 1938 Pound said that the history of Jews had been inimical to rational values, and in the following year he wrote "I begin to doubt that yidd (sic!) fluence has ever been anything but a stinking curse to Europe" (p. 141).

The psychiatric/ poetic cabal that saved Pound from the consequences of his treason and forced his stay in St. Elizabeths Hospital for the insane, remains a disgrace both to literature, to psychiatry, and to justice.

In a celebrated essay, "*Politics and the English Language*", George Orwell brilliantly and ethically advanced an opposite view: "If thought corrupted language," he wrote, "language can also corrupt thought." (1946) He fought consistently against "the slovenliness of our language", particularly with reference to "political language . . .

that is designed to make lies sound truthful and murder respectable and to give an air of solidity to pure wind."

To present Pound in the same vein with Orwell profanes the lesson that the fascist poet, and a re-examining of his obscene role as anti-semitic propagandist for Mussolini and Hitler, can yet bequeath to our literary ethic, and would make the libertarian Orwell turn over in his grave.

1991
Religion, War And Prayer
Freethought Today

At this moment of euphoria and self-congratulations over our victory in the Gulf War, it might be instructive to re-examine the relationship between war and religion, or more broadly, the use to which religion is put in the most crucial of secular affairs.

More than one million men and women (1.2 million, according to Allied estimates) were arrayed against each other in the Persian Gulf. Half were persuaded by their leader and by their religious orientation that no more rewarding death could be theirs than to die in a holy war (a Jihad), first against the Western infidels and then against the usurping Jews in Israel. Such a glorious death, Allah promised them, was a sure ticket to salvation and eternal bliss.

On the other side, the American President and his spokesmen never missed an opportunity to invoke God's name as their ultimate moral authority, and to urge universal prayer as the most important contribution ordinary Americans could make in support of the troops. Television images of wives and parents and families of the men and women at war inundated our home screens, as with an uncanny uniformity they all said, "We pray for their early return," responding, it seems, both to the President's exhortations and to their own all-explaining religiosity.

In an internationally-televised briefing heard around the world, General Norman Schwartzkopf, commenting on February 27 about the success of the ground war, said that the weather was perfect for the event because "God loves the infantryman"!

Do all these millions of people on both sides really believe in the God-given sanctity of their cause and in the efficacy of prayer? If so, why the war? Why the brutal fighting? Why the scuds and the patriots and the biological and chemical threats and the tanks and the bombings and the fearful destruction and the tens of thousands of human mutilations and death?

Anthony Lewis of the New York Times suggested that approximately 50,000 Iraqi lives were lost. The figure, others suggest, may be many times more. On our side we were lucky: the figure at this writing is about 400 dead. *Was this due to our superior technology and war-making skills, or to the superior strength and moral virtue of our God and our prayers over theirs?*

If we truly believe that God in His heaven, in His infinite mercy and wisdom, (selectively) blesses and supervises earthly events, why do we need guns and missiles and bombs? Why not amass the huge multitudes of believers on all sides, organize the greatest prayer meetings ever seen and pray and beseech and exhort God to do the right thing, to "drive out the infidels," to "bring our troops home safely," to restore goodness and mercy and justice to all? Incidentally, since this is the original purpose imputed to an all-knowing, all-powerful, all-seeing, just and merciful divinity, why does He have to be exhorted at all by mere mortals?

When we put more faith in developing a superior technology in mass killing and destruction, we demonstrate in fact that our "faith" is riddled with doubt, with creeping uncertainty, and that we would rather rely on our military-industrial complex than on religious imprecations and universal prayer.

The scenario, facetious in today's world of Orwellian "doublethink," of huge prayer meetings facing each other, instead of huge armies, would explode the hypocrisies inherent in the pious calls on both sides for religious legitimacy to their murderous endeavors.

William James, the apostle of pragmatism, once wrote: "the ultimate test for us of what a truth means is the conduct it dictates or inspires." (*The Meaning of Truth*, 1909)

What sort of conduct, we might ask in the Jamesian tradition, did religious ideology and religious teaching inspire in the Gulf War ?

June 19, 1991
Sound ground for no exemptions!
The Times Herald Record

A spate of letters has appeared recently in the Record for and against tax exemptions for religious institutions. None, however, addressed the pivotal issue of the *First Amendment to the Constitution:* "Congress shall make no law respecting an establishment of religion." It is significant that, before the colonists accepted the Constitution, they insisted on the first 10 amendments, which became known as the Bill of Rights. And the first clause of the First Amendment, the concern uppermost in the minds of our forefathers, was what became known as the "wall of separation between church and state," a phrase coined by the far-seeing Thomas Jefferson, spokesman of the revolution.

When tax exemptions are granted religious institutions, does that not breach the "wall of separation?" Are not tax exemptions clearly a form of tax support?

When religious properties are freed from tax obligations does that not force a compensatory involuntary tax increase for the rest of the taxpaying public? (In New York City alone, according to the New York State Board of Equalization and Assessment report of March 1989, religiously owned real property in the amount of $3 billion was tax exempt! How many social services would be spared the cuts now being ordered if these uncollected tax revenues were retrieved?)

When the taxpayers' money is used for religious purposes does that not promote the entanglement of church and state, precisely what the framers of the Constitution warned against?

When tax money is used for religious purposes, does not private religiosity enter the public domain, contrary to the letter and the spirit of the Constitution?

It is worthy of note that in the Mini Page of June 1, designed to inform and educate our younger readers, devoted this date to "Freedoms in the Bill of Rights," the page begins, inexplicably, with "the last two freedoms in the First Amendment." The first freedom, the Establishment Clause, the freedom from state interference in religion, does not even get a mention! Ignorance, prejudice, or editorial oversight . . . or is the Constitutional position on religion being deliberately distorted?

Let us keep the First Amendment alive!

August 15, 1991
Letter to the Editor
The New York Times

City College students of the thirties will resonate with the passionate and forceful column of A.M. Rosenthal (THIS UGLY ECHO, Aug. 13) on the retrograde obscenities of Prof. Leonard Jeffries. "I hope," Mr. Rosenthal writes, "that City College students of all pigmentations will renounce this man by boycotting him and his classes. I hope his peers will not accept him any longer . . ."

When I attended CCNY in the mid-thirties, the intellectual and moral climate of the College was informed by the wisdom and humanism of such teachers as Morris Raphael Cohen and by Dean Morton Gottschall, whose breadth and scholarship and intellectual honesty stand in sharp contrast to the Neanderthal crudities of Prof. Jeffries. And an alert and socially conscious student body would by now have had open-air meetings around the flagpole, marches and petitions, appropriate pressure and intellectually responsible dialogue as antidote to the racism, anti-semitism and bigotry that have no place in the University.

Last year, when this same "expert" argued that skin pigmentation, melanin, caused a clear superiority of blacks over whites, his pretensions to a "scientific" objectivity were blasted by fellow CCNY teacher, Prof. Leonard Kriegel (Letter of May 3, 1990), and by Harvard Prof. Alvin F. Poussaint (May 16, 1990). Their analyses and their passion (Dr. Poussaint stated then that Jeffries had "vitiated his qualifications to teach") still ring out as an unrepentant Prof. Jeffries continues to spread hatred and bigotry.

CCNY's anti-fascist students of the thirties would not for a moment tolerate faculty-sponsored racism. Theirs was a vigorous concern for the civil liberties movement that foreshadowed the activism of the sixties. For this, and for their attempts to rouse a then indifferent nation to the dangers of Hitler and Mussolini, they were dubbed by later historians as "premature anti-fascists"! It turned out that history was on their side, as it will be on the side of those who speak up now against the bigotry and racism of the Leonard Jeffries of today.

One Hundred Second Congress
Congress of the United States
Committee on Foreign Affairs
House of Representatives
Washington, DC 20515

July 25, 1991

Mr. Meyer Rangell
P.O. Box 183
Bloomingburg, New York 12721

Dear Mr. Rangell:

Thank you for sending me a copy of your May 16, 1991 letter to the editor regarding the Saudi refusal to honor Senator Frank Lautenberg's United States passport because it contained a visa stamp from Israel. I appreciate your taking the time to share your views on this issue.

As you may know, this issue has been a point of contention between us and the Saudis for years. It is particularly egregious because of the Gulf crisis. Please be assured that I shall continue to broach this issue with the Saudis as well as other Arab nations which, thus far, have failed to recognize Israel's right to exist.

I appreciate your thinking of me. Please do not hesitate to contact me again on this, or any matter of concern.

With best wishes,

Sincerely,

BENJAMIN A. GILMAN, M.C.
Ranking Republican Subcommittee
on Europe and the Middle East

Fall 1991
Threats to Church-State Separation
Free Inquiry

I read Alan M. Dershowitz's "Upholding the Wall of Separation" (*FI*, Spring 1991) with an increased regard for his wit, brilliance, clarity of expression, and superb articulation of the principles of religious liberty contained in our Constitution. I was disappointed, however, that Dershowitz did not confront the most obvious method by which "back door establishment" manifests itself—the ubiquitous tax exemptions that religious institutions enjoy across the nation. Do they not breach the "wall of separation"? Are not tax exemptions clearly a form of support, forcing a compensatory, involuntary tax increase on the taxpaying public? Is this not an egregious use of taxpayers' money for religious purposes, thus promoting the entanglement of church and state?

St. Patrick's Cathedral, on prime New York City, Fifth Avenue, real estate, has an assessed valuation of $45 million; its real property tax exemption costs the beleaguered taxpayers of New York approximately $4 million per year. How many libraries, to mention only one of the sacrifices now being ordered in the current fiscal crisis, or homeless shelters could be spared cuts and closings with that single tax revenue? More than $3 billion worth of real property is owned, and exempted from taxation, by religious institutions in New York City alone!

Finally, do not tax exemptions for religious purposes violate the Lemon test (*Lemon v. Kurtzman*, 1971) in all the three particulars set out by the Supreme Court: (1) The exemption does not have a secular purpose; (2) The exemption is favorable exclusively to religionists; (3) It fosters excessive government entanglement with religion. Does this not add up to a violation of the First Amendment and the Establishment Clause?

March 1, 1992
Excesses In Journalism
Mexico City—The News

In 150 BC, Cato the Elder set the ultimate and enduring standard for the "non-sequitur" when he indulged his consuming hatred for Rome's number one enemy by ending every speech he gave in the Roman Senate with the passionate cry, "*Cartago Delenda Est!*" "Carthage must be destroyed!," he shouted, finishing his every oration on any subject whatsoever, no matter how irrelevant, with his patriotic, war-mongering jingoism. And he finally succeeded Carthage was indeed destroyed in the Third Punic War in 147 BC—not only destroyed but crushed, leveled, pulverized and razed to the ground.

William F. Buckley Jr.'s all consuming passion against the Kennedys—living or dead—leads him to excesses in journalistic non-sequiturs that rival the historic Cato Case in point.

Discussing the problems of Governor Bill Clinton and the accusations against him (column of Jan 29) Buckley cannot resists another attack on President John F. Kennedy, whom he accuses of "adultery on a truly grand scale" (!) and whom he sneeringly describes as the "Perfect American." That his mind should rush at once from Gov. Clinton (whom he tries and finds immediately guilty) and the problem of current political morality to the martyred President; whose private life should at long last cease to be grist to the mills of the sensationalist press and its sleazy columnists; is typical of Buckley's dark obsession. "Cartago Delenda Est!," cried Cato. "Kennedy Delenda Est!," bellows Buckley.

The comparison of the Clinton/Flowers putative liason with the murky Whittaker Chambers/Alger-Hiss relationship is another such non-sequitur, one so wild as to call Buckley's intentions, not to mention his journalistic honesty into question. The tortured linkage of these two disparate situations (the Chambers/Hiss case had to do with questions of treason and national security; the Clinton/Flowers brouhaha at its worst concerns private indiscretions), reveals more about William F. Buckley's reckless disregard for decency than it does about the search for truth.

March 29, 1992
On William Buckley's 'Non-Sequitur'
Mexico City—The News

That William F. Buckley Jr. plays fast and loose with the "non-sequitur" should be apparent to anyone who tries to absorb many of his columns. But he is equally adept at polluting a premise to pander to his prejudice in another of his precious ploys.

In his column of March 7, Buckley tosses off the following with the unflappable certainty of a grand Panjandrum: "Life in Spain," he writes, "was certainly better under Franco, and in Chile under Pinochet; than under the democratic regimes that preceded them."

This, dragged in with blithe irrelevance, provides a noxious premise to a non-sequitur in reverse, while permitting Buckley to get in a snide attack on democracy in general and a good word for the world's dictators. In like manner he has in previous columns come to the support of the gracious Marcos in the Philippines and to Somoza in Nicaragua.

That life was "certainly better under Franco" (our marauding "maven" always writes with certitude, of course!) would be a "certitude" vigorously challenged by those who fought against his grab of power in the Spanish Civil War of 1935-37. Backed by the murderous mercenaries of Hitler and Mussolini, Franco's rebellion cost the Spanish people one million lives as he violently overthrew the legally-elected democratic government.

At the war's end hundreds of thousands of refugees poured into France to escape the "better times" ushered in by his totalitarian regime.

The terroristic air bombing of the Basque town of Guernica (immortalized by the famous Picasso mural) stands as a symbol and a metaphor to the Franco ethic, while Spain's return to democracy had to wait for the dictator's death.

What all this has to do with our own election campaign, only Buckley can tell us—with another tortured non-sequitur, no doubt.

May 23, 1992
Protesting rise in school taxes
The Times Herald Record

Articulate and voluble citizens in the Town of Mamakating raised their voices at the monthly public town board meeting in Wurtsboro on May 7 to protest the sharp rise in school taxes that appear to be projected for the coming year. Estimates vary from a 20 percent rise to as much as a 37 percent increase!

Senior citizens on fixed incomes view with alarm this addition to their already overburdened tax obligations. Some say that, unable to meet these growing expenses, they are in danger of losing their homes.

Along with representatives from the Ellenville district, plans are being drawn for a march in Albany to protest to our legislators.

This writer raised the relevance of tax exemptions which decrease the tax base, and force higher taxes on the rest of us in consequence. (The June 1991 report of the State Board of Equalization and Assessment, reports, for example, that religious organizations in New York state own more than $10 billion worth of real estate that enjoys complete tax exemption). I submitted a resolution to the Town Board requesting an in-depth study of the total amount of tax exemptions under the Real Property Tax Law, and what effect they have on the prospect of increases in school taxes this year. We look forward to their report at the next meeting.

July 20, 1992
Church lands should be taxed
The Times Herald Record

The Supreme Court decision banning prayers at public high school graduations was a significant step toward restoring Thomas Jefferson's "wall of separation between church and state." (It is germane to recall that the Constitutional Convention of 1787 did not include opening prayers either). We ought now to consider an even more consequential step toward church/state separation: That is the separation of the church from the financial bonanza it receives from the state in the form of tax exemptions. The loss of their special privilege to indoctrinate the young in public schools will pale into insignificance, I suspect, when compared to the loss of the special tax privileges they enjoy at the expense of the taxpayers.

The latest report of the New York state Board of Equalization and Assessment (June 1991) informs us that in New York state alone more than $10 billion worth of real estate is owned by religious organizations and exempt from real property taxes. Do these exemptions not violate the spirit, if not the letter, of the First Amendment? Does not a tax exemption granted specifically to one group of citizens who form religious establishments, only to have that additional burden foisted upon all citizens regardless of their religious or non-religious persuasions, violate the Establishment Clause?

How much revenue is lost to the public by unfair and perhaps unconstitutional religious tax exemptions? How far could this uncollected revenue go toward ameliorating the budget crisis problems that almost closed down New York City last year? How many homeless shelters, drug-abuse programs, desperate school budget cuts, libraries and firehouses could be saved by the simple expedience of having religious organizations pay their fair share of taxes?

Should the public interest be denied while the private interests of religion are served?

From the highest office, the president of the United States, Ulysses S. Grant, said in his annual message to Congress in 1875: "I would also call your attention to the importance of correcting an evil that, if permitted to continue, will probably lead to great trouble in our land . . . it is the accumulation of vast amounts of untaxed church property . . . I would suggest the taxation of all property equally, whether church or corporation." His warning is still, if not more, applicable today.

The school prayer decision may have created the climate in which to dare to address the more consequential issue of preferential tax treatment enjoyed by religious organizations at the expense of the taxpaying public.

July 3, 1992
Tax reform would relieve homeowners' education burden
The Times Herald Record

Our present problem with regard to the school tax derives from the fact that we have failed to address the issue of basic tax reform. It is a complex problem, but until we face it we'll have the same crisis of rising taxes and lower services year after year.

Question: Why, of all the services government provides, are schools singled out for a separate budget, and a separate tax? Why are policemen and firemen and the correction system and prisons and the judiciary and a host of other municipal and state services, funded by the general tax revenue (which draws on a wide array of taxes—income tax and sales tax and highway taxes and property taxes), while the school budget is supported primarily by the real property tax? What is the logic and the justice of thus placing the burden of providing quality education to our children mainly on the backs of homeowners in each school district?

Local assessments and mystifying equalization rates result in some districts paying high taxes for their schools, while others pay less, in what is seen as a capricious exercise of guesswork and political pressure. Mamakating taxpayers are justifiably up in arms when they compare their estimated school tax rate increase for 1992-1993 of 37.7 percent with that of Wallkill for example, of 1.2 percent.

The real property tax is not only an unfair method of meeting school obligations, it is also unjust in the way in which it is administered. Consider the matter of tax exemptions: Fully one-third of real property in the state of New York is exempt from property taxes (a total of $278 billion in value)! Remember that each and every exemption has the effect of raising the tax for each and every homeowner. Tax exemptions range from forestry and agricultural exemptions, through religious exemptions, to business investment exemptions and many others.

Tax exemptions need careful scrutiny: The latest report (June, 1991), of the state Board of Equalization and Assessment, for example, reports that religious organizations in New York state own more than $10 billion worth of real estate that enjoys complete tax exemption. Should all the taxpayers bear an extra burden to help support the private religiosity of others? Should clergy's residences be free of taxes? What other homeowners have the privilege of a tax-free home? Should not the category of business investment exemptions, and agricultural forestry exemptions be looked at more carefully? How do these exemptions impact on the school taxes that each locality must face in order to educate our children properly?

These are long-range concerns. They involve long-range solutions. They involve basic tax reform for a more effective and a more equitable tax system.

Almost a year ago The Record stated in an editorial (July 5, 1991) "The statute governing religious exemptions is outdated" and that the "taxpayers' frustration over tax-exempt properties should be directed at Albany, where tax exemptions are born."

The time to act is long overdue. If there is ever to be change, the process of change must begin NOW.

Fall 1992
Secular Humanism
Free Inquiry

Since the basic conflict between secularism and religiosity is the seminal struggle of reason versus unreason, science versus myth, freethinking versus superstition, rationality and adherence to observation and evidence in the search for truth rather than blind acceptance and faith, the answer to your question "Will Secularism Survive?" must, in the long run, be in the affirmative. The question is how long? How long will the unreason of religious mysticism block mankind from bursting through to the clear light of reason? The history of man's intellectual progress suggests that a tradition-bound and unthinking majority and a manipulative minority of power-seekers combine to perpetuate outdated archaic views and attitudes. Ritual, prayer, and myth still maintain an enormous hold on the fears and anxieties of multitudes around the world. No matter how close they might be to the mark, Bertrand Russell stated: "my own view on religion is that of Lucretius. I regard it as a disease born of fear and as a source of untold misery to the human race."[1], Sigmund Freud said: "Thus religion would be the universal obsessional neurosis of humanity . . . and the abandoning of religion must take place with the fateful inexorability of a process of growth, and that we are just now in the middle of this phase of development.[2], and the other freethinkers are, in today's environment, more likely to offend rather than to illuminate the thinking of most.

One of the problems is the pusilanimous posture of our leaders in government, politics, and academia, a posture that is closer to pandering to popular prejudices and misconceptions than one of leadership toward a new plateau of understanding. *Secular humanism will live as religious thought outlives its usefulness.* The speed of the process will depend on the courage and the steadfastness of the freethinking minority, as has been the case at all major junctures along the path of human progress.

August 21, 1991
Church/state issue
The Times Herald Record

The editorial ("Debate over ashram gains fire, loses focus") has the merit of calm reasoning over emotional rhetoric, but fails to address the political, philosophical and moral issue that is central to the problem: that is, the relationship between church and state, as defined in the *First Amendment to the U.S. Constitution*:

"*Congress shall make no law respecting an establishment of religion . . .*"

Thomas Jefferson, whose magnificent Declaration of Independence was celebrated just recently, said: "Religion is a matter which lies solely between man and his God . . . I contemplate with solemn reverence that act of the whole American people which declared that their legislature should 'make no law respecting an establishment of religion, or prohibiting the free exercise thereof,' thus building a wall of separation between church and state."

James Madison, sharing the same opinion, wrote: "A just government has no need for the clergy . . . Religion and government should never be mixed together."

This was the opinion of all 13 states. In Connecticut, one discussant, a clergyman as it happens, said, "Why should all the people be taxed for the support of one sect? We should disconnect the church and state." (In Jefferson in Power, by Claude G. Bowers). What could be more clear? Religion had no place in government and government had no place in religion.

To consider the question of tax exemptions for religious institutions without regard to this basic proposition, demanded by our first colonists before they ratified the constitution, is to ignore a solemn, fundamental facet of American life.

The tax function of government is a primary expression of its relationship with its citizens. It is, therefore, pertinent and inescapable that we ask whether a tax exemption granted to one group of citizens who form religious establishments, only to have that tax burden added to citizens outside that establishment, does in fact violate the separation of church and state that Jefferson and Madison proposed and the First Amendment mandated.

This goes beyond SYDA and its opponents. It goes to the heart of our secular state. To say, "So why pick on SYDA?" when there are other religious groups that also get exemptions is querulous and shallow, and misses the point. To argue whether SYDA does or does not bring enough money into the county to offset the tax losses it creates is to reduce a moral issue to crass commercialism. The question is not is religion profitable? Is it big business? Does it pay? If SYDA, or any religious group, attracted lots of money would that make it right to exempt them? Expedient, perhaps, but not right.

The question, rather, is how do we best handle this aspect of man's relationship to his god? Should it be private, as our constitution rules, or subject to the giving, or withholding, of tax favors by the state?

Your editorial avoids this basic issue, or skirts it, with the comments that the problem "belongs at Albany, where tax exemptions are born." If that is the case, and it is Albany that violates the First Amendment, direct your criticism in that direction. It may be difficult, and a long road, but adherence to principle remains the first step in redressing injustice.

Let us keep the First Amendment alive! No government in religion and no religion in government.

September 16, 1992
Letter to the Editor
New York Times Magazine

What leaps out of Miller's article is the frightening fact that in 1992 the Republican Party finds its staunchest support among right-wing, fundamentalist and evangelical religious groups that are vociferously urging an agenda that would cancel out the separation of church and state, invade our privacy, and, as Ann E. W. Stone, chairwoman of Republicans for Choice, put it, pursue "a trend towards church fascism." That a prominent Republican sees fit to use a word so strong in its implications sends a chilling message, not only to the Republicans, but to us all.

September 17, 1992
But Congress opens with prayer
The Times Herald Record

In a contradiction that is both curious and revealing, the Supreme Court ruled in the recent Lee vs. Weisman decision that prayers at public high school graduations violate the First Amendment and the Establishment Clause. "The First Amendment's religious clauses," it declared, "mean that religious beliefs and religious expression are too precious to be either proscribed or prescribed by the state . . . if citizens are subjected to state-sponsored religious exercises, the state disavows its own duty to guard and respect the sphere of inviolable conscience and belief which is the mark of a free people."

But, hold on! The court further declared that it does not address whether that reasoning is applicable "if the affected citizens are mature adults!" When I asked my Congressman (Benjamin Gilman, R.) about this, he responded that sessions of Congress were routinely opened by prayer and that "it did not seem to do us any harm"! Leaving aside for the moment whether high school graduates, many of whom are old enough to vote and to serve in the military, must be protected from "state-sponsored religious exercises," and whether or not Congresspeople fall under the definition of "mature adults," an egregious double standard is sorely in evidence; what is required constitutional protection for high school seniors is not important, or required, for Congress.

In this connection it may be germane to recall that the Constitutional Convention of 1787 did not include opening prayers and this calculated omission did not do the founding fathers "any harm" either. In fact it provided the atmosphere in which was born the essential concept of "the wall of separation between church and state" that remains a hallmark of our democratic, secular society.

The Lee vs. Weisman decision directs attention to just the tip of the problem. What is needed is a thorough-going separation of all the entanglements between church ritual and government functioning that cast a pernicious aura of tacit acceptance of religiosity as a permanent fixture in our public life.

October 3, 1992
Letter to the Editor
The New York Times

Mr. Wayne Biddle's Op-Ed piece (Science, Morality and the V-2, 10/2) makes one wonder, forty-seven years after the defeat of Nazism and fascism, whether our moral compass and our historical memory have disastrously degenerated or are suffering a terminal illness.

What is one to make of the "quandary" posed here: "whether to applaud him (Wernher von Braun) as a space pioneer . . . or to condemn him as a Nazi"? Mr. Biddle informs us that "Historians continue to plumb his innocence or guilt, just as they ponder whether the Manhattan Project's physicists, who created the atomic bomb, were saints or sinners." What historians is he talking about, who cannot distinguish between the Nazi scientist, whose efforts at Peenemunde cost thousands of deaths and injuries in London, as well as the lives of 20,000 slave-laborers, a scientist who supported the Nazi atrocities at Lidice, Auschwitz and Treblinka, who supported Hitler in his rape and murder and genocide in the lands he conquered, who saw his future in the slave-world Hitler almost succeeded in establishing, as opposed to the scientists who used their knowledge and skill to oppose the fascist threat?

Those of us whose memories are still intact and whose morality has not been terminally damaged, will have no problem in recognizing the difference between the two groups. Manhattan Project scientists, Leo Szilard and Robert J. Oppenheimer, following the revered Albert Einstein, spent the rest of their lives educating and campaigning against atomic war.

A popular satirist and songwriter, Tom Lehrer, said it well over 25 years ago when he sang of von Braun that he was "a man whose allegiance is ruled by expedience." The following Lehrer quatrain says it all:

"Once the rockets are up
Who cares where they come down,
That's not my department,
Says Wernher von Braun."

Morality, decency, concern for the future of mankind? Mr. Biddle may see a linkage between von Braun and the scientists of the Manhattan Project, but his reasoning is tortuous and his assumed blindness to the opposite goals of the two groups is preposterous and insulting.

November 14, 1992
Buckley Not Right
(Responding to a column by William F. Buckley, Jr., titled "THE LAWRENCE WALSH MESS, MESSIER" (11/14/92).)
Mexico City—The News

The Grand Old Party can always depend on William F. Buckley Jr. to come to its aid in moments of crisis. From Watergate to Irangate to Iraqgate—from Richard Nixon to Reagan and Bush—Buckley uses his fabled skill at obfuscation to pretend that he cannot differentiate between the firefighters and the arsonists.

Once again, in his column, "The Lawrence Walsh Mess" (Nov. 14), he turns his wrath not upon the alleged malfeasants but upon the agents of justice. He does his performance here once again, as he did during Watergate, when he supported Nixon and attacked mercilessly those who sought exposure and justice.

The title gives the game away. It is not "The Lawrence Walsh Mess," Mr. Buckley, that has cast a pall of corruption on the body politic. It is the Reagan-Bush mess, within which Reagan's men, as Nixon's before him, violated the law (the Boland Amendment), then lied to Congress, covered up, and corrupted the Constitution. The mess is the North-Poindexter-Secord-Hakim-McFariane mess. Having given public testimony under the cover of immunity, Oliver North and John Poindexter's convictions were overturned by appeals courts. Buckley knows, however, as we all know, that the legal technicalities did not reverse the facts of their lying to Congress and sending arms. To make Lawrence Walsh the villain of the piece is to villify the firefighter to get the arsonists off the hook.

The re-indictment of Caspar Weinberger, in the due course of a proper legal investigation, scares the pants off Buckley and his mentors because it might lead to Bush and even to Reagan. Buckley makes much of the fact that this came four days before the election. The timing, he suggests, is more evil than Weinberger's alleged guilt or innocence. Would it have been more proper to suppress the indictment, for political reasons? "Should we really care?" asks Buckley finally, whether Weinberger lied, whether Bush was "in the loop" at the time, whether the legal processes of government were being undermined by a cabal that assumed dangerous power unto themselves at a time of crisis? Of course we should care! The Lawrence Walsh investigation is important because it provides a mechanism that may prevent this sort of extra-legal power-wielding in the basement of the White House from happening again.

Imperially, Buckley advises the lame duck President Bush to "grant amnesty to everyone involved in Irangate/Iraqgate and tell Walsh et al. to go home and mulct someone other than the taxpayer!" Thus would Bush join President Ford, who pardoned Richard Nixon while his men went to jail, and saw to it that the American people would be forever denied the legal verdict on Watergate's top player.

As a parting shot, Buckley sneeringly libels Mr. Walsh as one who "mulcts . . . the taxpayer!" The real mulcting of the taxpayer resided in the millions of dollars in arms illegally sold by North's arms dealer Hakim, and the millions involved in the transfer of government property through the illegal North-Secord axis.

Come clean, Mr. Buckley, "the central figure" in this "mess" is not the prosecutor assigned to ferret out the trail of illegality and malfeasance, but the alleged violators, who are well known to the American people.

December 27, 1992
Humane Policy
Mexico City—The News

Today's issue of *The News* contains abundant evidence of the seminal significance of the U.N. and U.S. action in the Somalia crisis. On the Opinion pages, Jeane Kirkpatrick and Henry Kissinger offer long-range analyses, while Thomas Friedman, on the news pages, echoes the philosophic/political/moral implications.

None, however, emphasizes sufficiently the central significance of this action as a new dimension in the future foreign policy of the United States and, indeed, in the future international relationships among nations.

The end of the Cold War signifies a new era. It is both an ending and a new beginning. At this historic juncture, the new Clinton administration has it within its power to usher in a new set of principles for the civilized world.

Ms. Kirkpatrick concedes that "the goal of feeding hungry people is clear enough" but worries about "non-intervention in the internal affairs of states," a concern echoed by both Kissinger and Friedman. Kissinger acknowledges the need for "humanitarian intervention," but warns of the danger of "assuming the role of world policeman."

As the Clinton administration prepares to take office and begins to formulate its own vision for the future, the time is propitious to think in new terms for our foreign policy and new paradigms for international relations.

The Cold War dictated a foreign policy for the super-powers, and those dependent upon their favors, that was based on national self-interest almost to the exclusion of moral, humane considerations. What served the cause of anti-communism on one side and anti-capitalism on the other was at the core of foreign policy. Humane considerations were secondary. At this watershed in history, with the Cold War over and new administrations both in Washington and in Moscow, the time is at hand for basic change: It is time, long overdue, for humane concerns to take a proper precedence over purely selfish, national goals and interests.

The interests of humanity, all humanity, must be served, or the interests of the human family, everywhere, will suffer. The consequences of ignoring the hungry and the sick anywhere in the world will be felt eventually by everyone everywhere in the world.

The United States, as the only remaining superpower, must set an example of compassion and concern, not in the spirit of the self-interest generated by the Cold War, but in the spirit of the wealthy and powerful sharing with the least advantaged. It should no longer be permissable that under-consumption and starvation are tolerated for some peoples, while over-consumption and plenty are accepted as normal for others.

The politics of self-interest, geared to the geopolitics of ideology, must give way to a new politics that recognizes the needs of the whole human race. No one country should be "policeman of the world" but all countries must recognize that "we are our brothers' keepers."

January 10, 1993
Pardons Were Wrong
Mexico City—The News

The pardon by lame-duck President George Bush of the Iran-Contra conspirators represents a brazen affront to the American people and a dangerous and arrogant attack on the U.S. judicial system.

The legal ethic is based on the principle that no one is above the law. This pardon, as did President Ford's pardon of Richard Nixon, sends out the signal that powerful men and well-placed officials are exceptions to that rule.

President Bush justifies the pardons on the basis that the conspirators acted "for patriotic reasons." By the same reasoning, the assassins of President Kennedy, Robert Kennedy and Martin Luther King, (as well as John Wilkes Booth, the assassin of Abraham Lincoln), also deserved pardons. They also performed their heinous acts for what, in their opinions, were "patriotic reasons."

With an unintended irony, Pres. Bush elevates Samuel Johnson's pungent comment that "patriotism is the last refuge of a scoundrel" to the level of judicial principle!

Of course, as Lawrence Walsh was quick to point out, the transparent excuse of "patriotism" may be a cover-up for Bush's own involvement in the criminal aspects of the Iran-Contra scandal, which had every prospect of being made public if Caspar Weinberger sang at his trial, or if Bush were called as a material witness.

As it now stands, breaking the law, lying to Congress, and obstructing justice are all OK, as long as you do it in the name of "patriotism" and have the proper powerful connections! Accountability for one's actions, legal or illegal, we are now informed, is a concept only for ordinary citizens.

January 24, 1993
Year Of Decision
Mexico City—The News

The winds of change are sweeping over the world.

From Europe to Asia to the Middle East and Africa, to Central America and the United States, multitudes have raised their voices to demand new horizons. Old regimes have been voted out where possible (Poland, Czechoslovakia), or were abandoned by mass migrations as people voted with their feet (East Germany, Haiti), or took up arms in bloody frustration (Yugoslavia, Central America, the Middle East, Africa). The common dominator was a cry for change, for an end to distant control and tyranny, for access to a better life. Political leaders everywhere scramble to place themselves in synch with that demand, less they suffer the same fate as their predecessors.

All these ingredients for basic change come together as we enter this Year of Decision. The challenge to our political leadership is more sharp, more demanding, and more critical than ever before. Old answers will not do. New outlooks, new paradigms, new perspectives and new understanding are necessary for the survival of the human race and, indeed, our common home, the planet Earth.

With the end of the Cold War, with new administrations in Washington and Moscow, both the challenge and the opportunity are at hand for some basic rethinking of the human ethic. The times demand a leap forward, a giant leap of faith, from concern for narrow national interests to global concern for the whole human family. Interdependence in the modern world must be recognized as the new dimension, the sine-qua-non of the new thinking which alone can save us.

How long will it be before we recognize the obscenity that food consumption in the human family is so imbalanced that overconsumption causes disease and death in developed countries, while millions starve in the developing world. According to the United Nations Food and Agricultural Organization (FAO) there are 786 million undernourished people in the developing world. "Almost 13 million children under the age of five die each year as a result of hunger, malnutrition and infections." (*The World Paper*). The horrors of Somalia that we see on television are only the tip of the iceberg!

Ironically, the FAO also reports that "the world's food supply is adequate to feed all humankind, despite a doubling of Earth's population since 1955"!

If individual families operated with such callous indifference and imbalance, civilized society would shrink with horror. That the human family on a global scale operates this way, in 1993, must sink into human consciousness as the disgrace and shame that it is . . . and as the problem that faces us in this Year of Decision.

The requisite changes can only be initiated with the full recognition of the concept of the human family, the whole human family all over the globe and its interdependence.

Global perspectives must be achieved or we all lose the fight for survival, this is both a moral imperative and a practical one. It is the major challenge of the coming Year of Decision.

It is a challenge we ignore at our own peril.

February 14, 1993
Buckley's Wrong
Mexico City—The News

William F. Buckley's reputation for ideological virtuosity and the dazzling intellectual pyrotechnics of an unreconstructed conservatism are well known, but in his columns on the pardons of the Irangate conspirators (Nov. 14, 1992 and Jan. 14, 1993) he outdoes himself as he hovers between the specious and the meretricious. "Specious?" "Meretricious?" The definitions in Webster's New Collegiate Dictionary are as follows: "*specious* stresses colorability with always a clear suggestion of dissimulation or fraud." "*meretricious*: alluring by false show; gaudily and deceitfully ornamental."

In his first column, written as advice to President Bush *before* the Christmas Eve pardons, he pilloried Lawrence Walsh, the special prosecutor, as the prime villain of the piece and urged the president to pardon "everyone involved in Irangate/Iraqgate," and to fire Walsh. In other words, he advised, get rid of the firefighters, and let the alleged arsonists off the hook! His reasoning was that North, Poindexter, Abrams, Weinberger, et al, may have been "bound by executive loyalty" and therefore had no obligation to be perfectly truthful to "congressional fact-finding authority." Pardon them all, Mr. President, he urged with the sanctimonious passion of the true apologist, for they acted only out of patriotism and loyalty! So what if they lied, conspired to obstruct justice and undermined the Constitution? Fire the prosecutor, Lawrence Walsh! And pardon the alleged culprits!

As we know, the president took his advice. But after the pardons, Buckley felt obliged to answer the "uproar" of opposition (Jan. 14). Here he finally "acknowledges that laws were broken." In his first column he had conceded only that "misjudgments" had taken place (despite the guilty plea of Abrams, and the convictions of North and Poindexter). Now Buckley grudgingly concedes that "laws were broken." But so what? he cries, it is a "moot point" and a fault of the prosecutor that he is "so taken with a strict interpretation of the law." "Those who cooperated with the Reagan-Bush White House had nothing personally to gain from doing what they thought was their duty," he explains, so why should they be held responsible?

With a wild irrelevance and illogic, Buckley goes so far as to compare Bush's moral posture in this sleazy affair with the immortal Lincoln, Jefferson and Franklin D. Roosevelt. That assessment would best be left to future historians. Most of us have our contemporary doubts.

Did Webster have William F. Buckley Jr. in mind?

January 29, 1993
Harlot's Ghost Illuminates History with Mailer's Fictional Imagination
Atencion San Miguel

A few years ago I read Gabriel Garcia Marquez' magnificent novel, *One Hundred Years of Solitude*, on the tawdry beach of Manzanillo and felt that an illuminating dimension was added to the experience. It was reading, as it were, "in situ:" the hustle and bustle, the dirt and grime and sleaze of this oily town, the unceasing movement, this sea of agitation as if nothing was finished or ever would be, the incomplete houses, the sense of a pulsating life that was always striving but never achieving completion, seemed to be synchronous with the tumult that thronged the pages of Marquez' mythical Colombia.

I was now reading Norman Mailer's weighty tome of a novel, *Harlot's Ghost* (1300 pages!), again on Mexico's Pacific shore. This time it was, to coin a phrase, "in oppositu." The calm of the Pacific sea lapping a small strip of isolated beach, its tranquility punctuated here and there by low-flying gulls swooping down to snare a flying fish, was in startling contrast to the seething emotion and violence, the "sturm und drang," the murder and mayhem, the cross and double-cross and triple-cross, the clash of principles and ethics, the pain, euphoria, debasement, the pop-psychology, the pitiless searching the surgery of the soul, the exploration of meanings, of good and evil, right and wrong, that inhabit the pages of this lush, sprawling, verbose, prolix, unsparing, outpouring of Norman Mailer's prodigality. This reader's calm milieu—a universe of sea, sky, and pristine sand—was not unlike a blank white canvas on which Mailer's *Harlot's Ghost* rode roughshod, passionately, mercurially, like the violent explosions of the fantastic entwining of colors and hues with which Jackson Pollack changed forever the *tabula rasa* of an innocent plane.

But solitude was made to be broken; communion to be jarringly interrupted. Two friends walk the beach. Follows the obligatory greeting and conversation:

"Reading Norman Mailer?" The book cover's large print was electric.

I look up. "Yes."

"You like it?"

Tentatively, "Yes."

"I would not waste my time on that macho sexist pig." The depth of heat and passion in that declaration tears me from the pages of *Harlot*.

"Why is that?" I ask softly. "Have you read it?"

"No, I don't have to, Mailer's not worth it. I wouldn't waste my time," said again with a passionate intensity that somehow included me in the encompassing accusation. I feel I have to defend myself for reading Mailer! But I am in the mood for *Harlot*, not for irritating prejudgments. Without opening the book's cover, I thought, the superior condemnatory posture of a strident "feminism" dictated a ready-made prejudgment that required no verification. Captive of a posture of spurious intellectual certainty, reading before critical reaction becomes unnecessary and ignorance of the work and its content need not prevent *a priori* condemnation. How much easier it is to argue by *ad hominem* insult and epithet.

I go back to *Harlot*. Another interruption, an acquaintance from our time-share. The beach is sparsely peopled, but I am by nature gregarious and talk to anyone.

"What's that you're reading?"

"Norman Mailer's latest, *Harlot's Ghost*."

"Why do they call it *Harlot's Ghost*?"

"Well, it's about the CIA, and Harlot is the cover name for the main character."

"Yes, I heard about that. Is he for or against it?"

"For or against what?"

"The CIA!"

"Well, it's a big book. I'm only on page 700 and would not want to give a two-word review, at least not until I have finished all 1300 pages."

"But he is writing about the CIA, isn't he?" he persists. A pugnacious, almost nasty edge now creeps into his voice. I am hooked I am not a difficult man to provoke.

"Yes," I reply. "In fact, Mailer presents the results of some prodigious research. He took seven years to write the book, and he discusses and explores the ways in which the CIA operates, its morals and ethics, its goals, its relationship to government and to foreign policy. It's like history," I continue, "with all its warts, seen through the fertile imagination of a great novelist, but with a scrupulous adherence to what one may call 'historicity,' ever true to the reality of events, with true historical actors on the stage in what Mailer sees as their true dimensions and their real life characterology, often using their real words, relying on real, authenticated sources."

My "friend" bristles. He had not expected serious answers to his casual condemnation. "But the CIA is supposed to be secret," he explodes. "When you reveal those secrets you are acting for the enemies of our country. Do you remember the book, some years ago by Philip Agee, in which he named CIA agents'. As a result, at least one agent was murdered in Greece. I think Agee ought to be assassinated!" There is no longer any casualness about the conversation.

"You mean arrested, tried, and then, if found guilty, punished by law?"

"No. I mean just what I said. Assassinated! A traitor like that does not deserve the niceties of a trial." His beady eyes, humorless lips curling more easily into a sneer than a smile, reveal with clear certainty that he indeed meant what he said.

"How about law and order, the Bill of Rights, trial by jury, and all that?" I murmur.

"You fight fire with fire," he responds. "Those traitors need assassination."

"You mean like when the Ayatollah ordered the death of Salmon Rusdie also without reading his book?"

"Khomeni was evil and acted for evil reasons. I act for good. That makes all the difference." He is certain, pontifical.

"And you include Mailer, along with Agee? Or will you read the book first?"

"I don't have to read it. I would not waste my time." The grim implication is by now all too clear, and I am not sure I haven't talked myself into inclusion on the hit list. Like a rock star attracts groupies. Mailer attracts enemies from the left to the right—even on the beach in the sleepy Mexican village of Bucerias Aficionados of Norman Mailer will see in Harlot's Ghost another example of his pre-eminence in the uses of fiction and history. As in The Armies of the Night, Miami and the Siege of Chicago, The Executioner's Song, and the slim and under-appreciated novel, Why Are We in Vietnam?, Norman Mailer in Harlot's Ghost proves again his giant fictional imagination while remaining true to essential historicity. Call it fiction as history or history seen with a heavy dose of fiction. For this reader at least, it works.

Mailer takes us through events with which we are all familiar, casting new light on old problems that are still with us. The questions he raises anew are as fresh as today's headlines: the ugliness of the Cold War, on both sides; the ethical and moral morass of the intelligence community; the rationalization of evil cloaked in the self-righteousness of ideology are seen mercilessly in this dissection of the CIA. Berlin, Cuba and the Bay of Pigs, the missile crisis of 1962, the on-going fiasco of attempts to assassinate Fidel Castro, Latin America as a school for spies, the assassination of John F. Kennedy, the megalomania of CIA officers and agents and contractors and informers, the hatred and enmity between the CIA and FBI (each stopping at nothing to discredit and destroy the other) as well as Army Intelligence and NSC Intelligence, each concerned with its own private agenda, are explored and exposed to the light.

Real people stride across these pages: Howard Hunt before Watergate, Richard Nixon, Richard Helms, J. Edgar Hoover, the brothers Kennedy, Guy Burgess and Kim Philby, Frank Sinatra and Sam Giancana, a cast of politicians and prophets, philosophers and philanders, gangsters and self-seekers, love goddesses, mobsters and their molls—it's all here, larger than life, a Hollywood epic with a cast of thousands to fill the giant screen. Life, in all its contradictions and passions, its greed and ambitions, its grasping and groping for fame, money, recognition, and power—ideology always a vehicle for other, less noble purposes—is the subject of Mailer's eye and his art.

Through it all, Mailer writes with that love of words and that passion for language that inform all of his writing. His images erupt on the page like a volcano pouring its molten lava without restraint or inhibition. The verbal virtuosity, the felicitous imagery, the outrageous metaphor that we have come to expect from Mailer are here in sufficient abundance to satisfy every Mailer buff at the same time that they drive his critics and detractors up the wall.

In the February, 1992 issue of *Vanity Fair*. Mailer wrote: "Let us commence with what is needed for a great history (as opposed to a great movie). Such a work not only would require a comprehension of the forces and tides that shape and convey an era, but would be obliged to possess a special species of pointillism; its thousand diverse points of light ought to be details chosen well enough to buoy the history with resonance . . . a great film may be epic, operatic, panoramic, stoic, and certainly it can be mythic and embody the more powerful legends of our lives." He was writing about Oliver Stone's JFK, but he could as easily have been writing about his own book, *Harlot's Ghost*.

On the JFK assassination, Mailer writes: "Did Castro have a hand in it? No, of course not, he had too sure a sense of the consequences—is the reflexive reply, but then, who can be certain that individual members of the DGI, Castro's intelligence service, had not been engaged in some mutually deceptive game with Cuban exiles in Florida and Texas?"

In *Harlot's Ghost*, Mailer had written about "MONGOOSE, an operation subsequent to the Bay of Pigs to destabilize Cuba by a variety of covert means." An agent writes: "I cannot tell you what a shock the Bay of Pigs has been for those of us in the Agency who merely looked on. If we do not know how to steer a course through history, then who can? (sic!) We are supposed to serve the President, but most of our Presidents have had an inner light so dim that we have been obliged to take the lead ourselves."

Such was the cynicism and arrogance of the Intelligence community. The operation against Cuba, headquartered in Florida, is described thusly: "Perhaps the best way to give you a conception of our power and emplacement here is to note the state and national laws we are ready to bend, break, violate, and ignore. False information is given out routinely on Florida papers of incorporation; tax returns fudge the real sources of investment in our proprietaries; false flight plans are filed daily with the FAA; and we truck weapons and explosives over Florida highways, thereby violating the Munitions Act and the Firearms Act, not to speak of what we do to our old friends Customs, Immigration, Treasury, and the Neutrality Act."

The CIA brags and expatiates on "How to steal a country with three hundred men, a la Guatemala." And Howard Hunt is quoted as saying: "Ethics has to be subservient to the mosaic." He was referring, then, to the covert activities against Cuba ("each night boats were going out with Cuban exiles, some to plant explosives, others to infiltrate a few people back into Cuba where they could link up with underground organization.")

That was the Howard Hunt of the anti-Cuban operation, but it jibes neatly with the later Hunt of Watergate fame. From Mongoose and the illegal efforts to destroy

Fidel Castro, by any and all means, to Watergate, the operative morality remained unchanged. In the final analysis (although Mailer can never be "finally" analyzed), more questions are raised in *Harlot's Ghost* than answered. Lifted from the front pages into literature, however, Mailer guarantees that the questions will not go away, and he thus does history a not inconsequential service. Obscurity will not be the fate of these significant events, nor will they lapse so easily into the cobwebbed mists of a forgotten past.

When Mailer ends his huge book with the notice: "TO BE CONTINUED," one is sure somehow that it will be, either in another blockbuster sequel or in life itself (just follow the daily headlines!), seen by any reader of *Harlot's Ghost* in a new, more illuminating, multi-dimensional light.

March 7, 1993
Gelb's Courage
Mexico City—The News

Bravo to Leslie H. Gelb for his courage and his journalistic honesty in re-evaluating his initial negative response to President Clinton's address to the joint session of Congress. He now says that it was a "stunningly honest and realistic economic speech," and "that it was pure pleasure to hear a presidential address on the economy that seemed to make sense and wasn't riddled with baloney." (*The News*, Feb. 25). He thus distances himself from reckless critics like TV's Robert Novak and John Sununo and Congressional critics like Senator Dole and Congressman Michel, who "are ready to nuke Clinton at the slightest provocation," and whose venom and mean-spiritedness are equaled only by their intellectual dishonesty.

What unmitigated gall for political "experts" who sat still for the 12 years of the Reagan-Bush social and economic disaster, the paralyzing slashes in every meaningful social program from education to welfare to drug-abuse management, who, as Paul Tsongas stated on the same page, "lay dormant as Ronald Reagan and George Bush racked up 3 trillion dollars of debt," to leap like angry hyenas on a one-month old president because he did not solve all our problems in one speech.

"World Leaders Praise Clinton's Speech," stated Gelb's headline. I would venture that the American public (Gelb astutely remarked that he "felt that the president talked to the American people as adults"), also reacted with a positive sense of new directions and new, honest answers to America's problems, in sharp contrast to the pejorative melancholia so hypocritically assumed by the wounded Republicans and their nay-saying sychophants.

March 14, 1993
White House Newspeak
Mexico City—The News

I have privately vowed not to be hooked once more by William F. Buckley, Jr.'s bait. After all, he makes a living by being outrageous. One gets the impression that he is more interested in the shock-value of his vocabulary and rhetoric than in their credibility.

But once again I am provoked into a response; this time by his column of March 6, (*"White House Newspeak Wearing Thin"*). What is wearing thin is the level of criticism to which Mr. Buckley sinks. The dripping sarcasm, the snide innuendoes and the nasty, mean-spirited *ad hominem* nature of his argumentation seem always to reach a new low.

He calls the new president a "con man"; his supporters are "shills"; he stoops to a McCarthy-like red-baiting as he slyly pins a Norman Thomas label on Bill Clinton; he attacks the president's concern for "fairness" by misrepresenting his position insofar as taxes are concerned (the president did not say "the more you tax the wealthy, the fairer you are . . ."; that was Buckley's weakness for the *reductio ad absurdum* technique . . . only the absurdum is more Buckley than Clinton).

Buckley even invokes, favorably, the memory of "Tricky Dick." Anyone not born yesterday will recall that Buckley supported the disgraced and almost-impeached Richard Nixon all through Watergate and for many years afterward.

Mr. Buckley even fails to properly attribute the word "newspeak" to its author, George Orwell, who coined it in his famous attack on totalitarianism, "1984". Orwell was an outspoken liberal and self-declared socialist. As to who is using deceptive speech and deliberately misleading rhetoric, the chances are overwhelming that George Orwell would be on Clinton's side and not on the side of the conservative trickery, in language and in logic, of William F. Buckley, Jr.

March 28, 1993
Learn From The Truth
Mexico City—The News

One of the 20th century's greatest philosophers, George Santayana, provided us with the insight that "those who do not learn from history are doomed to repeat its mistakes."

This profound teaching is brought to mind with the release of the report of the United Nations-sponsored investigation into the atrocities committed by the Salvadoran government during the recent civil war.

Significantly called the "Commission on the Truth", the investigation "found that the U.S.-backed military committed most of the killings, massacres, and tortures the commission investigated." (*The News*, March 16). When American volunteers, observers, photographers and reporters testified in the past to these atrocities, they were dismissed as "communist sympathizers and apologists for the guerrillas."

The Reagan and Bush administrations were determined to insure continued support to the death-squad Salvadoran government to the point of repressing and denying human rights abuses. They (we) spent a million dollars a day, more than 6 billion dollars during the long war, and looked the other way when our proteges murdered, tortured and violated thousands of non-combatant women and children.

It is all in the open at last: "Salvadoran exiles living in Miami helped administer death squad activities between 1980 and 1983, with apparently little attention from the US government." (*The News*, March 16). The massacre of up to 1,000 men, women and children in the village of El Mozote, which the officials of the Reagan administration disputed ever happened, is "attributed to the U.S. backed military". The list goes on and on, including the murders in 1989 of six Jesuit priests and the slaying of Archbishop Oscar Romero, among others, by officials who are to this day not only unpunished, but in positions of authority in the Salvadoran government.

Do we learn from history? Are we even willing to face up to our complicity in these dreadful events and their moral and political implications? Will Ronald Reagan and George Bush re-evaluate the nature of the Salvadoran policy carried out under their watch, in the light of the grim revelations of the Commission on the Truth? Or do we sweep it under the rug? Santayana's message is critical: Will we learn from history, or are we doomed to repeat its mistakes?

The American people have a right to hear from Reagan, Bush, and those in their administrations who formulated Salvadoran policy. Their silence in the face of this report would be unconscionable. Past history, present policy, and a future morality we can live with demand our urgent attention.

April 18, 1993
Buckley Vs Cuomo
Mexico City—The News

Like the punch-drunk fighter who comes out wildly swinging and slugging at the sound of the bell, William F. Buckley Jr. just can't wait. He has to get his licks in first! Foaming at the mouth, he comes out fighting at the very mention of Governor Mario Cuoumo's name as a possible nominee for the Supreme Court. He uses once again his well known sneer-and-smear technique, enveloped in his legendary verbal bravura (Opinion pages, April 2).

Dripping with sarcasm, he calls New York's popular thrice-elected governor a "brooding omnipresence in Albany", the "Big Figure," King Arthur", a "liberal heavy", and an "evangelist". Then, with a sudden solicitude for his target's happiness, he counsels paternally that Governor Cuomo, "would not be happy in the eremitic halls of the Supreme Court" anyway!

If this is the kind of right wing, conservative argumentation we can expect in a forthcoming confirmation hearing, in the event of a Cuomo nomination, it will be a pleasure to hear the urbane and erudite Cuomo counter this know-nothing, mud-slinging drivel. But by then, we can fully expect Mr. Buckley to take off his gloves, no longer the punch-drunk slugger, but the clever in-fighter that he is on the Republican right.

May 26, 1993
Cal's got it all wrong
The Times Herald Record

Your excellent, well-reasoned, editorial (April 29) in support of equal rights for homosexuals stands in sharp contrast to the rabid ranting of columnist Cal Thomas on the same page. Mr. Thomas, spewing an out-of-control rage, hatred and prejudice, abandons all logic as he accuses gays and lesbians of every crime in the book and blames them for every social problem under the sun: "30 million abortions" (give us a break, Cal, you can't be accusing homosexuals of being responsible for millions of unwanted pregnancies!) . . . "broken families, drive-by shootings, riots, drug abuse, a pornography explosion, overflowing prisons, teen suicides . . .", all are linked by the apoplectic Mr. Thomas to homosexual practice!

The Bible-thumping Thomas sanctimoniously quotes from scripture to bolster his prejudice: Homosexuals "disconnect from a personal God," he pontificates, arrogantly assuming that he can be judge and jury of other peoples' spirituality, and "the nation abounds with biblical illiterates and disobedient apostates," by which he means those who disagree with his own narrow fundamentalist religious posture.

Mr. Thomas also forgets that this country formulated its social and personal ethic in the Constitution, and is governed by the Constitution and its Bill of Rights, and not by the Bible or any of its many conflicting personal, individual interpreters.

Your editorial had it right: Gays and lesbians are entitled to "the same basic civil rights enjoyed by other Americans" . . . but, "they are still denied basic civil rights that are guaranteed to all citizens of this nation." Cal Thomas had it wrong when he delivered a passionate, prejudiced, hate-filled sermon, full of rancor, innuendoes and lies, whipping up emotional misinformation that does nothing to solve our social problems.

June 14, 1993
First at the Wall
The New York Times

    Your report of President Clinton's appearance at the ceremony before the Vietnam Veterans Memorial (front page, June 1) contains the remarkable observation that he was the first President to attend Memorial Day services there in the 12 years since the wall's construction.

    I wonder how many caught the irony that President Reagan, in 1985, found the time to travel to the German cemetery in Bitburg, where he honored the graves of Waffen SS Nazis? Senator Daniel Patrick Moynihan said at the time that Mr. Reagan displayed "a measure of moral insensitivity that we must not permit in our Presidency." Elie Wiesel, Nobel Peace Prize winner, implored Mr. Reagan not to go to Bitburg, and 53 senators joined in appealing to him, in vain, not to lend his presence there.

    I wonder how many of those who shouted obscenities at President Clinton at the wall raised their voices then against the moral obtuseness of Ronald Reagan at Bitburg?

    Mr. Clinton is to be commended for his courage and his attempt to bind the nation's wounds. He honored the Vietnam dead, while not retracting his opposition to the failed foreign policy that sent them there.

    Our new, young President shows again that he has the courage of his convictions, a precious rarity in a cynical capital.

April 4, 1993
Seniors Abroad
Mexico City—The News

With America's health care system under the most careful scrutiny in history, under the able guidance of Hillary Clinton, the time is propitious to address a mistake that visits a grave injustice on our senior citizens. I refer to the policy that excludes seniors from the benefits they would otherwise enjoy under Medicare if they become ill while traveling or residing in a foreign country.

What is the logic of denying medical benefits to those who have paid their social security taxes all their working lives, and are now, additionally, paying for Medicare, if their illness strikes while they are abroad? Social security benefits are paid to Americans residing abroad, as they should be. Why are medical benefits withheld? The logic escapes me.

How many thousands of retired Americans are fearful of traveling for fear that they might require expensive hospitalization due to sudden and unexpected illness while abroad?

Traveling is one of the long-awaited bonuses of retirement, and this impediment (they must sacrifice their important health coverage) is both unfair and, it seems to me, contrary to the spirit, if not the letter, of the Social Security philosophy.

Americans living abroad, either permanently or for a part of each year, or traveling briefly, should not be penalized by being expelled from the Medicare system. It is neither wise, nor logical, nor justified. It is blatantly discriminatory.

THE WHITE HOUSE

WASHINGTON

August 4, 1993

Meyer Rangell
P.O., Box 183
Bloomingburg, NY 12721

Dear Mr. Rangell:

On behalf of the President and Mrs. Clinton, I would like to thank you for your interest in health care reform.

As you may know, on January 25, 1993, the President announced the creation of a Task Force on National Health Care Reform. The President asked the Task Force to provide him with proposals for comprehensive health care reform. The President also announced on January 25 the creation of an interdepartmental working group which would gather and analyze information and options for the Task Force.

In over twenty meetings held during April and May, the Task Force reviewed materials it received from the interdepartmental working group and policy suggestions such as yours, formulated proposals and options for health care reform, and presented those proposals and options to the President. Each of those Task Force meetings was announced in the *Federal Register*.

Having completed its mission, the Task Force was terminated on May 30, as provided in its charter. The President is now in the process of reviewing the proposals received from the Task Force and choosing from among the policy options that were presented to him.

I appreciate your participation in this vital endeavor. Your ideas have been very helpful during the deliberations on health care reform. Again, on behalf of the President and Mrs. Clinton, I thank you for your interest, time and support.

Sincerely,

Carol H. Rasco
Assistant to the President for
Domestic Policy

June/July 1993
One Person's Cult . . . Another Person's Religion
Freethought Today

In the thousands of words and hundreds of columns by pundits and columnists, talk show hosts and "expert" guests, one looks in vain for serious discussion of the central issue of the Waco tragedy: That is, to what extent does religious teaching, or what I would call *religious thinking*, bear responsibility for the tragic end-result that was enacted in the Branch Davidian compound?

Where is the religious leader who faces up to the connection between religious training, religious indoctrination, the inculcation of a religious way of looking at life, and the excess of religious dogma and belief that informed David Koresh and his followers? Can the tragic suicides and death at Waco be written off as the result of insanity, one man's abnormality, one man's mis-interpretation and distortion of religious thinking? Do not the official, institutional bastions of our powerful religious forces that cast such a wide net of influence in the United States, and have in their power the instruction and indoctrination of young and vulnerable minds, bear at least some responsibility when the outcome of religious zeal is the death and destruction at Waco?

Yet, we see nothing that might even remotely be described as evaluation, or re-evaluation, of the religious training that leads to the dogmatic *religious thinking* that characterized the Branch Davidians or the hundreds of other cults that, we are now told, exist throughout the country. It is as though theism, the concepts of Armageddon and Apocalyptic thinking, and the many other assumptions of religious thought, *and their consequences*, have nothing to do with the case! They are mad, insane, "cultists," not true religionists, we are told.

Aside from the (relevant) witticism that "one person's cult is another person's religion," what, it is pertinent to ask, is the difference between a religion, a sect, and a cult? And what do they all share in common? They all share the belief in theism (the existence of a Supreme Being); they differ only in interpretation. Above all, it would seem, they differ in the intensity of their dedication and belief. The cultist is most literal, most certain, most vulnerable and most dedicated to the charismatic leader.

Religious adherence flows along a continuum of belief, from what can be an almost casual acceptance of a vague religiosity to the all-consuming dedication (fanaticism?) of the cultist.

But the common denominator of *religious thinking* is present along the continuum: it consists of the abandonment of individual reasoning and blind acceptance of the assumptions of religious theism. The proselytism and indoctrination that is part and parcel of the every-day activities of religious institutions squelch individual, independent thought, create the atmosphere within which religious dogma goes unchallenged, and ordinary rational, scientific, everyday common sense evaluation of the evidence of one's senses and human reasoning are abandoned and ignored.

Can religious institutions escape their responsibility in the creation of this state of mind, upon which "leaders" like David Koresh and Jim Jones can build a life-view that results in 900 of Jones' followers drinking fruit punch laced with cyanide in Guyana and Branch Davidians accepting fiery deaths at Waco?

How much responsibility does organized institutional religion bear when religious teaching and religious thinking result in too much unquestioned and unexamined belief? The religious mode of thought encourages obeisance, loyalty, faith and respect that is non-questioning, and a total adherence to the authority of the theological leader.

How much is the religious community willing to examine the Koresh and Jones phenomena as predictable outcomes of such religious fervor and belief? What is the difference, except in degree, between religionists who practice occasionally, or regularly, or even devoutly, and the followers of Koresh and Jones who swallow the whole religious premise passionately to its ultimate conclusion: *If eternal bliss is the reward of a temporary life of virtue here on Earth, why not embrace an early death and an early entry into Heaven?*

Of course, such an examination leads to confrontation with the basic tenets of religious cosmology and belief, and is more likely to be avoided by the clergy of all denominations than to be addressed up front.

But without such an examination, all attempts to "understand" Waco and David Koresh and Jim Jones will founder on the shoals of pre-conceived assumptions and prejudices. Religious thinking and its consequences stare us in the face.

It is not a pretty sight.

Meyer Rangell is a subscriber to Freethought Today and a freelance writer living in New York.

Rejected by the NEW YORK TIMES and the CHRISTIAN SCIENCE MONITOR (I wonder why!), this was happily accepted by my favorite atheist journal:Freethought Today

August 18, 1993
Evidence abounds for gun control
The Times Herald Record

It is difficult to understand why good and well-intentioned people like Jim Eggleton (Letters, July 6) should so passionately leap to the aid of criminals and potential criminals by opposing efforts at gun control. "Gun control laws don't help to reduce crime," he states, with more fervor than evidence.

But each day's newspapers do, in fact, give ample evidence of the tragic consequences of too many guns in the hands of too many unstable, irresponsible people.

Ask the family of the elementary school principal who was shot down by kids who had no difficulty getting the guns they needed for their drug-war violence.

Ask the families of the two youths killed in Brooklyn by another teen-ager, "the deadly consequence of teen-age disputes in an age of easily accessible guns." (The New York Times, July 8).

Ask Mrs. Frances Davis ("Bullets Wipe Out Three Sons," Times Herald-Record, July 9). "We have more shoot-em-ups here than anywhere in the world," their grieving grandmother lamented.

The New York Times informs us (July 11) that "law enforcement authorities estimate there are tens of thousands of guns on the streets of New York . . . Already this year, 170 New Yorkers have been hit by so-called stray bullets . . . many of the victims were children."

Setting up a convenient straw man, Mr. Eggleton states that "more strict gun laws are not the problem." He advocates "tougher sentencing and prison reform . . . and parole boards and probation departments that actually do their jobs." Of course, but why does he assume that these reforms are antithetical to sensible programs that would make it more difficult for kids and criminals and drug dealers to get weapons? Gun control and other crime-prevention programs are not mutually exclusive!

I cannot fathom why sensible action to keep guns out of the hands of troubled kids, violence-prone teen-agers and potentially criminal adults should so fire up otherwise sensible people.

September 2, 1993
Church shouldn't shelter pedophiles
The Times Herald Record

If anyone helped a pedophile avoid identification and capture, or assisted a repeat child molester evade law enforcement authorities, he would be legally guilty of "aiding and abetting." Under ordinary circumstances this is a crime for which you can go to prison.

In the case of Father Edward Pipala, however, the "aiding and abetting" was done, not by an ordinary citizen or accomplice, but by the full authority of the Roman Catholic Archdiocese of New York, and the process was not stopped until it was faced with loud public outcries and the threat of civil action and million dollar lawsuits. Now, the public is expected to be reassured because the church promises that its Office of Priest Personnel will, in the future, keep a sharper eye to sexual misconduct by its priests. They even promise to provide "treatment" and to reassign erring members to jobs not involving children!

But, there is still no commitment to report the felonious abuse of children to the police authorities. The church knew about Father Pipala as early as 1977. It not only did nothing to report his illegal misconduct to the proper authorities, but instead, camouflaged his conduct and transferred him from parish to parish where his record of repeated molestation was unknown and where new groups of children became vulnerable to his approaches. This is "aiding and abetting" with a vengeance!

Should the clerical collar protect a felon—for years and years, as in the case of Father Pipala—at the peril of the community, while his church superiors arrogate to themselves the right to judge him privately, to "treat" him as they see fit, to keep him on the job and to shield him from proper law enforcement? It is unconscionable. To this day, the public does not have an unequivocal answer from responsible church officials.

September 8, 1993
Demjanjuk decision 'bone-chilling'
The Times Herald Record

Was he Ivan the Terrible, "among the most brutal of the Holocaust's war criminals?" Or was he "just" an ordinary guard, a simple man who gently packed naked men and women and children into the gas chambers, gently latched the doors, and gently pulled the switch that shot in the gas that killed millions in the "final solution?"

Such is the obscenity to which the discussion of John Demjanjuk has sunk. Holocaust deniers and Nazi sympathizers gleefully seize upon the terrible honesty and integrity of the Israeli court that decided that there was not sufficient evidence to convict Mr. Demjanjuk of being the actual Ivan the Terrible of Treblinka . . . although "there is now overwhelming evidence that he served at the Sobibor death camp, where 250,000 Jews were murdered, and at other Nazi concentration camps" (New York Times, 8/4).

Fifty years after the event, it is a bone-chilling, soul-searching assault on our conscience that the most heinous crime of the 20th century, and perhaps of world history, should be reduced to the question of the quality of the evil of whether or not he was Ivan the Terrible or just an ordinary guard; is to stand justice on its head, to desecrate the memory of 6 million victims, even in an oblique and obscene way to legitimize the Holocaust and to acquit its workmen of death.

Let not a narrow judicial determination by a scrupulously legal and courageous court obscure the enormity of the Nazi crime, nor vindicate any of its perpetrators and participants, nor dim the vigilance we must maintain to see that it never happens again.

December 4, 1993
Clinton's health care address strikes home
The Times Herald Record

There was a certain appropriateness, I thought, to listening to President Clinton's seminal address on health care on Sept. 22 from a hospital bed, where I was awaiting a cardiac procedure, I hung on every word of that magnificent speech. From my bed, facing the activity in the Intensive Care Unit, it seemed to me that the president was addressing my particular situation, and the problems and anxieties of every sick person in the country. Despite the negativism of the nay-sayers ("it sounds good, but how will we pay for it?"), the president seemed to me to be articulating an overarching vision for "giving every American health security."

I wanted to call in the busy doctors and nurses who hurried past my room to share with me this historic occasion. But, they were busy with their tasks and I was left to exult over the speech alone. I was happy to read later that my enthusiasm was shared by others: Brookings Institute economist, Josh Wiener, said, "It would be one of the truly landmark pieces of legislation in the history of the country . . . It's certainly of the magnitude of the passage of Social Security and Medicare."

Among the vicissitudes of hospitalization, anxiety and boredom play leading roles. Eliminating either would go far toward coping with the other. So, I decided to pass the time by conducting an informal poll, asking every doctor, intern, resident, nurse or nurses' aide who came to visit me what he or she thought of the Clinton speech. Most said they had not heard it, nor had they read it with any care in the newspapers the next day. And most shrugged off my enthusiasm with cynical comments that "it was all political and would not come to anything." "Wait and see" seemed to be the prevailing tone. They were busy, too busy to talk. They took my blood pressure, checked the IV tubes, drew blood and left.

One young resident, however, did show emotion as he angrily stated that the trouble with the speech was the mistake Clinton made in assuming that "Health care is a right!"

"Shouldn't it be?" I asked.

"Of course not," he replied. "Health care is not a right. It is something you buy, like anything else."

"What do you think of free public education?" I asked. "Is that a right?"

"Public education stinks," he replied. "It should be private, like medical care." Our conversation could not go further. He had patients to see and I was left alone with my hospital thoughts.

I was not surprised a week later to read that "Doctors Rebel Over Health Plan" (New York Times, front page, 9/30), or that the "AMA Says Its Move Reflects Patients' Interests" (ibid, sub head). The doctors' official organization, we are informed, is placing a budget of $7 million at the disposal of its lobbyists to begin a "lobbying blitz" on Capitol Hill, sanctimoniously declaring, as always, that they act not in their own special interests but in those of their patients, (recalling the unforgettable remark of another altruist who once said that "what's good for General Motors is good for the country.")

I understood the doctors' opposition more concretely when I received my bill for hospitalization. Only Medicare, plus a private insurance policy, stood between me and terminal shock! Five days in a major New York City hospital, in the Intensive Care Unit, was $28,055.50! Itemized, this included $2,560 per day for "basic hospitalization," plus $3,899 for the use of the operating room, plus $8,905 for cardiac catheterization. Recovering from shock, I rationalized that, if an athlete can get millions for his expertise in twirling a basketball into a distant hoop, why shouldn't the magnificent talent of the heart man who delicately and exquisitely maneuvered his instrument into my narrow arteries to clean them out and perhaps save my life be worth $8,905? How can one judge these things? Later, I received another bill from the surgeon for $5,500. The $8,905, it appears, was just for the hospital, bringing the total to $33,555.50.

The president said that there were "over 37 million Americans with no health insurance at all." How would they face the kind of bill I received? What happens when financial disaster is added to the medical anxiety? (Dr. C. Everett Koop, former surgeon general told Hillary Clinton that "an uninsured person who enters a hospital with the same problem as an insured person is three times as likely to die than the insured person," NYT, 9/29). Why?

President Clinton said that our present system must be fixed because "it is too expensive, too bureaucratic, and too wasteful . . . it has too much fraud and too much greed."

Hillary Clinton told a congressional committee that "the same coronary bypass operation cost $21,000 in one hospital and $84,000 in another." Why? (The Intensive Care Unit in the large New York City hospital where I was treated cost $2,580 per day. The ICU in a small hospital upstate where I was initially seen, cost $600 per day.)

The AMA sent letters to 670,000 doctors and medical students to pressure Congress against Clinton's proposals. The AMA, it will be remembered, fought against Medicare in the 1960s. And now, they boo and hiss Donna E. Shalata, secretary of Health and

Human Services, when she appears before them to promote the Clinton plan. "We are troubled by the degree of centralized regulation," they said in their urgent appeal to all doctors.

All, of course, as they "reflect patients' interests

December 12, 1993
The Vision
Mexico City—The News

It did me proud to listen to U.S. President Bill Clinton this morning on *CNN* as he spoke before an enthusiastic audience before signing the North American Free Trade Agreement into law. After all the arguments, the pros and cons, the demogoguery of Ross Perot and his unconcealed racial slurs on the Mexican people, it was Bill Clinton who cleared the air, cut through the self-serving rhetoric of an ill-conceived protectionism, and articulated a vision of the future with clarity, common sense, and vigor.

As with all other fateful junctures in history, it is the vision of the future, articulated and impressed on the national consciousness, that sets the over-arching tone, and determines the nature of the details that must follow. George Bush sneeringly referred to "this vision thing" . . . Bill Clinton increases his stature and does a service to us all, and to all the world by raising the "vision thing" to its proper position in the art of governing. Along with his penetrating evaluations and over all formulations in the Health Care Act, Bill Clinton demonstrates that he does not fail to see the forest for the trees, that he is capable of orchestrating the many strands that comprise policy, that he is creating policy and extending "vision," that he is approaching a philosophy of government that eluded his short-sighted predecessors.

December 19, 1993
Child Slavery
Mexico City—The News

Jeane Kirkpatrick's column of Dec. 12 on child slavery was a stunning, wrenching, soul-churning eye-opener! Coming from one who is a certified "conservative" (not a bleeding heart, over-indulgent, soft-headed, mushy "liberal" she) it had even more impact and bears the stamp of authentic truth. When she stuns our comfortable lives with the astonishing fact that "more than 200 million children, 8 to 14 years old, work as virtual slaves, 12 to 14 hour days, seven days a week, under sub-human conditions" she jolts us out of our complacency, rekindles our lagging moral indignation and challenges our indecent apathy.

That this comes from Ms. Kirkpatrick also says something about the lazy and unfortunate "intellectuality" that is wont to pigeon-hole writers and thinkers and to stick them with labels that have outlived their meaning. "Conservative? "Liberal?" They have less and less meaning as history moves to confound those so labeled with its own unpredictable dynamic. As meaning and content and individual thought are given their appropriate ascendancy, stereotypical thinking will fade away. Pre-judgments, based on previous modes of thought and the intellectual baggage that surrounded past issues and past conditions will give way to new judgments based on the content of one's ideas, not the invidious reputations of an already-judged past.

So hurrah to Jeane Kirkpatrick! She is neither "conservative" nor "liberal." The labels do not apply. She breaks the mold as she directs attention to an unconscionable horror.

She boldly challenges the sleeping "morality" of the more comfortable nations of the world and calls us all to an accounting in the name of humanity.

January 9, 1994
New Threat
Mexico City—The News

One of the most dangerous developments in the post-Cold War world is the emergence in the former Soviet Union of a bold spokesman for fascist ideology such as has not been heard since the days of Adolph Hitler. Anyone whose historical memory is still intact will have no trouble in recognizing the rhetoric of Vladimir Zhirinovsky. In strident terms he calls for a Russian revanchism, expanding the Russian empire to territory in Europe and beyond, while appealing to ultra nationalism and a scurrilous anti-semitism at home (see The News article, Jan. 3, page 6). It is frightening to witness his party's recent electoral success.

As Hitler did in the thirties, within the context of the poverty and disorder of his time, Zhirinovsky plays on the confusion, dislocation, and the economic and political vacuum created by the collapse of a failed Communism and the unsolved problems of mistery and want that followed.

What is even more frightening is the apathy with which the international community is reacting to this malignant development. Hitler's atrocities at home were ignored, while his foreign policy of divide and conquer disarmed opposition from Munich where Chamberlain deluded himself and the world that he had achieved "peace in our time" to Hitler's nearly successful campaign to conquer all of Europe: *The League of Nations failed to build a successful anti-fascist coalition while there was still time, and the rest is history.*

Zhirinovsky and his current success can be ignored only at our own peril. Whatever support, morally, economically and politically, that the United States and the European Community can render to bolster and unite the pro-democratic forces in Russia should be mobilized and brought to bear before it is too late. This may mean support for Boris Yeltsin now, but support should go beyond him as the situation develops. *Our focus should be on a policy not on a person.* The forces for democratic growth should be sought out and encouraged in every way. The vacuum that encourages wild, pro-fascist, dangerous and emotional excess, should be understood and addressed without delay.

January 16, 1994
Ending Violence
Mexico City—The News

Violence, or the study of violence, is the next frontier. I refer not to the violence of nature, but to what Darwinians might call "intra-species" violence—in this case, the violence of man to man.

The uncontrolled violence of the human race, however, directed toward each other under a variety of rationalizations, has escalated to such alarming proportions as to endanger not only our species, but the planet as an inhabitable environment.

In witness, it takes only an examination of one day's news in one newspaper in one country: *The News* of Jan. 7 includes *"Army Continues To Bomb Chiapas Rebels . . . Armed Rebellion A Warning . . . Rights Groups Ask Army To Stop Bombing . . . Airport Bombing Threat . . . Thirty Years Of War In Guatemala . . . Fighting In Guinea . . . 12 Croats Killed In Algeria . . . Assassination In Pakistan . . . Rebel Attack At Togo Army Base Leaves 40 Dead . . . Israel, PLO Stand-Off Threatens To Undermine Peace Process . . . Murderer Executed . . . Heiress Beaten . . . Secrecy's Left Us With A Radioactive Legacy . . . TV Violence Can Be Cut . . . Skating Champion Attacked After Workout."*

The list could go on and on, every single day all over the world. Violence is killing the human race.

The urgent task of the best brains of mankind—in science, medicine, anthropology, sociology, psychology, philosophy, political science, in fact in every branch of knowledge concerned with the human condition—is to study man's propensity to violence, to learn why reason is being abandoned to unreason, why we can find all kinds of rationales, from ethnic to nationalistic to religious to economic to political, to justify mass slaughter in bloody wars and individual violence in human relations.

This is the urgent task of these last years of the 20th century, and the crucial factor in determining whether the human race will survive in the 21st.

January 30, 1994
Genes And Violence
Mexico City—The News

There is good news and bad news in the article "Fear Clouds Search For Genetic Roots Of Violence (*The News*, Jan. 10). The good news is that some of the nation's most prominent academics are studying every aspect of the problem of violence in America. The disquieting news is that there seems to be an emphasis on biomedical research, on "how genes affect behavior, including violence." Many reputable experts feel that this is not only a blind alley, and a distraction from the social causes of crime and violence, but a dangerous path toward abusive control of children and minority groups.

I agree with Dr. Paul Billings: "We know what causes violence in our society: poverty, discrimination, the failure of our educational system . . . It's not the genes that cause violence in our society. It's our social system."

The most glaring lack in the article, however, is the failure to address the most dangerous, the most significant, and the most deadly violence of all. I refer to the violence of modern war. It is the group violence of people against people, nationality against nationality, religion against religion, country against country, that threatens us all with death beyond numbers, and the possible destruction of our planet. Can "behavioral genetics" explain this behavior? Does "biomedical social control" offer a remedy? Can the ultimate violence of war be studied and remedies sought in further biomedical research? The questions answer themselves.

The ultimate violence of man against man, modern warfare in the nuclear age, can be addressed only in the social sphere, in the combined wisdom of the entire spectrum of the social sciences. This includes political science, diplomacy, anthropology, international relations, religion and its unwanted consequences. It must embrace new and bold exploration into the fields of problem solving, conflict resolution, racial relations, the effects of poverty, disease, over-population, mass starvation and stagnation in a world where the distribution of resources is so lopsided as to create plenty and over-consumption in the developed countries while hundreds of millions die of starvation in the Third World. These are the roots of division and ultimately of war. They are social, not genetic. They are man-made, not biologically determined. And their solutions lie in understanding them in our lives and in our social relations, person to person, and nation to nation, and not in laboratory experiments.

The genetic answer may sound exciting and appealing because it offers a quick fix. But there is no Ehrlich's magic bullet to cure the complex ills that lie at the root of the deadly violence of war! War is a man-made disaster, and will be overcome only by the greatest man-made effort of all of us, individuals and nations . . . if it is to be overcome at all.

February 6, 1994
Buckley's Sarcasm
Mexico City—The News

William F. Buckley, Jr. decided long ago that he had hit a vein of solid gold with the discovery that a heavy dose of sarcasm could be a major ingredient in his columnar recipe. Sarcasm, he found, could eclipse analysis. If your opponent was obviously wrong, you could undo him with logic. If he appeared to be right, however, there was nothing like sarcasm to cut him to the quick. Sarcasm became the *sine qua non* of the Buckleyan recipe.

In his column on President Bill Clinton's State of the Union address, Buckley dares not attack the stirring quality of the over-arching vision for a more just America that millions across the nation heard and applauded. Instead he uses his well-honed skill with his ready-at-hand stiletto-of-sarcasm. Health care? Of course everyone wants it. Why not also "endorse free food, guaranteed housing, and full employment" too?, Buckley smirks. The "reductio ad absurdum" falls flat. Anyone without food, shelter or a job would not appreciate the well-fed sneer.

Where others saw a masterful, powerful confrontation with the real problems of the nation—health care, welfare reform, crime and violence—passionately and effectively delivered, Buckley could only splutter that it was "a meal consisting entirely of marshmallows."

For one who exalts logic and analysis when it suits his purposes, Buckley's column on President Clinton's address, was, to continue his own unfortunate metaphor, a mixture of such bile and spleen as to turn one's stomach.

February 11, 1994
NATO Partnership For Peace
Mexico City—The News

In a peculiar confluence of ideological criticism, President Clinton's "Partnership For Peace" came under sharp attack by Mikhai Gorbachev (in his article from *La Stampa*, The News, Jan. 15) and a short time later by Henry Kissinger (Op-Ed, *The News*, Jan. 24).

Ironically, both of these political gurus are left-over from discredited regimes; Kissinger from the Nixon regime, where he was able to avoid any responsibility for the Watergate miasma. Despite his importance as leading mentor to the president and his closeness to the White House, he knew nothing of the lawbreaking and the moral scandal! And Gorbachev who, although brought up, educated and toughened in the dubious moral environment of the Russian Communist Party, Stalinism, and the ensuing Brezhnev years, could now write with an unflappable lack of personal responsibility that "the problem is that three generations were formed in a certain type of environment in which it is impossible to apply the classical models of the IMF that were developed to restore health to free market economies."

And he writes as though he were not there at all, not a powerful member of the Communist elite, not involved in the formation of that "certain type of environment" he now deplores. Is there anyone, or any ideology, that was responsible? What lessons does history teach us? Whatever happened to accountability, as Gorbachev, through his Gorbachev Foundation, bids to become the Kissinger of Russia?

If a man is defined by the enemies he makes, President Clinton can take some solace as his policies are simultaneously attacked by ideologues with the credentials of Henry Kissinger on the one hand, and Mikhail Gorbachev on the other.

In his most recent column (Jan. 15), Gorbachev scoffs at the notion that the Czech Republic, Slovakia, Poland and Hungary might see Russia as a "threat," or a "menace," or as "aggressive," and that they might, therefore, seek the "protection of NATO." Is his historical memory so short as to forget Hungary's valiant uprising in 1966, or the Prague Spring of 1968 when Alexander Dubcek aspired to "socialism with a human face" in Czechoslovakia? Or the fate of the Rumanians under Couseauscu, or the squalor and tyranny forced upon nations from Estonia to Albania under the boot of the Soviet colossus?

Gorbachev fliply writes off that experience and those fears with a propagandistic swipe at U.S. policy: "With the pretext of a presumed return to imperialism in Russia," he writes, "the United States is feeding suspicious about its own imperial intentions." Why does Gorbachev find it necessary to advance such a transparent smokescreen? Does he really think that the countries on Russia's rim, freshly liberated from the brutal foreign domination of the Soviets, fear Clinton's "imperial intentions"—or are those fears legitimately centered on revanchism in Russia, fears fanned by the recent successes of the right-wing, fascist demagogue, Vladimir Zhirinovsky and his followers?

To fail to understand such fears, and their legitimacy, or to attempt to deflect them by references to U.S. "imperial intentions" is either a total mis-reading of recent history and present reality, or a deliberate and transparent propaganda ploy. Neither does credit to the man who bravely sponsored the then hopeful development of Glasnot and Perestroika!

Mr. Gorbachev can make a real contribution to the development of democratic institutions and democratic modes of thought in Russia only by abandoning the wornout clichés of the old regime, clichés overly-used to justify the bankrupt Soviet foreign policies of the past. The re-incarnation today only muddies the water and prevents the growth of those relationship of trust, honesty and equality between former enemies that alone can form the basis of future cooperation and peace.

February 24, 1994
New Political Boundaries Dictate New Foreign Policies
Mexico City—The News

The peace of Europe, and of the whole world, depends on a geopolitical restructuring that recognizes the new realities of the post-Cold War period.

This means, first and foremost, not only the end of the "buffer-state" as a peace-keeping mechanism, but the end of the "buffer-state" as an acceptable political concept.

In the end, the so-called buffer-state "solution" was immoral, illegal, anti-democratic, invasive and tyrannical. And it did not work. The buffer-state was seen, countenanced, and justified as a safety zone between warring super-states, and in peacetime as a means of keeping the antagonistic interests of the super-powers at bay, free from the pressure of geographical confrontation at their borders.

The moral obscenity of this arrangement was, obviously, that it took no account whatsoever of the needs, aspirations, and well-being of the peoples of the states so designated.

The sovereignty of the buffer-state and its inhabitants was of the least concern.

The socio-economic system, as well as the foreign policy of the controlled "buffer," was completely dictated by superpower interests and control.

Flowing from the decisions taken by the Allied triumvirate (Churchill, Truman and Stalin) at Potsdam, when the map of Europe was re-drawn in recognition of the relative positions of the armies of the three powers at that time, the buffer-states from Estonia through Albania were established and sanctified, ("Spheres of Influences" was the preferred term) until a final peace treaty would be drawn.

But the "temporary" lasted for over 45 years, (the peace treaty between the Soviet Union and Germany was not actualized until 1989!).

And the buffer-states remained until the Berlin Wall fell and the Soviet Union disintegrated.

As soon as the opportunity presented itself, all the buffer-states reclaimed their independence, changed their economic systems, and began the difficult task of establishing their own foreign policies.

This is the task of the moment, one in which they need and deserve the help from other sovereign states.

The guiding principle to which we must all return is that which recognizes that the foreign policy of a sovereign state reflects the national interest, safety and aspirations of the people of that state.

No longer should the foreign policy of any state, large or small, be determined by the interests and requirements of another state, no matter how powerful.

If the history of the last few years—from Czechoslovakia to Poland to Hungary—has taught us anything, it is that the "buffer-state" syndrome was both immoral and dangerous.

The end of the Cold War gives the world an opportunity to change that thinking and to chart a new, more moral and more productive course.

The "Partnership For Peace" is a step in that direction. It is interesting, in this regard, to note the positions of three leading political commentators on this pivotal issue: Henry Kissinger, Mikhail, Gorbachev, and Ian Brzezinski, as they respond to the proposal to have the so-called Visigrad nations—Poland, Hungary, the Czech Republic and Slovakia—gradually incorporated into the NATO framework.

Kissinger thinks it is wrong because NATO, he says, is the wrong venue; he prefers the European Union.

Gorbachev is more propagandistic, even vitriolic as he attacks U.S. policy as having "imperial intentions" of its own; in his latest column (*The News* Feb. 20) he darkly states that "the United States, France and other countries are involved in pursuing their economic and geopolitical interests on the great chessboard of world politics." (An unfortunate metaphor, since in chess only two players pursue their selfish, antagonistic goals, and to hell with the luckless pawns!)

Brzezinski alone enthusiastically endorses the "Partnership for Peace" program. "The extension of NATO membership", he writes (*The News* Feb. 17), "to the Visigrad Group, consisting of Poland, the Czech Republic, Slovakia, and Hungary, is another important step toward this end."

He goes further to encourage Ukraine's participation as well. "The decision to postpone NATO expansion only legitimates their claim that Moscow holds the right to determine the geopolitical alignment of other states." Clearly, that should not be our goal.

Buffer state thinking must be relegated to the ashcan of history!

March 13, 1994
Religion And Violence: An Ongoing Unholy Alliance
Mexico City—The News

SAN MIGUEL DE ALLENDE, Gto.—"Religious violence." Is the phrase an oxymoron? Would that it were.

In the minds of millions of church-goers, religious thought is firmly linked to the "Prince of Peace." And in temples, churches, and mosques, prayer for the most part goes hand in hand with feelings of brotherhood and peace. Astonishingly, a recent report stated that nine out of 10 Americans pray frequently and even more believe that God has answered their prayers" (*The News*, Feb. 23).

Judaic thought has been most eloquently expressed by the revered Rabbi Hillel, who, when asked the central meaning of Torah, answered, "What is hateful to you, don't do to your fellow man; the rest is commentary." And "Proverbs" says, "The ways of wisdom and understanding are ways of peace."

Non-violence, peace and brotherhood would seem to be the hallmarks of religious thinking. "Religious violence," it would seem, is surely a contradiction in terms: an oxymoron.

Yet, the linkage, in fact the co-existence of violence and religion haunts us. It screams down the corridors of history and in the headlines of today's newspapers.

From the time when Romans threw Christians to the lions, to the time when Christians threw Jews into the ovens, violence has been no stranger to religion and its institutions. The Crusades, the Inquisition, the religious facade under which Hernan Cortes raped and conquered Mexico, the Holocaust, are only historical highlights in the long process of religious violence and terror.

Around the globe today, religious warfare takes its terrible toll, as Catholics and Protestants kill each other in Northern Ireland, Muslims and Christians murder and rape in Bosnia-Herzegovina, Arabs and Jews slaughter each other in the "Holy Land."

Hezbollah and Hamas and Meier Kahane's Kach are testimony to the violent possibilities of religious zeal. And religious components form part of the rationale of regional wars and conflicts on every continent.

When Dr. Baruch Goldstein killed 39 worshippers in Hebron as they prayed on their holy day, Ramadan, (just as the Arab states murderously invaded Israel on the Jewish Yom Kippur holy day in 1973), his fanatic followers in Kahane Chai praised him as one who "sanctified God's name"!

To the vast majority of Jews, however, both in Israel and in the United States, it was a hideous and repellent act, totally repugnant to both their moral and religious sensibilities.

Israel's Prime Minister Yitzhak Rabin called it a "loathsome and criminal act by a deranged man" (*The News*, Feb. 26).

But does that explain it? When David Koresh led his followers to a fiery death at Waco, Texas, and when Jim Jones induced 900 followers of his People's Temple to cyanide deaths in Guyana, they were also characterized as fanatic and "insane."

When kamikaze pilots crashed their planes into American warships in World War II for the glory of their emperor and their country, was their nationalistic fervor "insane"? Baruch Goldstein, David Koresh and Jim Jones went willingly to their deaths too, in a violence that took hundreds of other innocent lives, for the "glory of God." Can we simply put that out of our minds as "insane" also? Can we really buy the "insanity defense"? Or were they, in a way, "religious kamikazes"?

Do not the official institutional bastions of our powerful religious forces and organizations, which cast such a wide net of influence over the instruction and indoctrination of young and vulnerable minds, bear at least some responsibility when the outcome of religious zealotry is wanton death and destruction? Must we not take another look at proselytism and indoctrination and their effect on individual reasoning and behavior?

There is much to be explored in the area of "religious violence," or violence and religion, not only by religious leaders and their institutions, but by social scientists, philosophers and statesmen the world over, if we are ever to understand the horror of Hebron (and the multitude of atrocities committed in religion's name) and its implications for religious thought and behavior.

Where, at this very moment, are future "religious kamikazes" being formed, nurtured and developed? It is not an idle question.

March 20, 1994
Nyet Nixon, Nyet
Mexico City—The News

We are constantly being reminded these days of the unpredictability of history, of its ironies and bizarre twists and turns.

Who would ever have thought that the inventor of "guilt by association" in his heady days as a young and unknown Congressman on the House Un-American Activities Committee and who parlayed his invention to national fame—ultimately to the presidency—would one day be slapped down with an uncompromising "NYET!" by the ex-Communist President of Russia because he had "associated with Communists!"

That is exactly what happened to Richard Nixon! (*The News*, March 10). Hoist by his own petard, Nixon was snubbed because he had met with Yeltsin enemy, Alexander Rutskoi, and Communist Party leader Gennady Zuganov.

Had Yeltsin been reading Nixon's old Committee records as he researched American political customs, or has he developed his own ideas about "Un-Russian" activities? In any case, the unflappable Richard Nixon turns out not to be the best representative of Russian-American relations, and ought to be encouraged not to roil the difficult diplomatic waters as he enjoys his well-deserved removal from political office.

March 23, 1994
Whatever Happened To Moral Codes?
Mexico City—The News

Whatever happened to morality? That inner core of truth? The "moral compass" that some Watergate conspirators claimed, a trifle too late, to have lost?

Whatever happened to principle, and a consistent moral code?

Has it been lost to expediency, to political partisanship, to cynical party gains as the Outs gleefully exploit the alleged wrongdoings of the Ins?

These thoughts are brought to mind as "Whitewatergate" unfolds, the clever and insidious language manipulation by means of which the incumbent president is immediately linked in the minds of the public with the disgraced "un-indicted co-conspirator" and almost impeached ex-president as birds-of-a-feather!
This is semantic skulldudgery.

It is the means by which Republicans still smarting from the Nixon moral disaster can at last assuage their grief and their never-expressed remorse, by pointing the finger at a new president (see, they chortle, Democrats do it too!). Add "gate" wherever possible—Iran/Iraq-gate, Whitewater-gate—and, in a manner of speaking, the original Watergate burglary and cover-up, and dirty tricks, and lying to Congress, and stonewalling, and crashing psychiatrists' offices, and destroying tapes, and withholding evidence, and obstructing justice . . . was not as bad as it seemed!

But where is that inner moral core?
Republicans who defended Richard Nixon in 1973, who did all they could to block any kind of hearing and any kind of special prosecutor, who defended "executive privilege" to the end, now sanctimoniously demand that hearings must be held at once on the Clintons' Whitewater dealings.

Or the Democrats, who demanded a no-holds-barred investigation of Richard Nixon and now use all their power to prevent Congressional hearings on Bill Clinton.

Isn't there some consistent principle here? Some moral core that rises above partisanship and the political gains of the moment?

Or is it simply a matter of whose ox is being gored?

The spectacle of that moral arbiter, Senator Al D'Amato, pulling out all the stops as he shrilly attacks the president—as though this were indeed another evil, conspiratorial web of Watergate proportions—is hardly likely to con New Yorkers who know him better.

D'Amato's sudden shift to the side of the moral angels will not erase his past career in the corrupt Nassau County Republican machine, or his use of HUD to reward family and cronies in his town on Long Island, or his allowing his office to be used by his brother for his private enrichment, or HUD officials to profit by favoritism, graft and corruption. The Senator himself narrowly missed censure by the Senate Ethics Committee.

His posture now, as moral apostle in battle with a new president (who happens to be of the other party) is, at best, an infelicitous choice of standard-bearer for the Republicans in their newly found moral crusade.

If "Whitewatergate" exposes anything, it is the vacuum of moral fortitude at the center.

Republicans form a solid block as they seek to discredit a Democratic president, suddenly discovering virtues and principles that had eluded them before. Through 12 years of Reagan/Bush, they succeeded in blocking any public knowledge of the covert Iran/Iraq/Contra policies of two Republican administrations, and the lies and deceit and cover-up that characterized the illegal arming and directing—of the Contra war against the legal government of Nicaragua.

The chief miscreant, Oliver North, pardoned by the Republican president, now even has the gall to run for the Senate, not only without apology or remorse for his lawbreaking, but actually reveling in his felonious past.

"Whitewatergate," so called, is surely not Watergate. It is not even in the same league. But it starkly reveals that there is something missing in U.S. national political life, on both sides of the aisle. That is an inner moral code, one that is consistent, principled, above personal political gain and corrupt partisanship, and true to the real meaning of the word "moral," which is simply a concern for what is right and what is wrong.

Morality does not come with the convenience of a party label.

April 2, 1994
The Meaning Of Passover
Mexico City—The News

The following is from a March 26 talk given by Meyer Rangell at the Community Passover-Seder Service in San Miguel de Allende, Gto.
Ma Nishtana Ha Lila Hazeh?
Why is this night different from all other nights?
Addressing this question might be the best way to begin to explore the meaning, the underlying significance of the Passover we celebrate today.

We might all ask, as individuals and as a group, what our answer to that *Ma Nishtana* might be. I have a feeling that there would be many different answers, as each of us examined his or her own Jewishness.

I use that term carefully and deliberately. Because Jewishness is the over-arching experience. Jewishness subsumes, and is not defined by, religiosity alone. It is quite the other way around. Jewishness includes ethical, moral, cultural and traditional values.

Jewishness is inclusive, not exclusive. That is its beauty! Our answers to the *Ma Nishtana*, our answer to the question "What it means to me to be Jewish," would be as varied and as personal as the individuality expressed by each and every one of us in this celebration.

The mythical, the historical, the traditional, and the personal, each has its place. And all come together here under the umbrella of the Jewishness that we all share.

For me, the answer to *Ma Nishtana*, what it means to me to be Jewish, is on two levels.

First, the inspirational story of Exodus itself, one of the earliest expressions of man's yearning for liberty, and freedom against the forces of slavery and oppression.

The long march across the desert, out of the bleak years of bondage and slavery in Egypt, rings down the corridors of history.

As do other long marches that have inspired man and changed the course of history:

The fight of America's black slaves along the underground railway was such a march.

The freedom riders in the '60s; during our own civil rights struggle was such a march, and let us not forget the contribution of Jewish heroes like Michael Schwerner and Andrew Goodman who gave their lives for that cause.

The march of father Hidalgo's and Ignacio Allende's ragged army down from Dolores Hidalgo through San Miguel, over to Comonfort and on to Guanajuato, where their severed heads were hung by the Spanish oppressor, was such a march.

And let us never forget the march of the remnants of the holocaust from the death camps to the new Jewish state of Israel. How moved we were when Steven Spielberg at the Academy Awards implored educators, in the name of the 350,000 survivors, not to allow the 6 million who died to be forgotten or the lessons of the holocaust to be lost in an historical footnote.

There were other struggles and marches for freedom that I am sure you can supply. Exodus is proud to be one of them. That is what we celebrate today.

On a second, and perhaps a deeper level, the *Ma Nishtana* represents the ongoing intellectual curiosity and the intellectual honesty that is the Jewish/Judaic tradition: The *Ma Nishtana* and the traditional *"Fier Kashes"* ("The Four Questions") are symbolic of the questioning nature of Jewish thought.

Question, question, question! It is the Talmudic as well as the Socratic method for getting a truth.

Ask the why of prejudice, the why of injustice, the why of war and the why for violence.

And then go a step further and ask what can we, all of us, do about it?

Never be afraid to challenge the status quo, be ready and brave enough to challenge authority. Previous authority is not carved in stone, but is subject to the reasoning power and the honesty-in-questioning of each generation.

The political theorist, Edmund Burke, once said "All that is necessary for the success of evil, is that good men remain silent."

The Jewish tradition cries out against such complicitous silence. The Jewish tradition encourages us to speak out and to involve ourselves wherever we see injustice or a threat to freedom.

The great Hebrew sage, Rabbi Hillet said it all when in response to a student's question to "Tell us what Torah means, the entire five books of the Pentateuch, but briefly, while standing on one foot!" Hillet replied: "What is hateful to you, don't do to your fellow man. The rest is commentary. Now go study."

Centuries later, right here in Mexico, Benito Juarez said the same thing when he said: "Respect for the right of others is peace."

From Rabbi Hillet to Benito Juarez to Martin Luther King, Jr., the message is the same.

It is the message of our *pesach*.

???

April 17, 1994
Syndicated Columnists:
The Arrogance Of Pen And Punditry
Mexico City—The News

What's with the U.S. syndicated columnists? Ever alert to pounce mercilessly on the "arrogance of power" that they perceive in politicians and elected officials, they assume an arrogance of pen and punditry of their own at every opportunity.

Witness three examples in as many days, as Kirkpatrick, Safire, and Buckley outdo themselves as they ply their trade:

On March 27, Jeane Kirkpatrick resorts to name-calling and the use of pejorative buzz-words in her shrill attack on President Clinton's Health Plan ("Clinton's 'Socialist' Health Plan Will Cause Harm To Americans.") She finds it easier to attach scary labels, like "socialism . . . nationalize one-seventh of the U.S. economy . . . a step toward collectivism . . . statist economics," etc., rather than face the health-care issues that confront us.

Ms. Kirkpatrick knows that these labels will distract from the real issues, and that they are expressly calculated, in fact, to frighten the American people, to obscure the problems rather than to illuminate them.

If by "socialism" one means the attention, direction, and action of government on social issues that affect the country as a whole, then "socialism" indeed exists, and to our benefit, in many areas:

Social Security can be called a form of socialism, as well as Medicare, and free public education, and free libraries, and government subsidies to farmers, and tax abatements to corporations, and tax exemptions to religious organizations, to name but a few.

Why, in one of the most important fields of all, the health of the people, should government concern, government input, and government action to secure the health security of all the people, be greeted by such outrage and hostility? "Socialism . . . collectivism," Kirkpatrick bellows, pulling out all the emotional and linguistic stops.

President Clinton opened his campaign for health care for all Americans on Sept. 22, 1993 before a joint session of Congress because "37 million Americans have no insurance at all" and because the current U.S. system is "too expensive, too bureaucratic and too wasteful . . . it has too much fraud and too much greed," he said.

Former Surgeon General Dr. C. Everett Koop told Hillary Clinton as she appeared before a Senate committee that "an uninsured person who enters a hospital is three times as likely to die than the insured person." (*New York Times*, Sept. 29, 1993).

President Clinton articulates with passion and integrity his goal for universal health security for all Americans, a goal to which all of us aspire, despite the fulminations of those who parrot the self-interest of special groups, such as the American Medical Association and the fat-cats of the insurance industry.

On March 29, in "Reading Hillary's Mind . . ." the usually lucid William Safire goes from columnist to mentalist, with no discernible additional qualifications. A neat leap. And a great ploy. He is able to "enter Hillary's mind," place words and thoughts there without the benefit of quotation marks, and with no fear of contradiction, or of libel. Innuendo leads to an exercise in character assassination, as Safire repeats unfounded accusations, giving them a curious credibility by placing them ingenuously "in Hillary's mind," her very secret thoughts, now made public by diviner Safire!

On March 30, William F. Buckley, Jr., not to be outdone in the field of character assassination, ("Solarz Dumping . . .") comes to the aid of Stephen Solarz as his name is withdrawn by President Clinton for consideration as ambassador to India.

With sarcasm dripping like venom from the fangs of an aroused cobra, Buckley writes: "The poor, precocious gentleman (he's talking of Solarz, whom he's come to defend!) was early in life afflicted by a virus that refined taxonomists identify as Eastern Seaboard liberalism."

He goes on to repeat charges that Solarz had had a relationship with a Hong Kong businessman "of bad reputation," although the FBI, after investigation, found no grounds for action against him. So why does Buckley give the wide publicity of his syndicated column to unfounded accusations? With friends like that, Solarz must wonder, who needs enemies?

Buckley's hatred for Clinton, almost equal to his hatred for all the Kennedys, leads him to attack both the appointer and the possible appointee . . . two "liberal" birds with a single conservative stone.

Arrogance of power is bad. Arrogance of pen can be equally bad. Character assassination is vile.

Are we looking at an occupational disease of the pundits?

April 24, 1994
Who's On First?
Mexico City—The News

Which do you think is the more important job—associate justice of the U.S. Supreme Court or commissioner of Major League Baseball?

As a Supreme Court justice you have input into such problems as women's rights, the right to privacy, labor relations, the maintenance of the First Amendment rights to free speech, the problems of upholding the Constitution and the direction of the country in the crucial years ahead.

As baseball commissioner, you get to decide who's on first and other such world-shaking problems on the baseball diamond.

The issue arises because, as reported in *The News* of April 13, U.S. Senator George J. Mitchell turned down the offer of President Clinton to appoint him to the vacancy created by the retirement of Justice Blackmun amid speculation that Mitchell might be more interested in becoming the baseball commissioner.

Of course, one must take into account that the salary of a Supreme Court justice is 164,000 dollars. The job of baseball commissioner "will very likely pay 1 million dollars or more per year." That's no small consideration!

But what does it say about the values and priorities both of individuals and the nation? Where should the special talents of an experienced legislator, senator, legal scholar and constitutional expert go in these crucial times? Where can they serve the nation best? On the nation's highest bench or in the ballpark?

May 15, 1994
No More Cover-Up
Mexico City—The News

    Congratulations on today's editorial (*The News*, April 24, "Nixon: An Expatriot's Sentiments"). It took an uncommon courage, rare political honesty, and the highest degree of editorial probity, for Patricia Nelson to avoid sentimentality and not to join the army of writers, columnists, and TV commentators as they wallow in the "Nihil Nisi Bonum de Mortuis" syndrome (Say nothing But Good about the Dead).

    Ms. Nelson calls the shots as she sees them. We owe her a debt of gratitude for recalling the dismal record of Richard Nixon as he attempted to subvert the U.S. Constitution. Ms. Nelson refused to take part in the final Cover Up!

    With "break-ins, bugging, plumbers, perjury, secret tapes, 'smoking guns' and slush funds", Nixon undermined for a whole generation the credibility and the good-faith of government. Cynicism and the expectation of corruption at the highest levels constitute the Watergate legacy that he bequeathed us and that still prevails. His administration gave an almost fatal blow to the essential morality that must be at the core of democratic society.

    Ms. Nelson does us all a service by reminding us that our democratic fabric can be fragile indeed, as the Watergate criminals, operating under the cover of a corrupt White House, demonstrated. It must not be permitted to happen again.

THE WHITE HOUSE
WASHINGTON

June 2, 1994

Mr. Meyer Rangell
Post Office Box 183
Bloomingburg, New York 12721

Dear Mr. Rangell:

Thank you for sharing your thoughts about health care and for expressing your support for the President's health care reform proposal. The President's proposal responds directly to the crisis our nation now faces in health care. At some point during the year 58 million Americans go without insurance, and 2 million Americans lose their insurance each month.

In an effort to give Americans the health security they deserve, the President wants to strengthen what's right about our health care system and fix what's wrong. The President's proposal works the following way:

> Guaranteed private insurance. Every American will be guaranteed private comprehensive insurance coverage that can never be taken away.

> Choice. All Americans will have the right to choose their own doctor and health plan. It will be the individual, not the employer or insurance company, who will make this important choice.

> Outlaw unfair insurance practices. It will be illegal for insurance companies to drop coverage or cut benefits; increase rates because of sickness; use lifetime limits to cut off benefits; or charge older people more than the young. This will help make it possible for all Americans to obtain dependable and affordable insurance.

> Preserve Medicare. Older Americans have a right to depend on Medicare and choose their own doctors. The President will protect and strengthen Medicare by

covering prescription drugs and providing new options for long-term care in the home and the community.

Health benefits guaranteed at work. Every job should come with health benefits. The government will provide discounts for small businesses and help cover the unemployed.

This nation now has a historic opportunity to change our health care system to make it work for all of us. I hope you will work with the President to make health security a reality for all Americans.

Regards,

Ira C. Magaziner
Senior Advisor to the President for
Policy Development

July 13, 1994
Tax-based health care is sensible solution
The Times Herald Record

    The debate on health care has reached such complexity it is no wonder that the average citizen is confused. The sheer weight of words and the variety of proposals, counter-proposals, criticisms based on self-serving partisanship and transparent political motivation, printed almost daily by "experts" of every stripe—doctors, lawyers, sociologists, politicians, social theorists, management professors, health-care "providers," has the average citizen without a Ph.D. or other credentials overwhelmed, frightened and bamboozled, unable to get his thoughts onto op-ed pages and made to think that the whole field is too complex for him, or her, to even hazard an opinion. Leave it to the "experts," we are told.

    As an average citizen, what I do know is that President Clinton's aim, to provide universal health care to all Americans, is the most significant reform to come out of Washington since Social Security and Medicare. For articulating that goal and or placing it on the front burner, he deserves our applause and support. Every American, President Clinton asserts, whether young or old, employed or unemployed, poor or rich, should be assured of proper health care. Maybe we cannot understand, we are told, the complexities of "managed care," "managed competition," "employer-paid insurance," "health maintenance organizations," "single-payer proposals," 'employers-employee contribution" plans, and more.

    But we do not find it difficult to understand that the most sensible, cost-effective, practical, efficient and fair proposal is what has come to be know as the "single-payer" plan. Under this plan, the federal government undertakes to pay all the bills for all the medical care for all the people. Every citizen would be covered. The plan would not be tied to one's job or to one's age, or to one's income. Simplicity in both concept and implementation is its greatest virtue: Medical, hospital, and drug bills would be paid for by the government. Its as simple as that!

    But, where would the money come form? From taxes, of course. Taxes would cover the people's health, just as taxes now cover their Army and Navy and Air Force, as well as the criminal justice system, public transportation, public libraries, to name but a few of the responsibilities that our government undertakes for the welfare of our people. Is the health of our people less important than these?

    But that would be "socialized medicine," one hears. No more than the defense establishment is "socialized," or the legal system, or the educational system. Early in the debate, this bugaboo was raised by Jeane Kirkpatrick, when she darkly warned of "socialism," "nationalizing" the economy, and the specter of "collectivism." The American Medical Association quickly followed suit. Isn't it strange that no one complains of "socialism" and "collectivism" when the government provides for the security and welfare of our nation through the defense forces, public education and welfare? Is not the cry of "collectivism" when used exclusively against health care somewhat suspect?

The three major opponents to this sensible, efficient and fair system, geared to the needs of all Americans, are predictably, the insurance industry, the pharmaceutical industry, and the American Medical Association. Their reasons are transparent.

1. The insurance industry would be deprived of its enormous profits if it were denied the millions in premiums that privately based insurance premiums. The advantage, of course, is that tax programs are accountable, through our representatives, while insurance companies, with their own bureaucracy and six-figure executives, are most difficult to regulate.

2. Pharmaceutical companies, which now gouge the public with obscene charges, would be regulated and prices brought down to reasonable levels if the government were their chief customer.

3. Doctors would be paid fair and reasonable remuneration, again under an accountable and fair system that would be the result of doctor-government-consumer cooperation. This might be a problem to the AMA and to the highest paid specialists it represents, but it need not be bad news for the thousands of practitioners in rural towns and in the inner cities where medical care is delivered under difficult conditions of poverty and scarce resources. Under the present system doctors are lured to practice where the money is. A government health plan would spread the wealth of medical care wherever it is most needed.

The present health-care system, in President Clinton's words, is "too expensive, too bureaucratic, and too wasteful. It has too much fraud and too much greed."

A privately administered system, dedicated to universal coverage, might eliminate much of this scandal.

But our best hope is in a single-payer government plan, one that recognizes the moral and practical responsibility of government to stand up and be counted in what has become the most important aspect of a people's well-being—the health of all its citizens.

August 19, 1994
Don't encourage moral terrorists
The Times Herald Record

Cal Thomas' column of August 5, offering a defense of the man accused of taking the life of Dr. John Bayard Britton at his Pensacola clinic is abominable both in its "logic" and in its conception of what is and what is not moral. Paul Hill is accused of taking it upon himself to judge and to kill. Thomas calls this an act of "pro-life;" apparently, the "life" that is yet unborn is the only life to be revered, while the life of a dedicated and compassionate human being can be viciously snuffed out.

Thomas' comparison of the values of an anti-abortionist killer with the values of John Brown shows an obtuseness that is almost beyond belief. It is an insult to all those, from John Brown to Abraham Lincoln, who fought and died to wipe the stain of slavery from American history. Those who fought slavery rediscovered our country, one might even say reinvented it in the true image of the Declaration which stated that "all men are created equal."

Those who would deny the established right of women to decide their own autonomy have nothing in common with the heroes of the freedom movement of the past century. To equate the struggle for human freedom against human slavery with the ill-conceived violence of the abortion-foe fanatics is to desecrate the memory of those who stamped out the greatest evil in American history, and to offer encouragement to arrogant and murderous moral terrorists.

September 3, 1994
Echoes from the 'Monkey Trial'
The Times Herald Record

The Record's resident fundamentalist bible-thumper, Cal Thomas, hits a new low in his Aug. 19 column with language that has not been heard in serious discourse since Clarence Darrow squared away with William Jennings Bryan in the famous, or infamous, Scopes ("Monkey Law") trial in 1925.

"Wright can believe," Mr. Thomas writes, referring to a new book on evolutionary psychology, that "his nearest relative is downtown at the zoo and that's why he likes bananas on his cereal!" This sounds eerily like the leading fundamentalist religious spokesman in 1860, Samuel Wilburforce, Bishop of Oxford, who, addressing the eminent biologist and Darwin supporter, Thomas Huxley, "begged to know, was it through his grandfather or grandmother that he claimed his descent from a monkey?" Huxley's famous reply was "I would rather be the offspring of two apes than be a man and afraid to face the truth."

This is 1994, not 1860, and one would think that the passionate arguments of early fundamentalist religion against scientific evolution had long been settled. But not, apparently, for Thomas, who leans on an outdated Bishop of 1860 and on fundamentalist William Jennings Bryan in 1925 to defend the religious bastion once more against rational scientific investigation.

Required reading for Mr. Thomas should include not only some of Charles Darwin, but also the dramatic "Inherit the Wind."

October 14, 1994
Shame on Congress' inaction
The Times Herald Record

Shame on the Congress of 1994 as they packed their bags and went home without passing health care reform—any health care reform whatsoever, even a beginning of health care reform, even a small start toward the eventual goal of full health care reform.

Shame on those congressmen and women who placed political expediency ahead of the health of our people.

Shame on those Republicans who cravenly followed the advice of their guru, William Kristol, who brazenly advised Republicans to prevent Congress from doing anything this year, even to the taking of small incremental steps, because any change would lend "retrospective legitimacy" to President Clinton!

Shame on a Congress that won't even consider a minimum bill designed "to insure all children and pregnant women, providing community and home-based long term care for the elderly and disabled, and making a number of widely supported changes in insurance laws," as some mainline Democrats propose. Such reforms, minimal as they are, would run against the Kristol doctrine: Don't pass anything that might redound to President Clinton's credit! Better to kill all health reform this year and wait for a Republican year.

Shame on those who, they would have us believe, sanctimoniously would not vote for a "good" bill because it was not a "perfect" bill. Baloney! They used every excuse at hand to buckle under to the financial and political clout of the lobbyists of the pharmaceutical, insurance, and medical conglomerates. Party and politics were their main concerns, not the people's health.

Shame on Republican leader Robert Dole, who led the pack that killed health reform for the express purpose of shafting President Clinton in order to politic toward '96 and the presidency.

November 27, 1994
U.S. Elections
Mexico City—The News

While the pundits, politicians, pollsters and assorted well-paid "experts" engage in the usual Monday-morning quarterbacking, "explaining the meaning" of the election to the voters they strove so hard to mesmerize, they overlook—or deliberately ignore—what may be the most significant statistic of the election:

That is, only 39 percent of the nation's eligible voters turned up at the polls. Put another way, 61 percent of the voters were unimpressed by the multi-million dollar blitz, and showed their disgust with the meanness, the nastiness, the obvious appeal to negative emotions, the avoidance of real debate, by saying: "A plague on both your houses. Your election stinks, and we'll have no part of it!"

Since the vote was closely split between Republican and Democrats (a 4 to 5 percent difference was enough to decide the outcome in many cases), it appears that the victorious candidates could boast the support of about 20 to 25 percent of the electorate: 61 percent stayed away altogether, while almost 20 percent of the 39 percent voted for the other party.

With all the hoop-la, all the fund-raising, the TV spots that dominated the airwaves, the multi-millions devoted to advertising, pollsters, media consultants, well-paid advisers and ad agencies, only one in four eligible voters actually went into the voting booths to elect the winners.

If a teacher reached only one in four students, if a doctor helped only one in four patients, if a lawyer helped in only one in four cases, would that be cause to cheer?

But the winning candidates in this election shout that the "American people have spoken."

The American people have indeed spoken. A better case can be made, however, that what they said was that they were disenchanted and disgusted with an electoral process that was an insult to their intelligence, that they were turned off by the lack of honest debate, by being treated as brainless, gullible consumers in the same way that crafty professionals induce them to buy a brand of auto or a more effective deodorant.

Tarring the opponent has taken precedence over the exploration of ideas and programs for the common good.

Securing the office by any means, fair or foul, is seen as the primary, indeed the only goal. What should be the finest expression of a democratic society, a national celebration of the freedom of choice that allows a free and uncoerced people to select their best and their brightest to lead and to shape their government, has turned instead into a nightmare of mean-spirited, perverse mud-slinging.

The fault lies in large part in the confusion between the art of getting elected and the art of governing.

Charisma, stage skills and the winning smile (the art of getting elected) play a larger role than demonstrated integrity and significant skills in the social, economic, diplomatic and legislative arenas.

It is not even the fault of the candidates, although a rare few do rise above the petty and the venal to display the required statesmanship.

The system, as it is now practiced, places the candidates in the hands of professionals who package them like any other product, selling them to vulnerable audiences and consumers with 30-second TV bytes calculated to appeal to the lowest common denominator.

Negative advertising and low-punching, the pundits of politics assure their clients, are a better way to go than positive discussion.

In this milieu, it is money that counts. TV costs plenty, repetitive messages calculated to press the right buttons, emotionally, if not intellectually or ethically, are more important than truth or substances.

A candidate in California spends 30 million dollars. In New York candidate Golisano spends almost 10 million dollars. Even the wealthy and privileged Edward Kennedy takes out a mortgage of 2 million dollars on his home to help his campaign. Oliver North spends 20 million dollars to get a seat in the Senate, his only claim to fame being his previous felony before that very body!

What is a poor candidate to do?

The compelling message of this elections is that 61 percent of the electorate were disgusted by the travesty and stayed home on election day.

The "meaning," which the pundits do their best to cover up (after all, their jobs are at stake!), is that the electoral process must be restored to a semblance of decency and fairness. It should not require million-dollar assets to be a candidate for office.

The "experts," apparently, feel comfortable with the appalling tact that less than half our citizens bother to exercise the most important right, and the responsibility, of our democracy, and that one quarter determine the electoral outcome.

They like to blame it on "apathy". But whom can we blame for the apathy? Clearly, an electoral system that requires millionaries candidates, that squeezes out promising aspirants with good programs but without deep pockets, a system that depends more on expensive packaging than on developing programs for the common welfare, is part of the problem.

But the major problem lies with a political, ethical and intellectual vacuum in our national life that fails to involve, energize, stimulate and educate our citizenry.

Citizens don't vote because there is too little leadership to capture their imagination and to stir them to participate.

Do we face up to the problem? Is our leadership up to the challenge? Do we reform our electoral system now? Or must we wait until there is an election and no one shows up?

June/July 1995
Tax Solution Is At Hand
Freethought Today

Every year, just as surely as the Ides of March are followed by the budget battles of April, New York's Mayor, Democrat or Republican, trots out the "budget gap." Right on schedule, Mayor Giuliani announces (NYT 4/26), that the shortfall "exceeds $3 billion" and proposes slashing spending by city agencies by nearly $400 million more than he proposed two months ago. In the next two months we can look forward to more political manipulation and economic sleight-of-hand.

There is a solution at hand that does not cut jobs or essential city services:

The last time I looked, the value of religiously owned land in New York State free from all property taxes amounted to $13 billion, according to the New York State Board of Equalization and Assessment for the year 1990. The New York City figure was over $4 billion! The figures for 1995 are no doubt even higher.

The solution to the "budget gap" is still available: Eliminate the tax-exemptions enjoyed by religious institutions. One prominent church alone, St. Patrick's Cathedral, on prime Fifth Avenue real estate, costs the city over $4 million per year in forgiven taxes! The elimination of tax-exemptions on religiously owned property would go a long way, perhaps all the way, towards solving Mr. Giuliani's shortfall.

Why, year after year, do politicians avoid even addressing this issue, while the media scarcely mention it? Is religion still a "sacred cow"?

Removing privileged tax-exemptions from religious institutions would:

1. Correct the inequity whereby the taxpaying public is forced to subsidize religious thought and practice.
2. Require religious institutions to pay their fair share for city services (fire, sanitation, et. al) that they now receive for free.
3. Re-establish the spirit of the First Amendment and the Jeffersonian separation of church and state. A special state-given freedom from taxes rewards what should be private religious enterprise with public funds.

Let organized religion pay its own way, no special favors asked or granted. That's the democratic way.

December 4, 1994
Helms At The Helm
Mexico City—The News

The *New York Times* editorial of Nov. 24 ("Helms Should Step Down Now") and the Kansas City Star editorial of Nov. 25 ("Helms Doesn't Deserve Seat") hit the nail squarely on the head!

This is the first, and perhaps the most crucial test of whether the Republicans, who have shown their skill in the art of getting elected, can also demonstrate that they have skill in the art of effective government.

Thus far the Republican leadership, including Robert Dole and Newt Gingrich, have waffled on the issue, preferring to minimize the significance of Helms' utterances as off-the-cuff remarks that don't mean very much.

But when any senator, not least the future chairman of the crucial Foreign Relations Committee, states that he has no confidence in the president as commander of the armed forces, and that he "better have a bodyguard and watch out if he comes down to North Carolina," he not only undermines the president in his conduct of foreign policy, but sows seeds of discontent and disloyalty in the military.

If his remarks mean that he is aware of a conspiracy to attempt harm to the president, he should be promptly investigated, as any other citizen would be.

If it is sheer hatred and distrust, he should be censured without delay.

His remarks, at the very least, encourage disloyalty in the rank and file and can easily be interpreted by any wild, unbalanced ego as an encouragement to violence.

They surely disqualify him for the post of chairman of the Foreign Relations Committee.

The senator's irresponsible ranting can place the president in a vulnerable position when he meets with heads of state, whether allies or potential enemies.

Influenced by Helms, might politicians abroad conclude that the U.S. president does not have the support of his own military? What does that do to his negotiating posture?

The seniority rules in the Senate are not writ in stone.

When seniority combines with irresponsibility and senility, it surely deserves a closer look.

The majority Republicans are duty-bound to consider political posture, appropriateness and the ability to contribute to the nation's welfare and security in their choice of this chairmanship.

The Senate, in the interest of its own moral posture, ought to censure Helms for his unconscionable statements, whether they approach the treasonous or are simply unworthy and stupid.

One hopes that there is at least one senator who has the courage and the wisdom to introduce such a motion-to-censure.

It would restore the American people's faith in that august body and assure the senator who does it a place for himself in history's "Profiles In Courage."

December 18, 1994
Time For A Censure
Mexico City—The News

"... false in their facts, incendiary in their temper, disunion in their object, high treason in their remedy, and usurpation in their character ... The whole concept ... perfected by fraud."

No, these are not the words of a courageous United States senator condemning the recent outrageous utterances of Sen. Jesse Helms. Though they might be! They were the words of another senator in another time at another critical juncture in American history, when the fate of the country hung on the issues of slavery, secession, union or disunion, and when the question of loyalty to principle versus loyalty to party faced every political leader on both sides.

The words were those of the flamboyant Thomas Hart Benton, senator from the slave-holding state of Missouri, as he fought against the spread of slavery to the Western territories and for the preservation of the union against the seccessionists. Benton staked his political career on what he thought was right, not on popular beliefs he considered wrong. "I despise the bubble popularity that is won without merit," he said, "I value solid popularity—the esteem of good men for good action." Because he adhered to principle, against an overheated public, Benton lost and was driven from office. But even in defeat, his powerful impress was largely responsible for the fact that the key border state of Missouri did not join the Confederacy in 1861.

Is there a lesson here for today? Perhaps. By all the signs, the Republicans are poised to elevate the loose-lipped, undisciplined embarrassment that is Jesse Helms to the chairmanship of the Senate Foreign Relations Committee ... because of his seniority (or is it because Robert Dole does not want to alienate his southern flank as he prepares for 1996!)

But it is not too late for a courageous senator, in the mold of Thomas Hart Benton, to put principle ahead of expediency, to champion a cause because it is right, if not popular, to raise in the Senate a forceful opposition to Jesse Helms becoming the chairman of the Foreign Relations Committee.

And even to censure him for his incendiary statements against the president!

The man to do this may be Senator Patrick J. Moynihan of New York, or Christopher Dodd or Edward Kennedy of Massachusetts. Such a motion-to-censure would be a breath of fresh air on the political scene, like the censure years ago of the infamous Joseph McCarthy, a censure supported at last by senators of both parties.

January 8, 1995
Ethical Conflicts
Mexico City—The News

Anthony Lewis touched on it in his column (*The News*, Dec. 20, 1994).

John F. Kennedy wrote a whole book on it: *Profiles in Courage*.

President Clinton travels the razor edge of it, especially since the last election.

Politicians and statesmen are always confronted with it, no matter how hard they try to avoid it.

I refer to the conflict between principle and expediency, between the requirements of getting elected and facing up to the ethics and problems of our times.

The conflict is between careerism and the welfare of the country, between personal ambition and the needs of our people, between honor and compromise.

How this conflict is resolved determines the differences between statesmen and mere politicians.

How politicians and office-holders view their role says much about whether they are politicians (professional office-holders, legislators or aspirants) or statesmen.

Do office-holders, legislators and elected officials (together they are the government) follow the whims and currents of popular opinion, or do they lead to a new plateau of political consciousness and understanding?

Followers, or leaders?

The ascendancy of pollsters and their ubiquitous public-opinion polls, the new and highly paid profession of political adviser, without whom no aspiring candidate dares go to the polls, would indicate that following the changing winds of popular preference, is more important, and prudent, in today's politics than vision and leadership.

And that is the difference between statesmanship and the frenetic pursuits of political charisma.

Abraham Lincoln did not have a poll-taker, or ghost-writer when he wrote the Gettysburg Address.

Nor did he take a sampling of the current opinion of his day before tackling the ethical and moral problems he so illuminated and ennobled in that seminal speech.

Thomas Hart Benton, Sam Houston, George Norris, Governor Peter Altgeld, among others, each risked their personal careers to support unpopular causes, championing what they though was right rather than expedient, choosing conscience over political gain, even when it meant opposing the views of their party and their constituency.

Is there such courage in the United States Senate today? Can Senator Jesse Helms be permitted to go unchallenged as he demeans and insults the president, challenges his ability to command the military and warns him not to visit North Carolina without a bodyguard?

Is there not one senator to speak up, one with the courage, conscience and adherence to principle, irrespective of party, to lift senatorial debate to the heights it once enjoyed?

A motion to censure would do it.

At the very least, a move to prevent Jesse Helms from being rewarded with the chairmanship of the Foreign Relations Committee.

Will it be Moynihan, or Dodd, or Kennedy, or someone else ready to "seize the day," and the opportunity?

February 19, 1995
Eroding Cancer
Mexico City—The News

Editor: Any day's reading of *The News*, or any other newspaper, is enough to drive home the conclusion that the understanding and control of violence remains the central problem of our time.

In the remaining five years of this century man must begin the process of peaceful progress toward sane co-existence of all peoples or face uncurbed violence and destruction in the next century. *Violence is the eroding cancer of our society.*

From state-sponsored violence and the slaughter of millions by "civilized" governments in wars that represent their perceived national interests as against the interests of others, based on ethnic, religious, economic or ideological differences, to the wide gamut of personal violence, criminal violence, violence against children, sexual violence, violence against women and their right to control their own bodies, every day's news brings ample new evidence of an endemic violence across the world. It is a violence that destroys the life of our cities, the community values of our neighborhoods, corrupts our youth, degrades our educational system and makes a mockery of our search for a sane society.

The striving for love and brotherhood, which is at our hearts' human core, and which nourishes our deepest sense of a caring humanity, has never been so threatened as by this spreading, all-pervasive, ubiquitous evil of violence that seems to engulf us and threatens to destroy us all.

Violence destroys our caring instincts and our aspirations toward altruism and human brotherhood.

In this tumultuous century man has reached new pinnacles of achievement . . . and has plumbed new depths of depravity and despair. We have put a man on the moon, made the world a global village with a wizardry hitherto undream of . . . and have also slaughtered our fellow-man with ever-improving death-machines with an efficiency previously unimagined in numbers formerly unthinkable. We have developed science and medical knowledge to unprecedented levels, wiped out polio and smallpox and other childhood diseases . . . but millions around the world still die of malnutrition, poverty and disease.

The New York Times reports (2/5/95) that "According to the World Bank 700 million of the world's 5.6 billion people now face endemic hunger."

Man's unavoidable new frontier as we enter the 21rst century is the study of violence and the concomitant problems of war, hunger, poverty and disease. These are our moral imperatives. We need to mobilize the best minds of our time, in social thought, medicine, psychiatry and psychology, in statesmanship and political theory, in philosophy and ethics and in government, to study and develop a new science of peace rather than the skills of war, and to explore the ground from which the evil of violence springs. We must develop new insights and new values and above all a new sense of the community of the human race.

March 12, 1995
Disaster At Hand
Mexico City—The News

Editor: "Christian Coalition Spells Disaster For GOP" (March 4) is the headline, but it is out of synch with the content of the column by William F. Buckley, Jr. as follows:

In the face of uncontested documentation of Pat Robertson's anti-Semitic views and the attempt of his Christian Coalition to black-mail the Republican Party, Buckley blandly responds that, despite some of his "cuckoo ideas" . . . "I rather like Pat Robertson . . . and invite him to be reborn historically"!

It is a little like "inviting" the anti-Semitic authors of the Protocols of Zion to please, please change their minds about the Jews.

The growing influence and boldness of the Christian Coalition was, in fact, highlighted just a few days before in *The News* on March 2, when it reported that Robertson's front man, Ralph Reed, had declared that if both halves of the Republican ticket in '96 are not pro-life, "the Christian Coalition will stay home."

To bolster his argument, Buckley gleefully cites Midge Decter, writing in the conservative magazine, *Commentary*, as she attacks the Anti-Defamation League (which Buckley cannot resist smearing as "an engine of the political left") for its recent in-depth report on the intolerance of the "Religious Right."

Decter tries to turn the table as she complains that it is the ADL that shows "bigotry against conservative Christians."

Talk about twisting words!

"Bigotry" is associated generally with prejudice and oppression by a powerful majority against a weak minority.

To turn it the other way only invites obfuscation. It is like saying that a survivor of Auschwitz is a "bigot" because he hates Nazis.

Pat Robertson and his Christian Coalition reveal themselves more and more as dangerous ideologues, not just harmless "cuckoos."

Your headline is more persuasive and to the point than is Buckley's mealy-mouthed column.

Yes, the "Christian Coalition Spells Disaster For GOP," and, one might add, for the United States as a whole.

March 19, 1995
Still Time
Mexico City—The News

Editor: Is it yet possible for President Bill Clinton to make an electrifying appearance before the U.N. World Summit for Social Development in Copenhagen?

Could President Clinton yet save this most idealistic and morally significant gathering of nations since World War II from what the *AP* reported (*The News*, March 10) as a "lukewarm ending"—in other words a dismal failure? The delegate from Bangladesh said, "It's just talk, not backed up by substance . . . a waste of our time and money!"

A total of 193 nations and almost 13,000 delegates assembled in Copenhagen to discuss the pressing issues of poverty, the imbalance between rich and poor nations, the problems of starvation and disease among one-fourth of the world's population. According to the U.N., 1.3 billion people of the world's total of 5.5 billion live in poverty. And every minute of every hour, 47 babies are born into a life of grinding poverty.

President Clinton sent Hillary, who gave a stirring speech on International Women's Day on the problem of illiteracy. And Vice President Al Gore, who is yet to speak. But demonstrators threw stones before the U.S. Embassy in Copenhagen to express their frustration at President Clinton's failure to lend his presence and his authority. His "skipping the summit raised the question of poorer countries around the world."

But there is still time. President Clinton's appearance even now would stun the world. A meaningful message from the American president that would include proposals for significant U.S. aid for development, social improvement and anti-poverty funding, could re-vitalize the conference and set the example the world so desperately needs.

President Clinton could electrify the summit, and the world. The moral weight of the United States, delivered directly by its most important spokesman, could turn the summit around.

Bold, effective, dynamic leadership by President Bill Clinton might still be able to rescue the summit from a disappointing "lukewarm agreement" to a bright beginning of hope, a beacon for the desperate and hungry around the world.

If there ever was a "moral imperative," this is it. There is still time.

March 26, 1995
Medicare
Mexico City—The News

Editor: A group of us in San Miguel de Allende have been trying to get a campaign started to change what we perceive to be an unfair, inconsistent, and self-defeating aspect of Medicare as it pertains to senior citizens who live or travel abroad.

As it now stands, Medicare subscribers, while paying their full share of Medicare premiums (it is now 46.10 dollars per month) are cut off from all benefits while they live, or travel, out of the States.

Thus, a couple, retired in Mexico or elsewhere, who maintain their Medicare status for purposes of emergency, pay 1,106.40 dollars per year, and receive no coverage, or even a re-adjustment of their premium, while they are abroad.

Thus, while Social Security recipients are permitted to receive their checks wherever they reside, as indeed it should be, seniors who wish to travel or to live abroad for part of the year are penalized by the threat of uninsured illness, despite their standing in Social Security and their paid-up Medicare premiums.

This is not only patently unfair, but in practice results in vastly higher costs to the Medicare system and to U.S. taxpayers.

When seniors are forced to return to the United States for medical and/or hospital care when they can receive such care at a fraction of the cost right where they are, here in Mexico, it is the Medicare system that loses.

For example, in a recent emergency, treated in a first-rate hospital in Guadalajara, emergency surgery, plus hospital costs, were astonishingly lower compared to costs for similar services in the United States. (A major New York hospital charges 2500 dollars—*that's dollars*—per day in their Intensive Care Unit; we paid 350 new pesos (that's 58 dollars) per day, plus an additional moderate charge for Intensive Care). Yet Medicare would pay the high cost of the U.S. hospital, while refusing to pay for the much lower costs here.

(Incidentally, the facilities at the hospital in Guadalajara, San Javier, were state-of-the-art, the premises immaculate, the treatment, concern and tender-loving-care by everyone—surgeons, nurses the entire staff—were par excellence! I take this opportunity to thank them all!)

Covering senior citizens here and elsewhere abroad while they are in good standing under the Medicare system, allowing them to receive quality care, in qualified hospitals, by qualified physicians, saving them the cost and the difficulty and sometimes the danger of traveling home when ill, makes both good sense, good morality and good fiscal policy.

The Medicare system would save, the elderly would receive care when needed and in time; and morality would be served by a policy that does not discriminate against our older citizens when they are abroad.

Write to your congressman and senator, and to the White House in support of this change.

Senior citizens should be covered under Medicare wherever they are treated in qualified facilities abroad.

They have earned this, as they have earned their Social Security, and they are paying for it as well.

April 2, 1995
What Contract?
Mexico City—The News

Editor: What is all this brouhaha about the "Contract With America" that permeates the media, is shouted from every Republican rooftop and now screams at us from the Dome of the Republican Congress? Just what is this "Contract"? Who negotiated it? Who signed it?

I had always thought that a "contract" signified an agreement reached by two adversarial parties after much negotiation and discussion and was sanctified finally, and legalized, by the freely-given signatures of the parties involved: Like a marriage contract or a divorce agreement, or an agreement between buyer and seller, or a union contract between workers and employers, binding on two sides. In each case there is the final signature at the bottom line, signifying mutual consent by two parties and a commitment to the terms of the contract.

But what is this "Contract With America"? Who negotiated it? Who agreed to what? Who gave mutual consent? The only signatures at the bottom seem to be the right-wing cabal that attained control of the Republican Party. Who signed for the American people? Who agreed with the contents? What kind of "contract" is this, anyhow?

Ah, the Republicans will reply, the results of last November's election can be read as the people's "mandate," the people's approval of the "contract." Their signature is implicit.

But is this so? Sixty-one percent of the electorate stayed away from the November elections; of the 39 percent who did vote, only slightly more than half voted for the Republican candidates; that leaves the much heralded "mandate" at about one-fourth of the electorate. And even they had only a faint glimmer of what the Republican program entailed.

Is this really a "Contract"? And between whom? Certainly not between the majority of the American people and the Republican power-holders.

Did the American people sign a contract to cut 600,000 summer jobs for youngsters across the nation?

Did the American people sign a contract to humiliate and oppress the unemployed and the disadvantaged through a welfare bill that provides "budget cuts on children and the elderly . . . to fund a tax cut for the privileged few," as Rep. Richard Gephart recently described it.

Did the American people agree to sign a contract to provide the rich with a bonanza in tax relief through capital-gains tax reductions?

What kind of "contract" is this, that has only one signature, on one side, no mutually consenting partner, and brazenly presumes to speak as though it had the authority of a worked-out agreement between adversaries?

The answer is that this is no "Contract" at all, in the usually accepted sense of "contract"!

Woman, children, the elderly, the poor, are being stripped of whatever safety-nets have been constructed over the decades, to create a mean-spirited government and a mean-spirited society, where human values, compassion and concern are lost. "Balancing the budget" is seen as more important than caring for the poor, as the Newts chase the almighty buck and serve the interests of the wealthy.

This is no "Contract," but a calculated political sham, and a shameful assault on the social fabric.

April 16, 1995
Deadly Warning
Mexico City—The News

Editor: In the brilliant interview conducted by Global Viewpoint (*The News*, April 3), Mr. Alvin Toffler reiterated and under-scored the major concerns expressed in this space in my letter of Feb. 19: "Man's unavoidable new frontier as we enter the 21rst century is the study of violence . . ." (M.R.).

Mr. Toffler poignantly stated that "all of us today live with a kind of floating fear in the background of our lives."

Much as it is important to state the problem as clearly and unambiguously as Mr. Toffler does, it is disheartening that he does not point to possible solutions.

Maybe there is no one certain solution.

The recent nerve gas attack in Japan points up the complexity of the problem and the difficulties that lie in the way of control of materials of mass destruction and the terrorist groups that might use them.

Nevertheless, it is essential that a pessimistic vision of inevitable doom be avoided. Violence is a human problem.

It is man-made.

We must believe that it can be solved by human intelligence.

But this solution can come only from the most extensive scientific investigations, study and effort by our best minds in every field of human thought.

Coming up soon, the Nuclear Non-Proliferation Treaty renewal discussions offer an opportunity for re-defining the ends and goals of that treaty; the dismantling of the 30,000 nuclear weapons that still exist, and the destruction of the nuclear materials in such a way as to prevent their finding their way into terrorists' hands.

Further, every nuclear power must accept the responsibility for research into the origins and control of violence and the development of the skills of peaceful negotiation, problem-solving without violence and the capacity of nations and peoples to live together on this, our only planet.

The challenge is immense, but not unachievable.

It is perhaps the greatest challenge in the history of man.

It will require the greatest understanding and cooperation of peoples of all nations.

Or will we succumb to a paralysis of fear, awaiting extinction?

May 9, 1995
Humanity imperiled by violence
The Times Herald Record

If the ghastly events at Oklahoma City have taught us anything, they drive home the point, nay they pound home the point like the nails in the coffins of the 19 innocent children, that the central problem of our time is the understanding and control of violence.

Violence is the eroding cancer of our society.

From the individual violence of terrorists and fanatics to the state-sponsored violence of "civilized" governments in wars that kill millions as they pursue their perceived national interests against the interests of others, to the wide gamut of personal violence at every level of society—criminal violence, sexual violence, violence against children, violence against women and their right to control their own bodies. Everyday's news bring new terrible evidence of an endemic violence in human affairs across the world.

It is a violence that bids to destroy our caring instincts and our aspirations toward altruism and brotherhood.

It is a violence that destroys the life of our cities, the community values of our neighborhoods, corrupts our youth, degrades our educational system, and makes a mockery of our search for a sane society.

The striving for love and brotherhood, which lies at our heart's human core and which nourishes our deepest sense of caring humanity, has never been so threatened as by this spreading, all pervasive, ubiquitous evil of violence that seems to engulf us and threatens to destroy us.

Man's unavoidable new frontier as we prepare to enter the 21st century is the control of human violence and the concomitant problems of war, poverty, hunger and disease. This is not only a moral imperative, but a practical imperative, if the human race is not to go the way of the dinosaur and the dodo bird.

We need to mobilize the best minds of our time, in social thought, medicine, psychiatry and psychology, in statesmanship and political theory, in philosophy and ethics and government, to study and develop a new science of peace and problem-solving, rather than the skills of war, and to explore the ground from which the evil of violence springs.

Above all, we must develop a new sense of community of the human race.

June 7, 1995
Don't ax treatment programs
The Times Herald Record

Among the issues being debated in Albany today, as the budget slashers wield their axes on one social program after another, is an item that merits our deep concern: The Pataki budget proposes to cut $11.7 million from prevention programs and another $8.5 million from treatment programs in the field of drug and alcohol abuse. There are also proposals to eliminate six state-operated Alcohol Treatment Centers.

If there were ever an example of penny-wise and pound-foolish, this is surely it. For every cent we would save now as we abandon this unfortunate population of teenagers, youth, and adults in every sector of our community, we would pay 10 times over down the road—in broken lives, destroyed families, deteriorated neighborhoods,—and in the spiraling cost of hospitals (to treat AIDS and related illnesses), in the prisons, where so many of them would land (at a cost of about $25,000 per person per year, not to mention the huge costs of new prison construction), in welfare costs (because the addicted do not have the best employment potentials!).

Cutting prevention and treatment budgets would be a sorry case of saving now and paying later, while condemning thousands to misery and despair.

Not only a decent sense of morality, but a practical sense of reality, should tell us what recent experience has proven over and over: treatment works, while abandonment and default lead only to more disintegration and despair.

member, Alcohol and Substance Abuse Committee,
Sullivan County Department of Community Services
Bloomingburg

August 3, 1995
Religion no test of democracy
The Times Herald Record

Your editorial, "Common ground on school prayer" (July 18) overlooks two significant aspects of the president's Virginia speech: one is contemporary, the other historical.

Contemporary: The president shamefully caved in to the religious right and its attempt to turn back the clock in an important area of American life. Their brazen goal, through Pat Robertson and others, is to destroy the religious diversity guaranteed by the First Amendment and to tear down the historic wall of separation between church and state.

To say, as the president did, that it is "necessary to protect religion from being inappropriately burdened by government action" is to lose a major argument by default. The majority religions do not need protection. Majorities never do. It is the minority that requires protection from an overbearing majority and its tendency to proselytize in order to increase its dominance.

The magnificence of our Constitution and the Bill of Rights lies in their concern to protect the less-powerful minority and their right to their religion, or non-religion, free of the pressure and prejudice of the safe majority. That is the significance of the Establishment Clause and of Article VI of the Constitution, which states that "No religious test shall ever be required as a qualification to any office."

Historical: Perhaps the most egregious abandonment of principle is the president's assertion that "Our nation's founders knew that religion helps to give our people the character without which a democracy cannot serve."

There is nothing in the record to substantiate that our founders "knew" any such thing. On the contrary, their effort was to establish a secular nation, free of the divisiveness of contending religious beliefs.

The Constitution begins with, "We, the people," does not mention God at all, not even once, and public prayers were deliberately omitted at the Constitutional Convention of 1787. This was a calculated demonstration of their determination to establish a government of an indisputable secular character. Their motto was "E Pluribus Unum" (one out of many).

"In God We Trust" was not installed on our currency until 1955, the result not of our forefathers thinking, but of the hysteria and jingoism that characterized the

McCarthyism of the '50s. What the founding fathers did know was that religion does not provide a litmus test for democratic thought and allegiance: Hence the First Amendment and Article VI.

September, 1995
Religion Bears Responsibility
Freethought Today

Re: Waco. Why is there no meaningful discussion of the key role played by organized religion, both mainstream and fundamentalist, the TV evangelists and the enormous network of proselytism and indoctrination with which they blanket radio and TV, overwhelming the country with an ever-increasing propaganda that reaches more and more into our socio/political life?

David Koresh and his Messianic vision may be viewed as a corruption of accepted religious thinking, and his "revelations" contrary to standard Biblical interpretations, but can the religious community absolve itself completely of any responsibility for the surround of religious (supernatural, non-rational, faith-dependent) thinking out of which a David Koresh can emerge?

Where is the line that separates "legitimate" religious hierarchies and their devoted and devout followers from a Koresh, who can induce his followers to accept fiery deaths, or a Jim Jones, who led 900 devotees to cyanide suicide in Guyana, in their blind acceptance of their leader's vision?

Do not the official institutional bastions of our powerful religious forces and organizations bear at least some responsibility when the outcome of religious zealotry is wanton destruction and death?

What other cult madness is even now being nurtured among the variety of religious groups that proliferate of all sides? What understanding can religious leaders, as well as sociologists and philosophers, bring to this phenomenon? It isn't enough for Chairman Bill McCollum, of Florida, to say on television that, "Of course, Koresh was a monster." But where did this "monster" spring from?

The silence of the religious community, and the philosophic and academic and sociological communities, does not speak well for them. There is a vacuum of that intellectual leadership that is necessary to first understand, then to cope with, the deep malaise, the social and cultural crises, and the absence of humanistic, reality-based, rational movements toward friendship and non-violence untainted by religious, mystical, thinking and its unpredictable consequences.

October 28, 1995
AMA not so altruistic on health care
The Times Herald Record

Although I agree with Dr. Charles Strober's passionate attack on the insurance industry ("Insurance game not in patients' best interest." My View, Oct. 11), his article might have been more persuas8ive if, in the context of the ongoing debate on national health care, he had also addressed the motives and behavior of his own profession and their "union" spokesmen, the American Medical Association.

"A year ago," Dr. Strober recalls, "when the Clinton administration proposed a universal health-care bill, the insurance industry spent approximately $63 million to defeat it. Why? Because they had discovered large profits in health care and therefore had the most to lose." What he fails to tell us is that his own organization, the American Medical Association, also opposed the universal health-care bill and placed a budget of $7 million at the disposal of its already well-heeled lobbyists to begin an intensive "lobbying blitz" of its own on Capitol Hill. The AMA also sent letters to 670,000 doctors and medical students to pressure Congress against the universal health plan. And when Donna Shalala, secretary of Health and Human Services, appeared before an AMA audience to promote the bill, she was hissed and booed by the altruistic MDs.

The insurance industry defended its own. And the organized doctors of America did precisely the same. Between the two of them, President Clinton's vision for a universal health-care plan to serve the medical needs of all Americans, young and old, poor or rich, employed or not employed, was defeated.

At the time, one expert, economist Josh Wiener of the Brookings Institute, said of the proposed legislation: "It would be one of the truly landmark pieces of legislation in the history of the country . . . It's certainly of the magnitude of the passage of Social Security and Medicare." Doctors and insurers both saw to it that it never happened.

It is ironic that on the same day that Dr. Strober attacked the insurance industry (properly, in my view) his own organization, the American Medical Association, was dickering with Newt Gingrich and his fellow Republicans on their plan to cut Medicare by $270 billion over the next seven years. "DOCTORS' GROUP SAYS G.O.P. AGREED TO DEAL ON MEDICARE," read the page one article in the New York Times, (Oct. 12). Were the doctors trying to protect the patients, to keep their costs down, to reduce the draconian Republican cuts? Not at all. The AMA was trying solely to protect doctors' incomes, and they succeeded before they officially supported the Republican plan.

As the New York Times reported, "The American Medical Association said today that they had received a commitment from House Republicans not to reduce medicare payments to doctors treating elderly patients." Representative Bill Thomas, a California Republican who is chairman of the Ways and Means Subcommittee on Health, "said the concession to doctors would cost no more than $400 million over seven years." Premium up for the elderly patient, but doctors' incomes protected all the way! A sweetheart deal between the AM and the GOP, at a cost of $400 million to the taxpayers.

It is interesting to note that the major answer to the for-profit insurers "raking off an additional 15 to 20 percent as pure profit for their shareholders an inflated chief executive officer salaries," that Dr. Strober so properly deplores, is the plan known as the "single-payer plan," briefly considered in last year's debate and totally forgotten in this year's Republican-dominated discussion.

This plan would place the responsibility for the people's health care on the government, as is the case in Canada, England, France and most other industrialize nations. The program would be administered by the government, its cost paid through taxes, not through insurance premiums that are too high, paid to private conglomerates whose major goal is not health but the generation of profit.

In fact, such a single-payer plan is in effect right now for members of the armed forces, for government employees and for the very congressmen and senator who are covered by plans subsidized by tax dollars while they threaten cuts to seniors on the one hand and support the insurance lobby on the other.

Last year, President Clinton said that the present health-care system is "too expensive, too bureaucratic and too wasteful. It has too much fraud and too much greed." He was right and still is.

A doctor friend once remarked to me that traditionally, the "best and the brightest" of our youth were attracted to medicine and its lofty goals of service an healing. That is still the case. Our society, and our political and professional leadership, bear the responsibility of providing the moral ambience within which that ethic can serve to the best advantage of all our people.

November 1995
Re-Visit Churches' Exempt Status; "KIDS ARE SEATED ON FLOORS IN OVERCROWDED SCHOOLS WHILE WE SUBSIDIZE CLERGY'S PRIVATE HOMES"
Freethought Today

At a time when "budget-cut" is perhaps the most widely used phrase in political discussion and tax-consciousness is at an all-time high, some astonishing revelations can be glanced from an otherwise tedious tome, *Exemptions from real property taxation in New York state*, recently issued by the New York State Board of Real Property Services (May, 1995, reporting for 1993):

While Mayor Giuliani and the Board of Education are at each others' throats, scrambling to find funds to make up a $230 million shortfall that threatens our schools with chaos, the state and city are giving away millions in exemptions on religiously-head property. In New York City alone, church-owned property in the amount of $5.8 billion are free of 93.60% of the real property tax. In addition, residences for the clergy, totaling $3.4 billion, receive a 47.14% exemption.

In New York State as a whole, the staggering sum of $13.8 billion of church real-estate receives almost complete exemption (97%) from the real property tax, while $4 billion of clergy residences receive 55% exemption. (In much of the state, exemptions in both categories reach 100%.)

What morality permits deprivation and disaster in our public schools while tax give-aways favor private religiosity? Are kids seated on the floor or on radiators in overcrowded classrooms (*New York Times 9/15/95*) less important than subsidizing private homes for clergymen at the expense of over-burdened taxpayers? (What other class of workers or professionals enjoy such tax-privileged homes?)

Aside from the vexing question of constitutionality (do not religious tax exemptions violate the spirit if not the letter of the Establishment Clause and the First Amendment, and the Jeffersonian principle of separation of church and state?) the tax exemptions force the general taxpayer, religious or otherwise, to support religious institutions that may be contrary to his/her own beliefs. Should not religiosity, a private matter, be supported privately?

At time of crucial tax-crunch in the city, state and nation, when a budget cut of only $93,000 jeopardizes a crisis nursery (*NYT 6/11/95*), and schools, welfare, health programs, and children's programs, are lost to the budget-knife, is it not time we revisited the exempt status of establishment religion and the public usage to which these recouped revenues could be applied? Should not the social good and public need take preference over private religiosity?

December 3, 1995
In The Name Of God
Mexico City—The News

Editor: It has become fashionable of late among some of our most distinguished legal scholars and criminal defense specialists, when all else fails, to advance the "abuse excuse" (Alan Dershowitz' phrase) in defense of murder, violence and assorted mayhem . . . More deadly and more morally destructive is the widespread use of the "God excuse," the consequences of which are devastating to moral philosophy and to the maintenance of an ordered society.

Yigal Amir murdered Israel's prime minister "in the name of God."

David Koresh, in Waco, Texas, led his followers to fiery death "in the name of God."

Dr. Baruch Goldstein, in Israel, mowed down 39 Arab worshipers at Hebron "in the name of God." (It is chilling in retrospect to recall that Prime Minister Yitzhak Rabin, destined to be the ultimate target, at the time, called it "a loathesome and criminal act by a deranged man").

Jim Jones, in Guyana, induced 900 of his followers to accept death by cyanide "in the name of God."

Followers of Hezbollah and Hamas and Meier Kahane's Kach kill and prepare to kill more "in the name of God."

How many more heinous crimes must we live through and suffer before attention is seriously addressed to the nexus of religion and violence?

Do not the official institutional bastions of established religion of all faiths bear at least some responsibility when the outcome of religious zealotry is wanton death and destruction? Religious leaders and institutions cast a wide net of influence as they indoctrinate young and vulnerable minds. Where is their teaching and influence when devoutness crosses into fanaticism, when belief in "God" becomes a license to kill?

The malignant consequences of all-consuming religious belief are now, as always, unexplored in any depth by official religious authority and its leadership as they rush to "explain," or to explain away, the horrors of murder and violence, and the attempts to destroy the national, rational, secular fabrics of nations "in the name of God."

The religious-activists-in-murder are always viewed as "insane," in no way representative of the religious mainstream. That may often be so. But what about the soil—the religious surrounding and the indoctrination that stresses faith over reason—

from which the fanatic impulse is born and nurtured? When faith is chosen as superior to reason, should it surprise us that reason is often in danger of being abandoned or lost?

There is much to be explored in the area of religion and violence, and religious leaders bear a major responsibility to initiate such exploration. It is also the responsibility of social scientists, philosophers and statesmen to join such a study to broaden its scope and depth, merging scientific ethical, moral and spiritual values.

Violence in all forms is the social cancer that threatens to destroy our society. As we head into the 21st century, our major effort must be in the direction of understanding that violence in order to control it, and to turn man's direction and behavior toward that loving-kindness of which he is capable, toward the Greek concept of *agape*, toward the nurturing of peace and brotherhood, on which, ultimately, our survival depends.

December 10, 1995
Cut—Off
Mexico City—The News

Editor: The budget battle rages. Republicans insist that their planned cuts in Medicare are not cuts at all, only a reduction in future increases. The Democrats maintain that future increases will be kept under control. But both agree that the premiums paid by senior citizens must go up, while services go down. In this atmosphere, no one, but no one, not even the AARP, addresses the plight of the senior citizen who lives or travels abroad and, despite his continuing payment of premiums, is cut off from Medicare cover-age.

Present rules deny seniors who become ill abroad from receiving covered medical care unless they travel back to the United States for treatment. If they are too ill, or unable to fly home, their treatment costs here are their own out-pocket problem . . . This despite their continued Medicare payments (which will rise considerably no matter who wins the budget debate).

As yet, no one has stepped forward to rectify this injustice, or to address the fiscal stupidity. Treated here in Mexico, in state-of-the-art hospital facilities, costs are usually one-fifth the cost of similar treatment in the United States—which Medicare will refuse to pay. Yet, if the stricken senior is able to make it back, Medicare would pick up a tab that is about five times higher than would be the case if treatment were secured, without travel or the dangers of delay, here in Mexico. It should not take a brain surgeon to figure out that this would save, not cost, the Medicare system millions.

Covering Social Security recipients who are also paying Medicare premiums while abroad is fiscally sound, and morally proper. We are still waiting for a courageous senator or congressman to step to bat on the issue.

December 24, 1995
What Revolution?
Mexico City—The News

Editor: When will a serious historical scholar come forward to puncture the pompous pretentions of Newt Gingrinch as he pontificates about his Republican "Revolution"? Gingrinch, a one-time history professor himself, surely is aware that students of history reserve the word "revolution" for those cataclysmic events that change forever the social-political-economic conditions of mankind, ushering in an irrevocable new reality. Such were the Industrial Revolution which changed our economic reality; the American Revolution, which sounded the death knell for colonial rule; the French Revolution, which destroyed monarchy and the divine right of kings; the Russian Revolution, which ultimately failed but which overthrew the tyranny of the Czars; the Mexican Revolution, which overthrew foreign rule and affirmed once again the principle that people have a right to determine their own destiny.

When Gingrrich clothes his retrograde program in the garb of "Revolution," he perpetrates a deliberate scam, trading on the charisma of a concept that he distorts and traduces. If anything, Gingrich's Contract With America is essentially counterrevolutionary. It poses not a new understanding or new and invigorating program for our current ills, but a return to the old, discredited values of Hoover Republicanism, when the only remedy for the evils of unemployment, poverty, despair, a flawed educational system and lack of opportunity, was the hallow call for "rugged individualism." Government, that philosophy contended, had no responsibility for these conditions and should remain aloof. Since then we have come to value the accomplishments of compassionate and practical involvement of government at every level, especially at the highest federal level, in the form of Social Security, Medicaid, welfare, unemployment insurance, college student loans and special programs designed to bring excellence to our public education system, to name but a few. Government, in other words, said that it was responsible and accountable for the quality of life of our people.

The whole thrust and philosophy of Gingrich and his minions, on the other hand, is to gut these efforts at human betterment or at least to get government out of the people-helping activities. "Rugged individualism" once again!

Future historians will no more confuse the retrograde Gingrich program with "revolution" than they will dignify his demagogic Contract With America as a modern Magna Carta.

December 31, 1995
Disingenuous
Mexico City—The News

Editor: Ms. Jeane Kirkpatrick in her article "Entitlements Impact Voting Worldwide" (*The News*, Dec. 24) is nothing if not disingenuous when she tearfully laments the fact that "Bill Clinton's approval ratings are above 50 percent and climbing: confidence in his judgement is up," while "public confidence in the Republican Congress and its leader Newt Gingrich have declined." She is clearly chagrined! "What is going on?" she plaintively asks. "Why do the voters feel such little enthusiasms for the 'Republican Revolution'?"

Clearly Ms. Kirkpatrick believes her stature as one of the country's most seasoned conservatives, or, hard to believe, she just doesn't get it. Or she refuses to see the plain answer to her query, which is that the American people have seen through the Gingrich "flim-flam." There is no "Republican Revolution," there has never been a "Republican Revolution" and there never will be a "Republican Revolution." There is only a cynical hypocritical exploitation of people's fears in a political grab for power by the right-wing of the Republican Party.

What there is is a confrontation between two concepts of government. One, championed by President Clinton, asserts that government has a responsibility for the welfare and the quality-of-life of its citizenry, a responsibility that transcends balancing the budget in a precise time frame. The other, championed by Gingrich, denies government responsibility and would turn back the clock to old-fashioned Hooverism, whatever its consequences in human suffering.

Ms. Kirkpatrick sneers at the humanist Clinton program by insulting its supporters as demanding "the immediate gratifications of statism!" What a put-down! The fact is she is mortified that the poor, the underprivileged, the aged, the medically deprived, have begun to see and to think through the basic practical and philosophical issues involved, and, lo and behold, prefer "immediate gratifications" (which means their safety nets in Social Security, Welfare, Medicaid, Medicare, AFDC for their children, et al!). The result is what Ms. Kirkpatrick fears and laments: Clinton's star rises, while the demagogic Gingrich falls from grace.

"What is going on?" Ms. Kirkpatrick wails: The people are waking up and doing some thinking, that's what is going on. They see that the Republicans are no 1995 version of the Sons of Liberty, that there is no "Republican Revolution," and that Newt Gingrich is no Thomas Paine.

January 7, 1996
Introspection
Mexico City—The News

Editor: It is that time of year again . . . *feliz año nuevo, Feliz* the lucky ones, not so *feliz* for the millions here in Mexico and around the world who suffer hunger, poverty, disease and the ever-present scourge of violence.

It is a time for introspection, retrospection and a look into the future.

A time for the New Year's resolutions made to be broken, and a time for serious decisions about where we are going.

In the new year we are entering we will be making decisions about our society and our governance for the last presidency of the 20th century. In so doing we will be laying the basis for the type of world we want in the new century to come.

"According to the World Bank," the *New York Times* reported in February of last year, "700 million of the world's 5.6 billion people now face endemic hunger." At the U.N. World Summit for Social Development in Copenhagen last March, it was reported that 1.3 billion people live in poverty. Surely, the improvement of this bleak and impoverished existence, visited upon almost one-fourth of the world's population amid an unprecedented opulence for the favored few, is of the highest priority.

But first on my list is the problem of violence. *Violence remains the eroding cancer of our society.* From individual violence (the obsession of millions of people with the O.J. Simpson trial), to widespread domestic violence, to the state-sponsored organized violence of war all over the globe, to the ethnic/religious violence that murders millions and is as common as each day's morning headlines, murder and violence have become almost accepted human phenomena, part of the human condition.

We have become inured, too, to the horrors of genocide. Almost forgotten is the example of Rwanda, where, "of an original population of 7.7 million, at least 800,000 were killed in just a 100 days." Up to a million Rwandans were murdered by their own fellow-countrymen, according to a special report in the *New Yorker* of Dec. 18.

Whatever the scale, from a single murder, to the mother who drowned her two children in South Carolina, to the murder of millions in the name of ideology or religious zealotry, the problem of man's propensity for violence and killing remains unaddressed.

The 20th century saw man reach unprecedented heights. We have put a man on the moon, made the world a global village with a technological wizardy hitherto undreamed of, wiped out many childhood diseases (polio, smallpox), but millions around the world still die of poverty, disease and malnutrition. Science and technology have reached new pinnacles of achievement, while inventing new methods of human slaughter previously unimagined. And we have come not one whit closer to solving the overriding problem of man's violence toward his fellowman. *The world remains a killing field.*

Man's unavoidable new frontier as we prepare to enter the 21st century is the study, understanding and control of man's violence. It is not only a moral imperative, but a practical imperative if we are to maintain the progress that we have achieved and avoid a return to barbarism, or the ultimate penalty, our extinction in an orgy of man-made destruction.

We need mobilize our best minds in every field of human endeavor, in philosophy and social thought, in science, medicine, psychiatry, biology and genetics, in statesmanship and diplomacy and problem-solving, to study the root causes of violence in man and in his social organization, to explore the ground from which the evil of violence springs.

We must learn how to replace man's propensity for violence with his capacity for love and brotherhood, which lie at our hearts' human core. We must develop new insights and new values, and above all a new sense of the community of the human race—the whole human race, all over our common planet, not only in our own small corner.

It is the major challenge of these last years of the century, and we must address it, lest it become the scourge of the next. Our survival depends on it.

January 14, 1996
Beneath Contempt
Mexico City—The News

Editor: William Safire, in his column of Jan. 9, loses his cool and reputation as American's leading word "maven" in one fell swoop, as he descends to the level of our unspeakable Speaker of the House when he (Gingrich) called the first lady a "bitch." Allowing his spleen to take the place of his brain, Safire rivals Gingrich in vituperation and name-calling when he solemnly asserts that Hillary Clinton "is a congenital liar."

Webster's New Collegiate Dictionary, 2nd edition, defines "congenital" as "existing at, or dating from, birth . . . acquired during development in the uterus . . . ." Although Mr. Safire may have established himself with his "On Language" column as a preeminent logodaedalian, he hardly qualifies either as a pathologist or as a psychiatric diagnostician. His attempt at medical etiology with respect to Mrs. Clinton is beneath contempt.

As to the "facts" he adduces to substantiate his shrill, frenetic outburst, Safire adds nothing to the well-publicized interpretations and opinions of Clinton's public and private behavior. He would do well to express his own opinions, labeling them for what they are worth, his opinions among many. Instead he has revealed his own bottomless animus against this presidency and has chosen to wallow in the intellectual swill that has unfortunately characterized so many of its current critics.

January 15, 1996
Divided Societies
The New Yorker

    Your coverage of the Rabin assassination, by Michael Walzer, David Remnick, and Amy Wilentz (November 20th), although wide-ranging, failed to address the central question it raised: When will serious thought be given to the notion of killing "in the name of God"? From Jim Jones, in Guyana, to David Koresh, near Waco, and on to Baruch Goldstein, in Hebron, and Yigal Amir, in Tel Aviv, such killing threatens the maintenance of ordered society. Don't the official bastions of organized religion, of all faiths, bear at least some responsibility when belief in God becomes a license to kill? Religious authorities make lame excuses about "lone killers" and "fanatics," but they owe us some serious reappraisal of religious indoctrinations that lead to murder.

the original letter

Meyer Rangell apdo 167 San Miguel de Allende GTO, Mexico 37700

November 28, 1995

"IN THE MAIL"
The New Yorker
20 West 43rd. Street
New York, New York 10036

Dear Sirs:

Your coverage of the Rabin assassination by Michael Walzer, David Remnick and Amy Wilentz (Nov. 20), although wide-ranging, failed to address the central issue that this heinous murder catapulted to the forefront: that is the nexus between religion and violence. When will serious thought, study and exploration be addressed to the question of killing "in the name of God"? From Jim Jones in Guyana, David Koresh in Waco, Baruch Goldstein in Hebron, to Yigal Amir in Jerusalem, not to mention the "holy wars" of Hezbollah and Hamas, and Meier Kahane's Kach, killing "in the name of God" has become an apologia that threatens the maintenance of ordered society.

Do not the official bastions of organized religion, of all faiths, bear at least some responsibility when the outcome of religious zealotry is wanton death and destruction, when belief in "God" becomes a license to kill?

Is it enough to plead "insanity", the loss of reason? But it is precisely religious indoctrination and proselytism that undermine reason as they inculcate Faith. When the result is that Faith is chosen as superior to Reason, should it surprise us that Reason is often abandoned, or lost?

Religious authorities owe more than lame excuses of "lone killers" and "fanatics." They owe us some serious re-appraisal of the consequences of a religious indoctrination that leads to and justifies murder and that threatens the secular, social fabric within which we all must live.

January 17, 1996
Hillary Comes Under Safire
Mexico City Times

Your article, HILLARY COMES UNDER SAFIRE, by *The Economist*, (January 13), is not only unfortunately skewed toward Mr. Safire and unfairly snide toward Mrs. Clinton, but misses the general tone of slander and vituperation in Safire's allegations.

As you state: "Mr. Safire is a distinguished columnist, regular commentator on language, lexicographer of American politics . . . he of all people picks his words carefully." It is all the more reprehensible that such a language expert, such a careful chooser of words, should call Mrs. Clinton a "congenital liar"! Not just a "liar," but a "congenital" liar. In so doing, Safire descends to the level of the unspeakable Speaker of the House when he (Newt Gingrich) called Mrs. Clinton a "bitch."

Mr. Gingrich never denied nor expressed regret for his gutter expression, and now Mr. Safire similarly revels in the shock value of his vulgarity and intemperance.

Webster's New Collegiate Dictionary, 2nd. Edition, defines "congenital" as "existing at, or dating from, birth . . . acquired during development in the uterus . . ."

Although Mr. Safire may have established himself as a pre-eminent logodaedalian he hardly qualifies either as a prenatal pathologist or as a psychiatric diagnostician. When this careful chooser of words sloppily attempts medical etiology with respect to his target, Mrs. Clinton, he abandons legitimate criticism and embraces the viciousness of deliberate slander.

As to the facts he adduces to substantiate his shrill, frenetic outburst, Safire adds nothing new to the well-publicized interpretations and opinions of Mrs. Clinton's public and private behavior. He is entitled to his own opinions, and should stick to his style of expressing them, but he should be able to see them for what they are, "his opinions," among many. He would also do well to stick to the political model of behaviour, in which he has standing, rather than wander into the disease model with wild biological interpretations, in which he is a babe in the woods.

But Mr. Safire chose here to reveal his own bottomless animus toward this presidency and to wallow in the intellectual swill that has unfortunately characterized so many of its critics.

Bill Safire blew it this time!

January 21, 1996
U.S. Budget Battle
Mexico City—The News

Editor: Perhaps the most disgraceful episode in recent American history, perhaps, in its way, in all American history, is the recent shutting down of important sections of the government. Closed, shut down, we have no money to run, was the message!

The richest and most powerful country in the world thus presented to the world a spectacle of abject impotence, of inability to perform the essentials of governance for which its political leaders were elected. Not only was it the almost 300,000 government employees who were suddenly faced with payless weeks, (while the congressional "budgeteers" continued to receive their pay without delay!), nor the various services, from passports to college loan applications to public parks, which were suddenly not available, but the stunning realization of our people that Government, upon which we rely for stability and civic cohesiveness, can fail to meet its obligations.

Confidence in our government and in orderly process received a blow from which it may never recover.

The Republican Party and its leadership in both the House and the Senate must bear the major responsibility for this paralysis. They used the demagogic cry for "a balanced budget in seven years" as a bludgeon to force through congress their version of social policy and to blackmail the President. It's either our way, they said, on Medicaid, Welfare, Medicare, Aid to Dependent Children, or we shut down government operations. Like children who threaten to pick up their marbles and go home unless the rules of the game were changed, they eschewed the regular legislative process through which changes can be legitimately accomplished and instead used their power to fund to bring government itself to a screeching halt.

The issue, at bottom, is not the budget, or whether it can be balanced in 7 years, (or eight, or six.) The issue behind the smokescreen is the kind of governing philosophy that is best for America: A philosophy that asserts federal government responsibility for the poor, the aged, the very young, through supportive programs like Medicaid, Welfare, Medicare, Aid to Families with Dependent Children, educational encouragements and support, or the abandonment of the poor by government at the federal level, cutting down or eliminating government aid for the least advantaged among us, while giving huge tax breaks to the very rich.

President Clinton champions the former, and uses his legitimate veto power to prevent the cutting of programs for the poor. Messrs. Gingrich and Dole represent the other side, but, unable to secure that votes necessary to override a presidential veto, they resort to the tactics of the bully: we'll have our way or shut down the government!

The good news is that Gingrich and his spoilers may have finally over-stepped their limits. Latest polls show their popularity in sharp decline, as the public reacts in fear and disgust—fear of losing their safety nets in an uncertain economic climate, and disgust at the bullying tactics so nuthlessly employed.

February 4, 1996
Hopeful Sign
Mexico City—The News

Editor: One of the more hopeful signs on the political landscape was buried on the inside pages last week, and then given a welcome boost in President Clinton's State of the Union address: I refer to Senator Bill Bradley's sponsorship of a legislative package that "would give elections back to citizens" and "would free democracy from the power of money." President Clinton in his address "called for passage of bipartisan legislation that would sharply restrict the large donations that are now legal, including those to party committees that critics complain are used to skirt federal election laws." (*New York Times*, Jan. 28).

The recent phenomena of multi-million dollar campaigns for public office is a disgrace, an insult to the general electorate and a threat to fundamental democracy.

Expertise at fund-raising, or personal fortunes that permit wild spending on a barrage of media brainwashing on non-issues calculated to appeal to the emotional rather than to the rational, has become central to the process of getting elected. The real issues that confront the nation—jobs, poverty, racism, foreign policy, the protection of the less advantaged, crime and justice—take second place to the advertising skills of highly paid image makers, whose only goal is to package the candidate and to sell him, like soap or detergents or automobiles. This means money, not principle, media masters not social/political/philosophical thinkers intent on addressing the nation's problems.

In the 1994 election, a senatorial candidate in California spent 30 million dollars on his campaign. The discredited Oliver North spent 20 million dollars in his unsuccessful campaign to join the Senate, before which body he had committed the felony that brought him national fame! Even the wealthy and privileged Edward Kennedy had to take out a 2 million dollar mortgage to help his campaign for re-election. The result of his money-directed campaigning was that only 39 percent of the electorate showed up at the polls. The remaining 61 percent showed their disgust with the mud-slinging, perverse, (and expensive) 60-second TV slots by staying away from the voting booths altogether. Money may have driven the election, but a smaller number of citizens were stirred up enough to participate.

"Campaign spending this year is expected to reach a stratospheric 100 million dollars for the presidential race alone," reports the *New York Times*. In these circumstances, it is the power to invest money, or the power to raise it, that assumes more importance in the selection process than the qualities of leadership. Candidates like Arlen Spector, among others, drop out, not because of failure of will or lack of program or promise, but because they cannot meet the insurmountable financial obstacles required for the campaign. While millionaires like Steve Forbes flaunt their ability and their willingness to spend themselves into office. Legislation such as proposed by Senator Bradley, and endorsed by President Clinton, would ban large contributions by the wealthy, support a constitutional amendment to give Congress the power to limit campaign contributions and spending, and "take power away from the special interests and return it to the voters."

Something to consider and to take action on, before election fever takes hold again and turns 1996 into another exercise in mud-slinging by those rich enough to afford the luxury price, while serious thinkers are forced out by the corrupting influence of money.

At a time when a budget-minded Congress is poised to cut 250 billion dollars from programs for poor children and poor families, the spending of hundreds of millions in the election process is obscene and unconscionable. The time for reform is long overdue.

February 16, 1996
A Cowardly Attack on the Clintons
Mexico City Times

I had to read and re-read the article, "Clintons Brought To Book," (Jan. 30) three or four times to fathom why I felt annoyed at first, then irritated, and finally infuriated at what was supposed to be a book-review, but which turned out to be yet another shameful, scurrilous attack on the Clinton presidency just in time for this elections year!

Although the book, Primary Colors, showing the true color of its brave author hiding under the veil of anonymity, is presented as fiction, your reviewer presents the novelized "facts" as though they were real; not only real, but proven, acceptable and true. He slips easily into designating the characters as Bill and Hillary, rather than the fictional names used in the novel, so that the reader gets the impression that, of course, the wild charges of "obsession with women", "willingness to unzip his trousers at the slightest provocation" (!), are well known and true of the president, while Hillary is "revealed" by unimpeachable sources as "icy calm" in bed, just as she is "the woman who creates terror in the White House."

Far from any pretense of objectivity, your writer not only accepts the fiction as fact, but adds his own anti-Clinton bias, his own interpretations of the Clinton presidency, full of an animus that seems reinvigorated by the "revelations" he so happily finds in this tabloid-intended, semi-pornographic, melange of gossip, slander, vilification and character-assassination.

It is unfortunate that you nor only dignify this "expose" with so much coverage, but that you fail completely to apply the least bit of critical judgement to its contents. Instead, your writer laps it up with alacrity, as though it reinforces what he had always felt about the Clintons, and uses it as a springboard to air his own opinions and prejudices about President and Mrs. Clinton, now bolstered and supported by this no-name purveyor of abuse and scandal. The fictional novel (is this a way to avoid libel suits and the scrutiny of historical truth?) thus achieves its objectives. Who can argue with fiction? And as "fact", who is there to refute it?

If this is the kind of electioneering we can expect in the 1996 campaign, buckle your seat-belts, folks, and hold on to your hats. We are in for a wild and bumpy ride!

March 3, 1996
War Crimes
Mexico City—The News

Editor: As doubts swarm about U.N. plans to arrest and try the war criminals responsible for the atrocities, mass murders, tortures and "crimes against humanity" committed in the war in the former Yugoslavia, and as Jeane Kirkpatrick, in her column of Feb. 18, makes an impassioned plea that "War Criminals Can't Be Let Off Scot-Free," we would do well to read, or re-read "Nuremberg; Infamy on Trial," written by our own *sanmiguelense*, Joseph E. Persico.

Mr. Persico (whose recent collaboration with General Colin Powell is a national bestseller), explored in "Nuremberg," in riveting detail, the moral, historical, legal and philosophical implications of the horrors of Nazism as has no other writer before him. Who was responsible? Was the "Nuremberg defense" (I was only following orders!) legally and morally acceptable? What moral degeneracy brought ordinary human beings to plan, or to acquiesce in, or to take part in, or to actively endorse and promote the horrors of mass extermination in the camps, the brutality of the occupations of Poland, France, the Netherlands? The enslavement under inhuman conditions of 5 million foreign workers in the armament factories of Germany, the Holocaust and the "final solution"?

Hannah Arendt broke ground and coined a memorable phrase with her seminal work, "The Banality Of Evil." Joseph Persico illuminated that ground with the combined skills of historian, legal scholar, philosopher, psychologist and moralist. His book might have been accurately sub-titled, "an exploration of the anatomy of evil."

The questions Mr. Persico raised about the nature of man are still to be answered. But they provide a guideline to the problems of crime and punishment, responsibility and law, and what constitutes "civilization" even during wartime. These problems still face us today, 50 years later in the War Crimes Trial soon to come up in The Hague.

"Nuremberg" might help us to remember the lessons of the past, reminding us of the philosopher George Santayana's famous dictum: "Those who do not learn from the errors of history are doomed to repeat them!"

This might be a good time to reset our moral compass, and, in Persico's words, strive so that "Law that supercedes nations, and justice that penetrates frontiers may yet be achieved."

March 17, 1996
It Can't Happen Here
Mexico City—The News

Editor: Fifty years ago Sinclair Lewis wrote a novel called "It Can't Happen Here."

Listening to Pat Buchanan and the sorry collection of used car salesmen vying with each other in a desperate display of venal verbiage for the Republican nomination for the U.S. presidency, one cannot be that sure.

Lewis was referring of course to fascism, or to that particular variety of fascist mentality which might find root in American soil.

One is reminded of this by the character of the Republican primary debate, as a talk-show host with delusions of grandeur and a magazine publisher born with more money than he knows how to spend vie with unsuccessful politicians to fill the vacuum created by a party that has only the funereal Bob Dole to advance its interests.

In a crescendo of raucous cacophony, they play on the fears, prejudices, xenophobia, racism and sense of hopelessness that they unearth (and foster) in American life.

With a cynicism born of unbridled ambition and a yearning for power, each strives to outdo the other to exploit what they see as a vulnerable despair, which, with proper manipulation, can be turned into votes.

So we hear, preferably in the alliteration that Buchanan honed in his days as speech-writer for the infamous "unindicted co-conspirator" of Watergate, of "vital vision" and "politics of the past" and "moving America forward."

This seems by far the favorite ploy: "Get America moving!"

Where?

"Forward" of course, we must move forward, not backward, or even sideways, but forward . . . not upward or, heaven forbid, downward.

Moving "upward" is given priority mainly by Buchanan as he tries to emulate Burt Lancaster as another Sinclair Lewis immortal in "Elmer Gantry," passing the hat in his evangelical tent as he plans his getaway hustle to the next town.

Technology, of course, has improved the evangelical business mightily, so that the Christian Coalition and Pat Robertson can now use the magic of television to reach the kind of take Elmer Gantry could never even dream of.

Pat Buchanan, aware and bold, audaciously dreams that this could take him from Crossfire to the White House! While the sedate Dole promises to be "whatever you want me to be," even "Ronald Reagan."

If you like!

Such is "principle," bereft of leadership.

The only real "principle" shared by all the aspirants is the principle that asserts that what is right is what-gets-you elected.

As we enter the 21st century, America needs more than that.

It needs commitment to face our problems at home and abroad.

It needs to combat the racism that still divides us, and the poverty and disease that still afflict so many; and to establish a government that assumes more, not less responsibility, for the quality of life of our people.

The blatant demagoguery of this primary season shames us all.

March 31, 1996
Home-Grown Problem
Mexico City—The News

Editor: Your *New York Times* editorial, published in *The News* on March 8 under the title "Poor Approach To Combating The Drug Trade", did not reach the heart of the problem until the very last paragraph, when it finally conceded that "As long as the United States is the largest consumer of illegal drugs in the world, suppliers will find a way to do business here."

For years, drug officials in the United States have pointed to "foreign suppliers" as the villains, as they expended millions of dollars in eradication of crops in other countries, erected barriers at points of entry, and lambasted the "foreign cartels", while paying lip service to the problem of reducing the demand at home through prevention, treatment, rehabilitation and basic research. Predictably, drug usage has shown little change through a succession of drug "czars" whose emphasis remained consistent: more prisons, more arrests of low-level pushers, little success in apprehending the real drug lords in the United States, (drug cartels were always in foreign countries!), and no real effort to change the prevailing drug culture in our neighborhoods and in our society.

Another report cogently states that "The street value of cocaine consumed in the United States adds up to 36.5 billion dollars a year. Of that, only 10 billion dollars returns to the producing countries. The lion's share stays in the United States."

But to our "drug czars" the villains are still abroad and, in today's issue of *The News* there is still the headline! "Republicans Seek Reversal Of Anti-Drug Certification", as Sen. Alfonse D' Amato and others poison our foreign policy as they continue to try to punish Mexico for what is essentially an American home-grown problem.

Yesterday still another drug czar was sworn in (why do we still call that important official a "czar", the only office in the country to use that hated reference to tyranny?), who stated that the United States "will not arrest our way out of the drug challenge". But there is still little indication that the arrest/punishment/prison regimens of past "czars" will be replaced by serious efforts to study and research the problem of the addictive personality and the addicted society that provides the culture within which he flourishes.

Until prevention, treatment, research and rehabilitation take the place of "blame the foreign cartels" in the formulation of our anti-drug policies, drug "czars" will come and go, but the problems of an over-narcotized society will still be with us.

"Peanuts" once said "We have met the enemy and it is us!"—an insight that has eluded a succession of powerful "czars"

April 7, 1996
Pundits' Trifecta
Mexico City—The News

Editor: In his column of March 15, "Three Shaky World Leaders," William Safire pulls his rank as Pundit Extraordinaire with a bold foray into the perils of political prognostication, as he bets on the defeat this year of Shimon Peres, Boris Yeltsin and Bill Clinton. It is difficult to tell whether this is a result of his special crystal ball, or simply an exercise in wishful thinking (none of the above are particular favorites of Mr. Safire!) In any case, I hope that he did not bet the family farm on his "Pundits' Trifecta". May I offer a trifecta on my own, based in part on analysis and, in part, I admit, on hope, because I think that the victory of all three will offer more hope for a better and a safer world.

Peters will win in Israel, despite the devastating effect of the Hamas murders and terror, because Israelis will, when the chips are down, support the difficult path of peace pioneered by their martyred leader, Yitzhak Rabin, rather than return to the policies of confrontation and war. By a narrow margin, perhaps, they will vote for a possible peace in the future, rather than for perpetual war.

In Russia, Yeltsin will win, because the Russian people are determined not to return to the terror and tyranny of communist rule, but are also fearful of the crime and anarchy brought on by the unfettered introduction of a free market economy. They will vote for the centrist position represented by Yeltsin, in the hope of retaining some of the advantages of the previous economy—job security, health benefits, education—without taking the risks inherent in the right-wing extremists' wild swings. Gorbachev had his chance and missed it. He won't make a dent.

In the United States Bill Clinton will be re-elected, also perhaps by a narrow margin, because the Republicans revealed themselves in the primaries as without credible, not to mention charismatic, leaders, and will be seen by most voters as endangering the safety net in social security, health care and education that is clearly associated in the public's mind with Democratic politics.

Of course, Safire hedges his bet with the caveat that if his predictions prove wrong, it is because "in presidential politics, hands across the sea can wash each other." I suggest, on the other hand, that if I am right, it is because the people in all three countries see their safety and their future better served by thoughtful centrist politics

385

driven by domestic needs in the interest of the daily trials and tribulations of the majority.

It will be an interesting year!

June 29, 1996
Why Israel turned to Likud
The Times Herald Record

The two most significant facts that emerge from the Israeli elections, not sufficiently explicated in the press, are:

One: the indisputable fact that Israel stands out as the only state in the Middle East that has a vibrant democracy. Such a democracy provides an elected leadership that must be accountable to its people and that provides a forum for the conflicting agendas of a multi-diverse population. Clearly, Israel is the only state in the Middle East to provide this!

Two: The election was, in the final analysis, determined by a foreign player, Yasser Arafat, whose inability to restrain the thugs of Hamas and Hezbollah, as well as his failure to apprehend and punish them after their murderous sorties into Israel, provided the razor-thin margin with which a security-conscious Israeli electorate turned to Likud. As Conor Cruise O'Brien, a persuasive United Nations presence, and author of the highly regarded "The Siege: The Saga of Israel and Zionism," put it (New York Times, June 5) "Mr. Arafat has shown that he cannot deliver peace because he cannot control the armed Islamic factions that regard themselves at war with Israel."

In this climate, fear and distrust won out over that mutual trust that needs to be established before true co-existence between Israel and its neighbors can become a reality. The PLO and its Arab allies still fail to provide that peace-leadership that can match their Israeli counterparts. Only in this context can the victory of Benjamin Netanyahu be understood.

July 1, 1996
Letter to the Editor
The New York Times

Francis X. Clines' excellent article (It's a War of Words (Say What?, 6/30) is witty and informative in his examination of "Clintonspeak vs. Dolespeak", but in all fairness he ought to acknowledge that his forerunner in this type of endeavor is George Orwell, to whom we owe the earliest analysis of the political phenomena of "doublethink", and of the use of language for political obfuscation.

"Doublethink," Orwell wrote, "means the power of holding two contradictory beliefs in one's mind simultaneously, and accepting both of them" (In "1984").

Before "Clintonspeak" and "Dolespeak", there was "Newspeak": In his shattering novel, "1984", Orwell wrote that "Newspeak (the official language) was designed not to extend but to diminish the range of thought . . . . the special function of certain Newspeak words . . . was not so much to express meanings but to destroy them . . . . ultimately it was hoped to make articulate speech issue from the larynx without involving the higher brain cells at all"! Thus, the weight of political authority could convince people that "War is Peace, Freedom is Slavery, and Ignorance is Strength."

Even prior to "1984", in a celebrated essay titled "Politics and the English Language" (1946), Orwell wrote that "Political language . . . is designed to make lies sound truthful and murder respectable, and to give an appearance of solidity to pure wind." Fifty years later, alas, how those words ring true! And what an army of ghost-writers and speech-writers and speech-consultants are now being so munificently employed to assist the politician (who is assumed to be an incompetent mumble-mouth without such help), to give a speech that "if it can't be electrifying, must at least not be stultifying and, above all, must be revealing of the speaker's human identity." Imagine that! "The speaker's human identity" is the goal, not of the speaker, but of his hired flack.

George Orwell, where are you when we need you?

July 17, 1996
Letter to the Editor
The New York Times Book Review

Wendy Lesser's problem with "The T. S. Eliot Problem" (Book Review, 7/14) is that she is sucked into the kind of verbose, turgid, prose that characterizes the tug-of-war among the literati who pontificate endlessly on the significance of the anti-Semitic writings of Eliot (as well as his revered colleague-in-anti-semitism, Ezra Pound). "Is it ART?," they adoringly ask. And if so, is not their anti-Semitic garbage someone else's fault, or the fault of the society in which they live? They are artists, after all! And "Is it ever possible for good art to have evil meanings, or intentions, or results?" Who's kidding whom?

Ockham's razor propounds that the simpler and shorter answer to a problem is probably the best. The fact is that Eliot and Pound wrote vile, filthy anti-Semitic stuff. Did they lead to the death camps? Of course they did, in the sense that they contributed to the moral and philosophic climate in which the death camps and "final solutions" were thinkable and made possible.

Eliot helped provide the Jewish stereotype with which Julius Streicher later poisoned a nation.

Pound propagandized for Mussolini at the very moment American boys were dying on the beaches at Anzio.

So why need we agonize over whether Pound's cantos were ART, and stretch literary criticism and intellectuality and ethics to the breaking point to "understand" Eliot's vile outpourings? Modern, post-Holocaust, posturing logodaedelians must surely have better things to do than cudgeling their brains over the supposed tendency of "Jewish readers to tolerate (Eliot's) insults in order to get what they could from the work." After Auschwitz and Dachau it is simply obscene to speculate whether Eliot's (and Pound's) poetry was "ART" or the deadly plantings of fascist seed.

July 28, 1996
Safire needs a new crystal ball
Sunday Record

This is to duly record that, with the victory of Boris Yeltsin in Russia, William Safire has lost his "Pundit's Trifecta," boldly put forward in his column of March 15, in which he predicted the defeat of Peres in Israel. Yeltsin in Russia and Bill Clinton this November in the United States.

Safire's loudly professed partisan opinions clearly indicated that his bet was based more on wish-fulfillment, and in particular on his animus toward the Clinton administration, rather than on any special qualities of his crystal ball.

He was not merely predicting, in fact he was rooting for, the defeat of all three, whom he characterized as "running mates," and suggested that "the weakness of any one of them (will) drag down the other two." His transparent goal, of course, was to saddle Clinton with responsibility for the outcome of the other two elections. If Peres and Yeltsin won, it would be because of Clinton, nefariously and wrongly, supporting them. If they lost, Clinton would also be a loser and go down with them.

History, however, defeated Safire's propaganda ploy. Peres lost by a razor-thin margin because the Israeli voters were more influenced by Yasser Arafat's potential threat than by President Clinton. And Yeltsin won because the Russians voted on purely domestic issues, refusing to return to the tyranny of a discredited Communist Party. In both cases, Clinton's supposed influence took second place to domestic concerns.

William Safire was wrong on both counts.

August 2, 1996
Where Is Our Political Courage on Health Care?
The New York Times

"Finally, a Health Bill" (editorial, July 27) indicates that the noble efforts of President Clinton (and intensive explorations of Hillary Rodham Clinton) in 1993 to achieve universal health care for Americans ended as his "greatest legislative fiasco."

Note, however, that the almost total victory of commercial interests over considerations of public health is revealed in the fact that universal health care, and its possibilities under what was known as the single-payer plan, does not merit a mention in today's climate, or in your editorial.

You stress that legislation should not harm "the insurance market," that insurers remain profitable. Just look at what has disappeared from the debate: the possibility that health care might be addressed by government itself, supported by general tax revenue instead of by "inflated premiums" that enrich executives and stockholders; and the idea that the health of the people is as much a moral responsibility of government as the maintenance of a public defense establishment, public schools or a public criminal-justice system.

August 3, 1996
Bosnia's disgraceful farce
The Times Herald Record

It boggles the mind that Mike Wallace can walk calmly and without challenge into the office of the indicted war-criminal Radovan Karadicz, interview him without any apparent restrictions, give him a worldwide audience to plead his case (in the face of seemingly overwhelming evidence of rape, torture and murder), while all the power and authority of the War Crimes Tribunal at The Hague are thwarted in their attempts to bring him to trial. If he refuses to turn himself in voluntarily, or the government he controls at Pale, Bosnia, refuses, he can, apparently, walk free, thumb his nose at the international community, and make a mockery of the U.N. proceedings.

It is as though the trial at Nuremberg, which established the legal and moral precedent of "crimes against humanity," depended on the acquiescence and cooperation of Goering, Streicher, Jodl, Hess and the rest of the Nazi butchers. If Hitler had survived his last bunker and controlled a small piece of Germany with loyal supporters, would the Allies have courteously waited until he deigned to present himself for trial?

How long can the United States and NATO and the U.N. itself continue this disgraceful farce? The arrest of the indicted war criminals, Radovan Karadzic and Gen. Ratko Mladic, is a moral imperative, a vindication (or an abandonment) of the principles established at Nuremberg, and a challenge to the conscience of the world.

August 21, 1996
Letter to the Editor
The New York Times

Regarding William Safire's "San Diego Speech Scorecard" (column, Aug. 19), how could a first-rate logo-daedalian overlook the week's most egregious oxymoron; Gov. George E. Pataki's praise for what he called Jack Kemp's "progressive conservatism"? A visit to Webster might have deterred the Governor from sacrificing linguistic integrity to political expediency.

September 13, 1996
Gov. Pataki needs a wordsmith
The Times Herald Record

Gov. George E. Pataki is surely the hands-down winner of the Oxymoron of the Month competition with his fulsome praise of Jack Kemp's "progressive conservatism" (!) at the Republican Convention. He would have done well to consult Noah Webster first before he sacrificed linguistic integrity for political expediency.

August 9, 1996
Tax Exempt Property to Blame
Sullivan County Democrat

On the same page in your edition of August 2, Assemblyman Jake Gunther is featured as sponsoring a bill to provide "much needed tax relief" for Sullivan County homeowners while State Senator Charles D. Cook is pictured as he offers his "School Property Tax Reduction Act" to Governor Pataki.

Although both these legislators recognize, and are quick to blame, the "lost tax dollars on tax-exempt property" which is a major factor in our ever-increasing tax burden, neither pays any attention to an important area of tax exemptions that puts a crimp in our tax picture:

I refer to the exemptions from real property taxes on billions of dollars of real property owned by religious organizations in New York State (and, indeed, around the country). These exemptions, while benefitting the religious propensities of a portion of our people, cause the tax rate for the entire population, religious or otherwise, to soar in order to make up for the tax revenue lost.

A recent report issued by the New York Board of Real Property Services, titled "Exemptions from Real Property Taxes in New York State," may not make the most exciting reading, nor will it make the New York Times bestseller list, but its dense statistical tables, carefully studied, provide some nuggets of information relevant to our problem. The latest report, issued May, 1995, covers the year 1993, and reveals the following:

In New York State, real property held by religious organizations, a total of 22,367 parcels, is valued at $13,774,594,000. These holdings are almost completely exempt from the property tax (97.23 percent).

In addition, 4,353 "clergy residences," valued at $4,018,274,000 enjoy tax exemptions of over half (55.35 percent) their value (What other class of workers, professional or otherwise, one might ask, enjoy such tax privileged homes?)

In Sullivan County, the same report tells us, 387 parcels of real estate valued at $113,208,000 are almost completely exempt from taxes (99.65 percent) while 22 parcels of "clergy residences" valued at $1,883,000 receive 100 percent exemptions!

Billions of dollars of tax frees, we are informed, shift the burden of community taxes to all the taxpayers, forcing the public to pay for the private views of the religious.

Aside from the vexing question of constitutionality (do not religious tax exemptions violate, in spirit if not in letter, the Establishment Clause of the Bill of Rights First

Amendment and the principle of separation of Church and State by favoring so egregiously the religious taxpayer over the free-thinking or non-religious?), it is the shifting of this tax-burden from the exempt group onto the backs of the general taxpayer that results in the enormous increase in taxes that overburdens our average homeowner, particularly here in Sullivan County where so many live on fixed incomes, or, are dependent on Social Security.

Although the necessary long-range tax changes can be made only in Albany, where budget negotiations were unconscionably delayed this year at additional costs to the taxpayers, religious organizations can, under existing law, make voluntary contributions from their tax-exempt bonanzas by paying PILT (Payment In Lieu of Taxes). It would be only fair to all the other taxpayers that they do. (In his recent letter to his constituents, our Assemblyman Jake Gunther alerts us to budget cuts planned by Governor Pataki in health care, but makes no mention of the revenue lost by the unfair property tax exemptions.)

Our forefathers fought a revolution because they thought that "Taxation Without Representation" was wrong. It is ironic that the religious establishment and its constituents today demand and get, representation without taxation.

Tax reform to correct the inequity whereby the general taxpayer is forced to subsidize the religious community is long overdue.

Should not the social good, and public need, take preference over private religiosity?

September 20, 1996
Religious Exemptions Going Up
Sullivan County Democrat

 In his letter of September 10, Senator Charles D. Cook proudly puts forward, once again, his "School Property Tax Reduction Act," which would have the staggering effect, if passed, of reducing our local school tax "by an average of 5%!" This is supposed to bring joy to the hearts of our over-burdened county taxpayers as they receive still another increase in their school tax bill for the coming year.

 Although he pays lip service to the concept of tax reform ("The existing inequitable system used to fund local schools is no longer practical or acceptable," he writes), Senator Cook totally ignores the inequitable (and arguably unconstitutional) tax exemptions, detailed in my recent letter of August 9, given to the religious establishment, which are a significant factor in the total picture of tax revenues versus tax requirements.

 Since my last writing, "Tax Exempt Property to Blame," (Democrat, August 9), I have received the latest report of the New York State Board of Real Property Services, titled "Exemptions From Real Property Taxation in New York State," issued June 1996 for the year 1994. This informs us that religiously-held real property in Sullivan County reached $115 million, up almost $2 million from the previous year. Thus, our tax loss through exemptions goes up; our tax liability goes up proportionately. Incidentally, "clergy residences" in Sullivan County, listed at $1.8 million, receive a 100% exemption, while the state-wide exemption is only 55 percent. Why, when every penny counts?

 Assemblyman Jake Gunther wrote (Democrat, 8/2), that an important tax issue resides in the fact "that Sullivan County residents have been making up for the lost tax dollars on tax-exempt property," but he, along with Sen. Cook and our other legislators, assiduously avoid the issue of the tax bonanzas enjoyed by the religious establishment at the expense of the taxpayer at large. With state-wide religious exemptions at a level of $15 billion, this is no small matter.

October 20, 1996
Safire showed his true colors
Sunday Record

In his column of September 19 (in Other Voices), William Safire gamely adheres to the ancient Latin "dictum, NIHIL NISI BONUM DE MORTUIS" (say nothing but good about the dead) as he reminisces about Spiro Agnew. In fact, he leans so far backward in his defense of the crooked, small-time pol turned national figure by that other examplar, Richard Nixon, that he not only loses his equilibrium but falls flat on his face. It is one thing to be kind to the dead, but quite another to rationalize the deleterious impact that Agnew had on the political scene at a crucial moment in our history. He was a corrupt governor, a sleazy bribe-taker (his plea of "nolo condere" was a tacit admission of guilt) and a disgraced vice-president. He sullied political discourse with an irresponsibility seldom seen in high office, and set a tone of shameful rhetoric that was not only an embarrassment but a dangerous example of the depths to which demagoguery and bigotry can reach.

Perhaps there is no small amount of self-serving here on Safire's part, for was it not Safire himself who penned the words, "nattering nabobs of negativism," among others, with which Agnew attempted to cover his own uncouthness as he viciously attacked the liberals of his day? Now Safire refers to this shameless crook as a "personable partisan" and "a thoughtful controversialist!" Safire reached a low point, finally, when he snidely compared the corrupt and felonious Agnew with the current president of the United States. Thus does the unbridled Safire hone his serpent's tooth on both the past and the present in order to preserve his own prejudices.

October 2, 1996
Letter to the Editor
New York Times Book Review

William Julius Wilson, we are informed (WHEN WORK DISAPPEARS, review 9/29) has discovered, or should it be re-discovered, what welfare workers have known for at least fifty years: that continued joblessness results in a loss of self-esteem, from which many never recover, a deterioration of family life, and a consequent social disorganization that destroys communities and neighborhoods. Caseworkers in New York's Home Relief Bureau in the thirties, the precursor of the Welfare Department, understood this basic as a given, and concentrated on the re-employment, as soon as possible, of the breadwinner in the family, recognizing that the crucial element in the family's rehabilitation was the restoration of the self respect that goes with holding down a job.

We knew then what is now presented as a remarkable new discovery, that "the real problem . . . is not that poor people don't want to work. It's that no work is available". True in the thirties; still true in the nineties. We seem always to be re-discovering the wheel!

Those whose memories are long enough will recall that the much-maligned WPA performed miracles in restoring individual faith and self-reliance, while at the same time producing lasting values for the community. It is to Prof. Wilson's credit that he now proposes similar remedies. Sometimes, we can actually learn from the past.

December 8, 1996
Cancer Of Violence
Mexico City—The News

Editor: Howard Kleinberg's article on the Holocaust, ("So Just When Did It Begin?" Nov. 28) serves an important and timely purpose by keeping before the conscience of the world the most heinous crime in modern history.

But the emphasis of the piece ("What did you know and when did you know it?"), as applied to the people and the governments of the civilized world, is secondary, it seems to me, to the more significant inquiry: What was the environment, the milieu— the social, political, economic, philosophic, religious soil—which nurtured the moral degeneracy from which the Holocaust grew?

What was the nature of the society that permitted an entire nation to stand by, acquiesce or participate in a crime so unthinkable that even now, 50 years later, ordinary people as well as trained scholars are at a loss to "explain" it? How could the official leadership of a modern civilized nation concoct a plan which boggles the mind and the conscience, a plan to systematically exterminate Europe's 10 million Jews? And how could the rest of the world, and the governments of the Allied coalition, stand by and permit it to achieve three fifths of its goal, killing 6 out of 10 million European Jews before the slaughter was ended?

Mr. Kleinberg confirms once again that the "final solution" was conceived and adopted as Nazi policy as early as 1938; that "the British, the United States and most of the world knew of escalating Nazi atrocities against Jews well before September 1941." But no action was taken by the Allies, such as the bombing of the railroad tracks to the extermination camps, as was urged by many, to prevent the ongoing slaughter.

The deepest questions remain, not only for those who committed or acquiesced in the crime, but for the rest of the world to ponder, examine and try to understand.

Why is this important now? Because, as the philosopher George Santayana stated in his famous observation, "Those who do not learn from the errors of history are doomed to repeat them."

The violence and killing derived from racism, religious intolerance, bigotry and chauvinism, still manifest themselves all over the world. The horrors of genocide and racial and religious violence are still very much with us: In Rwanda, where 800,000 people were killed in just 100 days; in Ireland where the killing of Protestant-Catholic adversaries continue year after bloody year; in Bosnia, where Serbian massacres of

Muslims in an orgy of "ethnic cleansing" has gone on relentlessly, with only a pathetic and ineffectual U.N. effort to stop it. (The major criminals are still at large, although we all know where they are, while an underling is at last found guilty and sentenced to 10 years in prison by the International War Crimes Tribunal at the Hague for the most ghastly crimes of murder and torture!)

A serious and multi-disciplinary study of the Holocaust, its genesis and its lessons for mankind, is the only way to confront the issues which it poses.

As we enter the 21st century, we still carry the cancer of violence that plagues man and threatens to destroy us. In the years ahead, our best brains in every field—in philosophy, science, psychology, medicine, biology, statesmanship, religion—must be harnessed to find paths to replace the racism and bigotry and intolerance that lie at the root of mass aggression and violence, and strive to make the next century, at long last, the one in which we realize man's dream of peaceful coexistence and harmony.

December 15, 1996
Set Of Beliefs
Mexico City—The News

Editor: In his article, "Germany Responsible For Its Own History" (Dec. 7), reviewing the penetrating work of Daniel Goldhagen, William Pfaff curiously does not mention the revealing and instructive name of Goldhagen's book, "Hitler's Willing Executioners: Ordinary Germans and the Holocaust".

Goldhagen's thesis, as Mr. Pfaff points out, was that "German society was itself, long before Hitler, dominated by an 'eliminationist anti-Semitism', and that Hitler merely authorized the Germans to do what they wanted to do, and had long been waiting to do." Mr. Pfaff also refers to the Goldhagen theme that "factors in German civilization itself were responsible for the crime of the Holocaust." But he fails to explicate just what those factors were, or to suggest where we might look for them.

Mr. Goldhagen himself, in a letter to the *New York Times* written coincidentally at almost the same moment (Dec. 8) stated that "it was a set of beliefs about Jews that was at the root of Germans' willingness to kill Jews . . ." But he also failed to address the origin of that "set of beliefs", where it came from, where its roots were.

Why is there such an avoidance of the seminal role played by the dominant religious establishments in the creation of the "set of beliefs" Mr. Goldhagen refers to? Was it not the accumulation of religious indoctrination, religious propaganda, religious lies about Jews that created that "set of beliefs", and with it the moral environment within which the unspeakable crimes of the Holocaust became possible?

Where else did this "set of beliefs about Jews" spring from? Indeed, where else could it spring from?

For one cogent answer we might look to the electrifying work, "The War Against the Jews, 1933-1945", by Lucy S. Davidowicz, who casts a scholar's unsentimental eye on Germany's unsavory anti-Semitic past: She writes: "A line of anti-Semitic descent from Martin Luther to Adolph Hitler is easy to draw . . ." "Know, Christian," wrote Luther, "that next to the devil thou hast no enemy more cruel, more venomous and violent than a true Jew."

"German anti-Semitism," Davidowicz writes further, "drew part of its sustenance from Christian anti-Semitism, whose foundation had been laid by the Catholic Church, and upon which Luther built . . . Modern German anti-Semitism was the bastard child of the union of Christian anti-Semitism with German nationalism."

To avoid this look into historical antecedents is to limit fatally any understanding of the Holocaust. "The national problem," Mr. Pfaff states, "has to be dealt with." And Mr. Goldhagen writes in his *Times* letter that "these beliefs (about Jews) are no longer dominant in Germany"—an optimism many will take with a large grain of salt, especially as long as the sources of those beliefs, and their continued influence, remain uninspected and largely papered over.

December 22, 1996
Prophet
Mexico City—The News

Editor: I always enjoy reading Meyer Rangell's letters, but at times he is like a prophet. He predicted the foolishness of the government policy on the lack of Medicare for residents in Mexico, who pay taxes. This last year, my mother, who is 92, visited me here and got a slight case of asthma. I wanted her to check into one of our excellent hospitals here at my expense but she found out she didn't have Medicare here so she went back to San Antonio.

I was stunned by what happened next. The charges were outrageous. Once when I was with her, a man came by and asked, "How was the food?" She answered, "Terrible!" He said, "It's just hospital food," and left. She was charged 85 dollars for that as he is the dietician. She complained about the padding and was asked by the hospital administrator, "What are you upset about? You don't pay for it." She said, "But I did, I pay taxes." The episode cost 40,000 dollars to the taxpayers and would have cost 3,000 dollars maximum here in Mexico.

Meyer was so right, but he did make one mistake: Mentioned in his letter was something about "honest politicians;" that's oxymoronic. Keep up the excellent letters, Meyer.

JOE STEWART
Mexico City

December 19, 1996
Obscene
Mexico City—The News

Editor: What could be more obscene and revolting in the aftermath of the ultimate obscenity of the Holocaust than the recent revelations that Swiss banks "had profited from business with gold plundered by Nazi Germany," as reported in *The News* of Dec. 14?

It is as though the conscience of the world, saturated by the evil of the concentration camps and the moral dimensions of the "final solution" can receive this bit of grisly information with a degree of equanimity that places it in a brief *AP* news item, obscurely, on an inside page. It is no longer real, front-page news, even as we note the 50th anniversary of the liberation of the camps and the defeat of the Nazi monstrosity. The conscience of the world can stand just so much.

While Jean-Pierre Roth, vice president of the central bank, admitted that "the bank made an estimated 20 million Swiss francs profit from its dealings with the German central bank during the World War 11 years," and "the Germans did rob gold from the countries it occupied and transferred it to the Swiss central bank," he denies that "gold from concentration camps was among this"!

Jewish groups document however that the Swiss still hold 7 billion in assets and interest belonging to Holocaust victims.

Although nothing can erase the depths of depravity of the crime, or atone in any way, or satisfy the descendants of the victims, the spectacle of bank authorities, 50 years later, still hiding the plunder of the marauding Nazi criminals should be too much for a society that would call itself civilized to bear. Our conscience should not be hobbled by a statute of limitations.

December 29, 1996
Indecent Proposal
Mexico City—The News

In his column of Dec. 22, "Churches Evading Responsibility for the Poor," Cal Thomas seems to be advocating a kinder, more socially conscious posture on the part of churches, (a position with which it is hard to disagree), but beneath this noble sentiment lies a dangerous and retrograde attack on the role and the responsibility of government, at the federal, state, and local levels to fight poverty and to institute programs for the welfare of the least advantaged among us.

The history of the development of the welfare system in the United States, and indeed in Western Europe as well, is the story of the gradual recognition that the victims of economic depression, the unemployed and under-employed, the aged and the sick, the disabled and the unemployable, the children in families without a viable wage-earner, cannot be assisted and cared for by the private sector, the religious establishment included.

If Mr. Thomas is inclined to quote Charles Dickens, he would do better to refer to the miserable conditions of the poor in Oliver Twist, and other works, where the plight of the poor thrown to the mercy of private charity was amply, and not so favorably, described.

With the recognition during the Great Depression that social responsibility for the poor was a legitimate, if not an urgent, problem for the government, which alone had the resources to meet a problem of such magnitude, the moral, as well as the financial obligation, shifted from the private sector. Indeed it could be said that this shift took place precisely because it had become abundantly clear that the private sector, including the religious establishment, could not and would not adequately meet the challenge. Soup kitchens and shelters in church basements could not meet the needs of the millions of deprived families, or the homeless, or the unemployed. They couldn't during the Depression; they cannot now.

It is ironic that Mr. Thomas supports the federal and state governments' "reducing their levels of welfare funding," the most egregious mistake of the Clinton Administration without even addressing the problem of where the churches are supposed to get the funding to take up this tremendous responsibility. From their members? Or does Mr. Thomas suggest that federal funds be channeled through the churches? The first is quixotic and impossible. The second is simply wrong, violating the principle of separation of church and state and placing a social set of secular problems in the hands of clergymen with their own agendas, and without any professional expertise in social welfare.

Returning welfare to the churches is to take a step backwards. The answer to the needs of the poor is to further develop public policies, under government auspices, that would alleviate the hardships of unemployment, train the employable for entrance into new job markets, and make provisions for the aged, the sick, and children. A decent sense of morality demands no less.

January 5, 1997
New Year's Message
Mexico City—The News

Editor: It is that time of year again: when prophets and pundits are wont to pontificate and prognosticate; time for the 10-best lists made so popular by comedians and mass circulation magazines; especially this year as we head into the penultimate years of the 20th century and look ahead to the next millennium . . .

What is our "wish list" as we end this century and prepare for the next?

Here is mine: I wish that

1. man bends every energy and all his finest resources of hand and brain to find an answer to the scourge of war ending the most evil aspect of our social existence at the end of this, the most murderous century in history.
2. man makes a beginning toward solving the problem of violence on all levels: personal violence, group violence, religious violence, national violence, terrorism, the violence of racism and persecution, rape and sexual violence.
3. man takes effective steps to solve the world's hunger problem. In an era when technology can put a man on the moon, and explore the planets, we still tolerate widespread deprivation and hunger on Earth. The World Bank reports that "700 million of the world's 5.6 billion people face endemic hunger", while "1.3 billion people live in poverty."
4. we heed the plight of millions of children around the world, who suffer starvation, disease, malnutrition and exploitation. The International Labor Organization reports that 400 million children work worldwide, under abysmal conditions, deprived of care, of education and of childhood itself. Child labor is an international obscenity!
5. we give the highest priority to the study of diseases and their cure, rather than to developing further the techniques of mass murder and destruction. The removal of the crushing burden of armaments which now consumes the largest portion of our national budget at home and in governments around the globe, could open the way to a new renaissance of study, research and achievement in fields that benefit mankind rather than threaten to destroy him.
6. we finally pay more to expert scholars, scientists, educators, philosophers and leaders in the field of democratic government, than we do to "experts" who can

throw a basketball into an elevated hoop, or place a little ball in a hole with a special stick.
7. we develop a value system that places personal morality and responsibility above the unbridled accumulation of wealth.
8. we build a society in which ethical values supercede personal greed. The good of the many must finally be of greater concern than the "success" of the few.
9. we heed the dictum of Edmund Burke when he warned that "all that is necessary for the success of evil is that good men remain silent," and, finally,
10. good men, and women, vow never again to remain silent in the face of evil.

January 19, 1997
Congratulations
Mexico City—The News

Editor: Congratulations to William Pfaff on his powerful article, "Time To Eliminate All Nuclear Weapons" in today's paper. It is not only timely; it is long overdue!

Mr. Pfaff's argumentation is persuasive and beyond refutation. The sad thing is that nuclear weapons have piled up obscenely even after the end of the Cold War, even after it had become clear to military analysts around the world that its "rational employment" was an oxymoron, a delusionary impossibility reminiscent only of a Dr. Strangelove, that none of the world's problems could be solved by nuclear explosions.

The recent call by General George Lee Butler, former head of the Strategic Air Command, and 60 other retired officers for total nuclear disarmament should be the number one priority of our government and of our new secretary of State, Madeleine Albright.

The upcoming hearings for confirmation in the Senate of Ms. Albright's nomination would be a wonderful opportunity for her to articulate this goal, and to build up support for its realization.

In this connection, we should also be in the front ranks of those who work for the strengthening of the United Nations, both as a moral force in the world and as an instrument through which international support for nuclear disarmament can be achieved. This might also be the time for the United States to quit undermining the only world community that has a chance, and to finally pay its dues, now over a billion dollars! Our failure to do so has long been an international disgrace.

The new State Department under Madeleine Albright ought to give the United Nations the support it requires, make nuclear disarmament its first priority, and in so doing, re-establish our moral authority around the world.

January 26, 1997
Fib Or Lie?
Mexico City—The News

Editor: Doesn't Tony Snow read the papers? In discussing the case of Newt Gingrich in today's column, Mr. Snow writes as though he is totally unaware of the gravity of the charges against the erring speaker, describing the case against him as based on the fact that he had "fibbed about something important!"

Thus does Mr. Snow obfuscate the issue by a semantic ploy: Gingrich only "fibbed," (fib is "a falsehood concerning a trivial matter," according to Webster). The consistent Snow, ever loyal to his right wing constituency, simply could not bring himself to say that his disgraced, amoral idol, had *lied*. Not simply fibbed, or committed a peccadillo, but *lied* to the Ethics Committee, to the Congress and to the American people, as he pursued his ruthless program of self-advancement and raw political ambition by any and all means at hand.

One doesn't have to have inside information on this matter. A day before Snow's column, we were all informed in *The News* of Jan. 22 that Mr. Gingrich's Republican House had voted by a stunning majority of 395 to 28 to reprimand the speaker and to fine him 300,000 dollars! It is significant that 195 Republicans voted in favor of this punishment. Hardly the reaction to a simple "fib," or a minor peccadillo.

The facts, as everyone who reads the papers knew were that Gingrich cheated on taxes to the extent of 1,660,000 dollars, in order to elect Republicans, and in the process to advance his own heady ambitions.

In the end, even his Republican colleagues could not stomach it and deserted him.

But not the ever-loyal Tony Snow. To him, it was all about a negligible "fib," as he used his column to defend the liar and to attack and defame Bonior and those who blew the whistle and produced the truth.

That Gingrich was allowed to remain as speaker speaks volumes about the state of morality in American politics.

February 2, 1997
Who Needs Enemies
Mexico City—The News

Editor: If President Clinton read William Safire's "Preserve, Protect, Defend" column on Jan. 24, I can see him muttering, with reason, "With friends like Safire, who needs enemies?"

In a burst of patriotic "chauvinism" (his own word), Mr. Safire comes to the defense of Clinton's Inaugural Address against the attack in Britain's *Daily Telegraph*, which had called it "banal". In a classic example of damning with faint praise, Safire countered the *Telegraph* by stating, "Banal it was not," then describing the address as "a respectable effort, forcefully delivered."

Having thus chided the *Telegraph*, Safire feels free to return to the calumnies of the election campaign: the president was "a demagogue . . ." a "rental agent of the Lincoln bedroom . . ." "he paid more than the usual obeisance to the black community . . ." "the second Clinton term will reveal the tawdry secrets of the first," ad nauseam, as he rushed to supply the *Telegraph* with ammunition the British public might have missed!

Give us a break, Bill! The election is over. The American people chose Bill Clinton over the slanders of Bob Dole and the rantings of Newt Gingrich, whose own Republican House denounced him with a reprimand and a 300,000-dollar fine, but not before they showed a fine sense of schizophrenic dissociation by electing him to the speaker's job despite the moral lapse that impelled them to punish him!

In his Second Inaugural Address, President Clinton articulated the hopes and aspirations of the American people.

Most Americans applaud his goals.

And if Bill Safire cannot get over the blow he endured when his candidate lost, he can at least desist, at long last, from the deplorable mudslinging that characterized the campaign and move on to a more positive approach to the problems that confront the nation . . . at least until the next campaign!

February 9, 1997
Albright's Blueprint
Mexico City—The News

Editor: Madeleine K. Albright's "Blueprint" (*The News*, Feb. 2) for foreign policy in the second Clinton administration merits comparison to a State of the Union address in its eloquence, its clear outline of the direction of future foreign policy, and its enunciation of the principles of American behavior on the world stage.

Her call for bi-partisanship in the realization of America's goals in world affairs should resonate in Congress and in the nation.

Her ringing call for American leadership "as peacemaker and problem-solver" and as "a model for strengthening democratic forces," will be welcomed abroad and at home by all who look forward to a new era of peace and cooperation among nations.

Disappointing, however, was her avoidance of the crucial issue of nuclear disarmament. If this is because of a desire not to ruffle the feathers of Republican opposition in Congress, it is a mistaken concession, made too soon.

A forceful statement in support of the recent call by the former head of the Strategic Air Command, General George Lee Butler, and 60 other retired officers, for "total nuclear disarmament" would have been more in keeping with the general tone of the rest of her programmatic statement.

A clarion call for the final elimination of this dangerous remnant of the Cold War could have provided a rallying point for those around the world who yearn for a nuclear-free atmosphere and a world free at last from the threat of nuclear destruction.

The continued retention of nuclear missiles by the five nuclear powers, and the piling up of plutonium, represent a danger to the world that is inexcusable in the post-Cold War era. No credible military analyst envisions the use of nuclear arms in today's conflicts.

"We want to halt the spread of weapons of mass destruction and to combat terrorists," Ms. Albright cogently states. A primary step in this direction, a first step in fact, would be to disarm and destroy the present nuclear stockpiles, as General Butler proposes. Their threat to the world would thus be removed, along with the source of stolen supplies which rogue states depend upon for their terrorist, illegal armamentarium.

Further, Ms. Albright's statement, made almost in passing, that the United States ought to pay its debts to the United Nations, could have been stronger. We owe over a billion dollars in dues to the U.N. Our failure to honor that obligation weakens our credibility in the world body and undermines the moral authority both of the United Nations and the United States in their quest for peaceful solutions to the world's conflicts.

Even now, Republican forces in Congress, Jesse Helms in particular through his chairmanship of the Senate Committee on Foreign Relations, represent a stumbling block, as indicated in the hearings on the nomination of Representative Bill Richardson as the next American delegate to the United Nations, (as reported in the *New York Times* of Jan. 28). Opposing Helms and those who would continue the international disgrace of our refusing to pay our U.N. dues should be of the highest priority.

February 16, 1997
Not Just Banter
Mexico City—The News

Editor: Like a punch-drunk fighter answering the bell, William F. Buckley Jr. (in his column "Nixon's Anti-Semitism All Foam, No Teeth") comes swinging into the arena to defend his once-and-forever-hero, Richard Nixon.

This time it is to defend and "explain" the incontrovertible evidence of Nixon's anti-Semitism as revealed in newly released tapes of his White House conversations.

To Buckley watchers over the years, this comes as no surprise. Buckley supported and defended Nixon during the Watergate hearings. He supported him even as evidence piled up attesting to corruption, obstruction of justice, lying to Congress, breaking into Democratic headquarters, burglarizing a psychiatrist's office, organizing "dirty tricks", maintaining an "enemies' list", and on and on.

He supported him even as the weight of the moral corruption in the White House forced Nixon to resign rather than to face certain impeachment.

He continued to support him after the resignation, never once repenting or indicating a change of mind about the disgraced president, whose moral imprint on the high office he swore to uphold still lingers.

And now Buckley rushes to Nixon's defense in the matter of his anti-Semitic utterances, declaring, without apology or a sense of shame, that Nixon "managed to bestride his own failings sufficiently to serve as an effective president!"

Buckley, significantly, offers not one word of doubt about the authenticity of the taped conversations. It is as though he was not even surprised when the president said to his most trusted aides: "John, we have the power. Are we using it to investigate the Jews? . . . I can only hope that we are doing a little persecuting." (!) Or "Please get me the names of the Jews . . ." Or, "How about the rich Jews? The IRS is full of Jews, Bob." (!)

Buckley, as lawyers are wont to do when all else fails, resorts to the "insanity defense". Nixon, he unflappably asserts, was "a paranoid" and "His anti-Semitism . . . was only "a psychological buzz". We are invited to accept this as "understanding" and even to sympathize with a beleaguered president "who felt threatened." And anyway Nixon's anti-Semitism was "all foam, no teeth" and was not "translated into anti-Semitic activity." It was only "anti-Semitic banter" after all!

What Buckley misses, or deliberately obfuscates, is the fact that words *are* a form of *action*. Especially when they come from the most powerful man in the United States (the "leader of the free world"). At Nuremberg, the accused Nazis were defended by some of their lawyers with the insanity defense also and the plea that they had simply used words, they never touched a Jew themselves. It didn't work, it was clear that their words led to the gas chambers.

Nixon's words didn't kill anyone, either, but they led to a dangerous ambience, a philosophical no-man's-land, a moral gutter in which anything could happen.

Language, the semantic philosophers (Korszybski, Hayakawa, and others) have postulated, is the mold into which we pour our thoughts. The language we use is the best indicator of our thoughts and our purposes.

Why, then, it is asked, did Messrs. Henry Kissinger, William Safire, and Herb Stein choose to work for a president with such views? (Buckley concedes that it is "unlikely" that they did not know of Nixon's anti-Semitism.) That is the best question raised here, and one that can only be answered by Kissinger, Safire and Stein themselves.

It may very well be that their yearning for power, their positions at the pinnacle of success and status, overrode their moral sensibilities, convinced them not to rock the boat in which they all shared such glory.

Not, finally, to bite the hand that fed them. Their responses now would be illuminating!

February 23, 1997
Twin Evils
Mexico City—The News

Editor: Twin evils threaten the existence of ordered human society.

They are the evils of pervasive *violence* and *corruption*. They are growing geometrically at the same time that the power and the peril of mass destruction continue to haunt us (thousands of nuclear missiles still remain poised and ready for cataclysmal use). Together, not only human society, but the world as a livable environment remains vulnerable.

Violence continues at every level, from personal to national to international, increasing in ferocity and in human consequences. Pundits casually refer to the last two years as the "era of O.J. Simpson", when personal violence ran amok and unpunished, largely due to the endemic prejudice, racism and ineptitude of our criminal justice system. And violence on a grand scale continues on every continent, from Rwanda to Zaire, from Bosnia-Herzegovina to beleaguered Ireland from the West Bank to the embassy in Peru, and in the streets of New York and Bogota and every major city where the drug lords and their satellites battle it out over the corpses and the broken lives of our shattered youth.

The international community represented by the United Nations, the only force that can possibly deal with international violence, is undercut at home as we, inexplicably, refuse to pay our dues; while Senators like Jesse Helms obstruct its functioning at every opportunity.

The international drug trade continues its trillion dollar business, corrupting governments and law enforcement around the world. Pathetically ineffective police and military measures are offered as a sop to an outraged public, while the disease of addiction, which lies at the root of the human problem, (the insatiable demand for drugs, with the largest market in the United States, fuels the entire enterprise) goes largely uninvestigated.

Addicts languish without treatment, we fill our jails, meaningful research into the root causes that lie in a crumbling immoral society is lacking.

Violence and corruption are the twin results, both cause and effect.

Corruption is the daily diet offered by the press to a world in which integrity, honesty and commitment seem like abandoned virtues from another time and place.

Hardly a government in the world is free of scandal, misgoverning or worse, a situation repeated in our biggest and most powerful corporations, as the grab for power for its own sake, greed, avarice and the lure of great wealth, overcome moral sensibilities and personal integrity.

The world stood in awe this week as an unimaginable technology repaired the Hubble Space Telescope hundreds of miles above the Earth, so that we can search the stars. Are there better worlds out there? More rational? More sane than ours? Perhaps, but at home millions still starve in the midst of "net surpluses": "In fact, it is estimated that 800 million people in the developing world are undernourished" (*The News*, Feb. 16). And we have made little or no progress in understanding and curbing man's propensity for violence, or how we can organize human affairs free of the cancer of venality and corruption.

Whether corruption breeds violence, or the other way round, whether violence is a genetic trait of the human species or a product of social institutions out of control, it should be abundantly clear by now that, unchecked, these twin evils represent the greatest danger to our survival. Our scientific and social endeavors to address these issues may well determine the quality of life in the coming millennium . . . or, indeed, whether there will be human life at all.

It is the responsibility of all of us . . . and the urgent task of the new Clinton administration. The risk is too high and the consequences of failure too unthinkable for the challenge to be ignored.

March 13, 1997
The Reasons Behind 'Poor' Health
Mexico City Times

Richard A. Shweder's article, "It's Called Poor Health for a Reason" (Mar. 9 *New York Times Weekly Review*) overlooks an important factor in the assessment of socioeconomic status and health. "No one knows why people with high social status are more healthy and less crazy", he states, posing statistics that would indicate that being poor is not a sufficient answer.

The factor not discussed is anxiety. The relationship between body and mind, psychosomatics, has been explored for many years, with the conclusion almost universally accepted that anxiety affects health adversely. It is by now a given that diseases like ulcers, headaches, and many others, in addition to the obvious emotional illnesses caused by free-floating anxiety, are closely related to anxiety levels.

Are these studies to indicate that the anxiety levels of the poor, realistically related to job insecurity, inadequate housing, a much more limited access to proper health care (despite public clinics and welfare resources), the fear of unemployment, the inability to provide proper care or nourishment for their children, the threat of family breakup, problems that are less pressing as one ascends the economic ladder, produce more anxiety, and thus more anxiety-caused health problems than among the wealthy?

If the body's auto-immune system is weakened by anxiety, and strengthened by its opposite, hope would this not offer at least one explanation? Anxiety levels among the poor are higher than among the rich. And hope, positive thinking, and realistic aspirations, factors which would strengthen the autoimmune system, as proposed in the writings of Norman Cousins, are signally lacking in the culture of poverty and the hopelessness of the ghetto.

Should we be surprised that "people with high social status are more healthy and less crazy?" And are the reasons really that hard to find?

March 16, 1997
No Price War
Mexico City The News

Editor: Mikhail Gorbachev ("Western Growth Causing Russian Fears" in the Feb. 27 edition of *The News*) makes a cogent case concerning the dangers of "expanding the Western military alliance up to but not beyond Russia's border." He quotes the scholarly and knowledgeable expert, George F. Kennan to the effect that "A decision to expand NATO could well be the most fateful error of American policy in the entire post-Cold War era."

His arguments cannot be dismissed easily. NATO was a child of the Cold War; its function was to guard against Soviet aggression. It was a necessary safeguard for the security of Europe at a time when Soviet expansionism was the main threat to the independence of nations. With the end of the Cold War and the removal of the threat from the former USSR, NATO as a military enterprise in defense of nations threatened by the Soviet collossus must be examined in a new light: the light of changed conditions.

(On the same page, Russia's ambassador to England, Anatoly Adamishin, urges that a new approach, such as the creation of a treaty between Moscow and NATO, would be more conducive to the development of "a genuinely collective security system", than the expansion of NATO's military might to Russia's borders.)

Regardless of what he calls "evasive denials", Gorbachev emphasizes that the widening of NATO is in "the same direction as during the Cold War". This continuing war-preparation toward the old Cold War enemy, he warns, risks dragging the world back "into something much more senseless than the Cold War."

Gorbachev's arguments have much merit. But his credibility is considerably lessened when he looks back at recent history and offers the same stale rationalizations for the flawed and fateful foreign policy of Joseph Stalin, and the Soviet's brutal trampling on the independence of the Eastern bloc of nations: Czechoslovakia, Poland, East Germany, Hungary, Rumania, et. al.

He actually urges that we believe "the responsibility of the West for its part in provoking Stalin's extreme reaction on the world stage" (he is too delicate to call the infamous Nazi-Soviet pact of 1939 by its name, and resorts instead to this oblique reference!) And he blames the Churchill Iron-Curtain speech in Fulton, Missouri, for the aggressions and the plunder and the brutal repression and subjugation by Stalin of the Eastern Bloc states.

In fact, Gorbachev states, "The West was also in no less measure responsible"!

Gorbachev still peddles the old and discredited Soviet "explanations" for Joseph Stalin's ruthless policies.

Such retroactive support of the infamies of the Stalin regime do not serve to build the confidence and mutual respect that is necessary today to undo the dangerous hostility of the Cold War era.

We must learn from the errors of history. But we gain nothing when we engage in re-writing history in order to sustain our past prejudices.

March 18, 1997
The Conscience Of Humanity
Mexico City Times

Reed Brody's article "Time for a lead on human rights", on today's editorial page (March 7), is an eye-opener and raises some interesting and intriguing questions concerning the United Nations.

Secretary-General Kofi Annan plans to name a new high commissioner for human rights. The fact, alas, is that this most important post, representing a significant aspect of the purpose and function of the UN, is all but unknown to the general public.

The function of the high commissioner, a post established in 1993, we are informed, was to "take an active role in preventing the continuation of human rights violations throughout the world". Yet how many of us are aware of his activities, or even of the existence of his office?

Human rights, including child labor, the exploitation of women, the violation of personal freedoms, so bravely outlined in the memorable Universal Declaration of Human Rights, pioneered by the unceasing labors of our own Eleanor Roosevelt just 50 years ago, blazoned the way for the most noble aspects of the family of nations in its formative years. It is to the shame of succeeding generations that this goal, this aspiration by the best in our national and international leadership, was never fulfilled, or energetically pursued.

The high commissioner, Mr. Brody points out, was a "cautious career diplomat", who failed to recognize the high responsibilities, and the high possibilities, of his office . . . with the result that little has been accomplished. The result is that few of us have been made aware of the problem, and the world-wide revulsion against abominable human rights violation has not been mobilized. The UN World Conference on Human Rights, in Vienna in 1993, sought to correct this and, at long last, to focus the world's attention on the egregious violations of freedom and the rights of peoples the world over.

Mr. Brody uses a wonderful and ringing phrase when he calls for the UN, and in particular its high commissioner, to become "the conscience of humanity." That expresses, it seems to me, the United Nations' essence and its ultimate purpose: to be nothing less than "the conscience of humanity."

The role of the United States ought to be as primary supporter of this development. It is in line with our democratic traditions and our national ethos. Our first step in this direction ought to be the immediate payment of what has become a national shame before the international community. How can we exert our maximum influence within the UN, in directions like the human rights issue, when we arrogantly refuse to pay our dues as loyal and rightful participants?

The statesmanship and the vision of the new UN Secretary-General Annan will be tested when we see whom he appoints to represent this "conscience of humanity." Will it be another "cautious career diplomat", or someone with the highest reputation for integrity, philosophic leadership, international vision, and a sense of commitment to all of mankind? Perhaps someone like Jimmy Carter, or Vaclev Havel, or someone from the arts and sciences, or academia? Anyone but another "cautious career diplomat!"

April 5, 1997
Where Roosevelt Left Off
Mexico City Times

Martin Walker's excellent article, "Clinton cleaves to Roosevelt's dream" (*Guardian Weekly*, Mar. 23), breaks the cycle of dreary reporting on who slept, and for how much, in the Lincoln Bedroom, and reveals a profound aspect of President Clinton's philosophy in welcome, serious reportage on important issues.

The recollection of the never delivered speech of Franklin D. Roosevelt, written just before his death, and little, if at all, known to the American public, is sensational. What President Roosevelt so eloquently said on April 11, 1945 ("Today we are faced with the preeminent fact that, if civilization is to survive, we must cultivate the science of human relationships—the ability of all people, of all kinds, to live together and work together, in the same world, at peace.") is as relevant today as it was 52 years ago. It is to President Bill Clinton's credit that he resurrects those ringing words at this important juncture in world history.

It is worth pondering that the world might have been different, as some historians have suggested, "if only Roosevelt had survived to deliver (this speech) and to act upon its sentiments." The "what-ifs" of history are intellectually challenging, and speculation of what might have been is a fine cerebral pastime, but the problem addressed and so eloquently articulated by Roosevelt is still with us. Clinton suggests that it is not too late, in fact it may be urgently on time, to address this problem now.

"The science of human relationships", President Roosevelt said in 1945, must be "cultivated."

Alas, in the 52 years since then, that science has been neglected, while the science of war and the preparation for war has been indefatigably pursued. Our energies, our resources, our thinking, have been directed toward ever-increasing capacities of mass destruction. Confrontation has been the order of the day rather than developing a science of how to "live together and work together". "Star Wars" was seen as our salvation, rather than solving the riddle of man's propensity toward violence and destruction. The Start II treaty, still not ratified, still permits nuclear missiles of 3000 to 3500 on each side, enough to destroy us all, while "the science of human relationships" shows no appreciable advance.

Just what this "science of human relationships" consists of is not explored by Mr. Walker in this interview. But its very mention opens a broad field of theoretical and practical pursuits, and indicates a dimension of President Clinton's thinking that is significant and replete with profound possibilities.

Surely "the science of human relationships" would cover the study of man's violence, its root causes, the part played by genetics and the part played by social forces, poverty, discrimination and environmental decay. It would cover man's need for cooperation and love, the "agape", brotherly love, described by the ancient Greeks, as opposed to the "ignorance and the greed which made this horror (of war) possible".

"The science of human relationships" would study the sources of human strife in religious differences and fundamentalist bigotry, in racial hatreds and oppression, in national rivalries and the horrors of genocide, in the "crimes against humanity", to recall what we learned at Nuremberg.

The "science of human relationships" would also explore the endemic violence on every level of society—personal, national, international—and how to mobilize the forces of modern knowledge and understanding to counteract that violence and to set mankind on a new path of cooperation and mutuality.

But we still spend billions, or trillions the world over, to increase our capacity to assault and kill one another (in the name of defense against the other side), while only a pittance is expended in the study of peace, cooperation, and how to live together.

Roosevelt's words, his unfulfilled aspirations, ring down the corridors of history. President Clinton does us a service to recall them. How he, and the rest of the world, pick up where Roosevelt left off, will determine the quality of the 21st century.

April 6, 1997
Heaven's Gate
Mexico City—The News

Editor: The sickening and ghastly events at the Rancho Santa Fe, where 39 people, most of them in the prime of their lives, chose death over life in order to reach "Heaven's Gate" as they blindly followed a charismatic Messiah, must alert us once again to the dangers of all-consuming, dogmatic, uncritical religious belief.

How many more heinous acts of violence, directed at oneself or at others, must we endure before serious attention is paid to the nexus between religion and violence?

It is only when unbelievable events such as the suicides at Rancho Santa Fe (or the deaths of the Branch-Davidians in Waco, Texas, as they worshipped David Koresh, or the 944 deaths by murder and suicide led by Jim Jones in Guyana, or the assassination of Prime Minister Rabin in Israel by a religious zealot, who killed "in the name of God", or the murder of 39 Arab worshippers in Hebron by Dr. Baruch Goldstein, also "in the name of God", or the wanton; terrorist murder of innocent women and children by the followers of Hamas and the Islamic jihad, who are assured of a "holy death" by their religion; or the recent suicides of the followers, of the Solar Temple) that attention is drawn to the lurking malignant consequences of uncritical, irrational religious belief.

After each grisly occurrence, there appear a flurry of "explanations" by pundits, but there has not been any evidence of serious thought by the theoreticians and the spokesmen of organized religion concerning the responsibility of religious indoctrination for these unexpected outcomes.

Is it enough to dismiss these "excesses" as "fanaticism", or "personal insanity"?

Do not the official bastions of our powerful organized religions bear at least some responsibility when the result of religious proselytism and indoctrination lead to death and destruction, when belief in God becomes a "license to kill"?

Is it "insanity", the loss of reason? But it is precisely religious thinking that inculcates faith over reason, stressing the magical in lieu of the reasonable. When the result is that faith is chosen as superior to reason, should it come as a surprise that reason is abandoned or lost?

Religious authorities cannot evade their responsibility in creating the soil, the surroundings within which the "fanatic" impulse is born and nurtured. Religious leaders and institutions cast a wide net of influence as they indoctrinate young and vulnerable minds. Where is their teaching and influence when devoutness crosses the line, when belief in God becomes a "license to kill"? They owe society a profound responsibility to examine in depth the malignant possibilities of pervasive religious, non-rational, superstitious modes of thought that often lead to irrational behavior, a blurring of the line between reality and unreality and the propensity to commit violence upon oneself and others "in the name of God." Otherwise, we face more Wacos and Guyanas and Rancho Santa Fes in the future.

April 10, 1997
Stamping Out Seeds Of Fanaticism
Mexico City Times

In his article "A Religion Of Special Effects" (New York Times *Weekly Review*, March 30) David Gelertner starts off auspiciously enough when he states, of the Rancho Santa Fe suicides, "You cannot help but conclude that this story is about religion, nor technology." If one expected from this that there would follow a serious discussion of religious belief and its possible consequences, or a serious attempt to address the responsibility of the religious establishment when religious indoctrination and proselytism lead to suicide, murder, and violence, one is sadly disappointed.

Instead, Mr. Gelertner, without a word of criticism of the possible malignant consequences of all-consuming religious belief based on blind faith, engages in a tirade against the principle of the separation of Church and State, by inference laying the blame for "weird cults" on those who support our Constitution's mandate to keep religion out of "the public sphere". He joins the extreme right-wing fundamentalists in their attempts to tear down Jefferson and Madison's "wall of separation" between private religiosity and public policy, as he calls for more religion, under public as well as private auspices, rather than addressing the social consequences of the spread of irresponsible religious dogma.

The fact is that the more and more frequent malignant consequences of all-consuming, dogmatic religious belief—the result of years of indoctrination by religious authorities of all faiths—are unexplored in any depth by our religious hierarchies.

What has been the response of organized religion when violence and murder take place "in the name of God"? Yigal Amir killed Israel's Prime Minister "in the name of God", and later stated that he would be happy to spend the rest of his life in prison studying Torah.

Baruch Goldstein, an educated medical doctor, killed 39 Arab worshippers in Hebron, "in the name of God." David Koresh led his followers to fiery deaths in Texas, "in the name of God." Jim Jones, and his People's Temple, induced 900 followers to accept death by cyanide "in the name of God".

How many more heinous crimes must we live through before attention is seriously addressed to the nexus of religion and violence? Philosophical pundits and religious leaders rush to put the blame on the excesses of "fanatics", or on "insanity", the loss of reason. But it is precisely the indoctrination of religion that undermines reason as it inculcates blind Faith. When the result is that Faith is chosen as superior to Reason, should it surprise us that reason is abandoned or lost?

What is required is not, as Mr. Gelertner proposes, a further erosion of the separation of Church and State and the extension of publicly sanctioned religious indoctrination on young and vulnerable minds, but, to the contrary, a multi-disciplined investigation into the malignant possibilities of pervasive religious, non-rational, superstitious modes of thought, developed within the religious establishment, that lead to irrational behavior, a blurring of the line between reality and unreality, and the propensity to commit violence upon oneself and others "in the name of God."

Above all, religious authorities cannot evade their responsibility in creating the soil, the religious surroundings within which the fanatic and irrational impulse is born and nurtured, and their responsibility is to examine the line between Faith and Reason and to see to it that their teachings do not lead to a "license to kill" "in the name of God."

May 20, 1997
Letter to the Editor
The Times Herald-Record

It is curious, and instructive, that not a single spokesperson of the local Republican Party saw fit to comment on the sweetheart deal between Newt Gingrich and Bob Dole—a deal that stood the principle of fairness and of equal-treatment-before-the-law on its head as it thwarted the process of Congressional "justice".

Under the "Dole Plan" (I can't resist punning about Gingrich on the "dole") the errant Speaker, who was punished by the House Ethics Committee after lengthy and careful deliberations with a fine of $300,000 for his moral lapses (read "lying" to Congress and the Committee) is conveniently rescued by Mr. squeaky-clean Republican Dole with a painless solution: an immediate loan, with not a penny due in payment for eight years, when Gingrich, no longer in office, will be easily able to repay with the millions he expects to earn from book and speaking contracts.

Does not this largesse from the pre-eminent moral arbiter of the Republican Party send a message of acquiescence, if not support of the Speaker's immoral behavior (the $300,000 fine deemed appropriate by the Ethics Committee is not exactly the punishment meted out for a traffic violation!)

And to add insult to injury (to the American taxpayer!) the unflappable Newt has the unmitigated gall (an egregious example of modern "chutzpah") to ask for a tax deduction for his repayment of the loan!

Is there a local Republican who will speak to this?

May 9, 1997
A sweetheart deal for Newt
The Times Herald Record

    A fine, we have always thought, issued by a court or by the House Ethics Committee, is a form of punishment for law-breaking or for other illegal activities. Were we being naive?

    When Mr. (squeaky-clean) Republican, Bob Dole, rushes to the aid of (rogue) Republican Newt Gingrich to make it oh-so-easy for him to pay for the punishment that the House Ethics Committee, after lengthy deliberation, decided he deserved, does not the pre-eminent leader and moral arbiter of the Republican Party send a signal of approval, or at least of acquiescence in the speaker's illegal political behavior?

    Mr. Gingrich, under the "Dole plan," escapes all punishment in the present; he does not have to pay one penny for eight years, his first payment is due in 2005, when presumably, he will be able to use his $900,000 campaign fund, and the millions he expects to earn from book and speaking contracts. Gingrich gracefully opined that this was "right, morally and spiritually!"

    It is difficult to see how breaking the law and avoiding meaningful punishment is "moral," or how he can cover up his material gains with "spiritual" appeals.

    But Bob Dole, despite the findings of the committee (a $300,000 fine is hardly meted out for a traffic violation!) still calls his friend Newt a man of "impeccable integrity," putting party loyalty above considerations of probity, honesty, and decency.

    Dole's action disgraces his party, as he supports the old boys' club no matter what and adds further to the public's cynicism with regard to the political process. Our local Republicans ought to speak up.

May 14, 1997
City College's Flavor
The New York Times

Your May 8 news article on the 150th birthday of the City College of New York does not mention the extraordinary flavor of the college in the 1930's, when it was a leading center of scholarship and the country's foremost campus for social and political consciousness. The campus was the hub of student activism, rallying against fascism, war and racism, earning its students the appellation "premature anti-fascists."

A delegation of Fascist students from Mussolini's Italy was booed off the stage in the Great Hall; Mussolini's invasion of Ethiopia was condemned, and the democratic Government of Spain was supported against Hitler and Mussolini's mercenaries. The 1960's earned a reputation for social activism on the campus. But the 1930's at City College was its predecessor.

June 1, 1997
The Philosopher-King Is Mortal
The New York Times Magazine

What leaps out of Paul Berman's article on Vaclav Havel is the simple, but in these days extraordinary, concept that democracy requires a certain kind of citizen—one with backbone ("The Philosopher-King Is Mortal," May 11). At a time when paralyzing cynicism and a lack of respect or trust in politicians and governments is at an all-time high, Havel's clarion call for nonparty politicians who will speak the truth and stand on principle is nothing short of revolutionary.

(*the original letter*)

Dear Editor:

What leaps out of the piece on Vaclav Havel (May 11) is the simple, but in these days, extraordinary, concept that "democracy requires a certain kind of citizen . . . . citizens with backbones . . ." At a time when a paralyzing cynicism and a lack of respect or trust in politicians and governments is at an all-time high, Havel's clarion call for "non-party politicians who will speak the truth and stand on genuine principles" is nothing short of revolutionary. In this era of Gingritch chicanery, and a supine Congress that reelects him to the Speakership despite his moral lapses; when millions of campaign dollars, legally and illegally, corrupt the political process, Havel's clear call for politicians to have "the courage to be oneself and go the way one's conscience points" comes as almost revolutionary, even in its simplicity, or perhaps because of it.

"But who in the late 20th. century was the poet of democracy", Mr. Berman asks, who will carry the torch for these "lofty ideas"? His answer, of course, is Havel himself. Without detracting from Havel's stunning articulation of the nexus between true democracy and individual authenticity, another poet, almost 100 years earlier, wrote:

"Creeds and schools in abeyance . . . .
"Whoever degrades another degrades me,
And whatever is done or said returns at last to me."

Havel speaks of "authenticity", of "democracy as the individual's responsibility to himself and to the universe". In many ways he is the literary and spiritual heir to our own Walt Whitman.

June 28, 1997
TV Spectrum Giveaway
The New York Times

"Another Broadcast Giveaway" (editorial, June 25) raises the timely question of the ongoing disgrace whereby the television broadcasters are "in firm control of old and new frequencies without competition and without paying a dime into the Treasury." In turn, this power of the broadcasters serves to corrupt the political process by requiring huge sums to be raised by both political parties for political advertising.

An obvious solution to both problems would be requiring the television industry to provide free air time to legitimate candidates. It could thus repay the public for its year-round privileges and counter the process by which the political parties are corrupted in their continuous and costly fund-raising.

July 21, 1997
Letter to the Editor
The Times Herald Record

> *We asked for readers'*
> *opinions on school taxes.*
> *Here are some of your*
> *solutions and comments.*

Your editorial of July 16 (Keep local control of school tax rise) properly raises the question of school taxes and the burden they place on local property owners. You fail, however, to face some of the central questions involved.

Of course, we all want quality schools and quality education for our children and qualified and dedicated teachers and quality equipment (like computers) to provide a meaningful educational experience. There is no more important goal for our troubled society. The problem is: How do we pay for it? For years many of us have been writing about the basic inequity of paying for schools primarily through local property taxes. Aside from the fact that local property owners face many inequities (such as differences in assessment from county to county, even from school district to school district, and the effect of tax exemptions for religious and other properties that shrink the tax base at the expense of the community at large), why should the school budget be treated separate and apart from all the other services that are traditionally assumed by state government? Why should we not, as an important priority, pay for good schools out of the general tax base, using all of the government's sources of revenue (including income taxes, sales taxes, as well as property taxes)? Would not this make more sense than the complex juggling from district to district ("Byzantine school finances," you called it) that now prevails?

Case in point: Relying on the property-tax method, taxpayers face the glaring inequity caused by tax exemptions, which shrink the tax base and cause higher taxes for the rest of us. A report issued by the New York State Board of Real Property Services, dated June 1996 for the year 1994, informs us that more than $15 billion of real property held by religious institutions in New York are almost completely exempt (97 percent) from taxes. In Sullivan County alone, religiously held real property increased to $115 million, up almost $2 million is the year before! Our tax losses through these exemptions add additional burdens to school taxpayers, or force cutbacks in school services. Not only is this a violation of the spirit of the First Amendment and the time-honored principle of keeping church and state separate, it is also an inefficient and unfair way to pay for schools. Billions of dollars of tax exemptions increase the burden of taxes in order to support institutional religion, forcing the general public to pay for the private views of the religious. At least one state legislator, Assemblyman Jake Gunther, has indicated his agreement, and is introducing legislation that would put most of this exempt acreage back on the tax rolls. A good, if belated, step in the right direction.

Our education system is our best hope for creating future citizens capable of facing the challenges of a rapidly changing world. It is up to our generation to face the challenge of maintaining and improving that system. That means basic changes in our approach and basic changes in how we meet the economic problems it presents. The archaic system of small local districts competing with each other for scarce funds in a patchwork of jurisdictions, with unfair property-tax bases, needs to be re-evaluated and changed. It is a reform that is long overdue.

August 10, 1997
New Era
Mexico City—The News

Editor: In my Mexican experience, having talked with Mexicans of many classes and persuasions, (taxi-drivers and low-wage workers, as well as teachers, doctors, lawyers, business people and professionals), I had always been discouraged by the widespread sense of futility in the face of what was seen as the "inevitable" and never-to-be-corrected corruption on the part of their government and political leadership.

Corruption, they seemed to say, was endemic and, with a sigh, "it will always be thus!"

In my diary during a previous election (1982) I had noted the soft spoken remark of a waiter, "The outcome," he said, "is certain, Portillo and the PRI guarantee the victory of their selection . . . and the *mordida* will continue as always."

Octavio Paz, one of Mexico's most insightful writers, wrote in his brilliant "Labyrinth of Solitude" (1961) of the "masks behind which the Mexican hides" and of the Mexican characteristic of "resignation."

This year's election flew in the face of this pessimism, opening up a new era of hope and promise, and giving encouragement to the hitherto silent (and silenced!) people of all classes who yearn for true democracy. It is all the more fitting that this historic breakthrough should be led by the son of one of Mexico's most dynamic presidents, Lazaro Cardenas, and that he should bear the name Cuauhtemoc, significant of Mexico's irrevocable ties to its Indian past.

July 31, 1997
The Pondering Jew
Slate

Herbert Stein's "*On Being A Jew*" reveals more about Stein's survival tactics in the face of anti-Semitism than it does about the centrality of the Jewish experience. Stein obviously chose to remember on which side his bread was buttered rather than address the larger issue of the Jew in a Christian world.

Of Richard Nixon's disgraceful anti-Semitic utterances, made public in recently revealed tapes, Stein can only meekly remark, "Apparently, Mr. Nixon said some things that I wish he had not said." Surely an entry for the understatement of the year.

As reported in the press, at long last, President Nixon, in the privacy of the Oval Office, said to his trusted aide, "John, we have the power. Are we using it to investigate the Jews? . . . I can only hope that we are doing a little persecuting." Further, "Please give me the names of the Jews." And, "How about the rich Jews? The IRS is full of Jews, Bob."

Even such a staunch supporter as William F. Buckley Jr. squirmed in embarrassment as he defended his hero Nixon, calling him "paranoid" and dismissing his anti-Semitism as "all foam, no teeth," pointing out that Jews like Henry Kissinger, William Safire, and Herb Stein continued to support him although it was "unlikely" that they were "unaware" of his anti-Semitic tendencies.

Yet Stein can now write: "But I know of nothing in his behavior to me, to my family, to Israel, or to Jews in general that entitles him to anything less than my total loyalty."

Loyalty? To a president who can mouth (and therefore think) such dangerous anti-Semitic dynamite? Stein's posture is that of one who puts self-interest above principle, opportunism above ethics. In so doing he fails the Jewish people, and does a grave disservice to the sense of fairness and decency to all.

August 21, 1997
Letter to the Editor
The New York Times Magazine

If the August 17 MAGAZINE should fall into the hands of a future sociologist, say a hundred years from now, or, later, into the research of a 21st. century anthropologist, what a picture he would get!

He would find full page advertisements in which a sullen, angry-looking model with an electrified hairdo shows off a "wool top trimmed with swan feathers" for $3,170 and a matching skirt at the bargain price of $1,500. A knit dress is shown for $2,240 (it sports maribou feathers). This is followed by a "beaded crepe mousseline" dress for $2,070, and an angora sweater for only $800. A mohair dress is the next offering at $1,370, followed by a neat coat at $2,005, a velvet jacket for only $600, and a skirt with fake-fur-trimmed underskirt for $450. That these are popular bargain-prices is underscored by the news, on page 47, that a jet-setter had just purchased a Givenchy gown for "about $50,000". The lucky lady was pressed for time, or she would have bought about 20 such pieces, as she normally does, but she just had to rush off to Antibes to launch her new 243-foot yacht and she was simply exhausted by the details of closing her homes in Los Angeles, Manhattan, and Paris for the summer.

A lengthy article on food and eating out reveals that one can get a great dinner in downtown New York for $165 for two people. A bargain-hunter can avail himself of a "special four course menu" for only $65, featuring such delicacies as "Thyme-Honey Glazed Duckling With Fresh Artichokes, Cippolini Onions and Green Potato Gratin." In case our future historian should think this is extraordinary, he is assured that the demand is so great that the restaurant received 4,000 calls in one day and that a reservation for a choice table must be made two months in advance! He might also be intrigued to know that a co-op apartment in the restaurant's building sold for $3.7 million.

An interview, page 17, with a young entrepreneur titillates the reader with details of his new "medieval-style castle" that cost nearly $10 million and sports such necessities as "an underwater sound system in the swimming pool, indoor and outdoor hot tubs, a tennis court, 80 gilt mirrors and six suits of armor." Doesn't everyone?

Page 19 provides the exciting and welcome announcement that you can get a fun-ride in a two-seater MIG-21 for only $3,500. "Let Yourself Go", the enthusiastic entrepreneurs advise, and they expect lots of takers.

Looking for a place to live? The real-estate ads have much good news: You can get a lovely house with breathtaking views of the Hudson for only $7.5 million, or, if you prefer town, you have a choice of coops in Manhattan's finest buildings "incredibly priced in the $1,000,000" range.

What goes on here, our future historians might ask, as, indeed, do we!

Of course if our future researcher should be lucky enough to discover a yellowed and mildewed few pages of any daily newspaper that managed to survive, he might also find that in addition to the shenanigans so loudly trumpeted in the glossy pages of the Magazine, there were also some people who were engaged in a strike (185,000 UPS workers, for example) to secure a living wage; that our Congress spent months recently in a serious debate on whether we could afford to raise the minimum wage from $4.75 per hour to $5.25. (Those are dollars and cents, not like the figures in the Magazine!). And thousands of poor people were being transferred from Welfare to work at wages that caused alarm on the part of private-sector workers. And thirty million people, without health insurance for themselves and their children, face economic disaster if illness should fall.

What goes on here? For whom is the Magazine printed? Never mind the conclusions as to the kind of society we live in that will be drawn by future researchers. What are regular folks here and now to think of the options open to the rich and famous (or more accurately to the simply rich and favored), while real problems of living and coping beset the vast majority in our country—not to mention the starving millions (gaunt children and undernourished populations are nowhere in evidence in this week's MAGAZINE) around the world.

What goes on here?

Thorstein Veblen, where are you when we need you?

October 1, 1997
Letter to the Editor
The New York Times

Progress is where you find it!

In front-page headlines we are informed today that the Roman Catholic Church of France has issued an apology to the Jewish people "for its silence in the face of French collaboration with the Holocaust".

"The time has come for the church to submit its own history, during this period in particular, to a critical reading, without hesitating to acknowledge the sins committed by its sons, and to ask forgiveness from God and from men . . . . Today we confess that silence was a mistake. We beg for the pardon of God, and we ask the Jewish people to hear this word of repentance", said Archbishop Olivier de Berringer, in what, even at this late date, stands as an extraordinary document in Church history.

It took only 57 years for the French Catholic Archbishop to acknowledge the Church's complicity in the round up of 76,000 French Jews to be deported from Drancy, France, to the death camps at Auschwitz!

This is surely an improvement over the 359 years it took for the Roman Catholic Church to admit that it was also wrong when, in 1633, it sentenced Galileo Galilei to be burned at the stake for insisting upon the (then) anti-religious notion that the Earth revolved around the Sun, not vice versa as the Bible taught. The Vatican officially acknowledged that "mistake" in 1992, 359 years after the event.

(It is worthy of note that the present Pope, and the Vatican, have yet to acknowledge not only the French "mistake", but indeed the Church's role in the evils of the Holocaust in general.)

If indeed "the time has come for the church to submit its own history to a critical reading," can we now also expect apologies for the Crusades, which also began in France, in 1095, when Pope Urban 11 exhorted Christians to war against the infidels, starting with a massacre of Jews?

Or an apology to the Mexican people for the rape, slaughter and murder visited upon them by the invading conqueror Hernan Cortes for gold and glory, with a religious rationale provided by the Church, which condoned the killing of those who would not be converted?

Or for the hideous massacre of the Cholulans, one of many graphically described by William Prescott in his "History of the Conquest of Mexico," (he referred to this, one of the many atrocities of the Christian Conquerors as "the work of death"). Cortes' men were "soldiers of the cross", fighting "a holy war . . . . against the infidel".

And long before Prescott, the historian and participant in the Conquest, Bernal Diaz, in his seminal work, "The Discovery and Conquest of Mexico", described the Conquest with all its gory details of atrocity piled on atrocity, replete with references to the Christian God who encouraged them and in whose name they fought.

Or is there a statute of limitations on churchly "mistakes" and "the sins committed by its sons" in the name of God?

October 13, 1997 1:03 AM
On "France's Bishops Apologize".
The New York Times

Your editorial, FRANCE'S BISHOPS APOLOGIZE (Oct. 12) is far more benign than the acid comments of Russell Baker in his column of Oct. 7, that "hollow apologies . . . make the apologizer feel good about his liberality" . . . but have the effect of "trivializing" heinous behavior. I'm all with Mr. Baker!

How can an "apology" even begin to serve as a moral equivalent to the monstrosity of the Holocaust?

It took 57 years for the official French Catholic Church to acknowledge its complicity in the rounding up of 76,000 French Jews to be deported from Drancy to the death camps at Auschwitz. (Even at this late date the Vatican has still not apologized for the French "mistake" or for its role in the evils of the Holocaust in general. It is still "studying the possibility".)

But the church, one will remember, was also tardy in acknowledging that it was wrong when it condemned the Italian scientist, Galileo Galilei, to be burned at the stake for insisting that the Earth revolved around the Sun, not vice versa as the Bible was said to have taught. That "mistake" was officially acknowledged by the Vatican in 1992, only 359 years after the event!

If indeed, as the French Bishops stated, "The time has come for the church to submit its own history to a critical reading", can we also now expect apologies for the Crusades, which began in France in 1095 when Pope Urban II exhorted Christians to war against the "infidels", starting with a massacre of Jews?

Or an apology to the Mexican people for the rape, murder and slaughter visited upon them by the invading Hernan Cortes for gold and glory, with a religious rationale provided by the church? Both William J. Prescott, the historian of the Conquest, and Bernal Diaz, historian and participant in the Conquest in his seminal work "The Discovery and Conquest of Mexico", described Cortes and his followers as "soldiers of the cross", fighting a "holy war against the infidel".

Or is there a statute of limitations on churchly "mistakes" and the "sins committed by its sons", in the name of God?

October 24, 1997
Letter to the Editor
The New York Times

It is "apology" time! The French Roman Catholic Archbishops apologize "for their silence in the face of French collaboration with the Holocaust". The Red Cross apologizes. The French police, "who did much of the Nazis' dirty work", apologize. Even the French Medical Association, which "barred Jewish doctors from their profession", now apologizes. (NYT 10/12). Finally, we are told in a Letter (Jonathan Kwitny, 10/22) that we may expect the Pope himself to apologize "for past errors", but we have to be patient and wait for the year 2000 for that!

Curious that these belated "apologies" should come at the season of Yom Kippur, the Jewish Day of Atonement, as though the virulent enemies of Judaism and the Jewish people have caught the spirit and beg for forgiveness, not only from the Jewish people, but from God!

But apologies just won't wash. As Russell Baker said (column 10/7), heinous behavior and unspeakable agonies "are trivialized by hollow apologies that make the apologizer feel good about his liberality". The horrors, bestiality, and obscenity, the monstrous evil of Hitler's "final solution" can never be obscured or mitigated by the ineffectual hand-wringing of those who collaborated in its execution—either in France or elsewhere.

Nor will the church establishment gain surcease from conscience as long as it continues to avoid its grim history and its contribution to the moral decay that prepared the soil in which anti-Semitism flourished, and from which the Holocaust derived.

The depths of German depravity at every level, a depravity that was all-pervasive, mainly due to the anti-semitism fostered by church propaganda, is nowhere more painfully and exactingly described than in Daniel Goldhagen's recent book, "HITLER'S WILLING EXECUTIONERS . . . . ordinary Germans and the Holocaust". This most revealing analysis of the roots of the Holocaust should be studied by everyone, especially by the belated "apologists."

Some brief excerpts: ". . . antisemitism has been a more or less permanent feature of the western world. Without a doubt, it is the all-time leading form of prejudice and hatred within Christian countries."

"European antisemitism is a corollary of Christianity." . . . "The Catholic Church as an institution remained thoroughly and publicly antisemitic" . . . "The German churches cooperated wholeheartedly . . ."

It was this all-consuming and pervasive antisemitism, nurtured by years of religious lies and propaganda against the Jews, that led to the Nazis' "final solution", the carefully planned attempt to annihilate an entire people. Further, as Goldhagen chillingly states as he discusses "eliminationist antisemitism as genocidal motivation:, "That the perpetrators approved of the mass slaughter, that they willingly gave assent to their own participation in the slaughter, is certain."

Before accepting "hollow apologies", read Goldhagen, and ask what evidence there is that the apologists now plan meaningful and effective changes in their programs and practices, and in their role in society that would prevent the horrors that they helped produce from being repeated in the future. Apologies are not enough!

October 28, 1997
Letter to the Editor
The New York Times

"Oops! I'm sorry!", said the French Roman Catholic Archbishop, Olivier de Berringer, as he confessed to his church's complicity in the rounding up of 76,000 French Jews, including 12,000 children, to be shipped to Auschwitz and certain death.

"Oops. We're sorry!", now say the leaders of France's biggest police union for having "done most of the Nazis' dirty work" during the occupation.

"Oops!, We're sorry!", say the Red Cross for having collaborated with the Nazis while they were torturing and exterminating Jews.

"Oops! I'm sorry!", says Dr. Bernard Glorion, leader of the French Medical Association, for our having "violated the basic values of our profession", and our "shameful operation of discrimination and exclusion concerning Jewish doctors."

And, further reports the New York Times, "a succession of occupational groups and organizations have asked for forgiveness in recent weeks for their roles during the occupation years", (10/12).

The Pope himself is said to be still "studying the possibility of an apology" and might have a statement soon—"in the year 2000"!

All of which brings up the question of moral equivalency as well as moral sensitivity. How, in Heaven or in Hell, can an "apology" even begin to be an appropriate response to the monstrous evil of the Holocaust? Is it an "apology" that we want for the tortured and slaughtered six million? Can their suffering and their martyrdom be mitigated in any sense by belated expressions of remorse by those who participated, in any way, in the "final solution"?

If not "hollow apologies", as Russell Baker called them, then what do we want? Hard to say, since nothing will suffice. But surely it is not the crocodile tears of the apologizers, who now go about their-business-as—usual.

The problem is moral change, for individuals as well as for the larger society.

When we see plans for meaningful education for tolerance, acceptance of diversity, the replacement of hostility toward other views with a new emphasis on love, understanding, and brotherhood rather than on hate, divisiveness and violence, we will have a beginning.

Thus far, we have plenty of "apologies", but little in the way of changed attitudes toward "the other". The somber observation of Blaise Pascal in 1670, in his "Pensées", that "men never do evil so completely and so cheerfully as when they do it from religious conviction", still holds. Anti-semitism still flourishes. Racism is still the number one social/moral problem in the United States. And ethnic-religious fanaticism continues in blood baths from the Middle East to Ireland, from Asia to Africa.

Apologies are just not enough. Moral leadership toward a broad, new community of peoples living in justice and peace and mutual harmony, is still conspicuous by its absence. Religious, social, and political institutions and their leaderships are yet to construct patterns of education for this and coming generations that would bring about real change and would render "Oops! I'm sorry!" the inadequate, ludicrous, insulting response to man's evil behavior that it is.

(Meyer Rangell is a free-lance writer. His Letters have appeared in the New York Times, the New York Times Magazine, the New Yorker, the Mexico CityNEWS, The Times-Herald Record of Middletown, NY)

November 11, 1997
Apologies will never be enough for genocide
The Times Herald Record

Your Oct. 1 report "Repentance . . . church apologies to the Jews," informs us that the Roman Catholic Church of France has issued an official apology to the Jewish people "for its silence during the systematic persecution and deportation of Jews by the pro-Nazi Vichy regime" from 1941 to 1944. Thus it has taken only 57 years for the French Catholic archbishops to acknowledge the church's complicity in the rounding up of 76,000 French Jews, including 12,000 children, to be held in filthy camps at Drancy before being packed into cattle cars for the trip to the death camps at Auschwitz, where only a handful survived.

An "apology," now? "Better late than never," some will say. Or, "Justice deferred is justice denied," others might reply. But how, at any time, whether sooner or later, can an "apology," official or otherwise, even begin to serve as an appropriate or adequate response to the monstrous evil of the Holocaust? The unspeakable horrors, bestiality and obscenity of Hitler's "final solution" can never be obscured or mitigated by the hand wringing of those who collaborated in its execution, in France or elsewhere.

Nor will the church establishment gain surcease from conscience as long as it continues to avoid its history of shameful involvement at the very top. The Vatican, one will note, has yet to acknowledge, even at this late date, not only the French "mistake" (what a pale euphemism!), but indeed the church's role in the evils of the Holocaust in general (The Vatican is reported even now to be "studying the possibility of an apology!). A report from the Vatican of Nov. 1 described a symposium of "about 60 Christian theologians of different denominations" considering the matter. Not a single Jew was included. And the "long-awaited apology" was not forthcoming. (The Record, Nov. 1)

But the church's tardiness in recognizing its "mistakes" is a matter of historical record.

It took 359 years, for example, to recognize its "error" in the case of the scientist Galileo, who was sentenced to burn at the stake for his insistence that the earth revolved around the sun, contrary to church doctrine. It was not until 1992 that the Vatican officially acknowledged that "mistake"—359 years too late!

While "apologies" are in the air, are we now to expect apologies for the Crusades, begun in France in 1095 when Pope Urban II urged war against the "infidels," beginning with a massacre of Jews?

Or an apology for the terrors of the Inquisition?

It was not until 1965 that the Second Vatican Council condemned anti-Semitism and announced that the Jews had not killed the Christ, after all. How long was that "apology," and "mistake," in coming? And after how much blood was shed?

Or is there a statute of limitations on churchly "mistakes" and "the sins committed by its sons," in the words of the French archbishop?

All of which brings up the question of moral equivalency as well as moral sensitivity. How, in heaven or in hell, can an "apology" even begin to be an appropriate response to the monstrous evil of the Holocaust? Is it an "apology" we want for the tortured and slaughtered six million? Can their suffering and their martyrdom be mitigated in any sense by belated expressions of remorse by those who participated in any way in the "final solution?"

If not hollow apologies, then what do we want? Hard to say, since nothing will suffice. But surely not the crocodile tears of the apologizers, who even now, in the main, go about their business as usual.

The problem is moral change, for individuals as well as for the larger society. When we see plans for meaningful re-education for tolerance, acceptance of diversity, the replacement of hostility toward other views with a new emphasis on love, understanding, and brotherhood rather than on hate, divisiveness and violence, we will have a beginning.

Thus far, we have plenty of apologies, but little in the way of changed attitudes toward "the other." The somber observation of Blaise Pascal, in 1670, in his famous "Pensees," that "Men never do evil so completely and so cheerfully as when they do it from religious conviction!" still holds. Anti-Semitism still flourishes. Racism is still the number one social/moral problem in the United States. And ethnic-religious fanaticism continues to produce blood baths from the Middle East to Ireland, from Asia to Africa.

Apologies are just not enough! Moral leadership toward a new community of people living in justice and peace and mutual harmony, is still conspicuous by its absence. Religious, social and political institutions are yet to construct patterns of education for this and for coming generations that would bring about real change, and render even the consideration of belated "apologies" the inadequate, ludicrous, insulting response to man's evil behavior that it is.

November 23, 1997
Premature
Mexico City—The News

Editor: David Amato (in his column of Nov. 16) is somewhat premature, to say the least, when he leans over backwards to praise Pope John Paul II for "condemning firmly the anti-Semitic beliefs and feelings of many Christians."

At a time when the Holocaust and its roots are being reexamined in many quarters, including the religious sector, the Pope's condemnation appears too little and too late.

Too little in that he addresses "the anti-Semitic beliefs of many Christians" rather than the pervasive institutional anti-Semitism inherent in church teachings that provided the soil from which the murderous hatred of the Holocaust derived. And too late—52 years too late, after the monstrous "final solution" was promulgated by Hitler without any official church opposition.

Even now, after the French archbishops officially apologized to the Jewish people and to God for the church's complicitous silence as 76,000 French Jews were rounded up and sent to certain death in Auschwitz, the leadership of the Catholic Church in Rome is still only studying the question of an apology. The recent high-level gathering at the Vatican (news reports Nov. 1) to study the meaning of anti-Semitism and the Holocaust did not include a single Jew. Nor was the long-awaited apology forthcoming. Instead we get another exhortation, while Mr. Amato blames the press and 'media failure' for not giving the pope Amato seems to be saying, thus avoiding the profound deficits in the message.

All of which brings up the question of moral equivalency and moral sensitivity. How can an apology, or a new papal exhortation, even begin to be an appropriate response to the monstrous evil of the Holocaust? Is it an apology we want for the tortured and slaughtered 6 million? Can their suffering and their martyrdom be mitigated by belated expressions of remorse by those who participated in any way in "the final solution?"

If not hollow apologies or yet another exhortation, then what do we want? Hard to say, since nothing will suffice insofar as the depth of past evil is concerned.

Surely not the crocodile tears of the apologizers who, even now, in the main, go about their business-as-usual.

The problem is profound, requiring moral change for individuals and their leaders, as well as for the larger society. When we see plans for meaningful reeducation for tolerance, acceptance of diversity, the replacement of hostility toward other views with a new emphasis on love, understanding and brotherhood rather than on hate, divisiveness and violence, we will have a beginning.

Thus far, we have plenty of apologies but little in the way of changed attitudes toward the "other." The somber observation of Blaise Pascal, in 1670, in his famous Pensees, that "Men never do evil so completely and so cheerfully as when they do it from religious conviction!" still holds. Anti-Semitism still flourishes. Racism is still the number one social/moral problem in the United States. And ethnic-religious fanaticism continues to produce blood baths from the Middle East to Ireland, from Asia to Africa.

Apologies and exhortations are just not enough! Moral leadership toward a new concept of people living in justice and peace and mutual harmony, is still conspicuous by its absence.

Religious, social and political institutions are yet to construct patterns of education for this and for coming generations that would bring about real change, and expose the solemn consideration of belated apologies, and ineffectual exhortations, as inadequate, ludicrous, even insulting responses to man's evil behavior. We must do better than that!

November 30, 1997
On the Right
William F. Buckley's Internet WEB page

As usual, it is difficult to determine just what William F. Buckley, Jr. is trying to say in his column of Nov. 22, CAN CHRISTIANITY AND JUDAISM COEXIST, on the occasion of the establishment of a new Jewish Center on the campus of Dartmouth College.

Buckley's customary turgid prose and confusing circumlocutions have to be carefully dissected and analyzed to get at his point. Does he look with nostalgia on "the original mandate" of Dartmouth College, which was to "Christianize its students", or does he truly welcome the more recent policy of "abolition of religious and ethnic discrimination from admissions policy"? A little bit of both, it would appear.

Buckley quotes, without criticism, the words of a previous Dartmouth President, Ernest Hopkins, to the effect that a quota system (designed to keep out all but a few token Jews and other undesirables), was necessary because "Dartmouth is a Christian college founded for the Christianization of its students." He further asks us to consider whether "an effort to inculcate Christian values and Christian teachings is a morphological (!) act of anti-Semitism", and whether those who carried out such a policy (through unfair admissions policies, among other practices on campus) should be judged as anti-Semitic. Buckley thinks not. President Hopkins, in this view, administered an anti-Semitic program, to be sure, but does that mean he was an anti-Semite?

Buckley is often hard to follow, but he seems here to be confused himself as to the relationship between anti-Semitic behavior, an evil ipso facto, and those who (innocently?) practice it. It is a little like drawing a distinction between the planned killing policy of the Holocaust and the (untainted?) characterology of those who carried it out.

Far fetched, you say? But in the post-Holocaust era no one can look without fear upon the possible consequences of an undefined "Christianization". Recent scholarship, like the study by Harvard professor Daniel Goldhagen, in his book 'HITLER'S WILLING EXECUTIONERS', traced the roots of the Holocaust to decades of anti-Semitic propaganda by the church. ("European anti-Semitism is a corollary of Christianity", he wrote.) Buckley does not say what he means by Christianizing, but, as my Grandmother used to say, it doesn't sound good for the Jews!

But it is not until the final paragraph that Mr. Buckley gives himself away: He, reluctantly it seems, accepts the end of the quota system, but adds his own caveat, that this "shouldn't require the abandonment of the ideal of Christianizing those susceptible to Christian mores."! Just what he means is not too clear, but post-Holocaust shivers should give us pause. And his final word is that "Judaism and Christianity can go hand in hand at Dartmouth, with the conventional deferences to the majority".

Hold it, Mr. B! Most of us thought that the elimination of the discriminatory quota system had as its goal the teaching of American values of equality, mutual respect and understanding among different ethnic and religious groups. Not "deference", repeat, but equality and mutual respect. That is a far cry from "deference", which implies the superiority of one group and its mores over all others . . . surely not the goal sought by a new admissions policy that finally put merit above prejudice. Or did that thought just sneak up on Mr. Buckley as he breathlessly belabored and obfuscated the issue?

December 28, 1997
The Microchip
Mexico City—The News

Editor: In a way, *Time* magazine reflected the value system of our times when it selected Andrew Grove, CEO and chairman of Intel Corporation as the *Time* "man of the year."

The selection represented our obsession with technology and paid homage to the stunning advances in high-tech information gathering and storage and dissemination.

Mr. Grove and, his company developed the microchip, which revolutionized modern communication in ways never before dreamed of, and with consequences that are still unforeseen. In that sense, one cannot quarrel with the choice.

But the niggling critic in me leaves me unsatisfied. Technology at any stage of development represents, after all, only a tool. In and of itself it is effective or ineffective, inefficient or magnificently efficient and breathtaking, or, as in the microchip, represents a new opening of such staggering proportions as to take one's breath away.

But, it is still only a means to an end, its impact on the world and on civilization will be determined in the final analysis by the goals that this new technology sets for itself, or that society sets. Mr. Grove said it best himself when he said to Time, "Technology happens. It's not good, it's not bad. Is steel good or bad?"

Aye, there's the rub. Steel is neither good nor bad; technology, in and of itself, is neither good nor bad. What makes it, steel or technology, good or bad, is the use to which it is put. Steel can build bridges and life-saving surgical instruments; or make bullets that maim and kill. Technology can save life, or destroy it. The "information explosion" can bring people together as never before, or it can spew hatred and bigotry.

In an era of explosive violence, corruption and immorality on all levels of society, from the inter-personal level to the community level to the relations among peoples and among nations, the world cries out for a moral leadership that would use our immense advances in technology for humanitarian purposes and goals.

The homage paid to technological genius, as represented in the selection of the chairman of Intel, would be in better balance if there were, also, the selection of a representative of moral leadership, a leadership that would direct us to an understanding of the "good and the bad" that Mr. Grove speaks of, of the right and the wrong. This may be an even harder task than calling attention to the information explosion.

Who is there, on today's horizon, who speaks to the aspiration of mankind to a world free of discrimination, racism, religious bigotry, poverty, violence and war? Who can claim the moral mantle of a Thoreau, whose concepts of right and wrong and civil behavior have infused our philosophy, or of a Mahatma Ghandi, who utilized those concepts in a moral leadership that inspired mass action that changed the course of history?

Perhaps, next year, our man of the year will be one who will represent the finest goals of peace, brotherhood, non-violence and harmony that might, if we have the wisdom and the courage and the will to change our ways, be made more possible by the stunning advances in human relationships that are opened up with the microchip and its vast potentialities.

January 4, 1998
New Year
Mexico City—The News

Editor: As we say "Happy New Year" and "*Feliz, Año Nuevo*" today, it is a sober and disquieting thought that since we uttered those hopeful words a year ago, mankind has made little, if any, progress toward addressing the central problem of our time, a problem that threatens the very existence of humanity and of life itself on our planet!

I refer to the endemic and unchecked violence that characterizes our society—a violence that is an eroding cancer on our personal and social lives, a violence that grows alarmingly in its intensity and its ubiquity.

Criminal violence, sexual violence, violence against children, violence against women and their right to control their own bodies, violence "in the name of God" and religion, ethnic violence, national and regional violence the world over—every day's news routinely bring terrible evidence of a continuing endemic violence from all corners of the globe.

It is a violence that bids to destroy our caring instincts and our aspirations toward altruism and brotherhood.

It is a violence that destroys the life of our cities, the community values of our neighborhoods, corrupts our youth, degrades our educational system, and makes a mockery of our search for a sane and "civilized" society.

The striving for love and brotherhood, for what the Greeks called "*agape*," which lie at our hearts human core, has never been so threatened as by this evil of violence that seems to engulf us and threatens to destroy us all.

Violence as "entertainment" (did you see De Niro's "Casino"?), strives to exceed the violence of actuality, as the media poisons our children with ever-increasing images of human bestiality. But the real news from the real world is worse.

Recent hearings of South Africa's Truth and Reconciliation Commission revealed unspeakable tortures practiced routinely by South Africa's former white government.

Here in Mexico, brutal bloody attacks in Chiapas massacred 43 Indian refugees, including women and children. Its sources are being "investigated."

In Rwanda, murder and bloodshed continues as over 300 Tuti refugees were hacked to death, reminiscent of the genocidal slaughter of over a half-million people in the murderous rampage of 1994.

Further killings occur in Bosnia, while the accused war criminal, Radovan Karadicz, remains at large, thumbing his nose at the United Nations War Crimes

Tribunal which has indicted him for war crimes, torture, and crimes against humanity.

Hamas, and its supporters, continue to wage a *"Jihad,"* their "holy war" to destroy the state of Israel.

Unconscionably, President Clinton continues to reject a ban on land mines that has been endorsed by 89 countries.

And, according to our Secretary of Defense William Cohen, Saddam Hussein is very likely the possessor of enough virulent biochemical weapons to destroy the world!

The list could go on and on.

Meanwhile, our own Carol Bellamy, executive director of the United Nations Children's Fund, informs us (*The News*, Dec. 17), that "malnutrition kills 6 million to 7 million children every year." Astonishingly, in the affluent United States, "more than 13 million children cannot get enough to eat!"

Man's unavoidable new, and perhaps last frontier as we prepare to enter the 21st century is the control of violence and the concomitant problems of war, poverty, hunger and disease. This is not only a moral imperative, but a practical imperative if the human race is not to go the way of the dinosaur and the dodo bird.

We need to mobilize the best minds of our time, in social thought, medicine, psychiatry and psychology, in statesmanship and philosophy and political theory, in ethics and government, to study and develop a new science of peace and problem-solving, rather than the skills of war and destruction. We need to explore the ground—social, psychological, ethical, biological and developmental—from which the evil of violence springs. Such research is practically non-existent. Its importance cannot be overstated.

Above all, we must develop a new sense of the community of the human race.

January 20, 1998
Violence
El Independiente (Bilingual Periodical)

Violence

Is

Our eroding deadly cancer,

Looming over us, a sword of Damocles

Erasing reason,

Negating the immune system of rationality of a

Caring human society.

Extinction yawns.

January 23, 1998
Letter to the Editor
The New York Times Book Review

I searched in vain, in Alan Wolfe's review of "PILLAR OF FIRE: America in the King Years" (Book Review, 18), for some explanation of why the Kings, father and son, chose to perpetuate the name of Martin Luther.

In his extraordinary work, "HITLER'S WILLING EXECUTIONERS.: ordinary Germans and the Holocaust", Harvard Professor Daniel J. Goldhagen wrote: "Martin Luther's antisemitism was ferocious and influential enough to have earned him a place in the pantheon of antisemites."

Further, "One leading Protestant churchman, Bishop Martin Sasse of Thuringia, published a compendium of Martin Luther's antisemitic vitriol shortly after Kristallnacht's orgy of anti-Jewish violence. In the foreword to the volume, he applauded the burning of the synagogues and the coincidence of the day: "On November 10, 1938, on Luther's birthday," he wrote, "the synagogues are burning in Germany." The German people, he urged, ought to heed these words" of the greatest antisemite of his time, the warner of his people against the Jews."

Why did the Kings, learned theologians both, choose to perpetuate that name?

February 17, 1998
What Means Globalization?
The New York Times

A sword of Damocles hangs over mankind!

Humanity is threatened with extinction!

The earth as an inhabitable environment is in peril!

Every day's news from around the world brings new evidence of the reality of this dire assessment. Yet there is an astonishing refusal to face up to it, as though people in positions of power, as well as the general public, have lulled themselves into a massive state of deliberate anomie and denial.

It is not the spread of disease that threatens us, nor untreatable cancer or heart disease or AIDS. Medical science and research are alert to such problems and are working, albeit not sufficiently, to address them.

I am referring to the overriding problem of man's propensity to violence. I refer to the endemic and unchecked violence that characterizes our society—a violence that grows alarmingly every day in ubiquity and intensity, a violence that is the eroding cancer of our society.

Criminal violence, sexual violence, violence against children, violence against women, violence by devout religionists "in the name of God", ethnic violence, national and regional violence, the ultimate violence of war and terror by "civilized" governments—every day's news brings additional evidence of a continuing and endemic violence that has come to characterize human behavior in these last years of a murderous century.

It is a violence that bids to destroy our caring human instincts and our aspirations toward altruism and brotherhood.

It is a violence, ranging from the personal to the social to the world stage, that destroys the life of our cities, the community values of our neighborhoods, corrupts our youth, degrades our educational system, makes a mockery of international relations, and is the ultimate stumbling block in our search for a sane and "civilized" society.

The striving for love and brotherhood, for what the Greeks called "agape", which still lie at our hearts' human core, has never been so threatened as by this evil of violence that seems to engulf us and that threatens to destroy us all.

Violence as "entertainment" (among others, note DeNiro's recent film, CASINO), strives to exceed the violence of actuality as the media poisons our children with ever-increasing images of human bestiality. And the violence reported in the world's daily press and on television, always selected over more benign news items, continues to inure our children as well as the population as a whole, to the obscenity of a violence run amok.

But the real news from the real world is worse:

Recent hearings of South Africa's Truth and Reconciliation Commission revealed unspeakable tortures practiced routinely by South Africa's former apartheid government.

Here in Mexico, brutal bloody attacks in Chiapas massacred 45 Indian refugees, including women and children. Its sources are still being "investigated"!

In Rwanda, murder and bloodshed continue as over 300 Tuti refugees are hacked to death, a still lingering aftermath of the genocidal slaughter of over a half-million people in the murderous rampage of 1994.

Further killings occur in Bosnia; Hamas and its fanatic supporters continue their "holy" war, their Jihad, against the state of Israel; the death toll in Algeria is over 26,000; a "Catholic killing spree" (AP 1/24) is admitted in Northern Ireland.

Organized religion, whose original intent was defined by the "Prince of Peace", has blazed a bloody path of violence and cruelty from the Crusades to the Inquisition to the Holocaust. To this day, bloodshed and violence "in the name of God" continue around the globe.

And the world has not as yet come to terms, to understand the ultimate meaning of the horrors of the HOLOCAUST, the nadir of the 20th. century experience of the supremacy of violence and prejudice over reason and sanity.

As though this were not enough, U.S. Secretary of Defense William Cohen has stated that Sadam Hussein is very likely the possessor of enough "VX chemical agent alone to kill every person on Earth" (Reuters, Nov. 26, 1997)!

Man's unavoidable new frontier as we prepare to enter the 21st. century is the control of violence and the concomitant problems of war, poverty, hunger and disease. This is not only a moral imperative, but a practical imperative if the human race is not to go the way of the dinosaur and the dodo bird.

Perhaps, at the highest level, there ought to be convened a "WORLD CONFERENCE ON VIOLENCE" to mobilize the best minds of our times, in social thought, medicine, psychiatry and psychology, in statesmanship and diplomacy and philosophy and political theory, in ethics and government, to study and develop a new science of peace, conflict-resolution, and problem-solving, rather than increase still further our capacity to annihilate each other.

We need to explore the ground—social, psychological, ethical, developmental—from which the evil of violence springs. Such basic research is practically non-existent.

Above all, we must develop a new sense of the community of the human race . . . . BEFORE IT IS TOO LATE! Time is short!

February 8, 1998
New Low Level
Mexico City—The News

Editor: Even for William Safire, whose legendary career is replete with columnar lows, his column Jan. 27, titled "Speechwriter's First Draft," sank to a new low level, more worthy of the salacious tabloid press than of the august *New York Times*, or the *NEWS*. It was surely a nadir, one of a long list, reeking of innuendo, sarcasm, prurience, double-entendre, and a meanness of spirit difficult to exceed. Even for an inveterate hater of Bill Clinton, Safire reached a new low as he all but chorded with glee, unable to contain his delight at the President's dilemma.

The best answer, on the same day, was the magnificent State of the Union address delivered by the President. Despite the intense pressure upon him, President Clinton was presidential in every sense of the word as he ignored the Safire crowd and addressed the pressing problems of the nation and the world. His far-ranging, informed, and constructive comments on social security, welfare, child care, education, taxes, a balanced budget, NATO and the world crisis created by a dangerous Saddam Hussein, all exhibited a hands-on leadership of the highest quality. He tackled his responsibilities as leader of the nation, and of the world, with rare skill and brilliance. . . . leaving to Safire his role as "gnat."

Safire's pathetic application to resume his role as presidential "speechwriter" was more appropriate to the time when he filled that role for his hero, Richard Nixon, with whom he was totally in synch, than with President Bill Clinton, for whom he bears only a malevolent hatred.

February 15, 1998
Media 'Feeding Frenzy'
Mexico City—The News

Editor: Watching the joint TV press conference of British Prime Minister Tony Blair and President Bill Clinton and the question period that followed, one could not help observing the differences between the British reporters and the American.

The British asked substantive questions about the issues so clearly addressed by both leaders—on domestic policy, welfare, standards of living, and foreign policy, particularly the crisis created by Saddam Hussein.

The Americans—you guessed it!—all but ignored the pressing problems of policy and crisis as they concentrated once more on Monica Lewinsky. Fulfilling all the descriptions of the "feeding frenzy" on TV and in the press, reporter after reporter outdid each other in formulating questions that were provoking, insinuating and disgracefully crude toward the President, while ignoring the repeated statements in which he denied all the allegations of his accusers, and his insistence that the Grand Jury had ordered his silence while the investigation was under way.

The usually even-handed Wolf Blitzer continued the needling and the provocateur-posture as he snidely asked: "What would you say to Monica Lewinsky, now?" The President put him in his place like a thoughtful college professor to a callow freshman upstart.

These proceedings bring to mind the challenge of the soft-spoken gentle Boston lawyer, Welch who, no longer able to stomach the vile tactics of Senator Joseph McCarthy during the infamous hearings in the fifties, asked: "At long last, sir, have you no decency?"

It was perhaps the most memorable line of the hearings. One may ask, now, of the reporters and their masters in search of ratings and circulation and money and competitive position in these disgraceful media attacks on the President: "Sirs, at long last, have you no decency left?"

When will the press and the TV talking heads recognize their crudeness and their unfairness? When will the press turn its attention to the task of exploring and illuminating the crucial issues of the day, as both Tony Blair and Bill Clinton did in their joint conference—rather than try to outdo each other as they dig for dirt?

Or, does anything go in the sleazy scramble for headlines?

Sincerely

February 26, 1998
Netanyahu and the press
The Jerusalem Post

Why does Israeli Prime Minister Benjamin Netanyahu get such bad press?

"NETANYAHU OFFERS MODEST PULLBACK" in his talks with President Clinton, reports THE NEWS (Mexico City, Jan. 21), "We made a decision to go for peace," he told the President. Concerning withdrawal from the West Bank he said "only it WAS A WITHDRAWAL THAT WILL ASSURE OUR DEFENSES . . . AND NOT JEOPARDIZE ISRAEL'S SECURITY." Like any other responsible head of state, he placed the security of his people and his country above all other considerations. What other head of state would do otherwise?

For this, Anthony Lewis took him to task in his column of Jan. 20, with a blaring one-sided streamer, "HOW NETANYAHU BLOCKS THE WAY TO MIDDLE EAST PEACE." All criticism of Netanyahu; not one word of censure for Yasir Arafat.

And the usually fair-minded Thomas L. Friedman even-handedly excoriates both Netanyahu and Arafat for not living up to the "ANWAR SADAT STANDARD" (column, Jan. 21.). But that standard (of accommodation to and recognition of Israel) was destroyed not by Netanyanhu but by fanatic Arab extremists still bent on annihilating the State of Israel. The infamous clause in the PLO Covenant that calls for the destruction of Israel has still not been repudiated or amended.

And Yasser Arafat and his Palestine Authority are still unable (or unwilling?) to curb the terrorists in their ranks who are determined to destroy the peace process through violence and bloodshed in Jerusalem and Tel Aviv.

Under these circumstances it is naive, if not deliberately provocative, to place all the blame for the current impasse on Benjamin Netanyahu, or to fault him for attempting to steer a path that would protect Israeli security and that would finally lead to a Palestinian State dedicated to mutual recognition and peaceful co-existence.

Toward this end, the policies of the PLO, the Palestinian Authority, and Yasser Arafat, must be credibly altered. Holding Benjamin, Netanyahu's feet to the fire, while ignoring the very real threat of a continuing Arab intransigence and terror, is no solution, either practically or morally.

March 8, 1998
On Certification
Mexico City—The News

Editor: For balance in the current drug-war debate on "certification," U.S. drug authorities would do well to heed the headlines in today's *The News*: "Latin States Blame U.S. For Drug Scourge"; "OAS urged to impose certification check unless consumption is cut." (*The News*, March 4).

Americans ought to take seriously the fact that at the meeting of the Inter-American Commission for the Control of Drug Abuse, sponsored by the Organization of American States (OAS), convened in Mexico City yesterday, it was the failure of the United States to reduce the demand for illicit drugs that dominated the discussion, rather than the culpability of the supplying nations. Mexican Health Secretary Ramon de la Fuente voiced the prevalent opinion when he said that "the growing demand for illicit drugs is most to blame for narcotrafficking." And "the country where the demand is most concentrated is the United States."

It follows, he persuasively argued, that it is wrong policy "to separate production from consumption because consumption is the most powerful lever that activates the chain of narcotrafficking."

Simply put, it is ironic, if not arrogant and self-defeating, that the United States, where an insatiable demand for illicit drugs fuels the entire illegal enterprise both here and abroad, should be pointing the finger of blame at other countries rather than take the necessary steps to reduce demand at home. That means, of course, a renewed emphasis, long overdue, on programs for prevention and treatment, whatever it takes, rather than the current emphasis, at huge costs, on interdiction, border patrols, and reliance on the criminal justice system.

It is not inappropriate to ask, from a moral, ethical and practical point of view, who should be "certifying" whom?

March 23, 1998
William Safire: The Death of Outrage
The New York Times

William Safire's column of March 20 resurrects an important element in the social/political environment as he comments on "THE DEATH OF OUTRAGE". He posits that outrage—more specifically I would call it "moral" outrage—is conspicuously absent in the public reaction to the alleged White House sex scandals.

The trouble with this formulation is that Mr. Safire has the object of his sermon all wrong. The fact is that the general public IS outraged, but not toward the President's behavior, as Safire would have it, (as is shown in poll after poll that give President Clinton the highest acceptance ratings in history) but at the vindictive, vitriolic, unrelenting hounding of the President by television and press pundits like Mr. Safire himself.

In this column, as in so many previous ones, Mr. Safire denies the President that presumption of innocence that all Americans are granted in a court of law, and instead assumes a presumption of guilt, without trial or jury, or any of the legal protections accorded citizens accused of alleged crimes. Without evidence or a proper examination of credibility, Mr. Safire irresponsibly repeats his incendiary phrases, "the cover-up crew", "criminal conspiracy in the White House", "hanky-panky with an adoring young intern", "witness tampering", "central abuse of power", "apparent criminality at the top", "lying about adultery", ad nauseam, even going so far as to compare the President with the infamous Jimmy Hoffa! With an unremitting hatred of the President, Mr. Safire uses the power of his Op-Ed position to declare President Clinton guilty as charged. Tried in Judge Safire's "court", Clinton is found guilty and sentenced: Jail him! Hang him! And, of course impeach him forthwith!

The public is not without outrage, Mr. Safire, but it is increasingly directed toward those in the press and on television who persist in "trying" the president, not in a court of law, but in vicious columns like yours and those of Cal Thomas and others, and, endlessly, on Larry King and The Capital Gang and Crossfire and Geraldo, where accusation and innuendo fly unchecked and simple decency is sacrificed to shock value and "entertainment".

Moral outrage is indeed here, and growing, but it is against the salacious press and a television mentality that grows more wildly irresponsible every day.

March 28, 1998
Letter to the Editor
The New York Times

President Clinton's request that "Attorney General Janet Reno convene experts to study what might be done in the future" to prevent the ghastly violence by children of 11 and 13 in the Jonesboro, Ark, middle school comes as too little and too late. (Editorial March 26)

We need, and have needed for a long time, a serious, well-thought out and well-prepared WHITE HOUSE CONFERENCE ON VIOLENCE to mobilize the best and most creative minds of our time, in medicine and psychiatry and psychology, in philosophy and political and social theory, in ethics and philosophy, in biology and anthropology and sociology, in all the behavioral and social sciences, in order to explore the ground—social, ethical, environmental, biological, and developmental—from which the evil of violence springs. Such basic research is practically non-existent. Its importance cannot be overstated if we are to stem the endemic violence that, like a malignant cancer, grows unchecked and threatens to destroy the very fabric of our society.

April 5, 1997
... An Explanation?
Mexico City—The News

Editor: If you were "LOOKING FOR AN EXPLANATION TO JONESBORO" (*The NEWS*, March 31) you will have to look elsewhere. Stephanie Salter, alas, is far more skilled at non-explanatory banalities than she is at any serious attempt at profundity or even a hint of new understanding.

All Ms. Salter can tell us, with the air of offering stunning new illumination, is that we would be wrong to concentrate on gun control or on the consequences of a pervasive environment of violence or other explanatory social characteristics that come readily to mind. With numbing intellectual insight she suggests that "we are no further out of the cave than anyone else. We have not managed to escape the negative, destructive aspects of humanness that have bedeviled individuals and their social systems since Cain slew Abel." Finally she breathlessly informs us that "Americans have been inclined to kill in small numbers for individual reasons," and that "we continue to kill!"

That such drivel passes for new insight underscores the pressing need for serious attention by serious scholars to the problem of violence in our society. A good beginning might spring from the request by President Clinton, as reported in the *New York Times* of March 26, that "Attorney General Janet Reno convene experts to study what might be done in the future" to prevent the ghastly violence by children of 11 and 13 years of age in the middle school at Jonesboro, Ark.

An idea that deserves attention is that a serious, well-thought out and well-prepared WHITE HOUSE CONFERENCE ON VIOLENCE be organized without delay in order to mobilize the best and most creative minds of our time, in medicine and psychiatry and psychology, in philosophy and political and social theory, in ethics, in biology and anthropology and sociology, in all the behavioral and social sciences, in order to explore the ground—social, ethical, environmental, biological and developmental—from which the evil of violence springs.

Such basic research is practically non-existent. Its importance cannot be overstated if we are to stem the endemic violence that, like a malignant cancer, gows unchecked and threatens to destroy the very fabric of our society.

We must surely go beyond the glib and unproductive "explanations" of Ms. Salter.

April 12, 1998
Church And Holocaust
Mexico City—The News

Editor: As specifically stated in the headline, "Separating Church From Holocaust" (*The News*, April 2). Marc Saperstein attempts to exonerate the official Church from any culpability both in the creation and nurturing of the vitriolic, widespread anti-Semitism that made the Holocaust possible, as well as its specific role in the execution of the Holocaust itself. His arguments fall short on both accounts.

Referring to the recent Vatican statement, a document that took 10 years to produce and that came 53 long unconscionable years after the bestiality of the death camps was revealed to a stunned world, Mr. Saperstein states, "I believe that the Vatican statement is correct in asserting that Nazi anti Semitism "had its roots outside of Christianity, that it was not derived from the anti-Jewish doctrines of the church . . ." His arguments is not nearly as compelling as the results of recent scholarship on the issue:

In an electrifying work, "The War Against The Jews, 1933-1945," Lucy S. Davidowicz, in an exhaustive and detailed study, states: "A line of anti-Semitic descent from Martin Luther to Adolph Hitler is easy to draw. Both Luther and Hitler were obsessed by a demonologized universe inhabited by Jews. 'Know, Christian,' wrote Luther, 'that next to the devil thou hast no enemy more cruel, more venomous and violent than a true Jew.(!)' . . . Luther's protective authority was invoked by the Nazis when they came to power, and his anti-Semitic writings enjoyed a revival of popularity."

With no waffling like that of Mr. Saperstein, Ms. Davidowicz states unequivocally that "modern German anti-Semitism . . . drew part of its sustenance from Christian anti-Semitism, whose foundation had been laid by the Catholic Church, and upon which Luther built . . . modern German anti-Semitism was the bastard child of the union of Christian anti-Semitism with German nationalism . . ."

In a more recent work, hailed by scholars here and abroad, Harvard professor Daniel J. Goldhagen ("Hitler's Willing Executioners: Ordinary Germans and the Holocaust," 1996) flatly states: "European anti-Semitism is a corollary of Christianity . . . The Catholic Church as an institution remained thoroughly and publicly anti-Semitic . . . The German Churches cooperated wholeheartedly." Professor Goldhagen's scholarship reveals in stark, uncompromising terms what the current apologists refuse to face; that it was a pervasive anti-Semitism, deliberately created, fostered and nurtured by the Catholic Church, and by almost all Christianity, that poisoned society in Germany and in all of Europe for hundreds of years and that provided the soil that made the Holocaust possible, and that made "ordinary Germans Hitler's willing executioners."

Unlike the forthright apology issued last year by the Roman Catholic Church of France, which asked forgiveness "for its silence during the systematic persecution and deportation of Jews by the pro-Nazi Vichy regime" (76,000 French Jews, including 12,000 children, were held in filthy camps in Drancy before being packed into cattle cars for the trip to Auschwitz, where only a handful survived), the current statement by the Vatican offers no apology whatsoever for its failure to speak out against Hitler. "Long passages of the text," writes the Guardian Weekly, ("Vatican Statement Disappoints Jews" 3/22/98) "smack of self-justification . . . Many Jews will be appalled by the document's insistence that Nazi anti-Semitism had its roots outside Christianity . . ."

Israel's chief rabbi, Meir Lau, said he expected an unequivocal apology from the Vatican for Pius XII's "shameful attitude." And the chairman of the Holocaust Educational Trust in Britain, Lord Janner said, "I am deeply disappointed at this unworthy document."

Try as he might, Mr. Saperstein does not succeed in "Separating the Church from the Holocaust," but his discussion may have some value if it directs attention to the moral issue of man's responsibility in the face of evil, especially of the magnitude of the Holocaust and genocide, and the responsibility of all sectors of society.

April 29, 1998
Letter to the Editor
The New York Times

It is of more than passing significance that, on the same day that your positive editorial, ISRAEL TURNS 50, (April 26) praised Israel for its stunning economic accomplishments and its "vibrant democracy", while acknowledging that it still "must maintain the military might to defend itself . . . against an array of Arab enemies", on that very day Israel's former Prime-Minister, Shimon Peres, reiterated his support "for the creation of a Palestinian state by May, 1999" (NYT, 4/27). Two peoples must have two separate states; Mr. Peres re-confirms his far-reaching and thoughtful statesmanship when he articulates this goal at this time.

What your otherwise excellent editorial failed to point out, however, is that the major obstacle to the creation of a Palestinian state is the legitimate fear within Israel caused by the failure of Yasir Arafat and the Palestinian Authority to carry out their pledges to curb terrorism, and the terrorist organizations in their midst that maintain to this day their determination to destroy Israel.

The prime requirement now is for Yasir Arafat and the Palestinians to fulfill their promise to curb that terror and to start by removing, at long last, that clause in the PLO Covenant that still calls for the destruction of the Jewish State.

April 24, 1998
Letter to the Editor
The New Yorker

The stark revelations of "The Klemperer Diaries" (April 27) represent, inadvertently, a chilling confirmation of the major thesis of Harvard Professor Daniel J. Goldhagen's recent work, "HITLER'S WILLING EXECUTIONERS . . . ordinary Germans and the Holocaust" (1996):

"There's not a sound from anyone, and everyone's keeping his head down," writes Klemperer of life in Dresden during the Nazi years . . . "And there is the constant pointless tyranny" . . . . "In Ulm, the rabbi was chased around the market fountain with his beard alight—chased by a 'mob' (that is by 'people', and not just by Storm Troopers carrying out orders!)." . . . Of other behaviors, Klemperer writes, "to me they confirm the claim of the National Socialists to express the true opinion of the German people."

All of which validate Professor Goldhagen's conclusion that "ordinary Germans" were "Hitler's willing executioners", who participated in the wholesale slaughter of the Holocaust without saying "no" and, in many cases, with obscene enthusiasm.

May 7, 1978
Civility in the Stars
The New York Times

Ian Tattersall gives only a hint of an answer to the question he raises—"is incivility in our genes?"—when he suggests that "genes are deceptive indeed" (Op-Ed, May 4). His gentle reminder that "good ideas should not be caricatured by excessive zeal" calls to mind another dolorous dictum: "No good deed shall go unpunished."

Is incivility genetic? I don't think so. Long before Gregor Mendel, Shakespeare was on a better track when he said, "The fault dear Brutus, is not in our stars, but in ourselves." And, he might have added, in our society.

May 31, 1998
Subject: child abuse and violence
The Times Herald Record

Bravo and congratulations on today's stirring front-page coverage of the issue of child-abuse. It is the kind of pro-active journalism that seeks to awaken its readers to a crucial social issue, rather than merely report events that are so ghastly and destructive.

Marie Szaniszlo and Mike Levine not only report, but also, with decisiveness and effectiveness, point to "solutions" in the face of our "outrage" at the pusillanimous behavior of our do-nothing political leaders. .

The outpouring of letters on the tragic death of Christopher Gardner attests to the impact of this event on our town and its people, and the sense of urgency that is now felt about our children and their welfare, as well as the general increase of violence in our society.

The school killings in Jonesboro, Arkansas, and in Springfield, Oregon, by kids in their teens, have stunned the nation. This is a time for serious thinking, and action, about the problem of ubiquitous violence by children and toward children, from Oregon to Bloomingburg. Attention must be paid! We put it off at our own peril.

Many experts are of the opinion, based on social studies, that there is a direct line of causation between children who are abused when very young and children who act out violently while still in their teens. President Clinton seemed to grasp this when, following the Jonesboro killings, he requested that "Attorney-General Janet Reno convene experts to study what might be done in the future" (New York Times, March 26) to prevent such child violence. This might be a good beginning. But nothing has been done since. Was the President serious, or was it just an appropriate off-the-cuff remark?

It is clear, from the many remedies proposed, from gun control, to moral teaching, to more psychologists in schools to detect and to counsel troubled young people in time, that the problem is complex, and that there is no one single answer. If there ever was a problem that required a multi-disciplinary approach, this is it.

On every level, and from many vantage points, we need attention to the issue: In Bloomingburg, tomorrow, there will be a town meeting on child abuse. It should be well-attended.

On a national level, it would be appropriate if there were convened, as soon as possible, a "WHITE HOUSE CONFERENCE ON VIOLENCE . . . . it's causes and remedies", (as was done in the past on health care, child care, drug abuse, etc.) in order to mobilize the best and most creative minds of our time, in medicine and psychiatry and psychology, in child care and development, in ethics and philosophy, in religion and social theory, in biology and sociology, in all the behavioral and social sciences, to explore the ground—social, ethical, environmental, biological and developmental,—from which the evil of violence springs.

Such basic research is essential if we are to stem the endemic violence that, like a malignant cancer, grows unchecked and threatens to destroy the very fabric of our society.

June 1, 1998
Violence in Schools
The New York Times

There has been yet another outbreak of violence at a school, this time in Oregon. Two students are dead and 22 more were wounded; the suspect, Kip Kinkel, is also accused of killing his parents before going to the school.

Have school shootings in this country become an epidemic? What is to blame for this violence?

(1031 previous messages)

    —02:18pm Jun 1, 1998 EST (# of 1063)

June 1, 1998

Following the horrendous school-yard murders by teen-agers in Jonesboro, Arkansas, President Clinton, responding to the nation-wide outpouring of concern, dismay and outrage, suggested that "Attorney-General Janet Reno convene experts to study what might be done in the future" to prevent such obscene violence. (Editorial, March 26). In the short time since then, we have had school-yard murder and rampage in Edinboro, Pennsylvania, Fayetteville, Tennessee, Onalaska, Washington, and Springfield, Oregon. Nothing, so far, about an "expert study". Will the President's suggestion to the Attorney-General be taken seriously, and acted upon, or was it just an appropriate off-the-cuff remark, appropriate to the occasion?

>From the variety of remedies proposed, from "moral guidance" to "more psychologists in schools" to the need for effective gun-control, it is evident that this is a complex problem, that there is no one single answer. Nothing short of a comprehensive, multi-dimensional, inter-disciplinary approach will do.

But attention must be paid. We procrastinate at our own peril.

One answer, or the beginning of one, is the immediate preparation of a WHITE HOUSE CONFERENCE ON VIOLENCE—ITS CAUSES AND PROPOSED REMEDIES, to mobilize the best and the most creative minds of our times, in medicine, psychiatry and psychology, in child-care and development, in ethics and philosophy, in religion and social theory and state-craft, in biology and sociology, in all the behavioral and social sciences, to explore the ground—social, ethical, environmental, biological and developmental-from which the evil of violence springs.

Such basic research is essential if we are to stem the endemic violence that, like a malignant cancer, grows unchecked and threatens to destroy the very fabric of our society.

June 11, 1998
Thoughts at a tree-planting
Sullivan Weekly Opinion

It was only a small group of people that gathered in Mamakating Town Park today, neighbors, and some children, too, to dedicate the planting of a tree as a memorial to Christopher Gardner, who lived a stone's throw from here and whose brutal murder, as Supervisor Duane Roe said, "impacted on the people of this small town more than any event he could remember."

It was a somber group, quiet, thoughtful, still in shock that such a thing could happen in this sleepy community. There wasn't a dry eye among the rapt listeners, as Town Justice Marcelle Matthews spoke of the little boy who was the victim of such heinous child abuse, and of the responsibility of the community at large to see to it that this does not happen again.

A few children, with their small spades, helped tamp the ground for the new tree to take root, while the adults stood around trying to make some sense of it all.

But the only sense to be made, as Supervisor Roe and Ms. Matthews emphasized, was for us all to be alert, aware, responsive to our children and to all the children, and to recognize the importance of a shared responsibility for their healthy growth and development. They are all our children, the responsibility of us all, and the kind of lives they lead will determine what kind of society the future holds for this country.

Coming at a time when violence screams out at us almost daily, and when, specifically, violence toward children and violence by children assault us obscenely, this is a time for serious thinking, and acting, about a problem that we put off at our own peril.

There is, many experts think, a direct line of causation between children who are abused and children who act out violently while still in their teens. The school killings in Jonesboro, Arkansas, where an 11-year-old and a 13-year-old, killed five and wounded 10, and in Springfield, Oregon, where a 15-year-old killed two and wounded 25, electrified the nation, stunned us all into a sense that something must be done, that more attention must be paid.

President Clinton, after the Jonesboro killing spree, requested that "Attorney General Janet Reno convene experts to study what might be done in the future" to prevent such ghastly deeds. (New York Times, March 26). This might be a good beginning. The problems of child abuse and child violence, and their linkage, cry for more serious attention and study.

We need, and have needed for a long time, a professional, well-thought out and well prepared *White House conference on violence . . . its causes and remedies*, to mobilize the best and most creative minds of our times, in medicine and psychiatry and psychology, in child-care and child development, in ethics and philosophy, in religion and social theory, in biology and anthropology and sociology, in all the behavioral and social sciences, in order to explore the ground—social, ethical, environmental, biological and developmental—from which the evil violence springs.

Such basic research is practically non-existent. Its importance cannot be overstated if we are to stem the endemic violence that, like malignant cancer, grows unchecked and threatens to destroy the very fabric of our society.

A major study, sponsored at the very highest levels of our government, to spur our understanding of child violence and to begin to formulate long-range programs to deal with the issue, would be an outcome of hope born of the despair of Springfield, Oregon, and Jonesboro, Arkansas, and Bloomingburg, N.Y.

June 14, 1998
Letter to the Editor
The New York Times

Your front page story, "From Adolescent Angst To Shooting Up Schools, 6/14), by the very nature of its wide-ranging coverage, strengthens my conviction that there is a fatal lack of serious, in-depth scholarship and research directed to the problem of violence in general and violence toward and by children in particular.

Timothy Egan's report is good journalism. But its very topicality points up the need for extensive scientific study. President Clinton expressed that need when, after the ghastly school killings in Jonesboro, Arkansas, he suggested that "Attorney-General Janet Reno convene experts to study what might be done in the future" to prevent its repetition. (March 25, New York Times). Will the President's suggestion be taken seriously, and acted upon, or was it just an off-the-cuff remark, appropriate to the occasion?

It is evident that this is a complex problem, that there is no one single answer. Nothing short of a comprehensive, multi-dimensional, inter-disciplinary approach will do.

The beginning of an answer might be sought in a professional, well-thought-out and well-prepared "WHITE HOUSE CONFERENCE ON VIOLENCE—ITS CAUSES AND REMEDIES", where we might mobilize the best and most creative minds of our time, in medicine, psychiatry and psychology, in child care and child development, in ethics and philosophy, in religion and social theory, in biology and sociology, in all the behavioral and social sciences, in order to explore the ground—social, ethical, environmental, biological and developmental—from which the evil of violence springs.

Such basic research, with the moral authority of the highest levels of our government, is essential if we are to stem the endemic violence that, like a malignant cancer, grows unchecked and threatens to destroy the very fabric of our society.

June 26, 1998
Letter to the Editor
The New York Times

Herbert Mitgang's book review of "Daimler-Benz in the Third Reich", by Neil Gregor (June 26) reveals nothing new when he tells us that the Mercedes-Benz was Hitler's favorite car, but he does drive home the chilling information that the Daimler-Benz company "like other companies producing arms for the Third Reich, became one of the way stations to the death camps." And that "its relatively healthy position down to the end of the war was at least partly at the expense of the health and indeed in many cases the lives, of thousands of victims of forced labor." He informs us that "Mercedes-Benz was a transit point for people going to the death camps."

The Chrysler Corporation, of course, looked only to the bottom line in their current merger. The one and only criterion is PROFIT. But I wonder how many investors will still cast a long look into history. Can it be that cupidity will always overcome morality? Is there a difference between "unforgiving" and massive "rewarding"? Or is there a statute of limitations on history's butchers?

July 3, 1998
Study abuse further
The Times Herald Record

Congratulations on your continuing front-page coverage of the issue of child abuse, following the tragic death of Christopher Gardner.

At a time when killings by children in Arkansas, Oregon and elsewhere have stunned the nation, this heinous murder in our own Bloomingburg has heightened our sense of urgency about child violence. Following the killings in Jonesboro, Ark., President Clinton requested that Attorney General Janet Reno convene experts to study what might be done to prevent such violence. There have been more kids killing kids since then, but no action by either Reno or Clinton.

A beginning might be made if there were convened a White House conference on violence, to mobilize our best and most creative minds to explore the ground from which violence springs.

Such scholarly, scientific research is essential if we are to stem the violence that threatens to destroy the fabric of our society.

July 13, 1998
Science and Religion
The New York Times

With a wave of new books, a forthcoming PBS special, and a much-publicized conference recently in Berkeley, these are metaphysical boom times. The focus of the effort: to reconcile science and religion. Do these two very different ways of explaining the world have anything in common? Or are they fated to stay apart? I gave my thoughts on this in a *Science*. Please take a look and give us your own opinion.

Postscript: You might also want to take a look at my piece in Sunday's (7/11) *Week in Review*.

(679 previous messages)

—10:55pm Jul 13, 1998 EST (# 670 of 817)

Meyer Rangell July 6, 1998

Editor The New York Times

Dear Sir:

In a Letter to the New York Times, printed on July 5 under the title "When Religion and Science Collide", Mr. Clay Williams urges scientists to "give up their stranglehold on empirical truth as the only form of truth that matters".

But what other form of truth is there?

Webster defines "empirical" as "relying or based solely on experiments or experience", and "truth" as "the quality of being in accordance with experience, facts, or reality."

Thus, theological, or religious "truth", implied by Mr. Williams as deserving equal consideration to that based on experience, facts or reality, is surely the ultimate in confounding oxymorons.

July 19, 1998
Letter to the Editor
The New York Times Book Review

In his review of "Explaining Hitler" (July 19), by Ron Rosenbaum, Mr. Michael R. Marrus states that "the great quest has been to find the source of his (Hitler's) anti-Semitic obsession." Although he quotes from the estimable work of Lucy Dawidowicz ("The War Against the Jews"), Rosenbaum, and Marrus, inexplicably overlook Ms. Davidowicz' historic insight into the seminal ideological link between Hitler and the Christian theologian, Martin Luther, whom Harvard Professor Daniel J. Goldhagen, in his equally ground-breaking work, "Hitler's Willing Executioners", called "the greatest anti-Semite of his time". Marrus denigrates Davidowicz' work by calling her evidence "problematic". Yet there is nothing "problematic" with the unambiguous, forthright prose that Ms. Davidowicz brings to the problem, as she writes:

"A line of anti-Semitic descent from Martin Luther to Adolph Hitler is easy to draw. Both Luther and Hitler were obsessed by a demonologized universe inhabited by Jews. 'Know, Christian,' wrote Luther, 'that next to the devil thou hast no enemy more cruel, more venomous and violent than a true Jew.' . . . Luther's protective authority was invoked by the Nazis when they came to power, and his anti-Semitic writings enjoyed a revival of popularity."

And Professor Goldhagen wrote, "Martin Luther's antisemitism was ferocious and influential enough to have earned him a place in the pantheon of anti-Semites."

So much for the "great quest" to find the source of Hitler's fanatic anti-Semitism!

August 13, 1998
Drug Policy
The New York Times

Your editorial of August 8 ("Changing the Drug Laws") correctly highlighted the moral stupidity, as well as the practical ineffectiveness, of treating the crime of "being caught with four ounces of cocaine" with punishments equal to the crimes of murder and rape. The Rockefeller laws which mandated such an approach surely need revision, if not outright repeal.

However, you do not go far enough. The real answer is to transfer the problem of drug addiction from the criminal justice system, where it is "treated" like a crime to be addressed by prisons and punishment, to the health-care delivery system, where it would be treated as a disease. Research and rehabilitation cannot flourish in the atmosphere of a criminal "justice" system that lacks the resources as well as the philosophical background that must be brought to a problem that is clearly a health problem and not a problem (read "crime") for ill-equipped and ill-trained policemen and prison guards.

August 19, 1998
Clinton's Speech to the Nation
The New York Times

In 18 Letters on President Clinton's "mea culpa" in today's paper, the word "moral" was mentioned in only two, and the word "integrity" not at all, while your lead editorial stressed "Betrayal and Embarrassment", with only a passing mention of the "moral proportion". Yet the major damage in this sordid affair is precisely and overwhelmingly the moral loss to our country set in motion by our leader-in-chief and the inevitable cynicism that is already metastasizing like a rapidly spreading cancer into the entire fabric of our body politic.

The President, having demonstrated his lack of both morality and integrity, ought to resign before he can do further harm, and disappear into the kind of total oblivion usually reserved for malfeasants by the Federal Witness Protection Program.

Aug. 27, 1998
Drug cause is traffic, not addiction
The Times Herald Record

Nancy Reagan said, "Just Say NO."
Bill Clinton has upped the ante. At a cost of $1 billion, with Newt Gingrich in tow, he plans to convince our troubled youth with the ultimate in advertising exhortation, a la Mel Brooks. "Don't tear paper!" the well-compensated ad-biz hucksters will scream. In this scenario, selling the anti-drug message is no more a problem than selling deodorants or toothpaste or the new model cars. Where Nancy failed, Bill, with a cool billion, hopes to prevail.

How many more children will have to be killed?
How many more families destroyed?
How many more schools made useless and unfit for education?
How many more lives with no future but violence?
How many more prisons to be built and filled with hopelessness and despair?
How many governments corrupted?

How much more corruption in our body politic, here and abroad, can we tolerate . . . before we recognize that the cause is not the epidemic of drug addiction per se, but the illegal drug traffic that supplies that need and poisons everything and everyone with which it comes into contact?

Isn't it time that we recognized that there are two problems here? One is the disease of drug-addiction, which we are at long last beginning, however tentatively, to understand and to make progress along the lines of meaningful, innovative approaches to treatment and prevention.

The other problem is the scourge of the drug-trafficking empire, the magnitude of which is swept under the carpet, certainly not adequately fought, although it is the source of a major assault on our social fabric. When we separate the two, we'll be on the way to some solutions. As long as we refuse to recognize the need for such a separation, drug abuse, encouraged by the traffickers, will continue unabated, along with the rapid decline of stability and integrity in our social institutions.

At this time, the primary threat is from the drug trafficker, not from the drug user. It is the illegal, multi-billion-dollar international drug-trafficking industry that is the enemy. (I heard drug czar Barry McCaffrey inform us on a TV show that 12 million drug users in the United States spend $50 billion a year on illegal drugs). Like the gangsters in the Prohibition era, they feed on the illegality that drives their industry, and the desperation of their addict customers, just as the Capone gang fed on the illegality of alcohol.

The only answer is the decriminalization and selective legalization of the drug market. The murder, violence and gangsterism that characterize our drug culture will not be brought under control until drug marketing and distribution are transferred from criminal gangs and powerful illegal cartels to legitimate legal (and taxable) channels. Just as the criminality and violence associated with booze was not eliminated until the Volstead Act was repealed and alcoholism brought into proper perspective as a social/health problem to be addressed by the healthcare delivery system rather than by the criminal justice system, so will the drug problem not be productively addressed until the Harrison Narcotics Act of 1914, and its consequences in repressive "drug-war" legislation, are repealed. If the repeal of Volstead has taught us anything, it is the validation of the wisdom of philosopher George Santayana in his well-remembered insight that those who fail to learn from the mistakes of history are doomed to repeat them.

In a recent in-depth analysis, author Mike Gray ("DRUG CRAZY, how we got into this mess and how we can get out") wrote: "Americans will have to take the drug market out of the hands of the Tijuana Cartel and the Gangsters Disciples, and put it back into the hands of doctors and pharmacists where it was before 1914."

That is not to say that legalization, under proper government controls, will end drug abuse. But it is to say that until our energies are redirected, away from multi-billion-dollar, ineffective "war on drugs" that has benefited nobody more than the drug trafficker, and effectively directed toward the problems of research, treatment and prevention of the problem of drug abuse as a treatable disease, no progress will be made. The billions now being spent in the useless effort to combat the powerful and well-connected gangsters of the drug cartels should be directed toward the field of treatment and research, within the parameters of the health-care system, and not the hopelessly out-maneuvered criminal justice system. Legalization will cut the ground from under the illegal traffickers, whose huge profits derive from the illegal status that creates their huge, victimized market and the unconscionable returns it provides.

August 30, 1998
Is Impeachment an Option?
The New York Times

Assuming Starr does submit a report to Congress, should they consider impeachment proceedings? Or is this simply a private matter that has been blown all out of proportion?

(1607 previous messages)

—06:51pm Aug 30, 1998 EST (# of 1609)

Meyer Rangell August 25, 1998

The New York Times To The Editor:

Thomas L. Friedman's crucial question, "'can' he be President anymore?" (Op-Ed, Aug. 25) was answered in part only the day before when a White House aide said, "there's a sense of frustration that we can't focus on issues that really mean something to people day to day" (NYT, 8/24, "Federal Officials Shaken By President's Admission.")

>From his own Administration officials to the public at large, President Clinton's shameful abandonment of morality and integrity has spawned a terrible cynicism that is felt not only in a creeping paralysis in governance but is spreading like a metastasizing cancer into the very fabric of our body politic.

President Clinton has delivered a body-blow to our government's ethical posture and to our national MORAL ENVIRONMENT, with consequences as yet unforeseen.

Without the bedrock of morality and integrity that must be central to the Presidency, Bill Clinton ought to resign before he can do further harm. His influence on our country and on our youth should be ended forthwith. His lack of contrition as he tries to brazen it out only exacerbates and prolongs the evil. Perhaps he could follow Hamlet's advice, "Get thee to a nunnery!" (or in his case, to a monastery) Or, even better, having disgraced the "bully pulpit" of the Oval Office, he should disappear into the kind of total oblivion reserved for malfeasants through the courtesy of the Federal Witness Protection Program!

September 29, 1998
Citizens, Not Enablers
The New York Times

President Clinton's transgressions are described in some quarters as being a result of "addiction" or "disease" and the people who elected him as being "enablers" (Week in Review, Sept. 27). Such obfuscating nonsense results when the problem is transferred from the social-political realm to psychopathology, a process deplored over 30 years ago by Dr. Thomas Szasz, who warned of the psychiatric tendency wherein "moral and political values may be redefined as health values."

The people who elected Mr. Clinton are not "enablers" but free and responsible citizens exercising their electoral rights. In this sense, the evangelist Robert Schuller's unctuous comment that "we all share part of the shame" is neither helpful nor factual.

October 10, 1998
Clinton should resign
The Times Herald Record

My conviction that the president ought to resign is strengthened by Starr's revelations and its consequences for the following reasons:

- Clinton's admitted lying and has continued flimsy, legalistic "defense" of the indefensible.
- The almost undeniable commission of perjury by the president.
- And, most important, Clinton's loss of any moral stature as well as his inability to provide effective political leadership in the new circumstances. The public defection of leading Democrats like Lieberman, Gephardt, Moynihan, and others who won't let him near their election campaigns, amply demonstrate that he has become an albatross to his own party, and an obstacle, rather that a leading force, to the advancement of the liberal Democratic programs that he formerly led.

For these reasons, among others, he ought to resign before he does further harm to the presidency and to his own party.

October 25, 1998
Letter to the Editor
The New York Times Magazine

"The experts weigh in," we are solemnly informed, with the startling discovery that "sexual boredom is the most pandemic dysfunction in this country." Wow!

Not one "expert" has even one word to say about our real "dysfunction"—the willingness, even eagerness, with which we allow sex and its mystifications to obscure our real problems: health care, child welfare, education, racism and the need to protect the elderly and the Social Security System.

Sex is the ultimate cover-up.

November 6, 1998
The Books of Slavery
The New York Times

The recent spate of Letters to the Editor on the Thomas Jefferson/Sally Hemings affair prompted this comment:

Meyer Rangell November 4, 1998

To the Editor:

It is ironic and instructive that the Letters on "Rethinking Jefferson . . ." (Nov. 4) revealed a revulsion toward Thomas Jefferson's taking his slave, Sally Hemings, as a concubine that ran more deeply than any similar revulsion toward the institution of slavery itself.

It is as though a slaveholder, Jefferson among others, who could and did buy and sell human beings, work them to death for profit, and countenance the utmost of brutality toward them as "normal", is suddenly reviled because he also took his sexual pleasure as he pleased,—a common practice among slaveholders known to historians for a hundred years and now suddenly discovered to be reprehensible. Not the slavery, mind you, but the sex suddenly arouses our sleeping conscience.

November 9, 1998
Letter to the Editor
The New Yorker

Mr. Rangell did not say, but this letter was apparently sent to *The New Yorker* magazine on 27 September 1998. He wrote the magazine again 20 October 1998 with this comment: "Was I naive to expect that you might print my Letter of September 27 (below), while Chanel #5 [is] advertised heavily in the magazine?" He sent it to this page as an item of criticism of John Updike's point of view in his *New Yorker* book review. He has a point worth noting.

9 November 1998

To the Editor:

It is astonishing to read John Updike (not a man to be careless with words) suggest that Coco Chanel might be "the greatest French woman of the century" (Sept. 21 issue). Or to read his cavalier dismissal of the pro-Nazi behavior of Chanel during World War II: her "attempted use of the Nazi anti-Semitic laws to wrest control of Chanel No. 5 from her (Jewish) partner"; her protected position in Paris during the war because of her friendship with the traitor Pierre Laval, her love affair with a Nazi spy both during and after the war. To view these events as forgivable peccadillos in an oh-so-glamorous life is particularly repulsive at this time when Nazi crimes against Jews and all humanity are being freshly recalled (as in the hypocritical dealings of Swiss and Italian banks and insurance companies as they reaped huge profits at the expense of Holocaust victims).

Updike's literary skills are hardly in evidence when he casually refers to Chanel's "attempted exploitation of the Holocaust as not becoming". "Not becoming"!

"Greatest French woman of the century" . . . or Nazi collaborator?

November 11, 1998
Campaign Fund-raising
The New York Times

The most important fact to emerge from this election is not about the issues, or the "character" of the candidates, or the candidates' qualifications to lead, or the state of mind of the electorate.

None of the above!

It is the ugly fact that MONEY has a lethal stranglehold on our electoral system.

The electoral process as it is now exercised is dominated by money from beginning to end.

>From the time when candidates are selected by the major parties, throughout the long campaign, and particularly during the frenetic few weeks prior to Election Day, it is the ability of the candidate to provide money, or to raise money, or to attract major contributors to what is, ironically but accurately called his "war-chest", that determines almost everything. "How much money can the candidate raise?" is the first question asked. The high cost of campaigning, getting higher every year, is the major corrupter of our electoral process and represents a blight and a danger to our most cherished institution: the free election of independent, un-bought candidates under a system of free, honest choice based on relevant issues by a free citizenry that is not manipulated or brain-washed by the new class of highly-paid, shrewd, purposeful political professionals, who will sell anything from cars, deodorants, and cat-food, to political candidates . . . . as long as the fee is right!

The high costs of campaigning conspire to make the aspiring candidate's ability to raise funds more important than his capacity for legislative leadership. It has become a truism that the first responsibility of a candidate is to get elected (whatever the cost!), and the second to get re-elected (at any cost!); any good he may accomplish in between is purely accidental. Perpetual campaigning is his first priority.

Efforts to put a brake on campaign spending, the Shays-Meehan bill in the House and the McCain-Feingold bill in the Senate, were defeated this year by a Republican-controlled Congress. The result in this election is a wild increase in political spending, using the euphemistically called "soft money", i.e., Party money raised by energetic continuous fund-raising and arm-twisting to create huge funds for the support of candidates by skirting the Federal Election Commission's spending limits. "Both parties are expanding their use of issue advertisements to make use of their soft money. Republican Party committees have taken in $100.2 million in soft money this election cycle, compared with about $35 million in the 1994 cycle, while Democrats have received $75.6 million, up from about $40 million" (New York Times, Oct. 26). The pressure on candidates to help generate this kind of money is enormous.

The Federal Election Commission reports that "combined donations to all national party committees have risen by more than 50 percent from the same date in 1994. Republican committees have raised $284 million, compared with $185 million in 1994; Democrats have raised $174 million, compared with $111 million" (NYT, Oct. 24). "A party committee set up to help Republican Senate candidates is taking in $300,000 a day, and a fund-raiser it sponsored few weeks ago to celebrate the Republican Senate majority took in $7 million!"

In New York, the mud-slinging campaign between Al D'Amato and Chuck Schumer will cost in the range of $40 million. For this outlay the public is treated to the edifying spectacle of Senator "pothole" calling his opponent a "putzhead" while the ubiquitous ex-Mayor Ed Koch prates on TV that it could have been worse, he could have been called a "schmuck"!

Independent candidate Thomas Golisano is spending $20 million of his own money in the race for Governor.

Across the nation the costs of elections have grown to astronomic proportions. The Presidential election of the year 2000 will probably go into the billions. "War-chests" are even now in the making.

It is a scenario under which only the paid hucksters and television magnates get rich. The rest of us will pay the cost and reap the harvest of political corruption, low-level name-calling TV bytes, the absence of serious meaningful debate on the issues, and elected officials who are beholden to their wealthy contributors.

Another disturbing aspect of this fund-raising frenzy is the significant fact that candidates seeking re-election, or election to a higher office, do their electioneering on OUR TIME and at OUR EXPENSE. From the President down (Mr. Clinton has already made over 100 campaign trips to support local candidates), to Congressmen and Senators, all are on the campaign trail while on the public payroll, when they should be in Washington passing legislation and doing the job they were elected to do. The pressure of re-election is a continuous problem that prevents significantly their full-time attention to their jobs as elected officials. There must be a better way!

Electoral reform is an issue that must be faced, lest our democracy is further tarnished and shamefully corrupted.

November 12, 1998
The Books of Slavery
The New York Times

The continuing discussion of the Thomas Jefferson/Sally Hemings liaison (Letters, Nov. 9) runs the risk of trivializing the horrors of slavery and its permeating effects on American life and history in the same way that anecdotes of individual kindness tend to trivialize the stupendous iniquity of the Holocaust. Perhaps it is a human trait to seek out a shred of humanity within the landscape of Hell. How else can one assess the comment that "Jefferson stepped over what should have been a boundary of decency in the master-slave relationship" (Letter, Nov. 9)? That there was indeed a "boundary of decency' in any sense of the word within the institution of slavery itself is a far leap of wishful thinking—like assigning some "decency" to the oven-keepers of Auschwitz.

To even begin to "understand" the monstrous evil that was slavery, as well as the monstrosity of the Holocaust, one must not be de-railed by the all-too-human effort to discover a "boundary of decency" that may tend to paper over the depths of depravity inherent in both instances.

November 29, 1998
Electoral Reform A Must
Mexico City—The News

In his column of November 23, Tony Snow asks the relevant question, "Why should I care about politics?" But he assiduously fails to address the crucial fact of the last election: that is that the public showed its disgust with the political process as now practiced by staying away in droves. According to the Committee for the Study of the American Electorate, only 36 percent of eligible voters bothered to vote, the lowest turnout since 1942. (*New York Times*, 11/6). "The largest number of eligible Americans in history opted not to vote, estimated at 119.45 million!" (ibid).

The sorry fact is that elections today are not about the issues, or the "character" of the candidates, or the candidates' qualifications to lead, or the state of mind of the electorate. It is the ugly fact that MONEY has a lethal stranglehold on our electoral system.

The electoral process as it is now exercised is dominated by money from beginning to end.

From the time when candidates are selected by the major parties, throughout the long campaign, and particularly during the frenetic few weeks prior to Election Day, it is the ability of the candidate to provide money, or to attract major contributors to what is, ironically but accurately called his "war-chest", that determines almost everything. "How much money can the candidate raise?" is the first question asked. The high cost of campaigning, getting higher every year, is the major corrupter of our electoral process and represents a blight and a danger to our most cherished institution: the free election of independent, unbought candidates under a system of free, honest choice, based on relevant issues by a free citizenry that is not manipulated or brain-washed by the new class of highly-paid, shrewd, purposeful political professionals, who will sell anything from cars, deodorants, and cat-food, to political candidates. . . . as long as the fee is right!

The high costs of campaigning conspire to make the aspiring candidate's ability to raise funds more important than his capacity for legislative leadership. It has become a truism that the first responsibility of a candidate is to get elected (whatever the cost!), and the second to get re-elected (at any cost!); any good he may accomplish in between is purely accidental.

Efforts to put a brake on campaign spending, the Shays-Meehan bill in the House and the McCain-Feingold bill in the Senate, were defeated this year by a Republican-controlled Congress. The result in this election is a wild increase in political spending, using the euphemistically called "soft money," i.e. party money raised by energetic, continuous fund-raising and arm-twisting to create huge funds for the support of candidates by skirting the Federal Election Commission's spending limits. "Both parties are expanding their use of issue advertisements to make use of their soft money. Republican Party committees have taken in 100.2 million dollars in soft money this election cycle, compared with about 35 million dollars in the 1994 cycle, while Democrats have received 75.6 million dollars, up from about 40 million dollars." (New York Times, Oct. 26). The pressure on candidates to help generate this kind of money is enormous, and takes preference over almost all other considerations.

The Federal Election Commission reports that "combined donations to all national party committees have risen by more than 50 percent from the same date in 1994. Republican committees have raised 284 million dollars, compared with 185 million dollars in 1994; Democrats have raised 174 million dollars, compared with 111 million dollars." (New York Times, Oct. 24). "A party committee set up to help Republican Senate candidates is taking in 300,000 dollars a day, and a fundraiser it sponsored a few weeks ago to celebrate the Republican Senate majority took in 7 million dollars!"

In New York, the mud-slinging campaign between Al D'Amato and Chuck Schumer cost in the range of 40 million dollars. For this outlay the public was treated to the edifying spectacle of Senator "pothole" descending to the vulgarism of calling his opponent a "putzhead"!

Independent candidate Thomas Golisano, spent 20 million dollars of his own money in the race for Governor, proving once again that if one is rich enough one can indulge in the lust for fame and political power.

Across the nation the costs of elections have grown to astronomic proportions. The Presidential election of the year 2000 will probably go into the billions. "War-chests" are even now in the making. It is a scenario under which only the paid hucksters and the television magnates get rich. The rest of us will pay the cost and reap the harvest of political corruption, low-level name-calling TV bytes, the absence of meaningful debate on the issues, and elected officials who are beholden to their wealthy contributors.

Another disturbing aspect of this fundraising frenzy is the significant fact that candidates seeking re-election, or election to a higher office, do their electioneering on OUR TIME and at OUR EXPENSE. >From the President down (Mr. Clinton made over 100 campaign trips to support local candidates), to Congressmen and Senators, all are on the campaign trail while on the public payroll, when they should be in Washington passing legislation and doing the job they were elected to do. The pressure of re-election is a continuous problem that prevents significantly their full-time attention to their jobs as elected officials. There must be a better way!

Electoral reform is an issue that must be faced, lest our democracy is further tarnished and shamefully corrupted.

December 20, 1998
The Scourge Of Drugs
Mexico City—The News

Today's report that Mexico's Foreign Relations Secretary Rosario Green is in Washington to discuss the drug problem with top American officials, and that President Zedillo expressed his concern over the significant consequences of an American "decertification" on Mexican/American relationships, (*The News*, Dec. 15), emphasize the relevance of the following comments, submitted last week:

Dec. 10, 1998

It is that time of year again. Once again, in what has become a yearly ritual, Congress is poised to decide whether or not Mexico is to be "certified" as an ally in the war against drugs.

The outcome of the debate in Washington will have serious consequences on the relationship between the United States and Mexico, going well beyond the problem of drugs to the entire range of our relationship. "Decertification means aid is cut partially or completely. Mexico, according to a local newspaper, is in danger of being decertified." (*The News*, Dec. 9).

An important aspect of this "certification" process is the not-so-subtle manner in which it deflects our understanding of the scourge of drugs in the United States. The fault, this policy infers, is not in the United States and its own social problems, but in the foreign supplier. The villain, the prime causative agent of drug abuse, this argument runs, is abroad, in the nations that raise and supply the nasty stuff, rather than in the social problems in the United States that create the largest single market for mind-altering drugs in the world. Earlier this year, U.S. anti-drug czar, Barry McCaffrey stated that there are 12 million illegal drug users in the United States who create a market of 50 billion dollars per year! It is that huge active demand, many suggest, that generates the supply. The profits, however illegal, have proved too rich, too enormous, too available, for foreign cartels and native drug dealers to abandon.

Greater attention to addressing and reducing that demand at home through rehabilitation programs, widespread and meaningful educational efforts at all levels of our educational system, and a wide array of social programs to address the poverty, discrimination, and frustration among the youth in our ghettos, would be more in order than the easy route of "Blame the Foreign Supplier".

One cannot help but agreeing with Mexico's Foreign Relations Secretary, Rosario Green, ("Mexico Denounces Certification Process" . . . and "Green Defends Nation's Sovereignty" . . . *The News*, Dec. 9), when she denounced the process thusly, as "the U.S. government's unacceptable and unhealthy practice of judging and certifying other countries' efforts in the fight against drug trafficking." Green added that this type of policy "only presents obstacles for cooperation between nations and creates animosity between the United States and the country it decertifies." (ibid)

"Physician, heal thyself", would be a more appropriate motto for us to consider. CURB THE DEMAND AT HOME BEFORE YOU SHIFT THE BLAME TO THE CULPRIT ABROAD.

December 27, 1998
Educating For Peace
Mexico City—The News

We are indebted to David Amato (column Dec. 20) for directing our attention to the unusual, if not extraordinary step taken by a leading university in Mexico in the furtherance of world amity and good will: "Anahuac Univ. Practices The Golden Rule," we are informed, as it names its new cultural center after Yitzhak Rabin. (*The News*, Dec. 20).

It is indeed remarkable that a country thousands of miles away from Israel, with a small population of Jews (Mexico's Jewish population numbers only 40,700) should see fit to honor the martyred Israeli Prime Minister at this time and in this lasting way. In creating The Yitzhak Rabin Cultural Center, Anahuac University establishes a significant remembrance that will stand through the years as a permanent reminder of the philosophy not only of a great Israeli, but of a great and practical peace-maker in the troubled history of the Middle East.

Mr. Amato aptly describes this enterprise as an application of the "Golden Rule" as a guide for human behavior in modern times. One will remember that the most celebrated expression of that Rule is that of the Hebrew sage, Rabbi Hillell, who was asked by a student to "tell us what Torah means, the entire five books of the Pentateuch, but briefly, while standing on one foot!"

Hillell replied, "What is hateful to you, don't do to your fellow man. The rest is commentary. Now go study." Centuries later, right here in Mexico, Benito Juarez voiced the same opinion when he said: "Respect for the right of others is peace."

Yitzhak Rabin did indeed represent that "Golden Rule" in today's world. Peace with justice in Israel and the entire Middle East may very well depend on the emergence of someone of his stature, integrity, and philosophy to re-invigorate the foundering peace process before it is too late.

In distant Mexico, an institution of higher education furthers that process in more than symbolic ways with this remarkable dedication.

January 10, 1999
Faith In Human Character
Mexico City—The News

Poised at the brink of the penultimate year of the 20th century, approaching the year dubbed by our new class of reigning technocrats as the last before the fateful "Y2K"—hailed by many as the dawn of a new era for mankind, dreaded by others as the onset of Armageddon, predicted by many serious futurists as the day of unmeasured disaster in the financial world and in economic and government circles as our computers fail and crash, the year we are about to enter, by any calculation, will be pivotal, unpredictable to say the least, and the last opportunity for 20th century man to hone his legacy for future generations.

Although it may be all too sanguine, even Pollyanish, to expect that this last year can change the murderous characteristics of the expiring century—the most violent century in the recorded history of man, committing unheard of violence to the ecology, altering forever our natural environment, reaching new levels of violence of man to man, perhaps we can usher in, in this last year, a period of new and unprecedented thought, of introspection and re-examination of our priorities. Thought, after all, and the daring to contemplate basic change, are the forerunners of human renewal. That is, perhaps, the burden and the challenge of the coming year. BEFORE Y2K.

Is it possible, at long last, to grasp the deadly continuum of irrational hate-bigotry-intolerance-cruelty to others-murder-violence-slaughter—genocide that has seemed to permeate the human condition and that has characterized, with increasing intensity, this past century?

While man has demonstrated the most astonishing break-throughs in science and technology—men on the moon, space vehicles in orbit, the unleashing of the awesome power of the atom, computers that think and disseminate knowledge more efficiently than man, our technical wizardry has been equaled, even surpassed, by an unparalleled destructiveness, while our conscience no longer seems to be human as we become inured to horrors unimaginable: the Holocaust, slaughter in Rwanda, Kosovo, Cambodia, the former Yugoslavia, Chiapas, ubiquitous "religious" murder and terror "in the name of God," domestic violence, children killing children in schoolyards around the country, world-wide violence in drug-obsessed society.

It is, perhaps, no accident that the American people were so easily distracted from the large-scale immorality and violence on a world scale to immerse themselves in the saga of "sexual McCarthyism" and "sex-drenched politics" at home.

Violence, its origins and causes, needs to be studied as never before. We must mobilize the best and most creative minds of our time, in medicine and science, in psychiatry and psychology, in child care and child development, in ethics and philosophy and religion, in social theory and biology and sociology, in all the human behavioral and social sciences, in order to explore the ground—social, ethical, environmental, political, biological and developmental—from which the evil of violence springs.

Such basic research, with the moral and financial authority of the highest levels of government (perhaps it is time for another White House Conference On The Causes And Remedies Of Violence) is essential if we are to stem the endemic violence that, like a malignant cancer, grows unchecked and threatens to destroy the very fabric of our society.

In a prescient and far-ranging study, "Our Violent Society" (1970), psychiatrist David Abrahamsen wrote of the prevalence of "hidden violent aggression" and of the "anger generated by fear" leading to violence. The climate is described by Matthew Arnold as:

"We are here as on a darkling plain
Swept with confusing alarms of struggle and flight
Where ignorant armies clash by night."

Re-evaluations, research, renewed efforts to understand our humanity and to chart a new course for mankind may be the essential components of that fabled "bridge to the 21st century," much maligned metaphor that it is. We may find that our problems, and their solutions, lie not in the realm of technology but in the deeper and more determining realm of human character.

Feliz Año Nuevo!

January 17, 1999
What "Conscience?"
Mexico City—The News

In the recent debate in the House of Representatives and now in the Senate "trial", no word has been more over-used than the word "conscience," as speaker after speaker solemnly averred that his/her vote would be driven by his/her "conscience", above all other considerations.

Webster's New American Dictionary (1995) defines "conscience" as "consciousness of the moral right and wrong of one's own acts and motives."

Note that it is the MORAL quality, THE RIGHT AND THE WRONG of it, that lies at the heart of our understanding of "conscience." Not partisan, or political, or practical, or convenient, or expedient, but MORAL.

Is it not confounding, therefore, to observe that the "conscience" which drove the voting in the House on impeachment expressed itself strictly along party lines: only five Democrats found their conscience among the 225 Republicans who voted for impeachment, while just two Republican "consciences" were among the 186 Democrats whose consciences told them to vote against?

Is it not strange that the dictates of "conscience" were so unfailingly partisan and political—and predictable? Or is it more than "conscience" that is the issue? Can it be that political considerations of power, re-election, control of Congress, strivings for a Republican White House—all the elements of naked political goals that were there long before Clinton's abominable and indefensible sexual behavior, now form the dynamic of this all-out "BOOT-OUT-THE-PRESIDENT-CAMPAIGN, guised in the sacred name of "conscience"?

"Conscience makes cowards of us all," warned Shakespeare. At this crucial juncture, let us not permit hypocritical calls to a suddenly-aroused "conscience" to mask the political realities that confront us.

Sunday, January 24, 1999
Clinton Psychoanalyzed
Mexico City The News

Who is this man, William Jefferson Clinton?

Behind this fair-haired boy with his charismatic smile, his winsome, *princely demeanor* and his dashing good looks, we see at a closer glance *a complex and obscure psyche*.

Though he defies *a definitive character profile*, it is irrefutable that this man is no dummy. Despite his lustful nature, he knew exactly what he was doing when Monica Lewinsky came into his life. He knew how to read people, and she was as transparent as glass. His powerful political machine had helped him sidestep the Jennifer Flowers, the Paula Jones, the Kathleen Willey dalliances (and countless others), but Monica Lewinsky was his Waterloo, or better yet, his "coming out."

I propose that William Jefferson Clinton willingly, though *perhaps not consciously* created this *bizarre scenario*. He wanted to get caught. There is simply no other explanation. He had everything going for him . . . but life was too good, so he sabotaged himself!

Despite his undisputed brilliance and statesmanship, this man is *sadly flawed. In his maturation process, he failed to develop any sense of self esteem. He is a hollow shell*. Without going into a full *psychoanalytic dissection*, it is clear that despite a life of countless successes, *he remains a lonely, frightened child*. He has *been crying out for help for a long time. Monica Lewinsky heard him*, and it would appear they deserve each other.

In his *progressive sickness*, he continues to display total denial of his dark side. How else could he present himself before his legislative peers to deliver a State of the Union Address on the same day that these very statesmen are deciding his ultimate political and personal fate? It is the *Theatre of the Absurd*, and he has engaged us all as players in his surreal morbid drama. God help us.

Sincerely,
S. J. Wichterman
Bucerias, Nayarit via e-mail

February 7, 1999

Mr. (psychoanalyst?) S.J. Wichterman's Jan. 24 Letter to The Editor ("Clinton Psychoanalyzed") is proof again of the perils of long distance psychiatry and a rush to "psychoanalytic dissection."

It is a long way from Bucerias to Washington, and, without troubling to make the trip or see the "patient," Mr. Wichterman offers, up a lyrical description of President Clinton that is more suitable to the simplicities of Hans Christian Andersen or the entertaining fairy tales of the Brothers Grimm than to the realities of today's bitter, bruising politics and one of its major players.

Without the benefit of couch or interview, Mr. Wichterman describes the President as of "princely demeanor," but plagued by "a complex and obscure psyche" (whose isn't?), who "defies a definitive character profile" (although Mr. Wichterman is not above making the attempt), who has a "lustful nature" and who, "perhaps unconsciously" is "sadly flawed" because his "maturation process failed to develop any sense of self-esteem." He is "a hollow shell . . . who remains a lonely frightened child . . . crying out for help for a long time." And, lo and behold, "Monica Lewinsky heard him," and rushed to his rescue!

In sum, we are solemnly informed, President Clinton suffers from "a progressive sickness," although Mr. Wichterman modestly declines to offer a specific diagnosis, or to explain how it affects his "performance as President (a performance still approved by almost three-quarters of the American people, according to the latest polls).

The only statement close to the bone here is that this entire fiasco is "Theater of the Absurd" and a "surreal morbid drama." But the sad part is that Mr. Wichterman adds to this sense of absurdity and unreality by his attempts to "explain" the President and the impeachment mania in psychoanalytic terms. (That may be another story, to be sure, if approached seriously and scientifically in therapeutic treatment in a proper therapeutic setting). But it does no service to present-day realities and to the complex problems of constitutionality, democracy, impeachment politics, and the issues of presidential performance and the popular will, to transfer the problem from the public arena to the murky field of psychiatry and psychoanalysis.

The problem, as members on both sides of the aisle have said, is political. Impeachment is a political proceeding; it is a matter of power politics, of political gain or loss. It is politically motivated, as the naked partisanship in every vote in the House or Senate proves beyond the shadow of a doubt.

The issues of public importance and significance will ultimately be decided in the political arena—and not on the analyst's couch.

Mr. Wichterman's long distance "analysis" only muddies the waters and produces more obfuscation than illumination to the present "bizarre scenario."

February 28, 1999
Drug Policy
The New York Times

Will the continuing debate on drug laws lead to a more reasoned approach to America's drug problem, or is the citizenry convinced that any loosening of the reins will result in a gallop to social ruin? November's midterm elections saw four states and the District of Columbia approve medical marijuana measures—bringing to seven the number of states that have reexamined and significantly changed their approach to this controversial substance, despite harsh Federal criticism. Are the medical marijuana and industrial hemp initiatives clever diversions designed to change public perception? Drug Czar Gen. Barry McCaffrey thinks so. What do you think?

—06:52pm Feb 28, 1999 EST (# of 10759)

To the Editor New York Times

Your editorial of February 15, reprinted here in "The NEWS" of Mexico City under the title, "Judging Mexico's Drug War In The Age Of Certification", correctly characterizes the certification process "as an annual exercise in hypocrisy" that should be stopped. As the Mexican Foreign Relations Secretary, Rosario Green, said, "the US government's unacceptable and unhealthy practice of judging and certifying other countries . . . only presents obstacles for cooperation between nations and creates animosity between the United States and the country it decertifies."

However, although you do concede that "the use of illegal drugs in the United States fuels the problem", you make no mention of the extent to which efforts to reduce demand at home have not kept pace. It is still easier, apparently, to blame the foreign supplier rather than face addiction's root causes—underlying conditions of poverty, discrimination, and frustration among the youth in our ghettos. Rehabilitation and meaningful educational efforts at all levels to re-claim the addicted and to reduce the demand are still inadequately supported.

Yes, repeal the hypocritical "certification" of a friendly, sovereign country, but also face the disquieting truth that the problem is us.

March 8, 1999
Letter to the Editor
The New York Times

Today's editorial (A New Speaker Errs on Reform) is a timely, not-too-early reminder that the corrupting influence of money is already tainting the Presidential election of the year 2000. Candidates in both parties are being made keenly aware that they must be able to raise at least $20 million, or more, in the primaries alone if they are to be serious candidates in the general election. To accomplish this, candidates must rely on far more than the legal limit of $1,000 individual contributions as mandated by the Federal Election Commission. As in the last election, "soft money" is their answer and their salvation.

The Shays-Meehan bill would effectively prevent the escalation of big-money contributions and should be acted upon with all due speed, before the electoral process wends its weary and costly way from New Hampshire, with money-bags calling the shots, and the candidates.

The public is clearly tired of money-driven elections. If the presidential election of the year 2000 is to be more responsive to the public interest the time to act is now . . . or let the new Speaker Hastert go the way of his obstructionist predecessor. Electoral reform cannot wait!

March 17, 1999
Drug Policy
The New York Times

For the past three administrations the War on Drugs has been fought on many fronts, from the jungles of Peru to the streets of every American city. The social ramifications have been huge. Americans have become accustomed to submitting tissue or fluid samples when applying for jobs. Small towns have their own SWAT teams. The U.S. will soon surpass Russia as the country with the most citizens behind bars. At what cost will this war be won?

—01:00am Mar 17, 1999 EST (# of 11903)

March 13, 1999

Letter to the Editor:

At long last, today's cogent editorial, "The Drug War Backfires", states unequivocally and forcefully what drug-rehabilitation experts, penologists, and thoughtful people in all the social sciences have suggested for at least 20 years; that the so-called war-on-drugs is a failure and that, in General McCaffrey's words, "We have a failed social policy and it has to be re-evaluated."

You are, finally, right when you state that "The best hope for controlling illicit drugs lies in treatment." It must be emphasized that this requires a major change in thinking and in programming, not only for the "hundreds of thousands of people in prison with drug problems", as you suggest, but in society at large. We need a complete U turn from the policies of incarceration and blaming the foreign suppliers, (and the policies of cutting treatment and rehab facilities as was done during the Reagan administration when cuts as high as 40% almost crippled the treatment front), to policies of broad anti-drug education at every level in every school across the country, examination of the root causes of addiction in the discrimination, frustration, and hopelessness that pervade our ghettos, and in a renewed and re-invigorated treatment network, not futile incarceration, using the enormous funds now being spent, uselessly, on prisons.

March 21, 1999
GOP Needs Modern Ideas
Mexico City—The News

In his column of Feb. 16, William F. Buckley, Jr., who has earned a deserved reputation as America's leading architect of modern conservatism, had to reach back over 200 years to seek a theoretical buttress for his theories: Writing on the "Rich Legacy Of Great Communicator" (Ronald Reagan), Buckley lectures us on the late 18th century philosophy of Adam Smith, who, we are informed, "taught us that there are three legitimate uses of public money: the maintenance of justice, the cost of military defense and the preservation of public monuments."

This, apparently, still remains the basis of the Republican Party's concept of the uses of government, and forms the core of its opposition to "Big Government" and "Spendthrift Democrats."

Anyone who is even dimly aware of the differences between the social structures of 1776, when Smith wrote his seminal "Wealth of Nations" (in which he asserted the principle that "unrestricted market forces are self-regulating, that is, one can do as one pleases in the market") and the complexity of today's economic system both domestically and globally, will have no trouble concluding that today's government has far more tasks and responsibilities than the simple "three legitimate uses" postulated by an 18th century economist.

All over the industrialized world, responsible government has come to mean concern for the general welfare of its people. Conditions of employment, problems of unemployment, discrimination, health care, available education, welfare, the requirements of ecology, among many others, are accepted provinces of responsible, and responsive, government.

Only someone with complete amnesia as to the development of society in the last 200 years would need to look to the Adam Smith of 1776 for theoretical sustenance and for a model for the conservative posture urged by the right wing on today's beleaguered Republicans. It would be far wiser to look for other platforms, and other more up-to-date theoreticians.

April 5, 1999
Show Them the Money
The New York Times

Your March 31 front-page article "Fund-Raising Deadline Poses Early Test of Candidates' Strength" highlights dramatically the consequences of Congress's failure to act on campaign reform.

With a little more than a year before the conventions and a year and eight months before the 2000 elections, the candidates' energies are almost exclusively directed toward campaign contributions. And this is only the beginning.

In a March 8 editorial ("A New Speaker Errs on Reform"), you said that "there is a window of opportunity to do campaign finance reform in April and May," with a further consideration of the Shays-Meehan bill.

It is still not too late to prevent the next election from being corrupted by a process dominated by money instead of illuminated by principles and issues.

April 6, 1999
Letter to the Editor
The New York Times

Your cogent editorial of April 3 ("Partisan Churches") correctly states that churches that engage in "blatantly partisan activities" ought to be stripped of their tax-exempt status. A good first step! But why not go the whole hog? In the broadest of senses, aren't churches also engaging in "blatantly partisan activities" when each preaches its particular brand of religion? Why should non-religionists and freethinkers be saddled with higher taxes in order to subsidize their religious fellow-citizens? Should freethinkers be discriminated against, tax-wise, for their philosophical/ethical differences with religionists?

True religious freedom would be better served by non-discriminating tax laws, under which all citizens, religious and otherwise, would be treated equally, each sharing equally in the common tax burden.

May 4, 1999
Let's brainstorm on violence
The Times Herald Record

One answer, or the beginning of one, to the horrendous school murders is the immediate, careful preparation of a White House conference on violence . . . its causes and remedies.

Nothing short of a comprehensive, inter-disciplinary, multi-dimensional approach, with the supportive authority of the highest level of government, will suffice.

A White House conference would mobilize the best and most creative minds of our time in medicine, the behavioral sciences, ethics and philosophy, religion, and government to explore that from which the evil of violence springs. Such basic research is essential and critical if we are to stem the endemic violence that, like a malignant cancer, grows unchecked and threatens to destroy the very fabric of our society. We procrastinate at our own peril.

May 18, 1999
'We Procrastinate at Our Own Peril'
Sullivan County Democrat

It has happened again! The unthinkable has reoccurred. Once again the nation is shocked by violence and murder by kids in school. And once again the Monday-morning quarterbacks are back in the press and pontificating on television as the "experts" try to "make sense" out of horrendous events that make no "sense" and to "explain" a violence that is so inadequately "explainable."

One lesson, states the *New York Times* (editorial, 4/21) "is the urgent need for concerted action by Congress, state legislatures and gun manufacturers to keep guns out of the hands of troubled youngsters. Guns are still too readily available."

"Experts," after the fact, solemnly opine that "parents, teachers and students themselves ought to be receiving training in the early detection of depression and violent tendencies." (*New York Times*, 4/22).

It is as though the public has to be reassured, and at once, that our leaders and our society are confident and in charge and have a handle on the problem, as they "round up the usual suspects" and trot out the usual "experts"—school administrators, psychologists, psychiatrists, social theorists—to inform us, after the damage has been done, of its "significance" and how thoroughly they "understand" it. They offer, once again, the probable "causes" along with quick remedies to prevent a recurrence. But recur it does, as little or nothing is done in the breathing spaces in between.

How many will recall that President Clinton, just a year ago—reacting to the shocking murders by two boys, aged 11 and 13, who shot to death four classmates and a teacher in a middle school in Jonesboro, Arkansas (March 24, 1998)—requested that "Attorney General Janet Reno convene experts to study what might be done in the future" to prevent further violence? (*New York Times*, March 25, 1998) To date, we find no evidence of such a serious study.

Only a few months later, more kid-killing occurred: in Springfield, Oregon, where two students were killed and more than 20 people injured in another schoolyard rampage. No "expert study" yet by Janet Reno's Department of Justice or by any other responsible agency. Other killings took place in Fayetteville, Tennessee (May 19, 1998) and in Edinboro, Pennsylvania (April 24, 1998). Still no "expert study" by the White House or anyone else.

Now, following the most horrendous outbreak of them all, the President is quoted as suggesting that Janet Reno and the Department of Justice do all it can to "assist local law enforcement" (*New York Times*, 4/21). "There will be time enough for analysis . . . we don't know yet all the hows or whys of this tragedy," the President said. "I think after a little time has passed, we need to have a candid assessment about what more we can do to try to prevent these things from happening."

Still the same handwringing and good intentions, but no "expert study" yet.

Time is short, as the violence continues and the process of "understanding" lags. Attention must be paid, not after each shocking and "senseless" event, not on the unbearable Monday mornings after the killings are over, but now. We procrastinate at our own peril.

From the variety of remedies proposed, from "moral guidance" to more psychologists in schools" to the urgent need for more effective gun control, to the role played by intolerance, and bigotry and race-hatred, it is evident that this is a complex problem—that there is no single answer.

Nothing short of a comprehensive, multi-dimensional, inter-disciplinary approach will do, supported and given respect, prestige, and authority at the highest level of government.

President Clinton's hastily convened meeting at the White House on May 10 was a good beginning, but must be seen as ONLY a beginning. This "summit" lasted just three hours, with 50 speakers—a good start but not nearly enough for the ongoing study and in-depth investigation that is needed. One of the most important outcomes, at long last, was the call for the Surgeon General to conduct just such a study.

One answer, or the beginning of one, is the immediate and careful preparation of a White House conference on violence, its causes and remedies, to mobilize the best and the most creative minds of our time in medicine, psychiatry and psychology, in childcare and development, in ethics and philosophy, in religion and social theory, in state-craft and government, in biology and sociology, in all the behavioral and social sciences, to explore the ground—social, ethical, environmental, biological, and developmental—from which the evil of violence springs.

Such basic research is essential, even critical, if we are to stem the endemic violence that, like a malignant cancer, grows unchecked and threatens to destroy the very fabric of our society. We procrastinate at our own peril.

May 28, 1999
The violence summit
The Times Herald Record

President Clinton's long-awaited White House "summit" on youth violence, held on May 10, heard 50 speakers and lasted three hours. It doesn't take a rocket scientist to figure out that, given a 30-second breathing spell between speakers, each had just three minutes to present his/her contribution to this complex, many-sided problem.

By contrast, the White House Conference for a Drug-Free America, in 1997, conducted six regional meetings around the country, capped by a three-day national meeting in Washington, and issued a 288-page report in June 1988. Total attendance was about 5,000 across the country, while the national meeting was led by 127 high-level, expert "conferees." In all, every shade of opinion from every walk of life was represented, in a diversity of disciplines and occupations.

Is such an in-depth study and exploration now being planned on the issue of violence? If not, why not?

June 8, 1999
The Saint and the Holocaust, June 7
The New Yorker

Although a Vatican official is quoted as saying, "We do not accept any cure as a miracle unless we are scientifically, humanly certain that the cure has been instantaneous, not expected, and complete", the Church has officially accepted as a "miracle" the recovery of a two year old child from a Tylenol overdose after (and presumably because) her parents and a circle of friends "prayed to Sister Benedicta", formerly Edith Stein. This, despite the fact that the eminent toxicologist on the case stated unequivocally that, given the proper antidote, the child's recovery was "what was to be expected" and that "ninety-nine percent of the time children with Tylenol overdoses fully recover." His one word response as to whether it was a miracle was a resounding, "No". He was not invited to Rome.

The attending doctor, who traveled to Rome to "provide the needed testimony" upon which the Church's finding was based, himself stated that "When I think of applying the scientific method to things of faith, you end up with something that is not satisfying as science and not satisfying as religion." If so, one is permitted to wonder why he lent himself to these proceedings in the first place. Surely he did not act in the spirit of the century's greatest scientist, Albert Einstein, who wrote, "In their struggle for the ethical good, teachers of religion must have the stature to give up the doctrine of a personal God, that is, give up that source of fear and hope which in the past placed such vast power in the hands of priests." (Albert Einstein, "OUT OF MY LATER YEARS," (1956), p. 26.

June 23, 1999
Gun Control
The New York Times

The House has passed an amendment to permit the display of the Ten Commandments in schools and government buildings in an effort to deter juvenile crime. Is the amendment a positive step toward the prevention of tragedies such as the Colombine high school shootings, or does it violate the separation of church and state? Should gun control be treated as a "moral issue," or are stricter regulations on gun sales needed?

—11:13am Jun 23, 1999 EST (# of 19273)

In today's discussion on youth violence in the House of Representatives, (New York Times, June 17, p. 26) majority whip Tom DeLay declaimed that "our school systems teach the children that they are nothing but glorified apes who are evolutionized (sic!) out of some primordial soup of mud." To which an incredulous Barney Frank was moved to respond that "I just heard the majority whip say it (i.e., youth violence . . . MR) was Charles Darwin's fault"!.

This in the enlightened year 1999, 139 years after the famous debate between Samuel Wilberforce, Bishop of Oxford, and T. H. Huxley, scientist and ardent supporter of Darwin: The year was 1860. The indomitable Reverend Wilberforce, addressing Huxley, had "begged to know was it through his grandfather or his grandmother that he claimed his descent from a monkey?" To which Huxley made his famous reply, "I would rather be the offspring of two apes than be a man and afraid to face the truth."

After 139 years, and 74 years after the Scopes trial, we still witness an unabashed Tom DeLay/Barney Frank exchange on the same subject! Tempus does fugit, but, "Plus ca change, plus c'est la meme chose."!

July 5, 1999
William Safire
The New York Times

It is lamentable to see William Safire, logodaedelian extraordinaire, lend his prominence to the disrespectful if not downright pejorative phrase "geezers" to describe our elderly. He not only stereotypes them (us) with a patronizing sneer (anticipating criticism he sneers again as he smears the more sensitive among us as "whining") as he trivializes the problem of the high cost of drugs not covered by Medicare. He ends, again, with a patronizing," raise your voice, Gramps"!

Old age, even young/old age by today's standards, is a condition devoutly aspired to by all (considering the alternative!), and the problems of the elderly are the problems of us all. Cultural attitudes, like the respect for age in Chinese and other cultures, are shaped to an extent by opinion-molders like Safire, and his sneering reference to "geezers" contributes to mindless prejudice, harmful to all of society, the elderly and those who would hope some day to be elderly themselves.

As to appropriate drug-coverage, we must all raise our voices, not only "gramps". Our elderly deserve that from us all.

July 8, 1999
There's no one answer to violence
The Times Herald Record

Since Littleton, Colorado, and Conyers, Georgia, an anguished country is asking once more, why are school kids killing school kids? The answers are confusing.

Ask a psychiatrist and he'll say that the killers are mentally ill. Ask a psychologist and he'll inform us that they are alienated, confused loners seeking identity. Ask a social worker and he'll explain that it is a result of family breakdown, a loss of family values. Ask a sociologist and he'll say that they are the products of a culture of violence, spawned by a pathological environment. Ask a religionist and he'll insist that it comes from a lack of moral values, a loss of faith in God, religion and the church.

Ask a policeman and he'll say it is a lack of cops.

Ask a biologist and he'll blame it on genes, heredity and the forces of genetics.

Ask a Freudian psychoanalyst and he'll suggest that aggressive instincts in the unconscious ID overwhelmed the civilizing restraints of the ego and the superego.

Ask an educator, he'll say it is the impossible, overwhelming burden placed on the schools: overcrowding, large classes.

Ask anyone but the gun lobby, (or Rep. Tom DeLay, who pronounced that "guns have little or nothing to do with juvenile violence"!), and he'll say it is the easy availability of guns. Ask an ethicist, he'll emphasize the blurring of the concepts of right and wrong in our culture.

Ask a parent and he/she will blame it on TV, movies, rock music, and video games that are full of sex and violence. Ask the entertainment industry and they'll blame it on irresponsible parents or on the gun industry.

Ask me and I'll say "all of the above." Each is right . . . partially. But each suffers from a sort of tunnel vision that sees the problem through the narrow prism of his/her particular specialty. It is a bias of discipline, a tendency to limit one's sights to the Procrustean bed of a single viewpoint. What is needed is a unified approach, a joint search for what might be called a "unified theory of social behavior," much like the "unified field theory" postulated by Albert Einstein and his colleagues to unite a "fragmented physics" in order to bring together the various strands of understanding of the physical universe.

A daunting enterprise, to be sure, but the only one likely to bring order out of chaos. Toward this end, a White House Conference on Violence . . . Its Causes and

Remedies, should be convened. Not a three-hour "summit" where 50 speakers are allowed three minutes each, as on May 10, but one which would mobilize the best and most creative minds in all the disciplines above, and then some, to explore the ground—social, ethical, biological developmental—from which the evil of violence springs.

Such basic research is essential, even critical, if we are to stem the endemic violence that, like a malignant cancer, grows unchecked and threatens to destroy the very fabric of our society.

July 19, 1999
How Profits Affect Patient Care
The New York Times

At the core of the Senate debate on health care (front page, July 16) lies a profound moral issue: Should the United States remain the only modern industrial country that does not provide basic universal health coverage to its citizens? That is not even addressed in the current discussion.

Even the modest attempts of the Democrats to inch forward toward more extended coverage are defeated by a Republican majority that places cost above the people's health.

Neither addresses the plight of the 43 million Americans who do not have health insurance. Neither challenges the morality, and the practicability, of placing the country's health care in the hands of private insurance companies, which, by their very nature, value profitability over quality care and the public good.

Note:: due to limitations of space, the following final paragraph was omitted:

> "Only a universal health care plan, known as the single-payer plan, would cover all our citizens, and the moral responsibility of government would be served as the public good is placed before private profit."

M.R.

August 1, 1999
Writers and Ideology
The New York Times Book Review

How has the study of ideology changed the art of writing both fiction and nonfiction? What makes writing ideological—and why do so many critics disagree about it?

(1072 previous messages)

—11:10am Aug 23, 1999 EST (# of 1077)

The otherwise penetrating review by Mark Lilla of Francois Furet's insightful "THE PASSING OF AN ILLUSION—The Idea of Communism in the Twentieth Century," (Book Review, July 25) reflecting Furet's passionate and informed search for the truth behind the Marxian experience, or the experience of Marxism, in the United States and elsewhere, is disappointingly and crushingly marred by his (the reviewer's) last sentence: When Furet, ("wistfully", says Mr. Lilla, but perhaps "hopefully" would be more appropriate to Furet), states "that our destiny as modern men 'creates the need for a world beyond the bourgeoisie and beyond Capital, a world in which a genuine human community can flourish'", he, Mr. Lilla, sounds a pessimistic death knell as he adds: "A need that no society can ever satisfy"!

But it is precisely that aspiration and that hope for "a genuine human community" that inspired the best leaders and thinkers in every era, from Plato to Spinoza, from Mahatma Ghandi to Martin Luther King, Jr. to Nelson Mandela, from Henry David Thoreau to Albert Einstein. "I believe in the brotherhood of man", said Einstein, speaking perhaps for all of them. Not one believed for a moment that "no society can ever satisfy" that aspiration.

August 29, 1999
On Language, 8/29
The New York Times Magazine

In "Fancy Speak", August 29, Charles Harrington Elster sells himself short by adopting the monicker, "Grandiloquent Gumshoe"; it's good, but not quite good enough for his eloquence and fecundity. He deserves better. Borrowing from the elegant locution of rarified diplomacy, which sports the likes of "Ambassador Extraordinary and Minister Plenipotentiary" (or was it Gilbert and Sullivan?), I offer "Logodaedelian Extraordinaire" for one so uniquely talented as Mr. Elster. His gibe at the posturing pontifications of William F. Buckley, Jr., who uses language to obfuscate rather than to illuminate, was delicious.

August 28, 1999
RE: Op-Ed by Melvin Maddocks, Aug. 27
The New York Times

You've got the headline wrong ("Let's Hear It For Decrepitude", Aug. 27). Mr. Melvin Maddocks' real, and poignant, message is not of "decrepitude" but of "the fullness of life in all its mystery, its sweetness, its terror."

Cicero, in his famous essay, "De Senectute" (On Old Age), stressed that age brought with it pure reason to replace the irrationality of youthful lust and passion.

I don't know what Freud meant by "strange, secret yearnings" (we can only guess!), but as an 80-something I venture to suggest that we all yearn deeply for meaning in relationships, meaning in life, and a meaning to our having been here:

MAN SEEKS FROM BIRTH
FOR MEANING ON EARTH
AND TO HIS LAST BREATH
THE MEANING OF DEATH.

September 17, 1999
The Uses of Wealth, Public and Private
The New York Times

Re "Elder Gates Takes On the Role of Philanthropist" (front page, Sept. 12):

When we are informed that Bill Gates's foundation has $17 billion in assets—not a startling amount for the charity of a man worth $100 billion—it forces us to rethink what may be the central political and moral debate of our time: Where is the line between public and private responsibilities, between the domain of government and that of the private sector?

It is mind-boggling to think that in areas where government is often bogged down to the point of paralysis by red tape and the differing agendas of competing politicians, one man can get things rolling with a nod of his head or the stroke of his pen.

Kurt Vonnegut Jr.'s philanthropist hero in his satiric novel "God Bless You, Mr. Rosewater" asked, "How can we help you?" The question remains, for those with accumulated wealth, for the Government and for all of us.

October 14, 1999
Who has answer on tax exemptions?
The Times Herald Record

It is that time of year again. Our school tax bill has arrived. As Yogi Berra would say, "It is deja vu all over again!" as angry taxpayers raise anguished voices over yet another increase. In a spate of letters in The Record (9/6) one reader complains that "school taxes just get higher and higher each year" while another calls for a "tax revolt." An official letter from the Pine Bush Central School District tries to explain away a 12.94 percent increase over last year by pointing to the "elimination of fund balance to offset taxes" . . . !

As in previous years, no one calls attention to the direct, disastrous effect of property tax exemptions that shift the burden of school costs, exclusively, to the property owner.

A glaring example, as I outlined in this space just two years ago (July 21, 1997), is the tax exemption granted to religiously held property. The June, 1996 report issued by the New York State Board of Real Property Services for the year 1994 informed us then that more than $15 billion of real property held by religious institutions in New York state received almost full exemptions (97 percent) from taxes.

In Sullivan County alone the figure was $115 million. Thus, billions of dollars of tax-frees increased the tax burden of the rest of the community and compelled the general public to pay, in part, for the private views of the religious.

At that time, Senator Charles D. Cook said, "The existing inequitable system used to fund local schools is no longer practical or acceptable. (Sept. 10, 1996).

Assemblyman Jake Gunther wrote (Aug. 2, 1996) that "Sullivan County residents have been making up for the lost tax dollars on tax-exempt property" and promised action.

And The Record characterized the method of school-tax financing as relying on "Byzantine school finances" (editorial July 16, 1997).

Fast forward a few years. Has anything changed? The latest Report of the New York State Office of Real Property Services, issued April, 1999 for the tax year 1997, reports the familiar figure of $15.5 billion for religiously owned property in New York state, almost totally exempt from taxes, and $119 million for Sullivan County, slightly higher than in 1994.

So much for the politicians' promises and public posturing, while our school tax is up another 12.94 percent.

Plus ca change, plus c'est la meme chose!

The exemptions continue, even go up, while the tax burden on the beleaguered property owner continues to increase. This is not only patently unfair, but, in the opinion of many, a violation of the time-honored principle of the separation of church and state, and an archaic way of paying for our schools.

It would be illuminating to hear from our current political leadership on this issue: Senator Cook? Assemblyman Gunther? Legislator Gordon MacKinnon? Supervisor Duane Roe? And The Record?

Can principle yet prevail over politics?

October 25, 1999
An Election Sonnet
The New York Times

When I observe the Presidential scene,
The blatant self-interest, the grab for power,
The lies, half-truths, the slick obscene
Pandering to prejudice, the warp of the hour,
Bush and Buchanan regaling the right,
Their minions obsequiously complying,
Humane leadership nowhere in sight,
While Justice and Honor and Truth lie dying,
Then I think of America past,
Of Lincoln and Jefferson and Thomas Paine;
Their words and deeds were of stuff that would last,
Enduring, eschewing the pandemic stain
Of temporal interest and fraudulent phrase.
Is nothing left of those heroic days?

September 27, 1999
Letter to the Editor
The New York Times

Re: "Hitler's Pope" by John Cornwell (9/26): In a stunning understatement your reviewer writes that "he (John Cornwell) believes that religious anti-Semitism, with its ancient roots in the church, constituted but one motive for the Pope's silence . . ." Compare this with the unequivocal conclusion of Harvard Professor Daniel J. Goldhagen in his penetrating work, "Hitler's Willing Executioners: Ordinary Germans and the Holocaust (1996): "European anti-Semitism is a corollary of Christianity", he wrote." The Catholic Church as an institution remained thoroughly and publicly anti-Semitic . . . The German churches cooperated wholeheartedly."

In October, 1997, 57 years late, the Archbishops of the Roman Catholic Church of France, issued an official apology "for its silence during the systematic persecution and deportation of Jews by the pro-Nazi Vichy regime."

Just this week, New York's Archbishop offered his "abject sorrow" (New York Times, 9/19), but refrained from any specific mention of Catholic complicity in the Holocaust.

Pope John 11 has yet to offer any meaningful apology for the "deafening silence" that your reviewer states "was crucial to the rapid consolidation of the Hitler dictatorship".

In this climate the proposed canonization of Pius X11, the architect of the policy of silence during the Holocaust, will not further the kind of reconciliation and mutual respect so necessary today.

October 1, 2002
Iraq, the U.N. and Us
The New York Times

Thomas L. Friedman's Sept. 29 column, "You Gotta Have Friends," is incontrovertible, as is his admonition that any United States action against Iraq must have the backing of the United Nations and important allies. But the fact is that we are a member of the United Nations. We not only need its backing, we also need to act as a loyal and responsible member, through its legal and established apparatus. Above all, we need to support, not undermine, the United Nations Charter.

As Bruce Ackerman of Yale writes (Op-Ed, Sept. 21), the Bush plan is nothing less than the repudiation of the United Nations Charter, which makes collective, multinational security measures the norm.

Our policy should be one of a responsible internationalism rather than a unilateral machismo that would destroy the United Nations and with it the hope of an international ethic of the rule of law for all countries.

November 28, 1999
Money And Elections
Mexico City—The News

The Presidential sweepstakes in the United States are off and running! As a direct result of the failure of Congress to enact meaningful legislation on campaign reform (such as the McCain-Feingold bill in the Senate and its House counterpart, the Shays-Mcchan bill) the campaign opens with a frenzy of money-raising. The over-riding concern is money, money, and more money. Millions of dollars are sought, and obtained by the lucky aspirants, while others, no matter what their politics, drop out of the race for lack of finances.

Money, not social policy, is the chief obsession of all the candidates. Obscene amounts are raised, even in this early stage, as we look forward to a long, divisive, campaign that the *New York Times* predicts will cost 2 billion dollars!

Money, not social issues, drives the process, as corporations, financial institutions, and special interest groups pour their millions in, creating candidates who will be bought now and beholden later, while the campaign is saturated, ad nauseam, by mischievous sound bytes, repetitive and benumbing TV spots, and benumbing oratory designed to mesmerize the voters while pleasing the money-bag contributors. With money calling the shots, issues get lost, and democratic process withers.

In this milieu, may I be indulged a lapse into poetry, with an election sonnet:

When I observe the Presidential scene,
The blatant self-interest, the grab for power.
The lies, half-truths, the slick obscene
Pandering to prejudice, the warp of the hour,
Bush and Buchanan regaling the right,
Their minions obsequiously complying,
Humane leadership nowhere in sight,
While Justice and Honor and Truth lie dying,
Then I think of America past,

Of Lincoln and Jefferson and Thomas Paine;
Their words and deeds were of stuff that would last,
Enduring, eschewing the pandemic stain
Of temporal interest and fraudulent phrase.
Is nothing left of those heroic days?

December 9, 1999
Letter to the Editor
The New York Times

It is a sad commentary on the state of our socio/political mores that our leaders' behavior is judged not on its MORAL content but on whether it is advantageous or disadvantageous in the pursuit of electoral careers.

Thus, Mayor Rudolph Giuliani's mean-spirited and unproductive policy toward the homeless, punishing them for their plight rather than planning for their rehabilitation, is viewed in the context of his ambitions for the Senate rather than on the moral test of right and wrong.

The Mayor's approach is simply wrong. The homeless need compassionate, realistic programs that address their urgent problems: re-education for employment, treatment for mental illness and drug-abuse, family counseling, subsidized housing and/or assisted-living group homes.

You don't cure a disease by punishing its victims.

December 6, 1999
Brotherhood Of Man
Mexico City—The News

As we approach the holiday season—Christmas and Chanukah—it is disheartening to read Howard Kleinberg's column of Dec. 1, in which he gives us a cold dose of the reality of the religious violence and hatreds that still disgrace society.

Instead of the peace, good will and brotherhood, preached and desired by, most religionists, he points up, sadly but truly, "the feverish religious fervor that has set people against each other, the present one between Israelis, Muslims and Catholics among the most aberrant."

He writes of the religious acrimony that has been going on for centuries, of the "Middle East quandary," "the malice there is between Hindus and Sikhs in India, between Protestants and Catholics in Northern Island and between Christians and Muslims in the former Yugoslavia."

He writes of "God-inspired mayhem and religious division" and "religious zealots" and despairs that any solution will be found even in the next century. He seems to be repeating the dour dictum of Blaise Pascal, 'Men never do evil so completely and so cheerfully as when they do it from religious conviction."

Despite Mr. Kleinberg's pessimism, a major challenge to us all as we enter the 21st century will reside in our capacity to devise the means and to acquire the courage, the will and the intelligence to face this problem of religious violence—indeed of all violence of man to man—that threatens to destroy the very fabric of, our society.

Surely the intelligence, skill, and the amazing developments of human discovery and inventiveness that have distinguished our century in science, the arts, medicine, productivity, scholarship and philosophy, have the possibilities of researching, understanding and controlling the pandemic violence that could destroy us all.

If we can put a man on the moon, explore space, crack the genetic code, shatter all previous records of human communication with the miracles of the computer and the internet, surely the combined wisdom of our best minds can find the solution to man's propensity to violence—religious violence, personal violence, domestic violence, and above all the hideous violence of war in its most lethal modern forms.

The greatest, indeed the ultimate challenge of the next century is to lead mankind from its anachronistic prejudices and the hatreds that divide people, to establish the overriding recognition that we are all one, all fellow passengers on this Earth-ship of ours, all bound together striving for our common survival. Every human institution must contribute to such an understanding, or it fails the requirement of humankind and will inevitably wither and disappear. One of the greatest minds of our time, Albert Einstein, said it all when he said, "I believe in the brotherhood of man."

That is, perhaps, the most significant message that the 20th century can send on to the next.

December 26, 1999
Good News, Bad News
Mexico City—The News

In an ironic, but instructive, juxtaposition, Mr. Tomas Eloy Martinez' devastating article ("LatAm Children Are Born Into Dark World Of Violence, *The News*, Dec. 19, 1999) appeared on the same page as my letter, "The Brotherhood Of Man." His terrible indictment seems to come as a pessimistic reply to the possibilities of that "brotherhood."

The article by Mr. Martinez, whose writings on Latin-America have always been incisive and illuminating, contains good news and bad news.

The good news is that, at long last, a serious conference was held in Cuernavaca under the auspices of the newly formed Hemispheric Studies Center, and that "social scientists, authors and experts from Brazil, Columbia, Mexico, the United States and Venezuela" addressed the issue of "urban violence." Such a conference should be front-page news and should be replicated all over the world. Attention is, at long last, being paid!

After the school-boy massacre in Jonesboro, Ark, in March 1998, President Clinton was widely quoted as requesting that "Attorney General Janet Reno convene experts to study what might be done in the future" to prevent further violence (*New York Times*, March 25, 1998). A year later, after the even more horrendous killings in Columbine, Colorado, President Bill Clinton said "There will be time enough for analysis. . . . We don't know yet all the hows and whys of this tragedy." But there has still not been a serious attempt at the highest levels of government and academia, to study this ghastly phenomenon in the depth it requires and deserves. Still wanting, I suggest, is the convening of a White House conference on violence, its causes and remedies. Such a Conference would mobilize the best and the most creative minds of our time, in medicine and psychiatry and psychology, in childcare and development, in ethics, and philosophy and religion, in social theory and state-craft and government in biology and sociology and all the social sciences, to explore the ground—social, ethical, political, environmental and biological—from which the evil of violence springs. Mr. Martinez' Cuernavaca Conference could be one of the seeds for such a continuing, far-ranging study.

The bad news is that Martinez' description of the findings of the Conference is pessimistic to the point of paralysis. He points to no paths for remedies. He may be right when he says that "Today thousands of those who belong in this category (the poor) are meaningless beings lacking a place in society, people to be forgotten" . . . and that "The free market has blindly created a new form of slavery at this century's end, more terrifying than the one abolished 100 years ago in that the human being who then was regarded as merchandise, now has been reduced to a non-being, a zero, a nothing, the discardable piece of an infinite machine."

If this is so, as is so passionately argued here, then the conclusion seems to be that poverty is the root cause of the social disintegration that results in widespread violence. A reasonable conclusion, and one that alone justifies the Cuernavaca deliberations.

There are other causes, of course, and understanding them and researching their origins, is the only path to a consideration of possible remedies. A White House conference, at the highest levels, is still in order.

January 2, 2000
Letter to the Editor
The New York Times

In your editorial, "Two Visions on Health Care" (Dec. 27), you fail to even mention a third vision, that of universal health care for all, known as the single-payer-plan, administered and regulated by the government and supported by the nation's taxes.

By having the public pay for the nation's health through taxes rather than through insurance premiums (which low-paid workers and the unemployed cannot afford, hence the disgrace of 45 million uninsured and uncovered), the profit-driven insurance companies, whose take for administration, the maintenance of a highly overpaid private bureaucracy, and the need for ever-rising profits for their shareholders, boost the cost of health care for us all, would be eliminated. Additionally, such a plan would force the pharmaceutical companies, whose prices have risen astronomically, to provide its largest customer, the government, with drugs at reasonable costs.

"Socialized" medicine, you say? I suppose so, just as our defense system, army, navy, and airforce are "socialized". As is free public education, and the criminal justice system, our courts and jails, and free public libraries, and the leveling and collection of taxes through the IRS, and the Social Security system. Why not health care? Or is the health of our people less important?

January 5, 2000
Letter to the Editor
The New York Times

Your admirable group of letters (12/31) heralding the new century needs the addition of a most significant dimension: THE PLIGHT OF THE WORLD'S CHILDREN. It is a moral obscenity that, at century's end, at a time of unprecedented prosperity, millions of children around the world go to bed hungry, or die of malnutrition or preventable diseases, while millions more of robbed of childhood by the hideous institution of child labor.

The exploitation of children is an unconscionable blight on "civilized" society. It is an obscenity that reveals much about the morality of our profit-driven times. The cliche that "the future lies in our children" is a pale avoidance of the reality that how we treat our children TODAY is a reflection of our present value system, the state of our present mores. The next century must free our children from exploitation, want, and disease, for its own moral sake, or we stand to lose our humanity.

January 15, 2000
Letter to the Editor
The New York Times

Commenting on Peter Steinfels' "Beliefs" column (Jan. 8), Andrew Sprung's letter (Jan. 15) offers the stunning "insight" that "the development of religious expression is contiguous with language, and as fundamental to the emergence of human consciousness"—an egregious error in logic of the "post hoc ergo propter hoc" variety.

To Mr. Steinfels' bland assertion that "The big news, in religion, is often that there is no news", I would offer the news he prefers to overlook, by three 20th. Century thinkers who cannot be overlooked:

BERTRAND RUSSELL, winner of not one but two Nobel prizes, wrote long ago, "My own view of religion is that of Lucretius. I regard it as a disease born of fear and as a source of untold misery to the human race." ("HAS RELIGION MADE USEFUL CONTRIBUTIONS TO CIVILIZATION?" (1930).

Or SIGMUND FREUD, who wrote, "Thus religion would be the universal obsessional neurosis of humanity . . . and the abandoning of religion must take place with the fateful inexorability of a process of growth, and that we are just now in the middle of this phase of development" ("THE FUTURE OF AN ILLUSION" (1928).

Or ALBERT EINSTEIN, recently named TIME'S "Man of the Century", who stated, "I cannot accept any concept of God based on the fear of life or the fear of death or blind faith . . . . I believe in the brotherhood of man and the uniqueness of the individual". (in "EINSTEIN", by Ronald W. Clark.)

Perhaps the changes brought about by science, rational thought, and the rise of secular humanism, are not as "glacial" as Mr. Steinfels presumes. They may very well be the wave of the future in the next millennium, or even the next century. Russell, Freud, and Einstein are hardly a trio one can ignore.

January 16, 2000
World Revolution
Mexico City—The News

William Pfaff's article ("Nations Still Rule Global Community," Jan. 8) was thoughtful and provocative but left me with niggling caveats. Although Mr. Pfaff takes a stab at prognostication ("I would myself argue," he writes, "that the nation-state remains the most efficient and effective agency of self-government for a community of people united by a common history and culture." And further, "The nation state's obituary remains to be written.") My discomfort lies in his failure to distinguish between prognostication and aspiration.

Prognostication is fraught with uncertainty and can be turned upside-down by unknown and unknowable variables. Who in 1800 (when slavery and bloody, swashbuckling empire-building seemed like permanent fixtures) could predict the world of 1900? Who in 1900 could predict the amazing developments of science and technology by the year 2000?

And who today can predict the marvels, and the dangers, yet to come by the year 3000? Prediction is an exercise in futility, or perhaps in science-fiction. So it is with the future of the nation-state, now still ruling the global community, as Mr. Pfaff states. But who knows?

Aspiration, on the other hand, is another matter. Aspiration, spurred by innovation and the march of ideas, is that which fuels the engine of change. The aspirations of our best minds provide the nursery of change and progress.

In a glaring omission, Mr. Pfaff does not even mention the greatest failure of the nation-state system; its inability to address the hideous violence of war. The nation-state system in the past century was awash in the blood of millions, spilled in wars between and among nation-states, and within nation-states. In these relatively "peaceful" times, we still suffer the obscenities of Rwanda, where 800,000 people were slaughtered in just 100 days, the bloodbaths of Yugoslavia's Kosovo, Russia's Chechen, Northern Ireland, the Middle East, to name but a few. What is the role, and the responsibility, of the nation-state system in his ongoing orgy of blood-letting?

We may not be able to predict the future, but we can, and must, aspire to change for the better. In the atomic age such change is essential if mankind is to survive the possibilities of destruction made possible by nuclear weapons (in the hands of nation-states.)

Albert Einstein, scientist, pacificist and humanist, well-named in my opinion as

Time's "Man Of The Century," pointed the way. After his contributions to the development of the atomic bomb (his famous letter to President Roosevelt was the initial stimulus) Einstein passionately devoted the rest of his life to curbing and destroying nuclear weapons and to the need for world government.

He wrote, "Unless another war is prevented it is likely to bring destruction on a scale never before held possible and even now hardly conceived, and little civilization would survive it. "This must be prevented at all costs, he continued, "if man is to prove himself worthy, at least to some extent, of the self-chosen name of Homo Sapiens."

Toward this end, Einstein became an advocate of world government, declaring that national sovereignty is an anachronism in the nuclear age and that supranational government our only hope. "Our situation is not comparable to anything in the past," he wrote, "We must revolutionize our thinking, revolutionize our actions; and must have the courage to revolutionize relations among the nations of the world . . . We must overcome the horrible obstacles of national frontiers."

The whole world now accepts Albert Einstein's contributions to science, the result of this century's greatest thinker and innovator, who changed forever our concepts of space, time, and man's place in the universe. Can we afford to ignore his warning and his seminal thinking on the greatest social-political issue facing the next century?

January 22, 2000
**RE: "Election's Barometer: Barbs of Late-Night TV",
(News Item, Jan. 19)**
The New York Times

Let Letterman and Leno tell their jokes. Let Gore and Bradley bore us to death. The American voters will laugh and yawn, as the case may be. But we still have the most open democratic expression of a people's freedom in the world.

So what's missing? What's missing is dedication, inspiration, a dynamic leadership that energizes, stimulates, involves and stirs the imagination.

In the 1998 election only 36 percent of the eligible voters turned out to vote, according to the Committee for the Study of the American Electorate (New York Times, 11/6/98). The rest apparently laughed and yawned . . . and stayed away from the election.

When will Gore and Bradley and Bush and McCain learn how to grip us with the intensity of a Lincoln, or a Roosevelt, or a Kennedy? When will they summon up the courage to grapple with the burning issues of our time? When will they involve us on the deepest levels of our aspirations, and our fears? When will they address questions like these:

Will the hideous face of war still be with us in the next century?

Will the wide gap of injustice and unfairness between the haves and the have-nots, here and abroad, be addressed?

Will society address the urgent need for research into disease and famine and malnutrition, . . . or will we continue to spend billions on improving the means of mass destruction? Will we lead the nations toward removing the nuclear threat that still hangs over the world?

When the discussion takes this turn, NO ONE WILL LAUGH OR YAWN.

February 19, 2000
Letter to the Editor
The New York Times

As reported by Peter Steinfels (Beliefs, Feb. 19), Lincoln scholar Professor Allen Guelzo "emphasized Lincoln's notion that politics is about right and wrong, not just about fixing things." A truism with which all would agree, and, it would seem, should go without saying.

"Right and wrong", however, seem to have been all but lost in this year's frenzied war for votes, conducted not by political and philosophical theorists, by candidates or their ideological supporters, but by legions of high-paid media and advertising "experts", whose expertise is not in a special understanding of "right and wrong", but on how to use the most modern techniques to manipulate, persuade, mesmerize, cajole and brainwash the voting public. To search for truth? To seek the "right and wrong"? Unfortunately, no! TV bytes, at astronomical costs, are designed to turn votes by any means that work for the candidate who pays the piper. The New York Times recently reported (Jan. 23) that an obscene $3 billion will be spent on this years' elections. Today's report is that in South Carolina alone, "Mr. Bush's strong showing came at a price: He overwhelmed McCain by pouring more that $3 million in an advertising blitz into the state."

Only the naive believe that the goals of "right and wrong" have anything to do with the goals of the media manipulators who today control the process.

"Honest Abe" Lincoln would be dismayed.

February 27, 2000
Doubting Thomas
Mexico City—The News

Why is it that Cal Thomas in his column entitled "Old Dixie Debate Driven By Dirty Politics" (*The News*, Jan. 27) reacts with uncontrollable knee-jerks wherever issues of what he conceives to be left/right ideology are concerned, bypassing his normal powers of reasoning?

Insofar as South Carolina's insistence on flying the Confederate flag on the dome of its capitol is concerned, it is just plain wrong. It is as though the Republic of Germany chose to fly the Nazi flag with its hated swastika over Berlin. It is true, as Thomas says, that "in an election year all appeals to facts and common sense are put aside in favor of demagoguery division and appeals to constituencies."

Nothing confirms this more than his own column.

That being said, it is dismaying to see Thomas use the issue, the transparent issue of the flag itself and its symbolism, not to criticize those who would resurrect the abominable representation of slavery and black oppression, but to attack its victims.

He saves his venom to attack Jesse Jackson and NAACP President Kweisi Mfume and black sociology, rather than address the obvious, ill-conceived insult to all of us, black and white, inherent in honoring the flag that led thousands to their deaths in defense of history's worst abomination.

March 4, 2000
Tax Cuts
The New York Times

When Pastor Gregory J. Dixon, of the Indianapolis Baptist Temple, took the position that his church did not have to collect, or pay, withholding, Social Security, and Medicare taxes according to federal law, (news article, March 3), he may have opened a Pandora's box he and other churches will regret.

"We will not comply", he said, "because we are subject only to the authority of our Lord Jesus Christ." As to real estate taxes, he added, "the property belonged to God", who, as everyone knows, is not subject to mortal taxation.

Thank goodness, Federal Court Judge Sarah Evans Barker ruled otherwise, and the IRS is taking steps to collect $5.9 million in back taxes and penalties. Her ruling, however, pertained only to the payroll taxes, and not to the property tax, which enjoys exemption in every state across the nation.

Now, to be consistent, if churches must collect and pay on their payroll taxes, is it not time we reviewed the huge bonanzas they enjoy, at the public's expense, through their property tax exemptions?

The property tax loss to us all through religious tax exemptions is of a magnitude that dwarfs the $5.9 million owed by the Indianapolis Baptist Temple on their payroll tax dodge. In New York State alone, the latest report of the New York State Office of Real Property Services, issued April, 1999 for the year 1997, informs us that religiously held property in the a mount of $15.5 billion is tax-free. And that is only one state.

Judge Barker's decision on the payroll taxes should call attention, at long last, to this inequity, wherein the public is forced to pay in part for others' private religious views.

March 5, 2000
Peanut Farmer Makes Good
Mexico City—The News

Bravo to Jimmy Carter! Once again he proves that he is the outstanding ex-president of our time, perhaps of all time. Not content to accept an obscure post-presidential retirement, he uses his not-inconsiderable talents and his passions, his knowledge of world affairs and his well-earned reputation and experience in peacekeeping and statehood, to address pressing worldwide concerns that our current presidential candidates shamefully avoid.

In his timely and important article ("Deal With Nukes Before It's Too Late," *The News*, Feb. 24) former President Carter alerts us and the world to the dangerous state of our nuclear predicament.

"I think," he writes, "It can be said that the world is facing a nuclear crisis. Unfortunately, U.S. policy has had much to do with creating it."

Carter goes on, with a persuasiveness that is refreshing in this year of candidates' political double-talk, to stress that the nuclear non-proliferation treaty (NPT) is due for reassessment, and that "the current state of affairs regarding nuclear proliferation isn't good." He alerts us to the continued existence of up to 200 nuclear weapons in Western Europe alone; and that American and Russian nuclear missiles are on "hair-trigger alert." He points to the regrettable rejection recently of the Comprehensive Test Ban Treaty by the U.S. Senate.

President Carter's clear-headed and forceful reminder of the gravity, indeed the urgency, of these issues, makes the current presidential candidates—all of them, Gore and Bradley, Bush and McCain,—look irresponsible in their avoidance and their "debates" shamefully trivial by comparison. They could all learn some important lessons from the indomitable President Carter.

March 12, 2000
Criticizing William F. Buckley
Mexico City—The News

The Republican Party is blessed to have William F. Buckley, Jr. on its side. They should give him an Oscar for "life time achievement." Through Richard M. Nixon and Watergate, Ronald Reagan and Iran-Contra, Oliver North and his illegal arming of the Contras, Buckley was always ready with his virulent vocabulary, his intellectual virtuosity and his tele-venomous presence, to turn logic on its head in support of any Republican position in language cleverly designed to obfuscate rather than illuminate, and always, always, no matter what, to come to the aid of his party.

Case in point is the Buckley column, "Even Southern Bigots Are People Too" (Feb. 29, *The News*).

Buckley has always believed that a good offense is the best defense. He thus hastens to violently attack those who criticized George W. Bush's appearance at Bob Jones University, rather than question the propriety of Mr. Bush lending his presence and, by his silence, his seeming approval of that University's well-known policies of racism, anti-Catholicism, and general intolerance toward non-fundamentalist positions in either religion or politics. He even excoriates his fellow-conservative, William Safire, for calling the Bush performance at BJU a "surrender" to the Christian Right.

To a Republican like Buckley, who never surrenders, this was treason. It is germane to recall that in July, 1974, just before the Nixon resignation, Buckley, in a desperate last-minute attempt to rally the Nixon forces, wrote that "at this moment his (President Nixon's) stock is rising, very fast." And a month later, August, 1974, even after the deluge, he still could write that Watergate was "a little scandal in his household." He similarly defended Oliver North's lawbreaking in his arming of the contras, in a column on Dec. 17, 1987.

It is entirely characteristic that Buckley now violently attacks those candidates who differ from Bush, even questioning their "honor," and expresses dismay that there are "ignorant people in America" who do not like Bush's revealing moral gaffe at BJU, while praising Bush as simon pure as he quested for votes in that unsavory racist forum.

Even Bush himself recognized his error when he wrote a letter of apology to Catholic Cardinal John O'Connor in New York, acknowledging that he had been mistaken in not speaking up at his BJU appearance. This seems to suggest that Bush decided that his critics were more right than Buckley. Could this be because Bush saw the need to mend fences for the upcoming New York primaries? Did he suddenly realize that what played in South Carolina might not play in New York? What has Buckley to say of Bush's own self-criticism? Whatever happens, William F. Buckley Jr. can be depended upon to come up with some "explanatory" logic, with his usual obfuscating rhetoric.

March 17, 2000
Letter to the Editor
The New York Times

At last our brave legislators in Washington have awakened to a profligate and spendthrift America and with courage and fortitude have taken a stand and dug in their heels. Millions, nay, hundreds of millions, on electioneering? Billions for bombers? Billions for foreign aid? A cool billion and a half to eradicate the coca plant in Colombia? Trillions for future defense? This has got to stop somewhere! So they resolutely put their collective finger in the dyke and took a stand—resolutely against another reckless raise of seventeen cents an hour for minimum wage workers! (News story, March 9). Now that's political bravery! President Clinton wants to raise the hourly minimum wage by one dollar in two years by fifty-cent yearly steps; Congress wants to do it in three years by thirty-three cent steps. That's a seventeen cent difference in two years, and by golly, Congress just won't give in to such wild spending. You have to put your foot down somewhere!

March 19, 2000
Analyzing An Apology
Mexico City—The News

It is "apology" time again. In a small article on an inside page we are informed once more that the "Pope Apologizes For Past Crimes" (The News, March 13). It is hardly electrifying news, coming as it does almost three years after "apologizing" for the Holocaust became fashionable for the church and other organizations, fifty-five years after the event.

On October 1, 1997, the Roman Catholic Church of France issued an apology to the Jewish people "for its silence in the face of French collaboration with the Holocaust."

"Today we confess that this was a mistake, "Archbishop Olivier de Berringer declared, (New York Times, Oct. 1, 1997).

Thus it took 57 years for the French Catholic hierarchy to acknowledge its complicity in the round-up of 76,000 French Jews, including 12,000 children, to be shipped to Auschwitz and near-certain death.

The Red Cross followed with an apology for having collaborated with the Nazis while they were torturing and exterminating Jews. Even the French Medical Association apologized for having "violated the basic values of our profession . . . and our shameful operation of discrimination and exclusion concerning Jewish doctors."

The Pope remained silent. Another two and a half years would pass before today's apology, in which the Pope "asked God's forgiveness for the sins of Roman Catholics through the ages, including wrongs inflicted on Jews, women and minorities."

Significantly, he did not "mention the Holocaust or other infamous wrongs such as the Inquisition or the Crusades," provoking Israel's chief Rabbi, Meir Lau, to characterize it as "deeply frustrating."

All of which brings up the question of moral equivalency, moral sensitivity and moral requirements. How, in any reckoning whatever, can an "apology" even begin to be an appropriate response to the monstrous evil of the Holocaust, or the cruelties of the Crusades or the horrors of the Inquisition? Will an "apology" suffice to remember the slaughtered six million? Can their suffering and their martyrdom be mitigated in any sense by belated expressions of remorse by those who participated in any way in "the final solution"?

If not "hollow apologies", then what? Hard to say, since nothing will suffice. The problem is complex, it calls for nothing less than deep moral change, for individuals as well as for the larger society. When we see plans for meaningful re-education for tolerance, acceptance of diversity, the replacement of hostility toward differing views with a new emphasis on love, understanding and brotherhood rather than on hate, divisiveness and violence, we will have a beginning. Thus far we have plenty of apologies, but little in the way of changed attitudes toward "the other."

June 20, 2000
Letter to the Editor
The New York Times

"Bravo" to your editorial (6/20) and to the Supreme Court for its decision that: Student Prayers Must Be Private . . . (front page, 6/20). The wall of separation between Church and State is thus, once again, upheld and the secular character of our society re-affirmed.

A niggling caveat, however, disturbs me. As in the landmark Lee v Weisman decision, which outlawed prayers at high school graduations, today's decision, outlawing prayers at high school football games for similar reasons, avoids the greater issue of prayers by adults in more significant public venues, such as Congress. Sessions of Congress are routinely opened by prayer; indeed, Congress employs a religious Chaplain, paid for by public funds. The rationale offered in both Lee and the present decision is that "susceptible adolescents" need protection because "the delivery of a pre-game prayer has the improper effect of coercing those present to participate in an act of religious worship". Does not the same apply to Congress? Does not a public prayer before Congressmen and Congresswomen, before they deliberate on public laws, represent a "mechanism encouraging divisiveness along religious lines in a public . . . setting, a result at odds with the establishment clause"? Should not adults get the same protection of their First Amendment rights as "adolescents"? If an "act of religious worship" is prohibited at high school graduations and at high school football games because they are "coercive" to those present, should not "religious worship" also be prohibited in Congress? Especially in Congress!

March 26, 2000
Buckley's Ignorance
Mexico City—The News

When I wrote a few weeks ago ("Criticizing William F. Buckley," March 12), a friendly critic said that my flamboyant phraseology was Buckleyism at its worst, unrestrained and unworthy hyperbole. ("designed to obfuscate rather than illuminate," M.R.) I cannot resist noting that only a few days later Buckley himself ("Quickie Debates Serve No Intelligent Purpose," March 18) amply confirmed my remarks, even justified my hyperbole.

The background: One of the first actions taken by Al Gore after nailing down the Democratic nomination was to challenge the Republican winner, George W. Bush, to a series of ongoing debates, no holds barred, on all issues, answering all questions, two debates a week, from now to election time. Bush promptly rejected the challenge out-of-hand apparently with no more than a second's thought. Gore, in the opinion of most, was clearly one-up. He was unafraid of any confrontation, before the largest audiences on national TV, while Bush trotted out lame excuses.

As usual, the Republican intellectual backstop, the aforementioned Mr. Buckley, hastened to the aid of his logic-deprived candidate, offering practical theoretical sustenance to Bush's weak-kneed posture of refusal.

Consider these nuggets of Buckleyan expository prose:

Debates, declared Buckley, would "serve no intelligent purpose," because "quickie responses" would be "pretty asphyxiative," offering "one to two minute responses" that would require too much "concision" and "encourage an expeditiousness of formulation that can undermine their complexity." So much for "obfuscating rather than illuminating."

Apparently, according to Buckley, one-line bumper stickers, or 30-second TV spots would serve greater "intelligent purposes," and the millions of dollars required for such emotionally charged and brainless electioneering would be more worthwhile. Hence, Bush was right to avoid debates and stick to the money-bags that would support the more "intelligent" bumper-sticker approach. There is nothing wrong, Buckley advises, with the "objurgative mode." He demonstrates again his confidence that verbal virtuosity and a smug assurance that his readers will not be able to follow closely the involutions of his "logic" will get his man, once more, out of an unpleasant and revealing corner.

March 26, 2000
RE: Germany and the Jews (Mar. 13)
Newsweek

Your page on "Germany and the Jews" (March 13), was most illuminating and timely. The historians' antipathy to the unsparing analysis of German anti-Semitism by Harvard Professor Daniel J. Goldhagen seems to me to be carping and disingenuous. The indisputable fact is that "ordinary Germans" did carry out the grisly details of the Holocaust slaughter. Without such cooperation the Holocaust would have been impossible.

Historian Eric A. Johnson states that this was done "more from a lack of moral concern . . . than from active anti-Semitism." But how did this "lack" express itself, and what was its breeding ground, and why specifically against the Jews? Professor Goldhagen's explanation of a virulent anti-Semitism, introduced and sustained over hundreds of years by the Christian Church, and supported even during the slaughter, is the most plausible explanation. The rest is hair-splitting.

March 25, 2000
Letter to the Editor
The New York Times

As long as a putative apologia remains the central issue of Pope John Paul II's "hadj" to the Holy Land, the reality of that journey and its significance will remain obscure. That reality resides in the continued failure of the Catholic Church to face up to the challenge delivered by Olivier de Berringer, the Roman Catholic Archbishop of France, when, apologizing "for the silence of the Church of France in the face of French collaboration with the Holocaust", while 76,000 French Jews were rounded up for shipment to Auschwitz, declared that "the time has come for the church to submit its own history to a critical reading." (New York Times, Oct. 1, 1997). That, the church has still not done—55 long agonizing years after the death camps were revealed to a horrified world.

The problem is that the religious establishment cannot bring itself to examine the religious thinking that made possible the execrable excesses of religious behavior that has spilled rivers of blood down the corridors of history. How can they submit the cruelties of the Crusades, the horrors of the Inquisition, the monstrosity of the Holocaust "to a critical reading"? Can religious leadership (of all faiths) re-examine the unexpected consequences of passionate proselytism (which still erupts today), the inculcation of faith above reason, the dogmas, anti-Semitic and otherwise, that permeate the religious mode of thought and provided the sub-soil that permitted "ordinary Germans" (as Harvard Professor Daniel J. Goldhagen so eloquently described in "Hitler's Willing Executioners" (1996) to cooperate with or acquiesce in the butchery of the Holocaust?

Apologies will not and cannot suffice. Nor should we bank on them. What is required is deep moral change, for individuals, for institutions, and for society. When we see plans for meaningful re-education for tolerance, diversity, and the replacement of hostility toward differing views with a new emphasis on love, understanding and brotherhood rather than on hate, divisiveness and violence, we will have a beginning. Thus far we have plenty of apologies but little in the way of changed attitudes toward "the other". The somber observation of Blaise Pascal in his famous "Pensees", in 1670, that "Men never do evil so completely and so cheerfully as when they do it from religious conviction" still flourishes.

Moral leadership toward a new community of people living in justice and peace and mutual harmony is still conspicuous by its absence. Religious, social and political institutions have yet to construct patterns of education, for this and for coming generations, that would bring about real lasting change and render the consideration of belated "apologies" the inadequate, ludicrous, and essentially insulting response to man's evil behavior that it is. It is a challenge for all of us.

April 9, 2000
Crazy Zealots
Mexico City—The News

Re: "Ugandan Cult Deaths Surpass Previous Worst" (The News, April 1).

Once again, this time in Uganda blind faith based on religious zealotry has overwhelmed reason, with ghastly results.

How many more deluded and misguided men, women and children must we lose to what amounts to a slaughter-of-the-innocents before we heed the warning signs and address the problem? How many more abominations must we witness like Heaven's Gate in California (39 dead), the Branch Davidians, in Texas (81 dead), the Peoples' Temple in Cirvana (913 dead), and now the Movement for the Restoration of the Ten Commandments, in Uganda (925 dead and still counting)?

How many more must die while religious sophists debate the difference between acceptable mainstream religions and cults, refusing to face the issue of where one begins and the other ends? Is one man's religion another man's cult?

The bastions of organized religions, of all faiths, steadfastly avoid the question of responsibility when the outcome of proselytism, indoctrination, and the constant inculcation of a religious mode of thought that places faith above reason is wanton murder, or suicide, or a license to kill "in the name of God."

Yigal Amir murdered the Prime Minister of Israel, "in the name of God."

Dr. Barich Goldstein invaded an Arab temple and killed 39 Arabs "in the name of God."

The followers of Hezbollah and Hamas killed Jews again and again "in the name of God."

Jim Jones and David Koresh, and now Joseph Kibwetere and Credonia Mwerinde, "who claimed direct contact with the Virgin Mary" (New York Times, April 2) all acted on "divine" instructions.

The common denominator in all these horrendous events is the acceptance of what might be called the "religious mode of thinking," a mode that places blind faith above reason. The unexpected consequences of such an abandonment of reason is precisely what religionists of all faiths refuse to explore. Perhaps because it might undermine the very pillars of their philosophical system.

But if faith is to be maintained above the evidence of reason can we be surprised when reason is abandoned?

Religious thinking ultimately embraces the abandonment of individual reasoning and the blind acceptance of the assumptions of religious ideology. The proselytism and indoctrination that is part and parcel of the every day activities of religious institutions squelch individual, independent thought, create the atmosphere within which religious dogma goes unchallenged and foster the readiness with which converts, trained to follow unquestioned and unexamined beliefs, are easy prey to charismatic, manipulative, and dangerous "gurus."

The malignant consequences of an all-consuming, dogmatic, religious belief system, the result of years of consistent indoctrination by religious authorities molding the minds of the young and the vulnerable, enforcing the principle that faith is to be maintained above the evidence of reason, are unexplored in any depth by our religious hierarchies.

Jones, Koresh, Kibwetere and Credonia Mwerinde how many more "Leaders to Salvation" are even now in the wings, easily manipulating the easily brainwashed? How can religious leaders, as well as the rest of us escape responsibility."

April 30, 2000
Elian Is No Joan Of Arc
Mexico City—The News

Once again, William F. Buckley Jr. ("Gov't Bends to People's Will—Especially in Election Year," April 12) indulges his formidable talent in flights of fancy circumlocutions and off-the-wall historical analogies that approach the oxymoronic.

This time our foremost conservative comes to the aid of "200 proof populism," (which merits an oxymoron citation in and of itself), as he seeks historical justification for mob rule over the rule of law in the service of his political preferences in the case of Elian Gonzalez.

Those who support the grand-uncle who wishes to keep the six year old Elian in Miami against the wishes of his father, are hailed as heirs to the "Cossacks who refused to fire on the people in St. Petersburg." They represent a "whiff of independence," and, Buckley darkly hints, foreshadow "the revolution." Against whom; Fidel or the U.S. Government, Buckley does not say.

The 6-year-old Elian himself is compared to Joan of Arc, in Rouen, no less, and to Martin Luther King, Jr., in Montgomery, while in a wild reversal of historical accuracy, Attorney General Janet Reno, who is trying to enforce the law, is compared to Gov. George Wallace, who was trying to violate it. The head reels as Buckley juggles ideas and tactics, right and wrong, and what should be the role of a "functioning democracy," while the reader tries to keep score and to decide who is on which side and why.

Through it all, his tongue firmly in cheek, Buckley uses the sorry occasion of an unruly mob attempting to keep a bereaved child from the love and comfort only his father could provide, in order to strike a blow; no matter what the cost for his own conservative political causes.

May 31, 2000
Consumption, 100 Years Later
The New York Times

In Los Angeles, a satisfied customer of Ginza Sushiko (" . . . And $300 Fed a Crowd?", May 17) says that, not having a psychiatrist, "this is our therapy." What could the diagnosis be? Incurable narcissism?

It was just 100 years ago that a more persuasive explanation was offered in "The Theory of the Leisure Class," which suggested vanity and "see how rich I am" and coined the memorable phrase "conspicuous consumption." Thorstein Veblen, where are you when we need you!

May 18, 2000
RE: "Dining Out", May 17
The New York Times

New Yorkers will undoubtedly be thrilled to read (DINING OUT, May 17) that a strip steak, "with just a dusting of chopped parsley", or a dover sole, "garnished", are popular restaurant dishes at only $49.95 or $46.00 respectively. While in Los Angeles, at the GINZA, "the Most Expensive Restaurant in America" you can enjoy a luncheon for one at $300, not including wine, tax and tip.

Restauranteurs offer explanations like "Garnishes aren't cheap", or, "you're renting a piece of real estate", or "it's the ambience, the rent, the total experience". In Los Angeles a satisfied customer raves that "it's so sublime" . . . not having a psychiatrist, "this is our therapy". (What could the diagnosis be: incurable narcissism?)

It was just one hundred years ago that a more persuasive explanation was offered in THE THEORY OF THE LEISURE CLASS (1899), which suggested vanity, look-a-me-look-a-me, see how rich I am, and coined the memorable phrase, "conspicuous consumption."

Thorstein Veblen, where are you when we need you!

June 1, 2000
Letter to the Editor
The New York Times

Two comments on Mary Gordon's Op-Ed piece (WE ARE ALL SPENDTHRIFTS NOW, May 29): First, the title is misleading, if not incorrect: Even in this gung-ho economy millions of poor and the near-poor must spend more than they can afford for the bare necessities (food, shelter, clothing) not because they are "spendthrift" (a personal pejorative) but because they are forced to bear the burden of inflation caused in part by 6 or 7 digit CEO salaries and the need to provide continued dividends for shareholders. They must, indeed, be carefully "thrifty", not "spendthrifty" just to keep afloat.

Second, in an egregious oversight, Ms. Gordon refers, without attribution, to the most insightful explanation of the current "extravagance" in spending, namely, "CONSPICUOUS CONSUMPTION". In fact it was Thorstein Veblen, just 100 years ago, who coined the phrase in his seminal work, "THE THEORY OF THE LEISURE CLASS", (1899). Veblen wrote, further, with an uncanny prescience, that "conspicuous expenditure . . . must be an expenditure of superfluities. In order to be reputable it must be wasteful". In other words, the spenders' concern is not "is it worth it?", but sending the message, "look-a-me, look-a-me, see-how-rich-I-am"! What better explanation of the $1000 bottle of wine or the $60 boiled sole? Thorstein Veblen had it right!

June 27, 2000
The lost cause: campaign reform
The Times Herald Record

The lost cause of the 2000 election is the cause of election campaign reform.

Despite lip service paid by all the candidates before, during, and after the primaries, money-rising has been their principle preoccupation. All make the same claim: They must have the money to counter their opponents' money.

In August of last year, The New York Times predicted a stunning total of $2 billion for the 2000 campaign, then, five months later, upped its estimate to $3 billion! Even the estimable Sen. John McCain, author of the McCain-Feingold campaign reform bill in the senate, engaged (he was forced he said) in energetic fundraising to run against the well-heeled Gov. George W. Bush.

Governor Bush was reported in The New York Times to have raised a record $78.6 million, while Vice President Al Gore had taken in a total of $40.4 million to that date. Having spent prodigiously in the primaries (Bush poured in $3 million to win in South Carolina alone), he had, then, only $6.8 million in the bank.

Gore, likewise, ended March with only $3.8 million on hand. But the big spending still lay ahead, and Gore raised a whopping $2.8 million in a single Hollywood night in April.

Further evidence, if any were needed, of the power of money, was offered in the New Jersey senatorial contest, where a multi-millionaire political newcomer was able to snare the Democratic nomination by spending a record $35 million (and that, for starters only, in the primaries). On the same day, Gore was reported as planning to spend $25 million in the next ten weeks to "redefine" his image.

The money race continues. The Record reports (June 21, page 22) that "Bush sets $90 million fund-raising landmark and that both he and Gore plan to spend about a million dollars apiece a week before the conventions this summer.

The figures boggle the mind. Mr. Average Citizen is benumbed and has lost count. Even in a nation as rich as ours the amounts spent on electioneering have gone beyond the obscene, when one considers the social programs, in health care, education, medical research, and others, that could serve the public more effectively with such funding.

Money still precedes principle in the current political process.

Money decides who will run and money will decide who will win.

Back in 1978, Vice President Gore wrote that "changing the campaign finance system is one of the most important steps we can take to return government to the people."

That still holds, but Gore, along with the others, is still engaged in the frantic, money raising sweepstakes, TV moguls and the media fill that coffers in this, their most lucrative season, while the public foots the bill for deliberately deceptive 30-second sound-bytes that brainwash them, a political honesty and integrity bite the dust.

To top the irony, candidates have the effrontery to ask for our contributions now, as they solemnly promise to fight for campaign-spending reform later . . . after they get elected.

No one talks any more of spending reform or of the insidious effect of the big contributors' hold on candidates and their future policies.

The big challenge to our democracy, the need to keep our democratic process in the hands of all the people, and not descend to a struggle for power and control in a game played by the super-rich, is perhaps the crucial issue of this election period.

June 30, 2000
RE: "House Approves a Medicare Prescription Benefit" (6/29)
The New York Times

It is disheartening to see both the Republican and the Democratic bills on prescription drugs for the elderly unimaginatively, if not cravenly, offer the profit-swollen insurance industry still another opportunity to make millions selling drug insurance policies to the elderly, PLUS a huge free subsidy from the government, i.e., out of taxpayers' pockets.

Rejected out of hand was President Clinton's more sensible plan "to offer drug benefits through Medicare".

Profit-making by insurance companies' HMOs has been the main source of the ills of the current health-care delivery system. Let us not introduce the same dangerous ingredient into plans for prescription drugs for the elderly. The insurance companies ought not be given still another area into which to expand its lucrative domination.

June 30, 2000
Letter to the Editor
The New York Times

The logic of your editorial ("Mr. Nader's Misguided Crusade, 6/30) would imply that a third party candidacy is almost always "irresponsible", except in the rare circumstances that both major parties are incurably corrupt. Yet it is clear that the two party system does not fully express the wide range of public interests and attitudes in our diverse society. Hence the validity of broader political expression. Is not the inclusion of a "conscience-driven crusader", as you describe Ralph Nader, better than a restricted choice of the "lesser of two evils"?

July 11, 2000
Letter to the Editor
The New York Times

In the article, ("AIDS Forum Opens in South Africa Amid Controversy, July 10), South African President Thabo Mbeki is reported as stating that "The world's biggest killer and the greatest cause of ill health and suffering across the globe, including South Africa, is extreme poverty." He is also reported as being opposed to the opinions of the world's leading scientists that H.I.V. causes AIDS. Is it not possible, even probable, that these views, those of President Mbeki and the scientists', are not antithetical or mutually exclusive? Extreme poverty, or H.I.V.? Which is the culprit? Perhaps both. The one problem, poverty, requires long-term planning, the other, AIDS needs immediate attention. Should theoretical concerns block appropriate actions, necessary NOW, to combat the epidemic that threatens an astounding 4.2 million people in South Africa alone who now have H.I.V. and who need remedies NOW?

It is paradoxical and unconscionable that the required action NOW is stymied by what appears to be more a political and theoretical dispute than a scientific one.

July 14, 2000
RE: "Slavery's Fellow Travelers", July 13
The New York Times

Professor Eric Foner's comments ("Slavery's Fellow Travelers", Op-Ed July 13) on "retrospective apologies" for slavery bring to mind the spate of "apologies" a few years ago by Roman Catholic leaders and others for their complicity in the monstrosity of the Holocaust. In October, 1997, the French Roman Catholic Archbishops apologized "for their silence in the face of French collaboration with the Holocaust". The French Red Cross followed, as did the French police, and even the French Medical Association, which had "barred Jewish doctors from their profession." (New York Times, October 12, 1997). The heart of the Christian world, however, the Vatican itself, has still, unconscionably, failed to do the same.

Professor Foner is absolutely right in his bitter criticism that "apologies make the apologizer feel good without doing anything concrete about the enduring consequences of past injustices." True for slavery and true for the Holocaust. The first obligation, of course, "is to acknowledge the full truth" (still not done either in regard to slavery or to the Holocaust), and "to own up to the past". But more than that, the continuing struggle against the consequences of slavery, and against the continuing dangers of anti-Semitism, must be reinvigorated in each generation. It is a moral and practical obligation for all of society.

August 24, 2000
What is Cheney up to?
The Times Herald Record

Far from being a serious instrument for the deliberative selection of a candidate, the Republican Extravaganza was a tasteless "infomercial," designed with all the hoopla of a circus. More insidiously, it was an opportunity for lobbyists of major corporations to angle for influence.

Even more significant is the revolving door—from government employment to big business and back to government—exemplified by the vice-presidential choice of Dick Cheney: From Secretary of Defense to CEO of the oil-giant Haliburton Company and now back to government as vice-president. Why would one give up a yearly salary of $1.3 million (plus a stock package now worth $43 million) to seek an office that pays $181,400? Is it because a stint in public office is now the career-builder and contact-maker that leads to big money in the private sector?

Wasn't this precisely what a distinguished Republican President Dwight D. Eisenhower, warned against, the noxious collaboration between government and big business, when he identified the "military-industrial complex"?

August 18, 2000
Letter to the Editor
The New York Times

In his stirring acceptance speech, Vice-President Gore included a pledge to pass "a law against hate crimes". He specifically honored the memories of Matthew Shepard, Joseph Ileto, and James Byrd.

He might also have added the names of Andrew Goodman, Michael Schwerner, and James Chaney, two Jews and one Afro-American, who were brutally murdered in Philadelphia, Mississippi in June, 1964 as they worked to register blacks to vote. It was the same year that another Jew, Joseph Lieberman, also traveled to Mississippi to serve in the same cause. Al Gore's selection of Lieberman, and his passion to do more against bigotry and hatred, resonates a symbolism that cuts deep for those whose historic memories are still intact.

September 24, 2000
Letter to the Editor
The New York Times

If anyone doubted that the profit-driven insurance industry was NOT the best way to provide health care for the American people, such doubt was reinforced by the frank admission of the spokesman of the Health Insurance Association of America ("The Cost of Insurance", Sept. 24). Charles N. Kahn 111, speaking for his insurance constituency, warns (or is it threatens?) that "patients rights legislation . . . would significantly raise the cost of health insurance, raising the number of uninsured Americans." What more evidence is needed that health care "through insurance channels" (as promoted by letters of 9/19 and 9/21) is self-limiting, morally blind, and of value primarily to the insurance industry?

A government-run plan, the single-payer plan for universal health insurance, is morally superior and fiscally more equitable (as has been demonstrated by the best health-care delivery system in the country, MEDICARE), and would place our wealthy country alongside all those other nations in the modern industrial world that consider the public's health a public priority, not a private-profit business deal through profit-driven insurance conglomerates.

September 17, 2000
RE: Howard Raines' "Editorial Observer", Sept. 17
The New York Times

Howell Raines' assertion that Senator Joseph Lieberman has had what may turn out to be a decisive effect on "Christian voters", that he has significantly moved the "evangelical-fundamentalist group" to the Democratic side, ("When Devotion Counts More Than Doctrine", Sept. 17), is disconcerting, even threatening, news to our secular citizenry. We are, after all, a secular nation, not only in spirit, but in our basic law: Article VI of the Constitution states, without ambiguity, that "NO RELIGIOUS TEST SHALL EVER BE REQUIRED AS A QUALIFICATION TO ANY OFFICE OR PUBLIC TRUST UNDER THE UNITED STATES." Thus, if religion may not be a litmus test, or a "qualification" for office, the public posturing of piety ("I am holier than thou!") can only be seen as unseemly pandering to majority prejudice.

- PUBLIC POLICY SHOULD TAKE PREFERENCE OVER PRIVATE PIETY.

August 20, 2000
Letter to the Editor
New York Times Magazine

William Safire (On Language, Aug. 20) offers an erudite display of political obfuscation: "iron fist . . . inclusion . . . big tent . . . moderation . . . compassionate conservatism . . . mainstream." . . . (he failed to mention the oxymoron of 1996, by Jack Kemp at the Republican Convention, "progressive conservatism"!)

In all fairness, however, Mr. Safire should have acknowledged the primacy of George Orwell in this word-cleansing endeavor. Orwell had no peer in exposing the use of language to obfuscate rather than illuminate the political scene. In his shattering novel, "1984", Orwell wrote that "NEWSPEAK (the official language) was designed not to extend but to diminish the range of thought." Earlier, in 1946, in a celebrated essay, "POLITICS AND THE ENGLISH LANGUAGE", he wrote, "Political language . . . is designed to make lies sound truthful and murder respectable and to give an appearance of solidity to pure wind." Move over, Bill Safire; make way for George Orwell!

October 1, 2000
Bellow, Bubbles, and Me

The panic set in on Sunday night, forty-eight hours after the surgery.

The endovascular surgery, triple AAA (Abdominal Aortic Aneurysm repair) as it is called by the doctors, at Mount Sinai Hospital, had gone well, the doctors assured me, despite the fact that two hours after the operation I had blacked out, completely lost consciousness, while urinating, supposedly under the watchful eyes of two nurses, fell forward over the potty, painfully bruising my rib. It happened again a few hours later, again while on the toilet, I lost it, fell forward, cracking my head on the hard tile floor, and woke a few seconds later in a pool of blood around my head and nose with four or five doctors questioning me, neurologically, to see if I was still there! When I opened my eyes, stunned and disbelieving, my head was in the hands of my grandson, Lee, a newly-minted doctor, staring at me deeply and concernedly. Rushed to radiology for Xrays and a cat-scan, through endless corridors that linked the huge complex of Mount Sinai, more tired than I have been in all my life, just wanting to close my eyes and sleep, sleep, sleep. Lee, with his large beautiful eyes, eye-balling me with great intensity and repeating, "Grandpa, don't close your eyes, grandpa, do it for me, talk to me, don't close your eyes, please!" So I stayed awake, forcing my eyes open . . . just for him, as the gurney sped along.

The corridor was long, endless, closed doors on either side. Looming ahead I saw a "long tunnel" . . . to the "other side" I thought, with scenes from TV and science fiction running through my head, I was looking for a light at the end of the tunnel, a blinding light ala Rod Serling, or HG Wells, or H.P. Lovecraft, or Jules Verne, and wondering calmly what the "other side" would look like. I was curious, and wanted to close my eyes and sleep and find out.

But finally, and suddenly, abruptly, they found the right door, as Lee repeated continuously, "talk to me, grandpa, talk to me, don't close your eyes, please, grandpa, do it for me, grandpa!" . . . the gurney swung gracefully around and I was in a head—scan. No intra-cranial damage, the scan confirmed, and I was back in my room, in my bed, in a wink. They kept me in the hospital for another day.

I slept at home last night, happy to be in my own bed in my own sunny bedroom in the country . . . tired, tired, tired, but re-assured that I was, and would be now, alive.

The panic was in the dream.

My bedroom was a cube filled with bubbles blown from a hidden source. The bubbles floated along the ceiling and around the walls, filling the entire room's space, each bubble transparent, diaphanous, and each holding a single, capital, letter. They moved languidly, floated serenely, gradually filling all the available space, and leaving me, and my body, with less and less space to occupy, or to breathe! I opened one eye to see this right and to get away from the floating bubbles that now seemed to be threatening me . . . . if they filled the entire room, where would I be, how would I breathe? Terror began to seep in. The room was there, all right, just as it should be, the pictures on the wall, the ceiling as it should be, no bubbles . . . . but when I closed my eyes, I was back in the bubble-filled room, floating, menacing . . . .

The bubbles read: SAUL BELLOW AND HIS FAMOUS TRAVELING COMPANIONS, AND RAVELSTEIN. They read horizontally and vertically, like words neatly fit into a cross-word puzzle grid:

```
                        R
S A U L B E L L O W A N D H I S F A M O U S T R A V E L I N G C O M P A N I O N S.
                        V
                        E
                        L
                        S
                        T
                        E
                        I
                        N
```

The bubbles float all around, floating, floating, with an ethereal grace and serenity, gliding effortlessly, sliding and bouncing in perfect harmony, stately, as though responding to an eerie, but unheard, off-stage, music of the spheres. They move left and right, up and down, with inexpressible beauty; they are formed, but form—free, as though encased in and snugly protected by a gelatinous primordial goo.

I write:

Saul Bellow's a lit'ry fellow
Ideas just pop from his head,
Hume and Kant and Montesquieu
And philosophers live and dead.
Locke and Shakespeare and Aristophanes
And Thucydides too,
All seen through Ravelstein,
Himself a Wandering Jew!

So much stuff from his head,
So erudite is he,
A fount of knowledge,
Makes an illiterate of me.!

But when he goes from purges
To personal urges,
I think, with nasty glee,
He must do what we all do,
Rely on his prick to pee . . .
Just like you and me,
Just like you and me.

I write many more verses, scatological and otherwise. I vow to remember them for later, for when I wake up . . . if ever I do . . . . if the bubbles allow me. But they are lost!

I keep wondering, wondering, how I could survive in this bubble-filled space, how would this end . . . will I ever be able to breathe after the bubbles fill all . . . in what space . . . would there be space left over? I open my eyes, meaning to tell Evelyn who would surely have a reasonable answer and save me. She always does. She is coming into bed. She holds me. I tell her about the bubbles. She says it will be all right, come morning, the space will be there. But when I close my eyes I am in the bubbles again, this time with a balloon-like figure that is Evelyn, struggling but afloat as she tries to assert her right to space among the bubbles. She is a human figure, constructed of thin balloon material, in bubble-segments, head, breasts, belly, and legs, like I have seen the tricksters do in the Zocalo, in Mexico City, in the Jardin in San Miguel, in the square at Key West, Florida . . . a neat skill with a large balloon, blowing and tying and twisting with a magician's grace, delighting children and adults as well. Bubbled Evelyn swims, floats, in an air-space near me, trying to keep close, past the letter-bubbles that keep jostling, fighting for every available space. I try to make sense of the encapsulated letters. I write some more rhymes, even laugh out loud at my own humor, and finally fall asleep without any certainty at all that the ordinary air will be free and available in the morning. Or will the bubbles take over ... and fill everything?

Later I go back to Bellow and "RAVELSTEIN". Though not quite a tour-de-force, it certainly qualifies as a rare intellectual romp. Bellow, the narrator, himself, not through Ravelstein, says: "I had a good grasp of reality and of my defects. I permanently kept in mind the approach of Death, who might at any time loom up before you." And then, on the upbeat, Robert Frost's memorable lines:

"For I have promises to keep
And miles to go before I sleep."

Amen.

September 24, 2000
Letter to the Editor
The New York Times

Let's cut to the chase: the issue boils down to whether the government of "the richest country in the world" will accept the moral challenge of providing health care to all of its citizens, or whether it defaults and leaves the problem to private, profit-driven insurance conglomerates.

The problem of the public's health should not be couched in terms of "insurance needs", but in terms of the health and welfare of our people as seen by their democratically-elected, accountable representatives, rather than by hugely-salaried, profit-driven, self-motivated, unaccountable insurance executives. Senior citizens on MEDICARE pay $45.50 per month—one fair price to all—to a responsible government. Private insurance (where HMOs can reduce coverage and increase premiums at will) can cost $5,000 to $6,000 yearly per family, for those who can afford it.

It is time we joined the rest of the world's industrial nations with a compassionate public health policy that is responsive to the public's need, and BREAK THE INSURANCE INDUSTRY'S STRANGLEHOLD ON THE PUBLIC'S HEALTH.

October 7, 2000
The Race for No. 2: A Debate With a Difference
The New York Times

The most glaring omission in the Cheney-Lieberman debate was the failure of either to address the question of universal health coverage for all the American people under a government-run, single-payer plan (front page, Oct. 6).

With 43 million uninsured and with private health maintenance organizations cutting services to Medicare recipients, the candidates' policy of avoidance is unacceptable.

October 6, 2000
Faith shouldn't be a litmus test
The Times Herald Record

Bravo to Richard Cohen for his column in The Record on Sept. 13. The rush by candidates at every level to appear more "God-fearing" than their opponents, the unprecedented emphasis on religiosity and the insistence that morality is driven only by religion, is clearly contrary to the American spirit.

After all we are a secular nation! Our uniquely American principle of keeping church and state separate was established not only in the First Amendment, but also, firmly and unambiguously in Article VI of the Constitution, which states that "No religious test shall ever be required as a qualification to any office or public trust under the United States." Thus, if religion in any form may not be a litmus test, or a "qualification" for office, the public posturing of piety ("I am holier than thou!") can only be seen as pandering to majority prejudice.

Public policy should surely take preference over private piety. "Religion and government," James Madison wrote, "should never be mixed together." Let's keep it that way.

November 5, 2000
Letter to the Editor
The Times Herald Record

 A vote for the presidency is the most significant vote an American can cast. An overlong and much too expensive campaign has demonstrated clear differences between the candidates on health care, education, taxation, and Social Security among others.
 Al Gore prefers an expanded healthcare system, including prescription drugs for the elderly under Medicare and, eventually, full coverage for all children. Gov. Bush tends to favor a greater reliance on private health plans under private insurance programs.
 On education, Gore favors major public funding and more support for quality improvements in our public school system, while Bush proposes vouchers for private, including religious, schools, thus taking away from public school resources.
 On taxation, Gore proposes tax reductions for middle class and low-income families, while Bush favors the greatest tax relief for our richest segment.
 On Social Security, Gore favors the unambiguous protection of Social Security funds for the elderly, while Bush proposes a risky privatization.
 For all these reasons I support Gore. He is clearly superior in breadth of intellect and in experience to shoulder the tremendous responsibilities of the job. The presidency, after all, is not a place for on-the-job training.

November 12, 2000
RE: The 2000 election
The New York Times

Whatever the outcome of the 2000 election, it is clear, at long last, that the Electoral College is an anachronism and should be eliminated to make way for the supremacy of the popular vote. One man, (or woman), one vote, each with equal authority, better represents the "will of the people". As Professor Akhil Reed Amar pointed out in his excellent Op-Ed piece ("THE ELECTORAL COLLEGE, UNFAIR FROM DAY ONE," Nov. 9), the Electoral College had its roots in slave-America in order to appease the South, where slaves were counted ("albeit with a two-fifths discount"!) in order to augment their electoral votes. The Electoral College is as archaic today as slavery and should be abolished.

November 26, 2000
It Ain't Over Yet
Mexico City—The News

Who's he kidding?

Can it be that William F. Buckley, Jr., the legendary wordsmith and logodaedalian extraordinaire, whose skill at spinning and turning a phrase in multi-dimensional pyrotechnics is exceeded only by his prodigious power of purulent prolixity, is now informing us ("Florida Showdown: Somebody's Gotta Lose," Nov. 19) that the current election impasse can be reduced to just three simple words, "Procedure is king"?

And only three more to turn complexity to simplicity, "Nothing else counts"? Very un-Buckleyan, but in a way true to the same Republican consistency that put him, always, on the side of Richard Nixon, Ronald Reagan and George Bush, Sr. as the principal architect of ideological conservatism, the intellectual guru who always "came to the aid of the Party" no matter what. "Nothing else counts!"

Does Buckley really expect us to believe that "nothing else counts?" Not the direction of the country on the issues of health, education, taxation, and Social Security? Not violence and gun control, women's choice, the composition of the Supreme Court? Not campaign reform and the obscene spectacle of 3-billion dollars recklessly spent on the electoral process? Not foreign policy and the nature of U.S. participation in world affairs, a battle between involvement in worldwide peacekeeping efforts and a new neo-isolationism?

Does it "count" if we re-assess the Electoral College, if not for this election then for the future? In a penetrating article in the New York Times, ("The Electoral College, Unfair >From Day One," Nov. 9), Yale law professor-Akhil Reed Amar stated that the Electoral College is a "hopelessly outdated system . . . and we must abolish it." This method had its roots, he pointed out, in slave-America in order to appease the South, where slaves were counted ("albeit with a two-fifths discount!") in order to augment their electoral votes vis-a-vis the free states. The Electoral College is as archaic today as is slavery, and should be abolished.

Does it matter that the "will of the people" is more directly and unambiguously reflected by the popular vote rather than by the mystifications of a system devised 200 years ago as "a consciously anti-democratic system . . . to assure rule by property interests," a description offered, strangely enough, by a supporter of the College, William Pfaff (The News, Nov. 21)?

Of course, at the present juncture, where his Republican hero has lost the popular vote, Buckley comes forward to champion the old elitist method and to brush aside principle and issues. "Procedure is king," he bellows, "Nothing else counts!"

But, "It ain't over till it's over" (Yogi Berra?), or was it, "It's not over til the fat lady sings!" In any case, Buckley will have a hard time convincing the American people that "nothing else counts." A fair, transparent, honest election that is moved by issues and principles may still count more than a sterile, antiquated and outmoded "procedure" that can mischievously thwart the peoples' direct expression.

December 3, 2000
On Safire And Buckley
Mexico City—The News

With the juxtaposition of America's two leading Republican pundits, William F. Buckley, Jr. and William Safire, on today's Opinion Page, your readers, even the most partisan, were given more than enough food for thought. To digest this overdose of self-serving, conservative ratiocination in one day, however, will require a strong stomach.

In a considerable retreat from the rigid posture he took in his previous column (Nov. 19), Buckley now starts off by declaring in an unusual (for him) straightforward manner, that "In any normal country, Gore would be acclaimed the winner for the simple reason that he got a majority of the people who voted on Nov. 7." He goes even further to state that. "Even under the auspices (of the Electoral College system) there is a pretty good likelihood that Gore is the winner." So what's the problem? The problem, of course, is that Buckley simply does not want Vice-President Gore to be the winner, despite his victory in the popular vote. Hence his skillful spinning on subjects like the legitimacy of the election in Florida, the legality of the counts, the ineptitude, unfairness and/or corruption of the Florida electoral process (Jesse Jackson powerfully described the intimidation and disenfranchisement of thousands of Afro-Americans at the voting booths), the need-to re-assess the outmoded Electoral College system, etc.

Despite his opening remarks, Buckley goes on to calumniate Democratic voters as "types less accustomed to the disciplines of civic behavior" (does he mean "stupid"?), and to suggest that Al Gore benefits from a "more latitudinarian canvas"-(whatever that means!) He ends, having come full-circle from his beginning, with an encouragement for his party: "So just stick in there," he says, "It's going our way"! The fact that Vice-President Gore won the popular election by 300,000 votes suddenly no longer matters.

William Safire, the second batter in this mutual-admiration team, steps up to address the immediate political ramifications of a Bush, or a Gore, victory: i.e., the opportunistic partisan consequences, the effect on "committee staffs, jobs, budgets, committee assignments—in a word, power." He doesn't even touch on the long-range problems inherent in this flawed election caused by the Electoral College, its origins in an 18th century America of slavery and free-men, its skewing of the count to overturn the "will of the people" as determined by the popular vote. Neither Buckley nor Safire wants to address the Right and the Wrong of it. At every step along the way they both evaluated each twist and turn of the tortuous legal process only on the basis of whether or not it helped their Party and its candidate, not on whether the vote was clean and ethically administered, not on whether the count was proper and fair, not on who were disenfranchised. Party interest always superseded right and wrong.

Safire, whose fame began when he was a speech-writer for Richard Nixon and the infamous Spiro Agnew, sees his role in the election as another lawyer for George W. Bush, specializing in PR with his formidable skill as a word-spinner at the service of his client.

It would be more to the public interest if serious scholarly attention were paid to the electoral process itself and to its paramount position in our democracy, as in the non-partisan study recommended by New York Sen. Charles Schumer. Such a study would examine the causes of the present miasma, and seek remedies so that results actually reflect the expressed "will of the people" and even consider the abolition of the archaic Electoral College.

The election process needs to be re-invigorated, re-energized, and re-ennobled, so that the disgrace of more than half the eligible voters not even showing up to vote does not become a permanent feature of American politics. Buckley and Safire would do better to address themselves to this over-riding problem, rather than to the narrow, special interests of their chosen party.

November 29, 2000
U.S. State Of Mind: Healthy And Divided
Mexico City—The News

AN EXCHANGE OF VIEWS:
    1. A PSYCHOANALYTIC VIEW . . . AND 2. A RESPONSE

By PETER WOLSON
                      Los Angeles Times

    In this time of prosperity and with both political parties moving toward the center, how can we account for the 50-50 partisan standoff in America's body politic? Both houses of Congress are almost evenly divided between Republicans and Democrats, and the presidential race has come down to fewer than 1,000 votes in Florida.

    One might think that as the two parties moved closer to the center, the chances for political deadlock would have dropped. But the opposite has occurred. Why?

    Broadly speaking, in the American psyche, the Democratic Party's vision of government is roughly equivalent to a powerful, nurturing mother figure protecting and caring for the needy and downtrodden. By contrast, the Republican ideal embodies a *strong father figure* who rewards people for taking responsibility for their own lives and who supports independent initiative. The Democratic "*breast-mother*" government satisfies the basic human need to be taken care of by a loving, tolerant parent; the Republican father figure fulfills the need to break from parental domination, to have control over one's life and to pursue one's fortune.

    Psychologically, the basic human need of maternal nurturance often conflicts with the need for autonomy. During adolescence, this conflict plays out: Children struggle to liberate themselves from their need for parental care by rebelling against parental authority and trying to assume personal responsibility for their lives. However, even after the adolescent has attained adulthood and become more self-reliant, the psychological need to be taken care of persists to varying degrees and remains in conflict with the need for separation and autonomy. In the political arena, Americans try to resolve this personal conflict by voting for the party that represents their strongest internal need.

    Americans who have traditionally been more in need of help or care—women, the working class, the aged, the disabled, immigrants, certain racial and religious minorities, gays, etc.—and Americans who support them are more likely to vote

Democratic. For these voters, liberal means the generosity of a nurturing governing structure. In contrast, they view Republicans as uncaring, hardhearted and greedy, a party of the rich and powerful demanding that government support their aggressive, self-serving (often entrepreneurial) needs.

For liberal Democrats, conservative is often equated with depriving the hungry and poor of government support through tax dodges, paying employees the lowest wages and benefits they can get away with, exploiting "Mother Earth" for profit and risking gun violence for the "macho" preference to hunt. They view the Republican stance against abortion as a willingness to ruin a woman's life in favor of the right of a fetus to live, again supporting the vital interest of the "child" against a "murderous" maternal authority.

In contrast, Americans who live according to an ethic of self-reliance and subscribe to an individual's right to control his own life, money and property with minimal interference are more likely to vote for a paternal Republican government. For these voters, government represents a powerful, controlling parental figure, a necessary evil that potentially threatens individual autonomy by "stealing" earned money through excessive taxes. The ideal Republican governance does not spoil or infantilize the people with nurturing, protective handouts but requires them to be responsible for themselves and supports independent initiative through tax breaks.

If Democrats and Republicans signify, respectively, the human need to be taken care of vs. the need for autonomy and control, then the 50-50 split in campaign 2000 suggests that both basic psychological needs are exceptionally well represented in the American body politic. In other words, the American psyche is maximally healthy. Yet, as a result of this desirable balance, the political process seems deadlocked.

Will this continue, and is this bad or good for America? The current psychological stability of the country, perhaps more than at any other time, gives each party's politicians the choice of moving forward or remaining paralyzed. A 50-50 split means that the only way for each party to fulfill its political agenda is to compromise with the needs of the other. Ideally, this would lead to more balanced political programs and great psychological satisfaction for the American people.

But government might also remain stalemated by partisan politics. In other words, elected politicians might self-destructively choose not to compromise. This would frustrate the American people, having made the best psychological selection for themselves but electing politicians unwilling to make concessions necessary to fulfill their needs.

Unfortunately, America cannot avoid this conflict. U.S. politics will inevitably be divisive because of the inherent unconscious conflict between the need to be taken care of, as represented by Democrats, and the desire for autonomy and control, embodied by Republicans. It is the dynamic struggle between these two competing psychological needs that serves as a major catalyst for human growth, both individually and politically.

Ironically, the most representative election outcome provides the greatest opportunity to fulfill the psychological wishes of the American people, while also leaving them ripe for political deadlock.

Wolson is a psychoanalyst and past president of the Los Angeles Institute and Society for Psychoanalytic Studies.

December 17, 2000
Wolson's Analysis Falls Short
Mexico City—The News
A response by Meyer Rangell

If Peter Wolson ("U.S. State Of Mind: Healthy And Divided," Nov. 29) teaches us anything, it is that intellectual danger lurks when the basic assumptions of Freudian psychoanalytic psychology are glibly transferred from the exploration and treatment of individual behavior to the "state of mind" of an entire nation of 270 million people.

The transfer of metaphors from the individual to the social fabric does not work, as Dr. Wolson makes the leap from a framework of theory intended to identify and treat individual neuroses and psychopathology to postulate a "diagnosis" of the behavior of an entire population of varied, disparate, multi-dimensional, multi-ethnic, people. The results, predictably, are narrow, shallow, unsupported by any credible evidence and lead to an "analysis" of our "body politic" that is not only scientifically unconvincing but tends to discourage positive action for real social and mental health through positive socio/economic/political expression and the healthy exercise of our democratic rights and responsibilities.

To characterize the Democratic Party as the "breast-mother" and the Republicans as "strong father figures" is to confuse the broad canvas of political reality in all its complex dimensions with the strained and spurious metaphor of a Freudian procrustean bed. One hundred million voters defy such a reductio-ad-absurdum. Not to mention another 100 million whose "unconscious" prevented them from voting at all. Where were they when their "breast-mother" or their "strong father figure" called? Perhaps they were responding to real causes in the real world when they decided for "None of the above!"

Dr. Wolson views the split vote as evidence that "the American psyche is maximally healthy . . ." and is in a "desirable balance." This optimistic health report will surely come as news to the millions who even today live on the edge of poverty, who lack affordable housing, who have no health insurance or job security, and little prospects.

Are we "maximally healthy" when the divide between the haves and the have-nots has grown wider, when the nation consists of an excess of wealth and privilege on the one hand and dismal pockets of poverty and neglect on the other, evident in every ghetto and barrio from New York to Los Angeles? The Freudian metaphor describing the "psychic health of the nation" in terms of conscious/unconscious, nurturing mother and stern father, and the glib conclusion that "the basic psychological needs are exceptionally well represented in the American body politic" (!), grievously distorts the significant focus as it ignores the broad, socio-cultural environment within which human social behavior evolves.

The wealthy who strive to hold on to the status-quo and their entitlements will love, and welcome, Wolson's theoretical, ideological rationale: It is not in social policy that unfairness exists, but in the uncontrollable, unpredictable "unconscious." No one, after all, is to blame. And those who want to change for the better are just weaklings and whiners looking to the "breast-mother" for help. They (the Democrats) want to "spoil or infantilize the people," while the stalwart Republicans want them "to be responsible for themselves." George W. Bush could not have said it better!

But it does not require esoteric Freudian theory to understand why the well-born, the privileged and the moneyed will vote Republican to protect their entitlements and their interests, while the poor and the disadvantaged vote Democratic to keep their heads above water and to try to better their conditions of life. It is not the "unconscious" that explains it, but the nature of the surrounding environment, the cultural milieu, the ethos and values of a society with wide differences in birth-advantage, status and living standards. The choice is between government policies that promote equal opportunities for the millions of underprivileged and disadvantaged (an even playing field or as close to it as we can get), versus the hard-nosed protection of the entitlements of the wealthy, Freudian "explanations" notwithstanding.

The problem is a real one, to be fought and resolved in the grim arena of a conscious reality, not in the dark and murky realm of a speculative "unconscious."

January 1, 2001
Letter to the Editor
The New York Times

The one undisputed fact to emerge from this most-disputatious election is that we are about to install a President who is not the "undisputed choice" of the American people but the selection, by a single vote, of a shamefully politicized Supreme Court. The egregious failure of election 2000 lies in the outmoded Electoral College, whose method of winner-take-all in State contests resulted in the disastrous contradiction of the winner of the national popular vote losing to the flawed Electoral College count, thus thwarting the "will of the people".

Most scary, however, is the absence of any public outcry, or political leadership, to alter or abolish this archaic structure, originally conceived in 1787 in Philadelphia to appease America's slave-holders so that they could count their slaves (albeit at three fifths of a human being!) in the counting for electors. In fact, business-as-usual seems to be the order of the day as candidates lose no time to position themselves for 2004. Electoral reform is no longer in the air.

At this juncture, a supine continuance of the outdated Electoral College modality does a crucial injustice to our nation and to the American ethos. Our democracy calls at long last for a review of this 18th. century albatross in order to rise to the democratic demands of a new century and a new time.

January 15, 2001
Copenhagen Poses Moral Questions
Atención San Miguel

In presenting Michael Frayn's *Copenhagen* last week, Gerry Wodin and her Playreaders performed a magnificent service to the community of San Miguel. She and her fine players (Rick Davey, Marilyn Bulivant and Jerry Phalen) brought us meaningful, thought-provoking, socially conscious theater that stretched the imagination, challenged one's understanding of recent history and stirred up some deep moral questions.

The audience was mesmerized by this shattering exploration of the nexus between science and politics, as the morality of the race for the atom bomb between the Allied scientists at Los Alamos and their counterparts in Nazi Germany during World War II came under scrutiny by two extraordinary minds, both scientific and philosophical. Niels Bohr, Danish and half-Jewish and Werner Karl Heisenberg, a German patriot, grappled with the complex issues of the "duty" of science relative to the war effort on both sides versus the morality inherent in fashioning and unleashing the unimaginable destructiveness of the atom upon humanity itself. Bohr touched the core when he screamed with impatience and exasperation and anguish that "We must be first, or should we allow a homicidal maniac to attain and use this power?", while Heisenberg continued to work for the Nazi bomb project to protect his "beloved German homeland." Later, neither were without guilt.

Frayn, in Copenhagen, presents us with a disturbing morality play, exploring in excruciating detail what is perhaps the greatest moral problem of our time: Do we, and our generation, recognize the significance of the monumental breakthrough of modern science when it discovered and unleashed the hitherto unimaginably destructive power of the split atom? What are the consequences for mankind and for the life of the whole planet of this power that was used twice in World War II with devastating effect? Is it defining our international relations and determining the character of our security?

Even now, a new administration will have to face the problem, and already sharp differences appear in the crucial debate on our proposed national missile defense system. Should we commit ourselves and immense economic resources to this nuclear program (which many scientists insist just does not work), or should we stress international cooperation leading eventually to universal nuclear disarmament?

Sixty years after Copenhagen, this issue is still with us. Nuclear power and the nuclear threat hang over humanity like the sword of Damocles. Thousands of nuclear missiles are still poised and ready in Russia, the United States, in smaller countries that have the bomb and in uncontrolled rogue states. In *My American Journey*, written with San Miguelense Joe Persico, Colin Powell—a strong force on these issues—informs us that from "23,000 operational nuclear weapons in the armed forces . . . . between our own initiatives and the START treaties, we should be down to 8,000 warheads by 2003." Added to other nuclear arsenals, that is still a giant destructive power at large in the world today.

Albert Einstein, whose seminal letter to President Roosevelt sparked the Manhattan Project, and Robert Oppenheimer, brilliant leader of the project, as well as the eloquent Leo Szilard, all devoted the rest of their lives working for civilian control of nuclear weapons under international auspices, and, ultimately, for universal nuclear disarmament. They were afraid of the genie they had let out of the bottle. How this conflict is resolved, and how successful the better minds and the better natures of mankind confront the nuclear problem will determine the kind of world we will live in the century ahead.

BRAVO to Gerry Wodin, and to the trio of Davey and Bulivant and Phalen!

February 5, 2001
Further thoughts inspired by *Copenhagen*
Atención San Miguel

It is an exquisite irony, or, tragically, a testament to the manner in which the cultural milieu shapes our sensibilities and our moral priorities, that a furor has arisen around the use of weapons containing depleted uranium (DU) by NATO forces in Bosnia and Kosovo and by the United States in the Gulf War, while we remain almost inured to the vast destructive potential of "the real stuff," the thousands of nuclear missiles still poised and ready in our, and others' nuclear arsenals.

DU "comes from recycled nuclear fuel and contains traces not only of highly radioactive uranium-236 but of plutonium as well" (Mexico City NEWS, January 21). The report of cancer among handlers of these munitions, as well as environmental damage caused by their use, have caused justifiable alarm among our allies in Europe, even as "the Pentagon twice sent U.S. Army medical experts to NATO headquarters . . . to help it get 'hysteria' over the DU scare under control." (NEWS, January 23)

The "scare" is surely understandable, given the fact that "scientists have been quoted as saying that a particle as small as a millionth of an ounce (of plutonium), if inhaled, can cause a fatal cancer." (NEWS, January 22)

Amidst this furor, it is not inappropriate to note that the really big threat, which could destroy millions and devastate cities with a single nuclear bomb, is still with us. It is not the DU, which should scare the daylights out of us, but the continuing threat of arsenals of nuclear weapons around the world and their proliferation.

Yet the Comprehensive Nuclear Test Ban Treaty, which prohibits all "nuclear weapons test explosions and all other nuclear explosions," and whose preamble states that the treaty is intended to constrain "the development and qualitative improvement of nuclear weapons . . . and end the development of advanced new types of nuclear weapons," and which has been signed by 155 nations, *has still not been ratified by the United States*! (Mexico ratified in October, 1999). The treaty was rejected by the United States Senate in October, 1999. (New York Times, January 5, 2001)

General John M. Shalikashvili, former Chairman of the Joint Chiefs of Staff, recommended ratification, concluding that "the United States must ratify it in order to mount an effective campaign against the spread of nuclear weapons" (New York Times, January 5, 2001), as did General Colin Powell, now Secretary of State. But the Republican-led Senate refused to ratify, and President Bush opposed the treaty during his presidential campaign.

How does one explain the uproar over the use of depleted uranium weapons with its "limited" dangers and the silence by the public, political pundits and our political leaders on the continued threat of incalculable death and destruction by the "real stuff?" Can it be that we inure ourselves from even thinking about the worst evil while we generate moral outrage over a "small," but palpable by-product?

We must wait and watch President Bush as he decides between the advice of Powell, who said in 1993, that "the treaty is necessary for the safety and reliability of the world because it will reduce the threat of nuclear weapon attacks," and the advice of the conservative defense secretary-designate, Donald Rumsfeld, who has heatedly opposed the treaty.

This is an issue that must be kept alive by an alert public and by an informed public debate.

February 4, 2001
Election Reform Now
Mexico City—The News

Well, it's over! After gallons of printers ink, reams of learned articles, editorials, op-eds, letters-to-the-editor, and endless TV talk shows with their "talking heads," "experts," lawyers, journalists, political analysts, pundits, politicians, even psychoanalysts, and the expenditure of 2 billion dollars, an obscene record in U.S. presidential election history, to brainwash the public (even sub-liminally!), the verdict is in.

The candidate who won the election across the nation, even Florida, by a plurality of 337,576 votes (the New York Times, Dec. 20) was declared the loser. And the candidate who lost in the national vote, but won in Florida by a "certified" 537 votes while he prevented the recount of thousands of disputed ballots, was declared the winner (Even his staunchest supporter, William F. Buckley, Jr., wrote (Nov. 19), "Even under the auspices of the Electoral College system, there is a pretty good likelihood that Gore is the winner.")

The most disquieting phenomenon, however, in this tragi-comedy, is the speed with which the public, following the lead of politicians in both parties, appears willing to embrace a "spirit of conciliation," and "consensus," code words for ignoring the obvious lessons of this election, while the politicians return to business as usual. Already, positions are being staked out by ambitious aspirants for the next round in 2004, would be candidates and campaign strategists losing no time to heat the system next time.

In the wake of the 2000 election fiasco, common sense cries out for a thorough, and long overdue re-examination of our electoral process. First and foremost there is the ancient institution of the Electoral College, designed over 200 years ago in a United States vastly different from today's. It is clear that a system designed to favor the landed, the slave-owners and the privileged of that time has worked in 2000, to thwart the "will of the people," overturning the national choice by a method of state counting that, as Yale Law Professor Akhil Reed Amar stated, "is a hopelessly outdated system and we must abolish it (the Electoral College)" (New York Times, Nov. 9, 2000). "The Electoral College began as an unfair system, and remains so," he continued, "So why keep it?"

With the notable exception of New York's Sen. Charles Schumer and recently, Sen. Hillary Rodham Clinton, few have paid attention to this most significant aspect of the election mis-adventures. A federal commission to re-examine this and other aspects of our electoral process, as proposed by Schumer, should be a No. 1 priority of the new Congress.

The McCain-Feingold bill for election finance reform is still dormant, while President Bush seems to be relegating it to a back burner.

Modern, efficient, voting machines, in keeping with 21st century technology, should be uniform and nationwide.

Election laws that shorten the campaign period, and financing guide-lines that would prevent billionaires from buying elections with their personal fortunes (65 million dollars bought the Senate seat in New Jersey), should be enacted.

A re-ennobled process should be sought that brings in the 100 million eligible voters who expressed their disgust and distrust of the system by not voting at all. Small turn-out is a national disgrace.

Above all, the tainted election of 2000 must arouse and re-energize us all to rescue this crucial process of democracy to the central place it must occupy to continue government that is truly "of the people, by the people, and for the people."

The time to start the process of electoral reform is now!

February 4, 2001
DU Weapons Debate
Mexico City—The News

It is an exquisite irony, or, tragically, a testament to the manner in which the cultural milieu shapes our sensibilities and our moral priorities; that a furor has arisen around the use of weapons containing depleted uranium (DU) by NATO forces in Bosnia and Kosovo and by the United States in the Gulf War, while we remain almost inured to the vast destructive potential of "the real stuff," the thousands of nuclear missiles still poised and ready in our and others nuclear arsenals.

DU, or depleted uranium "comes from recycled nuclear fuel and contains traces not only of highly radioactive uranium—236 but of plutonium as well" (The News, Jan. 21). The report of cancer among handlers of these munitions, as well as environmental damage caused by their use, have caused justifiable alarm among our allies in Europe, even as "the Pentagon twice sent U.S. Army medical experts to NATO headquarters . . . to help it get 'hysteria' over the DU scare under control" (The News, Jan. 23). The News has amply covered the story on Jan. 11, 13, 18, 21, 22, and 23.

The "scare" is surely understandable given the fact that "scientists have been quoted as saying that a particle as small as a millionth of an ounce (of plutonium), if inhaled, can cause a fatal cancer." (The News, Jan. 22).

Amidst this furor, it is not inappropriate to note that the really big threat, which could destroy millions and devastate cities with a single nuclear bomb, is still with us. It is not the DU which should scare the daylights out of us, but the continuing threat of arsenals of nuclear weapons around the world and their proliferation.

Yet the Comprehensive Nuclear Test Ban Treaty, which prohibits all "nuclear weapons test explosions and all other nuclear explosions," and whose Preamble states that the treaty is intended to constrain "the development and qualitative improvement of nuclear weapons . . . and end "the development of advanced new types of nuclear weapons," and which has been signed by 155 nations. HAS STILL NOT BEEN RATIFIED BY THE UNITED STATES! (Mexico ratified it in October 1999). The treaty was rejected in a rebuff to President Clinton, by the U.S. Senate in October 1999! (New York Times, Jan. 5, 2001).

Gen. John M. Shalikashvili, former chairman of the Joint Chiefs of Staff, in a recent report to President Clinton recommended ratification, concluding that "the United States must ratify it in order to mount an effective campaign against the spread of nuclear weapons" (New York Times, Jan. 5, 2001), as did General Colin Powell now Secretary of State. But the Republican-led Senate refused to ratify it, and President George W. Bush opposed the Treaty during his presidential campaign.

How does one explain the uproar over the use of depleted uranium weapons with its "limited" dangers and the silence by the public political pundits, and our political leaders on the continued threat of incalculable death and destruction by the "real stuff"? Can it be that we inure ourselves from even thinking about the worst evil while we generate moral outrage over a "small," but palpable by-product?

We must wait and watch President Bush as he decides between the advice of Powell, who said in 1993, that "the treaty is necessary for the safety and reliability of the world because it will reduce the threat of nuclear weapon attacks," and the advice of the conservative Defense Secretary Donald Rumsfeld, who has heatedly opposed the treaty.

This is an issue that must be kept alive by an alert public and by an informed public debate.

February 11, 2001
Bush's Attack On Tradition
Mexico City—The News

In his first two weeks in office, U.S. President George W. Bush has earned the distinction of launching the most intensive, aggressive attack on one of the most hallowed traditions in American life—the wall of separation between church and state—since British Redcoats fired on American patriots at the "rude bridge" in Concord to preserve the British monarchy and its version of State religion. Never has the religious community had a better spokesman in the White House!

Going beyond school vouchers, which would divert much needed dollars from beleaguered public schools to "faith-based" (read, religious) private schools (a program put on the back burner for the time being due to public resistance). President Bush proposes the most sweeping change ever in the way in which a variety of social services are to be delivered. Caring for the poor and needy, the homeless, rehabilitation for drug and substance users, counseling for dysfunctional families, among others, in President Bush's view, should be the province of churches, synagogues, and mosques, not the responsibility of a compassionate and effective government. According to his plan, millions, even billions of taxpayers' dollars would be syphoned off from appropriate government agencies and public projects designed specifically to address and provide remedies for social ills, to be granted to church hierarchies—unelected, unaccountable to the general public and to the taxpayers, and to be spent in accordance with each church's unique theological vision.

This involvement of state and church, intertwining our elected officials with unelected church officials, and ignoring their responsibilities to ALL the people, religious and otherwise, who elected them, is a flagrant violation of the First Amendment and the most audacious assault on the principle of separation of church and state that has been a hallmark of U.S. society.

Taxpayers of every religious persuasion, or none at all, expect their government, their legally elected representatives, to spend their tax money on the nation's problems through responsible, accountable programs, and agencies run by accredited responsible professionals. They do not expect their government to default on its responsibilities by turning over the whole problem and its difficulties to non-governmental, non-elected, unaccountable, Church hierarchies, whose staff-hiring instincts and practices would tend more toward preference for those versed in theology (their particular brand!) than toward professional, well-trained, social work and social welfare experts.

Would we want millions, even billions of taxpayers' dollars granted to Pat Robertson, or Jerry Falwell, or Louis Farrakhan, with their special brand of "caring," based on religious dogma and divisiveness, and their fervid belief in their own, individual paths to salvation?

The principle that our elected government recognizes and faces its responsibilities to the nation's less-advantaged, regardless of religious belief or non-belief, must tell us that a responsible government does not shuck off its duties by transferring its problems to unelected and self-appointed hierarchies with their own primary religious agendas.

February 18, 2001
Buckley's Linguistic Tricks
Mexico City—The News

Editor: George Orwell, in his prophetic novel "1984," wrote of the way in which language can be distorted and deliberately manipulated to serve political bias.

"NEWSPEAK," was designed, he wrote, "not to extend but to diminish the range of thought . . . the special function of certain Newspeak words . . . was not so much to express meanings but to destroy them."

What could better describe William F. Buckley, Jr., especially his column of Feb. 12 in The News? Rushing to offer much needed support to U.S. President George W. Bush's plan to divert millions of taxpayers' dollars to the religious establishment, Buckley praises his "determination to use the reserves of religious institutions in the United States to forward charitable and educational work undertaken by the government." By a linguistic trick, Buckley turns the truth on its head. If there were, indeed, "reserves of religious institutions" sufficient to accomplish this task, there would be no need for huge government infusions of taxpayers' money! The fact is just the opposite: government is not "using" the religious institutions' "reserves." On the contrary, it is government "reserves" (meaning your money and mine) that are to be "used," to bolster religious hierarchies and to increase their power in an otherwise secular society. Who is "using" whom is perfectly clear.

Further, Buckley states, "The question before the house is, essentially, can one exploit the resources of a religious organization without violating the First Amendment?" The question, I suggest, is just the opposite: Should we allow, and does the First Amendment permit, . . . religious organizations to "exploit the resources" of the government, via official funding, to carry out what should be the government's responsibilities in the secular area of social services?

Buckley wants it both ways. He wants "smaller government," even "no government" in many areas of social services, while at the same time he wants huge public subsidies to permit private, unselected unaccountable "faith-based" groups to do the work which our government and its public officials are elected, and paid, to do.

February 20, 2001
**RE: "Bush's Call to Church Groups to
Get Untraditional Replies, Feb. 20):**
The New York Times

It is surely a curious development in the field of combating social ills such as literacy and drug-abuse that President Bush should concentrate on religious groups (including such questionable one as the Moonies and the Scientologists), holding out a most generous hand of public funds for their programs. Beside the question of violating the First Amendment and breaching the wall of separation between church and state, why are religious groups singled out for such generosity, at the taxpayers' expense? Why not civic and social groups and rehabilitation groups that are based on secular understanding and secular research, and are not basically beholden to any theological dogma? Most important, why are these funds, millions, even billions of dollars, not used to further government programs, through HEW or NIMH, where proper scientific standards can be applied and properly-trained researchers and therapists from the fields of social work and medicine and psychiatry are employed, rather than well-meaning, but essentially untrained religious devotees from a variety of conflicting metaphysical systems of belief?

February 25, 2001
Faith-Based Double Talk
Mexico City—The News

It's official U.S. President George W. Bush last week opened the White House Office of Faith-Based and Community Initiatives, giving the religious establishment the greatest boost of official support since the creation of our secular Republic. Not since state-approved official religions shared in, or even superseded, the power of the monarchies of medieval Europe has religious authority been granted such status: a partnership between the elected government and unelected church hierarchies, headquartered at the White House.

There are problems: The New York Times reported, "Devoting government money to selected religious programs also runs the risk of sparking conflict." (Feb. 20), as differing and competing groups line up for government largess. Hare Kishna, the Moonies, the Scientologists, among others, in addition to "mainstream" religions (who is to choose among them?) are already in fierce competition as the Church-State partnership gives them new-found status.

It is also a clear violation of the spirit and intent of the First Amendment and the Establishment Clause: ("Congress shall make no law respecting an establishment of religion"). In 1787, the original colonists refused to ratify the Constitution until this guarantee of Church-State separation was adopted, the first of the 10 amendments that comprise our cherished Bill of Rights. They believed the dictum of James Madison: "Religion and Government should never be mixed together."

Structures already in existence within the government might be better used: the Department of Health, Education and Welfare; the National Institutes of Health. Would not existing organizations be more effective than a Church-State partnership that is arguably unconstitutional and surely contrary to the basic pillars of our secular society?

March 11, 2001
Mexican Marshall Plan
Mexico City—The News

When the two millionaire presidents of the United States and Mexico met at their summit in Guanajuato recently there was no indication, at least in the press reports, that they addressed the basic reason for the vexing problem of illegal immigration that plagues both sides.

That reason can be seen in just one sentence: "The average minimum wage in Mexico is 40.35 pesos (4.21 dollars) per day in the best paid areas . . . elsewhere, like in Oaxaca, it is 35.83 per day." (The News, Dec. 23, 2000). In the United States the minimum wage is 5.25 dollars per hour!

It is this 10-fold difference that motivates impoverished Mexicans to leave their families, their villages and cities, to undertake the dangerous trip across the Rio Bravo, the scaling of the formidable Wall, and the danger of being shot as they traverse unfamiliar fields.

In my observation, Mexicans love their country, their families, their homes. They undertake the dangers of illegal immigration in the desperate attempt to earn 10 times more for their labor in the United States with which to feed their impoverished families.

The long-term answer to this problem lies in creating better conditions in Mexico. For the Mexican president, it means new and innovative economic policies to create higher wages, along with better housing, health and educational opportunities, as suggested in Tim Wiener's article, (The News, March 6). For the United States, it might suggest an economic policy toward Mexico that would raise its standard of living, something like the Marshall Plan that rescued the devastated economies of our former enemies after World War II. Why can't we do the same for our close neighbor, Mexico?

Aid from a combination of the government and private sector to raise the standards of living here in Mexico would be more efficacious in preventing what is essentially a flight from poverty than costly walls of separation and armed INS agents.

And besides the humanitarian aspect, a healthy Mexico would be a better market for U.S. goods. A win-win situation all around.

March 8, 2001
Letter to the Editor
The New York Times

Mr. Steven Waldman's Op-Ed article" (March 7), concerning President Bush's new "White House Office of Faith-Based Initiatives," concentrates, as its title suggests, on "Doubts Among the Faithful".

It would be more in keeping with our democratic, pluralistic, secular society if he included, also, some "doubts" among the secular "unfaithful" among us—just to be fair.

The basic insult to freethinkers and secular humanists is the arrogant elevation of church hierarchies to an unprecedented position of prestige and status at the very pinnacle of political power, the White House itself, with a partnership between the elected government and unelected church establishments, aimed at the funneling of public funds through religious institutions. This is not only arguably unconstitutional, but, of equal importance, would undermine social-service strategies based on reality-based scientific research from the fields of medicine, social work, and psychiatry in favor of questionable programs derived from metaphysical, unscientific, supernatural systems of belief. Taxpayer dollars were not meant to support religious agendas.

March 25, 2001
Madison's Legacy
Mexico City—The News

William Safire's column of March 21 (Happy Birthday, 'Little Jemmy') offered faint praise but did not nearly do justice to the magnificent contributions of James Madison to the structure of the U.S. Constitution and its lasting influence on U.S. life and values.

Madison's authorship of the first 10 amendments, the immortal Bill of Rights, was in itself an achievement of the greatest magnitude, setting the tone for U.S. democracy and continuing to this day to guard its primary allegiance to individual freedom and liberty.

The First Amendment ("Congress shall make no law respecting an establishment of religion") remains to this day a monumental and fundamental guide to the U.S. concept of diversity and freedom of conscience in a secular society, as it firmly establishes the principle of separation of church and state while preserving the individual's right to private religious belief and observance.

As U.S. President George W. Bush rushes to elevate religious hierarchies to an unprecedented partnership with the government in his "Office of Faith-Based Initiatives" at the very pinnacle of secular political power, he would do well to ponder Madison and his legacy: "Religion and Government should never be mixed together" he said.

President Bush should consider carefully Madison's passionate advocacy in the Virginia House of Delegates, described thusly in the Encyclopedia Britannica: "As a member of the committee on religion, he opposed giving special privileges to the Episcopal (or any other) Church, and spoke against a general assessment for the support of the churches of the state." Madison could not be more clear: "no special privileges to the church!"

James Madison, where are you when we need you?

March 30, 2001
Subject: LETTERS: On election reform in the U.S.
Mexico City—The News

U.S. voters, whether they reside abroad, in Mexico, or at home, are keenly interested in the Senate debate on the McCain-Feingold bill and in other proposals for election reform. It is clear that the country is fed up with an electoral process that is awash in money. Everyone, on both sides of the aisle, seems to want change. The debate waxes theoretical and ideological as it addresses the First Amendment "free speech right" of the wealthy to spend their money, politically, as they choose versus the corruption of the electoral process that, in effect, "buys" candidates and their future.

There is no doubt that a billionaire can "buy" a candidate and expect a quid-pro-quo in future legislation with greater ease than an ordinary citizen can influence his candidate with his one vote or even with his modest individual contribution. One answer, to even the playing field, is public financing of elections, TV regulations for equal free time for candidates, and a specific, time-limited campaign period, say 3 to 6 months.

A significant side-benefit of such an election would be the freeing of our elected officials from the burden of continuous fund-raising so that they could pay full attention to the legislative jobs for which they were elected rather than the shameless begging for money that now occupies so much of their time, at taxpayers' expense.

And while we're at it, doesn't anyone want to re-examine the archaic Electoral College system, which permitted a candidate with almost half-million more popular votes across the country to lose to the candidate who came in second?

Passage of the McCain-Feingold bill, reducing the stranglehold of soft-money on the campaigns, would be a step in the right direction. More basic reform still awaits stronger champions.

April 20, 2001
Separation of church, state fickle
The Times Herald Record

New York's Cardinal Edward Egan, in his first visit to Albany, revealed the essential contradictions of the church's posture vis-a-vis the government: While demanding state funding for Catholic, parochial schoolchildren, the cardinal was adamant in his opposition to a legislative package of women's health issues because it also included birth control coverage. "Government must not interfere with matters of religious faith," he said.

How then does the cardinal justify the huge government subsidy to institutional religion inherent in the ubiquitous tax exemptions for religiously owned property? In New York alone, $15 billion of religiously owned real-estate is free of taxes. And how does the cardinal view the new office for "faith-based initiatives" established in the Bush White House to specifically channel millions of taxpayers' dollars to religious organizations?

Are these not violations of our traditional church/state separation? Or does he want it both ways: Government aid to religion when it suits him, while he applies his considerable political clout and pressure for non-interference, even to the extent of sacrificing the health needs of all the women of the state, when it goes against his private religious agenda?

April 26, 2001
Why not use reality-based agencies?
The Times Herald Record

It's official!

President George W. Bush has opened the White House Office of Faith-Based and Community Initiatives, giving the religious establishment in the United States the greatest boost of official support since the creation of our secular republic.

Not since state-approved official religions shared in, or even superseded, the power of the monarchies of medieval Europe has religious authority been granted such status: *A partnership between the elected government and unelected church hierarchies, headquartered at the White House.*

But there are problems: As The New York Times reported, "Devoting government money to selected religious programs also runs the risk of sparking conflict," as differing and competing groups line up for government largesse. Hare Krishna, the Moonies, the Scientologists, among others, in addition to mainstream religions (who is to choose among them?) are already in fierce competition as the church-state partnership, at the highest levels of government, gives them new-found status.

How many religiously oriented groups will vie for rehabilitation funding in Orange and Sullivan and Ulster counties to compete with reality-based, scientifically oriented, secular groups based on the findings of social work, medicine and psychiatry?

A White House office that is aimed at the religious community is also a clear violation of the spirit and intent of the First Amendment and the Establishment Clause: ("Congress shall make no law respecting an establishment of religion.") In 1787, our original colonists refused to ratify the Constitution until this guarantee of church-state separation was adopted, the first of the 10 amendments that compose our cherished Bill of Rights.

They fervently believed in the dictum of James Madison: "Religion and government should never be mixed together." It is worthy of note that the new office in the White House is called "faith-based." Is this a euphemism, or a deliberate linguistic cover-up, meant solely to obfuscate and confuse? Everyone knows that "faith-based" means "religious." "Religious" is a clear, unambiguous, worthy word. So why not use it, and say what you mean? Or would that make the entire enterprise altogether too clear to the American people?

Finally, structures already exist in the government where the millions of dollars about to be diverted to religious groups might be better used: The Department of

Health, Education and Welfare, for example. Or the National Institutes of Health, or the NIMH, where proper scientific standards are applied and where properly trained researchers and therapists from the fields of social work, medicine and psychiatry are employed, rather than well-meaning but essentially untrained religious devotees from a variety of conflicting metaphysical, supernatural systems of belief.

Would not such investment in our reality-based democratic institutions serve all the people better and more justly than a church-state partnership that is arguably unconstitutional and surely contrary to the basic pillars of our secular society?

May 2, 2001
RE: "Why Not Try Vouchers?", Op-Ed April 27:
The New York Times

The major issues in the debate over President Bush's eagerness to spend taxpayers' money on religious social-service programs are: 1) Is it unconstitutional, under the First Amendment's Establishment Clause, and 2) is it more efficient, and moral, to use public funds for accountable public programs than for programs run privately by unelected and unaccountable religious hierarchies with their own religious agendas?

Mr. Wilson, offering advice as a shrewd lawyer for a religious client, suggests an end-run around the constitutional issue by suggesting that vouchers could accomplish the same results, thus avoiding the widespread sense that direct public funding of religious enterprises would indeed violate the principle of separation of Church and State. "Whether religious groups receiving federal aid should be allowed to hire only those who share their spiritual views ought not to be an issue", he declares. In other words, the widespread support for the principle of "equal opportunity employer" should be sacrificed in the case of religious programs—even those supported by taxpayers' dollars!

On the question of efficacy, there is simply no evidence that programs imbued with "spiritual" (read religious) content are more apt "to help drug abusers, juvenile delinquents and unwed mothers" than secular programs based on the scientific findings of social work, medicine and psychiatry, and there is no reason to abandon the wisdom of Thomas Jefferson and James Madison that "religion and Government should never be mixed together."

May 15, 2001
A Letter to the Editor
The New York Times

The appointment of John P. Walters as "drug czar" (article, May 11) is deja vu all over again! As long as we continue to put more effort into bombing the crops in Columbia and jailing the addict at home, rather than treating the disease of addiction, educating our troubled youth, and addressing preventive measures, the scourge of drug-abuse will continue to corrupt the nation, destroy our inner cities, and condemn our youth to the terrors of drug dependency.

The answer is not a futile continuance of a perpetual (and unsuccessful) "war on drugs" through military means and a lock-em-up-and-throw-away-the-keys mentality, but a recognition, at long last, that the problem must be transferred from the criminal-justice system to the health-maintenance system for a meaningful change in thinking and approach. We don't need still another "czar", but a compassionate, multi-disciplined, leadership that can put the drug-abuse problem into the proper context of social and environmental disorder.

May 18, 2001
RE: Op-Ed, "Congress's Virtual School Reform"
The New York Times

William J. Bennett and Chester E. Finn Jr. ("Congress's Virtual School Reform", Op-Ed, May 18) support a program for "school choice" (meaning vouchers that would siphon off funds from the public school system to the private, read "religious", sector, stress rigorous testing of the children, and give states more control over school spending. Nowhere do they address the real problems of under-funded public schools, crowded classrooms, the enormous burdens placed upon teachers by large class-sizes, and crumbling, and often dangerous school-buildings in our inner cities. To move public educational funds to the private sector is the exact opposite of what is needed for a democratic school system that would serve all our children: Better public schools, smaller pupil/teacher ratios that would give teachers the opportunity for one-on-one teaching, and higher teachers' salaries and incentives to attract "the best and the brightest" to this crucial profession. THE PUBLIC SCHOOL SYSTEM NEEDS STRENGTHENING, NOT ABANDONMENT.

May 21, 2001
Letter: On President Bush's Notre Dame address.
The New York Times

In his commencement address at Notre Dame ("Bush Pushes Role Of Private Sector In Aiding The Poor", front page, May 21), President Bush vigorously pursues his campaign to make organized religion his partner-in-government. His agenda is to transfer what have come to be accepted as government responsibilities to un-elected and unaccountable religious hierarchies. His program undermines, if not totally dismantles, the First Amendment's Establishment Clause and the principle of separation of church and state so passionately championed by Thomas Jefferson, James Madison and the founding fathers.

>From school vouchers that would cripple public education, to the unprecedented establishment of a "faith-based" office in the White House specifically designed to funnel taxpayers' dollars to religious authorities, and now to suggestions that anti-poverty funds be deflected to religious groups, the President's agenda is clear: *Government responsibilities to provide basic social services to all taxpayers through accountable government agencies are to be abandoned, losing by default to unaccountable private (read 'religious') institutions, a trend that runs contrary to the basic American secular society devised in 1787. Government responsibility, and secular accountability, must be re-affirmed to counter this retrograde tendency.*

May 22, 2001
RE: "Ford Wins Kennedy Award for 'Courage' of Nixon Pardon" (News article, May 22.)
The New York Times

It is a puzzlement! What are we to say when our children ask, "So, Grandpa, was Nixon good, or bad? And if he was bad, so bad that he had to resign the presidency, why do we give a medal now to the man who pardoned him?" Why is the "un-indicted co-conspirator" deserving of a nation's forgiveness while his "loyal men" (Haldeman, Ehrlichman, Dean, Mitchell, et. al.) deserved prison for having carried out his program? Or is pardoning evil itself deserving of a retroactive pardon, too? A political oxymoron!

The ill-conceived selection of Gerald Ford for the Kennedy medal for "political courage" robs us of the moral lesson of the Nixon/Watergate blot on the presidency. Re-furbishing the Nixonian image by a pardon for the pardoner is not the moral lesson we, or our children, need today.

June 9, 2001
RE: "Beliefs", June 9, 2001
The New York Times

It is dismaying to see Peter Steinfels (BELIEFS, June 9) dance around the subject of "faith-based programs" in a tepid confrontation of the issue of government funding for religious organizations for the delivery of social services. The obvious contradiction, in a secular society, is that religious organizations, "striving to maintain their religious identity" will tend to discriminatory hiring on the basis of religious faithfulness rather than professional qualification, in violation of Civil Rights laws as well as the First Amendment principle of the separation of church and state.

Simply put, secular purposes, such as the providing of public social services, should be supported by secular funds from all taxpayers, religious and otherwise, through secular, governmental programs and agencies, unencumbered by competing religious agendas or personal metaphysical systems of belief. An elected and accountable government must not be permitted to pass off its responsibilities to unelected, unaccountable religious hierarchies with private agendas of their own.

Mr. Steinfels might well profit from the direct and unambiguous counsel of James Madison, father of the Constitution, when, without pussyfooting, he said, "Religion and government should never be mixed together." A special White House Office for faith-based (read 'religious') initiatives, would have been anathema both to him and his colleague, Thomas Jefferson!

June 24, 2001
**RE: "Will Patients' Rights Fix the Wrongs?",
Week in Review, June 24**
The New York Times

RE: 'Will Patients' Rights Fix the Wrongs?" (Week in Review, June 24): If, as Michael M. Weinstein writes, "the Senate debate is a sideshow. The legislation being considered would fail to reach the roughly 40 million Americans without insurance, as well as the 15 million others . . . who buy stripped down coverage at exorbitant prices", and avoids "the real crisis", which is "the quality of care", then why is not a single voice being raised for the best alternative: universal health care, the so-called single-payer plan, run by a responsible, accountable, government rather than by private profit-driven insurance conglomerates? Instead, we see, ironically, a passionate emphasis on "the right to sue", a right that is a given to consumers in all other areas of American life, but strangely at issue where the nation's health is concerned. The issue is, clearly, the need to break the stranglehold of the insurance industry on the health-care delivery system and to return that system to the medical/professional health care system under public, responsible, accountable, governmental authority and financing, where the only criteria are quality and dedication, not profit, high executive salaries and stockholders' returns.

June 27, 2001
RE: "Bush Asks Mayors to Lobby For Faith-Based Social Aid" (June 26).
The New York Times

President Bush's statement to the United States Conference of Mayors (news article, June 26) that "we respect the separation of church and state, and the constitutional rights of religious people" is as astonishing as it is redundant. That the President feels the need to reassure us all that he "respects" what is a mandated constitutional principle is in itself revealing, but perhaps made necessary by his unprecedented establishment of a specific "White House Office of Faith-Based and Community Initiatives". Does he plan, in balance, to establish next door an equivalent White House Office for non-religious initiatives? Of course not: that function resides in Congress, in the House and Senate, in the various Cabinet departments and government agencies, all non-religious as the Constitution requires. That the President feels the need to compensate for, or to "correct" this, by special action for "the constitutional rights of religious people" is a dangerous sign that he "just does not get" the essence of our secular democratic form of government and that free-thinking people who want a government free of religious dogma and preference must fight once again the ideological battle that we thought was settled in Philadelphia in 1787.

July 8, 2001
Issue of the Week: The President's Agenda
The New York Times

RE: "Mr. Bush's 'Faith Based' Agenda (editorial July 8): The problem with President Bush's "speaking fervently of his religious faith" and embracing "the role of religion" is the simple fact that he forgets that he was elected by a diverse population to be the nation's political, not religious leader. He was elected to lead a country, not a ministry. Like all elected officials he is bound, regardless of his private beliefs, to be religiously impartial in the performance of his official duties. This is the essence of our secular society, the meaning of the Establishment Clause of the First Amendment, the core of Article VI of the Constitution ("no religious test shall ever be required as a qualification to any public office or public trust under the United States") and the dictum of James Madison, "Religion and government should never be mixed together." Or must we fight over again the battle of secular democracy versus religious dogma that we thought was settled once and forever in Philadelphia in 1787?

July 13, 2001
Letter to the Editor
The New York Times

RE: "On First Visit to New York, Bush Hews to Basic Themes" (front page, July 11): I wonder how many people thought it unseemly, to put it mildly, for the President of the United States, in his continued religious zeal, to mount a religious pulpit to echo a religious leader's opposition to the law of the land, as President Bush did yesterday at St. Patrick's Cathedral, where he praised the late Cardinal O'Connor's unremitting campaign against women's right to abortion (established by law and confirmed by the Supreme Court in Roe vs. Wade). Our two New York Senators applauded. Only the estimable former Governor Mario M. Cuomo, who courageously clashed with the late Cardinal on this issue in 1990, raised an eyebrow, as he saw the implications in the current debate on embryonic stem cell research.

June 15, 2001
Letter to the Editor
The New York Times

In "General Says Missile Shield Needs Money And Prudence" (news article, June 15), "Pentagon officials said that it would require billions or tens of billions of additional dollars" for "more ambitious testing" of antimissile weapons. This is on top of the $63 billion already spent on the program since 1985—a program that Senate Majority Leader Tom Daschle, among others, has doubted is "practical or even do-able" (CNN, 6/8/01). But where the Pentagon is concerned, money is no object . . . . millions, billions, even trillions, the mind boggles, and the average taxpayer is benumbed.

What if, instead, President Bush were to startle his European audiences by saying:

"The United States is prepared to put up $60 billion, through our United States Institute of Peace, to bring together the best minds in the world to research pathways to peace. And we urge your governments to do the same. (The US Institute for Peace is an under-budgeted research and study group, established by Congress in 1984, and little known even to the American public.) With such resources, and universal support by all civilized nations, we ought to be able to find a way to peace rather than to blunder into nuclear destruction!"

Billions for peace studies, rather than more billions for missile research. That should shake things up a bit!

July 02, 2001
RE: "A Changing World Is Forcing Changes On Managed Care", front-page, July
The New York Times

After the Senate huffed and puffed and exercised itself on the "right to sue" for those Americans lucky enough to have health insurance in the first place, it will be interesting to see, when the bill comes up in the House, whether anyone has the political and moral courage to address the real issues of health care in this country: the plight of the 43-million Americans who have no insurance at all, the 15 million who have stripped down coverage at prices they can hardly afford, and the 39 million seniors on Medicare who have no coverage for the prescription drugs they need to stay alive. Is there no one in Congress, at long last, to step up to bat for universal health coverage for all Americans in this, the wealthiest nation in history?

July 25, 2001
Aim should be 'universal' care
The Times Herald Record

Your passionate criticism of the HMO system of delivering health care (June 25 editorial) is right on the mark. The million-dollar salaries of HMO officials is obscene and morally repugnant when we see cuts in service, higher premiums to workers and employers and, most important the deteriorating quality of care.

But you fail to take the next logical step, which is to recognize that the peoples' health is much too important to be left to private insurance conglomerates where, inevitably, the emphasis is on profit, not on the public's welfare. With 43 million people uninsured and with another 15 million forced to "buy stripped down coverage at exorbitant prices" (New York Times, June 24), the Senate bill under discussion concentrates on "the right to sue," a consumer right that is strangely challenged where health is concerned!

The real issues are coverage and the quality of care. These can be addressed only in a system of universal health care, the so-called single-payer plan that would cover everyone, administered and financed by a responsible, accountable government and that would return the health-care system to medical professionals, where the only criteria would be quality and dedication, not profit, obscene executive salaries and stockholders' return on investments.

July 29, 2001
When Hospitals Shop Abroad
The New York Times

Of course we must be concerned about people in other countries who are ill (front page, July 23). But there is something wrong when our best facilities are blind to the 43 million uninsured Americans, and the millions in health maintenance organizations who are subject to limited care and bureaucratic regulations that can prevent a patient in one state from getting treatment in another.

Turkey's health care system, we learn, paid $300,000 for one citizen's liver transplant. When will the United States catch up and treat its own people as well?

August 11, 2001
Kelly, Gilman: Speak up
The Times Herald Record

The long campaign to save our electoral system from the corruption of big money is at a critical phase, and one man—House Speaker Dennis Hastert, with the support of a Republican majority—bottles up the Shays-Meehan bill, throttling it in committee. By a transparent procedural maneuver he is able to prevent this long-overdue reform from even being considered, or debated, by the full House.

Just a few brave Republicans have it within their power to prevent this outrageous assault on elementary democracy from happening—among them, our own Sue Kelly and Benjamin Gilman, who originally co-sponsored the bill in the House but have up to now, remained silent on Hastert's shameful obstructionism.

Meanwhile, election fund-raising is reaching obscene proportions. A New York business tycoon is trying to buy the mayoralty with a multi-million-dollar TV blitz. On the national level, both parties are engaged in unprecedented, frantic money-raising. Elections are awash in and besmirched by big money. The time to act is now—time for Reps. Kelly and Gilman to stand up, against their Republican leadership, if necessary, to restore and maintain elections that are fair, untainted and morally fit for a democratic nation.

August 27, 2001
Health-care reform vital
The Times Herald Record

Your news article ("Frustrated, Medical Society sues six HMOs," Aug. 6) offers the most compelling evidence yet that the nation's health ought not to be entrusted to the private insurance industry.

When doctors find it necessary to sue "six leading HMOs for allegedly faulty business practices," it should alert us all to the essential reality that the insurance industry is motivated only by profit (whether it insures cars or houses or health), and not by any special solicitude for the public's welfare. It is the search for profit, for their obscenely paid executives and for their investors, that drives the world of HMOs, and this is at the root of what the doctors' suit describes as "an utter disregard for patients and doctors."

The answer to the problem, however, may not be in an attempt to clean up and liberalize the insurance-driven system-for-profit, but to transfer the responsibility for the nation's health where it belongs: to our elected, responsible government, under a fair system of universal health care, administered and financed by responsible, accountable, governmental agencies and under the watchful eyes of the electorate and their representatives.

Meanwhile, bravo to the doctors in their campaign to protect their patients from rapacious insurance schemes.

But let us keep our eyes on the ultimate goal of complete coverage for all Americans under a fair, humanitarian, nonprofit system run by our government for the benefit of all and not for the enrichment of a few.

August 30, 2001
Letter to the Editor
The New Yorker

A first reading of Jim Holt's "The Life Of The Saint" (August 13) gave me a queasy feeling of painful un-ease and, after a careful re-reading, a keen sense of disquiet, even a welling anger, as though I had been intellectually assaulted, not unlike the rape victim who is challenged to defend his/her behavior as part perpetrator instead of victim. The "good guys", he seems to be saying, are not so easily differentiated from the "bad guys".

Indeed Mr. Holt, in an attempt that reaches the facetious at times, seems intent on taking down those who "do good", as he pretends that it is so very difficult to ferret out the difference between the socially desirable and the socially malicious. To do this he uses the age-old debaters' technique of "reductio ad absurdum" to muddy morality and to make it appear that what is "good" behavior and what is "bad" is difficult to ascertain and even more difficult to evaluate on a moral scale. Despite his display of erudite authority, such as the astonishing statement by the philosopher G.E. Moore that "no sufficient reason has ever yet been found for considering one action more right or more wrong than another" (!), most laymen, unencumbered by such philosophic profundity, would, in most instances, have no such difficulty. Who cannot tell the difference between those who prepared human beings for incineration, stuffed them into ovens and turned on the Zyklon B gas as they carried out the Final Solution—and those who risked their lives to prevent the ghastly genocide? Or, on a more pedestrian every-day level, does Mr. Holt pretend that it is so difficult to differentiate between acts of altruism, small or large, and behavior that is consistently and exclusively self-serving, even anti-social? To create such difficulty, and ambiguity, Mr. Holt introduces what he sees as a moral dilemma, i.e., a choice of "looking after those close to you rather than worrying about all humanity". As though the choice were all or nothing. And since very few of us would choose to give all, we who choose to give something are hypocrites, not "moral saints", (the sneer does not go unnoticed!). The argument is a straw man. "Philosophical" obfuscation notwithstanding, the need to serve one's own needs and the welfare of one's family, need not be incompatible with our instinct toward altruism, toward serving the social good, toward a recognition that we are, at least in part, "our brothers' keepers". The two are not mutually exclusive!

Henry Thoreau said it best, when he wrote, in "CIVIL DISOBEDIENCE": A man has not everything to do, but something; and because he cannot do EVERYTHING, it is not necessary that he should do SOMETHING wrong."

September 12, 2001
A Letter to the Editor
The New York Times

Everyone, from President Bush down, agrees that "we are at war." But no one is quite sure with whom! William Safire suggests that it is "religious zealots . . . seeking to find the path to paradise" (column, 9/11). Your editorial states that "We suffer from an act of war without an enemy nation with which to do battle" (editorial, 9/11).

But it is not only, or even primarily, an "enemy nation" we should be seeking. It is the "intensity of hatred" (NYT) that motivates the fanatic mind-set of religious belief and idolatry all over the world. In the West Bank city of Nablus, we read of "rejoicing Palestinians", chanting in the streets that "God is great!". In the United States, religious leaders view the carnage and also call on God, and urge prayer as a remedy. The President himself ended his speech with "God bless."

Religious leaders solemnly sermonize about the "love of God" and attempt to bring "spiritual healing" through prayer and worship, while violence in the name of God renders civilized discourse irrelevant, and, in an ultimate example of prejudice, arrogance and shameful bigotry, the Reverend Jerry Falwell blames the ACLU, abortion providers, and gay rights proponents for having so "weakened" the nation that it "left us vulnerable", so that "God lifted the curtain of protection" (NYT, Sept. 14)! The religious community does not contribute to our understanding when it tolerates such dangerous drivel!

When will we learn that our problem is man-made not God-given? The answer to blinding rage and violence lies in the realistic nurturing of man's innate capacity for kindness and love, in the support of the rational in the real world, not in the superstitious, paranoid, irrational thought processes of medieval religious thinking that has no place in our modern world, anywhere!

September 16, 2001
Reaction to terrorist attacks
The Times Herald Record

Congratulations on your magnificent coverage of the attack on America in your editorials, reportage, pictures and instant letters. It was great journalism, immediate and compassionate.

Everyone, from President Bush down, agrees that we are at war. But no one is quite sure with whom! The New York Times' editorial stated, "We suffer from an act of war without any enemy nation with which to do battle."

But it is not only, or even primarily, an "enemy nation" we should be seeking. It is the irrational, mindless, intense hatred that motivates the fanatic mindset of religious belief systems and idolatry all over the world.

When will we learn that our problem is manmade not God-given? The answer to blinding rage and violence lies in the nurturing of man's innate capacity for kindness and love in the real world, for compassion and concern for one another, for tolerance and the acceptance of differing world views in a common humanity—not in the superstitious, paranoid, irrational thought processes of medieval religious thinking that can produce consequences such as this loathsome act of violence. It should have no place in our modern world, anywhere.

September 17, 2001
Letter to the Editor
The Nation

I was dismayed, disgusted, and finally outraged by Alexander Cockburn's knee-jerk, immediate "analysis" (October 1) of the barbaric, loathsome terrorist attack on the United States and its people. He seemed to be champing at the bit, raring to go, more anxious to "explain" this monstrous, unprecedented assault on American civilian life and property rather than to reflect on the justified horror and anger of our people against the murderous perpetrators. Leave it to Cockburn to deflect attention and horror from the "prime suspect", Osama bin Laden and his anti-Semitic, anti-Western, anti-democratic private army of fanatics and religious zealots, by pointing the finger at, you guessed it, his perennial scapegoat, Israel. Not the terrorists, not the hijackers and their probable origin, but, Cockburn rushes to inform us, "Israeli rampages in the occupied territories" are to blame, a connection he is the first to (eagerly) proclaim, as he berates the more objective, professional TV reporters for not seeing this light.

Casting restraint to the winds, it took the "progressive" Cockburn in the "progressive" NATION not only to blame Israel for all Mid-East troubles, but now for this most heinous attack on America. Israel, constant victim of a continuing jihad (holy war) by Arab terrorists since the Arab coalition declared war to the death and invaded the new state in 1948, is now proclaimed the villain and perpetrator, not only in its own land, but in this terrible outrage on the United States by our common enemy. Cockburn's gambit is to "Blame the victim", carried to new depths, by his anti-Israel animus.

Cockburn is outrageous, and the NATION should be ashamed to have published his wild, incendiary, bigoted outburst. I can only respond, finally, by canceling my subscription, so as not to suffer my own small financial aid to this irresponsible, unconscionable, dangerous "journalism" at this pregnant moment.

September 18, 2001
Letters—On the Attack On America
The New York Times

In the thousands of words "explaining" the abominable attack on the United States and its people, by pundits, scholars and clerics, it is significant to note the studious avoidance of the single most compelling root cause: the pervasive and dominant influence of religious thinking (and its "unintended consequences"). What other motivation has the power to bring human beings to transform themselves into human missiles, to choose a fiery death over life, other than the promise of reward and glory in the hereafter? Even our indomitable Reverend Billy Graham, at the Washington National Cathedral, stated that our martyred dead are in a "better place" and would not want to return if they could! Only a pervasive religious philosophy that defies, indeed scorns reason, could so thoroughly implant this transfixing illusion of an Edenic future paradise that is preferable to earthly life.

Only when we free ourselves of such supernatural, irrational belief systems and embrace a secular, humanistic, rationalism will reality conquer illusion and free mankind to value life and human responsibility over death.

September 22, 2001
Letter to the Editor
The New York Times

In all the thousands of words from pundits and "experts" on the root causes of the abominable attack on the United States, no one has shown the integrity, or breadth required to re-evaluate the responsibility of organized, institutional religion and its widespread influence for what William Safire called the 'theological brainwashing" that provided the soil that nurtured and informed otherwise "sane" human beings to transform themselves into human missiles to kill themselves and thousands of others "in the name of GOD!" Our response, predictably, was a call for prayer on our side (witness the services at the Washington National Cathedral), calling on our God (over theirs, presumably) to sustain us and to bring about a more moral society.

When will we learn that the problem is secular, societal, not theological, and that the answer lies with responsible behavior by man, not by a "higher authority"; that we need to look into our ethics and value-systems, created and sustained by reason, logic, and reality, not by the supernatural, the unknown and unknowable "higher authority".

THE RESPONSIBILITY IS OURS, to change and to move ahead, discarding medieval modes of thought, into the new millennium. The thinking of the "flat-earth society" is no longer appropriate in the modern world.

September 24, 2001
RE: The Attack On America
The New York Times

I wonder how future scientists, or cultural anthropologists, reviewing the data of this historical era (if any remain), will "explain" or analyze the spectacle of 19 religious zealots, dedicated to their doctrine, willingly embrace a fiery death by suicide, even as they kill thousands of others with them, all IN THE NAME OF GOD,—and the response of a tragic and victimized society gathering in huge prayer meetings to appeal to the same God for justice and brotherhood? What schools of thought may emerge in a future "human studies department" in a future, more objective time, when science and reason will have superseded religious superstition and "faith"? This may be the central ideological and intellectual task of the coming century.

September 25, 2001
RE: Thomas L. Friedman, TERRORISM GAME THEORY, Op-Ed, Sept.25, 2001
The New York Times

Thomas L. Friedman ("Terrorism Game Theory", Sept. 25) describes the terrorists who pulverized the World Trade Center as "evil, educated, and suicidal", a combination difficult to understand because it lay "outside the boundary of my imagination". Why? Like the majority of our pundits and political theorists, Mr. Friedman inexplicably omits the most compelling causative characteristic of these terrorists: they are all convinced, religious zealots, "theologically brainwashed", as William Safire put it in a recent column. How else can one explain how even "evil and educated" human beings could willingly embrace a fiery death, and kill thousands of innocent people with them, were it not for their ideological conviction: the promise of martyrdom, glory and reward guaranteed by their religious beliefs? The widespread unwillingness to address this "unintended consequence" of religious indoctrination is apparent among our theologians of all faiths. But understanding will elude us until we face the dangers of blind "faith-based", irrational, supernatural motivation versus a social ethic based on secular reality, brotherhood and human responsibility.

October 17, 2001
**RE: "U.S. Weighs the Hidden Cost of
Its Pharmacy Bill", (front page, Oct. 17), and
"Hoarding Cipro" (editorial).**
The New York Times

Is there not something immoral, if not downright obscene in this situation?: While the President properly urges all Americans to sacrifice and to contribute in every way toward our national recovery from the September 11 calamity (even asking school children to earn and give $1); while our servicemen and women are patriotically putting their very lives on the line to strike at the terrorists' source; we tolerate the spectacle of giant pharmaceutical companies seeking to reap a profit, even a windfall, on the nation's terrible ordeal. In the anthrax threat, one company (Bayer) actually pays another company (Barr Laboratories) "about $30 million a year NOT to make a generic version of Cipro." (NYT, page 7), a tidy arrangement, designed to keep the price high, that would appear immoral in ordinary times, but downright unconscionable in times of national emergency. Should patent rights ever be place above human needs, now or at any time? Bravo to our Senator Charles Schumer for showing the way.

November 2, 2001
RE: "Our Commitment to You", Advertisement 10/24):
The New York Times

The full page ad by the Bayer Corporation (October 24) raises some questions:

To: Bayer: Does the order for additional Cipro from the United States Government—probably the largest single order from a single customer you are likely to receive—involve a profit? Would that be ordinary profit, or a lesser profit, or is it "at cost", your contribution to the fight against terrorism?

When school-children are urged by President Bush to earn and donate $1; when servicemen and women are patriotically putting their lives on the line to stamp out terrorism at its source; should you be making any profit at all on this terrible calamity to America and the world?

Are you still paying Barr Laboratories "about $30 million a year NOT to make a generic version of Cipro," as reported in the New York Times of October 17?

For the rest of us: Should patent rights ever be placed above human needs, now or at any time? Bravo to Senator Charles Schumer for showing the humanitarian way.

October 7, 2001
Letter to the Editor
The New York Times Magazine

Bravo to Andrew Sullivan ("This Is a Religious War", Oct. 7) for boldly confronting the great "denial" by our government and by most commentators, that this war is "not about religion"! The root motivation of the suicide bombers, bred into their very bones by their religious training and indoctrination, was clearly articulated by the alleged lead-hijacker, Mohamed Atta, when he said, "everybody should mention God's name (at his funeral) and that I died as a Muslim, which is God's religion" (N. Y. Times, Oct. 4).

Religious authorities of all faiths strain credulity as they try to distance themselves from "fundamentalists", those of "sharpened faith" and "intensified zeal" and the "violence that such zeal can lead to." Their refusal to accept any responsibility whatsoever for what some have called the "unintended consequences" of religious thinking does not add to their stature as moral leaders.

In the end, Mr. Sullivan's conclusion that "We are fighting for the universal principles of our Constitution—and the possibility of free religious faith" inexplicably overlooks the free choice of a non-religious, free-thinking, secular humanism (also guaranteed by our Constitution), based on reason, science, morality and human responsibility, unfettered by superstitious, supernatural, controls.

Reason and humanism may hold more promise for peace, justice, and brotherhood, than the dangerous possibilities of religious dogma, as the World Trade Center disaster so monstrously taught us.

November 5, 2001
RE: "Yes, This IS About Islam", Op-Ed Nov 2:
The New York Times

Salman Rushdie may be reaffirming his pre-eminence as a wordsmith and fiction-writer when he can coin what may be the oxymoron of the year as he asks us to hope for a "secular-humanist Islam . . . . if terrorism is to be defeated"!

It is like expecting the establishment of a chapter of the American Civil Liberties Union in Auschwitz, or a branch of Amnesty International in the gulags of Joseph Stalin's Russia.

Instead, clear-headed and without illusion, we must concentrate on defeating the reality of a terrorist, anti-Western, anti-Semitic, theocratic Islam, as it prevails today in Afghanistan, Iran, and elsewhere, and then work with all the tools at our command to educate the next generation in the modern principles of secular-humanism both in and out of Islam, for a future world of brotherhood and reason.

October 30, 2001
What Makes A Suicide Bomber, Oct. 28
The New York Times Magazine

Joseph Lelyveld's front page question, "What Makes a Suicide Bomber" (Oct. 28) was in fact previously answered by Andrew Sullivan on Oct. 7, when he said ("This IS a Religious War"), "The religious dimension of this conflict is central to its meaning." What is remarkable is that, although both acknowledge unequivocally the "use of religion for extreme repression, and even terror" (Sullivan), and that, as the professor Lelyveld interviewed in Tel Aviv said, "It's not a phenomenon of individual psychology. It's an organizational phenomenon", they both avoid the next logical step, which is to re-examine, in depth, established religious hierarchies and the consequences of their influence, here and abroad. Do not the official institutional bastions of our powerful religious organizations, which cast such a wide net of influence over the instruction and indoctrination of young and vulnerable minds, bear at least some responsibility when the outcome, however unintended, of religious teaching and zealotry is wanton death and destruction? It may very well be that, in the end, we might conclude that secular humanism holds more promise for a safe, sane and moral universe based on man's capacity for love, reason and brotherhood than the possibilities for evil of unfettered religious dogma, based on superstition and blind faith.

November 25, 2001
Redefining The United States' War
Mexico City—The News

With the Taliban driven from Kabul, and Osama bin Laden in hiding, it is time to examine in depth the core meaning of the attack on America and the ultimate objectives of our "War on Terrorism".

The name itself, "War on Terrorism," is a just and powerful rallying cry, both domestically and internationally, for all decent people to oppose the monstrous barbarity of the attack on civilian life in New York and the Pentagon in Washington. But it is perhaps a misnomer, or at best inadequate, not getting to the deep inner significance of the event and its consequences. It is like calling World War II a war against the German U-Boats that sank ships in the Atlantic, or a war against the Nazi rockets that terrorized and slaughtered London civilians in their blitz against England, or a war against the cannon that killed soldiers and civilians alike in the brutal siege of Leningrad. World War II was fought against those weapons, of course, but to be understood, it was never forgotten that it was FASCISM that was the enemy. It was Nazism, Fascism and the Axis powers that we were fighting against. Fascism was the enemy, its weaponry the means. It was as a "WAR AGAINST FASCISM" that it achieved its significance and its historic meaning.

The present enterprise will be more properly understood when we call it, properly, by the name of its underlying goals and characteristics, its philosophy and purposes, rather than by its chosen modus operandi, however obscene.

In this vein, the attack on America was motivated, inspired, and guided by what might be called RELIGIOUS FASCISM. Osama bin Laden is its Hitler.

The al-Qaida are its storm troopers.

The Bin Laden interpretation of the Koran is its Mein Kampf.

An unprecedented, immoral, barbaric reign of terror on peaceful civilian life is its modus operandi.

And its first targets are Americans and Jews.

Our goals and purposes in this war will be understood and effectively pursued only when we recognize the difference between means (a conscienceless terror) and ends (the political, moral, ethical, singular purposes of the enemy; the totalitarian aims of a religious fascism.)

Calling it a "War Against Religious Fascism" might be a good way to begin to understand the suicidal behavior of its faith-based "martyrs" and to sharpen and define our own ultimate goals. Such an exploration must be the primary, ideological, intellectual and moral responsibility of our leaders—political, theoretical, philosophical and religious in all hierarchies—to make sense of our military endeavors and to provide goals that are in keeping with our democratic, freedom-based, secular society.

December 3, 2001
Demonizing the U.S.
Atención San Miguel

I was in New York on September 11 and witnessed on television (along with millions of other people around the nation and world) the horrifying spectacle of the Twin Towers in flames and then collapsing and crashing to earth, incinerating 4,000 innocent people. Disbelief, fear, anger, dismay, a sense of events taking place that were beyond understanding, feelings of rage, fury, impotence crowded in on all of us. What was happening? Why? What could we do?

Later, I walked the streets, now different than ever before, and shared in the numbness and despair of so many. Then, in a miraculously short time, witnessed the rebounding of extraordinary energy on all sides as people came together to combat whatever evil had befallen us. New Yorkers, and the indefatigable Mayor Rudy Giuliani, poured out their caring and concern for the immediate victims, the firemen, policemen and emergency rescue workers who gave their lives to save others, and to help the families, widows, widowers, and orphaned children, suddenly bereft and in immediate need of life-sustaining assistance.

A great evil had suddenly smashed the rubric of ordinary life, killing ordinary people as they went about their ordinary tasks; service workers and CEOs, secretaries and executives, Wall Streeters and messenger boys, without discrimination, in an unprecedented assault on a civil society in a time of peace. Two months later, I arrived in San Miguel, and was chagrined, dismayed, and finally angered to read of an event in Atención. Anti-war petition signed in San Miguel, read the front page headline (November 19). Was there an outpouring of sympathy for the thousands of innocent lives lost in New York and Washington and on the hijacked planes? Was there any concern expressed for the thousands of innocent family members whose lives had been shattered forever? Not at all! The thrust, instead, was to protect the people of Afghanistan from the actions of the United States and its allies to prevent further terrorist attacks! One signator of the petition was concerned that "bombing will give . . . reasonable Arab people more reason to be righteous, indignant and angry with the United States."

After just one sentence of lip-service to "join the world-wide condemnation of those abominable acts of death and destruction on U.S. soil," the rest of the petition is directed to a one-sided attack on the United States. The extreme depth of animus toward American policy destroys any pretension of objectivity or impartial logic.

Unbelievably, the victim is castigated, portrayed as the prime evil-doer, while the perpetrators of this heinous deed are provided with a rationale and justification. Right and wrong are turned on their heads; good and evil confused and obfuscated; victim and criminal blurred. More so, the criminals here are protected from the deserved outburst of revulsion and condemnation for their evil, unforgivable act of barbarism and inhumanity, while the entirely understandable and just action of the United States in defense of its people and its society are condemned out of hand, in a rash knee-jerk reaction.

The September 11 attack on the United States was an unprovoked act of war, violence and terror by a dangerous movement of religio/fascists, to be fought against with every means at our disposal—just as we fought against fascism in World War II. If Pearl Harbor was a day that will live in infamy, and Nazi Germany and its Axis partners were the champions of genocide and totalitarianism, to be fought and vanquished at all costs, then this modern religio/fascism movement, whose primary spokesmen today are the Taliban, al-Qaida and their networks around the world, must also be fought and utterly defeated in order to maintain a civilized society that is freedom-based, democratic and secular.

A petition that demonizes the United States and offers a rationale for its enemies, at the wrong time, with the wrong message and with a wrong and flawed analysis of events, is not what we need in this pregnant moment of crisis.

December 9, 2001
Fascism Vs. Fundamentalism
Mexico City—The News

In Thomas L. Friedman's column of Nov. 29 (The True Cause Is The Defeat Of Religious Fundamentalism), he enlarges the debate and gets beyond the surface when he suggests the real war against Osama bin Ladin and the Taliban is about "religious totalitarianism," not simply "terrorism."

In last week's letter, I suggested a similar approach, but called our enemy "Religious Fascists." I think this is more than just a semantic quibble. Nomenclature can be significant Fundamentalism and totalitarianism, religious or otherwise, are dangerous, anti-democratic, anti-rational movements. But full-blown fascism is the ultimate evil. And it is surely full-blown fascism, delivered under a cloak of piety and religious dogma, we face today.

"Fundamentalism" usually refers to literal biblical interpretations, and those who passionately, even fanatically, endorse it are implacably hostile to what Friedman calls "modernity and pluralism." In this sense, they might also be called "totalitarian," intolerant toward other interpretations of the "holy word." But for the most part, these remain intra-religious debates, with consequences normally contained within the fold.

The Taliban is a wholly different enterprise, with its evil, repressive control over an entire society, and with its foreign aggression. Thus, "fundamentalism" changed radically into an aggressive fascism, a danger to the entire world. It's a slippery slope, but to the single-minded, committed biblical literalist it is not that illogical a progression. And it explains suicide-bombers and hijackers willing to die "in the name of God."

Clearly the immediate imperative is to defeat the Taliban fascists and their allies, as we did the political secular fascists in World War II. The long range cure, however, is not that simple. Friedman states "the generals we need to fight this war" are religious leaders who "embrace modernity" and possess a "multilingual view of God" against those with "exclusivist religious visions." Of course, if we are to defeat the aims of a future religious fascism, the institutional leadership of every religious hierarchy must accept the responsibility to insure their teachings do not lead to that slippery slope, toward killing "in the name of God."

On a deeper level, however, it may very well be the critical battle of the 21st century will be between blind faith without reason, the worship of an unaccountable "higher authority," versus a liberating humanist secularism that accepts human responsibility based on human morality and brotherhood.

December 16, 2001
Human Rights Misinformation
Mexico City—The News

International Human Rights Day was observed on Monday in San Miguel's lively Jardin with a "mesa informativa" (information table) that was used, unfortunately, to express more bias, hostility, and animus toward U.S. policy than toward the real enemies of human rights in the post Sept. 11 world.

With amazing and infuriating even-handedness the thousands of victims of the religio-fascist unprovoked, monstrous bombings in New York and Washington and the retaliatory bombing by the U.S. and its allies in Afghanistan in order to prevent further terrorist attacks are equally condemned . . . and the first demand of the "organizers" is "a halt to the military attack on Afghanistan"! Oblivious to the fact that the coalition bombing (which they vociferously opposed just a few months ago) brought down the repressive Taliban regime and restored more human rights to the beleaguered people of Afghanistan than they have had in the five years of Taliban rule, now, as the coalition hunts down the al-Qaida and Bin Laden to prevent their regrouping for further religious violence and murder, they call for "a halt to military attack"!

This in the name of "human rights"!

Throughout, the exercise of this small group criticizes not the criminal perpetrators and violent aggressors, but the United States, in a disgraceful display of bias and one-sidedness.

It is the United States they attack for not upholding "The Rule Of Law," not the Taliban fascists, whose contempt for civilized "rules" threatens all civil, secular society, just as the attack on Pearl Harbor and the Nazi blitzkrieg threatened all democratic society in 1941.

Similarly, the "information" dispensed suggested that "going after Hamas and Hezbollah would be a terrible mistake" since "neither is an exclusively terrorist organization (!), neither is attacking Americans.

With a terrible timeliness, the lie was given to this weak rationale just yesterday when Hamas-boasted of killing another 10 people in a bomb-bus attack in the West Bank. Not a terrorist organization, indeed!

A new Marshall Plan is urged for Afghanistan to help rebuild the country . . . but not a word about the rebuilding of devastated New York, or aid to the thousands of widows and widowers and orphaned children and their families who were left bereft, innocent victims of this first 21st-century fascist attack on democratic values and secularism.

Most of all, it is sad and disquieting to see the total absence of a sense of MORAL EQUIVALENCY, as victim and criminal perpetrator are assigned equal culpability, as good and evil are blurred, as the violent consequences of a fanatic religiosity are visited upon secular society and democratic, pluralistic values.

Suffice it to say the organizers of this display did not represent the best traditions of human rights, nor did they enjoy the support of most San Miguelians.

December 21, 2001
letter re: Fukuyama
Newsweek

Francis Fukuyama (Dec. 2001-Feb. 2002) is right, as far as he goes, when he states that we are fighting "Islamo-fascism". But he does not go far enough. The New York Times' Thomas L. Friedman went a step further when he stated that we are fighting "an ideology: religious totalitarianism". (New York Times, Nov. 29). I suggest that the most inclusive, comprehensive term would be "RELIGIOUS FASCISM", of which Islamo-fascism is a part.

How can Prof. Fukuyama speak of "the Christian doctrine of universal human equality" when the worst historical fascism, the Nazi genocide and the Holocaust, occurred in Christian societies with Christian acquiescence if not complicity, and when Christian history reeks with the bloody burdens of the Crusades, the Inquisition, the rapacious conquest of Mexico, all "in the name of God"?

Yes, Islamo-fascism is our current religious abomination, but all religious ideologists have the responsibility to examine the intense zealotry and passionate intolerance that may be nurtured in their midst, providing the breeding ground for the hatreds of "jihad" (holy war) and fascism.

December 30, 2001
Defending Patriotism
Mexico City—The News

The old saw, "Patriotism is the last refuge of a scoundrel" has been repeated so often it has given a good thing a bad name.

Historical U.S. examples—Alien and Sedition Law of 1798, Palmer raids of 1917, McCarthyism—have aroused skeptism when patriotism is offered as rationale. We suspect it's being used to conceal a less worthy agenda.

In the process, we've given in, allowing the "bad guys" to coopt the noble word. We've allowed "patriotism" to look bad! Except under rare historical circumstances (World War II), the "good guys" have been afraid to look too "patriotic!"

Webster defines patriotism as "love of country" and "public spirit." Perhaps because of a fear of over-sentimentality, the "good guys" have been afraid to assert they love their country.

In times of crisis, however, patriotic sentiment is revived.

When the first U.S. statesmen fought the tyranny of the English crown, they called themselves, simply, "patriots." "Patriotism" was nothing to be ashamed of.

When the Declaration of Independence was signed, at a time when the ragged colonial army was in retreat before the professional mercenaries of the king, they knew they were committing treason, at risk of death. As Benjamin Franklin supposedly said as they signed. "We must all hang together or most assuredly we shall hang separately."

Perhaps now is the time for the "good guys" to reclaim patriotism in its truest sense, not only to defeat religious fascists and preserve secular democracy, but also political fascists who threaten the original concepts of freedom and liberty. As the U.S. government pursues its immediate imperative of destroying the Taliban and their terrorist allies, we can reflect upon the original intentions of the founders of the United States, described thusly by John Adams, in David McCullough's biography, "Let us recollect it was liberty, the hope of liberty, for themselves and us and ours, which conquered all discouragements, dangers, and trials."

In that sense, let us not be afraid to be called "patriots" again.

January 27, 2002
Fascism Is The Enemy
Mexico City—The News

As students of the science of semantics never tire to point out, language is the mold into which we pour our thoughts, but the way in which language is used can itself be a potent molder of beliefs and public attitudes.

Thus, it is instructive to examine the language of the war in Afghanistan: Officially, it has been named the "War On Terrorism," a brilliant stroke of PR that resonated exactly with the public horror after Sept. 11 and rallied a world-wide coalition. But it soon became apparent it was insufficient to the full scope of the event.

William Safire, on the very day of the attack, called it a deed of "religious zealots" who had been "theologically brainwashed."

On Oct. 7, Andrew Sullivan stated in the New York Times what had been officially avoided up to then, "This is a religious war," he wrote.

On Nov. 29, Thomas L. Friedman came closer to the mark when he wrote, "We are fighting an ideology, religious totalitarianism."

Still later, the eminent Harvard professor, Samuel P. Huntington—author of the widely acclaimed "The Clash of Civilization and the Remaking of World Order"—wrote in Newsweek, "The age of Muslim wars had come home to America" in the form of a "holy war on the United States."

Finally, professor Francis Fukuyama of Johns Hopkins, came closest to reality when he wrote. "The present conflict is not simply a fight against terrorism . . . but rather with Islamo-fascism."

In this space, on Nov. 25, I used a broader, more inclusive term, Religious Fascism, a description still assiduously avoided by almost all officials, pundits, columnists and commentators.

It is a truism to state "to defeat the enemy, it is first necessary to know him." The imperative today, as the first phase of the "War On Terrorism" nears its end is to recognize terrorism is the means, the modus operandi.

The real enemy is fascism, this time delivered under the cloak of religion, but fascism nonetheless, with all its evils and its threats to freedom and to democratic, secular societies.

February 3, 2002
Bush's Questionable Domestic Agenda
Mexico City—The News

In his State of the Union Address Tuesday, U.S. President George W. Bush secured the overwhelming support of the U.S. people as he resonated passionately with their justified anger at the horrendous attack of 9/11 by religious fascists from abroad. His steely resolve, forcefully presented, was precisely what was needed, expressing the primary responsibility of government, any government, to protect its people from foreign enemies.

Whether President Bush succeeds, however, in using this new-found political capital to put across his domestic agenda, is another matter.

Forty million Americans, probably even more now due to the increased unemployment caused by Sept. 11, are without health insurance. A "patients" Bill of Rights" does not even begin to address this problem adequately.

Bush's uneven and unfair tax cut for the rich is seen by serious economists as no panacea that would "stimulate the economy."

The president still lends White House authority to "faith-based" views for the delivery of social services, and education, despite serious questions as to their constitutionality or effectiveness.

His obsession with a "star-wars" missile defense remains, despite evidence it is unworkable and costly to the point of threatening funding to other more traditional defense programs.

And electoral campaign reform, now finally under discussion in the U.S. Congress, does not even get a mention.

Although there is no doubt that President Bush deserves, and will get, vigorous support on the broadest level for his steadfastness and leadership in the War on Terrorism, on which almost all-Americans will back him, this should not diminish a principled and thorough examination of the merits and demerits of his flawed domestic agenda.

February 17, 2002
Church Vs. State
Mexico City—The News

A Feb. 2 New York Times article entitled "New Leader Picked for Religion-Based Initiative" reported that U.S. President George W. Bush has appointed a new director for his White House Office devoted to securing federal funds for "faith-based" programs in the administration of charities to the general public. How ironic that while we are in the midst of a bitter war against terrorists spawned by religious fervor gone amok and a burning hatred of our free secular society, President Bush should seek to revitalize and re-affirm his lagging, official program to link organized religion with government sanction as he provides public money to buoy religious influence.

A cardinal feature of U.S. society from the very beginning has been a clear separation of Church and State, promulgated by the founding fathers, and insisted upon by the 13 colonies before they ratified the U.S. Constitution.

It is, perhaps, the feature of the United States' free secular society and its Bill of Rights that enrages the Taliban the most. As the United States fights "religious fascism" abroad, the enormous strength of the principle of separation is more clear and important than ever.

It should be revitalized, not scuttled or whittled away, as the White House official "faith-based" use of public funds for religious purposes inevitably does. It is significant that, although ensconced in the White House itself, the program has not yet been approved by the U.S. Congress.

While the fight abroad against the dangerous consequences of control of government by religion continues, the United States must be careful of first steps that negate that principle at home and threaten the basic principle of separation of Church and State.

March 17, 2002
Six-Month Anniversary
Mexico City—The News

On the six-month anniversary of the Sept. 11 attack on the United States, many are casting a more reasoned eye on that horrendous event. What has transpired since and where do we go from here?

Despite its complexity in terms of socio-political considerations, the overwhelming response in the United States was, predictably, the anguished response of a people and a country invaded during peace time, with an unprecedented toll in human life and destruction on a scale never before experienced in that country. More than 3,000 civilians were killed in New York, Washington and Pennsylvania. More than 7,000 were injured. The devastation in New York was on a scale never before imagined possible.

U.S. President George W. Bush's immediate response, supported overwhelmingly at home and abroad; was to protect against another attack. Although some will quarrel about the political coloration of the coalition he put together, the U.S.-led coalition achieved its early objectives: The Taliban-controlled Afghanistan government was overthrown, the al-Qaida thugs were defeated and dispersed. A new interim government restored the basis for a renewal of human rights, women were liberated from the medieval tyranny of the repressive Taliban rule.

Above all, a necessary and seminal blow was successfully mounted against a religious fascism that was breaking out of its borders to threaten the rest of the world.

The United States, the "Great Satan," was chosen to be attacked first, because it represents all that religious fascism hates and fears: diversity, religious tolerance, democracy, popular representation, and, above all, the separation and precedence of a democratic state over an established church. This just could not be tolerated by a movement steeped in religious bigotry, what Thomas L. Friedman called "an ideology of religious totalitarianism."

Where do we go from here? Today, President Bush warned the war is "entering a new phase." He warned of the "growing threat of terror on a catastrophic scale," should nuclear weapons end up in the wrong hands. After Sept. 11, no one can afford to treat this lightly. The landscape of possibilities has suddenly widened. Without succumbing to a paralysis of fear, the problem is to organize the widest coalition of nations to combat the forces of evil. It is impossible to go back to our former complacency.

The problem is not only military. U.S. relations in every dimension with the rest of the world is suddenly on the table. Economics, politics and philosophies of government, and the place of religious thought and proselytism everywhere and its "unintended consequences," must engage us all. It is a truism, by now, to state "the world will never be the same" after 9/11. But how it changes depends on the willingness of global leaders, as well as political, civic and religious leaders, to rethink and reshape the way in which we live together, as individuals, as groups, and as nations, on this singular planet we all share.

March 14, 2002
Bill saves electoral system
The Times Herald Record

History was made in the House of Representatives with the passage of the Shays-Meehan bill, which, together with the passage of the McCain-Feingold bill in the Senate, rescues our electoral system from the corrupting influence of big money.

With shameful regularity, candidates of both parties have accepted huge contributions (more than $500 million in soft money last year) and pretended that they were not beholden. Public disgust with bought elections, finally, could no longer be ignored.

It is to be hoped that public pressure does not let up, that the Senate acts promptly and that President Bush signs the measure without delay.

Bravo, also, to our own Ben Gilman for challenging his Republican Party on this issue. It took 41 Republicans to defy their party and join the Democrats to achieve this major victory for democracy.

One caveat: Why; after a seven-year delay, should this bill, if passed and signed, not go into effect immediately, in time to clean up the November 2002 elections?

March 23, 2002
On New Revelations of Nixon tapes.
The New York Times

Mr. Leonard Garment's lame efforts (Op-Ed, March 23) to maintain a "distinction between private speech and public behavior" is either disingenuous or overly ostrich-like, or both! The question is not the "ugly consequences" of the taping or their publication, but the ugly consequences to the public weal of the anti-Semitism itself. His lugubrious, and questionable, assertion that "for individuals of his time and background the stain of anti-Semitism in private language was nearly universal" is as indefensible a "defense" as asserting that there is nothing to the "private use" of the N word to warn us of the true racial attitudes of the speaker. Mr. Garment seems to be more upset by the revelation of iniquity (in this case "raw anti-Semitism from the Reverend Billy Graham") than by the iniquity itself. When one exhibits such a conflict between "private speech and public behavior", he exposes what psychologists might term "cognitive dissonance", or what ordinary citizens would call simple "hypocrisy". This is especially dangerous in high places!

March 24, 2002
The Spirit Of Monterrey
Mexico City—The News

    Amid this week's depressing news of war, violence and the threat of more war, (even nuclear or biological war via Saddam Hussein), the very best news is headlined "The Spirit of Monterrey" and regards the continued inspiring leadership of U.N. Secretary-General Kofi Annan. The energetic Annan emerges as a leading force in the fight against poverty and it is to be hoped this summit of world leaders will prove a watershed in this area. As Annan so cogently put it, "It is time to recognize we cannot live in a world so unequal that it is like two worlds." Just the day before he reminded us "well over 1 billion people go to bed hungry every night."

    It is encouraging that, while overwhelmed by the War Against Terrorism, the U.S. government is not uninvolved in the war against poverty. The U.S. pledge of an additional 5 billion dollars over the next three years in foreign aid for poor countries is a welcome and significant move. U.S. columnist Thomas L. Friedman hailed it as a "substantive breakthrough for this administration."

    But it is only that, a "breakthrough," and not nearly enough. More than 1 billion people live on less that 1 dollar a day—an obscenity when an excess of luxury and over-consumption is commonplace in the "developed" world. Fifteen EU member-nations contribute one-third of 1 percent of their gross national product to aid poor countries and have pledged to increase that to 0.39 percent by the year 2006. The United States, according to former U.S. President Jimmy Carter, "gives one-thousandth of its gross national product . . . embarrassingly low." The U.S. pledge of 5 billion dollars more is a step in the right direction . . . but only a step.

    Above all, the U.N. International Summit on Financing for Development in Monterrey will focus attention on the rampant poverty that blights so much of our planet. It is a beacon, a moral uplift in a world that sorely needs it. This effort is not only right, moral, and humanitarian, but is also essential for all human society. It is clear poverty, disease, hopelessness, malnutrition, suffering, hunger and despair provide the breeding grounds that produce the excesses of terrorism and war we face today. We must address the basic evils of poverty and its consequences in order to solve the evils they breed. In the last analysis, to ignore these problems is to do so at our own peril.

April 14, 2002
Human Bombs Are Unjustifiable
Mexico City—The News

    Semanticists never tired to remind us that language is a potent force in the formation of attitudes and social thought. Words and phrases, repeated often enough, take on a life and meaning of their own, for good or for bad, to express phenomena, or, by constant repetition to render them emotionally harmless. Thus, words like racism, anti-Semitism, genocide, Holocaust, have entered our vocabulary in a sort of sanitized way. They roll off one's tongue, or leap from the printed page, with less and less emotional effect. The real horror, the evil, the obscenity of their actual meanings are lost as we are inured emotionally by repetition or by a self-protective resistance to deeper thinking.
    So it is now with the term, "suicide-bomber," repeated endlessly until it all but loses its stark, unbearable reality.
    If, instead of the by now sanitized expression, "suicide-bombers," reporters and newspapers were to write, more precisely and graphically, "Yesterday, still another 'KID WRAPPED IN DYNAMITE' was hurled at a cafe in Jerusalem, killing, etc., etc.", perhaps the revulsion of the civilized world would be sufficiently roused against this new form of human sacrifice to mobilize world opinion against this repulsive development in human warfare! Of course, the ultimate solution of the Middle East war will be achieved, if at all, at the negotiating table. But the civilized world cannot afford to wait the months, even years, that this might take.
    NOW is the time for leaders of all nations to come forward to mobilize the conscience of the world against this new form of human cruelty in warfare . . . KIDS WRAPPED IN DYNAMITE, adolescents WRAPPED IN DYNAMITE, girls WRAPPED IN DYNAMITE, women WRAPPED IN DYNAMITE, suicide and death by brainwashing and disregard for human life in the most vulnerable of youth . . . humans transformed into weapons, WRAPPED IN DYNAMITE!
    President Bush and Prime Minister Blair and President Fox and Secretary-General Kofi Annan, and leaders in religion, academia, philosophy and political science, in every civilized country, on all sides of this conflict, should meet at once to declare unequivocally that WRAPPING KIDS IN DYNAMITE as a new form of warfare is unacceptable to the human race. The unresolved and endless moral debate about when "the end justifies the means" has taken on new diabolical dimensions that cannot be ignored or swept under the rug.

"Political complexity", and "long range solutions" cannot be used as excuses for inaction in the face of this inhuman development that threatens the very fabric of human relations, as it re-defines, in a ghastly and amoral way, the value of the individual human being. There is no time to be lost! No one was ever meant to be "WRAPPED IN DYNAMITE"!

May 17, 2002
Costly tax exemption
The Times Herald Record

While the public still reels with ever-expanding evidence of sex-scandal and unconscionable cover-ups in the Catholic Church, another crisis in the state tax budget is announced as Albany reports a shortfall of $1.1 billion dollars. Unconnected? Consider this:

Settlements for victims of criminal child sexual abuse in the Catholic Church have reached into the millions.

Tax exemptions to the religious establishment continue, year after year, to provide huge bonanzas, at the expense of the general, taxpaying public. In New York state alone, according to the latest report of the New York state Office of Real Property Services (May 2001), more than $16 billion of religiously owned property is exempt!

Has anyone figured out how much revenue would be recouped simply by eliminating that exemption, while at the same time upholding the First Amendment and reinforcing the basic principle of separation of church and state?

Or should our tax-exemption codes be revisited, so they don't continue to give financial public support to disgraceful abuse and illegal behavior?

May 19, 2002
RE: "What's the Ostrich For? Politics" page one, Metro
The New York Times

I wonder if the budget protesters parading at City Hall to complain about "the loss of teachers and programs to budget cuts" (page one, Metro Section, May 18) are aware of the best kept secret in town, a secret kept by the political budgeteers in Albany as well as by the press: that is the loss of tax revenue by the city and by the state through tax exemptions to the religious establishment. According to the latest report of the New York State Office of Real Property Services, (May, 2001), over $7 billion of religiously owned property in New York City alone (and a staggering $16 billion in New York State) enjoy tax-free bonanzas, at the expense of ordinary (secular) property owners and taxpayers.

Will someone do the math? How much of New York's budget shortfall ($5 billion in New York City alone), and how many teachers and programs, could be saved by eliminating these discriminatory exemptions and upholding the spirit of the First Amendment's principle of separation of church and state? Or are policies rooted in religious bias too much of a sacred cow for either our politicians or our press to question?

May 21, 2002
Children are not meant to be wrapped in dynamite
The Times Herald Record

Semanticists never tire to remind us that language is a potent force in the formation of attitudes and social thought. Words and phrases, repeated often enough, take on a life and meaning of their own, for good or for bad, to express ideas or phenomena, or, by constant repetition to render them emotionally harmless.

Thus, words like racism, anti-Semitism, genocide, Holocaust, have entered our vocabulary in a sort of sanitized way. They roll off one's tongue, or leap from the printed page, with less and less emotional effect.

The real horror, the *evil* we cannot face, is lost as we are inured emotionally by repetition or by a self-protective resistance to deeper thinking.

So it is now with the term, "suicide-bomber," repeated endlessly until it all but loses its stark, unbearable reality.

If, instead of the by now sanitized expression, "suicide-bombers," reporters were to write, more precisely and graphically, "Yesterday, still another 'KID WRAPPED IN DYNAMITE' was hurled at a cafe in Jerusalem, killing himself and a number of innocent bystanders, etc., etc., perhaps the revulsion of the civilized world would be sufficiently roused against this new form of human sacrifice to mobilize world opinion against this repulsive, barbaric, and nihilistic development in human warfare.

Columnist Thomas L. Friedman, in the New York Times (April 17), said, aptly, "That is not martyrdom, that is ritual sacrifice" that "breaches all boundaries of civilized behavior."

Of course, the ultimate solution of the Middle East war will be achieved, if at all, at the negotiating table. But the civilized world cannot afford to wait the months, even years, that this might take, without addressing this new barbarism. Now is the time for leaders of all nations to come forward to mobilize the conscience of the world against this new form of human cruelty in warfare . . . WRAPPED IN DYNAMITE, adolescents WRAPPED IN DYNAMITE, girls WRAPPED IN DYNAMITE, women WRAPPED IN DYNAMITE, vulnerable youths brain-washed and transformed into human missiles, the ultimate in amoral weapons, WRAPPED IN DYNAMITE!

President Bush, Prime Minister Blair, U.N. Secretary-General Kofi Annan and leaders in religion, academia, philosophy and political science, in every civilized country, on all sides of this conflict, should meet at once to declare unequivocally that WRAPPING KIDS IN DYNAMITE as a new form of warfare is unacceptable to the human race. The unresolved and endless "moral" debate about when "the end justifies the means" has taken on new diabolical dimensions that cannot be ignored or swept under the rug.

"Political complexity" and "long-range solutions" cannot be used as excuses for inaction in the face of this monstrous, inhuman development that threatens the very fabric of human relations, as it redefines, in a ghastly and amoral way, the value of the individual human being. There is no time to be lost. No one was ever meant to be WRAPPED IN DYNAMITE . . . for any cause!

May 25, 2002
RE: "Pay the Victims, Protect the Church", op-ed May 25
The New York Times

In "Pay the Victims, Protect the Church", op-ed May 25, we are informed that the Catholic Church has already paid out at least $350 million in settlements for its abominable sex-abuse, according to its own United States Conference of Bishops, and as much as $1 billion according to estimates from plaintiffs' lawyers. A "staggering" figure in either case. What Mr. Olin fails to mention, however, is that part of this sum comes from the unwary taxpayer, Catholic, secular or otherwise, in the form of tax bonanzas enjoyed by the religious establishment. In New York State alone, according to the latest report of the New York State Office of Real Property Services (May, 2001) $16 billion of religiously owned property is exempt from taxes. Do the arithmetic for a nation-wide figure of such exemptions and figure out how much all of us are paying for the church's malfeasance! "Pay the Victims", of course . . . but the public has no obligation to "Protect the Church"!

May 29, 2002
RE: "New Arab Bombing in Israel Deepens A. Sense of Dismay", (front page, May 28), and "Six Wars and Counting", Thomas L. Friedman, (May 29)
The New York Times

One hopes that Thomas L. Friedman's naming of the 2002 attack on Israel the "Suicide War" will rouse the conscience of the world against this new form of human sacrifice and mobilize world opinion against this repulsive, barbaric and nihilistic development in human warfare. The overriding image of the present Palestinian offensive is that of brainwashed kids wrapped in dynamite and hurled as human missiles into civilian enclaves to "martyr" themselves and to kill as many innocent civilians as possible. The sheer obscenity of this "warfare" obscures whatever may be its purposes.

It is time that President Bush, Prime Minister Blair, and UN Secretary-General Kofi Annan, along with leaders in religion, political science, academia and philosophy . meet and declare unequivocally before the world that kids wrapped in dynamite as a new form of human warfare is unacceptable to the human race. The conscience of mankind demands no less.

June 7, 2002
Letter to the Editor
The New York Times

In your editorial of June 2 ("Staying Engaged in the Middle East"), you casually refer to the fact that "Suicide bombings have resumed", and then conclude that "Israel should act with restraint"! Thus you chastise the victims not the bombers, nor do you make any comment about the repeated horrors of this new form of amoral, inhuman addition to the "art" of human violence and conflict!

You further suggest that "curbing terror will be easier if there is renewed movement toward Palestinian statehood". It is the other way around: statehood would be advanced if Palestinian terrorism were curbed!

Most important, however, is the fact that an international peace conference is being delayed by the U.S., while the central obscenity of suicide-bombing continues unabated. The time is NOW for President Bush and our allies to declare unequivocally before the world that dynamite-wrapped kids as human missiles is unacceptable to the human race and must be denounced without delay. A common humanity requires it. The conscience of mankind demands nothing less.

June 8, 2002
RE: "In Israeli Bed, Failed Bomber Tells of 'Love of Martyrdom'" (front-page, june 8)
The New York Times

RE: "In Israeli Bed, Failed Bomber Tells of 'Love of Martyrdom'": This poignant front-page story screams out our failure to address the moral issue that is at the core of the current intifada: the successful indoctrination of Arab youth to embrace death and "martyrdom", the use of dynamite-wrapped human missiles as instruments of war in the pursuit of religio/political purposes, as ideological demagoguery continues to cynically and brutally destroy young lives. The failed suicide-bomber, Zaydan Zaydan, was more profound than he perhaps intended when he said that "we are the victims of our leaders"!

The time is overdue for President Bush and our allies in the "war against terrorism" to mobilize world opinion, to convene and to declare unequivocally before the world that dynamite-wrapping kids as human missiles is an obscenity unacceptable to the human race and must be denounced without delay. The conscience of mankind demands nothing less. A common humanity requires it!

June 13, 2002
RE: "Suicide Bombers"
The New York Times

With painful regularity, "suicide bombers" make the news almost daily. Today it is "In Suicide Bombings, the Taxi Man Got Away". Yesterday it was "Palestinian Suicide Bomber Kills a Girl and Wounds 8". Your editorial of June 2 informed us, if we needed the reminder, that "Suicide bombings have resumed". . . Let's be clear: the phrase "suicide bomber" is a euphemism for human beings wrapped in dynamite and used as human missiles for religio/political purposes, while the conscience of the world remains paralyzed, When will President Bush, Kofi Annan, and the world's leaders in religion, statecraft, philosophy and academia, convene to declare unequivocally that this new obscenity is unacceptable to the human race? A common humanity demands its condemnation. It is the least first step toward any reasonable solution and a requirement for the conscience of mankind.

June 18, 2002
RE: "Suicide Bombing on Bus in Jerusalem Kills at Least 14", news item, June 18:
The New York Times

When, at long last, will President Bush, Kofi Annan, and our allies, bring all their power and influence to bear, and convene a conference to rouse the world's conscience to the abomination of "suicide bombing"—a sanitized expression that means the wrapping of kids in dynamite to be hurled at civilian populations for religio-political objectives? Before we discuss Palestinian statehood in any form, as per "Powell's Trial Balloon" (June 17, William Safire) human missiles must be denounced before all the world for the obscenity such "warfare" represents. A common humanity demands it. It is the very least first step toward any reasonable solution and a requirement for the conscience of mankind.

June 19, 2002
RE: Israel's Pain and Arafat's Future (letters, June 19); *The New York Times*

Suicide Bomber Hits Jerusalem, (June 18); Powell's Trial Balloon, (Safire, June 17); and today, Explosion Goes Off in Jerusalem, (June 19): How long must the world wait before President Bush and Kofi Annan declare for all of us that wrapping kids in dynamite to be hurled at civilian populations is unacceptable to the human race? When, at long last, will the civilized world UNCONDITIONALLY denounce the obscenity of "human missiles" as an instrument of religio/political warfare? It is the very least first step toward a reasonable solution to the Mid-East problem and a requirement for the conscience of mankind. As Cicero would have put it: "QUO USQUE TANDEM ABUTERE NOSTRA PATIENTIA, O CATALINA?"

June 26, 2002
RE: A Plan Without a Map, Bush's speech, and today's *The New York Times*

It is a deplorable lapse that neither President Bush's speech ("Bush Says That Arafat Must Go . . .", June 25, nor your editorial, "A Plan Without a Map", June 25, nor any of today's Letters, addresses the central moral obscenity of the latest Palestinian intifada; the wrapping in dynamite of brainwashed youth and adolescents to be hurled as human missiles for religio-political objectives. President Bush referred to this ghastly monstrosity as "homicide bombings" (an inaccurate and patent redundancy!). The conscience of the world demands an unconditional denunciation of this latest debasement of human life. It is the very least first step toward a rational solution. A common humanity requires it if our moral paralysis is, at long last, to be lifted.

July 3, 2002
Letter to the Editor
The New York Times

In his long awaited speech on the Middle East President Bush opposed "homicide bombings . . . . and terrorist groups seeking the destruction of Israel." But he just missed the opportunity to take the real high moral ground: He did not effectively use the occasion to rouse the conscience of mankind to the obscenity of "suicide bombing", the wrapping in dynamite of brainwashed youth and adolescents to be hurled as human missiles for religio/political purposes. The world cries for an unambiguous statement that such barbaric monstrosities are unconditionally unacceptable to the human race. It is the very least first step toward a rational solution. A common humanity demands it if our moral paralysis is, at long last, to be lifted.

July 9, 2002
RE: Op-Eds of Kristof and Shikaki, July 9
The New York Times

It is significant that in two op-ed articles today ("Bigotry in Islam—And Here" and "How to Reform Palestinian Politics") neither Nicholas D. Kristof nor Khalil Shikaki addresses the central issue of the moral image presented to the world by Islam in today's crisis: the horrendous images of youths wrapped in dynamite and hurled as human missiles for religio/political purposes. This new form of "jihad", with its ultimate debasement of human life as it embraces a cult of death and "martyrdom", challenges the conscience of mankind and must be denounced as unacceptable to the human race. A common humanity requires it, if our moral paralysis is to be lifted. This monstrous "unintended consequence" of a pervasive and distorted religiosity cannot be swept under the rug or ignored, neither in "Palestinian Politics", nor in any consideration of "bigotry" as it takes this new and obscene form.

July 14, 2002
The Most Wanted Palestinian
The New York Times Magazine

What leaps out of Elizabeth Rubin's soul-wrenching article (June 30) is the frightening fact that fanatic religious dogma filled the vacuum and provided a raison d'être for aimless, desperate Palestinian youth, where secular, rational thought might have provided a more useful form of patriotism. A 5-year-old child says, "I want to meet Qeis in paradise." The cult of death wins over the love of life.

July 22, 2002
RE: "Dancing With Reform", Bob Herbert, July 22):
The New York Times

After decades of self-serving political palaver and dismal failure, the disastrous Rockefeller Drug Laws of 1973 must be abolished to make way for plausible approaches to the problem of drug-abuse. The lesson of the past, which Governor Pataki is determined to ignore, is that drug addiction and its consequences of personal deterioration, crime, and social disruption should be removed from the province of the criminal justice system, because incarceration without treatment has proved hopeless and ineffective, and placed in the health-care delivery system for treatment that is both hopeful and humane (drug-treatment programs, unlike prisons, have a proven record of accomplishment), and for the scientific research that is necessary to make long-range gains to bring this social scourge under control.

July 31, 2002
RE: prescription drugs
The New York Times

How much further can the richest country in the world embarrass itself by its callous healthcare posture? Alone among the industrialized nations, we consign 43 million of our uninsured citizens to health-care-limbo as we spurn universal health plans. Now, making matters worse, our valiant legislators quit and go home without passing legislation to provide prescription drugs even for our elderly poor, because "they blew all the money on tax cuts for the rich" (editorial July 23). Elementary fairness gets lost, without a spokesman, in a trillion dollar government that has lost its moral bearings. For shame!

July 29, 2002
RE: "George Washington: Mr. Excitement?",
The Arts, July 29, 2002
The New York Times

That a renewed interest in the magnificent achievements of our founding fathers is certainly in order, as the popularity of David McCullough's "JOHN ADAMS" and Joseph J. Ellis's "FOUNDING BROTHERS" attest, the fudging over of their singular, most egregious failure, *their inability to face the institution of slavery*, would not do justice to our country's revolutionary origin. Will *"pepping* up his image" include the fact that Washington, like Thomas Jefferson and at least one-third of Congress, owned slaves? Washington and Jefferson each owned about 200 slaves (in "JOHN ADAMS")! Will the new Mount Vernon include replicas of the slave-quarters, too, to remind us of the "tragic and perhaps intractable problem that even the revolutionary generation, with all its extraordinary talent, could neither solve nor face" (in "FOUNDING BROTHERS")?

July 29, 2002
RE: "Searching for a Drug Compromise", editorial July 29:
The New York Times

As Senators on both sides of the aisle throw numbers at each other, where is the courageous Senator who will say: *"Gentlemen, it's not the math that counts, it's the morality! Why does the richest country in the world not only fail to cover the basic health needs of 43 million uninsured, but cannot even provide affordable drugs for the elderly poor? This time, it's not the economy, stupid, it's the morality!"*

August 2, 2002
RE: "Drug Coverage Failure", editorial, Aug 1, 2002
The New York Times

When Congress recessed yesterday they abandoned our senior citizens, our elderly poor, and the rest of the American people, to the tender mercies of the rapacious, gouging pharmaceutical industry. Their huge, well-paid lobby was more effective than the social conscience of our legislators. But all need not be lost. We, the people, ought to declare the month of August *"SAVE OUR HEALTH CARE MONTH"*, and deluge our Senators and Congress people with letters, calls, telegrams, and personal visits, to insure that, when they return in September, they pass the necessary bills to rescue us from drug-debt with a program that is government subsidized. This is a first step toward a broader program of *UNIVERSAL HEALTH INSURANCE* that will bring us in line with all the other industrial countries in the world that value their citizens' health above private corporate profit.

August 17, 2002
RE: "Jack Grubman's Last Deal", editorial Aug. 17
The New York Times

What you fail to emphasize in this latest case of unconscionable greed in the marketplace is the obscene moral rot now surfacing in Wall Street. Along with the "news" of other huge raids on corporation assets at the expense of unwary shareholders (like the report of the Conseco fiasco (Business Day, August 10), in which the failing CEO is rewarded by a $1.5 million a year annuity for life while investors lose everything,) the Grubman deal that guarantees millions for one who acts as both "objective analyst" and super-salesman, should alert the victimized investor. The only national political leader to warn us of this rapacious trend was the indomitable RALPH NADER, who spoke up against this deplorable descent of corporation "ethics" when no one else had the courage. Ralph Nader, where are you now when we need you?

August 21, 2002
RE: "White House Denies Texas Session Is About Iraq", aug. 21
The New York Times

>From Crawford, Texas, to wherever Americans gather, the question is: Will we or won't we attack Iraq? The question is of world-shattering importance. What is extraordinary, however, is not that the question haunts us, but that it is, apparently, not being examined where it should be . . . *at the United Nations*. Whether Saddam Hussein is concealing nuclear, biological and chemical weapons of mass destruction is of crucial importance to all the civilized world. It follows that the United States ought press immediately for consideration of this threat where it belongs—before the world body. Inspection and control *under UN auspices* ought be undertaken without delay. If Iraq refuses, or places obstacles in the path of real appraisal of any presumed threat, or possesses illegal weapons, the United Nations ought to act to remove that threat. The United States, acting not as the unilateral "policeman of the world", but as part of the informed conscience of the world, will then be seen as a world savior, not as a hegemonic, arrogant, self-starting, super-cop.

August 28, 2002
RE: "Summons to War", editorial Aug. 28
The New York Times

The core proposition in your cogent editorial ("Summons to War", Aug. 28) is unassailable: The problem of Iraq pursuing nuclear, biological and chemical weapons of mass destruction is a critical problem for the entire world. As such it should be addressed by the world body of nations, the United Nations. The policy of the United States should be one of acting through the UN for international inspection. If military action is necessary because of the belligerence and non-cooperation of Saddam Hussein, that action should be under the auspices of the UN. Thus, the United States would be seen as acting in unison with the informed conscience of the world, rather than as self-appointed, unilateral, hegemonic world-cop. The consequences of nuclear and/or chemical warfare are too ghastly for all civilization to be either ignored or treated as a purely American problem.

August 29, 2002
RE: letters: "A Call for War: Will the Country Respond?, aug. 29
The New York Times

RE: "A Call for War: Will the Country Respond?" (August 29): Again, ten letters and not a single mention of the United Nations! Have your readers, as well as the Bush Administration, given up completely on the U.N. as an instrument for peace? The horrendous possibility that Saddam Hussein may be pursuing the development of nuclear, biological, and/or chemical weapons of mass destruction is a critical problem for the entire civilized world, and should be addressed without delay by the world body. It is not an exclusively American problem. We should be building a world response, through the U.N., not a unilateral approach based on American hegemony. In a crisis that threatens all civilized humanity, the world desperately needs international consensus and cooperation, not a U.S. super-cop.

August 30, 2002
RE: "France and Britain Press for Working with U.N." (front page, Aug. 30):
The New York Times

As Vice President Cheney plugs for a unilateral strike against Iraq, it is disheartening that there is no groundswell of public opinion urging us not to undercut the basic principles of the United Nations and the "vision of collective security that is based on cooperation among states, respect for the law and the authority of the Security Council." (French President Jacques Chirac).

Saddam Hussein's illegal pursuit of nuclear, biological, and/or chemical weapons, is a problem for all the world, the consequences of which are too ghastly for all civilization to be either ignored or treated as a purely American problem. Appropriate action should be taken through the U.N., representing the informed conscience of the world, rather than through a self-appointed, unilateral, hegemonic world-cop.

October 1, 2002
Iraq, the U.N. and Us
The New York Times

Thomas L. Friedman's Sept. 29 column, "You Gotta Have Friends," is incontrovertible, as is his admonition that any United States action against Iraq must have the backing of the United Nations and important allies. But the fact is that we are a member of the United Nations. We not only need its backing, we also need to act as a loyal and responsible member, through its legal and established apparatus. Above all, we need to support, not undermine, the United Nations Charter.

As Bruce Ackerman of Yale writes (Op-Ed, Sept. 21), the Bush plan is nothing less than the repudiation of the United Nations Charter, which makes collective, multinational security measures the norm.

Our policy should be one of a responsible internationalism rather than a unilateral machismo that would destroy the United Nations and with it the hope of an international ethic of the rule of law for all countries.

October 17, 2002
Will strikes a low blow against the United Nations
The Times Herald Record

"So who put the U.N. in charge of the world?" Asking this (rhetorical?) question, the conservative columnist George F. Will (column Sept. 21) astonishes even his most avid readers with the depth of his venom and vilification.

He is much too erudite not to know the answer to his question, but raises it with a sneer and a hatred that must surely represent a nadir in his writing.

The United Nations, of course, for those who need a refresher course in its importance for world civilization, was "put in charge," in April 1945, by a world still fresh in its abhorrence of the carnage of World War II, determined not to repeat the horrors of war and aggression and concentration camps and the monstrous civilian destruction and death caused by modern warfare.

Fifty-one nations, including the United States, thought this was a better way to address conflicts among nations. The Charter of the United Nations, aspiring to deliberative, peaceful methods of conflict-resolution, was considered a more civilized way to conduct international affairs than mindless death and destruction.

That most of us still think so is attested to by polls both here and abroad. Although aware of the dangers of Saddam Hussein's violations of U.N. resolutions, recent polls indicated that 60 percent of Europeans and 65 percent of Americans "would favor an American-led invasion of Iraq only if the United States first receives the support of allies and the United Nations.

If Mr. Will still needs to be reminded of the legal precedence of the U.N., not to mention its deep moral weight, he need only check with Professor Bruce Ackerman of Yale's law school, who stated unequivocally on the Times' op-ed page on the same day as Mr. Will's piece, that the Bush position "is nothing less than the repudiation of the United Nations Charter's effort to restrict unilateral uses of force to extreme cases, and to make collective, multi-national security measures the norm."

Mr. Will's outrageous invective comes at a critical moment in the struggle between the go-it-alone hawks in the Bush camp who would unleash a unilateral machismo, and those who would build a responsible world of nations governed by a civilized ethic and the rule-of-law, . . . what might be called a *responsible internationalism.*

Finally, it is beyond belief to read Mr. Will refer to the U.N. as "that tar baby"! For shame, George Will, how low can you get?

November 24, 2002
Unprecedented Times
Mexico City—The News

The times we live in are unprecedented in all of past history: the lull before the storm, pregnant with the most dire of possibilities, a pause while all the world holds its breath in horror on the brink of unimaginable devastations, war such as we have never seen before (chemical, biological, nuclear), and unpredictable acts of terrorism on civilian populations.

Or is there still time for a valiant, universal effort to prevent disaster and to establish a world order in which we all can survive in a civilized, world-wide peace?

As of the moment, President Bush and his administration proceed as though the war is "pending", already decided upon by the United States alone if necessary, like a scheduled prizefight just waiting for the opening bell! This despite the fact that recent surveys, as reported in the New York Times, indicate that "60 percent of Europeans and 65 percent of Americans "would favor an American-led invasion of Iraq only if the United States first receives the support of Allies and the United Nations."

President Bush's hawkish advisors notwithstanding, the fact is that under the U.S. Constitution war can be declared only by Congress. That it has not done, despite its recent action in support of the President's goals. The question that still remains is how do we defend ourselves best against the specific threat posed by Saddam Hussein, and the ever-present threat of random terrorism?

Both terrible threats are world-wide.

Whether Iraq possesses weapons of mass destruction, or al-Qaida is plotting further acts of terrorism, the threats confront all law-abiding countries, not only the United States, and should be addressed internationally. That is precisely what the United Nations was created to do. President Bush's recent forceful appeal for U.N. action (responding to overwhelming domestic and international pressure) was the correct first step. If legal inspection by the U.N. reveals weapons of mass destruction or other violations of U.N. resolutions in Iraq, action, military and otherwise, should be taken by the U.N. International action, undertaken by the world body of nations, with all the support that the United States can provide, with the consensus of the civilized world, is the only logical, appropriate, and effective way to counteract threats to the peace of the world.

The other course, unilateral action by the United States, in opposition to the Security Council, would satisfy the machismo posture of the hawks who surround

President Bush, but would alienate U.S. allies around the world, confirm U.S. enemies' view of the United States as aggressive world-cops seeking world hegemony, undermine the Charter of the United Nations, and destroy the U.N. itself as an effective instrument for peace.

If every nation takes it upon itself to launch "pre-emptive strikes" and to force "regime changes" by war and invasion (if the United States can do it, why cannot other nations do the same?) . . . we return to anarchy in world affairs, a condition in which no nation is ultimately safe.

In the long run, the only hope for a world governed by a civilized ethic and the rule of law, is the strengthening of the United Nations, and the pursuit of a truly responsible internationalism. THAT IS OUR BEST DEFENSE.

December 1, 2002
Bush's Mandate Questioned
Mexico City—The News

Amid the jubilant hoop-la of the Republicans, and the self-congratulatory assertions of talking heads on the boob tube to the effect that President Bush had been given a resounding "mandate," the recent elections showed once again that money, huge infusions of expensive brain-washing via TV bytes and shallow slogans, can turn an election, without reflecting a true national scenario.

What sort of national "mandate" can be expressed in an election in which less than 40 percent of eligible voters bother to show up? According to the Committee for the Study of the American Electorate (report of Nov. 8, 2002), only 39.3 percent of eligible voters turned up to vote. In total, 78.7 million people voted. And 121 million Americans did not cast their ballots!

Hardly anyone discussed in depth the urgent issues of President Bush's tax largesse for the rich, health care for the 40 million uninsured, prescription drugs for the elderly on Medicare, the crisis in education, the president's "faith-based" programs to turn aid to the under-privileged into the hands of an unelected clergy . . . and above all, the international crisis of Saddam Hussein and the obvious rush to a cataclysmic war.

The Republicans did not want to take these issues to the people because they felt that the surge of popular anger after 9/11 was in their favor; they could label "unpatriotic" anyone who dared to disagree with them.

And the Democrats, lacking in leadership and in guts, failed to engage them because their political experts, counting votes instead of addressing issues, foresaw a close election and decided to offend no one.

The result was a key election in which more than half (60 percent) of the eligible voters chose not to vote. And on the basis of a narrow victory, in which his party won only slightly more than half of a less than 40 percent voting turn-out, a President who himself was "elected" despite the fact he lost in the popular vote, can now claim a "mandate" for policies that are far from universally accepted. A "victory" based on winning slightly over 20 percent of the electorate should give us food for thought.

The recently-passed McCain-Feingold bill, designed to take soft-money out of U.S. elections did not work in this election. Perhaps next time. But meanwhile, it is imperative that steps be taken to rescue the electoral process (the central feature of U.S. democratic society) from the grip of big money and private interests.

An election dynamic is needed that is characterized by integrity of purpose, dedication, inspiration, and a leadership that stirs people, energizes their commitment to the public welfare, and dispels the apathy of the large majority that has stayed away in disgust. Only when such a leadership emerges will U.S. democracy take on a new lease, and the real American potential reveal what an informed and involved citizenry can accomplish.

December 15, 2002
U.N. Still Best Option
Mexico City—The News

Mr. Fred Hiatt ("Are Saddam's Lawyers Considering Moral Law", The News, Dec. 10), joins the widespread discussion of the Iraq problem with thoughtful considerations of the overriding "moral" dimensions. After a harrowing description of the monstrous persecutions practiced by Saddam Hussein, and his gangster methods of maintaining control, Mr. Hiatt poses the question of who has the "moral high ground"—those who would stick to the rule of law under the United Nations or those who would sanction a United States-led war of invasion even without the Security Council's approval.

Although he concedes "no one wants a world in which powerful countries feel free to go about smashing into weak ones," Mr. Hiatt ends up with the question unresolved: perhaps, he infers, Saddam's blood-curdling crimes of murder and torture justify the abandonment of the niceties of international law, and just perhaps, the United States might be more "moral" (than the peace groups) even if it flouted the United Nations and took it upon itself and its allies to do the job with unilateral invasion and war.

The best answer to this moral dilemma was given just a few days later by the estimable Jimmy Carter, when he said, in his Nobel Prize acceptance speech: "For powerful countries to adopt a principle of preventive war may well set an example that can have catastrophic consequences." An obvious warning to the Bush Administration and its headlong, impatient rush to war, even before Saddam's 12,000 page document has been analyzed, even before the U.N. inspectors have delivered their findings. As Ohio Democratic Rep. Dennis Kucinich put it, President Bush "prepares to engage in war no matter what the U.N. findings."

"Taking out" Saddam by a righteous but relentless Rambo, or a suave James Bond, or a vengeful Western posse under John Wayne, may be oh-so-soul-satisfying. The good guys triumph over evil. George W. Bush rides high in a Texan saddle. But it took former U.S. President Jimmy Carter to cast the current crisis in terms of our complex modern realities and, "as a citizen of a troubled world," to remind us that "the United Nations is the best avenue for the maintenance of peace."

December 29, 2002
Bile Over Brain
Mexico City—The News

Mr. Dewey Bowman's letter ("In Praise of Chomsky", Dec. 15) was a most egregious example of the triumph of bile over brain.

Mr. Bowman was "thrilled" with Noam Chomsky's views of U.S. history, as expressed in a previous column by Prof. Russell Jacoby ("United States Gets The Dissent It Deserves," The News, Dec. 8), in which Prof. Jacoby states that "For Chomsky, the United States is . . . the chief terrorist state"; that, in fact, "the United States regularly provokes bloodshed to further its ends"! That sweeping view of American history not only "thrilled" Mr. Bowman, he even enlarged on the accusation with hyperbole gone amuck, asserting that "even before its founding", the United States was an "outlaw terrorist state", and that he, as a "patriotic citizen" finds "this historic fact as a reason for deep personal shame."

Not satisfied with a vilification that includes tarring the United States for over 200 years of an unmitigated evil history, Bowman goes back into the womb, finding the United States guilty even pre-natally, a new wrinkle in criminal justice evaluation that would charge the victim one wishes to demonize for crimes committed even before he was born!

In a more reasoned comment, Prof. Jacoby had stated: "But, alas, Chomsky often sounds like U.S. President George W. Bush in reverse. For Bush, the United States can do no wrong. For Chomsky, it can do no right. Chomsky is a charter member of the 'told-you-so' school of leftism. The United States had the September attacks coming." (!).

Mr. Bowman not only enthusiastically endorses this view of the United States "deserving" 9/11, but takes it a step further to include Pearl Harbor also, where, again, it was the victim he accuses of not being "peace-loving" . . . not a word about the fascist attackers (presumably they were "peace-loving" and justified!) then, nor a single word of condemnation now of the religio/fascist murderers who attacked New York and Washington on Sept. 11. It is an example of uncontrollable animus and hatred-producing gibberish and splutter, not reason.

Dissent is a necessary and desirable component in democratic political life. It is precisely this aspect of U.S. society, from its very inception engraving these rights of speech in the Constitution and its seminal Bill of Rights, that continues to attract millions of oppressed to U.S. shores even to this day, despite the calumnies of a Bowman, whose example is dangerous only in that it gives legitimate dissent, and dissenters, a bad name!

January 17, 2003
Letter to the Editor
New Year's Resolution

As we enter 2003, a sword of Damocles, in the form of a threatening war with unpredictable consequences, hangs over us all. The voices of reason face the forces of unreason and prejudice. The outcome of this confrontation, the unleashing of violence in forms hitherto unimagined or the victory of non-violent deliberative measures designed to maintain peace, presents us with a challenge that is as immense as it is without precedence.

What course of action is the "right" course? What road ought "reasonable man" to take? What should be our number one New Year's resolution?

Should the United Nations, as a last resort, take military action to disarm Saddam Hussein in order to relieve the world of what is perceived as the threat he presents in the form of weapons of mass destruction?

Should the United States unilaterally by-pass the United Nations and the Security Council and invade Iraq with whatever other nations it can rally to join in, to destroy Saddam's weaponry and to effect a "regime change" we can trust?

As the debate rages, polls indicate that most Europeans, and a majority of Americans, would not support an invasion by the United States unless it had the support of the United Nations. Many view the United States as a bullying superpower, prepared to impose its values on the world by its overwhelming military superiority. In the U.S., a small but strident group, led by Noam Chomsky, go so far as to portray the United States as "the chief terrorist nation"(!) In this view, even Sept. 11 was justified, with the US getting "what was coming to it"(!)

If reason and peace are to prevail, these shrill voices of hate, prejudice and extremism must be overcome by the rational thinking of the majority of people around the world, who see the only hope of peace in deliberative consultation among the community of nations, as well as vigorous support of the United Nations, the Security Council and the United Nations' Charter. Neither the warped America-haters, those only too willing to place the entire onus on the US (as chief terrorist nation) nor the apologists for the brutal regime of Saddam Hussein, nor those who find "justification" for the religio/fascist terrorism of Al-Qaeda, contribute to the kind of political discourse required if we are to avoid a cataclysmic eruption of war and violence.

Former U.S. President Jimmy Carter struck the right note in his Nobel Prize acceptance speech, when he said, "The United Nations is the best avenue for the maintenance of peace". This is the most imperative of New Year's resolutions for all who would preserve the rule of law and an international ethic that we can all live by.

HAPPY NEW YEAR! PEACE!

G NOTICE OF A NEW U.S., POISED TO HIT FIRST AND ALONE," (News article, JAN. 27) confirmed our worst fear that President Bush is prepared to destroy the United Nations in order to establish the hegemony of the United States in what he grandiosely perceives as the American Century.

Playing on the real danger of religio/fascist aggression and the real threat of terrorism to the United States, President Bush, never a staunch believer in the United Nations, prepares to scuttle its power and influence, and to reduce it to irrelevance and impotence . . . in effect to destroy it. Secretary of State Colin Powell made that crystal clear in his speech today threatening "preemptive war" against Iraq, alone if necessary.

The consequences of the destruction of the U.N., a world returned to the anarchy of international relationships determined solely by military might, is too frightful to contemplate. An unrestrained arms race, including weapons of mass destruction, biological, chemical and nuclear, that would be unleashed upon the demise of the U.N., is not what the world needs now. Whatever its faults, only the U.N. and its Charter, and its promise of international norms and ethics for a civilized world, stands between us and international chaos. The civilized path to deal with the Saddam Husseins, and the Al Qaedas of the world, is to retain the moral unity of the United Nations, rather than succumb to the bigotry, prejudice and moral blindness that characterize the cycle of terrorism and retaliation.

January 31, 2003
Reader's Forum
Atencion San Miguel

Last Saturday's anti-war vigil would have been more effective if the petition we signed was less one-sided and directed its message of peace not only to the Bush Administration's headlong drive to war, but to the destabilizing forces of violence and terror around the world.

The threat to world peace resides not only in the reckless saber-rattling of hawks in the United States who would by-pass the United Nations, undermine its Charter, defy the Security Council and effectively destroy the community of nations. The threat to world peace is also in the rise of terrorism, both non-governmental and governmental, insofar as it is aided and abetted by nations that encourage, aid and provide safe haven for terrorist groups. We should also be petitioning, and rousing the nations of the world, against the dangers of Al Qaeda (with cells said to be re-grouping in more than 60 nations), to Hamas and Hezbolla and the Islamic Jihad, and to the nations that give them both open and covert support.

The quest for peace and justice will not be served by assigning all evil to the United States. Peace will be served only by recognizing its enemies around the world, not by unilateral recklessness as proposed by President Bush, nor by the venting of hatred against the US as it attempts to sort out the proper response to the unprovoked slaughter of September 11. The terrorists, and the threat of a Saddam Hussein armed with weapons of mass destruction, can be effectively dealt with only through the United Nations, and a worldwide consensus for peaceful co-existence.

February 23, 2003
Letter to the Editor
The Miami Herald

It is disgraceful to see Cal Thomas (column, Feb. 21) mercilessly rip into the United Nations as "pathetic," and as "founded on the dubious premise that flawed humanity can be perfected by flawed human beings," just at the moment when our only international body of nations dedicated to mutual cooperation and peaceful co-existence needs all the support it can get.

Mr. Thomas' wild rhetoric is as irrational as it is reckless. Of course, human beings are "flawed." That does not mean that a "flawed humanity" cannot aspire to peaceful problem-solving, if not to a sought-after "perfection."

The central issue is, as your editorial states, that the United States is "determined to act unilaterally in an era of international cooperation." Such American defiance of the five million people around the world who demonstrated on Feb. 15 against the war, and of the nations in the U.N. who clamor for consensus in the face of threats to world peace, would effectively destroy the United Nations and with it the only hope of an international ethic of the rule of law for future generations.

We must act through the United Nations. We must support the Security Council. We must bolster the moral authority of the United Nations Charter. We must re-invigorate, re-energize, strengthen the community of nations, and turn around the image of a self-appointed American super-cop imposing its will in a drive to singular hegemony.

We must prevent the destruction of the United Nations, as well as defeat the threats of Saddam Hussein, Al Qaeda terrorism, and the North Korean nuclear bomb build-up. These goals are mutually intertwined. Their long-range solution, in fact, may very well depend on the recognition that they can all be solved only through a strong international consensus, through a strong international unity, through a strong UNITED NATIONS.

February 24, 2003
Stories of September 11
Google.com

The "lesson" that was explosively forced upon us on September 11 was one that was philosophically and theoretically known but not truly understood: that we are indeed "One World", inescapably bound to one another, where inter-dependence has become more than just a theoretical concept. The condition of peoples on one side of the globe has profound influence on the other side. The prejudices, superstitions, and belief systems of distant peoples reverberate world-wide. The consequences of hatreds reach beyond state and regional borders. Three thousand Americans died because of the twisted misconceptions of a distant, uninformed, and manipulated "enemy".

Through a ghastly, cruel and tragic event, we learn that millions of people on the "other" side, see us as an "evil enemy", to be destroyed even at the expense of their own "martyrdom" and death. They have been taught to hate us with an intensity we could not understand . . . . by deliberate increments, from a brainwashed childhood to the all-encompassing religio-fascism that spawned today's monstrous terrorism. The "explosion" of hatred and suicide and destruction was almost beyond our comprehension.

The "lesson"? Beyond the immediate "remedies" to prevent a continuance of terror, only a new vision of mankind liberated from the shackles of inherited dogmas of hate, will provide the answers in the long run. Twenty-first century technology, which has made the world a "global village", needs to be matched by a new twenty-first century ethic that infuses us all, to the marrow of our beings, with the sense that we are all responsible for each other, wherever we live. National, regional, religious boundaries have become anachronistic and must be overcome as we recognize and respect our common humanity. That is not only the challenge of the new century, but the ultimate challenge of man on earth!

March 9, 2003
RE: Editorial of March 9, 2003:
The New York Times

The most compelling argument against a unilateral, pre-emptive strike by the United States against Iraq, is that such action would spell the beginning of the end of the United Nations.

An invasion by the United States in defiance of the Security Council would be a violation of the Charter, and would undermine, if not eventually destroy the UN as an instrument of world peace.

Just as the failure of the League of Nations to establish "collective security" against Hitler in 1939 led to its destruction and to World War II, so the present failure to give full and unconditional support to the Security Council will lead to the irrelevance, if not the end of the United Nations, and with it our only hope for a civilized international ethic and the rule of law among nations.

President Bush would gain a place in world history if he used this moment, this "United Nations leadership moment" (as in your editorial of Feb. 23) to return to and re-affirm basic U.N. principles. Declare a victory, President Bush (your threat of force accomplished its goal without the use of force) and give full support to the United Nations as the world's best hope to preserve the peace!

March 18, 2003
Letters to the Editor
The Miami Herald

In its penetrating editorial last Sunday, the New York Times resonated with the increasing anti-war sentiments expressed around the world this week:

"More discussion," it wrote, "is the only road that will get the world to the right outcome-concerted effort by a wide coalition of nations to force Saddam Hussein to give up his weapons of mass destruction. We need another debate, another struggle to make this the United Nations leadership moment."

The key, ringing phrase is "the United Nations leadership moment."

This is what Mexican President Vicente Fox meant when he said, "We want the only course to be through the United Nations and only through the Security Council, only multilaterally," as reported in The Herald of Feb. 20.

This is what your editorial of Feb. 21 reiterated when it stressed that "the central issue is that the United States is determined to act unilaterally in an era of international cooperation."

This is what more than 5 million protesters in cities around the world passionately declared on February 15.

This is surely "the United Nations leadership moment." It can be its finest hour, when leadership, courage and determination can forge a consensus of peace-seeking nations that will not only preserve peace today, but provide future generations with an international ethic they can live by and a rule of law for all peoples . . .

We must act through the United Nations. We must support the Security Council. We must re-invigorate, re-energize, and strengthen the universal message of the Charter.

The U.S., the most powerful nation on earth, must be a leader in this endeavor and must turn around the image of a self-appointed American super-cop imposing its will in what is perceived as a drive to singular hegemony.

This is indeed "the United Nations leadership moment!" How it is met may determine the character and the future of the new century!

March 29, 2003
Letter to the Editor
The New York Times

The attempt by PrimeMinister Tony Blair of Britain to heal the rift in the United Nations caused by Washington's unpopular, pre-emptive and unilateralist policy is of the highest importance if the world organization is to regain its stature and relevance (news article, March 27).

    The United Nations must not become a casualty of war. That is Mr. Blair's message. Let not victory be a Pyrrhic one, with the war won but the United Nations effectively destroyed.

March 30, 2003
RE: "With God On His Side", March 30:
The New York Times

With his usual penetrating erudition, Garry Wills explains why those who prepare and lead the nation into war find it expedient to ignore James Madison's passion to separate the state from religious influence. Madison notwithstanding, Wills reminds us, "There is ample precedent for . . . official religiosity in time of war".

It does seems pointless, in the "odd euphoria of war", as Mr. Wills puts it, to examine the rationality of the same God being fervently on both sides as each fights for good against evil "in the name of God"! This would be possible only if "God" suffered an advanced form of "cognitive dissonance", or, more likely, if the leaders on both sides cynically recognized the greater pull of faith over reason as a galvanizing tool.

The best way of putting it was that of Blaise Pascal, who wrote, "MEN NEVER DO EVIL SO COMPLETELY AND SO CHEERFULLY AS WHEN THEY DO IT FROM RELIGIOUS CONVICTION.". (Pensees, 1670)

May 3, 2003
RE: Albany Deal Lets City Raise Taxes To Limit Layoffs" (front page, May 3, 2003)
The New York Times

Faced with "a budget gap brought on by the city's worst fiscal crisis since the 1970's, which threatened to reverse New York's re-emergence as a livable metropolis", Mayor Bloomburg and Albany legislative leaders have cut a deal. Only 3,000 layoffs (it could have been 10,000!), raises in the sales tax (falling most heavily on lower income groups), and sundry cuts in services in education, health, child care. But even in this crisis, nothing is said about the give-away to religious organizations inherent in their tax-exemptions. According to the report of the New York State Office of Real Property Services (May, 2001) over $7 billion of religiously owned property in New York City alone (and a staggering $16 billion in New York State enjoy tax-free bonanzas, at the expense of ordinary (secular) property owners and taxpayers.

Will someone, please, do the math! How much of New York's shortfall and how many cuts and layoffs could be saved by eliminating these discriminatory exemptions and upholding the spirit of the First Amendment principle of separation of Church and State?

Or are policies rooted in religious preference too much of a sacred cow for our politicians (or our press) to question?

Yours truly

May 21, 2003
RE: "When Cities Go Broke the Options Are Few", April
The New York Times

In "When Cities Go Broke the Options Are Few" (May 20), Sam Roberts states that the only options are "either taxes or reductions in services". He further states that "Mayor Bloomberg has been lobbying . . . for wringing out about $600 million in productivity concessions from organized labor".

Completely, and astonishingly, overlooked is the area of tax-exemptions. The New York State Office of Real Property Services, reporting in May, 2001, informs us that $7 billion of religiously-owned property in New York City alone (a staggering $16 billion in New York State) receive almost complete tax exemptions, even including huge exemptions for the residences of the clergy. Might the elimination of these unfair, discriminatory tax bonanzas, be reconsidered in the light of our $3.8 billion short-fall in New York City (and 11.5 billion in the State)? The revenue thus recouped would certainly provide the $600 million Mayor Bloomberg seeks to "wring out from organized labor", if not millions more. Do not special tax concessions for the religious, at the expense of the secular taxpayer, violate the spirit, of not the letter of the First Amendment and the principle of separation of Church and State? Or should private religiosity take precedence over the public good?

May 25, 2003
A Letter to the New York Times
The New York Times

RE: "Six Firehouses Receive Order to Close by Sunday Morning, as Lawsuit to Save Them Proceeds" (news article, May 22); "Mayor Michael R. Bloomberg has said that the city needs to close the firehouses to balance its budget".

Some questions:

1. How much would it cost to keep these firehouses open?

2. How much revenue could New York recoup if it eliminated the tax-exemptions now granted religious organizations in New York City (According to the Report of the New York State Office of Real Property Services for May, 2001, over $7 billion of religiously owned property in New York City alone received almost full or partial tax exemptions. (In New York State the figure was a staggering $16 billion!).

3. Are special tax bonanzas for private religiosity, and for "clergy residences" more important than the public safety, if we had to choose? There is more than one way to "balance the budget"!

June 4, 2003
State should end all religious tax exemptions
The Times Herald Record

It's about time! I could say better late than never, but it is never too late to correct palpable injustice. So, congratulations on your front page treatment of Sen. John Bonacie's efforts to challenge the unfair, prejudicial, probably illegal, tax laws that give special bonuses to a variety of "causes" and especially to religious organizations.

While the cost of government has been skyrocketing, and the burden of taxation on all of us gets higher every year, any group that declares a religious orientation may receive a tax entitlement that increases the burden on the nonreligious, and is frequently abused, manipulated, and corrupted.

The major religious establishments get a free ride, tax-wise, that adds an unconscionable burden to the already over-burdened taxpayer. This is not only unfair on the face of it, but in the opinion of many violates the principle of the separation of church and state and the spirit, if not the letter, of the Establishment Clause of the First Amendment: "Congress shall make no law respecting an establishment of religion."

Tax law, it seems to me, is still "law."

This has been going on for years. I quote: "I would also call your attention to the importance of correcting an evil that, if permitted to continue, will probably lead to great trouble in our land . . . it is the accumulation of vast amounts of untaxed church property . . ."

The speaker was not a wild-eyed atheist reformer, but the president of the United States, Ulysses S. Grant, in his annual message to Congress. The year was 1875. The president was disturbed then because, in his words, "In 1850 the church properties in the United States which paid no taxes, municipal or state, amounted to about $83 million. In 1860, the amount had doubled; in 1875 it is about $1 billion. By 1900, without check, it is safe to say this property will reach a sum exceeding $3 billion . . . So vast a sum, receiving all the protection and benefits of government without bearing its proportion of the burdens and expenses of the same, will not be looked upon acquiescently by those who have to pay the taxes. . . . I would suggest the taxation of all property equally, whether church or corporation."

That was 1875. The president was fearful that religious tax-exemption would grow to the "vast sum of $3 billion by 1900" for the entire nation. History has shown that his fears were vastly understated: According to the report of the New York State Office of Real Property Services of May, 2001, there is more than $7 billion of religiously owned property in New York City alone and a staggering $16 billion in New York state, receiving almost complete tax exemption, and including even the residences of the clergy.

That is one city and one state. What might statistical research into the nation as a whole reveal in terms of this huge free-tax bonanza and its effect on our tax system?

You are on target when you headline your editorial, "N.Y.: Put the brakes on the free rides." (April 27). But, alas, neither you, nor Sen. Bonacie take on the special tax-frees of the religious establishment. In fact, Sen. Bonacie states specifically that "as a practical matter, 99 percent (of church properties) are not going to be touched" by his proposals.

Why not? The present budget in New York City alone was "brought on by the city's worst fiscal crisis since the 1970s," (New York Times, May 3) and homeowners and taxpayers throughout the state face crises in education, health, child welfare, hospitals, clinics, etc.

In the Record of May 5, columnist Douglas Cunningham calls the state budget "broken and bereft of new ideas." How about the "new idea" in this climate of rectifying the injustice of the free rides for the religious establishments? Do the math, someone, and figure out how many cuts in essential social services can be saved by eliminating the millions in tax revenue lost by these unfair exemptions.

If ever there was a time to confront and correct the long-standing inequity of tax-free rides for the religious among us, at the expense of the secular taxpayer now is that time.

The welfare of the community as a whole should take precedence over private religiosity. And true religious freedom would be served more equitably if believers carried their own weight and if religionists and nonreligionists shared equally in bearing public burdens.

Or is this too much of a sacred cow for politicians, and the press to challenge?

July 20, 2003
Letter to the Editor
The New York Times

I was dismayed that at this crucial moment in international policy-making, Prime Minister Tony Blair and President George W. Bush gave short shrift to the United Nations. President Bush did not mention the UN at all, while Prime Minister Blair gave it only a fleeting nod.

To "defeat the anti-Americanism that sometimes passes for political discourse", Blair asserts, "any alliance must start with America and Europe". A better starting point, I suggest, is the United Nations. After a unilateral pre-emptive strike that shattered the prestige and authority of the world body and produced a world-wide hostility to what was perceived as an arrogant, hegemonic thrust for world power by the United States, now is the time, if it is not already too late, to revive, re-invigorate, and restore the moral authority of the United Nations as the world's best hope for a true, responsible internationalism.

The rule of law, under the United Nations Charter, recognized by the world's community of nations, offers a better hope for the end of terrorism and tyranny, than a Pax Americana, based on the shifty soil of one nation's overwhelming military power and the subservience of a terrified world.

July 30, 2003
**RE: 'NURTURING A FRAGILE MIDEAST PEACE"
editorial, july 30, 2003**
The New York Times

It is exasperating to observe that, after years of "analyzing" the Israeli-Palestinian conflict, pundits and the press seem confused as to cause and effect, equating "building of fences' and the wrapping of kids in dynamite for suicide missions in Israel as equal evils to be overcome by reasonable negotiations. Even-handed observation cannot sustain the notion that these courses of action are moral equivalents. Ariel Sharon's statement that no solution is possible until "the Palestinians put a complete stop to the threat of Palestinian terrorism" (page one article) is the clearest, no-nonsense evaluation of the present impasse. It is also the number one moral imperative facing us all, as we contemplate the threat of terrorism in the modern world and its obscenity as an instrument of political policy.

August 13, 2003
No tax break deserved
The Times Herald Record

In an astonishing report (July 24), Thomas F. Reilly, attorney general of Massachusetts, exposed what he described as "the greatest tragedy to children in the history of the commonwealth," the clergy sexual abuse scandal in which over a thousand children were abused, while the church leadership "chose secrecy to protect the church" and "sacrificed the children for many, many years. "A moral indictment," your excellent editorial (July 25) called it.

Many will think that a charitable description. The sheer number of clergy involved (237 priests) and the selfish involvement of the hierarchy to protect their institution rather than show concern for the welfare of their young charges create an almost unbelievable picture of callousness and lawlessness (they illegally protected the child predators for years), and an almost inconceivable social negligence.

That this heinous behavior took place within a religious establishment, and under its protection, takes one's breath away.

It may not be insignificant to note further that unwary taxpayers help to support the church establishment, even in its unforgivable malfeasance, through religious tax-exemptions. In New York state alone, a staggering $16 billion of church-owned property is tax-exempt (report of the New York State Office of Real Property Services).

Aside from the fact that this may violate the First Amendment's establishment clause and the principle of separation of church and state, it should make us all even more responsible for this covert social, moral, legal abomination.

Such immorality should not have even a smidgeon of tax support.

August 23, 2003
RE: "The Illusions Of Progress", front page, August 23:
The New York Times

The problem is circular (suicide bombings in Jerusalem lead to reprisals in Gaza which lead to suicide bombings in Israel which lead to further reprisals, ad infinitum). The answer is simultaneity, through a joint bi-national officialdom, to stop the fanatics of Hamas and Jihad, and to dis-establish the illegal Jewish settlements *at the same time*. If a two-state solution is the goal of peace-lovers on both sides, they must start now to try a two-state methodology. A JOINT COMMISSION, consisting of Israelis and Palestinians, under United Nations auspices, supported diplomatically, materially and, if necessary, militarily, by the United Nations, could demonstrate before it is too late that the two sides can work together now to stop the "martyr" killings and to remove the most incendiary cause, i.e., Jewish settlements in Palestinian territory, simultaneously. Such a move, supported by the two prime-ministers, Sharon and Abbas, would demonstrate that both sides can work together now, on a common problem, as they must work together in the future as two independent states. Continued futile violence is the only alternative.

January 20, 2004:
Letter to the Editor
The New York Times

Thoughtful Americans were challenged tonight to choose between the considered opinion of the best minds in the country, represented by the prestigious National Academy of Sciences, who declared just this week that "it is time for our country to extend coverage for everyone" . . . through Universal Health Insurance (New York Times, Jan. 15), and the bland denial of this imperative by President Bush in one simple, unsupported, declarative sentence.

"It is time for our nation to extend coverage to everyone,. the academy's Institute of Medicine said ". President Bush may ignore this considered opinion by the nation's best and brightest, but 43 million uninsured Americans, and most fair-minded Americans will not so easily be put off forever!

January 15, 2004
Letter to the Editor
The New York Times

When, at long last, the prestigious NATIONAL ACADEMY OF SCIENCES issues a long-overdue call for universal health care (by 2010 !), stating that "It is time for our nation to extend coverage to everyone" (news article, Jan. 15), President Bush's secretary of health and human services, Tommy G. Thompson, responds immediately, with a knee-jerk reaction of opposition, saying that universal coverage by 2010 was "not realistic!" Was our health secretary equally reactive when his boss recently, in a moment of euphoria, promised full health care for all, rich and poor, . . . provided, of course, that they live in Iraq?

Universal Health Care is an issue whose time has surely come. It is shameful, not only for the 43 million Americans who are not insured at all, as well as the millions whose coverage is too costly and too inadequate, that none of the aspiring Presidential candidates is brave enough to face the issue squarely and unambiguously. The need is NOW. The issue is not one for 2010. Candidates in this year's election will be missing what is perhaps the most anxiety-producing problem in the country if they put off, once again, the widespread concern for the nation's health.

September 19, 2003
RE: "Germany Will Share the Burden in Iraq",
op-ed, Sept. 19, by Gerhard Schroder:
The New York Times

Not in a million years did I ever think that a German head of state would be lecturing America about international morality . . . . *and be right!* I cringed to read Chancellor Gerhard Schroder instructing us with the words "We must work together to win the peace", and "The United Nations must play a central role". And that "We must not forget that security in today's world cannot be guaranteed by one country going it alone"!

It is more than galling that an American foreign policy that thumbed its nose at the United Nations, defied the Security Council and the UN Charter, alienated our natural allies, and brought the moral authority of the world body to its lowest ebb, should have put itself in a position to be the subject of a lecture by a German chancellor. It gave me knots in my stomach.

There might still be just enough time to recoup: by a serious move to re-establish the UN and its authority as the world's international moral and humanitarian center, and by formulating an exit policy from Iraq that conforms to a "rule of law" under the aegis of the United Nations, thus turning the world toward a responsible internationalism and America toward a moral posture befitting the world's leading democracy.

January 6, 2004
Letter To the Editor:
The New York Times

Why, alas, especially in the social sciences, does each generation have to re-discover the wheel? Dr. Felton Earls' admirable research (at a cost of over $51 million so far) replicated to an amazing degree the findings of Saul Alinsky over fifty years ago.

Alinsky, who also worked in Chicago's slums, without expensive grants, came to the conclusion that "criminal behavior is a symptom of poverty and powerlessness". His recommendation was for "community organizing", his goal a vast national comprehensive "organization of organizations", strikingly similar to Dr. Earls' phrase, "community efficacy". Dr. Earls is so right when he says that "community is important". Saul Alinsky said the same thing 50 years ago. What is lacking is not millions more for reserach to confirm the obvious, but action, at long last, by an aroused citizenry and a compassionate, people-oriented social structure to bring substance too both Dr. Earls' and Saul Alinsky"s cogent messages.

August 30, 2003
RE: Pact to Help Poor Nations Obtain Drugs is Delayed, Aug. 29
The New York Times

Before these two news articles appeared, I wonder how many Americans knew that for years American policy has prevented the adequate provision of drugs necessary to treat the epidemics of Aids, malaria, and tuberculosis in the devastated and poverty-ridden countries of Africa and around the world. It is to our shame that, up to now, "the United States single-handedly blocked the deal (to provide cheaper generic drugs) citing concerns from the American pharmaceutical companies". (Aug. 29). The Bush Administration, as well as the press, which kept this abominable secret off the front pages for years, have yet to come clean on this disgraceful obeisance to the profit lines and the patent rights of the pharmaceutical companies at the sacrifice of the lives of millions of poor people as *cheaper, generic* drugs were withheld. The present reversal at the World Trade Organization is a late recognition of the humanitarian, moral demand of the poorest countries that human needs should override patent rides and corporation profits!

September 8, 2003
RE: "The President's Speech", Sept. 8
The New York Times

Most glaring by its absence in President Bush's speech and in your editorial, is the President's stubborn refusal to face the fact that his policy is *unilateralism*, as against a policy of responsible internationalism, is at the root of the present chaos and confusion in Iraq. His call now for "a multinational force in Iraq" is a tacit admission of the wrong-headedness of his policy of going into the war in defiance of the UN Security Council, thus bringing the moral and practical authority of the world body to its lowest ebb. The problem now is the complex one of re-invigorating the United Nations and restoring its moral authority. Turning Iraq around and continuing the war against terrorism are still international problems, requiring a strong international ethic. Now, more than ever, re-establishing the international rule of law, under the aegis of a strong United Nations, should be at the center of American foreign policy.

September 9, 2003
RE: David Brooks, "Whatever It Takes", Sept. 9, 2003
The New York Times

David Brooks' auspicious first column (Whatever It Takes, Sept. 9) discovers at last what most of his critics have known for at least two years, i.e., that "the leading Bushies almost never admit making serious mistakes". And his neo-con supports have never had the political courage to call him on that! Even now, Mr. Brooks fails to state unequivocally and forcefully that President Bush and his Rumsfeld-Wolfowitz teammates refuse to acknowledge that the policy of **unilateralism and war in defiance of the United Nations Security Council are at the root of the present chaos and confusion in Iraq.** That policy has alienated our national allies and has brought the moral and practical authority of the world body to its lowest ebb. Turning Iraq around and pursuing the war against terrorism are still international problems, requiring the re-invigorating of a strong international ethic. Now, more than ever, the re-establishing of the rule of law under the aegis of a strong United Nations, should be the center of American foreign policy. That is what the Bushies just don't get.

September 14, 2003
**RE: "An Unsustainable Policy on Iraq",
editorial Sept. 14, 2003**
The New York Times

The headline is appropriately bold, but your editorial today gives only one brief mention of that "unsustainable policy" in just one line: "Washington's . . . stubborn resistance to broader U.N. involvement, . . ." But that is the crux of it! President Bush and his Rumsfeld-Wolfowitz team-mates still adamantly refuse to acknowledge that the policy of unilateralism and war in defiance of the United Nations Security Council lies at the root of the present chaos and confusion. Turning Iraq around and pursuing the wider war against terrorism are international problems, requiring a strong international ethic, not the unilateral Bush policy that has alienated our national allies and brought the moral authority of the world body to its lowest ebb. Now, more than ever, re-invigorating the U.N., re-establishing the international rule of law, returning the United Nations to its position of the world's ethical guide, should be at the center of America's foreign policy. Now, before it's too late, before hatred of American "arrogance" and fear of American unbridled power destroy our effectiveness as leaders of the democratic world.

September 16, 2003
RE: "Veiled and Worried in Baghdad", September 16, 2003
The New York Times

Lauren Sandler's horrifying reportage of the condition of women in "liberated" Iraq adds the greatest of urgency to the need for the United States to formulate an exit strategy. While our formidable military superiority toppled the tyrant and his evil regime, our military is clearly not equipped, or trained, or experienced in the "nation building" skills necessary to turn our presence from that of "occupier" to that of "liberator". The United Nations is the only world body that possesses that possibility.

Our policy should be directed toward re-invigorating the U.N. and its agencies for international humanitarianism, re-establishing its position as the world's ethical, moral, center, the only avenue toward establishing the rule of law for the new century. Our "out" is the U.N and our enthusiastic and loyal participation within its Charter, thus turning the world toward a responsible internationalism.

October 9, 2003
**RE: "His name takes up the whole marquee"
oct. 9 editorial**
The Times Herald Record

Your editorial hit the nail on the head! The incredible California election revealed the idiocies of the "culture of celebrity", in which "name recognition", however irreverently achieved, is the biggest deal, trumping the values of informed debate and the integrity of meaningful political experience.

If one measure of insanity is the triumph of fantasy and wishful thinking over reason, then California's voters indicate a major epidemic of mental illness! I was in Los Angeles last week, where I talked with several "Ah-nold" supporters. They were disgusted, they explained, with Governor Davis's ineptness. Asked why they thought Arnold Schwarzenegger, with no experience whatsoever in the socio-economic complexities of state economics and management, was the answer to California's economic woes, they offered only a desperate faith in the can-do, macho, "Terminator". University of California Sociology Professor Arlie R. Hochschild called it a "rescue fantasy".

The idea that a Hollywood-honed image of body-builder par excellence, plus Conan the Barbarian, plus the indefatigable and inexhaustible "Terminator", with no experience or demonstrated skills in the art of governance, could sell himself as California's savior, is simply terrifying. Unthinking Faith, born of despair, conquers Reason! What next? On a national level, may we look forward to a "Rambo for President"—or do we already have one in Washington?

October 12, 2003
RE: "Government by Celebrity is Already Asserting Itself", WEEK IN REVIEW, October 12, 2003
The New York Times

Mr. Todd S. Purdum's perceptive article on "Government by Celebrity" (Week in Review, October 12) importantly reminds us that Governor-elect Schwarzenegger, lacking "a well-formed political ideology, is dangerous" and seems to be "after power for its own sake", in the words of columnist Charles Krauthammer. Mr. Purdum's quote of the witty Tom Lehrer brings to mind another pithy quatrain by Mr. Lehrer:

"Once the rockets are up
Who cares where they come down
That's not my department
Says Wernber von Braun."

With the "Terminator" in power, with no indication of knowledge or experience in governance, we have to worry that his political "rockets" do not come down too disastrously. How did California's voters ever permit Hollywood fantasy to triumph over reason?

October 21, 2003
**RE: "Waiting for Democrats on Iraq",
editorial October 20**
The New York Times

Isn't it an ironic and revealing commentary on the moral values of our society that "as American soldiers continue to die and the cost to American taxpayers continues to mount', you find it necessary to warn Congress not to pass legislation that "excessively enriches politically connected companies like Haliburton and Bechtel" with "taxpayer dollars"!

It is taken for granted, of course, that big business will be "enriched", i.e., make billions of dollars out of the Iraq adventure (supposedly undertaken in the name of democracy), while our soldiers die and our taxpayers make sacrifices. But let it not be "excessive", you plead! Justice, morality, integrity, equality of sacrifice for a noble cause? Indeed!

November 1, 2003
**RE: "Spending Bill Nears Passage In the Senate",
Nov. 1, 2003**
The New York Times

What goes on here? Doesn't Congress read the Times? Or are they so beholden to the big-business power-brokers as to defy common decency? Your editorial of October 20 suggested the very common-sensical notion that "as American soldiers continue to die and the cost to American taxpayers continues to mount", Congress ought not to pass legislation that "excessively enriches politically connected companies like Halliburton and Bechtel . . . with taxpayer dollars". (editorial, Oct. 20). Note, the editorial did not say they should not be "enriched", but please, not "excessively"! Who could disagree with that? But today's vote indicates not only that Congress, by a vote of 298 to 121, did not listen, they even went out of their way to knock out an amendment "that outlawed profiteering by contractors" (Nov. 1 news item). What goes on here?

February 11, 2004
Halliburton profits while U.S. soldiers die
Worcester Telegram & Gazette

A front-page story, "New probe confronting Halliburton" (Telegram & Gazette, Jan. 24), raises some profound moral issues for the body politic.

While our young men and women give their lives in Iraq in the name of democracy, a giant American conglomerate, Halliburton Co. (where Vice President Richard Cheney made his fortune and continues to reap profits through is extravagant retirement plan), overcharged the government, cheated the taxpayers to the tune of $6 million, bribed tax officials in Nigeria with $2 million and offered kickbacks for Army contracts in Iraq. Now it tries hypocritically to cover its malfeasance and polish its image with sanctimonious TV ads on CNN showing how it supplies hot meals, laundry and telephones for the troops. Taxpayers and all fair-minded Americans who must bear the heavy burden of President George W. Bush's multibillion dollar war should want to know:

Should private companies be making handsome profits, not to mention obscene, illegal bonuses, while our soldiers die?

Should Mr. Cheney, at the very least, come out with a public statement denouncing his company?

Should Mr. Bush demand that his vice president disassociate himself from Halliburton's misdeeds, or even fire the vice president to disassociate the administration from its abominable behavior?

Can a sense of decent morality be maintained, at the highest level, even as we pursue our democratic goals in Iraq?

March 2, 2004
Ezra Pound
The New York Times

It is astonishing that in this era of soul searching and intensive philosophical re-evaluation of the horrors of WWII, the monstrosities of the Holocaust, and the ominous re-emergence of anti-Semitism, both your reviewer (David Gates in "A Black Jacket for Old Ez,", Feb. 1) and your single letter-writer ("The Pound Era", Feb. 29) can casually dismiss the abominable anti-Semitism and the criminal treason of Ezra Pound and look forward to having "the controversies forgotten" because, after all, the lovable "Old Ez" was "one of the greatest American poets ever".

What if this traitor and anti-Semite were merely a workman, a carpenter or a plumber, or a radio personality (Tokyo Rose) or a statesman (Laval, or Quisling)? Or are there special dispensations for a poet that earn him pardon or forgiveness, as though it were somehow churlish to recall that he was a revolting, dangerous, fascist ideologue at one of history's most pregnant moments?

March 6, 2004
**RE: KERRY CAMP PLANS TO RAISE $80 MILLION,
March 5 news item**
The New York Times

Your News article, ("Kerry Camp Plans to Raise $80 Million", March 5) forcefully reminds us that the next phase in our quadrennial electoral process is not the serious and contemplative exploration of the contrary ideas of the two candidates, but a frenzied chase for the almighty dollar. Despite the reforms of the McCain-Feingold, Bill, the paramount energy of both parties will be directed towards raising money . . . $80 million for Kerry just for now to offset Bush's recent $144 million, with hundreds of millions sought before the campaign ends.

Kerry "will convene 85 top fund-raisers in Washington next week", as money supercedes the development of socio/political ideas. This frantic money-chase corrupts the electoral process at every turn. It enriches the television industry and short-changes the public, as sloganeers seek the magic phrase that will turn the voter instantly, trivializing complex issues with the adman's mesmerizing hyperbole. It would be more civilized and raise the electoral process to the level of a national educational exercise, if we employed the best minds in both parties for intellectual brainstorming and problem-solving, rather than enriching advertising wizards with eyes only on the buck. And hundreds of millions of dollars would be saved for more pressing needs in education, health, peace studies and a host of other urgent problems that beset the nation.

March 23, 2004
Letter to the Editor:
SECULAR-HUMANISM AND "CITIZENSHIP"
The New York Times

It is astonishing to see how, with one fell swoop, relying more on hyperbole and emotion than on evidence and reason, David Brooks wipes away the intellectual and scientific advances of a thousand and more years to declare that " biblical wisdom is deeper and more accurate than the wisdom offered by the secular social sciences"! Thus the ruminations of rabbis and their followers in an age when human knowledge was in a state of wonderment, and often bewilderment, are elevated to a greater understanding of " what human beings are like and how they are likely to behave", while the findings of sociology, psychology, historiography, philosophy, and the other social sciences, built upon and reflecting the revolutionary insights of the scientific revolution, are tossed aside with a sneer as a bad influence over "thoroughly secularized listeners." We poor " secularized " "utility-maximizes " just lack the mental equipment " (!) to understand Brooks' lofty, but opaque notion that old-fashioned religion is "citizenship".....a cheap shot at the rationalism that lies at the heart of secular-humanist thinking and informs our modern reality.

April 5, 2004
On religion and " compassion"
The Magazine, The New York Times

"Compassion . . . . it goes right across the board in all the world religions", Karen Armstrong informs us (Taking Religious Liberties, April 4). After the Romans threw Christians to the lions, after Hitler threw six million Jews into the ovens, after the "compassionate" Crusaders killed, maimed and slaughtered all the Jews and non-Christians they could find, after the bloody conquest of Mexico for loot and the cross, after all the blood and cruelty and genocide in modern times, after Rwanda and Bosnia, after the Catholic/Protestant wars in Ireland, after the "compassionate "suicide bombers in Israel! *All done in the name of God* ! And after this bloody swath down the corridors of history, "religious scholar " Armstrong can solemnly opine " Compassion is the key . . ." without raising a single caveat, and without your interviewer even raising an eyebrow . It's almost enough to turn reasonable people to atheism.

Yours truly

April 13, 2004
**Letter to the Editor
On Ralph Nader**
The New York Times

Ralph Nader is a national treasure. More than anyone else he symbolizes the American ideal of social responsibility and the uniquely American notion that one man, one voice, one determined advocate in a democracy can make a difference. Almost single-handedly he revolutionized the car industry, made driving safer, and defeated the giants of Detroit by his doggedness and persistency. His agenda in the presidential race is head and shoulders superior to any and all the other candidates . . . on women's rights, civil liberties, war and peace, the ecology, the struggle against the greedy and corrupt world of corporate conglomerates, etc., etc. So what's the problem? Simply that he is not electable. It isn't that he is not up to the presidency. It is, rather, that the present electoral process (driven by money), and the present mood of the electorate (misinformed and brainwashed by money), is not up to Ralph Nader. So what's to be done?

Nader ought to continue his courageous, issue-driven campaign with the persistence and incorruptibility that he has come to exemplify. He can thus educate the public as no candidate seems capable of doing, he can push the Democratic candidate to more forthright and responsive positions, and then, at or before the Democratic Convention, he must join the anti-Bush coalition, urge his followers to vote for the Democratic candidate, and continue, within the broadest coalition possible, to add his considerable weight and intelligence to defeat the worst president in modern times.

Yours truly